BAD
NEWS

*THE FOREIGN POLICY OF
THE NEW YORK TIMES*

Russ Braley

Regnery Gateway
Chicago

To Magda

Published by Regnery Gateway, Inc., 940-950 North Shore Drive, Lake Bluff, Illinois 60044.

Library of Congress Cataloging in Publication Data

Braley, Russ, 1921-
  Bad news.

  1. United States—Foreign relations—1945-
2. World politics—1945-   . 3. New York times.
4. Foreign news—United States. 5. Government and the press—United States. I. Title.
E840.B7 1983   327.73   82-42907
ISBN 0-89526-627-X

Acknowledgments

The author is indebted to a number of persons for their encouragement or assistance in this project.

During the early 1970s Henry P. Durkin, who acted as the author's agent, kept voluminous chronological files of clippings on the Pentagon Papers and Watergate. He donated 16 enormous file envelopes weighing 40 kilos, an invaluable research aid.

Rael Jean and Erich Isaac generously shared research they had done on the American New Left. Professors Anne Marie and Charles Poinsatte introduced the author to academic publishing by arranging an invitation to speak on the Iranian Revolution at Saint Mary's College, Notre Dame, Indiana. Managing Editor William Umstead granted a year's leave of absence from the *New York Daily News*. Barbara and Henry L. Trewhitt of the *Baltimore Sun* offered shelter in Washington, D.C. Thanks also are due to the staff of the Montclair Public Library and to all those who agreed to interviews and answered correspondence.

Without the encouragement of Henry Regnery, there would have been no book.

For permission to cite lengthy excerpts, the author thanks Anthony Moncrieff and Michael Charlton, authors of *Many Reasons Why,* Hill and Wang, New York, copyright © 1978; Edith Efron, author of *The News Twisters,* Nash, Los Angeles, copyright © 1971 (reprinted by permission of the William Morris Agency, Inc., on behalf of the author); and Harper & Row, New York, publishers of the late Marguerite Higgins' *Our Vietnam Nightmare,* copyright © 1965.

Montclair, New Jersey
November 1982

CONTENTS

Introduction

To those who remember World War II, isolationism is a grave offense. Because the United States was isolationist and unprepared, Japan was tempted to destroy the U.S. Pacific fleet at Pearl Harbor on December 7, 1941, abruptly changing everyone's life. On Monday morning, December 8, military recruiting offices across the country opened to lines of young men who had been isolationists, if not pacifists, on December 6. The nation literally became internationalist overnight.

After the war, for a dozen years Americans found themselves with a unique, privileged status in much of the world. The American news media and citizenry paid attention to the world as never before. Americans became citizens of the world, in a leading role thrust upon them by the circumstances of their comparative prosperity and security.

About 20 years after World War II, the United States drifted into a revolution at home—that it did not need—to correct social imbalances that already were being addressed. The revolutionary discontent appeared triggered by the assassination of President Kennedy, but it had been aroused by a series of disillusionments ranging from the intractable racial problem at home to foreign policy disasters.

Only 30 years after World War II, with the fall of Saigon to North Vietnamese Communists, the United States cancelled its world citizenship and reverted to the isolationism of December 6, 1941. As the United States was perceived to cop out, friendly leaders, factions, governments and parties fell to revolutions from Southwest Asia and the Middle East to Central America.

To examine the reasons for the hasty American retreat required considering several themes, including the historical context, the personalities of leaders, the communications explosion and the role of the media.

When this book was first outlined in 1976, a starting point was the striking disparity in the media's treatment of Presidents Kennedy and Nixon. Big media adored Kennedy and detested Nixon, so news commentators hailed as triumphs Kennedy's foreign policy mistakes and condemned as failures Nixon's tentative successes. (An early working title was, *KENNEDY AND NIXON, Their Foreign Policies, Their Media.*)

The public could be fooled, because foreign affairs is the area of news easiest to manipulate. A news consumer cannot run out to Tehran, to the Western Sahara or to Honduras to check if the media reports are true or not. Editors, whether in newspapers or broadcasting newsrooms, seldom have foreign experience of their own, and they hesitate to contradict the judgment of the Eastern Establishment's foreign affairs elite.

As research progressed, a minor player seized a major role, without the author willing it: The *New York Times*, along with its allies and its government-interchangeable men, increasingly turned up at the center of faulty foreign policy decision-making. *Times* intervention was not spotty or occasional, but continuous and pervasive.

It was commonplace to say that *Times* editorialist Herbert Matthews "created" Fidel Castro in the late 1950s, but who was Matthews, and how did he do this? Explaining the phenomenon stretched into two chapters. Since the *Times* midwifed Castro, it was not surprising that Timesmen could literally order White House actions both at the Bay of Pigs and during the Cuban missile crisis.

At the time of Castro's triumph, the *Times* also was at the center of charges that a Nazi revival threatened West Germany. A correspondent in Bonn who thought West Germany faced, instead, a threat from the Soviet-backed left, found himself powerless to refute the notion, which spawned a flood of articles and books on the neo-Nazi menace. Instead of neo-Nazis, Germany got the Berlin Wall, a Social Democratic regime edging toward neutralism and urban terrorists financed by East Germany but called "anarchists" in the Western press. Alone in the media, the *Times* knew instantly how the Wall came to be built, but it did not honor the public's right to know.

The Berlin Wall was a catastrophe for all of Eastern Europe, another installment on the Soviets' heavy grip. When the Soviets subsequently mobilized the Warsaw Pact to invade Czechoslovakia, the *Times* advised the Czechs, as it earlier had advised Hungarians, to grin and bear it; don't make trouble.

For many years news editors across the country used *Times* dispatches and commentary on the Middle East, confident that the *Times* must be a friend of Israel, and a particularly knowledgeable one, because of its Jewish connections. The degree to which many Israelis regard the *Times* as an enemy did not become clear until the *Times* began its long campaign to unseat Prime Minister Menachem Begin.

Times efforts to display even-handedness toward Arabs repeatedly led the newspaper into grotesque situations, such as alternating praise for Dr. George Habash and Yasser Arafat, depending on which terrorist happened to be on top at the time during Jordan's civil war. The *Times* counseled against rescuing King Hussein from Palestinian revolutionaries, and later it advised, through its favored ex-diplomat George W. Ball, ending aid to Israel and sending the money instead to Lebanon, although no one could form a government there to receive it.

As in the Middle East, nothing could have happened the way it did in Vietnam without the *Times*. Its Saigon correspondent in the early 1960s, David Halberstam, wrote later that he had been ready to join young Vietnamese officers in a coup against Ngo Dinh Diem by pretending to be kidnaped. A coup did occur, and Halberstam's engaged dispatches did much to set the stage for it, and for the ensuing American debacle in Vietnam. The *Times* did not turn against the Vietnam war as such until 1965, but when it did, it eventually dragged the rest of the media along with it, as documented by correspondent Peter Braestrup.

The deep involvement of the *Times* in Vietnam made allies of Daniel Ellsberg and a part of the radical New Left; it was leaders of the radical Institute for Policy Studies who helped Ellsberg plant the Pentagon Papers in the *Times*. It was, however, *Times* editors who published the rewritten papers in crassly manipulated form. Ironically, the Johnson administration was charged by the *Times* with conspiracy, in a conspiratorial *Times*-leftist action that was hailed as heroic by a majority of the Supreme Court and by the rest of the scooped and moribund media.

The clandestine publication of the manipulated Pentagon Papers led the Nixon administration to set up its own bungling security operation, but well before the White House plumbers went burgling, the *Times* and its far-left allies were calling for Nixon's impeachment over the incursion into Cambodia, while at the same time egging on demonstrators who turned violent.

The Watergate burglaries, occuring in this revolutionary atmosphere, sent more than two dozen men to prison for political offenses, while it proved impossible to make charges stick against demonstrators who, it turned out, later, had received directions from Cuban and Vietnamese Communists on how to disrupt the American political system.

By the time that the media and Congress combined to force the United States to leave Indochina and Nixon to leave office, editorial dissent on those subjects was forbidden in the United States, censored out by one's media peers. If an experienced reporter or editor wished to write a commentary disagreeing with the *Times* on a foreign policy issue in the period 1973 to 1980, he was free to write it, but as in the Soviet Union, there was no place to print it. The media had formed in lockstep behind the *Times* and the *Washington Post*.

In 1983, Public Television spent about $6 million to produce a manipulated series on the Vietnam war that simply reinforced earlier mistaken news coverage. It was intended for schools and libraries. The main author of the series was Stanley Karnow, who had earlier displayed open and rabid bias against Ngo Dinh Diem in publications ranging from the *Saturday Evening Post* to *The Nation*.

The most difficult area of foreign policy is national defense, and the most esoteric part of defense is strategic defense, especially control of nuclear arms. The *Times* is the only publication in the country that can offer a 5,000-word article on the defense budget or on strategic armaments options that will reach an audience of millions through the *Times Magazine*. The authors chosen to write these uniquely favored articles usually are people like Leslie Gelb, once chief editor of the Pentagon Papers and one of the custodians of the copy stolen by Ellsberg, or Earl C. Ravenal, a member of the anti-defense lobby who rose near the top in the Carter administration's Defense Department. Gelb can be counted on to cite his former partners in the Pentagon, Morton Halperin and Paul Warnke, while Ravenal for years has been selling an entirely isolationist defense establishment limited to 8 military divisions, with no deployment overseas. Both Gelb and Ravenal also hawk their wares on the *Times* Op-Ed page.

In recent decades, while the rest of the media fell in line behind the *Times* lead on foreign and defense affairs, United States credibility in the world and the media's credibility in the United States both declined. When did the deterioration begin, and when did the media begin committing credibility suicide? One watershed year was 1956, when two fatal American policy decisions were taken, one of them sanctioning the Soviet Union's introduction of heavy weaponry into the Middle East, and the other allowing the Soviets to consolidate their hold on Hungary and Eastern Europe. That is where our narrative begins.

Chapter I
Hungary and Suez

*"Internationally there is tumult; there is great disor-
der under heaven, and the situation is excellent."*

—*Slogan of China's Cultural Revolution*

On election night, 1956, Americans who followed world news felt a
dizzying schizophrenia at the events clamoring for their attention.
Election returns came over radio and television. Savage fighting continued in Budapest, where Soviet tank cannon answered a sniper by
blasting down the building he was firing from. British and French commandos landed under cover of naval bombardment at the north end of
the Suez Canal, to be met by Egyptian soldiers and teenagers firing rifles handed out from the Soviet consulate in Port Said. The United Nations, balked by great power vetos in the Security Council, was
meeting in an emergency session of the General Assembly.

The day before, Anglo-French paratroops had dropped on Port Fuad
and Port Said, following Israel's blitz across the Gaza Strip and Sinai Pe-
ninsula. The Hungarian Communist Party newspaper *Szabad Nép*
(Free People) had sent a last telex to Vienna: "The people are throwing

9

themselves on the tanks. Now they're shooting again. We're being hit. . . ."

On election day, November 6, the Soviet Union published messages from Premier Nikolai Bulganin to the leaders of Britain, France, and Israel—before the messages had been delivered—threatening "the use of force," perhaps with "every kind of modern destructive weapons. . .such as rocket technique," if they did not withdraw immediately from Egypt.

The fighting was far from the United States, but the air of confusion on election night was like that in a chaotic battle. The best place to turn for orientation was *The New York Times,* generally regarded as the nation's newspaper of record.

The *Times* was meticulous in fitting the size of its headlines to the worth of a story, and it seldom used a banner headline over all eight columns of Page 1. The banner headlines had been thundering for a week now, and that night there were four of them:

RUSSIA WARNS   OF FORCE   TO END SUEZ WAR;
LOSES U.N. BID FOR JOINT U.S.-SOVIET ACTION;
BRITISH, FRENCH COMMANDOS LAND IN EGYPT
Nation Goes to Polls With Big Turnout Indication.

A Page 1 story indicated that the Hungarian revolution was over:
SOVIET   MOPS UP
HUNGARY REBELS.

European newspapers played the news differently. In Europe, the Hungarian tragedy was closer, more immediate, and more agonizing than the Suez war, and the United Nations was a distant chimera. On November 4, Europeans had heard—first hand and repeated in English, French, and German—two messages from Budapest's Radio Kossuth.

One said, "This is Imre Nagy speaking, the president of the council of ministers of the Hungarian People's Republic. Today at daybreak Soviet forces started an attack against our capital, obviously with the intent to overthrow the legal Hungarian democratic government. I notify the people of our country and the entire world of this fact."

Two hours later: "This is the Association of Hungarian Writers speaking to all writers, scientists, all writers' associations, and scientific unions of the world. We turn to the leaders of intellectual life in all countries. Our time is limited. You all know the facts. There is no need to expand on them. Help Hungary! Help the Hungarian writers, scientists, workers, peasants, and intelligencia. Help! Help! Help!"

The Hungary and Suez crises did not go away after Dwight Eisenhower was re-elected President by a landslide. Both crises festered on for months, souring Eisenhower's second term and placing the West in a defensive and indecisive frame of mind.

Hungary and Suez overshadowed other crises going on at the same time that would prove to be transient, such as the upheaval in Poland and the Quemoy-Matsu affair. The two major crises were of a different order, sharp confrontations with definite outcomes, and each opened a new direction in history for their regions and the world. Both weakened American authority and the West, moving the Soviets to gamble on a Berlin ultimatum two years later and to range farther afield to Indochina and Cuba.

Washington, like most of the world, was caught off guard by the spontaneity of the Hungarian revolution, but the Suez crisis was not unexpected. It had been simmering and periodically erupting throughout Eisenhower's first term, moving unmistakably toward a climax, and John Foster Dulles had been enmeshed in it since May 1953, when he became the first Secretary of State to visit the Middle East.

Dulles walked into Middle East intrigue, where no one played with all cards on the table, bearing a gift for the wrong man. He presented a silver-plated pistol inscribed from Eisenhower to General Mohammed Naguib, the nominal head of the junta that had overthrown Egyptian King Farouk the year before. The real boss, Colonel Gamal Abdel Nasser, had Naguib placed under house arrest in November 1954, charging that a $12 million CIA bribe had been found in Naguib's home.

On his visit to Cairo, the anti-colonialist Dulles sided with the Egyptian revolutionary government against the British. His pressure speeded the Anglo-Egyptian Agreement of July 27, 1954, that would require Britain to vacate its Suez Canal military base within 20 months, while maintaining the base in readiness with civilian contractors. Dulles' diplomatic assistance, plus $40 million in economic aid, appeared to start the Eisenhower administration off on the right foot with the jealously independent Egyptians.

In February 1955, with Nasser alone in charge of Egypt, Soviet Ambassador David Semenovich Solod arrived in Cairo at about the time that a Czechoslovakian mission turned up to discuss a deal for cotton industry machinery. Agence France Presse reported that the Czechs really were negotiating a deal to sell Soviet-designed weapons to the Egyptians.

Nasser discussed weapons with U.S. Ambassador Henry Byroade on March 10. Dulles' announced policy was that the United States would not sell arms in the Middle East, and he had not permitted any to go to

Israel. Attempting to get a handle on the use of weapons in the Middle East, Dulles instructed Byroade to offer Egypt $27 million in arms for cash, on condition that the arms could not be used for aggression. The deal also would require sending American military advisers to Egypt. Eisenhower thought that the $27 million was "peanuts," and so did Nasser, who declined the offer.

The following month Nasser went to the conference of nations emerging as "the Third World" at Bandung, Indonesia—his entrance on the world stage. Chou En-lai advised him to request arms on credit from the Soviets, but Nasser did not need to be told.

In June Nasser called in Byroade to inform him that the month before, Soviet Ambassador Solod had offered him arms. The United States could not say Nasser gave no warning.

Dulles dismissed Byroade's report with an ear-burning lecture. He did not believe that the Soviets had arms to spare, or that the bankrupt Egyptians had anything to offer for them. Nor did the CIA, under Dulles' brother Allen, confirm that an Egyptian-Soviet arms deal was in in the works.

Dulles was occupied with the countdown of preparations for a big-league event. In July 1955 Eisenhower went to Geneva to meet at the summit Soviet Premier Bulganin, British Prime Minister Anthony Eden, French Premier Edgar Faure, and the fifth wheel, Soviet Communist Party First Secretary Nikita Khrushchev, who, under Western protocol, would be left out of photographs of the Big Four.

It was the Soviets' coming-out party after years of sealed borders under Stalin, and they were on their best behavior. The summit settled nothing, but it allowed Eisenhower to outshine the others with his "open skies" proposal to preclude surprise attack, and it handed over the central question of divided Germany to what turned out to be a series of foreign ministers' conferences, the first to begin in October. Dulles lost no opportunity to stress his skepticism of the exercise, but the media liked the spectacle. It was talking, not shooting, and we called it "the spirit of Geneva," a forerunner of Charles de Gaulle's detente.

During the conference Israel's Prime Minister Moshe Sharett visited Dulles in Geneva with a report from Mossad, Israeli intelligence, that an Egyptian-Soviet arms deal was going through, and with a request for American arms to counter it. Dulles was disturbed and set in motion his brother's CIA. Now the CIA confirmed the arms deal, but Dulles continued to say no to arms for Israel.

Outside the formal conference Dulles asked Khrushchev if the Soviets were selling arms to Egypt. Khrushchev grinned openly and assured Dulles that the Soviets were not.[1]

Khrushchev, who would later emerge as an ebullient extrovert, was subdued in Geneva, even dour as he stood aside to watch Western news photographers crowd around Eisenhower and the nobody, Bulganin. Never mind. Eventually Khrushchev would get their attention.

If Dulles did not accept that the Soviets were introducing weapons on a large scale into the Middle East, the British popular press was all over the story, although it had no hard facts. Sefton Delmer, of the *Daily Express,* watched a man floating with outstretched arms in the swimming pool of his Cairo hotel—Soviet Deputy Foreign Minister Dmitri Shepilov. A blazing African sun cast his wavering shadow on the tiled bottom of the pool, Delmer wrote, in the form of a spider, or perhaps an octopus. The Soviets, he reported, were moving in on Egypt as Britain abandoned its bases there. In Geneva, correspondents passed the *Express* around, smiling at the gaudy imagery.

On September 27, two months after Geneva, Nasser announced the Soviet-Czech-Egyptian arms deal. He became the instant hero of the Arab world.

A month later, at the Geneva foreign ministers' conference, Sharett again approached Dulles, who would only tell him that the United States would "look sympathetically" at a request for defensive arms, but that the United States would not contribute to an arms race in the Middle East. Sharett also saw Soviet Foreign Minister V. M. Molotov, warning him that the Soviet arms buildup in Egypt was bringing the Middle East to the flashpoint of war.

Months later the United States authorized Israel to order $4 million in small arms and light equipment, a drop in the bucket compared with the $200 million initial Egyptian-Soviet deal. When the Suez war broke out, the arms for Israel still had not been delivered, and they were held up.

Soviet arms poured into Egypt in November 1955. Until then, Middle East wars and skirmishes had been fought with weapons that a man could carry, and in 1950 Israel had improvised armored cars by welding steel plate to trucks. On paper, Egypt became a major military power with the arrival of 200 MiG-15 jet fighters, 60 Ilyushin-18 bombers, 200 T-34 tanks, 100 Stalin-3 heavy tanks, 200 armored personnel carriers, 100 self-propelled guns, several hundred field howitzers, 134 anti-aircraft guns, plus barrage rockets, antitank guns, two destroyers, four minesweepers, 12 torpedo boats, and quantities of Kalashnikov assault rifles. Egypt previously had inherited about 40 British Centurion tanks, about 100 Vampire and Meteor jets, and some obsolete World War II Sherman tanks. Nasser had so many weapons coming that he formed a new organization to use part of them, the

Palestine Liberation Army, drawn from his "Egyptian fedayeen."

The Israelis scrambled for arms but found no country would sell to them. Not until April 1956 did Israel receive a dozen Mystère jets and some AMX light tanks from France, and the promise of six Meteor jets from Britain. The Israelis set about remodeling old Sherman tank carcasses received from France.

Nasser's arms deal took the lid off. Eventually the Middle East would bristle with more conventional weaponry than the NATO nations possessed in western Europe. From Cuba to Indochina, arms would buy the Soviets a stake in nations around the world. Mozambique, when it threw off Portuguese colonialism, briefly made the Kalashnikov rifle the centerpiece of its national flag.

That this would happen was classic Dulles doctrine, yet he refused to believe it was happening until the Soviet-Egyptian deal had been months in the making and was irreversible.

Dulles thought he still could buy back into the Egyptian game. After conferring with allies at a meeting of the North Atlantic Treaty Organization, Dulles announced on December 16, 1955, that the United States, Britain and the World Bank would offer to help Egypt build the Aswan Dam. It appeared that the project would take about 15 years and cost around $1.3 billion. Two days later the Soviets offered to join in and were rebuffed. Eugene Black, president of the World Bank, traveled to Cairo and reported that Nasser would accept no advice on running Egypt's economy. Still, Black recommended going through with the dam project.

In February 1956, Black's International Bank for Reconstruction and Development announced agreement in principle to start financing the Aswan Dam with a loan of $200 million, contingent on pledges from the United States of $56 million and from Britain of $14 million. Loan conditions stipulated that Egypt could not accept Communist participation in building the dam.

Dulles intended to tie up Egypt's economy by demanding sound, long-term financing arrangements, so that Egypt would have nothing left over to spend for maintaining its military hardware. Nasser already had mortgaged to the Soviets and Czechs Egypt's crop of long-fiber cotton for the next decade.

In March 1956, Nasser told Byroade that Egypt might go to the Soviets to finance Aswan. Dulles was sure the Soviets couldn't do it. At the same time, King Hussein, under pressure from Nasserites in his nation, dismissed Jordan's Arab Legion commander, Sir John Glubb. Two months later Nasser recognized China, infuriating Dulles.

On June 18, 1956, the last of the British soldiers scheduled to leave the Canal Zone under the 1954 agreement slipped away early to avoid humiliation. Nasser, about to be elected president with 99% of the vote, arrived on the dot for the exit ceremony, accompanied by Shepilov, who had succeded Molotov as foreign minister. Together they watched an impressive parade of Soviet-designed arms under a flyover of MiG-15s.

Nasser was stuffing quite a bit down Foster Dulles' craw; on July 10, Dulles told a press conference that it was improbable that Egypt would get the Aswan loan.

Dulles was being pressed by his friend Adenauer, even in public statements, to authorize the Aswan Dam loan. The French Ambassador to the United States, Maurice Couve de Murville, told the State Department that denying the loan would be "very dangerous. . . it can affect the Canal Zone."[2]

Dulles told the British, without consulations, that the deal was off, and then called in the Egyptian Ambassador, Ahmed Hussein, on July 19. Dulles questioned the feasibility of the project and said he doubted that the Senate would authorize it, because Egypt was so heavily in debt to Czechoslovakia and the Soviet Union for arms. Hussein said he hoped Dulles was not going to withdraw the Aswan Dam offer, because he had a Soviet offer right in his pocket. Dulles told him in that case, he did not need the United States. Two years later the Soviets began work on the dam.

Nasser received news of the cancellation on the Yugoslav island of Brioni, with Marshal Josip Broz Tito and Indian Prime Minister Jawaharlal Nehru, pillars of the new Third World.

A week later, on July 26, Nasser seized the canal by having a handful of police occupy the International Suez Canal Company and announced the takeover in a flaming speech in Alexandria: "This, O citizens, is the battle in which we are involved. It is a battle against imperialism and the methods and tactics of imperialism. . . Arab nationalism has been set afire from the Ocean to the Gulf. . . ."

Eden that night was in London receiving the young King Faisal of Iraq and a personal friend of many years, Iraqi Prime Minister Nuri es Said. The dinner broke up early. Nasser was engaged in a propaganda war against Said, and the British believed he had been behind at least two attempts on Said's life.

Dulles was on a state visit to Peru, where he was reported shaken by the canal seizure. Nasser had gone to the brink, and perhaps over it.

In Israel, Defense Minister Moshe Dayan and his aide, Shimon Peres, had just returned from a secret mission to France. The jets they had received in April had alarmed the French foreign ministry, which had ordered a new arms cutoff. In three days of talks Dayan and Peres managed to wangle a promise of more jets and AMX tanks.[3]

Dulles flew to London on August 1 to discuss the crisis and set a date, August 16, for a London conference of 22 nations that would reply to Nasser's seizure of the canal. Dulles declared that a way had to be found "to make Nasser disgorge what he was attempting to swallow." Eden told him that half of Britain's oil imports came through the canal and would be subject to Nasser's whims. The canal already had been closed to Israeli shipping, in violation of the Canal Convention of 1888, which guaranteed its use to all nations.

Eden wrote in his memoirs that he had mentioned military preparations to Dulles.

> I did not wish to conceal anything from Mr. Dulles, and I told him that the United States Military Attaché had been asking for information about our military preparations. I said that we were quite ready to give this, but that I wanted first to make sure that the United States government really wished to have it. Mr. Dulles replied that the United States government perfectly well understood the purpose of our preparations, and he thought that they had a good effect. It was preferable that the United States government should not seek detailed information.[4]

Eden said that Dulles in his talks with the British and French in London did not rule out the use of force, but said it was the last method to be tried if all other methods failed. In his memoirs, Eden, one of the great losers in the Suez war, documented U.S. delaying actions over the next two months, including a refusal to withhold canal fees in blocked accounts and the proposal of a Canal Users' Club, a suggestion that amused Nasser.

French forces took up stations on Cyprus on August 28. In September, Britain began staging forces on Malta.

Eisenhower sent a message to Eden on September 3 saying that American public opinion rejected the use of force. Eden remarked it was the first such suggestion to come from the United States. He sent a long reply detailing the dangers to be expected if Nasser were successful in the seizure of the canal. By this time the British felt confirmed in their belief that the United States intended to replace the former British influence in Egypt, which made the Aswan Dam cancellation more baffling to them.

Both Eisenhower and Dulles were asked at press conferences later that month what the United States would do about its militant allies. Neither answered the question, for the good reason that they hadn't decided yet. Eisenhower said, "As you know, this country will not go to war ever while I am occupying my present post unless Congress is called into session and Congress declares war." Dulles also limited his answer to U.S. intentions: "We do not intend to shoot our way through. It may be we have a right to do it, but we don't intend to do it, so far as the United States is concerned."

Eden received a warning message from Bulganin. He informed Eisenhower on October 1 that "there is no doubt in our minds that Nasser, whether he likes it or not, is now effectively in Russian hands." He warned Eisenhower of plots in Libya, Saudi Arabia and Iraq.

On October 14, Britain and France brought a resolution to the UN Security Council to keep the canal open while respecting Egypt's sovereignty. The Soviets vetoed it. The British-French checklist of steps to avoid the use of force was running out.

The American media treated Suez as a clash between Egypt and Britain, in clandestine collusion with Israel. Britain had been expelled from Egypt, and Eden's fall would be dramatic. The French played a walk-on role without lines to speak, according to the media.

Actually, the French were prime movers in the attack on Suez. To Premier Guy Mollet, Nasser was a "megalomaniac" who would wipe out Israel if he could and was fomenting revolt in Algeria. Immediately after Nasser's seizure of the canal, the French and British governments agreed to take it back by force, if necessary.

As the French government watched the British-American maneuvering through August, it appeared to Mollet that the American-British special relationship was a handicap to action. Mollet believed the Americans did not understand the gravity of the problem Nasser presented. He would tell David Ben-Gurion, who had returned from retirement and became prime minister again in November 1955, that there always was a two-year time lag before the Americans understood any European problem, as in 1917 and 1941.[5] In September 1956, Mollet felt justified in his decision, just before Nasser's seizure of the canal, to give Israelis access to French weapons. Mollet, along with his defense minister, Maurice Bourges-Manoury, and his foreign minister, Christian Pineau, did not believe the Israelis would simply wait for an Arab attack. If the British backed out, the French and Israelis would go it together.

Dayan and Shimon Peres were invited to France on secret missions in September. At the end of the month a full-scale Israeli delegation slipped into France: Dayan, Peres, Foreign Minister Golda Meir, and Transport Minister Moshe Carmel.

Between secret visits to France, Dayan was supervising reprisal raids against Jordanian forts of the Arab Legion to blunt the mounting fedayeen raids into Israel. Britain, tied to Jordan by treaty, informed Ben-

Gurion that an Iraqi division was about to enter Jordan, and that if Israel should attack it, Britain would go to Jordan's aid with the Royal Air Force. Ben-Gurion replied that Israel would not accept Iraqi troops on its border, and the Iraqi move was called off.

Mollet invited Ben-Gurion to Paris on October 19. The Israeli delegation arrived secretly on October 22 and plunged into negotiations. Now, on the eve of war, the British were brought in. Foreign Secretary Selwyn Lloyd joined the talks that night, at first speaking only with the French in a separate room. When he finally met the Israelis, "His manner could not have been more antagonistic. His whole demeanor expressed distaste—for the place, the company and the topic."[6]

Nevertheless, the plot was concluded by October 24. H-hour for Israel would be Monday, October 29, 1956, at 5 p.m. Britain and France would demand that both Israeli and Egyptian forces leave the Canal Zone. Nasser had to refuse, and British and French planes would bomb Egyptian airfields on Wednesday, October 31. French troops would land in Egypt November 2.[7] Israeli pilots flew 24 Mystère jets to Israel, bringing Israel's combat plane strength to 94.

While the French, Israelis, and half-reluctant British planned "Operation Musketeer" in Paris on October 23, Egypt, Syria and Jordan announced a joint military command under Egypt, and Nasser sent a garrison of 2,000 men to Sharm el-Sheikh to close the Gulf of Aqaba to shipping destined for Israel's southern port, Eilat, an act of war.

That afternoon a demonstration assembled in Budapest at the statue of Polish General Jozef Bem, one of the heroes of the Hungarian revolution of 1848. The demonstrators, many of them students, set off from the statue for Parliament, not quite aware that they were marching into revolution.

Few Americans knew much about Hungary at the beginning of 1956. It was a forgotten country, almost sealed off from the West since the middle of World War II, first by the Nazis, then by the Soviets. Not many Western reporters passed through, just as none had been there when Hitler lost patience with Hungary's efforts to evade his grip and seized the country in 1944, installing a fascist government. When the revolution was over, a Hungarian refugee remarked that only one good thing had come out of it: "Now the Americans know that Budapest is not Bucharest."

Europeans knew more about Hungary; for decades they had traces of a guilty conscience about it. They knew Hungary as the civilized, one-time Western bulwark against the East that had, unaccountably, become the most-punished nation after World War I, deprived by the Treaty of Trianon in 1920 of nearly three-quarters of its territory, two-thirds of its population and one-third of its ethnic Magyar population to help to create Czechoslovakia and Yugoslavia and to reward Romania for joining the winning side in 1916.

The Hungarian revolution and the Suez crisis began building in parallel in February 1956, when the World Bank announced the Aswan Dam project and Khrushchev denounced Stalin before the 20th Party Congress in a speech intended to remain secret within Communist Party councils.

Khrushchev made his takeover bid for all of the powers once held by Lenin and Stalin on February 25, 1956, with an emotional denunciation of Stalin's crimes, a shocking heresy, to the Party Congress in Moscow, still a city almost closed to outsiders.

West Germany's Gehlen Organization quickly obtained the text of Khrushchev's speech.[8] This organization was financed by the CIA and still flew the American flag over its headquarters in Pullach, near Munich, not yet having become the West German *Bundesnachrichtendienst*. At the urging of Frank Wisner, the CIA's chief of covert operations, who had played a role in co-opting the Gehlen Organization after the war and had founded Radio Free Europe in 1949, the text of Khrushchev's speech was broadcast on RFE and on Radio Liberty, both headquartered in Munich.

Even before the decision to broadcast Khrushchev's speech there had been rumblings in Poland, Hungary and in East Germany, which had gone through an abortive uprising three years earlier following Stalin's death. By the time of the Hungarian revolt, the Soviets had slipped two divisions of reinforcements into East Germany.

Eastern Europe's unrest was most apparent in Poland, where Boleslaw Beirut, the Soviet-installed president and Communist Party leader, died in March, throwing open his succession. In June, just after the RFE broadcasts of Khrushchev's speech, workers in Poznan staged a general strike that grew into bloody riots. Poles demanded free elections, bread, and the departure of Soviet occupation troops. In August, the Poles got a compromise: the rehabilitation of Wladyslaw Gomulka, the World War II underground Communist leader who had been purged in 1948.

While Poles rioted for "bread and freedom" in Poznan, Hungary's government in June announced that László Rajk, the Communist interior minister who had been executed after a show trial in October 1949 during the Soviet-directed anti-Tito purges that swept Eastern Europe, had been rehabilitated secretly the previous December. Rajk's widow was made the heroine of the hour. Hungarians knew that Rajk had been as ruthless as the other Soviet-installed interior ministers in the East bloc, and they had little sympathy for him, but he had been juridically killed for the wrong reasons, and his rehabilitation was an occasion for raising other grievances against the Communists.

In late June, several thousand Hungarians jammed into the newly reopened Belvárosi Cafe and the building housing it to hear a discussion evening called by the Petöfi Circle, a literary branch of the Communist youth organization. Several members of the Communist Party Central Committee showed up and heard demands for the resignation of Party boss Mátyás Rákosi from speakers including Tibor Déry, a Communist author who had been expelled from the party during a writers' revolt in 1955 that had gone unnoticed in the West. The government radio warned that "counter-revolutionary attitudes" would not be tolerated.[9]

In July, Khrushchev dismissed Rákosi, the hated Party boss, and Rákosi went to the Soviet Union on an extended vacation. Soviet Politburo member Mikhail Suslov had visited Hungary and recommended that Rákosi be replaced by Ernö Gerö, a doctrinaire Communist. In Vienna, a CIA agent tipped Edgar Clark, a *Time-Life* correspondent, that events around Rajk's rehabilitation and the Petöfi Circle were worth looking into. Clark filed a dispatch that he said predicted the Hungarian revolution, but *Time* editors in New York spiked the story.[10]

On October 7 about 200,000 Hungarians marched in a macabre funeral procession. Rajk and three other Communists executed in the purge were exhumed and their caskets reburied in the national cemetery. Budapest radio issued another warning: Troublemakers were forming around Imre Nagy, the former Communist premier who had been expelled from the party in January.

A week later Nagy was readmitted to the party at a meeting of the Central Committee after he assured the members in a letter: "I declare myself in agreement with the Leninist principle of democratic centralism. I thereby regard Party decisions as binding on me, also when I am not in agreement with them in part or in whole."[11] Budapest radio announced that Nagy's expulsion had been illegal, and it quoted him as saying that political freedom would be the guarantee of progress.

In Warsaw, the Polish Communist Party's Central Committee met on October 19 to select a new leadership in the aftermath of the Poznan riots. A Tupolov-104, the Soviet Union's newest jet airliner, with Khrushchev, Molotov, Lazar Kaganovich and Anastas Mikoyan, appeared over Warsaw's airport, requesting clearance to land. The Polish flight controllers kept the plane flying in circles before authorizing a landing.

A furious Khrushchev was driven to an angry meeting with Polish Communist leaders in Belweder Palace. The Poles demanded equality and sovereignty as members of the Socialist camp, but they raised no challenge to Marxism-Leninism. They also wanted Gomulka, out of jail since April and readmitted to the party in August, on the Politburo. Once Khrushchev became convinced that Gomulka did not represent a threat to Soviet hegemony, he endorsed him as the new party leader and flew back to Moscow on October 20. Gomulka was made party First Secretary, and the Soviet overlord of Poland, Marshal Konstantin Rokossovsky, was dropped from the Politburo.

At about that time a large group of Czechoslovakian tourists arrived in Budapest, almost all young men, filling up the downtown Astoria Hotel. Everyone in Budapest knew they were STB, Czechoslovakian interior ministry police. They were in the right place, Hungarians remarked. The Astoria once had been Gestapo headquarters.

The Poles appeared to have faced down the Soviets. Could they be bolder than Hungarians? The ethnic remark went around Budapest: "The Poles are behaving like Hungarians; the Hungarians are behaving like Czechs, and the Czechs are behaving like swine."

So, on October 23, the Hungarian demonstration began at the monument to a Polish general. The crowd moved first to Parliament, where Gerö appeared, haranguing, threatening and insulting the crowd until it grew unruly. He was whisked away in a car. The demonstrators moved on to the building housing Radio Kossuth, with a list of 16 demands to be read over the air. A committee of students entered the building and did not come out. When the crowd shouted threats to come in and get them, the Ávo—Államvédelmi Osztály, the Soviet-trained secret police—opened fire at about 8:30 p.m.

The crowd scattered, some of them carrying the wounded. It was not a panic, said a 20-year-old Hungarian who was there. "There was a sense of deliberation and inevitability about it. We went to a police station, and nobody stopped us when we took rifles out of the racks." The armed men and boys, almost all young, returned to the radio station, hunting Ávo men. The Hungarian revolution had started.

Gerö called for help from Soviet troops in barracks on the city's outskirts. Tanks clattered through the city to the radio and Parliament buildings. In the next days, Hungarian youths learned to leap on the tanks and smash gasoline bottles over the engine intake vents. There were tentative standoff encounters that went unresolved. Some Soviet soldiers declined to fight and sold their tanks to Hungarians. Unpredictably, others appeared to be friendly and then opened fire. The Hungarian military stayed aloof until the Soviet counter-attack on the city, November 4.

In Washington, the Hungarian revolution touched off around-the-clock crisis meetings. Wisner of the CIA was one of the few who believed that the United States could act in Hungary. He had participated in creating the Special Forces, a Green Beret outfit trained semi-secretly at Bad Tölz, West Germany, its recruits mostly East European refugees or émigrés. The unit had been trained as a cadre for the day the Eastern European satellites rose in revolt, and that day had come. The unit had advanced equipment from sophisticated communications to grenades disguised in food cans. Wisner argued that the unit should smuggle antitank weapons into Hungary and take leadership roles in coordinating Hungarian groups fighting in the streets. He was rebuffed; neutral Austria, the only access route, had almost no defenses, and the Soviets had evacuated the eastern part of Austria only the year before.

In Israel, Ben-Gurion had just returned from secret tripartite talks in Paris with a timetable for war on Egypt. On October 25 Israel's cabinet ordered mobilization, its scope unannounced, ostensibly to meet the threat of Jordanian and Syrian troops on its borders, the Egyptian emplacement of 6-inch and 3-inch guns at Sharm el-Sheikh and the new Egyptian-Jordanian-Syrian joint military command. Then as now, Israel's armed forces were mostly reserves, and the United States could not ascertain whether the mobilization was partial and precautionary or total.

On the day Israel mobilized, Jordan brought a complaint before the UN Security Council because of a heavy Israeli reprisal raid at Kalikala, on the Israeli-Jordanian border, on October 11. The Security Council had been seized of the Suez Canal question since October 5, and the Jordanian initiative reopened the debate.

Suez preempted the United Nations agenda just as sketchy information from the revolt in Budapest began to reach the Western public. Some important news organs, including the *Times,* still were reporting that Soviet troops had put down riots there.

The United States government learned definitely on October 26 that Israel's mobilization was total, and the media reported that Hungary was in full-scale revolution.

For the next two days, with increasing urgency, Eisenhower cabled appeals to Ben-Gurion that Israel take no forcible action against Egypt. On both days copies of his cables to Ben-Gurion were sent to Eden in London and Mollet in Paris.

Eisenhower and Dulles had plenty of evidence that the Israelis, French and British were on the verge of an attack on Egypt, but Dulles was reluctant to believe it. Allen Dulles had reported that the attack was being planned for just after the November 6 election. As of October 20, French parliamentary deputies had been telephoning the U.S. Embassy in Paris with the news.[12] Dulles' disbelief had remained like that of Eden's initial reaction when Selwyn Lloyd had first told him of prospective French-Israeli collusion: "What? Israel attack Egypt? Don't be stupid."[13]

The British, French and Israeli governments and intelligence services almost managed to keep the secret from their American counterparts, but the long cooperation between American and British military men could not be denied. Leonard Mosley reported that "practically every senior general, admiral and air marshal in the British armed forces was keeping the U.S. Joint Chiefs of Staff informed of every move they were making."[14]

On October 27, as lightly armed Hungarians were tank-hunting in Budapest, Admiral Arleigh H. Burke, Chief of Naval Operations, stopped Dulles after a meeting of the National Security Council. Burke had spoken by telephone with Lord Louis Mountbatten, First Lord of the Admiralty, in London, and Mountbatten had told him that British preparations at Malta for the invasion were in a terrible mess.

Burke told Dulles that the British were ready to go, but they would not be able to invade properly because their ships were slow and their landing craft insufficient.

"For God's stake, let's give them the craft. Give them ours. They're over there. They've got to make this thing successful."

"We can't," Dulles said.[15]

Dulles and Eisenhower had been undercutting the French and British steadily since Nasser seized the canal in July, a holding action, impeding and delaying any military moves or overt threats, keeping the American position equivocal, but distancing themselves from the "colonial powers." Eden and Harold Macmillan, his Chancellor of the Exchequer, both wartime colleagues of Eisenhower, were given reason to believe that Eisenhower would not turn on them, and Macmillan had told U.S. special envoy Robert Murphy shortly after the canal seizure that Nasser would have to be chased out of Egypt.

No American decision had been made when Burke's report to Dulles brought it home to him that Egypt was about to be invaded. The Joint Chiefs met under Admiral Arthur Radford and, according to an officer present, "were all agreed that the Suez crisis was a good occasion to do nothing at all."[16] The Joint Chiefs had monitored and studied the crisis throughout its development. They were unanimous that the Soviets could not intervene at that distance, that Nasser should not have leverage on oil flow, Europe's financial structure or military-basing arrangements, and that toppling Nasser was an excellent idea. They were aware that Nasser was subverting Arab governments both on his own and as a surrogate of the Soviets.

At the news of the Israeli drive into the Gaza Strip and Sinai desert on October 29, the National Security Council met immediately under Eisenhower.

"Dulles wasn't there," said George Keegan, Jr., an Air Force officer and Eisenhower's military aide. "He came in later, his hair disheveled, collar unbuttoned, completely unlike himself. He was dying of cancer, but he didn't know it yet, and he went in to Eisenhower.

"I heard him say to the President, 'Ike,'—and I knew that meant something. He never addressed the President that way, except for that one time, as far as I know. He said, 'Ike, you have got to do something.' He went on, saying that for 170 years the United States had been a beacon of justice and independence in the world, not only to Arabs but to all the people in the world, and that Eisenhower had a responsibility to all the world to stop this attack.

"Eisenhower told him, 'By golly, you're right, Foster,' and that was it. Just like that. A disastrous decision we still are paying for."

Arleigh Burke had alerted the Sixth Fleet in the Mediterranean after Dulles had told him that the United States could not help the allies. When the Sixth Fleet commander asked, "Who is the enemy?" Burke could not give an answer.

On a troopship in the Mediterranean, a bright and eager young Marine officer was ready to fight anyone. Lieutenant Daniel Ellsberg was ordered to plan an amphibious landing—an invasion—at Haifa. Ellsberg's forebears were Russian Jews, but his parents had left the religion to become Christian Scientists, and he had no particular sense of Jewish identity or identification with Israelis. But, highly educated and politically aware, he knew that a landing at Haifa would be resisted with everything the Israelis could throw at the invaders. He was relieved when his troopship was diverted to evacuate American civilians from Alexandria.[17] The experience must have suggested to him that the President of the United States, being of doubtful sanity, had too much power, a theme he would develop later when he took world history into his own hands in a decision perhaps as fateful as Dulles'.

In West Germany, the U.S. 7th Army had denied to correspondents that any alerts were ordered because of the Hungarian revolution. But with the Israeli invasion of Gaza and the Sinai, the Armed Forces Network broadcast orders for soldiers and airmen on leave to return to their posts. The broadcasts specified that they were not being alerted over Hungary, but over allied designs on Suez.

Eisenhower, whose warm, easy grin charmed much of the world, was a general officer who could unleash searing anger and icy disdain, and he loosed both at Anthony Eden over the telephone to London. Eden had not informed him, and the United States would go directly to the United Nations Security Council.

On the morning of October 30 Ambassador Henry Cabot Lodge appeared before the Security Council to lash Israel, demand its withdrawal from the Sinai and to warn that no other nation "should take advantage of the situation for any selfish interests." Soviet Ambassador Arkady Sobolov took pleasure in agreeing with the United States, but he had news for Lodge. The news agencies, Sobolov said, had just reported that Britain and France had sent simultaneous ultimata to Israel and Egypt to stand back from the Canal, proving that "these aggressive circles" were in collusion with Israel.

In contrast with the meeting of the Security Council on October 14, when the Soviet Union vetoed the Anglo-French proposal for a Canal Users' Association, the United States now was in competition with the Soviets in demanding a ceasefire and withdrawal of Israeli forces, with explicit warnings to Britain and France.

Britain never had used its veto, harboring hopes that the UN would develop along the lines of the mother of Parliaments, but now it cast a veto—against a U.S. resolution. Worse, the United States cast the decisive vote in a procedural motion not subject to veto to move the debate to the General Assembly under a provision called "uniting for peace," which the United States had used to avoid Soviet vetos during the Korean war. The procedure purports to make General Assembly resolutions binding and not merely advisory. Of the two decisions the General Assembly would make, one turned out to be binding on Britain, France and Israel, and the other turned out to be nonbinding on the Soviet Union.

Dulles appeared before the special session of the General Assembly on November 1 to present the U.S. resolution on Suez, which urged an immediate ceasefire in Egypt and asked that the assembly remain in emergency session until compliance. It passed 64 to 5. Britain then reported that the Egyptian air force had been destroyed.

In contrast to the speed and decisiveness displayed by the Americans over Suez at the UN, nothing had been done about Hungary. When the Hungarian revolution broke out, the Security Council met immediately, heard Western condemnations and then adjourned without taking action.

As the General Assembly prepared to meet on November 1 over Suez amid tense talk in the corridors of World War III, the government of Imre Nagy in Budapest took an unusual step. Having no delegation in New York that he could trust, Nagy opened the first direct telex communication between a government and the UN Secretariat. The line was kept open for two hours while Nagy's cabinet met, drew up a proclamation repudiating Hungary's membership in the Warsaw Pact and asked that the General Assembly "consider the defense of Hungary's neutrality by the four great powers." Nagy sent the message shortly after noon, New York time, after repeated conferences with the Soviet Ambassador in Budapest, Yuri Andropov.

The Nagy appeal provided a legal basis for UN action, but it did not come up at the marathon General Assembly session. Cuba's UN delegate, Dr. Emilio Nuñez-Portuondo, attempted on his own to call a Security Council meeting to consider Nagy's appeal, but he was unsuccessful. He later received 11,000 congratulatory telegrams and letters.

While Dulles, "with a heavy heart," told the General Assembly that the United States would be compelled to vote against its allies on Suez, a long Soviet armored column rolled through Kisvárda, and another tank division took position 50 miles northeast of Budapest. The Soviet Embassy in Budapest announced that the tanks around three airfields near Budapest were there only to protect the evacuation of Soviet personnel.

The General Assembly still was meeting at 1:25 a.m. November 2, when a Reuters dispatch arrived with detailed information on Soviet troop movements into Hungary. Dulles, drawn and haggard, spoke again at 4 a.m., and in closing recalled that the matter of Hungary still was before the Security Council.

The next day Dulles was rushed to Walter Reed Hospital in Washington, where surgeons removed a section of perforated large intestine. Dulles would live three more years.

After the all-night session, UN delegates were to have a day of rest on November 2. But the United States, Britain and France, together for the moment, called a Security Council meeting on Hungary for the evening. Nagy sent a second direct telex appeal to Secretary-General Dag Hammarskjold: "I request Your Excellency to call upon the Great Powers to recognize the neutrality of Hungary, and ask the Security Council to instruct the Soviet and Hungarian governments to start negotiations immediately."

Lodge delivered a spirited condemnation of Soviet actions in Hungary, but he mystified reporters by failing to call for a special session of the General Assembly.

On the morning of November 3, nothing happened at the United Nations. A final General Assembly session on Suez was scheduled for the evening, when the dispatch of UN troops to Egypt would be considered. But the persistent Cuban delegate, Nuñez-Portuondo, insisted on an evening Security Council meeting on Hungary. The council met, and Lodge finally introduced an American resolution. Yugoslavia moved for immediate adjournment, on the ground that Hungary and the Soviet Union appeared to be negotiating.

Lodge agreed. "We believe," he said, "that adjournment for a day or two would give a real opportunity to the Hungarian government to carry out its announced desire to arrange for an orderly and immediate evacuation of all Soviet troops."

Britain, France, Australia and Nationalist China argued against delay in the face of the Soviet military buildup, but their procedural effort to schedule a Security Council meeting for the next morning failed when Lodge cast the deciding vote against it.

At 4:24 a.m. November 4, Hungary time, Soviet artillery and planes struck Budapest, concentrating on Hungarian army barracks. It was 10:24 p.m. November 3 in New York, where the Security Council had adjourned and the General Assembly still shook with a storm of debate over Suez. Shortly after midnight, a group of Hungarian exiles led by Monsignor Béla Varga tried to reach Lodge at the UN. After a scuffle with an American official, UN guards removed them.

In Budapest, the Soviet KGB chief, Ivan Serov, had arrested General Pál Maléter, Nagy's new defense minister, while he was negotiating at Soviet headquarters at Tököl, on Csepel island. Serov similarly would seize Nagy on November 22, as Nagy and his party left the sanctuary of the Yugoslav mission under a Soviet guarantee of safe passage. Maléter, Nagy and others would be executed secretly in Romania in June 1958.

At 1 a.m. November 4, Australia interrupted the General Assembly debate on Suez to report the Soviet attack and to demand an immediate Security Council meeting. The Hungarians would fight on in Budapest for days, and for two months in the provinces, but it was over. Now the Security Council took up Hungary's case, passed it to the General Assembly session, and the Soviet Union was duly ordered out of Hungary by a vote of 50 to 8, with 15 nations abstaining.

In 1956, no one doubted that Eisenhower would trounce Adlai Stevenson for the presidency again, as he had in 1952. The Hungary and Suez crises were an unwelcome bonus, bringing out voters to keep the experienced commander in office. Stevenson made his chances worse by advocating, at a time when the world appeared to be blowing up, an end to the military draft and the unilateral suspension of U.S. nuclear testing to see if the Soviets could be persuaded to follow the example.

Eisenhower ran an above-the-battle campaign, checking out of it entirely in September, when he suffered a heart attack. That left the campaign as the responsibility of Vice President Nixon. Nixon's role was to support administration policy whatever it was; stepping out ahead of Eisenhower with a policy pronouncement that would not have amused the general. As the prospective President if Eisenhower's labile health failed further, Nixon was more than ever Target No. 1 of Stevenson's liberals. Dulles was Target No. 2.

In a speech at Flint, Michigan, October 17, Stevenson called Nixon "a man of many masks," "shifty," "rash and inexperienced," "a demagogue. . . who spreads ill will instead of good will abroad" and "whose trademark is slander." Stevenson's attack went beyond any Presidential campaign invective in this century, and Stevenson was chided for it by the media, which, however gave the adjectives prominent display.

A few days before the election, Eisenhower surfaced in Philadelphia to deliver the *coup de grace*. He said that Stevenson's proposal for renouncing nuclear tests in a period of world crisis was "a design for disaster." The idea proved disadvantageous later, in calmer times, when the Soviets picked it up as their own.

Nixon that day distinguished himself by a statement that confirmed Stevenson's characterization of his shiftiness on foreign policy issues. Under American leadership, the UN had just condemned Britain and France, and Nixon said: "For the first time in history, we have shown independence of Anglo-French policies toward Asia and Africa which seemed to us to reflect the colonial tradition. This declaration of independence has had a clarifying effect throughout the world."

Nixon retracted that statement several times when he was out of office, but Anthony Eden did not forgive it. Nixon wrote in his memoirs: "Eisenhower and Dulles put heavy pressure on Britain, France and Israel to withdraw their forces from Suez. In retrospect I believe that our actions were a serious mistake. . . I have often felt that if the Suez crisis had not arisen during the heat of a presidential election campaign a different decision would have been made." Nixon also believed that the West should have retaliated for the attack on Hungary.[18]

Dulles had built an imposing reputation as Secretary of State when the world collapsed around him in October 1956. He had been born to the job, the grandson of John Watson Foster, Secretary of State of President Benjamin Harrison, and nephew of Robert M. Lansing, Secretary of State to Woodrow Wilson. His father, the Presbyterian Reverend Allen Macy Dulles, was not wealthy, but both he and Dulles' mother, Edith Foster Dulles, were at home among the foreign policy elite. Dulles grew up around diplomats, Senators, lawyers and bankers who made foreign policy.

At 19, Dulles had been permitted by his uncle to play a small role at the Second Hague Peace Conference, and during World War I, when Dulles was 29, he accomplished a mission to Central America to dampen sympathy for Germany there. After World War I, Dulles accompanied Bernard Baruch as an observer at the Versailles peace treaty negotiations and, along with John Maynard Keynes, warned that vengeful reparations would make of Germany a menacing nation.

During World War II, Dulles wrote *Six Pillars of Peace,* a treatise for the National Council of Churches, in which he proposed in 1943 a United Nations organization. He negotiated with Japan and its neighbors a peace treaty without crippling reparations in 1950, becoming a midwife to the rebirth of both Japan and West Germany as modern industrial giants. His warm friendship with Konrad Adenauer helped ease West Germany's entry into NATO, which would have been a hollow shell if West German Social Democrats had blocked it.

Dulles was respected but not loved; his Calvinist righteousness alienated many. Eisenhower bowed to his expertise but thought he was "a bit sticky" and "takes getting used to." Dulles had been a sponsor of Alger Hiss when he was nominated to be president of the Carnegie Endowment for International Peace, as was James Reston of the *Times.* When Dulles became convinced that Hiss was a traitor, he said so, at a time when Reston still believed Hiss' guilt had not been proven.

Although Dulles was a charter member of the bipartisan Eastern foreign policy establishment, he was not a State Department man; his frequent service had been *ad hoc,* on leave from his Wall Street law firm. When Republicans returned to power after 20 years in 1953, the pool of prospective Secretaries of State was a mere puddle, with Dulles and John J. McCloy the biggest frogs in it. Dulles was almost 65 when he took over a State Department full of Democrats.

The difficulty of ending the Korean war and the impending Communist takeover of Indochina had made Dulles a vocal anti-Communist in 1956, when Dulles came under heavy fire from the detente faction of the foreign policy establishment, including the *Times.* Dulles had shocked and appalled with his talk of "rollback" and "liberation" in

Eastern Europe, "massive retaliation" to meet any Soviet attack and his boasting in a *Life Magazine* interview that he was not afraid to "go to the brink."

In newspapers across the country, Dulles' brinksmanship was ridiculed by columnists and cartoonists taking their cues from the *Times* and *Washington Post* cartoonist Herbert Block, who portrayed Dulles as a not-very-bright war monger.

As the 1956 election approached, *Times* editors had a small problem of endorsement. The editors liked W. Averell Harriman, Stevenson's prospective Secretary of State, who was confident that he could deal with the Soviet Union on a basis of cooperation. *Times* editors opposed Dulles, charging that his strident anti-communism was destroying the bipartisan basis of foreign policy. The *Times* endorsed the Eisenhower-Nixon ticket for the second time, but it would be its last endorsement of a Republican ticket.

When Allen Dulles at CIA decided to broadcast Khrushchev's anti-Stalin speech, brother Foster published the speech as a State Department document, with minor deletions. The *Times,* more intimate with both the CIA and State Department than any other news medium, received the 50-page text in a leak one day early. The *Times* summarized Khrushchev's charges against Stalin on June 3, then printed the text over four pages on June 4.

Most of the media hailed the release as a propaganda coup and a devastating indictment of the Soviet system, but *Times* editors had misgivings at such a heavy dose of anti-communism. Even though the *Times* had a scoop, Reston denigrated the operation in a news-page commentary:

The Victory of Dulles
A Critique on His View that West Spurred
Reds' Woes and on His Gloating Over Rift.[19]

Reston charged that Dulles was taking too much credit for internal change in the Communist world, and he deplored that the State Department had released "the private speech of the political head of another government," a rare solicitude for a secret document. Reston noted that "It is a long time since Mr. Dulles has had any victories to claim." Reston did approve that Dulles had "praised the courage of Marshal Tito and thus encouraged the development of Titoism."

Some of the flavor of the liberals' feelings toward Dulles, the "card-carrying Christian," was preserved in 1973 by Townsend Hoopes in his *The Devil and John Foster Dulles,* which was strongly promoted by the *Times.*[20] By 1973, the Democrats could look back on a long string of foreign policy catastrophes of their own, and Hoopes found that the responsibility for institutionalizing the Cold War and getting the United States into Vietnam lay with Dulles. His book is a goldmine of quotations but also a treasury of the author's misjudgments.

Oddly, Hoopes believed, and cited British Labor MP Richard Crossman to prove it, that Nasser did not want offensive weapons in early 1955 because the Middle East was "drifting toward peace."

Hoopes reported: "On the night of February 28, however, there occurred a savage, unprovoked Israeli raid on Gaza which transformed the hopeful possibilities for Egyptian-Israeli relations and sent a long shock wave down the corridor of time that came to its smashing climax twenty months later in the Anglo-French-Israeli attack on the Suez Canal."[21]

The Gaza raid had been strongly provoked by "Egyptian fedayeen" raids that had killed seven Israelis and injured 24 in the previous six months. As Israel reported in the UN, between the 1949 armistice and the 1956 war, Israel had suffered 1,335 civilian casualties in such raids, all hailed in the Arab press. In the Gaza raid, commandos ambushed Egyptian soldiers rushing to the scene of a bomb blast, killing 37. Israel's policy was to retaliate against military targets, not villages. To suggest that the Gaza raid caused Nasser to seek offensive weapons and led to the ensuing wars is a breathtaking notion.

Similarly, Hoopes dismissed the Hungarian revolution as misguided. He believed that Khrushchev on October 30 "made the momentous decision to offer to negotiate the full withdrawal of Red Army units from Hungary and establish a new basis of Soviet relationships throughout Eastern Europe—i.e., 'noninterference in each other's internal affairs.' "[22] The Hungarians, Hoopes believed, "broke the cease-fire," ruining Eastern Europe's bright hopes.

About the same caliber of argument was being employed against Dulles before Hungary and Suez, but the liberals had him dead to rights on one point: he had boasted too much of what he was doing to the Communists.

When the Hungarian revolution exploded, the American government and people gave no thought to backing up Dulles' talk of rollback and liberation. Dulles found himself exposed as a fraud just as the foreign policy establishment he had grown up with was ranged in an accusing circle around him. The European perception of Dulles will do: He had been trying to soften his hard line image by cozying up to Nasser in disregard of the French and British, and when Hungary revolted, he felt a compulsion to act. Belying his image as a stoic, he turned the world's most powerful nation on its allies.

The man in the street knew that something was terribly wrong, but the events and personalities involved were complex. Much of the media, as always declining to accept a failure of nerve on the part of an American leader, accepted the liberals' explanation: the mistake had been made when Dulles reneged on the Aswan Dam loan.

There were eight daily newspapers in New York City in 1956, enough competition to keep the *Times'* anti-anti-Communist ideology from being set in concrete. The *Times* sent squads of correspondents to Central Europe and the Middle East to reinforce correspondents there and gave them generous space. The surprise of the two crises helped keep *Times* reporting straight, and there are no distortions in the *Times'* reports or commentary on Suez and Hungary.[23]

Times back numbers show, however, a discord between the *Times'* dislike of Dulles and its tacit approval of his inaction on Hungary and his actions on Suez.

Times editors believed strongly in detente, and they had been encouraged when Georgi Malenkov, Stalin's first nominal successor, called for "peaceful coexistence" in his speech the day after Stalin died in 1953. Staunchly anti-colonialist, the *Times* tilted toward Nasser and remained equivocal toward Israel.

The newspaper played the Hungarian revolution second to the Suez crisis throughout, in contrast with, for example, *Time,* which made the Hungarian freedom fighter man of the year.

There were some practical reasons. Communications with Hungary were chancy, and John MacCormac, the correspondent there, was not permanently stationed in Budapest. The *Times* in 1956 was fixated on Poland, where it had a stationed correspondent, Sydney Gruson, backed up by his bright wife, Flora Lewis. Facts from Poland blocked out sketchier information from Hungary, filtered through Belgrade or Vienna, and the *Times* often made Hungary the shirt tail to the Poland story.

The *Times* did not want to believe that Hungary was in revolt, and it declared the rioting over the day it began. Only much later did *Times* readers learn that the Hungarians drove the Soviets from Budapest in the first week.

The events in Poland, while menacing and even bloody at Poznan, still gave reason for optimism. Wladyslaw Gomulka was known to be bold, presumed to be a nationalist and might not be corrupt. Communists were, after all, people, and the *Times* was perennially on the lookout for "another Tito." (Poles also said that Gomulka was stupid, and in 1968 he, along with Walter Ulbricht and Pyotr Shelest, would lead the chorus demanding the invasion of Czechoslovakia.) The *Times* hoped for good Communists who would make the system supportable, now that Stalin was dead. Because of *Times* reports, Congress offered Poland $500 million in feed grains, on the theory that Polish farmers who could keep their livestock might also keep their independence—not a bad idea. Correspondents remarked that Gruson was the only one of their breed who had $500 million at his disposal.

When the Hungarians revolted against communism as such, in toto, this development was simply all wrong, and the *Times* didn't believe it.

Throughout the Hungarian revolution, Suez claimed the banner headlines more often, and when Hungary made it into the *Times'* heavy type, it usually was linked with Poland.

On October 24 the revolt was announced in a four-column, off-play headline:

> Police Fire on Hungarians
> Marching Against Regime;
> Poles Say Soviets Yield.

The next day Hungary got a banner headline, shared with Poland:

> SOVIET UNITS QUELLING REVOLT IN HUNGARY,
> BUT SOME RIOTING CONTINUES IN BUDAPEST;
> WARSAW STUDENTS   SHOUT AGAINST RUSSIA.

The *Times* ended the revolt again that day, in an editorial saying that the Russians had "won a battle but lost the battle for men's minds."

On October 27 *Times* correspondent MacCormac beat the communications problem and the *Times* finally had it right, days behind European publications: "What began here Tuesday as a demonstration turned that same night into a revolt and yesterday became a war that was still raging today," a classically neat catch-up.

Still, *Times* editorials continued to lament the lost revolt.

The attack on Suez October 29 knocked Hungary out of the top headlines until the Soviets returned to Budapest on November 4. The *Times* caught up again with a heartfelt editorial.

We Accuse

We accuse the Soviet government of murder. We accuse it of the foulest treachery and basest deceit known to man. We accuse it of having committed so monstrous a crime against the Hungarian people yesterday that its infamy can never be forgiven or forgotten. . . .

The sympathy was real enough, but the *Times* also was bitterly disappointed at Khrushchev, the hope of peaceful coexistence, and the *Times'* anger gradually cooled.

Since the *Times* disapproved of Dulles, yet approved of the policy of retreat as it unfolded, it found a solution in Henry Cabot Lodge, glorifying his essentially dog-in-the-manger role at the United Nations.

Years later, on January 16, 1961, Lodge wrote a defensive letter to Imre Kovács, editor of the *Hungarian Quarterly.* Replying to an attack on his actions at the UN by Senator Thomas J. Dodd (D-Connecticut), Lodge insisted that on November 3, 1956, he was acting in accordance with Nagy's wishes.

> Would Senator Dodd have the United States ignore the announced desire of the Hungarian government to arrange for an orderly and immediate evacuation of all the Soviet troops?...The fact that a short time later it became clear to the Hungarian government that the Soviet Union was lying does not alter the fact that on November 3 the Hungarian government had some hope that the Soviets were telling the truth. This was a decision which it was the Hungarian government's to make....

But Nagy's telexes had pleaded for UN help, and for talks under UN directives.

The *Times* stamped its approval on the U.S. decisions at the UN in an unsigned accolade to Lodge on November 6, 1956:

U.N. Counterpuncher
Henry Cabot Lodge, Jr.

The profile did not feature Lodge's accomplishments of preceding days. Instead, it dredged up an episode of some months earlier in which Lodge had bested a Soviet delegate, Semyon Tsarapkin (who later made monkeys of the U.S. negotiators of the limited nuclear test-ban treaty).

"For what purpose does the gentleman from the Soviet Union seek the floor?" the *Times* quoted Lodge as asking. The report went on to recount how Tsarapkin "flew into a great rage and bellowed: 'I'm not a gentleman; I'm a delegate!' "

The *Times* reported: "Mr. Lodge gave the angry Russian what might be termed the Back Bay, or codfish, deep freeze. 'I had hoped that the two were not mutually exclusive,' he remarked, gazing at the fingernails of his right hand."

While the *Times* was admiring Lodge, Hungarian refugees, including much of the border city of Sopron, fled into Austria. The Suez Canal was closed; Nasser had scuttled every ship in it. Israel, in a sharp, 50-

minute final battle, captured Sharm el-Sheikh. In the Sinai, Israeli troops found vast weapons parks, ordnance depots and workshops at El Arish and Rafah, in sophisticated Soviet-engineered defenses, awaiting a move at Nasser's discretion. Eden, ill and disgraced, resigned, leaving his successor, Macmillan, to struggle with the rejuvenated left wing of the opposition Labor Party.

Eden wrote bitterly that the U.S. resolution on Suez was stronger than the earlier Soviet resolution, on which Britain had abstained rather than veto. He believed that U.S. actions had encouraged Bulganin to threaten Britain with nuclear destruction.

"The course of the Suez Canal crisis was decided by the American attitude toward it," Eden wrote. "If the United States government had approached this issue in the spirit of a true ally, they would have done everything in their power, short of the use of force, to support the nations whose economic security depended upon the freedom of passage through the Suez Canal."[24]

Eden's predictions in his messages to Eisenhower and his talks with Dulles came true. On July 14, 1958, Brigadier Abdul Karim Kassem, a Nasserite, led a revolution in Iraq. King Faisal, his family, his cabinet ministers and friends were murdered and their bodies dragged naked through the streets of Baghdad behind truckloads of revolutionaries. Eden's old friend, Nuri es Said, was among the mutilated bodies.

That revolt aroused Eisenhower to land Marines on the beaches of Lebanon, where they picked their way between bikini-clad bathers to the amusement of the international press. The media notwithstanding, the landing was a success. In 1975–76 the revolt of roughly the same forces would reach Lebanon, but the United States, paralyzed by defeat in Vietnam, took no interest.

Nasser moved into Yemen in 1962, using MiG fighters and Ilyushin bombers against loyalists fighting back after a Nasserite revolt. His planes dropped mustard gas on the Saudi town of Najran. Britain abandoned its Aden base, and two Yemens evolved. South Yemen became the first Marxist Arab state wholly subservient to the Soviet Union, its society patterned after that of its East German insructors.

In 1969, Colonel Moammer Khadafy overthrew King Idris in Libya, as Eden had predicted some Nasserite would, and, in 1970, Khadafy evicted the United States from the key Wheelus Air Base as the British had been evicted from Suez.

Some of those who encountered Nasser's charisma believed it was an irresistible force on the side of history, and the Suez outcome was preordained. But Nasser attempted to leap from leader of an underdeveloped country to empire builder, aiming to become a Saladin, a fantasy. His insistence that Israel be eliminated put him on a collision course with all of the Western nations of his period. In 1967 he repeated precisely his actions of 1956: he stockpiled arms at El Arish and Rafah, cut off Israeli shipping to Eilat at Sharm el-Sheikh and sent troops to Israel's borders, with exactly the same results as in 1956.

Nasser was sure he would not fall under Soviet domination, but his imitators in Cuba, Yemen, Syria, Ethiopia and elsewhere did. At Nasser's death in 1970 he was highly dependent on the Soviets, and it was touch and go whether he would be succeeded by Ali Sabry, his close aide and the Soviets' man in Egypt. Anwar Sadat won out, foiled a coup by Sabry and jailed him, apparently permanently.

The great Middle East event of 1956 was not the seizure of the canal or the invasion of Egypt, it was the introduction of Soviet arms and influence into the Middle East and Africa via Nasser. The Israelis, British and French had every right to try to stop it. The United States had no moral right to ease the unrestricted spread of Soviet weapons.

If Suez still stirs feelings, they are mere twitches compared with the passions that Hungary still evokes in those who were close to the revolt. The Soviets cruelly punished Hungary.[25]

In failing to move against the Soviets, at least diplomatically and economically, the United States abandoned Eastern Europe, the marvelously different little nations that had so much to offer the world in talent, intelligence and variety of culture. Cultural accomplishment was blighted; no new Bartóks or Kodálys are in sight. Deserting the sorely tried, wrung-out nation of Hungary was an act of debasement that demoralized the United States more than it recognized.

Frank Wisner believed that if the Hungarians could have held out a few more days, an anguish would have mounted in the United States that would have made the pressure to support the revolt irresistible. He permitted Radio Free Europe to broadcast messages past the logical end of the revolt, including the infamous "Hold on! Help is coming!" on November 6. The United States denied that any such broadcast had been made, blaming it on a mobile transmitter of NTS—Narodnyi Trudovoy Soyuz, or National Labor Union—a Russian émigré group that the CIA dropped as irresponsible. But Hungarians knew the voices of RFE announcers as well as Americans knew the voices of Walter Cronkite or John Chancellor. The West German government conducted an investigation of RFE tapes, delayed its report and finally let the issue die with equivocations.

Wisner, one of the CIA's founders and a former OSS agent in the Balkans, alarmed his friends with bizarre behavior in 1959 before he resigned; in 1961 he committed suicide.

A colorful sidelight to an otherwise desultory election campaign was the emergence of Senator John F. Kennedy of Massachusetts as a national figure. Stevenson decided not to choose his running mate, but to throw the nomination to the Democratic Convention. Kennedy, still recovering from two major back operations in 1954, had been angling for the vice-presidential nomination, and with Stevenson's decision he unleashed a sophisticated campaign for it. Senator Estes Kefauver of Tennessee, already a national figure through his Senate hearings on organized crime, barely was able to hold Kennedy off.

As it turned out, Kennedy had the best of all worlds. He had not expected the nomination, so he had lost nothing. He was not involved in the crushing defeat of the Stevenson-Kefauver ticket and was well-positioned for the next election.

Kennedy had looked terrible on television—gaunt, hollow-cheeked, his left eyelid drooping from the after-effects of radical surgery—but he had come over on television with striking appeal. Little known as a Senator because of his illnesses, but still a decorated World War II hero and a best-selling author, he represented in one glance a fighter who came back from disability, a cheerful and cooperative loser, and an object of sympathy for his unfortunate physical condition.

And 1956 presented Kennedy with an issue he would ride in the 1960 presidential campaign, "the decline of American prestige around the world." Kennedy, too, would have to cope with a charismatic revolutionary who landed on the coast of Cuba a month after Nasser's triumph at Suez: Fidel Castro.

Chapter II
The Cuban Revolution

*"The perfect Big Con is when the mark never knows
that he was taken. When it's all over, you've still got
his con."*

—Theme of "The Sting"

In the spring of 1956, while crises were building in the Middle East and
Eastern Europe, Herbert L. Matthews was predicting an explosion in
Cuba, not immediately, but one day not too far away. A distinguished
member of *The New York Times* editorial board, author and editorial
writer, Matthews liked Cubans and liked keeping up his Spanish on
visits to Havana. He detested Fulgencio Batista and all other *caudillos*
as he had detested Francisco Franco during the Spanish Civil War.

Matthews belonged to the first generation of American correspondents to use wireless—a pioneer and a trail blazer for those who would
follow. In 1936, he was the first correspondent, foreign or Italian, to
receive the Italian War Cross for valor in accompanying Italian forces
in their invasion of Ethiopia. The anti-fascist Matthews was thereupon
charged with being pro-fascist. Four years later, Benito Mussolini ex-

pelled him from Italy for reporting that the Axis was out to defeat President Roosevelt in the 1940 elections, but Mussolini relented and readmitted him to Italy after two months.

Reporting the Spanish Civil War from the Loyalist side, Matthews was the first to report that Italian fascists were fighting alongside the Nationalists, and was furious when *Times* editors changed "Italians" to "insurgents," ruining his news beat. Western correspondents were overwhelmingly anti-Franco, but Matthew's pro-Loyalist reporting was controversial. He reported Loyalist atrocities on at least one occasion, but as an aberration, a blot on an otherwise noble Loyalist record, as opposed to Franco's "systematic terror." Others were reporting widespread atrocities on both sides. Matthews refused to concede that Communists dominated the Loyalist side and insisted that the Russians had left Spain in 1937, a position he clung to in a subsequent book on the war. In 1939, the Catholic Editors' Association in the United States protested when the *Times* named Matthews head of its Rome bureau, where he also would cover the Vatican. Seventeen years after the civil war he revisited Spain and wrote, "The facts are that there was precious little communism in Spain when the civil war started and the Republican Government was at no time 'Red.' "[1]

Herman H. Dinsmore, who spent 31 years at the *Times,* in part concurrently with Matthews' 35 years there, felt strongly about Matthews and kept a clipping of a Matthews contribution to *Collier's* magazine in 1945: "All they (the Soviets) want is security. By refusing to share the secret of the atomic bomb we are bolstering Russian suspicions."[2]

Cuban politics always had been unruly, and the possibility of revolution was enhanced in 1955 with the attempted coup by Colonel Ramón Barquín. Barquín was imprisoned, but his *golpe* was the first crack in military loyalty to Batista since 1933.

In May 1956, Matthews predicted the Cuban revolution in a commentary in the Sunday *Times* Week in Review:

> Cuba is like a live volcano. Every now and then it is going to erupt.... 'Something is rotten' in any state that is continually blowing up.... General Batista has what it takes in Cuba— personal charm, quick intelligence, courage and tolerance. The tolerance is a willingness to let supporters milk the Treasury and rig elections.... Yet he cannot relax and he cannot really feel safe. The reason lies in the character of the Cubans. They have not made good use of their liberty, but they love and crave liberty. They were slowly and painfully evolving a democracy, but General Batista smashed the delicate structure that was being erected. The focus of resentment is in the student body, as it has

been throughout Cuban history. Students wrote some glorious pages in the wars of independence. . . .[3]

Matthews got along well with the *Times* correspondent in Havana, Ruby Hart Phillips, and joined her in covering the election of Batista, unopposed, as president in 1954. Mrs. Phillips had been through the bloody overthrow of General Gerardo Machado in 1933, and was sympathetic to young revolutionaries, whom she called "the boys."

Matthews' May 1956 commentary was inspired by a hopeless attack by young rebels on a garrison post at Matanzas, in which at least 15 rebels were killed and others wounded. It was an imitation of an earlier attack, unanimously called senseless, on the Moncado barracks in Santiago on July 26, 1953.

In the 1953 attack a 26-year-old Fidel Castro led a sizeable group of raiders including two women, all dressed in sergeants' uniforms, against Moncado, with diversionary attacks on Santiago's Palace of Justice and a barracks at Bayamo. Accounts of the attack vary widely, and most histories written during the period of Castro's ascendency report that his 158 men and two women hoped to surprise about a thousand soldiers. According to Andres Pérez-Chaumont, who was the lieutenant-colonel commanding Moncado barracks in 1953, Castro's force numbered around 295, and because of a carnival going on at the time, there were only 49 or 50 soldiers in the barracks. Pérez-Chaumont said he lost 21 men, including his aide standing next to him, and Castro lost 190 to 195 killed; about 70 were captured and about 30 to 40 escaped.[4] Legends created by the 26th of July Movement were another example of the victors writing history, according to Pérez-Chaumont. Only 32 rebels survived as prisoners to face trial, and Castro surrendered through the intervention of a priest after hiding out several days.[5]

At his trial, Castro delivered a passionate courtroom plea—"History will absolve me"—that he later printed as a pamphlet, the manifesto of his 26th of July Movement. Castro was sentenced to 15 years, his brother Raúl to 13. They were freed from the Isle of Pines prison after less than two years on May 15, 1955, under a Batista amnesty.

Under Batista's curious dictatorship, the released Castro was able to make statements to the press, return to Havana, consolidate a core there of the July 26th Movement—M26-7—and attempt to co-opt into his organization some of the welter of underground and semi-underground movements in the Havana political cauldron. The others were wary of Castro, his armed bodyguards and his "gangster reputation."[6] In 1955, Castro was the hero of Moncado, but he also was the crazy one who had led scores of this followers to their deaths and to prison.

Castro, never short of funds, flew to Mexico in July 1956, leaving behind a statement for the press: "In 1956, we shall be free or we shall be martyrs." Mexican police arrested him training in the brush with about 50 exiles and passed along the information to the U.S. government that Castro had been meeting with Communists there.

Teresa (Teté) Casuso, writer and occasional actress in Mexican films, heard that some young Cubans had been arrested and visited them in Mexico City's Immigration Prison. She found them a crude lot, using coarse language, but one struck her as a thoroughbred: "Fidel, calm, noble of bearing, stood out among them like a tower among hovels."[7] Castro and his group found haven with her, and she later withstood arrest and police grilling, lying about the weapons Castro had stored in her house.

Cuban exiles in the United States had pronounced the time ripe for revolution, and Castro joined them on a fund-raising tour of American cities, learning to know the nation he resented. He conferred with Carlos Prío Socarrás, the Cuban ex-president thrown out of Cuba by Batista and grudgingly allowed to live in Miami by U.S. authorities. With Prío's money, Castro bought for $15,000 the leaky yacht *Granma,* moored at Tuxpan, Mexico.

Frank País, a young Baptist school teacher from Santiago, a traditional revolutionary hotbed, visited Castro in Mexico, and coordinated an uprising timed to give maximum publicity and impact to Castro's return to Cuba. On November 30, 1956, País led about 300 men wearing uniforms and M26-7 armbands against Santiago's police headquarters, the Customs House, and port headquarters, while another group seized the Boniato prison and freed political prisoners. País' men killed a number of police and soldiers, burned the Customs House and withdrew. The next day País attacked again, burning the port headquarters. His losses were three men. Santiago was left in a state of panic.

Castro, with 81 men on the *Granma,* including his brother Raúl and the Argentine physician, Dr. Ernesto (Che) Guevara, arrived two days late and at the wrong spot on the coast of Oriente Province. Castro ran the yacht aground on December 2 on swampy land at the Playa de los Colorados, near Belic. Strafed by a Cuban fighter plane, the invaders broke up into small groups, lost most of their equipment and then were led astray by a guide while trying to push into the Sierra Maestra. Batista's army patrols located most of them on December 5, killing 24 and capturing others. Hunted by the army and air force for the next days, only 15 survived to reach the mountains, among them Castro,

Raúl, and Guevara.

In Havana, United Press reporter Francis McCarthy was told on December 2 that the Castro party had landed and had been wiped out. He reported that the bodies of Fidel and Raúl had been identified and buried.

The Castro invasion was marked down as a failure, and revolutionary activity in Havana subsided. Castro's handful of survivors, more than 500 miles from the capital, was preoccupied with staying alive, saved from starvation by the mountain bandit Cresencio Pérez, who claimed to have fathered 80 illegitimate children.

Nothing was heard from Castro for two months, although País sent him reinforcements from Santiago. There were several other guerrilla groups in mountains throughout the 800-mile-long island, and the Batista government said they were surrendering in droves. Havana's newspapers were reporting bright economic prospects, with a new international sugar deal and a new wave of tourists packing new international hotels. Ruby Hart Phillips, in touch with her "boys," thought it "looked as though the revolution was going to fail."[8]

Faustino Pérez, a Castro man in Havana, contacted Mrs. Phillips in February with the information that Castro was alive and wanted to be interviewed to prove it. Batista had reimposed censorship, so Castro was not interested in seeing a Cuban journalist. Mrs. Phillips conferred with Ted Scott, columnist for the *Havana Post* and stringer for NBC, who told here that Herbert Matthews had written to him that he might visit Cuba. She cabled Emanuel Freedman, the *Times* foreign editor, asking that Matthews come immediately. Then she coordinated arrangements with a Castro follower, Javier Pazos, son of Felipe Pazos, Cuba's leading economist and later president of Castro's National Bank.[9]

Matthews, then 57, arrived in Havana on February 9 as a tourist, with his wife for a cover, and traveled to the mountains with Javier Pazos and Faustino Pérez on February 15. After an exhausting climb into the mountains and an overnight wait, Matthews met Castro at dawn, conversing for three hours in whispers although there were no Batista troops within miles, and then "created for North Americans the legend of Castro, the hero of the mountains."[10]

Castro had only 18 men, but he had them moved around his rendevous point with Matthews, changing shirts and hats, to give Matthews the impression there were many more. Matthews did not see their camp.[11]

Matthews' series of three articles began on Page 1 of the *Times* on February 24, 1957. It was loaded with phrases that would serve as revolutionary slogans:

> Fidel Castro, the rebel leader of Cuba's youth, is alive and fighting hard and successfully in the rugged, almost impenetrable vastnesses of the Sierra Maestra. . . .

> This is the first sure news that Fidel Castro is alive and in Cuba. . . . This account will break the tightest censorship in the history of the Cuban Republic. . . . Havana does not and cannot know that thousands of men and women are heart and soul with Fidel Castro. . . .

> Fidel Castro and his 26th of July Movement are the flaming symbol of this opposition to the regime. . . .

> It is a revolutionary movement that calls itself socialistic. It is also nationalistic, which generally in Latin American means anti-American. . . .

> From the looks of things, General Batista cannot possibly hope to suppress the Castro revolt. . . .

Matthews described the pride of guerrillas who could claim to be "one of the 82" original invaders, and his meeting with "Raúl Castro, Fidel's brother, slight and pleasant." Of Fidel, he wrote,:

> This is quite a man—a powerful six-footer, olive-skinned, full-faced, with a straggly beard. He was dressed in an olive gray fatigue uniform and carried a rifle with telescopic sights, of which he was very proud. It seems the men have something more than fifty of these, and he said the soldiers feared them. . . . The personality of the man is overpowering. It was easy to see that his men adored him. . . .

Matthews wrote:

> 'We have been fighting for seventy-nine days now and are stronger than ever,' Señor Castro said. 'The soldiers are fighting badly; their morale is low and ours could not be higher. We are killing many, but when we take prisoners, they are never shot. We question them, talk kindly to them, take their arms and equipment and then set them free. . . .'

> The government, he said with some bitterness, is using arms furnished by the United States, not only against him, but 'against all the Cuban people.'

Matthews was convinced that Castro paid cash for the food he received from the peasants, and that Castro ruled the Sierra: "His position seems almost invulnerable."

As Matthews left for New York with his story and photographs of Castro and himself in the mountains, Felipe Pazos had a discussion with Mario Llerena, a professor who had returned to Havana from the United States in 1952 to write freelance articles and join the Movimiento Nacional Revolucionaria, an intellectuals' protest group. Llerena was attracted by Castro's violent activism and had visited him in Mexico.

Pazos told Llerena that a *Times* reporter, Matthews, had just interviewed Castro. He asked Llerena to fly to New York, get Matthews' articles as soon as they came out, have them reprinted and airmailed to Cuba. Pazos had an airline ticket ready, along with a copy of the Havana telephone directory and the Havana Social Register for addressing the reprints.

The next day, Llerena was in New York, looking up Castro sympathizers and organizing the reprint-and-mail campaign.

Llerena reported:

> While I was in New York, I went to see Herbert Matthews at the *Times* offices. When he learned that I had just arrived from Havana on a mission for the Castro movement, he was delighted to see me. . . .
> It was evident that Herbert L. Matthews was most sympathetic toward the revolutionary cause in Cuba and toward Fidel Castro in particular. He was also willing to help.[12]

Llerena said that Mrs. Phillips earlier had put him in touch with visiting NBC correspondents in Havana, and he had been televised on Dave Garroway's *Today* show, silhouetted and with his voice disguised to protect him. Matthews called the Columbia Broadcasting System and arranged for an interview with CBS News. The interview fell through, because CBS also wanted Matthews on the show, and he declined, but as a result of the negotiations Llerena met CBS correspondent Robert Tabor.[13] Tabor made a trip to Cuba, but a Castro interview could not be arranged.

The arrival of several thousand copies of Matthews' articles in Cuba spectacularly revived the revolutionary movement, with Havana's Civil Resistance Movement, the students' Directorio Revolucionario and Prío's semi-gangster Organizacion Autentica springing to life.[14]

Soon after Llerena's return to Havana, Armando Hart, organization secretary in the capital for M26-7, called him to a meeting with instructions to find another American reporter to interview Castro. Hart said it should not be Matthews again. "Both Matthews and *The New York Times* could be considered practically in our pockets, so it was better to keep them in reserve for the future."[15]

Llerena, who had arranged a code with Tabor, flew to New York and set up a CBS project. The team of Tabor and Wendell Hoffmann, with all their equipment, was transported into the mountains. The CBS special, "The Story of Cuba's Jungle Fighters," was telecast in late May, and a Castro spread appeared in *Life* on May 27, 1957. The CBS venture "proved to be another tremendous propaganda boost for Castro."[16]

Batista was baffled by the attention the American media gave to Castro and even complained mildly about it to Mrs. Phillips. Castro's men, after regrouping, had fought only two engagements—an attack on a 12-man army post at El Plata on January 17 that killed five soldiers, and an ambush February 9 of an advance patrol of troops tracking the Castro band. Castro had killed one scout himself at long range with his telescopic-sighted rifle, and his band killed three others, at which Castro proclaimed the guerrilla doctrine of killing scouts first. Matthews' articles brought Castro his first strong reinforcements on March 16, 50 more men from País' Santiago organization, guided to the Castro camp by a sympathetic rice farmer, Huber Matos. Castro's band had grown to more than 80 men when they attacked an army post at El Uvero in June, killing 14 soldiers and capturing 14, with a loss of six Fidelistas. It was to be their biggest battle until the closing days of the revolution.

Far greater damage was being done by other revolutionaries revived by the Castro publicity. On March 13, José Antonio Echevarria, directing about 80 men from the anti-Communist Directorio Revolucionario, attacked the Presidential Palace in an attempt to assassinate Batista. Echevarria seized Havana radio briefly and announced that Batista was dead, before he was himself killed. The rebels lost 35 dead and killed five palace guards in a battle more fierce than any of Castro's.

The greatest uprising of the Cuban revolution, the seizure for one morning in September 1957 of the naval base at Cienfuegos, was not planned by Castro but by a coalition of revolutionary groups including naval officers. The officers called off their coordinated attack plans for Mariel port and Santiago, but Castro's M26-7 nevertheless gave the signal to attack to the other groups in the plot. About 300 of the 400 revolutionaries, mostly from Havana's underground and only loosely allied with Castro, were killed in Batista's counterattack in the shelling and bombing by B-26 bombers of Cienfuegos. Justo Carrillo, a former head of Cuba's Agricultural Bank, who would join Castro, suggested later that Castro wanted the naval mutiny to fail, because it might have put in power his rival, the imprisoned Colonel Barquín.[17]

On May 11, 1957, Judge Manuel Urrutia Lleó of Santiago, defying Batista, declared that all 100 Fidelistas before him, including 22 survivors of the *Granma* landing, should be acquitted. Two other judges sent the *Granma* men to prison. Castro declared that Urrutia would be president when the revolution was won.

Eisenhower's second inauguration on January 20, 1957, was accompanied by the routine resignation of all of his ambassadors. Ambassador Arthur Gardner wanted to stay in Cuba, but in March, just after Matthews' articles in the *Times,* Eisenhower accepted his resignation and he was recalled. The State Department was disengaging from Batista, and Gardner was frankly pro-Batista. He said publicly, "I don't think we've ever had a better friend."

The new ambassador-designate, Earl E. T. Smith, a Wall Street investment broker who had been a government consultant and a World War II Air Force colonel, went to see a friend, Ambassador to Mexico Robert C. Hill, for advice. Hill had been an Assistant Secretary of State for Congressional Affairs and knew his way around. Hill later told the Internal Affairs subcommittee of the Senate Judiciary Committee: "I said, 'Earl, I am sorry that you are going to Cuba. . . . You are assigned to Cuba to preside over the downfall of Batista. The decision has been made that Batista has to go. You must be very careful.' "

Under questioning, Hill clarified that he had learned that in the State Department corridors: "I'm not saying the decision at the top, but the decision down at the lower level."

Asked by committee counsel J. G. Sourwine if Castro would come to power, Hill replied: "That is correct. I told Ambassador Smith that he should request from the Secretary of State to take men that he had confidence in, to Havana with him, including his Minister, because if he was not careful, his reputation would be destroyed."

Hill said he suggested some Foreign Service officers to Smith, but none would go to Havana. He testified, "Some of the men told me privately, 'I don't want to go to Havana because Castro is coming to power.' "[18]

Smith never did see Secretary of State Dulles, who was recovering from his cancer operation and was absorbed in the aftermath of Suez and Hungary, including the revolt in Algeria and Soviet rumblings about Berlin.

Smith would be dealing with Roy Rubottom, Assistant Secretary of State for Latin American Affairs, and with William Arthur Wieland director of the Office of Caribbean and Mexican Affairs, who had grown up in Cuba and had a Cuban stepfather. Some Cubans knew Wieland as

Arturo Guillermo Montenegro, from the time when he had used his stepfather's family name.

In May, Wieland, with authorization of Rubottom, instructed Smith to get a briefing from Matthews, which Smith did. Such a briefing was not unreasonable, except that Smith increasingly came to believe that Wieland and Matthews held the same views and were in collusion. There was a great deal of information on Castro's background kicking around in the corners of the government, but Smith said he was given none of it by Rubottom, Wieland, or Matthews.

Castro had been Cuba's outstanding track and baseball athlete at the intermediate school level. At Havana University's law faculty, he had become a political gang leader, accused but never charged formally with complicity in the murder of a former student leader, Manolo Castro. He had joined a force of young Cubans staging to leave for an armed invasion of the Dominican Republic in 1947, escaping when the others were caught by swimming the Bay of Nipes, near his father's ranch. In April 1948 he joined a Peron-sponsored student protest in Bogotá, Colombia, timed to coincide with the foreign ministers' meeting at the Ninth Pan-American Conference. In Bogotá, Castro had had an appointment with the popular Liberal Party politician, Jorge Eliécer Gaitán, when Gaitán was murdered, allegedly by Juan Roa Sierra, said to be deranged. At Gaitán's murder, riots devastated Bogotá, with estimates of 3,000 dead. Castro later said he got a weapon and 16 bullets, offered to organize a group of rioters, and fired four bullets in the course of the "Bogotázo," although he did not say whether he killed anyone. William D. Pawley, former Ambassador to Peru and Brazil, testified later that he heard a voice on the Bogotá radio saying, "This is Fidel Castro from Cuba. This is a Communist revolution. The president has been killed; all the military establishments in Colombia are now in our hands; the navy has capitulated, and this revolution has been a success."[19]

Smith had not heard of these reports when he went to Cuba in July 1957, and he complained bitterly that both Rubottom and Wieland had been present at the Bogotázo without mentioning to him that Castro had been there.

Smith's arrival in Havana on July 15 coincided with an upsurge of violence, especially in the hotbed that was Santiago. Following Matthews' advice to get out and see the country, Smith announced that he would visit Santiago, the U.S. Navy base at Guantanamo and some major U.S.-owned industrial properties. On July 30, the day before Smith was to arrive in Santiago, 23-year-old Frank País, the region's revolutionary hero, was shot down by Santiago police chief Colonel José

Salas Cañizares.[20]

Smith, new on the job, arrived in Santiago to be greeted by a funeral procession and demonstration for País, women in black shouting, *"Liberdad!"*

Shocked when firemen knocked down the demonstrating women with hoses and police roughed them up, Smith at first avoided the demands of accompanying reporters for a statement, then scheduled a press conference. He said,

> I would like to make the preliminary observation that I feel some of the people of Santiago de Cuba took advantage of my presence here to demonstrate and protest to their own government.... Any form of excessive police action is abhorrent to me. I deeply regret that my presence...may have been the cause of public demonstrations which brought on police retaliation. I sincerely trust that those held by the police as a result of their demonstrations have been released.[21]

Smith's statement, mostly reported without the caveat that the demonstrators had been provocative, angered Batista and brought Smith his first and only congratulations from the *Times* in an editorial August 3. Two weeks later, *Human Events* criticized the *Times'* glorification of Castro in an article quoting former Ambassador to Cuba Spruille Braden, who said that Castro "is a fellow traveler, if not a member of the Communist Party, and has been so for a long time."[22]

Meanwhile, Castro met in the mountains with economist Felipe Pazos and Raúl Chibás, head of the Ortodoxo Party and brother of Eduardo Chibás, who had been the student Castro's idol. They issued a manifesto, the "Pact of the Sierras," that promised "a Cuba free, democratic and just," with guarantees of a free press and specific reforms. It was not a radical document, and it did much to bring Havana's moderates behind Castro when he later emerged the revolution's winner.

By the end of 1957, Castro still had less than 300 men and had fought only one major engagement, in June. His use of force was confined to stealing cattle for food and burning cane fields with phosphorus sent to him by Teresa Casuso. But the enthusiasm in the media was contagious; Charles Ryan, an American who fought with Castro in the El Uvero engagement, came out of the mountains with the news that Castro had 1,000 men, and Donald Hogan of the *New York Herald Tribune*, reported he had 2,000.[23]

In 1958, the *Times* had a new man interviewing Castro in the Sierra, Homer Bigart, a legendary reporter from World War II who had been on the front line in most of the wars and revolutions since. In 1956, Bigart had managed to get to the shooting in both the Suez and Hungary crises, although they were going on at the same time thousands of miles apart.

Bigart found Castro "much more conciliatory" toward the Batista government than he had been a year earlier. Castro had sent a proposal to Batista to end the civil war and allow elections, provided the Batista army left Oriente Province, where Castro's men would supervise the polls. Castro had sent the message via Cuban congressman Leon Ramirez, who had come to see him in the mountains to ask him to stop rustling his constituents' cattle. Bigart indicated some skepticism of Castro, putting in quotation marks that he had interviewed him "resting after a major battle." He dropped into the story the comment that "in fifteen days in the Sierra this observer saw no evidence of rebel strength sufficient to win a decisive action on the plains."[24]

Meanwhile, Ambassador Smith was attempting to persuade Batista to hold elections, with someone other than himself as his candidate, and with international supervision of the voting. In January, William Wieland visited the Havana Embassy with a paper he had written describing the Cuban economy as collapsing and predicting that the Cuban government would fall soon. Working with John Topping, head of the Embassy's political division, Wieland prepared a similar outline for an Embassy paper, which Smith vetoed as soon as he saw it. The Cuban economy had never been better.

Smith was so irritated that he telephoned Rubottom in Washington and said he was coming to report. Rubottom told him the State Department had no funds for the trip, and Smith responded that he would pay his own expenses. Rubottom then issued Smith's travel orders.[25]

When Smith got to Washington, Wieland had arranged a press conference, although Smith did not want one. At the press conference, he put off the record his answer to a reporter's question, saying that he did not believe that the United States would ever be able to do business with Fidel Castro, because he did not believe that Castro would honor obligations or be able to maintain law and order. Smith said that Castro and pro-Castro Congressmen in Washington learned of his off-the-record comment within 24 hours, in a distorted version that he had called Castro a Communist.

In early March 1958, Batista announced that he would not leave the presidency before his term expired on February 24, 1959, but he was willing to hold elections with United Nation and world press observers. He said he would cooperate with demands of the opposition, which included political amnesty, a return of exiles, reestablishment of constitutional guarantees and eligibility of candidates from the 26th of

July Movement.

Batista had lifted censorship in February 25, 1957, in time for Cuban newspapers to print the third of Matthews' articles on his Castro interview. But on March 12, 1958, Batista suspended constitutional guarantees again for 45 days.

The State Department responded, over Smith's protests, by suspending the shipment of 1,950 M-1 rifles that were on the docks in New York ready for shipment to Cuba. It was a gesture disowning Batista, and Castro announced in a statement that he was declaring "total war" on the regime, including a general strike, the classic means in Latin America of delivering a *coup de grace* to a weakened government.[26]

At about the same time Frank Sturgis, a Miamian, recruited a Cubana Airlines pilot, Pedro Díaz Lanz, to fly a C-46 loaded with weapons to Castro's group in the Sierra. Sturgis entered the revolution as an agent for Prío Socarras, who helped finance Castro's departure from Mexico but also financed rival insurgents, including other groups of invaders. Prío was arrested in February after a battery of complaints from Ambassador Smith, but he probably was involved in the March arms shipment to Castro. Sturgis later told reporter Paul Meskil that he was in effect a triple agent, for Prío, then Castro, then the CIA.[27]

Díaz was anti-Batista, but he also was Catholic and strongly anti-Communist. He landed the arms shipment in the Sierra on March 31, 1958, damaging the plane. Castro, who was starved for weapons and ammunition, welcomed him as a hero. Díaz later would become the first spectacular defector from Castro's regime.

Smith and Matthews, by this time adversaries, lunched together twice in March. Matthews was sure that Batista was about to fall, and he accused Smith of interfering in Cuban internal affairs by pushing for elections. At the second luncheon, after an interval of eight days, Matthews could not understand why Batista had not fallen, Smith reported. Matthews repeated his charge of U.S. intervention in pushing elections, and said no peaceful solution was possible because of the Cuban people's pent-up emotion.[28]

Homer Bigart was not entirely in agreement with Matthews, but he also turned angrily on Smith when Smith asked him why he wanted to interview a bandit like Castro. The general strike called by Castro for April 9 failed miserably when labor leaders remained loyal to Batista and the Communist party refused to join in.

Bigart wrote that the failure of the general strike left Batista "stronger today than at any time since Señor Castro, military commander of the 26th of July Movement, launched this guerrilla war in the Sierra Maestra."[29]

Bigart reported: "Batista now appears to have a good chance for bringing off his plan for general elections Nov. 30. He is not a candidate, but he is confident that the Government Coalition ticket will win and that he will be able to continue as the 'strong man' in Cuba. . . . As for Señor Castro, his chances of winning are now at lowest ebb."

Matthews was not defeatist. He was ready with advice and encouragement, as in a *Times* editorial of April 18, 1958:

Ebb Tide in Cuba

This is a period of ebb tide among the opponents of President Batista of Cuba and especially among the followers of Fidel Castro. . . . The weeks just gone by have seen Fidel Castro and his supporters, despite bravery and idealism, make disastrous tactical mistakes. . . .

It was a great tactical error on Fidel Castro's part to announce in March he was going to start 'total war' against the regime on April 1 and follow it with a general strike. . . . It gave General Batista plenty of time to take drastic counter-measures that included arrests and killings. . . . The army and police stood by General Batista and used their American arms to good purpose. . . .

However, to leave the picture like this would be like painting in only the black parts and leaving all other colors out. . . .

The opposition has lost a major battle . . . but Cuba is in the midst of a long civil war. There is one fight the Cuban people will not and cannot lose, and that is the fight for freedom.

Other things were going wrong for Castro. His revolution had created two innovations: the taking of American hostages and the hijacking of commercial airplanes. Castro had the kidnap victims—about 100 in all—released fairly quickly, attributing their capture to his over-zealous brother Raúl. Of the first three political skyjackings, one Cubana Airlines plane crashed, killing 17, in November.

Matthews had a curious explanation for the kidnappings. They were caused by Batista's censorship of the press. In a commentary in the *Times* Week in Review he explained:

A vast majority of Americans must have been surprised, shocked and angered this week at the news from Cuba. The surprise came because the most rigid censorship in Cuban history had for months clamped a curtain of silence over what was happening in the island, which is only 100 miles from our Florida shore.

The Havana Government blandly gave out army communiques. . . . Fidel Castro and his rebels were starved, hunted and being hounded to an imminent death. . . .

Suddenly the veil has been torn from this fiction—but in a way that has aroused American opinion against the rebel leader, Fidel Castro, who until now had considerable sympathy in this country. . . .

It was clear that Fidel (as he is universally known in Cuba) was doing three things. He was registering a protest against American policies which he felt favored the military dictator, Fulgencio Batista. He was showing that he and his followers were masters in the eastern third of Cuba. . . . Finally he was calling attention to himself and his cause in a spectacular way. . . .

What General Batista did was to clamp a lid down on violent, courageous fighting people who have proved they want liberty. Thanks to the censorship, it seemed to the outside world that President Batista was sitting calmly and successfully on this lid. Now Fidel Castro has blown it sky-high, unfortunately using a lot of innocent Americans to make his point.

Castro's fortunes were turning. The Communists, the Partido Socialista Popular, had taken no overt part in the revolution, and had sabotaged the general strike. But now they put a guerrilla force into the mountains under Félix Torres, and Carlos Rafael Rodríguez entered into negotiations with Raúl (who had joined the Communist Youth in 1953), then with Castro, on behalf of the Communist central committee. In the summer of 1958 Castro reached a pact with the Communists, and his guerrillas, now divided into several groups, won two major victories over Batista's demoralized forces.

On the eve of the November elections, Mrs. Phillips reported to the *Times:* ". . . none can deny that (Castro) at least exerts supreme authority over large areas outside the cities, which are held by Government troops. . . he could take the cities were it not for the fact that he would thus provide the Batista forces with specific targets." She reported that Castro had broadcast orders to all insurgents to shoot at any vehicle moving in Oriente Province from October 30 to November 4, to prevent elections.[30]

The *Times* also published a map with shaded areas of guerrilla activity that gave the impression Castro was almost everywhere in Cuba.

Batista's election was held on November 3, and his candidate, Rivero Agüero, was elected over Márquez Sterling and Grau San Martín. Castro had threatened that anyone taking part in the elections would receive 30 years in prison or death, and one Batista candidate, Aníbal Vega in Camaguey Province, was assassinated as a warning. But the election was recognized as a fraud, and Ambassador Smith conceded to Washington that Batista had to leave Cuba. Smith hoped that a junta, and not Castro, could take over.

Smith was recalled to Washington on December 4, and was asked by Under Secretary of State Robert Murphy if Castro's movement was Communist. He replied that he could convince any jury it was. Murphy told him that Batista was to be approached by someone else, a person with no official connection to the United States government, who would ask him to leave Cuba to a military junta that had been selected by U.S. officials.

The secret envoy, William Pawley, had known Batista for 30 years. He had founded Cubana Airlines in the 1920s and ran the Havana trolley system, as well as having served as U.S. ambassador to Peru and Brazil and helping to start the Flying Tigers airline in China. Pawley had offered his services to middle-level State Department officials and to Colonel J. C. King, head of the Latin American section of the CIA, at a meeting in Pawley's Miami home. Smith suspected all of the American officials to whom Pawley spoke of having given information to Castro supporters.

Pawley made his proposal reluctantly. He did not know that the State Department was withdrawing recognition of Batista's protege, Agüero, and told the Senate Internal Affairs subcommittee later, "the only possible result of that would be Fidel Castro would have immediately come into power, and I am convinced that there was enough noise made in the meetings of the Department of State and in CIA for enough people to be convinced that Castro could bring us nothing but disaster."[31]

Pawley spent three hours with Batista in Havana on December 9. He offered Batista an opportunity to live at Batista's Daytona Beach, Florida, home and protection for his family. He named for Batista the junta to be appointed, which included Colonel Ramón Barquín, leader of the failed 1955 coup, who was still in Batista's prison. Pawley said that Rubottom had told him he could not guarantee the offer to Batista as already having tacit U.S. government approval, and because he could only promise to press for U.S. approval, Batista declined.

Batista's collaborators were asking Smith to whom they should turn to survive the coming collapse. Cuba's economy now was being affected by the revolution, and the sugar crop could not be transported.

As Batista was being told he was isolated, the *Times* bought a freelance article from Andrew St. George, who had spent five weeks with Castro's guerrillas in the mountains and also published reports in *Look* and *Coronet* magazines. St. George, a former U.S. military intelligence agent, thought that Castro was "an egomaniac and emotionally unstable, but not a Communist."[32] His article in the *Times* said:

> Fidel Castro, Cuban rebel leader, is seeking to have a confidential United States diplomatic representative visit him at his headquarters in the Sierra Maestra. . . .
>
> Sẽnor Castro also appeared eager to explain to the State Department and disavow various anti-United States activities in the rebel zone commanded by his younger brother.
>
> High among these was the publication of a political paper by Raúl Castro's command. . . "the Call to World Youth." . . . The paper attacks the United States position in Cuba and throughout Latin America in terms hardly distinguishable from the Communist positions. . . .
>
> Fidel Castro has angrily disavowed the political line adopted by his brother. . . .[33]

Smith saw Batista on December 17 under orders to present a harder U.S. line. He told Batista that the United States had given up on his government and the new president, Agüero. Batista asked if he could visit his home in Daytona Beach, and Smith suggested he go to Spain instead.

A Castro column led by Major Francisco Cabrera took the small town of Congramaestre, the first town taken and held. Guevara's column then seized a series of villages and on December 28 captured an armored train with 350 soldiers and officers, ensuring the capture of Santa Clara, the first city to fall to the revolution.

Castro had been two years in the mountains, with only a gradual buildup to about 300 men, fighting little, politicking by courier and by radio, posing a psychological rather than a military threat. Now his forces suddenly swelled and were fighting a demoralized army that knew the revolution had been accepted by the world as a *fait accompli.* Hugh Thomas, in his encyclopedic *The Cuban Revolution,* calculated that at the beginning of December 1959 there were 1,500 to 2,000 men under arms in all the various rebel groups, and at the end of the revolution a month later there were 3,000 at most, many of them camp followers.[34]

Times correspondent Ruby Hart Phillips quoted Ramón Grau San Martín on the eve of the November elections as saying that he believed 25,000 persons had been killed during the 22 months of Castro's rebellion.[35] The American media adopted the figure of 20,000 dead. Thomas calculated that 1,500 to 2,000 died, mostly in the cities. The only lists of dead were published by *Bohemia* in Cuba, its lists making a grand total of 898 dead, including 12 executions by Castro forces.[36] The American media's exaggeration of Castro's forces about equaled its exaggeration of the revolution's casualties.

Batista left a New Year's Eve party on December 31, 1958, and flew with his wife and son Jorge to the Dominican Republic and exile. Two other planes took the rest of his children and close advisers to Florida. Early on January 1, General Eulogio Cantillo called Ambassador Smith to inform him that Batista had left and that he had been left in charge of the armed forces.

The collapse Matthews had been lingering in Havana to see had occured, but the *Times* assigned him to cover the looting instead. He reported mobs looting, but at the same time excused them.

> Years of pent up emotion exploded in Havana today....
>
> By 9 a.m. crowds of vandals and looters got going. Their first instinct was part destruction and part looting, and it took the form of destroying hundreds of parking meters.
>
> These had been recently installed by the Batista regime and were in that sense symbols of the hated men and of the Government whose leaders had fled....
>
> The next phase was one of demolishing the windows of shops, restaurants and hotels...it was noteworthy that the places choses were owned by known sympathizers of former President Fulgencia Batista....
>
> The first victim was the Plaza Hotel...which is connected in Cuban minds with the gangland figure Albert Anastasia, who was murdered in New York, and which is now run by an American named Joe Rogers Stassi....[37]

The report of the attack on the parking meters was not entirely satisfactory, so the *Times* ran a small sidebar reporting that fashionable homes also were looted.

From the Sierra, Castro called a general strike and demanded that Urrutia be installed as provisional president. He sent an advance party to Havana under Major Camillo Cienfuegos and delayed his own arrival in Havana, uncertain about what the military was doing. The Directorio Revolucionario, only loosely allied with Castro, patrolled Havana in commandeered jeeps and cars.

On January 3, Smith went to the Presidential Palace with five other ambassadors to see General Cantillo, seeking reassurance that embassies would be protected, especially Latin American embassies harboring refugees. Leaving the palace, Smith met Matthews, who asked what he had been doing there. Smith told him. Shortly thereafter, Smith was called to the Embassy telex. Wieland, on the Washington end, implied that Smith had been to the palace soliciting a military junta to keep Castro from coming to power. Smith said Wieland "admitted the source of his information was Matthews."[38]

Matthews meanwhile had left for Camaguey to meet Castro on his triumphant tour the length of the island. He reported that Castro had called for an end to the strike, and intended to assume power over the armed forces, making Urrutia "in legal terms the Commander in Chief, just as the President of the United States is." Matthews reported that "Camaguey was literally in a delerium of joy. It took Fidel, as he is known, about three hours to force his way in a tank through crowds estimated to total 100,000."

Matthews also reported that the rebels had arrested Cantillo in Havana because they did not trust him. Cantillo had been in Camaguey, where he had allegedly promised the rebels not to accept a Havana post from Batista, and they believed that Cantillo had been in touch with Ambassador Smith, Matthews reported.

"From that they deduced that Mr. Smith had played a role in the naming of General Cantillo as chief of the armed forces after General Batista's flight," Matthews wrote.

"According to Señor (Raúl) Chibas, Mr. Smith was working for two months on a plan to find some conservative traditional figures to take power. . .and they point to it as another example of the lack of understanding of the Cuban situation by the United States Ambassador and the State Department," he reported.[39]

Castro's arrival in Havana on January 8 touched off the greatest celebration the city ever had seen.

Two days later the White House announced the resignation of Smith, who wrote Eisenhower that he believed it was in the best interest of the United States. Eisenhower responded with the usual compliments for the dignity and dedication Smith had shown under unusually difficult demands.

From Havana, Mrs. Phillips filed a dispatch that the *Times* headlined, "MANY IN HAVANA GLAD SMITH QUIT." It said that many Cubans were openly delighted. It noted that Britain and France also had sold arms to Batista, adding:

> However, the Cubans recognize that the career diplomatic systems of Britain and France are quite different from that of the United States. Ambassador Smith was a political appointee. The British and French Ambassadors are experienced career diplomats, and it is believed they will face out this situation with aplomb.[40]

Matthews wrote on January 17 a triumphant commentary from Havana, carried by the *Times* Week in Review:

The hunted young man who for three hours whispered his passionate hopes and ideals into my ear in the gloomy jungle depths of the Sierra Maestra at dawn on Feb. 17, 1957, is now the chief power in Cuba. In the eyes of nearly all his compatriots, Dr. Fidel Castro is the greatest hero that their history has known.

In much of the American press there was an outcry against Castro's executions, and against the cry of the mob, "*Paredon*—to the wall!"

Matthews reported that the Cubans were convinced the executed persons were "torturers and killers under General Fulgencio Batista," and that "there is hardly a family in Cuba that did not have a member at least arrested and at worst tortured and killed by President Batista's soldiers and police. Moreover, in every city, town and village, the killers and torturers were known."

Smith, meanwhile, had gone to Havana's Campamento Columbia at 2 a.m. on January 5, without official orders, for his first confrontation with a rebel: Major Cienfuegos, head of Castro's advance guard. Smith had heard that General Cantillo, who had been replaced by Colonel Ramón Barquín, released from the Isle of Pines prison, was to be executed that morning, although he was not one of Matthews' torturers. Cienfuegos told Smith that Castro's orders could not be countermanded, but that he would delay the execution and relay Smith's request to spare the general. Cantillo survived because of Smith's intervention.

Smith returned to the United States and media charges of dilettantism, unwilling to be buried under the debacle in Cuba. His view that Castro headed a Communist regime installed by the United States quickly became known, particularly after he testified to the Senate Internal Affairs subcommittee:

The United States government agencies and the United States press played a major role in bringing Castro to power.

Three front page articles in *The New York Times* in early 1957 by the editorialist, Herbert Matthews, served to inflate Castro to world stature and world recognition. Until that time, Castro had been just another bandit in the Oriente mountains of Cuba with a handful of followers who had terrorized the campesinos, that is, the peasants throughout the countryside.[41]

But Castro was a winner, Smith a loser, and the American media treated his testimony with skepticism.

One of Castro's close collaborators agreed with Smith even as Castro won. Mario Llerena, who headed Castro's Committee in Exile in New York, and had been Castro's major liaison with the *Times,* had broken with the 26th of July Movement in August 1958, shortly after Raúl Castro's wave of kidnapping Americans. Llerena would later write a duplicate of Smith's theme: "It was American withdrawal of support for Batista that determined his fall—and cleared the path to power for Castro."[42]

Castro named himself armed forces commander and set about forming an attractive cabinet that contained no Communists and few radicals. Judge Urrutia was president; Miró Cardona, head of the Bar Association, was premier, and several classic ministries were held by middle-aged, anti-Batista moderates. In other cabinet posts were Castro's men, some in their 20s, including Defense Minister Agusto Martínez Sánchez and Education Minister Armando Hart. Leaders from the Civic Resistence in Havana included Manuel Ray, public works minister, and Faustino Pérez, minister in charge of confiscated properties.

Castro introduced another innovation: rule by television. From the beginning he was constantly on both Havana television stations in Havana, explaining, directing, condemning. He quickly collected the arms of the other revolutionary groups, starting with the Directorio.

In the first month, both Urrutia and Cardona attempted to resign over the issues of executions and retroactive justice. When Miró found he had no power, he made his resignation stick, recommending that Castro become premier. The defections began with Miró Cardona.

Four months in charge, Castro accepted an invitation of the American Society of Newspaper Editors to speak to their convention in Washington in April. Crowds met him at Washington's airport, the first of many to cheer him on his tour. Indignation over the executions evaporated, and Castro's moderate, witty and reassuring speech was well received by the editors, as were his speeches at Harvard and Princeton Universities and in New York.[43]

Eisenhower did not want to see Castro and was absent from Washington. Castro lunched with Acting Secretary of State Christian Herter and then had a talk with Vice President Nixon in his office. Nixon dictated a memo to Eisenhower, concluding:

> Whatever we may think of him he is going to be a great factor in the development of Cuba and very possibly in Latin American affairs generally. He seems to be sincere. He is either incredibly naive about communism or under Communist discipline—my guess is the former, and as I have already implied his ideas are less developed than those of almost any world figure I have met in fifty countries.

But because he has the power to lead to which I have referred, we have no choice but at least to try to orient him in the right direction.[44]

Castro left a favorable impression, even to some extent with Nixon, who later revised his guess and decided that Castro was more Communist than naive.

Castro had hardly returned to Cuba when his regime in May inaugurated a classic Communist program for agriculture. The Agrarian Reform Institute (INRA), under Núñez Jiménez, became the secret government. INRA divided the country into 28 zones, each with a rebel commander under its president, Castro. It established cooperatives, banks, hospitals and schools under doctrinaire control.

A month after the founding of INRA, most of the liberal cabinet ministers resigned, and before long M26-7 heroes defected, leaving Castro with the new and old Communists.

Major Pedro Díaz Lanz, who had flown weapons to the the Sierra, had been appointed air force commander, but he found that Che Guevara had brought in instructors for his embryo air force, mostly Chileans, who were giving political indoctrination. Díaz, while ill with typhus, issued an order discontinuing indoctrination classes. Hearing that Castro intended to dismiss him, he asked to see Castro but was refused. Nevertheless, Díaz issued a statement to the press saying that he was resuming his command, and that the rumor he was a prisoner was false. His statement said that Batista's dictatorship had imprisoned revolutionaries, but that could not happen under a democratic regime. "I am against every type of dictatorship, including the most inhuman system in the world, communism," his statement said.

Castro summoned him for a dressing down and dismissed him with the remark, "I will have to decide what to do with you."

Díaz boarded a sailboat with his wife and several others, leaving behind copies of his letter of resignation with the Cuban media. It protested Communists in prominent positions and the indoctrination of the armed forces. His defection unleashed a propaganda blitz in Cuba, Castro denouncing him on television as a traitor and reactionary.

Castro required Urrutia to denounce Díaz on television, but the president took the occasion to warn also of Communist influence. Castro was enraged. While Urrutia was a prisoner in the Presidential Palace, Castro appeared on television to charge that he "is blackmailing us with communism. Everyone who promotes this ghost of communism is promoting foreign aggression. The president is drawing up a plan exactly like Díaz Lanz. Maybe he will send for 15 North American agents and install them as his cabinet ministers." Castro then announced his resignation as premier (as Nasser also would do after the defeat of the Six Day War).

Mobs threatened to hang Urrutia, who resigned while Castro was still on the air and escaped into the Venezuelan Embassy. In response to public appeals, Castro reconsidered his resignation and withdrew it.

If Castro thought Díaz was an American agent, he was only premature. Frank Sturgis, who had worked for both Castro and the CIA, said later he organized the escapes of Díaz, his wife and his brother.[45]

To both the State Department and the *Times,* Díaz's defection appeared to be a catastrophe. The State Department was attempting to encourage moderates in the Castro government via the new ambassador, Philip Bonsal, and felt Díaz's defection and denunciation of communism cut the ground from under them.

Matthews leaped to attack Díaz and to defend Castro in a Page 1 article from Havana under the headline:

> Cuba Has a One-Man Rule
> And It Is Called Non-Red.

Matthews wrote:

> Cuba is in the midst of the first great social revolution in Latin America since the Mexican Revolution of 1910 . . . for all practical purposes (Castro) is the provisional government of Cuba. . . .
>
> This is not a Communist revolution in any sense of the word and there are no Communists in positions of control.
>
> The accusations of the former head of the Cuban air force, Major Pedro Luis Díaz Lanz, before the United States Senate Internal Affairs subcommittee yesterday are rejected by virtually all Cubans. It is stated here that before his resignation Major Díaz was removed from his high post for incompetence, extravagance and nepotism.
>
> The use to which his defection was put in Washington has aroused more bitterness and resentment against the United States than any event in the history of Cuban-American relations, according to the reactions in Havana today.
>
> The point of view among the most experienced and knowledgable Cubans is as follows:
>
> There are no Reds in the Cabinet and none in higher positions in the government or army in the sense of being able to control either governmental or defense policies. The only power worth considering in Cuba is in the hands of Premier Castro, who is not only not Communist but decidedly anti-Communist. . . .[46]

Matthews said that U.S. suspicions strengthened the Communists by making them appear important, and that most Cubans "today do not want elections. The reason is that elections in the past merely meant to them the coming of corrupt politicians seeking the spoils of power."

Three years later, the extraordinary viewpoint that Díaz's defection and charges "dealt a devastating blow to the moderates in the revolutionary regime who opposed the now visible Communist infiltration" was still held, after the Bay of Pigs, by Tad Szulc of the *Times* and Karl E. Meyer of the *Washington Post*.[47]

Howard Hunt, CIA coordinator of the later invasion force of Cubans, wrote that the U.S. media's sympathy for Castro was so great that the State Department might have deported Díaz to Cuba if the Senate subcommittee had not subpoenaed him.[48]

Díaz's appearance before the Senators was a media sensation. He convincingly answered Senators' detailed questions, pressing his point, "I had the complete conclusion that he (Castro) is a Communist."

He quoted in his slightly broken English a conversation he said he overheard in which Castro said, "I going to introduce in Cuba a system like the Russians had, even better than the Russian system. . . . Later on I going to take the land of everybody. Well, someday the banks will disappear. . . ."

Díaz said he was deposed as air force commander for refusing to fly a C-46 with an invading force to the Dominican Republic to topple the Trujillo regime, as well as for releasing his press statement. He named and identified by position a score of leading Fidelistas he said were Communists.

Three months after this Senate appearance, Díaz flew over Havana from the United States in a B-25 that had been sold to Batista but never delivered and dropped leaflets, touching off wild anti-aircraft fire from a Cuban frigate and a chase by Cuban fighters. Castro charged that the planes (sic) dropped explosives, killing 36 persons. Most authorities concluded that two persons were killed and 45 injured, probably from the anti-aircraft fire. Frank Sturgis later said he was co-pilot on the mission, indicating that it had at least CIA approval.

Ten days after the leaflet raid, U.S. authorities on November 4 jailed Díaz temporarily on the Cuban government's charges of murder. A Miami judge refused to extradite him.

The leaflet-dropping mission coincided with another major defection from Castro. Huber Matos, named by Castro "the lion of Camaguey," tried to resign as military chief of the province, unwilling to work with Communists. Camillo Cienfuegos, Castro's chief of staff, whom Ambassador Smith had found to be surprisingly reasonable, tried to talk Castro out of arresting Matos, but Castro personally led the arresting troops. Camaguey's leadership, 25 officers, resigned with Matos. Cienfuegos dutifully condemned Matos in a radio broadcast, and on his return to Havana vanished. The wreckage of his plane never was found, and many believed Castro had the plane sabotaged because Cienfuegos' popularity rivaled his own.

Matos' trial lasted six days. He testified that Communist infiltration of his troops started in the fall of 1958. Castro spoke on the stand for six hours, denouncing Matos. Without a specific charge against him, Matos was sentenced to 20 years and served it all. He was released to Costa Rica in 1979 and dedicated his life to overthrowing Castro.

Castro's relations with Cuba's shopworn Communist Party, the Partido Socialista Popular, had been distant at the start of the revolution, and most of the Havana revolutionaries regarded the Communists as moribund and compromised by their cooperation with Batista. But Castro needed the Communists after the failure of the general strike in early 1958, and by the fall of that year Communist indoctrination of his forces was general. With the revolution's victory, it was the Communists who advised against resuming diplomatic relations with the Soviet Union, to avoid inviting American intervention.

That changed with the arrival of Anastas Mikoyan in Cuba in February 1960 on a visit that had been negotiated over several months.

Mikoyan signed a contract to buy five million tons of sugar in exchange for barter goods, some cash, a pledge of $100 million in credit and technical advisers to take the place of Cuban technicians who were leaving the country.

Mikoyan's commercial deal opened up similar exchanges with Communist bloc nations, and Czechoslovakia became Cuba's arms supplier, airline partner and the site of a Little Havana in Prague. Coincident with Mikoyan's visit about 100 Spanish Communists who had been in exile in the Soviet Union since the Spanish Civil War arrived in Cuba. More technicians came from Chile and other South American countries, all speaking Spanish and most of them speaking Russian. In March the first of Mikoyan's technicians arrived, including Alexei Alekseyev, who later became ambassador, and personnel from the Soviet foreign ministry's Latin American section, who purged the Cuban foreign service, according to Dr. Nicolas Rivero, an official who fled.[49]

Mikoyan said in a speech during his visit that the secret of organizing an economy was to take natural resources (land) without compensation, a remark that jolted Cubans.

Mikoyan's visit had turned into full-scale infiltration of Cuba by March 17, 1960, when the CIA outlined it to Eisenhower and he accepted a CIA recommendation to train secretly Cuban exiles for guerrilla activity in Cuba aimed at toppling Castro. Nixon and Admiral

Burke had been advocating such a force for months.

Cuba resumed diplomatic relations with the Soviet Union in May, and Raúl Castro went to Czechoslovakia on an arms shopping mission. At the same time government harrassment of the Cuban press turned into a purge, with Communist printers smashing the plates of an editorial written by a majority of employees of the *Diario de la Marina,* whose editor fled to the Venezuelan Embassy. The government seizure of *Prensa Libre* marked the end of Cuba's free press.

Throughout the revolution Castro had been well informed of events in Washington, and he quickly heard of Eisenhower's secret authorization of a guerrilla force. In July, Raúl Castro declared that the Soviet Union would support with military force and missiles Cuban resistance to any U.S. attack. On July 9 Nikita Khrushchev spoke to the All-Russian Teachers' Conference in Moscow saying that "figuratively speaking," the Soviets could "support the Cuban people with their missile fire if the aggressive forces of the Pentagon dare begin intervention against Cuba. . .as recent tests have shown, we have missiles capable of striking accurately in a preset square at distances of 13,000 kilometers. That is, if you like, a warning."

On the same day that the Soviet media publicized Khrushchev's speech, 600 American companies in Cuba were ordered to prepare detailed inventories of their properties.

The Soviet and Cuban media paid close attention to *The New York Times,* conducting a dialogue with it as though it were a government. In July, the Soviet government newspaper *Izvestia* quoted with approval a *Times* editorial saying that U.S. economic pressure was pushing Cuba into Soviet arms and making Cuban Communists more influential. When Max Frankel, the *Times* correspondent in Havana, reported after the U.S. elections that the Soviets had told the Cubans to quit rattling Soviet rockets, the Moscow press reprimanded him. Similarly, the Cuban Communist *Hoy* disagreed with Seymour Topping, the *Times* correspondent in Moscow, who implied that the Soviets were trying to exert a moderating influencing on Castro.

In September 1960, two months before the American elections, Castro paid his second visit to the United States as Cuba's leader, speaking at the United Nations on September 18. He returned to the theme of an impending invasion from the United States, noting that Admiral Burke had expressed doubts that Khrushchev would fire his missiles if Cuba were attacked. Castro said, "But suppose that Mr. Burke, even though he is an admiral, is mistaken?" In the General Assembly audience, Khrushchev took off his shoe and pounded his desk, leading the applause.

Castro's visit was high theater, although he now faced a partly hostile U.S. press. During the UN session he walked out of the Shelbourne Hotel, ostensibly insulted by the hotel's questioning his credit, and moved to the Hotel Theresa in Harlem, where he was lionized by Representative Adam Clayton Powell and acclaimed by black crowds who apparently were unaware that Batista had been a hero to Cuban blacks. Teresa Casuso, Castro's UN ambassador who had been his protector in Mexico, reported that the hotel switch

> . . .had been planned beforehand. He had intended from the start to complain that he was being overcharged. . .to plant himself with his retinue at the United Nations and thus present a spectacle that they had no place to stay, and then to move to Harlem, to give the impression that it was only among the humble and despised people of the United States, the Negroes, that the humble and despised Cubans and their leader were able to find shelter.[50]

Casuso, one of Castro's early fervent supporters, defected while he was in New York. She later wrote, "What the Castro regime has given Cuba are hatred, fear, suspicion, greater economic instability, a police state and utter economic dependence upon Russia and the Soviet bloc. And critical silence." She believed that Castro was paranoid, "a man with a disordered mind, a man fortunate in war but inept in peace, an absolutist obsessed with power and personal glory."[51]

She was especially disillusioned that Castro had imprisoned Captain Jesús Yañes Pelletier, who had saved Castro's life after the 1956 attack on Moncado by refusing orders to poison him, and then spreading the word, so that no one else dared poison him.

As the heated U.S. election campaign drew to a close in the fall of 1960 there was little doubt that Castro was in the Communist camp, although the dispute would continue between American conservatives and liberals about whether Castro himself was a Communist.

In April of that year, Matthews had told the American Society of Newspaper Editors, "In my 30 years on *The New York Times,* I have never seen a big story so misunderstood, so badly handled and so misinterpreted as the Cuban revolution."

Matthews certainly was right. Both the State Department and the American media ignored the storm clouds over Cuba until one enterprising newspaper, the *Times,* discovered a dramatic revolution with Matthews' series based on his single interview. In a pattern that would be repeated for decades, the rest of the media then leaped to imitate the *Times,* instead of independently discovering and evaluating Cuban developments, while a section of the media broke off later to stress Communist dangers.

Matthews left out his own misinterpretations; he stayed angry that Castro's menace to the United States was exaggerated, and he found no sign that Communists dominated the Castro program.

Not everyone fell into the media pattern. Theodore Draper was irritated by the bland distortions of Castro's media sympathizers and also at the shrill and shoddy reporting of the anti-Communists. In a series of articles for *Encounter* and the *New Leader,* Draper unleashed his scholarship at the conclusions of such Castro sympathizers as Jean-Paul Sartre and Simone de Beauvoir, and also at the anti-Communist Nathaniel Weyl.

Draper concluded that the revolution was not proletarian but middle-class, that Castro had adopted Marxism-Leninism, that he "represents a Cuban variant in the Communist family of revolutions," and that "communism in Cuba will be what he says it is."[52]

Mario Llerena, Castro's media man in New York, who quit the revolution in 1958, agreed:

> It was a marriage of convenience by which Castro declared himself a Communist and the Communists agreed to grant him endless power. Without Castro, the Communists could never dream of a day when they would rule Cuba, let alone make the island a Soviet base; without the Communists, Castro would have become perhaps a revised version of Batista—for a time—but never the uncontested doctrinal dictator, with international influence besides, that he is now.[53]

Draper only grazed Matthews in a few paragraphs, but Matthews, *engagé,* initiated a letter exchange that Draper included in his book. In a friendly tone, but pulling rank as the battle-tested correspondent, Matthews suggested that Draper

> . . . did not know Cuba and the Cubans in the sense that you did not realize how the Cubans felt. . . you do not know Fidel Castro and therefore ascribe to him ideas and feelings which are almost certainly incorrect. . . you evidently forgot, or perhaps have not read Che Guevara's book on guerrilla warfare. . . . You also evidently do not know that at that time there was a powerful ground swell in Havana and throughout Oriente Province against Batista. . . . I do not believe you have at all proved your point that Fidel 'deceived those who had believed in him.' . . . I feel you are doing something of great value in your continuing study

of the Cuban revolution even though I disagree with much of what you have written.

Unintimidated, Draper wrote back that Matthews' articles had been misleading: "I strongly doubt that your articles would have had such an electrifying effect if you had not personally vouched for Castro's large and winning force." He noted that Matthews now claimed he had estimated the guerrilla force at only 40 men, but in his book, *The Cuban Story,* had admitted going wrong in thinking the guerrillas he saw were part of a larger force.

Draper noted Matthews himself had said that his articles "literally altered the course of Cuban history," so his responsibility was unusually great. He took Matthews to task for justifying Castro's condemnation of Matos, quoting from Matthews' book, "By the logic of the Revolution, Hubert Matos was a traitor. Those who condemned the outrageous way he was treated, had to condemn the Revolution."

Draper noted that Matthews endorsed whatever the revolution did, justifying the substitution of Che Guevara, inexperienced, for the experienced economist, Felipe Pazos, as president of Cuba's National Bank, "because there are no revolutionary bankers," then reversing and justifying the appointment of top Communist Carlos Rafael Rodríguez as president of INRA because "the only trained and prepared elements were the Communists."

In the letter debate Matthews conceded error, writing, "I agree that I also made some mistakes as I went along, which I tried to correct. . . ." But he did not so much as correct errors as justify or minimize them in his subsequent writing.

Matthews never did change his basic themes. His strong feelings about the Loyalists in Spain—where Ernest Hemingway said Matthews was "brave as a badger"—put him on a collision course with those who had strong feelings from other wars where the Communists won.

Deeply marked by the Spanish Civil War, he wrote: "The premise is that Fascism is an impractical and evil way of life; the argument is 23 years of Fascist history (in Italy). . . ."[54] He insisted that Communist influence in Spain was exaggerated by everyone else, until he finally got around to correcting that at the age of 73. He continued to insist that Franco had not won the unfinished war in Spain.[55] Toward the end of his life, in a kind of exile in Australia, he even conceded that, studying the Spanish Civil War in retrospect, "many of the criticisms and fears expressed about the Nationalists during the war were unfounded and unfair. One can no longer, in honesty, draw a black or white picture."[56]

Even at 73, Matthews clung to one notion about the Spanish war that had broader implications for the legacy he left the *Times*: he believed the Loyalists lost because of divisions in their ranks, specifically because of the anti-Communists among them. He wrote of the last phase of the war: "Anti-communism, always a powerful factor in the Republican camp, was now decisive, for one of the best fighting units in the central zone, the Fourth Army, was commanded by an Anarchist, Cipriano Mera. He went over to the (anti-government) camp."[57]

The theme that Communists are not the problem; anti-Communists are, dovetailed neatly with the *Times'* defenders of Alger Hiss at the beginning of the 1950s and with the brief McCarthy period they called an "era." This theme would be found in *Times* editorials after Matthews died in 1977.

Matthews would not accept Castro's being a Communist because it would unleash the anti-Communists, who would ruin everything. He would insist in *The Cuban Story* that Castro "was not and is not a Communist" just before Castro himself on December 2, 1961, announced on television that he had been an apprentice Marxist-Leninist since his student days and "will be a Marxist-Leninist until the last day of my life."

Whether Castro was a Communist or when he became one was not really the point. For Cubans the point was whether he would impose a totalitarian system, and that was well advanced in late 1960. For the United States, the point was that by election day, 1960, Castro had introduced the Soviet Union's influence into the Western Hemisphere in a way it never had been able to penetrate before. Just before the American election, Peru broke relations with Cuba because Castro was funneling funds through the Cuban Embassy in Lima to Communists and to the Peruvian Communist Party.

John F. Kennedy was about to be elected President, and he would later say, "I am one of those who can truthfully say, I got my job through *The New York Times*."[58] Maybe the sally came from a half-remembered cartoon in the *National Review* in 1959, showing Fidel Castro sitting on a map of Cuba saying, "I got my job through *The New York Times*."

Chapter III
The Bay of Pigs

"In view of the fact that God limited the intelligence of man, it seems unfair that He did not also limit his stupidity."

—Konrad Adenauer to Dean Acheson on Hearing of the Bay of Pigs Fiasco

There never had been a presidential election quite like the campaign of 1960. Both candidates were unusually young, and both aggressively wanted the presidency. They contrasted sharply in background, personality and outlook. Voters had a clear choice, and they split almost evenly. Kennedy, relatively unknown, fought his way to national recognition and victory through the primaries and election in a dazzling campaign that inspired a textbook on getting elected in the age of instant communication.[1]

The challenger, Kennedy, seized the initiative in outlining campaign issues, and Nixon, defending the Eisenhower administration, never got off the defensive. Kennedy charged stagnation in domestic affairs, including the economy and civil rights, neglect in defense by permitting the Soviets to develop a "missile gap," and loss of influence in foreign affairs because of a "decline in American prestige."

Both men, politicians to the core, sought a broad spectrum of voters and stuck resolutely to generalities, avoiding programs and specific commitments that might alienate any group. That dulled the high drama of their extremely sharp exchanges in four television debates.

People thought the debates were bland, shallow and repetitive, but they were daring political duels, the first and best of their kind. Both men knew television as a treacherous medium—one misstep and you're dead nationwide—so they disagreed aggressively on what seemed to the viewer to be insignificant points. Kennedy, a trailblazer in television communication, trained for the debates as would a virtuoso. Nixon, the introvert who forced himself to play the extrovert as a high school debating champion, and had the forced personality to show for it, still debated for points.

Kennedy won the debates on an innocuous question by Charles von Fremd of CBS News in the third debate. The press had made much of President Truman's calling a music critic "a son of a bitch" for his harsh treatment of Margaret Truman's singing, and his remark that anyone who voted for Nixon could "go to hell." Von Fremd, lightening the tense debates, asked jokingly if Kennedy had any apologies to make for that.

Kennedy, amusement at the corner of his lips, said, "I really don't think there is anything I can say to President Truman that's going to cause him, at the age of 76, to change his particular speaking manner. (An open grin broke through.) Maybe Mrs. Truman can, but I can't."

Nixon, knees weak at the sight of Kennedy's easy grin, rambled sanctimoniously in rebuttal that he had seen mothers hold up their babies to see the candidates, and "whoever is President is going to be a man that all the children of American will either look up to or look down to. . . ."

James Reston, at the height of his influence, seized on the remark with what passed for glee in his column: "Vice President Nixon has suggested this week that President Eisenhower is a man who doesn't cuss and, in an obvious bid for the 'mom' vote, has indicated that if he (Mr. Nixon) is elected President, he won't cuss either. This raises a couple of questions. First, is it true? And second, do we want a President who doesn't cuss?"[2]

Under the rules of etiquette before the new journalism, Reston had an earned right to an opinion column and a partisan expression of his views. It was not well known that his enemity toward Nixon went back to 1948, when he was reporting, not in an opinion column, that

Nixon's "acid" questioning of Alger Hiss was unfair and in contrast to his sympathetic treatment of Whittaker Chambers, Hiss' accuser, on the stand of the House Un-American Activities Committee.[3] Reston had been among those who recommended Hiss to become president of the Carnegie Endowment for International Peace. At the first mention of Hiss' name in the House hearings, the *Times* attacked the committee in an editorial: ". . . we have a precious heritage in this country of protection of the innocent against false accusations, of a fair trial even for the guilty. . . ."[4] The *Times* became a rallying point for Hiss' defenders, as in a radio forum composed of Professor Henry Steele Commager, Seth H. Richardson, publisher Hodding Carter and A. J. Liebling on the *Times*-owned station, WQXR, on October 23, 1948. There still are New York intellectuals, marinated in the *Times* over decades, who believe that Hiss was innocent.

The 1960 campaign was unusual in that both candidates were fascinated by foreign policy, a matter of least concern to most voters. Foreign affairs turned up in all four of the debates instead of one, as planned. Kennedy was a world traveler from his youth, when he visited his father's embassy in London and then toured Europe. He reported back that "the Poles will fight for Danzig," and later wrote a best-seller at age 22 from his father's papers, with help from Harvard Professor Bruce Hopper and Dr. Payson Wild, editing by Arthur Krock and with a foreword by Henry R. Luce, publisher of *Time*.[5] Nixon became absorbed with foreign affairs through the implications of the Hiss case, his close association with John Foster Dulles and his travels as a Senator and Vice President.

The debates were in the hands of reporters who asked the questions, and neither candidate could risk planting a question with a friendly reporter. Kennedy, with his sure hand in guiding the press, made Cuba a major campaign issue by speaking on Cuba in Cincinnati the night before the second debate, making sure the *Times* had advance notice. The *Times* gave his speech major play on Page 1 and ran a partial text inside.[6]

Kennedy told a Cincinnati dinner audience that he wanted to talk about "the most glaring failure of American foreign policy, about a disaster which threatens the security of the whole Western Hemisphere, about a Communist menace which has been permitted to arise only ninety miles from the shores of the United States."

Kennedy said, "The American people want to know how this was permitted to happen. . . . It is not enough to blame it on unknown State Department personnel. Major policy is made at the highest level, in the National Security Council and elsewhere. . . ."

He said that Nixon had told *Meet the Press* that the Castro takeover might have been averted if the United States five years earlier had produced economic progress in Cuba:

> . . . but what Mr. Nixon neglected to mention is the fact that he was in Cuba five years ago, 'gaining experience.' He saw the conditions, he talked with the leaders. . . . But his only conclusion, stated at a Havana press conference five years ago, was his statement, and I quote, that he was 'very much impressed with the competence and stability' of the Batista dictatorship. If this is the kind of experience Mr. Nixon claims entitles him to the presidency, then I would say the American people cannot afford it.

Kennedy's speech made it inevitable that the first question asked in the debate of October 7 was addressed to Nixon on his and the administration's responsibility for Castro's rise.

Nixon denied that Cuba was lost, saying, ". . . there isn't any question but that the free people of Cuba, the people who want to be free, are going to be supported."

In rebuttal, Kennedy repeated the charge of administration responsibility and noted that Ambassadors Gardner and Smith (a personal friend), both Republicans, had warned the administration that Castro was a Marxist and Raúl Castro was a Communist.

Kennedy would have scored the first coup of the debates, except for a slipup. In the same debate he was asked what he would do about threatened Quemoy and Matsu, the small islands off China's coast, outposts of Chiang Kai-shek. Kennedy replied that they were "not strategically defensible," and a defense line should be drawn at Formosa. He had been too specific.

Nixon leaped to the attack, saying that the defense of the islands was a matter of principle, that the United States "should not surrender one inch of free territory."

Thus, the obscure question of Quemoy and Matsu became a major campaign issue, a symbolic means of tagging Kennedy soft on communism, recalling Dean Acheson's blunder in leaving South Korea out of the nations the United States was prepared to defend in 1950. Kennedy, pressed on the issue, called Nixon "trigger-happy." The Cuba issue did not catch fire.

A week after the first Cuba debate, the Eisenhower administration, partly in response to Kennedy's charge, banned all U.S. exports to Cuba except food and medicine, and within two weeks Castro had seized all remaining American enterprises on the island.

Two days before the fourth and final debate, the Kennedy campaign fired its second salvo on Cuba. Richard Goodwin, running Kennedy's campaign, had the New York office issue a statement that the *Times* splashed as the leading story across three columns of Page 1, sign of a major event:

> Kennedy Asks Aid for Cuban Rebels to Defeat Castro;
> Urges Support of Exiles and "Fighters for Freedom."[7]

Nixon was stricken by the headline and the story. The Eisenhower administration had been planning for seven months a CIA operation so secret that only a few in Washington knew of it, although for months it had been headlined in the Cuban press and was routinely discussed in the Cuban barrios of Miami. Nixon asked his aide, Fred Seaton, to call CIA Director Dulles. Yes, Seaton reported, Dulles had briefed Kennedy on the CIA's world operations including Cuba, on July 23 in Hyannis Port. At the next Security Council meeting, Dulles confirmed that he had talked two and a half hours with Kennedy, saying he had kept the Cuba part general, mentioning the radio operations. Radio operations included the clandestine infiltration of radio operators, basis for the invasion plan, and Nixon hit the ceiling after the meeting, according to Robert Amory, CIA director of intelligence.[8-9]

The major story in the *Times,* unprecedented for a campaign handout without direct quotations from the candidate, threw the issue into the last debate, and Kennedy came on strong for U.S.-supported exiled Cuban intervention to overthrow Castro.

Nixon, unable to say that he was a prime mover of exactly that project, and unwilling to confirm Soviet and Cuban charges of such a plan, called Kennedy's proposal shocking and reckless, unlikely to succeed and an invitation to Khrushchev to promote civil war in Latin America.

It was an extraordinary role reversal. The *Times* chastised Kennedy and complimented Nixon, but politically the episode was a plus for Kennedy; he stood to pick up some anti-Communist votes; the liberals who abhorred Nixon had no place else to go.

While answering Kennedy, Nixon proposed instead a quarantine of Castro, pretending that such action had brought down the regime of President Jacobo Arbenz Gusmán in Guatemala in 1954. Every newspaperman in the country knew that Arbenz fell to a CIA-organized coup, and Nixon's credibility was further damaged.

Raúl Roa, Cuba's foreign minister, called on October 31 for a United Nations Security Council meeting to charge that the United States planned an imminent invasion from bases in Guatemala. Roa told Herbert Matthews that he knew the exact locations of training camps in Guatemala and Florida.[10] Castro at the same time mobilized 200,000 militiamen (compared with the Batista-era army of 40,000 men), and kept them on alert until Kennedy's inauguration.

In Cuba, a major defection failed when David Salvador, head of the Cuban labor federation and Castro's close friend, who had been an underground leader of M26-7, was arrested November 4 while trying to flee in a boat. He would be held until August 1962, and then sentenced to 30 years in prison. Earlier, his arrest would have been a major story, but the media was sated with Cuba defection stores, and the *Times* noted his arrest on Page 24, second to a story about Cuban trade problems.

Reston was pressing election commentaries both in his column and in another device that permitted opinion under the rules of etiquette, the "news analysis."

In his analysis of the third debate, Reston wrote:

> Mr. Nixon's presentation was general and often emotional; Mr. Kennedy's curt and factual. Mr. Nixon, whose campaign is based on his reputation for knowledge of the facts and experience was outpointed on facts. . . . He has gone beyond the President's position on Quemoy and Matsu, he has elevated what the State Department and Joint Chiefs of Staff regard as a tactical question into an issue of fundamental principle. . . the feeling here (in Washington) is that the Senator won the main point in the debate over the offshore islands. . . . [11]

A week later, Reston's analysis said:

> On balance, the feeling among the political pros is that Mr. Kennedy came out on top, primarily because he started these broadcasts far behind. . . . On the same screen with Mr. Nixon, he managed to reduce the 'age issue' and the 'immaturity' charge. . . . He had a grasp of specific detail that came as a surprise to many of his supporters. . . . [12]

In his column that week, Reston wrote:

> . . . the contrast between them now is even greater than when the contest began. The Vice President is still painfully self-conscious while Kennedy is increasingly self assured. . . . now (Nixon's) basic speech almost amounts to saying that a vote for Kennedy is a vote for war, and higher prices, and inflation, and fiscal disaster, and government by political and labor bosses. . . . Nixon is aiming lower and concentrating on stopping bad things, while Kennedy is concentrating on starting new things. . . . [13]

As the campaign neared its close, Reston commented:

President Eisenhower is now engaged in the greatest rescue operation since Bill Mazerosky of the Pittsburgh Pirates hit the ninth inning homer in the World Series. . . . It is true that before the 1956 election the President did talk to Mr. Nixon about leaving the Vice Presidency and taking a Cabinet post, but he did not follow through on his plan against Mr. Nixon's opposition, and this, the idea of building up a new and popular national figure to carry out the Eisenhower formula of 1952 was forgotten. . . . Maybe even now (Eisenhower's) popularity can turn the tide, but it is very late in the game to reverse the forces now moving with Senator Kennedy in New York, Pennsylvania and Ohio.[14]

That same day the *Times* published in detail a USIA survey, which had been stamped secret, indicating that the United States had suffered a decline in prestige around the world. Kennedy had given the survey to the *Times*.[15]

A news analysis two days later said, "It is perhaps significant that while Mr. Nixon has been talking about new reorganizations, Mr. Kennedy has been talking about new men, and new ideas." Reston quoted Professor Arthur Schlesinger, Jr., on great Presidents:

The 'greats;' says Professor Schlesinger, were entirely different in looks, personality and temperament, but resembled one another in these ways: Each was identified with some turning point in the nation's history. All of them 'took the side of progressivism and human betterment as understood in their day.' To their contemporaries, they 'appeared ahead of their times.' A striking personality and gifts of showmanship became indespensible conditions of Presidential leadership.[16]

Reston was working overtime, and in his column the same day commented, "There is general agreement here (in Washington) that Senator Kennedy is going to win the election. . . . "

There never was any question that the *Times* would endorse Kennedy, even disregarding its clear enmity toward Nixon. Kennedy was a personal friend of many of the executives, editors and reporters, and Arthur Krock, the venerable Washington bureau chief, had been a kind of godfather from Kennedy's childhood, vetting and editing all of the books written by both John and Robert Kennedy. It was, however, unusual that the *Times* endorsed Kennedy three times, on October 27, October 30 and on November 6, stressing that "his approach to foreign policy is more reasoned, less emotional, more flexible, less doctrinaire, more imaginative, less negative than that of Mr. Nixon." The *Times* pledged that if Kennedy were elected, "we still scrutinize his words and deeds just as we would those of Mr. Nixon and will exercise a citizen's right to blame as well as praise." It didn't work out that way.

Early on November 9, with returns not yet in but with the *Times* bannering, "KENNEDY APPARENT VICTOR," Reston had the satisfaction of writing the lead story: "Senator John F. Kennedy of Massachusetts, the cool young Democratic leader of a new generation of American politicians, appeared to have won election today as the thirty-fifth President of the United States . . . ."

Kennedy was elected with a plurality of 118,574 votes out of a total of 68,838,219, as reports of vote fraud began in Duval County, Texas, and Cook County, Illinois, and as Cubans were pouring out of their country.

In the closing days of the election campaign, Max Frankel reported from Havana that Eisenhower's cutoff of trade with Cuba had further pushed Cuba into the Communist camp:

> Cuba's shortage of dollars and gold makes survival dependent upon the trade with the Soviet bloc of more than 3,000,000 tons of sugar, formerly sold to the United States, in return for oil, machines, trucks, tractors, spare parts and consumer goods to fill empty shelves. . . . In effect, therefore, Cuba must volunteer to be included in the long-range economic plans of the Soviet Union, Communist China and their allies.

He noted that Guevara, Cuba's economic director and head of the National Bank, was in Moscow.[17] His theme echoed that of Tad Szulc earlier, who reported that "the refusal by the U.S. and most Western European exporters to grant credits leaves her (Cuba) with virtually no alternative (to trade with the Soviet bloc)"[18] *Times* editorials also had pressed the theme that Cuba was being pushed into the Communist bloc by Eisenhower's economic retaliation.

But the Soviet bloc trade and credit was not all for tractors and consumer goods to fill empty shelves. As Americans went to the polls November 8, Castro warned again that the United States planned an invasion, and said, "We have acquired arms, many arms, many more of them than the mercenaries and imperialists have imagined." His callup of 200,000 militiamen had coincided with the arrival of a vast shipment of light arms.

On November 18, Tass commented, "Everyone knows forces are being readied in Guatemala and Nicaragua for an invasion of Cuba." It added that "friends of Cuba . . . would help her keep her liberty and independence." In Cuba, the theme of impending American attack filled the media and decorated Havana in large cartoon posters.

That day, Allen Dulles and Richard Bissell briefed the new President on what Tass already knew but Kennedy's men said he didn't, and on November 19, Kennedy received a more detailed briefing on the invasion plans. He told Dulles to proceed. Eisenhower was told by Dulles on November 20, that is, two days after Kennedy, that the original guerrilla-infiltration plan had been expanded to a beachhead invasion on the pattern of the Anzio landing in Italy in World War II.

In December Raúl Castro returned from his latest Moscow trip saying that he had been buying arms. He repeated the warning that Soviet missiles protected Cuba. The CIA reported that the new arms purchases included MiG-15 fighters.

Before Kennedy could be inaugurated, the new heavy Soviet arms arrived, and Castro paraded tanks and artillery in Havana celebrating the anniversary of his takeover there. In a television address on January 2, 1961, Castro demanded that the U.S. Embassy be reduced to 11 diplomats. Cubans rushed the Embassy for last-minute visas, and Eisenhower broke relations with Cuba. His ambassador, Philip Bonsal, had been recalled months earlier after his efforts at conciliation had been rejected by Castro.

Guatemala's leading newspaper, *La Hora*, had published on October 30 a Page 1 editorial by its editor, Clemente Marroquín Rojas, saying that the invasion of Cuba was being planned there by the United States, not by Guatemala. Ronald Hilton of Stanford University, who published the scholarly *Hispanic American Report*, was in Guatemala City and picked up the story. *The Nation* quoted from his report in an editorial opposing intervention on November 19.

The *Times* twice sent Paul Kennedy, its Mexico City correspondent, to Guatemala to find the bases. Kennedy knew President Miguel Ydigoras Fuentes and on both trips accepted his assurances that the base in the hills was Guatemalan, built to train for an expected attack from Cuba, where the deposed Arbenz was an honored guest. Since Peru had broken relations with Cuba after finding that Cuban diplomats were smuggling money to Peruvian Communists via the Cuban Embassy in Lima, it was not implausible. On his second trip, however, Kennedy filed a dispatch from Retalhuleu pinpointing a busy airfield and guerrilla training camp in a remote coffee plantation belonging to the country's largest coffee producer, Roberto Alejo Argu, and said it was U.S.-financed and staffed with U.S. military officers. He noted the presence of some Cubans, but his story did not specify a Cuban invasion force.[19] Because it was a *Times* report, news agencies lost interest in the alleged Guatemalan bases. Harrison Salisbury regarded the correspondent as something like a traitor, saying that Paul Kennedy was not regarded as a top-flight reporter and his dispatches gave rise to a question of his motives.[20]

Two days after Kennedy's inauguration, Dulles and General Lyman Lemnitzer, head of the Joint Chiefs of Staff, briefed Dean Rusk, Robert McNamara and Robert Kennedy on the invasion plans and the range of alternatives. The CIA now planned a medium-scale invasion with a paramilitary force that numbered about 550 Cubans in training, with more being recruited, backed by armor and air support. Kennedy convened his White House Staff on the Cuba plan on January 18, bringing McGeorge Bundy and Walt Rostow into the informed circle.

The covert branch of the CIA had conceived the plan in January 1960 and kept it to a small circle under Bissell, cutting out the larger intelligence branch of Robert Amory. Bissell had the reputation of being a dynamic and driven genius. He had been a key economic planner for the Marshall Plan, produced the U-2 plane in three months and coordinated the first photo-reconnaissance satellite. When he introduced himself to Kennedy at a White House informal dinner of CIA men and White House staff, he said, referring to his reputation, "I'm your man-eating shark."[21]

Bissell had started with the idea of infiltrating 30 trained radio operators into Cuba to coordinate arms deliveries and directions to anti-Castro bands in the mountains, but it quickly grew to include 60 more trained guerrilla-instructors. Through 1960, as CIA plans advanced, Castro used tens of thousands of militiamen to track down guerrillas, including those of Manuel Artime's Movement for Revolutionary Recovery, which also was conducting widespread sabotage in the cities. Exiles said that 1,300 were killed by Castro's men in 1960, more than the total casualties of the revolution.[22] As guerrillas were wiped out, the CIA's plan grew to make up the difference, and Bissell continued to add to his requirements. In August Eisenhower had authorized a budget of $13 million. Richard Helms, nominally Bissell's deputy, called some elements of the project "harebrained," and he was dropped from the operation, with some strain between himself and Bissell.[23]

The plan presented to Kennedy was for a sea invasion, with a paratroop drop by about 1,400 Cuban exiles at the town of Trinidad, about 200 miles from Havana. It was to be supported by air strikes to knock out Castro's small air force. Trinidad's citizens were supporting about 200 guerrillas in the adjacent Escambray Mountains and could be counted on to join the invaders, possibly doubling their strength at the outset. The CIA would fly the Revolutionary Council to the site once the beachhead troops had captured the nearby airstrip and thereafter would supply the anti-Castro brigade until they won control of the island. Castro's untrained militiamen were expected to switch sides and go with the winners, given the degree of discontent reported by the CIA.

Democrats in Washington were euphoric that winter. Kennedy had decimated the faculty of his alma mater, Harvard, and the White House, State Department, Defense Department and many agencies were full of bright young academic newcomers to power who would stay in Washington, a new and permanent infusion into high levels of the bureaucracy.

Cuba was a potential, but not actual, scene of direct United States-Soviet Union conflict, and therefore not the top priority issue. The urgent foreign issues were in two places where the Soviet Union and United States already were nose-to-nose: Laos, where a Communist takeover threatening all of Indochina was underway, and Germany, where Khrushchev was threatening to force the Western allies out of West Berlin.

Kennedy had been in office only a matter of days when he called in Llewellyn Thompson, the ambassador to Moscow, who returned in early February to see if he would remain under the new administration. Kennedy also summoned Averell Harriman, Charles Bohlen and George Kennan, all former ambassadors to Moscow, and "wondered aloud" if he should not consider a meeting with Khrushchev.[24]

Nobody said the idea was a bummer. The four-power "spirit of Geneva" conference of 1955 had proved to be a cover for Soviet infiltration into Egypt that produced the Suez war. The Eisenhower-Khrushchev summit of 1960 in Paris had been a fiasco, to the *Schadenfreude* of the allied leaders, who were edgy about the two superpowers going over their heads. Khrushchev torpedoed it on the pretext that Eisenhower had sent Gary Powers spying on the Soviet Union in a U-2, although Khrushchev probably was ordered to do so by the Politburo and the military because Eisenhower was not going to give ground on Berlin. A glowering Marshal Rodion Malinovski was sent along with Khrushchev to make sure he followed orders.

Despite the demonstrated hazards of summitry and the opposition of Dean Rusk, who disliked personal diplomacy at that level, Kennedy instantly won endorsement from the four Moscow experts. He felt on fairly good terms with Khrushchev, despite the rocket rattling over Cuba. Harriman had asked Khrushchev early in the election campaign not to favor Kennedy for fear of driving anti-Communist voters to

Nixon, and Khrushchev had sent warm congratulations to Kennedy on his inauguration. Kennedy intended to propose to Khrushchev an end to the cold war, and he also wanted to make Khrushchev's acquaintance early in his administration. Accordingly, without preparation and without having become acquainted with his new Secretary of State, Kennedy sent Thompson back to Moscow with a letter dated February 22 proposing a summit in Vienna or Stockholm in the late spring. Kennedy had been in office 33 days.

Meanwhile, word of the Cuba plans went around quickly among the new players in Washington, after Bissell had succeeded in keeping the project compartmented within the CIA and JCS for almost a year. Arthur Schlesinger, Jr., a special aide to Kennedy, learned of the plan in early February. A series of Cabinet meetings studied the plan through February and March, adding more persons to the informed. The Joint Chiefs studied the plan repeatedly. General Lemnitzer thought the plan would work, but he was glad it was not his. General David Shoup, the Marine Corps chief, who took Tarawa and held the Congressional Medal of Honor, who abhorred war and believed that massive force saves lives, thought the plan was inadequate and dependent on a simultaneous uprising, air superiority and the good will of God. Admiral Burke, Chief of Naval Operations, said the plan was weak, sloppy and had inadequate logistics, but he became the most actively involved military leader, trying to shore up the plan as he saw Kennedy progressively weaken it.

For Kennedy, the die was cast to go ahead with the invasion at a meeting in the Cabinet Room on March 11, when Dulles and Bissell argued that the plan would work and it was too far advanced to call off. Soviet MiGs and Cuban pilots training in Czechoslovakia were expected in Cuba, and Dulles added that there would be a "disposal problem" in turning loose trained guerrillas to talk freely and to organize their own bands. Bissell argued for the landing at Trinidad, the site long studied, close to the Escambray if the invaders should have to revert to guerrilla war. Kennedy ordered a quiet night landing at a more secluded spot. The CIA came up three days later with the Zapata swamp on the Bay of Pigs, not knowing that Castro had made allies of the local population by starting to build there Cuba's first seaside resort, complete with an airfield for tourist traffic.

Kennedy also intervened to demand that the Democratic Front be enlarged to include Manuel Ray, and that any former Batista men be purged from the invasion force. The intervention disrupted the Front, which already had great difficulty holding itself together, being composed of men who were long-time political rivals. Bissell said later the

Cubans were "incorrigible" and incapable of acting together politically.

Ray, a brilliant engineer and architect, had spent seven years building the tunnel under the Almendares River, then joined the Havana underground against Batista in 1957. With Armando Hart, he became a head of the Havana underground that summer and led a sabotage campaign in the cities in 1958. Castro made him Public Works minister in the revolution's first Cabinet, and the exile leaders were suspicious of him because he did not resign over Castro's arrest of Matos. Castro persuaded him that Matos was anti-Communist, so Ray remained in the Cabinet until November 1959, then resigned to become professor of architecture at Havana University. In the summer of 1960 he formed a new anti-Castro underground called the Movimiento Revolutionaria del Pueblo, or Peoples Revolutionary Movement. It had no support from exiled Cubans and was one of several undergrounds in Cuba. Its slogan was "Fidelismo sin Fidel,"[25] or Castroism without Castro, a return to the early revolutionary goals before Castro's personality cult developed, but it was not anti-Communist. Ray rejected any contact with the CIA and tried to assemble disillusioned Castro supporters, including David Salvador, the union leader. Ray escaped from Cuba to Miami in November 1960, at about the same time Salvador was arrested trying to escape. It was late to try to integrate him into the invasion plan, and he was anti-CIA in any case.

Bissell did not want him on security grounds.[26] His underground was questioned by exiles in the United States, who said that if it existed it was infiltrated by Castro agents. Bissell said later he made the project an invasion rather than an infiltration because he had little faith in any of the underground groups in Cuba. Howard Hunt, alias Eduardo, the anti-Communist CIA man trying to hold the exiled Cubans together, distrusted Ray completely, accusing him of betraying his brother René, imprisoned by Castro. The Front leaders rejected Ray because he stayed with Castro too long, his slogan meant a leftist-Socialist program, and he somehow never was arrested by either Batista or Castro, as most intriguers had been, some by both.

In a meeting in Bissell's office, Hunt was told the Front had to accept Ray, Tracy Barnes telling him, "This is terribly important to the White House." Hunt also was told that with the integration of Ray, a new Cuban constitution would be written, with U.S. participation, while the Front leaders wanted a return to the Constitution of 1940. Hunt said he would rather resign from the project than tell the Front to accept Ray, and was jolted to hear that he had just resigned. James Noel, the former CIA station chief in Havana, regarded by Hunt as once soft on

Castro, took over, assembling a meeting of the Front leaders at the Skyway Motel in Miami on March 18. He ordered them to accept Ray or the U.S. would withdraw from the project. Hunt, transferred to Washington, believed that Kennedy's Cuba experts, Schlesinger and Goodwin, along with Under Secretary of State Chester Bowles, had sold the President on Ray.[27] Schlesinger continued to describe Ray as the most calm and reasonable of the exiled leaders after the invasion failed, but none of Ray's men had gone with the invasion force, so he had less direct reason for anguish than those who had sent their sons.

On March 22, dangerously near the invasion date, Manuel Antonio Varona signed for the Front an agreement with his old adversary Ray, making Miró Cardona, who had been Castro's first premier and the first to resign from the moderate sham government, head of the new Revolutionary Council.

The shakeups in Cuban political leadership and in CIA personnel contributed to the confusion. CIA personnel in Guatemala were telling the invaders they would get United States support all the way, including air cover. Kennedy was telling Cabinet meetings there would be no U.S. military intervention, but in less than forceful terms. Adolf Berle told Miró that the United States would back up the invasion with arms once it got a beachhead established, but not with men.

The Joint Chiefs attending the meetings apparently did not get Kennedy's message unequivocally that there would be no U.S. intervention at any point. Kennedy, after all, was a guerrilla buff. The Joint Chiefs had been glad to disband, as too elitist, the Green Berets of Bad Tölz after they were not used in the Hungarian revolution, but Kennedy made them revive the Green Berets. None imagined that Kennedy would put the Cubans on the beach and then leave them. Kennedy required Lemnitzer and Burke to endorse the invasion plan in writing.[28]

Schlesinger opposed the project entirely and wrote at least three memos to Kennedy warning that the United States would be held accountable by the world for whatever happened, and there was a probability of touching off a long civil war in which the Russians would call for volunteers in an attempt to make it another Spanish Civil War. Schlesinger wrote that his memos "looked nice on the record, but they represented, of course, the easy way out."[29] He reproached himself for not daring to speak out against the invasion in the Cabinet Room, as Senator J. William Fulbright had done in declaring that Castro was "a thorn in the flesh but not a dagger in the heart."

Adlai Stevenson, who had reluctantly become Kennedy's United Nations ambassador after almost upsetting Kennedy's sweep of the Democratic Convention the year before, took alarm at news reports and went to Washington on April 8 to ask what was going on. Tracy Barnes and Schlesinger briefed him—vaguely, as Schlesinger wrote—and Stevenson was left with the impression that no action would take place while the United Nations was discussing Cuba's complaint of planned American aggression. Stevenson also saw Kennedy and told Hugh Thomas that Kennedy said that "I could rest assured that whatever was being planned, there would be no question of U.S. involvement. I said I was greatly relieved at this."[30]

While Stevenson was relieved, the men running the project were not. Jacob Esterline, the CIA man running the project's operations in Washington, and Marine Colonel Jack Hawkins, who supervised the buildup in Guatemala, went to Bissell's home that night and said they were resigning. The President had watered down the project, and the change from Trinidad to the new landing site changed the character of the operation. Bissell talked them out of quitting. Later, Hawkins would say, "The President shot this thing down."[31]

Reston heard of the invasion plan not long after Schlesinger did—the date is uncertain—and went to the top for an explanation. Kennedy assured him that U.S. involvement would be minimal.

Times reporter Peter Kihss, who also had reported from Cuba, interviewed Roa at the United Nations on April 5. His report was the lead story: Roa charged that the United States was in an "undeclared war" against Cuba. Roa said the United States was supporting "a so-called liberation army of 4,000 to 5,000 counter-revolutionaries, mercenaries and adventurers" in Florida and Guatemala. He said he had photocopies of checks paid by the United States to dependents of guerrillas in training and spoke of U.S. plans to seize a beachhead in Cuba. The guerrillas, he said, were under the CIA-financed Democratic Revolutionary Front.[32]

Tad Szulc meanwhile had stopped off in Miami at the end of March en route from his post in Argentina to a new assignment at the *Times* Washington bureau. Within a day he had run into several Cuban friends who filled him in on the invasion, sponsored, as they joked, by the Cuban Invasion Authority. One gave him the telephone number of "Frank Bender," the *nom de guerre* of Gerry Droller, the CIA supervisor of the exiles. Szulc flew to Washington and New York to consult with his editors, then returned to Miami to flesh out the story, pooling his findings with Stuart Novins of CBS.

Szulc filed his story on the same day Kihss' story appeared, and it was dummied into Page 1 with a four-column headline—a blockbuster format—when publisher Orville Dryfoos had second thoughts and called Reston in Washington. Reston cautioned against playing the story heavily or tying it to the CIA. Dryfoos apparently called Kennedy, who said in equivocal language that the story was questionable and damaging. The publishing layout was revised. Managing Editor Turner Catledge cut out the word "imminent" and all references to the CIA and reduced the headline to one column placed low on Page 1. Salisbury reported that senior editors Theodore Bernstein and Lewis Jordan remained bitter for years over the tampering.[33] Szulc was dismayed that the story was emasculated. Kennedy was furious that it was published at all, complaining to Dryfoos that other newspapers followed the *Times'* lead.

At least two reporters had the full story when Szulc did. Howard Handleman of *U.S. News and World Report* conferred with Schlesinger and did not publish it. Karl Meyer sold the story to *New Republic*, using a pseudonym byline. Gilbert Harrison of *New Republic* sent proofs of the article, "Our Men in Miami," to Schlesinger at the White House, and Kennedy had the story killed.[34]

Szulc's story reported that an army of 5,000 to 6,000 exiles had been training in the United States and in two camps in Guatemala for nine months. The exile force included an air force, navy and commando infiltrators, supported by paratroops and saboteurs who had been landing in Cuba for months from the Florida Keys in cooperation with a growing underground in Cuba.

Szulc reported the exile political developments as well, describing the Democratic Revolutionary Front, which "enjoys the tolerance and the active cooperation of United States officials (changed by the editor from CIA)." He identified the Front leaders: Dr. José Miró Cardona, Dr. Manuel Antonio Varona, Manuel Artime, former Cuban President Carlos Hevia, Dr. Justo Carrillo and Dr. Antonio Maceo. He reported that the Front, had, however, been superseded. "Last month it was absorbed into the Revolutionary Council formed to unite all the factions opposed to the Castro regime and to any resurgence of a Batista-type dictatorship," Szulc reported.

"Until the signing of the unity pact last month and the establishment of the Revolutionary Council under Dr. José Miró Cardona, the military units of the Democratic Front operated separately from the groups of the People's Revolutionary Movement headed by Manuel Ray, Dr. Castro's former Minister of Public Works.

"The Ray movement is the foremost underground organization in Cuba, but it also has small military groups in the United States," he reported, adding that "there are deep differences in political views between Señor Ray and the leaders of the Democratic Front."

"Señor Ray, a soft-spoken engineer who studied in Utah, is opposed to any early military operation from abroad against Dr. Castro. . . . He takes the view that it would be better to strike through an internal uprising aided from abroad," Szulc reported.[35]

Following Szulc's story, the *Times* tacked on a shirttail: "Invasion Reported Near." It quoted Novins' CBS report, which he had coordinated with Szulc for simultaneous publication, to the effect that exile troops had been mobilized and were ready to go—using six paragraphs to replace the word "imminent" killed from Szulc's story.

Szulc's story, promotional of Ray, was accurate in saying that there were differences between Manuel Ray and the others. Szulc and Meyer later said in their book that "the idea of men like Ray and his companions was to restore the revolution to its original goals of political democracy and social justice. They stood firmly for the continuation of the social reforms initiated by Castro."[36] Six pages later they complained that some Americans and Cubans opposed Ray as "advocating 'Fidelismo without Fidel,' whatever that was supposed to mean."

Szulc had stopped off in Washington before writing his story, and Reston's doubts that Kennedy had leveled with him were confirmed. Reston went to Dulles' home and asked the CIA director what was going on. Dulles put him off as Kennedy had done, denying that the United States was deeply involved. Reston resented being lied to.

Reston's deputy, Wallace Carroll, went to Schlesinger, who told him it was "the hottest thing in Washington and is gathering momentum." Carroll then braced his close friend, Richard Helms, who told him he was keeping clear of the program, and if Carroll wanted to stop it he would have to act quickly.[37]

Reston set out to stop it. First he wrote the lead story in the *Times*,[38] a departure from his usual column and analyses: "Washington—A sharp policy dispute has developed within the Kennedy Administration about how far to go in helping the Cuban refugees overthrow the Castro government." Reston wrote that Kennedy was getting conflicting advice from his White House advisers, the CIA, Defense Department and State Department, the latter especially worried about the political consequences of using military force. Reston noted that Article 15 of the Charter of the Organization of American States, "which was signed by the United States and the other American republics at Bogotá, Colombia, in 1948, specifically forbids such action." He cited the treaty paragraph. Reston reported that Kennedy was being pressed to make up his mind because Cuban pilots were being trained in Czechoslovakia.

Kennedy the next day told a press conference, "There will not be, under any circumstances, an intervention in Cuba by the United States Armed Forces. . .and I understand this administration's attitude is so understood and shared by the anti-Castro exiles from Cuba in this country."

Reading Kennedy's press conference statement in Moscow, where Ambassador Thompson was sending Kennedy messages that Khrushchev was absorbed with Cuban developments, Khrushchev took it as a signal that Kennedy was in retreat, as his letter to Kennedy showed later. Moscow also had a sensation to jubilate that day: Yuri Gagarin became the first man to fly in outer-space, orbiting the earth in 108 minutes.

Reston pressed his offensive against the invasion plan. He published in succession two columns, "The Moral Issue-I," and "The Moral Issue-II."[39] No one had raised a moral issue directly, even Fulbright arguing in pragmatic terms that an invasion would alienate Latin America and the world, although a moral element was implicit in the warnings of Schlesinger and the unheard protests by Chester Bowles, Edward R. Murrow of the United States Information Service and others. Reston's columns warned that use of United States military force against Cuba was immoral because it would violate both the country's treaty obligations to the OAS and also the government's duty not to mislead its citizens. He asked, "If they get in trouble once they land, will (the administration) continue to supply them?"

Reston was late. As he wrote his columns, Brigade 2506, named for the serial number of an exile killed in training, was arriving by truck convoy at Puerto Cabezas, Nicaragua, from Guatemala. At Puerto Cabezas on April 13, Artime, the political leader, military chief Jose Pérez San Román, his deputy Erneldo Olivia and six commanders of 200-man battalions learned for the first time their destination and the plan of attack worked out by the CIA.

The brigade boarded the invasion fleet: four merchant ships chartered with their crews by the CIA—the *Río Escondida,* the *Houston,* the *Caribe* and the *Atlantico*—plus the landing ship LSD *San Marcos,* which carried landing craft, and two infantry landing ships carrying tanks, the *Blagar* and *Barbara J.* They sailed on their four-day journey to the Bay of Pigs, seen off by Nicaraguan President Luis Somoza, who was providing an airfield at Puerto Cabezas for their 16 B-26 light bombers and a dozen unarmed C-47s. The U.S. Navy had deployed a carrier-destroyer task force to turn back the invasion fleet if Kennedy should reverse his decision.

The original plan had been changed from a simultaneous landing and air strike to provide for an air strike on Castro's air force two days before the landing. Kennedy called Bissell on April 14 to ask how many planes would take part in the next day's first strike. Bissell said all 16 B-26s. Kennedy said that was too many; he wanted a minimal air strike.[40] Bissell sent orders to let six planes fly.

At dawn April 15, six B-26 bombers, a World War II obsolete type sold as surplus all over the world, including to Batista's Cuba, struck Cuban airfields at Havana, Santiago and the air force headquarters at San Antonio de los Baños. Castro had inherited from Batista about 19 B-26s, ten British Sea Fury jets and four U.S. T-33 jet trainers. Soviet MiGs had arrived in Cuba, but were still crated.[41]

A seventh B-26 flew from Nicaragua to Miami, where the pilot would pretend to be a defector from Castro's air force. Unexpectedly, one of the attack B-26s was partly disabled and flew to Key West rather than chance the long flight back to Nicaragua.

Kennedy went to his vacation retreat at Glen Ora, Virginia, that Saturday, with his brother-in-law, Stephen Smith, and their wives. In New York, Roa demanded an immediate meeting of the United Nations Political Committee, where Stevenson repeated Washington's cover story that Cuban defectors had done the bombing. Stevenson was scathingly attacked by Soviet Ambassador Valerian Zorin just as the cover story began coming unstuck. Reporters in Miami identified the B-26 as not one of Castro's because it had a different nose cone, and they doubted it had been in battle despite its bullet holes because its machine guns had not been fired and still were sheathed.

On Sunday in Havana Castro addressed a rally for the seven persons killed in the bombings of airfields the day before. He referred to the Revolutionary Council as the "council of worms" and ridiculed Kennedy and Stevenson. He charged that the United States had staged a Pearl Harbor attack because it could not bear a socialist revolution under its nose, and he warned that the bombings meant an invasion was underway.

Castro shouted, "Comrades, workers and peasants, this is a socialist and democratic revolution of the humble, with the humble, for the humble. The attack of yesterday was the prelude to aggression by mercenaries. All units must now go to their battalions. . . . *Patria o Muerte, venceremos!*"

At the same time Castro's *Direccion Generale de Inteligencia* (DGI) supervised the roundup of at least 200,000 persons, including all of the island's priests and a handful of North American correspondents (but not the *Times'*), who were held in jails, theaters, ballparks and even chickencoops. What was left of the underground was immobilized; in any case it received no radio instructions from the CIA.

That day an editorial in the *Times*, delivered as usual to Kennedy in

Glen Ora, issued a direct warning to the President: "...it must certainly remain true, as President Kennedy has promised, that no American military forces will take part in any attack on the island. Cuba is not going to become a Hungary in reverse."

At noon on Sunday, Kennedy passed the last no-go point, and the invasion could no longer be recalled. The Navy ships, including the carrier *Essex,* changed missions, and now became out-of-sight, over-the-horizon escorts of the invasion fleet.

Stevenson angrily protested to Rusk that he was dismayed at being lied to, that his credibility and that of the United States was being destroyed at the United Nations. Rusk relayed the message to Kennedy at Glen Ora. U-2 evaluation pictures showed that the first air strike had knocked out only five planes, and some of them may have been derelicts. Castro's air force was almost intact.

Late Sunday the CIA team in Washington prepared to signal a go-ahead to Nicaragua for the second air strike when General Charles P. Cabell arrived in the war room, in overall charge of the CIA in the temporary absence of Dulles. Howard Hunt, in the war room, watched his CIA seniors argue furiously that no particular authorization was required for the strike, but Cabell held up the go-ahead while he telephoned Rusk at the State Department.

Rusk called Kennedy in Glen Ora and received Kennedy's refusal to authorize the second air strike at the airfields. "I'm not signed on to this," Kennedy told Rusk.[42] Rusk told McGeorge Bundy to give Cabell the bad news, and then told Bundy to go to New York and pacify Stevenson. Cabell and Bissell visited Rusk at the State Department Sunday night to plead for the second strike, but Rusk told them they would have to make their appeal directly to Kennedy.

Rusk called Kennedy while Bissell and Cabell stood by, explaining again the CIA's concern, but at the end of the conversation advised Kennedy that the strike should be cancelled in view of what was happening in New York, where Stevenson was hard pressed at the United Nations. Kennedy confirmed that the strike was cancelled. Rusk held out the telephone to Cabell, who declined to press the President after his appeal had been twice rejected.

CIA headquarters called Bissell out of the meeting in Rusk's office to hear that the strike definitely was cancelled. Outraged and frightened, the CIA men sent orders to Nicaragua cancelling all air sorties except reconnaissance flights over the beachhead. Hunt forever put the blame for the invasion's failure on Cabell for not going ahead with the strike without first inviting trouble from Rusk and the President.

In the darkness of Monday morning, April 17, the invasion fleet arrived at the Bay of Pigs and began disembarkment over unexpected coral reefs. Frogmen who went ahead of the landing craft were spotted by two militiamen in a jeep, and opened fire, killing them both. At 4:30 a.m. Cabell called Rusk to propose a last-ditch way to protect the ships: if the fleet withdrew 12 miles to international waters, and then ferried the supplies by landing craft, would they be given air cover by the *Essex?* Rusk rejected the suggestion, and Cabell finally called Kennedy directly in Glen Ora. Kennedy rejected it, too.

At 6 a.m. a T-33 hit the *Houston* with a salvo of eight rockets, and the ship began sinking. At 9:30 one of Castro's Sea Furies hit the *Rio Escondido*, which had ammunition loaded next to aviation fuel for the B-26s, blowing it up with much of the Brigade's ammunition and its communications van. The 5th battalion's 200 men jumped into the sea from the *Houston*, about 30 of them drowning. A Castro B-26 was shot down, and so was a Brigade B-26 attempting to fly cover. The *Caribe, Atlantico, Blagar* and *Barbara J.* left the beachhead, the *Caribe* fleeing 200 miles south. An eighth ship, *La Playa,* under a CIA officer and Nino Díaz, who had fought in the mountains under Raúl Castro, found a surf running and failed to make a decoy landing in Oriente Province with 160 men.

Grayston Lynch, the ranking CIA officer at the beachhead, a former Green Beret officer, was refused aid from the Navy escort force, as he found himself directing operations, almost without communications, from the *San Marcos.* He had been the first man ashore, with the frogmen, despite Kennedy's orders.

When Kennedy finally authorized the second strike from Nicaragua for Tuesday at dawn, the B-26s arrived over Cuba to find the airfield targets covered with ground fog. Castro kept his air force.

Kennedy returned to Washington early Monday, as the *Houston* was sinking. He closeted with his aides in the Cabinet Room to hear alarming and sketchy reports from the beachhead. That morning Rusk told a press conference that the United States had no intention of intervening in Cuba. Kennedy received an angry message from Khrushchev that had been delivered to the U.S. Embassy in Moscow shortly after news of the invasion had been broadcast.

Kennedy asked Pierre Salinger to lunch with Reston, and Reston reported that day that it was overdrawn to speak of an "invasion." Rather, it was a supply reinforcement, involving a few hundred Cubans.

Khrushchev's note, put out to the media in Moscow, said in part,

> It is not a secret to anyone that the armed bands which invaded (Cuba) had been trained, equipped and armed in the United

States of America. The planes which bomb Cuban cities belong to the United States of America, the bombs they drop have been made available by the American government.. . .

Your statement of a few days ago to the effect that the United States would not take part in military operations against Cuba produced the impression that the top echelons of the United States are aware of the consequences of aggression against Cuba to world peace and to the United States itself.. . .

I earnestly appeal to you, Mr. President, to call a halt to the aggression against the Republic of Cuba. The military techniques and the world political situation are now such that any so-called 'small wars' can produce a chain reaction in all parts of the world.

As to the Soviet Union, there should be no misunderstanding of our position: we shall render the Cuban people and their government all necessary assistance in beating back the armed attack on Cuba.. . . [43]

On the same day the U.S. Embassy in Moscow received a far harsher government-to-government note, strengthening the threats of the Khrushchev letter. It charged that the United States had inspired and organized the "bandit" attack "under cover supplied by military ships and planes of the United States" and it could "place American lives in jeopardy." [44]

As bad news from the beachhead turned catastrophic on Tuesday, Kennedy had two priority men to answer: Khrushchev and Reston of the *Times*. He met with his crisis team, now including Soviet experts Bohlen and Foy Kohler, and then had lunch with Reston and Schlesinger at the White House.

Kennedy told Reston candidly that the invasion was going badly, but he said he would not send in the Marines. Defeat would be an incident, not a disaster, he said. Kennedy blamed the mess on the CIA. Dulles was a legendary figure, and it was difficult to deal with a legend. He told Reston that he should have replaced Dulles earlier, and that Bobby Kennedy should have been running the CIA. "We will have to deal with CIA," he said. [45-46]

Kennedy's reply to Khrushchev said that the Soviet leader was "under a serious misapprehension." Kennedy noted that 100,000 Cubans had fled their country because their liberty was suppressed, and it could not be surprising that Cubans would struggle for their freedom. He wrote, "I have previously stated and I repeat now that the United States intends no military intervention in Cuba. In the event of any military intervention by outside force, we will immediately honor our obligations under the inter-American system to protect against external aggression." He went on to suggest that Khrushchev could ease tensions as well in Laos, at the United Nations and in the Congo, and in concluding a satisfactory nuclear test ban treaty.

Khrushchev's previous threats to the West had been made when the action was over and decided, as in the Suez crisis. This time he made a threat while the action was undecided, and he received an immediate pledge from the President that the United States would not intervene.

As Khrushchev and Kennedy exchanged messages, the Brigade was surrounded by 20,000 Castro troops and militiamen, with tanks and artillery being drawn into positions.

Tuesday night Kennedy was host to the annual Congressional Reception at the White House. In white tie and tails, he mingled with his guests showing no sign of concern. At 1 a.m., he conferred with the crisis team, some of them guests in formal attire, some brought in. Bissell and Admiral Burke pressed him to give the invading force air support from the *Essex*, using unmarked planes. Kennedy already had pledged to Khrushchev—and to Reston—that the United States would not intervene. He finally authorized six unmarked jets from the *Essex* to rendezvous with B-26s flown from Nicaragua over the landing site, but only to protect the B-26s from Castro's Sea Furies and T-33s; the Navy jets could not seek targets either in the air or on the ground. A mix-up in timing brought the B-26s from Nicaragua over the Bay of Pigs an hour early and they were shot down, with four American pilots from the Alabama Air National Guard among those killed.[47]

Cuba sent a defiant signal, announcing the executions by firing squad of two Americans held as counter-revolutionaries: Howard F. Anderson, 41, who ran a chain of gas stations on the island, and Angus McNair, 25, who had been caught running a boatload of guns to Cuba.

The leaders of the Revolutionary Council, some of whom had sent their sons with the Brigade, were being held incommunicado by the CIA at the derelict airfield at Opa Locka, Florida. Kennedy sent Schlesinger and Adolf Berle to see them. Their recriminations were so strong that Schlesinger telephoned Kennedy to prevail on him to see them.

Kennedy met the Revolutionary Council sitting in his rocking chair at the White House on April 20 as Castro announced that the invaders had been completely defeated. His charm and *sang-froid* prevailed, but the experience left him shaken. He telephoned Nixon and asked him to the White House, telling him that facing the Cubans was the worst experience of his life. After venting his rage at the CIA, the chairman of the Joint Chiefs and his White House staff, Kennedy asked Nixon what he would do.

"I would find a proper legal cover and I would go in," Nixon said. "There are several justifications that could be used, like protecting American citizens living in Cuba and defending our base at Guantanamo. I believe that the most important thing at this point is that we do whatever is necessary to get Castro and communism out of Cuba."

Kennedy said that if he did, a cocky Khrushchev might act against Berlin, citing the advice of Walter Lippmann and Chip Bohlen. Nixon also advised Kennedy to use air power in Laos, and Kennedy demurred.

Kennedy said, "It really is true that foreign affairs is the only important issue for a President to handle, isn't it? I mean, who gives a shit if the minimum wage is $1.15 or $1.25, in comparison to something like this?"[48]

On the evening of April 19, the Brigade ran out of ammunition. It destroyed its heavy equipment and tried to disperse along the beaches and through the Zapata swamp. One man made it to asylum in an embassy in Havana. The Navy picked up 26 survivors from the beaches, and a passing ship rescued 12 far at sea.

Of the roughly 1,400 men involved, Castro's forces captured 1,189, 114 were killed in the fighting and disembarkment. Castro said his losses were 87 men, but credible witnesses said a single Brigade B-26 strike with bombs and napalm on a Castro column of troops and tanks bumper-to-bumper and three miles long caused an estimated 1,800 casualties.[49] The Brigade, citing a doctor in Cuba who was not named but treated casualties, said that Castro lost 1,650 killed and 2,000 wounded. The Brigade survivors were tried on television and sent to the Isle of Pines. Kennedy ransomed them a year and a half later for $53 million in medical supplies and baby food.

There is no count of those executed after Castro's massive roundup between April 15 and April 20. On April 20, Havana radio announced a list of persons executed from a raid that had taken place March 18, the date of the CIA's ultimatum to the Front to accept Ray at the Skyway Motel. Those executed included Rogelio Gonzáles Carso (Francisco), Artime's underground leader in Cuba, and Rafael Díaz Hanscom, who had combined several underground groups into the Unidad Revolucionario.

In the United States the Bay of Pigs triggered the first political demonstrations in decades at a dozen universities, and on April 21, Norman Mailer led a protest demonstration in New York City. It was the seed demonstration for those that followed through the 1960s, and participants in it brought Mailer back to lead the armies of the night against the Pentagon in 1967.

Kennedy brought General Maxwell Taylor out of retirement to lead an investigation that concluded, vaguely, that the project failed because the Brigade ran out of ammunition, and because the President was not completely informed about the necessity of air superiority and the impossibility of the force turning guerrilla and making it to the hills if the landing failed.

Kennedy publicly took the blame, but he soon fired Bissell, Dulles and all of the Joint Chiefs except General Shoup.

The media wants tomorrow's story, not yesterday's, and it accepted that since the invasion failed, it had to fail. In that spirit, David Halberstam picked up the story that Marine Corps General Shoup gave a demonstration that pleased Kennedy. He placed an overlay of a map of Cuba on the United States, showing its large size, and put a red dot on it, saying "That, gentlemen, represents the island of Tarawa, and it took us three days and 18,000 Marines to take it."[50] The comparison is specious, of course. Tarawa was a fortress, Cuba a paradise for invaders, with endless unprotectable beaches, just as the Japanese of 1942 fanatically died to the last man,[51] and the Cuban culture was a lighthearted one in 1961. Yet the specious illustration was so well accepted that Shoup became Kennedy's favorite general, and one author liked it so well he began his book with it.

The collapse of the Bay of Pigs invasion was quickly brushed off by the media. No one condemned the President, which astonished him. Reston kept his peace; after all, the President at their luncheon had practically told him he had been right all along. Arthur Krock, Kennedy's friend and mentor from childhood, wrote in his column before it was sure that the invasion had failed that "the threat of failure to American interests is so great that the American government and people can hardly allow it to fail."[52] But Krock had been cut out of the action by both Kennedy and the *Times*.[53]

There were magazine accounts, inspired by Kennedy and by the CIA, blaming everyone for the disaster from Adlai Stevenson to the war-mongering Joint Chiefs of Staff, but none blamed Kennedy. Except for Szulc and Meyer, no one rushed to publish a book on the fiasco. Their *The Cuban Invasion*, a polemical warning against American intervention in a changing and revolutionary world, is defensive of Kennedy, his White House men and Manuel Ray. It was called shrewd in political interpretation but "astonishingly short on facts considering the reportorial skills of the authors" by Peter Wyden, who finally pulled the story all together in *Bay of Pigs*. The first insider account was not published until 1965, in Schlesinger's *A Thousand Days*. It may be the best part of the book, as Schlesinger was personally involved, but it is marred by the author's straining to protect the President while revealing as much as he could to fulfill his duty as a historian.

The media as a whole adopted the *Times'* interpretation, echoed by Sorensen in his book, *Kennedy*: "With hindsight it is clear that what in fact (Kennedy) had approved was diplomatically unwise and militarily doomed from the outset."[54]

But the plan was not mad, it was sabotaged by Kennedy's changes. Kennedy was ill-equipped to conduct the Cuban invasion. His natural home within the foreign policy establishment was with the dominant group in the Democratic Advisory Council—called softheads by their Republican rivals—such as Stevenson, Harriman, Kennan, Bowles, Galbraith and Ball, rather than with the "tougher" Democrats (Schlesinger's word) like Dean Acheson and Paul Nitze. He was ambivalent toward the invasion plan from the beginning and watered it down repeatedly. He had committed himself to it as an election campaign ploy that was basically deceptive whether it was his idea or Richard Goodwin's; he went along with it as a means to election. Kennedy's failure of nerve at Glen Ora was almost pre-ordained.[55]

Bissell wrote to Schlesinger in 1965 that he was "unregenerate." He wrote, "If we had been able to drop five times the tonnage on Castro's airfields, we would have had a damned good chance."[56]

Sorensen also contended, "The President's postponement of the Monday morning air strike thus played only a minor role in the venture which came to so inglorious an end on Wednesday afternoon."[57]

Every military and CIA man involved disagreed violently.[58]

Lemnitzer: "absolutely reprehensible, almost criminal."

Burke: "horrified."

Brigadier General David W. Gray, the JCS-CIA liaison man: "There goes your operation."

Colonel Jack Hawkins: "This is criminal negligence."

Major General George R. Doster, commander of the Alabama National Guard at Puerto Cabezes airfield: "There goes the whole fuckin' war."

The fiasco left Castro powerfully strengthened in Cuba and on the world scene. It left the *Times* enormously strengthened too. How much it weakened Kennedy was not apparent from the favorable media treatment he continued to receive, but he would learn of it six weeks later in Vienna when he met Nikita Khrushchev.

Chapter IV
The Vienna Summit
and the Berlin Wall

The Potsdam Agreement of August 1945 decreed that "the transfer to Germany of German populations, or elements thereof, remaining in Poland, Czechoslavakia and Hungary will have to be undertaken." A census of June 6, 1961, registered 12 million expelled persons and refugees in West Germany.

In the spring of 1961, the girls of West Berlin adopted a grotesque uniform, as fashion-conscious women sometimes do. The elements of dress included a loose pullover a size too large, usually white, with sleeves pushed to the elbow; a short, tight skirt showing some knee and the straight Berlinerin legs, so uniformly perfect that they looked factory-tooled; four-inch stiletto-heeled shoes with pointed toes, and crowning it all an absurdly elaborate beehive hairdo, usually bleached blonde.

The contrast between the elegant and impractical shoes and hairdo on the one hand and the sloppy pullover and sassy skirt on the other was discordant, almost schizophrenic, although the costume had an undeniable appeal at the period. There is a theory that bizarre women's fashions forecast wars, natural disasters and stock market plunges, and Berlin in 1961 supported that theory. The Berlin Wall was about to be built.

Germans were increasingly apprehensive on both sides of the political lines that divided the country and the city. In November, 1958, Khrushchev had issued his Berlin ultimatum: the Soviets were "resolved to abolish the occupation regime in Berlin within six months." After nearly three years the threat still hung over the city. The United States, the only real guarantor of West Berlin's security, had a new President who had gotten off to a rocky start with the Cuban venture. A new drive to collectivize agriculture by East Germany's Walter Ulbricht, head of the Socialist Unity Party, was starting a renewed exodus of refugees.

The refugees could not cross directly from East to West Germany because the border, with its barbed wire and a plowed and mined death strip, stretched from the Baltic to Czechoslovakia, reinforced by a five-kilometer-wide forbidden zone on the East German side. Most refugees came out through Berlin, the four-power city where the Allies of World War II kept a measure of free passage between their sectors. West Berliners could visit East Berlin at will, subject to some harassment. There already was a border in the city, and many East Berliners crossed regularly to jobs in West Berlin. An East Berliner could visit West Berlin if he offered any approved destination, but there was little such casual traffic because West Germany currency was expensive, and harassment on return to East Berlin could be acute. It was a border of intimidation, not of physical barriers.

The elevated train lines running through the city belonged to East Germany, which inherited the central railroad system of the Third Reich. For 20 pfennings, then about five cents, a refugee from East Germany, arriving at the Friedrich Strasse railroad station in his capital, East Berlin, could buy a ticket across town to West Berlin and a different kind of life.

West Berlin maintained a refugee reception center in the outlying district of Marienfelde. Refugees were interviewed and registered there, providing a mosaic of data on conditions throughout East Germany and allowing the identification of some of the agents sent by East Germany's *Staatssicherheitsdienst*, or SSD. Then most refugees were sent along to West Germany by air to join relatives or to be put on their feet with welfare benefits and job referrals.

East Germany was being depopulated by the steady stream of refugees since the end of World War II, the only country in Europe with a declining population. The refugee drain threatened not only the grand design of building a Communist society; it threatened East Germany's existence. The population drop since 1950 had been from 18.4 million to under 17 million in 1961.

The dimensions of the four-year Berlin crisis, which lasted into 1962, were these:

In October 1958, in statements orchestrated with the Soviet Union's propaganda, Ulbricht began claiming all of Berlin for East Germany. In November, Khrushchev issued his ultimatum: remove the Western troops from West Berlin or he would sign a separate peace treaty with East Germany. Sovereign East Germany would take over control of the access routes to West Berlin which the Soviet military administered under Allied occupation agreements. Backed by 24 Soviet divisions and its own military forces, East Germany would be free to blockade the "free city" of West Berlin while Ulbricht carried out a promised purge of political elements unfriendly to communism.

During Eisenhower's administration, there were two conferences of Big Four foreign ministers in Geneva dealing with the Germany question. In the first conference following the 1955 Geneva summit, John Foster Dulles succeeded in focusing the issue on the reunification of Germany under arrangements that would guarantee European security. Dulles had little help from the British or French. French diplomats remarked that they wanted Germany reunified in the same way that they wanted to go to Heaven; not right away. Britain had adopted as a dictum Churchill's remark that Germans were either at your feet or at your throat. Dulles goaded Soviet Foreign Minister V. M. Molotov into returning to Moscow for instructions, and he returned to Geneva with what he described to correspondents as "better baggage," a polemical veto of the idea of German reunification that torpedoed the conference.

In response to Khrushchev's 1958 ultimatum, the Big Four foreign ministers reconvened in Geneva in May 1959 with a new cast of characters, this time pitting Secretary of State Christian Herter against Andrei Gromyko. The gentlemanly Herter found Gromyko "most difficult," but he too held off any change in the status quo, although British Foreign Secretary Selwyn Lloyd was willing to dilute allied troop strength in West Berlin and make other conciliatory gestures. That conference broke up after three months.

The Paris summit of May 1960, with Eisenhower, De Gaulle, Macmillan and Khrushchev, broke down with Khrushchev's cursing, table-thumping, threatening news conference[1] over Eisenhower's refusal to apologize formally for Gary Powers' May Day spy flight over the Soviet Union in a U-2. More important to the breakdown was that Eisenhower entered the conference pledged to permit no change in Berlin's four-power status in terms that were unequivocal and permitted no retreat.

After the Paris summit failed, the Berlin-Germany issue lay dormant while the Soviets awaited the outcome of the American elections.

To Konrad Adenauer, Eisenhower had been a solid ally and Dulles a trusted friend. Adenauer had awesome accomplishments behind him. The part of Germany he inherited, three zones run by different foreign armies with different rules, had problems that left visitors from the outside numb. Aside from the landscape of ruins, the decimated male population, the survivors in coats cut from army blankets and pasty-faced from a diet of starch and fat, Germans were demoralized to the point of being cowed by the occupiers. The mind could not cope with the enormity of questions of collective guilt for the Jewish holocaust and responsibility for the war, so Germans bent to rearrange the rubble, heads down, largely pacifist yet potentially revolutionary.

Adenauer had left solitary confinement in Brauweiler prison near Cologne in November 1944 as American troops approached, without waiting to be given back his shoelaces and suspenders, taken to prevent his suicide. Nearly 70, he had not been executed because his life was considered over. He returned to his home in Rhöndorf to be shelled and temporarily deafened by the Americans, who, at their next meeting, asked him to resume his post as mayor of Cologne.

The occupying authorities all believed that the long-established Social Democratic Party would dominate the three Western zones, but Adenauer, urging his chauffeur to drive at breakneck speed despite an earlier injury in a severe accident, traveled the country pulling together remnants of the old Centrists into the new Christian Democratic Union. In a stunning upset, Adenauer's party narrowly won the elections in August 1949. Adenauer was 73.

The New York Times at that period regarded Germany with a deep distrust that bordered on the hostility shown by most of the British press.[2] Its correspondents covering the 1949 elections included James Reston, Drew Middleton and Jack Raymond, all from the varsity team.

Reston, especially, doubted that the Germans were ready to control their own affairs. He reported that the State Department disapproved the indulgence shown the Germans by the American military governor, General Lucius D. Clay and the other Allied military governors who had wrangled for months over problems "that were settled by their three foreign ministers here in less than a week." Clay was "in a snappish argument with the State Department" over the use of Marshall Plan funds.³ The Germans' nationalist campaign oratory raised fears that "the Germans have learned nothing and forgotten nothing, and will go to any lengths, including another deal with the Soviet Union, to further their own interests." He added, "Few observers here are really prepared to reach such a pessimistic conclusion. (But) the Germans are still showing no signs of guilt about the history of the last thirty-five years. The quality of self-criticism in the German is still mighty scarce, if it exists at all."⁴

Accordingly, the *Times* was not encouraged by Adenauer's election victory, headlining, "West German Rightists Victors in First Free Elections Since '33." Reston's commentary again showed some anxiety that the Germans now would have more say over their future.⁵

Eight years later Adenauer's party still was winning, consolidating its position in the 1957 elections. Adenauer had absorbed into the economy more than 11 million refugees, ended British dismantling of industries, fought off the internationalization of the Ruhr, begun repairing relations with France's Maurice Schumann, preempted the Social Democrats with progressive social legislation, defused the right-wing Refugee Party by absorbing and then isolating it, single-handedly begun West Germany's defensive rearmament against powerful opposition in Europe and at home, pledged West Germany to the North Atlantic Treaty Organization and restored the half-nation's sovereignty and prosperity. His Christian Union parties won 50.2% of the vote and a commanding majority of 270 seats in the Bundestag in elections of September 15, 1957. The victory enabled Adenauer to govern without the fractious Free Democratic Party, which slipped to 7.7% of the vote, and to overwhelm the opposition Social Democrats of Erich Ollenhauer, which won only 31.8% and 169 seats in parliament.

Adenauer's steady success, without benefit of charisma but increasing recognition of his stature and integrity, contradicted the thesis of Professor Schlesinger that "the greats" had to be showmen.

Kennedy, then a Senator, commented in an article in *Foreign Affairs* that, "whatever elections show, the age of Adenauer is over."⁶ Kennedy belonged to that part of the American foreign policy establishment, as did the *Times*, that believed Americans had been too hypnotized by Adenauer and that U.S. relations with the Social Democrats had been neglected.

Kennedy wrote that the United States was too tied to Germany, to one party, and to one man there. "The giants of the postwar era—Churchill, Adenauer, de Gasperi—have left their imprint," Kennedy wrote. "The U.S. is ill-advised to chase the shadows of the past and ignore the political leadership of the generation which is now coming of age."

At that period the Social Democrats had not abandoned Marxism;

that happened in 1959 with the Bad Godesberg program of Herbert Wehner, who had renounced communism while in a Swedish jail as a Soviet agent during World War II. The SPD still voted against every defense budget, and in 1958 equated the United States with the Soviet Union in its "campaign against atomic death," in which Social Democrats demanded the withdrawal of foreign troops from Germany and neutralism. Although a general strike failed, the "campaign against atomic death" played a role in encouraging Khrushchev to issue his Berlin ultimatum.

Adenauer had little reason to look with enthusiasm on Kennedy's election to the Presidency three years after Kennedy had pronounced him washed up. He saw in Kennedy a young man, brash and naive, no friend of Germany.

During the debates with Nixon in 1960, Kennedy had sounded more encouraging to Germans. Kennedy said that the freedom of West Berlin "is a commitment that we have to meet if we are going to protect the security of Western Europe, and therefore, on this question, I don't think there is any doubt in the mind of any member of the community of West Berlin—I am sure there is no doubt in the minds of the Russians—that we will meet our commitment to maintain the freedom and independence of West Berlin."

Khrushchev's threat to Berlin was one of the most consequential problems Kennedy faced on election, and he downgraded it. He did not mention Germany or Berlin in his inaugural address on January 20, 1961. At his first news conference on January 25, Kennedy answered some of the threats made by Khrushchev on January 6, in which Khrushchev again threatened Berlin and praised wars of liberation, but Kennedy confined his remarks to Laos and the Caribbean, omitting Berlin. He did not mention Berlin in his State of the Union message on January 30, nor at his second press conference on February 1. In his answer to Khrushchev's threats over the Bay of Pigs, Kennedy mentioned Laos and the Congo, but not Berlin.

Shortly after Kennedy's election, Adenauer had seen a threat to Germany in reports from his embassy in Washington that Kennedy was interested in negotiating with the Soviets. Adenauer held a news conference for the sole purpose of saying that he had been invited to Washington in February by the private citizens' Atlantik Brücke/American Council on Germany, and hinting that it would be a convenient time for him to see the new President.

Kennedy rebuffed the hint when asked about it at a news conference on November 11, 1960: "I have not received any messages about the matter in February."

Adenauer did not go to Washington until April. Once there, Adenauer told Kennedy that he was not making use of the United States' "moral right" to lead NATO, which was drifting and without energy. "Leading is not ordering but persuading," Adenauer lectured. "Above all, it requires that a leader make his will known." He cautioned Kennedy not to encourage Khrushchev to believe that the Western alliance might fall apart in disagreement. "The Russian mentality is different," Adenauer said. "Only strength counts with them."[7]

Adenauer, 85, thought the meeting had gone well. He had picked up Kennedy's two-year-old son, and Kennedy remarked that was something he couldn't do with his bad back. Adenauer rather liked Kennedy, although he later concluded that Kennedy was irresolute and surrounded by too many advisors.[8]

Kennedy told Sorensen that there was more than a generation gap between himself and Adenauer, that Adenauer appeared to him to be from another century, another world. Adenauer left Washington on April 17, as Cuban exiles landed at the Bay of Pigs, and no one in Washington reflected on his visit.

Kennedy's plan for a two-man summit with Khrushchev was a new departure. Eisenhower never had considered a two-man summit because it would automatically downgrade Britain and France, change the world power relationship by stamping recognition on the idea that two superpowers ran the world and subject the Atlantic Alliance to new strain. The summit plan, codified on February 22, never leaked to the media before its announcement on May 20, when it was a *fait accompli* and therefore did not provoke a media discussion of its merits.

Although the Western Allies were told little of Kennedy's plan to go it alone with Khrushchev, the Soviets informed East Germany's Ulbricht shortly after Ambassador Thompson caught up with Khrushchev in Siberia on March 9 to deliver Kennedy's invitation. Ulbricht summoned his party's Central Committee on March 16 and informed them that he intended to stop the refugees with a wall built through Berlin.

Armed with the always-unanimous protocols of his Central Committee, Ulbricht went to Moscow on March 29. Germany was the main item on the agenda of a Warsaw Pact summit meeting in preparation for the superpowers' summit.

Khrushchev informed the East bloc leaders that any move on Berlin would not be a Soviet-East German affair; it would be a Warsaw Pact action. Ulbricht had made contingency plans for a wall through Berlin as early as 1958, but he did not specify a wall to the assembled East bloc leaders, rather, a barrier, a state border.

Poland's Wladyslaw Gomulka and Czechoslovakia's Antonin Novotný questioned him skeptically. Hungary's János Kádár, Bulgaria's Todor Zhivkov and Romania's Gheorghe Gheorghiu-Dej suggested that the barrier would damage the prestige of the socialist bloc. Ulbricht replied, looking at Kádár, that Hungary's state border with Austria, which had a plowed and mined death strip, was a model for his planning. Khrushchev did not announce a decision. He told Ulbricht that he could not authorize a drastic move against Berlin's four-power status until he learned from Kennedy how the new President's policies differed from Eisenhower's.[9]

Khrushchev was eager to accept Kennedy's invitation, but he did not answer immediately because of tension building up over the impending Cuban exile attack on Cuba. With the fiasco of the Bay of Pigs, Kennedy assumed the project was shelved, since relations with the Soviets were at a new low. On May 12, Kennedy received a letter from Khrushchev accepting the summit, unexpectedly, according to Schlesinger.[10] Less than four weeks remained to prepare the summit, and the simultaneous announcements in Washington and Moscow May 20 were a media sensation.

Rusk opposed a summit when Kennedy first proposed it, but, sensing Kennedy's determination, he did not make his opposition felt, the beginning of Rusk's withdrawal from policy-making. Kennedy did not rely on the State Department to negotiate the meeting but sent his brother, Attorney General Bobby Kennedy, to get assurances from the Soviet ambassador that progress was likely at the summit on Laos and a nuclear test ban treaty.

Most of Kennedy's entourage, including Stevenson and Harriman, were willing to make concessions in Berlin along the lines once proposed by British Foreign Secretary Lloyd. Kennedy recalled Dean Acheson from retirement as a consultant to add balance to the deliberations. Acheson opposed any hint of concession and endorsed contingency plans against any new blockade of Berlin that had been approved by the Joint Chiefs and the NATO Council. The plans included an airlift, a military drive up the Helmstedt autobahn, an ultimatum to Khrushchev and ultimate resort to tactical nuclear weapons. Acheson warned that Khrushchev would expect Kennedy to be demoralized after the Bay of Pigs, and would be out to humiliate the United States by forcing a backdown.

Before Khrushchev had replied to his invitation, Kennedy had made plans to visit President de Gaulle in Paris. The Paris trip became the curtain-raiser for the Vienna summit. Acheson went along and informed De Gaulle of the military contingency plans to defend access to West Berlin.

Kennedy had five long talks with De Gaulle, who advised him not to let Khrushchev upset him with the expected threat to Berlin. De Gaulle said that Khrushchev raised the threat regularly, every six months, and always backed away. He told Kennedy that no one could prevent Khrushchev from signing any number of documents with East Germany, but that no internal Communist document could change the Western Allies' rights and status in Berlin. If Khrushchev wanted to start a war, which was unlikely, then Western concessions in Berlin would not stop him; rather, concessions might encourage him as Neville Chamberlain had encouraged Hitler at Munich. If Khrushchev intended no war, there was no reason to be intimidated by threats to Berlin. Berlin was not so vulnerable, given Russia's need for Western trade and technology. De Gaulle said Khrushchev should be made to understand that there would be no skirmish over Berlin that would not widen to a larger war. De Gaulle also cautioned Kennedy not to become involved in Indochina, "an Asian morass."

Kennedy's first talk with Khrushchev was at the Vienna residence of U.S. Ambassador Freeman Mathews on June 3, 1961.[11] Kennedy intended to propose a standstill in the Cold War.[12] Khrushchev, after an amiable opening, went on the attack.

Chip Bohlen, who had favored holding the summit, reported that Kennedy made his first mistake by allowing himself to be drawn into an ideological discussion of colonialism and wars of liberation. Kennedy had been one of those in the Eastern establishment who had derided and ridiculed Nixon's kitchen debate with Khrushchev in 1959 in the intimidating atmosphere of Moscow. Now, in the friendlier atmosphere of a U.S. ambassador's home, Kennedy found himself put on the defensive by the Russian Bohlen had described as "not too bright." Bohlen reported that Khrushchev turned out to be a practiced dialectical debater, and "in the exchange, Khrushchev sounded like a libertarian, Kennedy a colonialist."[13] Kennedy was depressed after the first exchange, and Bohlen reassured him that "the Soviets always talk tough."

At the second meeting, held in the Soviet Embassy in Vienna on June 4, Khrushchev followed a scenario of mounting belligerence over Berlin. He told Kennedy that unless an interim six-month agreement were signed, he would sign with Ulbricht a separate peace treaty by the end of the year. The treaty would mean that Soviet officials would no longer be responsible for the access routes to Berlin. If the Western Allies did not make their arrangements with East Germany (recognizing East Germany and the permanent division of Germany), their routes to Berlin would be blocked. Khrushchev pressed the warnings increasingly in two conversations with Kennedy and his interpreter, one while strolling in the embassy garden and one after lunch in the embassy library.

Kennedy replied that the United States could not and would not hinder the Soviets from doing what they felt they had to do in their area of responsibility. But if the Soviets touched West Berlin or the access routes to it, the interests and rights of the United States would be violated, and the United States would not accept that without resistance.

Khrushchev said, "I want peace. If, on the other hand, you want atomic war, you can have it."

Kennedy replied, "You are the one who wants to force a change, not I."

Khrushchev said, "War or peace, that lies in your hand. The treaty will in any case be signed in December."

Kennedy: "If that is so, it will be a cold winter."

Kennedy was ill, suffering a recurrence of his back injury, for which he had undergone two severe operations in 1954. He received a painful cortisone injection into his spinal cord before the meeting, and would be on crutches for weeks after his return to the United States.

Kennedy had just given Khrushchev the answer to the key question posed by Khrushchev at the March 29 Warsaw Pact meeting: How did Kennedy's policies differ from Eisenhower's? Eisenhower had defended Berlin's four-power status. Kennedy had said the Soviets could do what they wished in their area of responsibility. Without realizing it, Kennedy had authorized the Berlin Wall.

Kennedy emerged from the Soviet Embassy and shook hands with Khrushchev under a giant chestnut tree. To correspondents held behind barriers across the street he looked drawn and tired, his left hand plucking nervously at the bottom button of his jacket. He flashed his smile only briefly to shouts of photographers.

The two press secretaries, Pierre Salinger and Mikhail Kharlamov, conducted an evasive and noncommital press conference. Kharlamov hinted at great progress. Salinger implied that nothing had been settled. At the end of it, Kharlamov stood up, looking elated, and clasped his hands over his head in a boxer's victory salute.

Kennedy had left Vienna when Khrushchev received Austrian Foreign Minister Bruno Kreisky, whom Khrushchev "knew to be a flexible politician who favored improving relations with socialist countries." Khrushchev also knew that Kreisky "was in close touch with Willy Brandt...both were Social Democrats." Khrushchev "recounted for Kreisky everything I'd told Kennedy. I knew that what I said would get back to Kennedy—and it would also be passed on to Willy Brandt. I hoped that by underscoring our determination not to abandon our intentions we might succeed in encouraging these leaders toward rational discussions and ultimately a reasonable agreement. . . ."[14] Gromyko gave Kreisky a six-page note to pass on to Brandt.

Western correspondents in Vienna did not know what to make of the summit, making it difficult to write a lead on the story. Salinger, Bohlen and Thompson briefed a crowd of American reporters ambiguously, beyond confirming that there had been an agreement to negotiate in Geneva over Laos. So everyone, even Reston, mentioned Laos in lead paragraphs—a red herring.

Correspondents were told that Khrushchev had been impressed with Kennedy's toughness, and that Kennedy had warned Khrushchev against war by miscalculation over Berlin. Khrushchev had not pressed the Berlin issue in the face of Kennedy's firmness. Bohlen did caution reporters against "optimistic speculation."

The correspondents felt that the meeting had gone badly, but they had no facts to work with, and the American briefers were essentially reassuring. Reston immediately knew what had happened, and the others were reduced to waiting for his report the next day in the Paris edition of the *New York Herald-Tribune*, picked up from the *Times*.

Reston's account spoke of a "sharp disagreement" on Germany and Berlin that "ended in hard controversy." The account's tone was soothing:

> There were no ultimatums and few bitter or menacing exchanges. . . . Accordingly, President Kennedy flew off to London tonight in a solemn, although confident, mood. . . . President Kennedy, if not pleased, has had his first major experience with 'cold war' diplomacy and has come out of it very well. He did not expect much and he did not get much, but he went away from here more experienced, and he now rates more highly in the estimation of the men who watched these exchanges than he has at any time since he entered the White House.[15]

The next day Reston reconfirmed that the Vienna summit had "ended in a scoreless tie."[16] In his column the day after that, he reported: "It is not that Mr. Khrushchev was personally disagreeable here. On the contrary, he was less quarrelsome than usual. Nevertheless, even he is trapped in the Communist sorcery, and had to be the agent of a series of proposals on Germany, Berlin, disarmament and inspection which no sensible man in the West could consider, let alone accept."[17]

Reston was under some strain. He had been slipped into the U.S. Embassy by a side door and talked with Kennedy on an off-the-record basis. He could not report that he had seen the President cracking up.

More than three years later, in an article commemorating the first anniversary of Kennedy's death, Reston wrote:

> It is impossible to be sure about this, but I was in Vienna when he met Khrushchev shortly after the Bay of Pigs, and saw him 10 minutes after his meeting with the Soviet leader. He came into a dim room in the American Embassy, shaken and angry. He had tried, as always, to be calm and rational with Khrushchev, to get him to define what the Soviet could and would not do, and Khrushchev had bullied him and threatened him with war over Berlin. . . .[18]

Reston's successive accounts of the Kennedy-Khrushchev meeting were progressively more disturbing. In the first, no threats or ultimatums and a confident Kennedy. Then a scoreless tie. Next, a nonquarrelsome Khrushchev. In the long-delayed final report, Khrushchev bullying and threatening, but still the "young leader" standing steadfast.[19]

What Kennedy told Reston had showed that he had abandoned Berlin's four-power status, the city's first line of defense. Throughout the Berlin crisis the *Times* knew how its acute phase started, but Adenauer's information was less complete. Foy Kohler, Assistant Secretary of State for European Affairs, flew to Bonn to brief Adenauer, but he did not report that Kennedy had broken down and was not intending to defend West Berlin. Adenauer's rival that year in Germany's elections, West Berlin Mayor Willy Brandt, had better information from Kreisky, relayed from the enemy camp.

Besides Reston, another American reporter quickly learned details of the Vienna summit but did not print them. Benjamin Bradlee, then *Newsweek* bureau chief in Washington, had a confidential relationship with Kennedy bordering on worship.[20] Jacqueline Kennedy had told Bradlee's wife Tony that they were the best friends the Kennedys had. Twelve years after Kennedy's death, Bradlee reported that when the President returned from Vienna he "carried excerpts from the official translation of his talks with Khrushchev around with him wherever he went, and read chunks of them to me several times." Bradlee wrote that Kennedy wondered why Khrushchev didn't liquidate (West) Berlin as he had said he would do in Vienna. "He said it over and over," Kennedy told Bradlee.[21]

The rest of the boobs of the media, like myself, relied on the briefings of Kennedy's aides, reinforced by the early reports of the insider Reston, and reported what became a slogan, that Kennedy "stood fast on Berlin."

As he left Vienna, Kennedy still was under shock from the brutality of Khrushchev's threats. He asked his staff, how could a statesman op-

erate so calmly with threats of nuclear war? On *Air Force One* he called
for a CIA study on Soviet nuclear capabilities. He studied the report
and closed it with the word, "Horrible."[22]

Arriving in London for a brief stopover, Kennedy went to No. 10
Downing Street and was relieved when Harold Macmillan suggested
they cancel a formal meeting "with the Foreign Office and all that,"
and instead have a drink. Kennedy related Khrushchev's threats and received sympathy and reassurance from the invariably poised Macmillan, the beginning of Kennedy's closest personal relationship with a
foreign leader. Eventually Kennedy relaxed with Macmillan to the
point of telling him of his active sex life, that every once in a while he
had to have a woman to relieve tension.

Macmillan and his predecessor Anthony Eden, both authentic war
heroes, had rejected with their usual aplomb the Soviet threats of nuclear destruction as the British withdrew from Suez in 1956, but the
Soviet threat had struck home in the opposition Labor Party, especially
in its left wing, so that Soviet threats constituted a political reality in
Britain.

Macmillan had been in Washington in April, meeting Kennedy and
hearing Acheson's hair-raising briefing on the possible use of tactical
nuclear weapons to defend access to Berlin. The popular British attitude toward dying for Berlin was akin to the French eagerness to die
for Danzig, and Macmillan urged Kennedy to seek a basis for Berlin negotiations with the Soviets. (De Gaulle, one-upping the British, would
reject any negotiations with the Soviets under duress.)

On his return to the United States, Kennedy gave a television report
to the nation on June 6, 1961. He said the Vienna meeting was "a very
sober two days...there was no discourtesy, no loss of tempers, no
threats or ultimatums by either side, no advantage or concession
gained or given, no major decision...planned or taken, no spectacular progress achieved or pretended."

A *Times* editorial on June 11 said: "Premier Khrushchev presumably
had hoped that the new Kennedy Administration would be more amenable to his designs than the previous one. That hope was dashed in
Vienna...."

While the American media continued to stress that Kennedy had
stood up to Khrushchev, the average German in east and west sensed
strongly the malaise that hung over the Vienna summit. The stream of
refugees from East Germany into West Berlin swelled to a tide.

Ulbricht held a rare press conference in East Berlin on June 15, to
which Western correspondents were invited. It was an unusual opportunity to question Ulbricht, and Annemarie Doherr of the *Frankfurter*

Rundschau asked Ulbricht if he intended to build a "state border" through Berlin, with all of the consequences that would entail.

Ulbricht replied, "I understand your question thus, that there are people in West Germany who wish that we would mobilize the construction workers of the capital of the DDR (German Democratic Republic—Ulbricht customarily used the initials in speaking) to erect a wall, yes? Ah, I know of no such intention. . . . . Nobody has the intention of building a wall."

Ulbricht said that when the state treaty with the Soviet bloc nations was signed, East Germany would control all access routes through its sovereign territory.

On the same day, in coordination, Khrushchev addressed the Soviet Union on television, saying that on the whole he was pleased with his talks in Vienna. He laid down a firm December 31 deadline for signing a treaty with East Germany, removing the ambiguity in the American press over whether a deadline had been set in Vienna or not.

The *Times* in an editorial called his speech "chilling," but Reston in his column called it bluster. Reston said that Khrushchev's "threats to use force sound brave enough, but actually mean very little." Reston pointed out Khrushchev's difficulties with the Chinese and other Communists, concluding that the speech was intended to impress them.[23] As Khrushchev's threats became unmistakable through July, Reston remained optimistic, commenting that Khrushchev actually was helping Kennedy get a strengthened defense through Congress. "What is developing in the capital is not a dramatic crash program to fight a conventional war for Berlin but an orderly series of political, economic and military moves to strengthen the alliance for a much wider test of will with the Communist bloc," he reported.[24]

What was developing in Washington was that Kennedy was in the process of rejecting Acheson's pleas not to give an inch on Berlin. Acheson argued that West Berlin was not a problem but a pretext. Khrushchev aimed to force the United States to back down on a commitment, weakening U.S. power and influence—essentially, the prestige issue on which Kennedy had campaigned.

Kennedy now was entirely concentrated on Berlin, as he had not been on Cuba. Rusk was told to produce a negotiating program; McNamara and the Joint Chiefs were told to devise new contingency plans that would not mean a quick escalation to tactical nuclear weapons. A large increase in defense spending and a tax hike to cover it was rejected as inflationary. Similarly, a declaration of national emergency was dropped as too extreme.

By July 25 Kennedy was ready to tell the Americans what he intended to do about the Soviet threat to Berlin, in a speech written by Sorensen. He declared that the United States "will not permit the Soviets to drive us out of Berlin, either gradually or by force." He announced a $3.8 billion increase in the defense budget that would not make itself felt for months, a callup of limited reserves and some National Guard units and a slightly enlarged civil defense effort. The media hailed the speech as a tough one, singling out the rhetoric, but ignoring a glaring omission: the speech did not mention the four-power status of Berlin.

Khrushchev meanwhile had heard that John J. McCloy, the first U.S. high commissioner to West Germany, was visiting in Moscow, and invited him to Khrushchev's villa at Sochi on the Black Sea. McCloy was on hand when Khrushchev received reports of Kennedy's speech, which he pretended to find belligerent. He asked McCloy to tell Kennedy that he hoped for peace, but he was worried that West Germany would obtain nuclear weapons, and he feared an uprising in East Germany, inviting a West German invasion there. The idea of West Germany invading East Germany was absurd, but McCloy cabled the information to Kennedy, who asked him to return to Washington immediately and report to him.

Shortly after Kennedy's speech to the nation, Senator Fulbright, chairman of the Foreign Relations Committee, said on television that he did not understand "why the East Germans don't close their border; I believe they have a right to do so. We don't have the right to demand that refugees can come out." Ulbricht would triumphantly quote Fulbright later.

East Germany's Communists took a series of actions against the background of a drumfire of threats during July. East Germans working in West Berlin were required to be screened and receive passes from the Socialist Unity Party. Ulbricht called West Berlin a "thorn in the German Democratic Republic and a center of war that must be removed." In a campaign against West German "head hunters" who allegedly lured refugees west, the East German press demanded that West Berlin, "a dirty sink, must be cleaned."

By August, East Germany's black-uniformed Transport Police (Trapos) were hauling suspected refugees off subway and elevated trains, threatening them with treason charges and a death penalty instead of the usual two to five years for "fleeing the republic."

The Allied commandants protested East German interference with workers crossing to West Berlin to the Soviets. The Soviet Mission replied that East Germany could take any measures it wished, since East Germany had not signed the four-power agreement.

Khrushchev assembled the Warsaw Pact leaders at an unannounced summit meeting in Moscow August 3. Ulbricht told them that "an explosion threatens" in East Germany. He said that alone in July, 30,415 refugees had gone West. The next day Ulbricht received a go-ahead from the Warsaw Pact for "measures to close the sector border of Berlin." For the first time Ulbricht detailed to the East bloc leaders his plans for a permanent, 46-kilometer-long wall through the city. Khrushchev already had moved reinforcement troops into Poland's Western Territories in April, and both Poland and Czechoslovakia now positioned divisions near German borders.

Ulbricht returned from Moscow August 5, looking grim to those who saw him arrive at East Berlin's Schönefeld Airport. That day 1,500 refugees checked into West Berlin's Marienfelde refugee center.

Khrushchev gave another television report to the Soviet Union on August 7, declaring that he would settle the Berlin problem unilaterally if necessary and announcing the callup of some reservists. In West Berlin 1,800 refugees reported to Marienfelde; the next day it was 2,000.

On August 10, the Soviets announced that Marshal Ivan S. Konev, the World War II conquerer of Berlin, was appointed troop commander in East Germany.[25]

Military movement was reported on highways throughout East Germany. On August 12, a Saturday, 2,662 refugees fled to West Berlin, bringing the total since the Kennedy-Khrushchev meeting to more than 70,000.

West Berlin had been full of Western correspondents since mid-July, although few British reporters made the trip from their stations in Bonn. Britain did not like the story, with a few exceptions such as the *Daily Telegraph* and *Reuters*, just as Britons were not impressed with the man the *Daily Express* called "Dr. Adenauer." Like other reasonable reporters in Berlin, I retired at the sensible hour of 1 a.m. on August 13, just minutes before a message ticked over ADN, the East German news wire, announcing that the Warsaw Pact had authorized the East German government to take extraordinary measures in Berlin. Dozing off at the Hotel am Zoo, I was brought half awake by the ringing telephone.

Without salutation, George Bailey[26] said, "They've done it. They broke their backs. They've got a goulash cannon at Brandenburg Gate, and they're stringing wire across Potsdamer Platz." He meant that the refugees had broken the backs of the Ulbricht group, which had sent soldiers and a field kitchen to Brandenburg Gate. Bailey's voice was elated and grim at the same time; the showdown had come, and he assumed that now all of the West's power and economic superiority would be brought to bear on the Communists.

Fifteen minutes later we met at Brandenburg Gate. Peoples Army soldiers were lined up at the goulash cannon. Soldiers with jackhammers were punching a line of holes across the concrete square to plant stanchions supporting barbed wire. An impatient captain grabbed a jackhammer out of a soldier's hands and leaned on it, making chips and dust fly. The soldier's face was ashen and expressionless. "So is it done!" the captain snarled at him, glaring at us.

Bailey said, "The taxi drivers had it first, on their radios. Probably as soon as the police."

"What do they say at the (U.S.) Mission?"

"I can't get an answer on any of the phones there."

"We'd better see if Allies can still go in."

We walked through Brandenburg Gate. The East German guard glanced at our passports and turned his back. We went down Unter den Linden, passing Serge Fliegers of *Hearst Headline Service*, ahead of us again, on his way out to report that he had been arrested by a detective in a Gestapo-style leather coat. A block from the dividing line the streets of East Berlin were dark and deserted, no military vehicles in sight.

Returning to the West we passed several B-girls coming home to East Berlin from West Berlin bars at their regular 3 a.m. end of shift, tripping along on their stiletto heels, their beehive hairdos held carefully erect. Some of them had husbands and children in East Berlin flats, and if they ever saw the West again, their youth would be gone.

On the West side, the U.S. Mission on Clay Allee was dark. No sentry came to the locked gate. McNair Barracks, home of the Sixth Infantry Regiment, was dark and silent too. Gate sentries shook their heads, answering no questions, refusing use of their telephone.

On the day the Berlin Wall was begun, Konrad Adenauer, 85, made one of his rare mistakes. He did not go to Berlin. He urged Germans on both sides of the borders to remain calm and believe that "the Allies will take the necessary measures." The next day, he kept an election campaign speaking schedule in Regensburg, telling a crowd of 25,000 that the Allies were ready to introduce "sensitive measures" against the Communists, implying that they would impose a trade embargo against the whole Communist bloc. Adenauer declared that Secretary of State Rusk "has shown himself in favor of economic countermeasures," and said that for West Germany's part, "we shall not contribute to the economic buildup of the Soviet Union if Moscow does not agree to reasonable negotiations with the powers of the North Atlantic Treaty Organization."

As Adenauer invoked the economic retaliation that De Gaulle had mentioned to Kennedy before the Vienna summit, the Foreign Office in London said that Britain opposed economic sanctions because it risked increasing unrest in East Germany. Adenauer continued to call for an embargo, especially of American and Canadian grain to literally starve out the Soviets.

Adenauer's coalition partners, the Free Democrats, divided on support of economic sanctions, some of them fearing it would bring on a new Berlin blockade, others representing businesses dealing with East Germany. Adenauer compounded his error in going to Regensburg by referring in his speech there to the beleaguered mayor of West Berlin by his original name, Herbert Frahm, an uncharacteristic slur on Brandt's illegitimate birth. Adenauer's mistake cost his Christian Union parties votes at the polls a month later, and it helped President Kennedy off the hook. It added distracting issues to the election campaign and gave the Social Democrats an opportunity to blame inaction on the Wall on Adenauer's waning influence with Washington.

Adenauer's failure to go immediately to Berlin reinforced the Social Democrats' contention that he did not care about the city or really about reunification. Adenauer's willingness to give up the Saarland to a European authority (his other mistake, rebuffed by Saar voters), his emphasis on NATO, his efforts to tie West Germany to a united Europe, his Catholicism as opposed to East Germany's mostly Protestant population, all pointed to Adenauer's disinterest in Berlin and East Germany, in the Social Democratic thesis. Actually, throughout Adenauer's 14-year tenure all of his foreign and intra-Germany policy efforts were directed toward "not voiding the option" of reunification. His spokesman, Felix von Eckardt, tirelessly explained that while German reunification could not be achieved immediately, it was inevitable eventually, and the day would be hastened if the option were not foreclosed.

Adenauer fought Kennedy's Berlin moves before and after the Wall was built, repeatedly urging that the West use its economic strength on Germany's behalf. Repeatedly he was rebuffed. At a press conference in Bonn, Rusk was asked later whether economic retaliation had been considered. Rusk snapped angrily, "What for? It never has worked. What would you expect to gain from that?"[27]

Brandt was campaigning in Hanover on the night of August 12-13, and he flew back to Berlin on the first plane in the morning. He convened the Berlin Senate (cabinet), then went to see the three Western commandants at 11 a.m. All three evaded his urgent questions, saying that they had no orders to send troops to the sector border. "You let yourselves be kicked in the behind by Ulbricht last night," Brandt burst out.

Kennedy was vacationing in Hyannis Port, where he had received reports that the East German Volkskammer on August 11 had voted powers to Ulbricht's State Council to take "decisive measures" to stop slave recruiting in Berlin and unmistakable reports that a showdown would occur over the weekend. The media was full of reports of mass arrests of East Germans along the sector border and on the transit system to West Berlin. Orders went to the Berlin garrison to avoid conflict.

With daylight on August 13 East Berlin came alive, seething with agitated Germans, circulating but not forming crowds. They went to see the sector border for themselves, held back by police at most points of the complex line that ran across hundreds of streets, alleyways, parks, warehouse areas, railroad yards, canals, gardens and even grazing areas for sheep and cattle. West Berliners drove into East Berlin searching for relatives, to lose their cars and be escorted back to the border or arrested. At an armory on Clara Zetkin Strasse rifles were passed out to Workers' Fighting Groups in baggy brown uniforms, brought in from Saxony.

On the West Berlin side of the line Germans shouted insults at workers and soldiers erecting the barbed wire barricades. On the east side a line of Peoples Police (Vopos) stood behind the workers and soldiers, and 20 yards back, a line of workers' militia watched the Vopos. Circulating between the lines, SSD men in civilian suits and blue shirts watched them all, but a soldier ran for it, leaping the barbed wire into West Berlin to the cheers of West Berliners, the beginning of an escape drama that would last for months.

About 10,000 West Berliners marched to Brandenburg Gate on the night of August 13, into an island of light from East German floodlights, chanting "Ulbricht must go!" West Berlin police turned them back after East German militiamen leveled rifles at the crowd.

Rusk reached Kennedy at Hyannis Port with a first full situation report at 11 a.m. on August 13, 16 hours after ADN had sounded the alarm with its dispatch. Rusk and Kennedy agreed it could have been worse; there was no indication that West Berlin was being touched. Kennedy boarded his yacht *Marlin* and sailed off for the day.

In Washington on the morning of August 13, Lothar Loewe, a gregarious television reporter with a legion of American friends, was getting calls from Bonn and Berlin, but he could get no information from U.S.

officials. He telephoned West Berlin to ask his friend Albert Hemsing at the U.S. Mission what was going on. Hemsing gave him a quick rundown. Loewe then went to State Department spokesman Roger Tubby, who took down everything Loewe told him. No report had come to the State Department through channels via Bonn, and Tubby was hearing from his man in Berlin for the first time through the German television reporter. Loewe, shaken by the incompetence, told Tubby, "You ought to send somebody immediately, like General Clay, so the Berliners will know you are behind them." Tubby relayed the suggestion to Rusk.

The *Marlin* put into Hyannis Port that evening, and the tanned President disembarked to find a furious friend waiting on the dock. Marguerite Higgins, of the *New York Herald-Tribune*, who had covered the 1948-1949 Berlin blockade, stood planted with the familiar Secret Service men.

As the President flustered, "Take it easy, Maggie," she told him, "There is not a single American soldier to be seen in Berlin! Some idiot in Berlin or Washington is not informing you fully. You can call it hysterics, but the Berliners are undergoing a terrible shock."

Kennedy asked what she suggested. She proposed that she sound out General Clay, to see if he would return to Berlin. Clay lived in nearby Cape Chatham, and she drove there immediately.

Clay said he was willing to leave his position as president of Continental Can Company, but he suggested that Higgins check first with Bobby Kennedy, with whom he did not get along. Higgins phoned Bobby, who told her that no one had touched a hair of a West Berliner's head, but if they wanted Clay, they could have him, "not as a commandant, but as a sort of moral rearmament."

Like Higgins, James P. O'Donnell, former *Newsweek* and *Saturday Evening Post* correspondent, had been receiving calls from friends in Germany, among them Peter Bönisch, an editor for publisher Axel Springer. Bönisch told him, "Wake them up in Washington, or they'll have lost Berlin by morning." O'Donnell called Higgins to confer, and she told him, "Tell them Clay is coming."

O'Donnell had joined the Kennedy administration to work for George Wildman Ball, Under Secretary of State for Economic Affairs, who was among those in Washington who hoped that the Berlin Wall might prove to be a stabilizing influence. Unsuited to work in a bureaucracy after an independent career, O'Donnell argued with his boss, whom he called "an anti-anti-Communist." Ball was glad to get rid of him, assigning him as an aide to Clay when the general was sent to Berlin as Kennedy's representative.[28]

Kennedy held his first emergency meeting on Berlin on Monday, August 14, with Rusk, McGeorge Bundy, Allen Dulles and Bobby Kennedy. Bobby advised against dramatizing the border-closing, which was not dangerous, but an uprising in East Germany would be dangerous. Bundy suggested offering negotiations to the Soviets as soon as the atmosphere calmed. Rusk cautioned that the United States should consult with Bonn first.

"What do you mean, ask Bonn?" Kennedy said. "Adenauer had better get used to the idea that I'm not Eisenhower, and he no longer has a veto over American foreign policy."

On Bobby's advice, Kennedy held up the Clay visit, so that the arrival of a cold warrior would not stimulate unrest in East Germany.

Edward R. Murrow, the radio correspondent who had set the pattern for American television news before becoming Kennedy's USIA chief, happened to land in Berlin on a world tour as the border was sealed. Murrow went to Brandt and showed the mayor a telegram he had sent to Kennedy saying that if Washington did not act quickly, "a political catastrophe threatens."

Murrow advised Brandt to write Kennedy directly. He brought in Allen Lightner, civilian head of the U.S. Mission, and with Brandt composed the letter, which Lightner telegraphed to Kennedy on Wednesday, August 16.

Pierre Salinger gave the Brandt-Murrow-Lightner letter to Kennedy, remarking on its "presumptious tone."

Kennedy read it scowling. Brandt's letter warned that inaction would cause a crisis of confidence, and the next act would leave Berlin a ghetto, cut off from both East and West, with severe psychological consequences. It closed, "I judge the situation as serious enough to write to you, honored Mr. President, with this ultimate frankness that is possible only between friends who trust each other fully."

Kennedy said, "Who does he think he is? . . . Trust! I don't trust this man at all. He's in an election battle with old Adenauer, and he wants to draw me into it. Where does he get off, calling me his friend?"

Brandt, in West Berlin, was absorbing a press statement by Rusk in Washington saying that the border closure was directed against East Germans and East Berliners, not against the position of the Allies or against access to Berlin. "Kennedy's throwing us into the frying pan," Brandt commented.[29] He ordered police to keep West Berliners back from the border.[30]

The *Times* was hard-pressed for headlines that would reflect credit on the United States or the President. One headline, strung across eight columns of an inside page, said, "U.S. is Drafting a Vigorous Protest to Soviets' Closing of Border Within Berlin." The Allied commandants made their vigorous protest to the Soviet commandant, who rejected it. "U.S. Sees Propaganda Gain," headlined the *Times*. A report from Washington by Max Frankel said,

> The Kennedy administration set out today to portray East Germany's closing of the border between East and West Berlin as a dramatic confession of Communist failure. The highest officials here indicated that this would be the extent, for the time being, of the Allied response to Communist moves in Berlin. As long as Western rights of access to the divided city are respected, the officials said, protest and vigorous propaganda will be the primary form of retaliation....[31]

Berlin remained in turmoil, with a considerable number of refugees still finding ways across the complicated border. On August 17, the barrier through the city began to become a wall. Long lines of trucks unloaded mountains of prefabricated concrete slabs hauled from throughout East Germany. No Soviet troops were seen, but a line of 25 T-34 tanks of the People's Army paraded down Unter den Linden and dispersed behind buildings and in courtyards near the Wall, emerging from time to time to support armored cars. Mounted machine guns on the armored cars dominated the borderline.

The saga of Bernauer Strasse began, the street of East German apartment houses bordering on the West Berlin working-class district of Wedding, where the residents never had stopped being neighbors. As the Wall went up, Vopos bricked up the windows on the ground floor apartments. Refugees leaped from second-story windows, so they were bricked up too. By the time the apartments were evacuated and sealed off from the Eastern side—they were too sturdy to be razed immediately—the sidewalk on Bernauer Strasse was dotted with creche flower memorials to East Berliners, usually elderly, who had died of injuries trying to drop from higher-story windows into blankets held by West Berlin neighbors. In the Teltow canal the first refugees were shot, trying to swim to West Berlin. Others were shot scaling the walls of a railroad freight yard.

At first there was little violence; rather, a collective holding of the city's breath. Berlin waited for the West's response. On August 16, Brandt addressed a union-organized rally of 250,000, saying he had just written Kennedy asking "political action, not words." He did not miss the occasion to invite Adenauer to "come to Berlin and see for himself the situation in this city where Germany's fate is being decided."

That day East Germany's newspapers headlined, "U.S. Will Not

Act," based on an AP dispatch from Washington.

Bild Zeitung, Axel Springer's often maligned boulevarde blatt, headlined, *"Der Westen Tut NICHTS!"* Under the headline in vertical order were portraits of Kennedy, De Gaulle and Macmillan, with readouts locating them at the White House, Colombey-les-Deux-Eglises and grouse-shooting in Scotland.

The United States finally reacted on August 19, sending Vice President Lyndon Johnson to Berlin with General Clay and starting a relief column of 1,500 troops in 250 vehicles up the autobahn to West Berlin. At the Helmstedt border-crossing point, the Soviets insisted that the U.S. troops dismount to be counted, and their troop commander, anxious to be on time to meet the Vice President, complied, in a concession that set a precedent.

In Berlin, huge crowds greeted Johnson, but he stayed in his car when it reached Brandenburg Gate and he made no effort to enter East Berlin to demonstrate the city's four-power status. The next day, Clay and Bohlen drove into East Berlin to make that demonstration, unchallenged. To the Berlin legislature, Johnson pledged "our lives, our fortunes and our sacred honor" to protect Berlin in a speech that turned the ears of his State Department escorts pink.

The next evening, Johnson visited Brandt in his home and found him wearing comfortable-looking slippers. Brandt protested that they were cheap, bought in the Kaufhof department store. The Kaufhof's night watchmen were surprised to see the store opened to allow the Vice President to shop for slippers.

Adenauer had asked to accompany Johnson on the plane to Berlin but was told, "This has to be a wholly American event." Brandt had warned that if Adenauer flew into Berlin with Johnson, "stones will fly." Adenauer and Refugee Minister Ernst Lemmer flew to Berlin in a separate plane, Adenauer privately referring to Kennedy as "this choirboy."

Clay, along with Air Force General Curtis LeMay, literally had saved West Berlin by beginning the airlift that broke the Soviets' 1948-1949 Berlin blockade. His presence guaranteed the success of Johnson's visit, but Kennedy did not yet permit him to stay on in Berlin.

On his brief trip with Johnson, Clay had seen that the Wall was a flimsy structure without a thorough engineering basis, as though the East Germans expected it to be replaced: a tentative wall. Doubtless Clay also was informed by the *Bundesnachrichtendienst* that East German contingency plans provided for building a permanent wall 100 or 200 yards deeper into East Berlin territory if an attack were made on the "temporary structure, which could have been withdrawn at the least sign of force from the three Western powers."[32]

Clay recommended that unarmed U.S. soldiers be sent to tear down the wall, and his suggestion was rejected. The permanent, engineered Wall was started only a year later, on the site of the temporary one.

On the day after Johnson and Clay left, Britain made the first show of force at the Wall, sending four tanks in response to East Germany's attempt to restrict Allied access to East Berlin to one crossing point. Now one of Clay's recommendations was followed, and U.S. tanks moved to the sector border at Checkpoint Charlie on Friedrich Strasse. It grew into a tense confrontation with East German armored cars, then tanks, on August 23. Kennedy ordered a withdrawal of armor from the immediate vicinity of the Wall. By the time Clay returned to West Berlin as President Kennedy's personal representative nearly a month later, the city's morale was at a low ebb.

Before Clay returned to Berlin, the Soviets introduced a new and powerful element of intimidation. On August 30, the Soviet Union broke an informal moratorium of almost three years on nuclear weapons testing, exploding a one-megaton hydrogen bomb. Kennedy, informed by his security adviser Carl Kaysen that the Soviets had broken the voluntary moratorium, commented, "Fucked again!" In the next two months the Soviets exploded nuclear weapons tests at least 26 times, almost one every second day.

A nuclear test ban treaty was one of Kennedy's most cherished goals, figuring in almost every speech and message he directed at the Soviet Union.

The United States, the Soviet Union and Britain had been engaged in nuclear test ban negotiations in Geneva since October 31, 1958, when talks started with a flurry of last-minute Soviet nuclear tests aimed at winning a practical and psychological edge. Then all three nations ceased tests voluntarily, at least in the atmosphere where they could be detected. The U.S. negotiators in Geneva had two aims: to get an over-all treaty that would also ban underground tests and thereby put an end to nuclear weapons development, and to win Soviet acceptance of on-the-spot inspection of suspected test sites. The second aim would bring the psychological bonus of opening up the closed and suspicious Soviet Union and set a precedent for cooperation. To this end, U.S. negotiators employed teams of scientists who set out elaborate criteria for a vast network of inspection teams.

The Soviet negotiator, Semyon Tsarapkin, accepted this nonsense with good humor, soberly dickering on personnel details of the never-to-be-realized army of scientific investigators and quotas of inspections per year as though the notion were not preposterous to the Soviets. Correspondents in Geneva liked him.

President Eisenhower, attempting to get negotiations off dead center, proposed in February 1960 that a treaty be signed banning tests in the atmosphere, leaving small-scale underground tests to be negotiated within a time limit under specific conditions of Soviet cooperation. The British were willing to go farther, a gentleman's agreement not to test at all for a period while methods were negotiated for verification (a word that was replacing inspection) that no cheating was occurring.

In March 1960, Tsarapkin picked up essentially the British idea and offered it as a Soviet proposal. David Ormsby-Gore, the British negotiator, who was a personal friend of then-Senator Kennedy, told correspondents at a closed meeting in Geneva that this was the last chance for the negotiations. Harold Macmillan, four years away from the Soviet threat to atom bomb Britain in 1956, was eager for progress. He flew to the United States to meet Eisenhower at Camp David and at Eisenhower's Gettysburg farm, urging acceptance of the Soviet offer.

Eisenhower demurred. A formal moratorium on underground testing would require the United States to dismantle what was left of its nuclear development team, while the Soviets, without a Congress to answer to, would keep their development team intact. The Soviet proposal would mean that the voluntary ban on testing would be made formal for five years, and Eisenhower was under pressure from John McCone, head of the Atomic Energy Commission and others to resume testing in view of suspected Soviet testing. But public opinion, aroused by Macmillan's urgent flight, required a response. Eisenhower and Macmillan issued a fuzzy one: If a treaty were signed, they would agree to a voluntary moratorium on underground tests, provided that the Soviets joined in a scientific search for ways to detect underground tests of a seismic magnitude under 4.75. The effect was to leave United States testing blocked, voluntarily and without formal commitment.

In June 1961 President Kennedy, in his turn trying to prod the Geneva negotiations into life, warned that the United States would not refrain from testing indefinitely. Khrushchev boasted at a reception on August 9 that the Soviets had developed a 100-megaton nuclear weapon that could "reduce Germany to dust." Kennedy told Arthur Krock off the record on May 5, 1961, that he believed that the Soviets had been testing secretly, and they were "supposed to have in the attic" a small neutron bomb.[33] That did not particularly worry him, but he wanted to keep the Geneva talks alive as part of an effort to keep China from developing nuclear weapons. Kennedy thought that neutron weapons were "foolish in the extreme."[34]

General Clay arrived in Berlin again on September 19, possessed of a direct line of communication with the President but no command authority. Laughing, weeping crowds of Berliners welcomed him, and by the time his limousine arrived at his Wannsee home he was knee deep in flowers thrown into the car windows.

For more than a decade, Clay had been out of touch with German politics. At an informal press reception on September 22 he chatted informally with reporters for more than an hour. Clay said it appeared to him that there were two Germanys, and West Germany eventually would have to recognize the reality and negotiate with East Germany toward reunification. That was an abrupt departure from official American policy, which had held that if Bonn negotiated with East Germany it actually would be negotiating at a disadvantage with the Soviet Union.

Answering hypothetical questions, Clay said that the United States would not give up protection of West Berlin's access routes, but that perhaps the (then unrecognized) East Germans might control the identification of travelers to and from West Berlin. Could they keep out Adenauer as a warmonger? No, Clay said, in that respect East Germany would have to give up some of its sovereignty. Such detailed answers from an emissary direct from the White House reinforced the impression that Clay was revealing policy.

As correspondents began leaving, Al Hemsing took Clay aside. Clay called for attention, then spoke of wanting to be open with reporters. Any information he had given was off the record, for use without attribution.

The story was a bombshell in Bonn and Washington because it appeared to confirm Adenauer's worst fears, that Kennedy had made a basic policy decision abandoning support for German reunification.

In Washington, West German Ambassador Wilhelm Grewe said that such a policy change would endanger NATO. Grewe had helped draw up the treaties and protocols by which West Germany had joined NATO, and he had written into the language formal Western commitments to German reunification.

Clay had, in fact, inadvertently revealed such a policy change, but not because Kennedy had briefed him to do so, rather, because Kennedy had not briefed him at all. The policy change was as Clay had stated it. The next major policy change would be taken when Kennedy visited West Berlin in 1963, and it would pass unnoticed by most of the daily press.

Clay's problems with the media were minor in comparison with those he had with the State and Defense Departments. Both Ambassador Walter Dowling in Bonn and General Bruce C. Clarke in Heidelberg resented Clay's activity in Berlin, with his direct line to Kennedy outside their channels. For the next seven months, Clay repeatedly took action to prevent the whittling-down of Allied access to West Berlin and between the sectors of the city. He seldom called Kennedy, except in serious cases such as Soviet air maneuvers in the air corridors to the city. Clay was reminded by Heidelberg that he had no command authority over troops, and the British protested formally in Washington when Clay helicoptered into the exclave of Steinstücken, in danger of being starved out by a mini-blockade.

Clay considered it his responsibility to draw the Soviets into conceding their responsibility in Berlin, rather than leaving the United States facing East German troops in a military version of recognition.

His chance occured on October 26, when East German border troops demanded identification from Americans in civilian clothing in American military vehicles. Clay sent five U.S. tanks to Checkpoint Charlie, the 90-mm gun of one tank overhanging the white strip that had been painted across Friedrich Strasse. That night 30 more Eastern tanks rumbled into East Berlin, parking in closed courtyards near the Wall. The August tank face-offs between Americans and East Germans had given the Soviets pause. An option for war had been placed in the hands of East German soldiers.

On the night of October 27, seven of the new tanks appeared on the East German side at Checkpoint Charlie, their gun muzzles about 50 yards from Clay's armor. They appeared to be different from the East German T-34s, and they carried no markings. Per Sjögren of *Dagens Nyheter* said, "They're Russian. I think they are the new T-54s. There's only one way to find out." We walked over the border and through the tanks. The tank captains, standing in their open turrets listening to lightweight earphones, wore an unfamiliar uniform, a black jumpsuit. "Look at those Slavic features," Sjögren said.

At the U.S. Mission, Clay had been informed that East German tanks had turned up at Checkpoint Charlie.

"Look again," Clay said. "Want to bet they're not Russian?"

A couple of bets were made when the telephone rang with the report, "They're Soviet tanks. We are monitoring their communications, and they're speaking Russian."

Clay collected a bottle of whisky and a carton of cigarettes. The tank confrontation lasted until October 28, when the Soviets withdrew. Clay had brought Soviet responsibility back into East Berlin, but Kennedy ordered him not to do it again.

Three days after Soviet forces reappeared in East Berlin, the Soviets reached the climax of their moratorium-breaking nuclear test series, exploding a gigantic weapon that Khrushchev claimed was a 100 megaton bomb. The largest known U.S. test had yielded 15 megatons. Fallout from huge Soviet tests showered down on Scandinavia and Japan, and several nations disposed of contaminated milk, accompanied by large headlines around the world. The Soviet tests continued into 1962, and the media gradually lost interest. Eventually a new Soviet test was reported in one paragraph with a small headline, "Another Soviet Test."

Clay kept some remnants of Allied access to East Berlin, and he kept the Berlin story alive in the American media after it had died out in Britain and France. He preserved some degree of credibility for the United States among Berliners, and without his actions Kennedy could not have visited Germany in 1963, yet an embittered Clay left in May 1962. When he visited Kennedy in Washington in April, the President had no time to discuss Berlin, and when Kennedy was asked what Clay would do after his resignation, he told a press conference that the general would go back to earning money on Wall Street. During his leave from the presidency of Continental Can, Clay had given up a half million dollars in income, and he told friends that Kennedy had given him a farewell kick in the pants.

Just before Clay's arrival in Berlin September 19, national elections reduced Adenauer's majority to a plurality, and his government became dependent on the unstable Free Democratic Party, led by Erich Mende, who later sold securities for the notorious Overseas Investors Services of Robert Vesco and Bernard Cornfeld. Mende demanded that Finance Minister Ludwig Erhard replace Adenauer as Chancellor, a move that Adenauer fended off for two more years. The Wall had crippled the Soviets' strongest adversary in Europe.

West Berlin did not come to rest. For more than a year it was the scene of spectacular escapes and sophisticated tunnel building.

The Wall put an end to talk of Germany's reunification. East Germans no longer had a way out, and they resigned themselves to making the Communist system work. People of other Eastern European nations realized that, if Germany, the traditional giant, was powerless, they too must come to terms with life in the socialist camp. The Wall proved to be an offensive weapon.

The Berlin Wall was an international watershed in ways that the Bay of Pigs was not. Kennedy did face a difficult problem. He had little support from Britain or France. The Germans themselves were unprepared for conflict either psychologically or militarily. Allen Dulles' report to Kennedy that East Germans were on the verge of revolt was mistaken, as a similar report had been in 1956, but neither Adenauer nor Brandt wanted to exacerbate the tense situation.

Khrushchev, however, had even more difficult problems; the key nation of his satellite empire was falling apart. Khrushchev had more pressing reasons to "negotiate" over Berlin than Kennedy did.

Kennedy had entered office with the intention of ending the cold war. The Berlin Wall would prove that it was too soon to end it; the other side wasn't ready. Kennedy had some hawkish inclinations, but except for Acheson, who was retired, Kennedy was surrounded by Adlai Stevenson's foreign policy groupies: Harriman, Bowles, Ball, Galbraith. Kennedy was not inclined to allow Germany its real weight in Europe, and neither was his conduit to the public, *The New York Times*. Kennedy experienced a second loss of nerve, and took the easiest way out of a situation that might have been an opportunity.

Winning the Berlin showdown gave the Soviet leadership a new lease on life because Germany counted in a way that Cuba could not count. The Wall accelerated Germany's move to the new generation of leaders Kennedy had awaited in his 1957 *Foreign Affairs* article. They included Brandt and his aide, Egon Bahr, who proposed instead of reunification, *Wandlung durch Annäherung*, or changing (East Germany) through friendliness, a version of neutralism.

In West Berlin, disillusionment with the West did not set in immediately, but it was on the march in 1964, at about the time that the American student revolt began. In Berlin, radicalism had more to feed on, and became far more virulent.

A few weeks after Berlin was divided, some of the former B-girls from West Berlin bars turned up at an East Berlin dance in a bare, undecorated school gymnasium. Their beehive hairdos were combed out, either hanging or braided, and they had run out of Western cosmetics. The blonde strands of hair were dark at the roots.

Chapter V
The Cuban Missile Crisis

*"To the south, the Union has a point of contact with
the empire of Mexico, and it is thence that serious
hostilities may one day be expected to rise."*

—Alexis de Tocqueville

The media demands solutions, but foreign policy problems are not
solved, only altered. A defeat leaves the original problem compounded
by new ones. Through 1962, Cuban exiles were killed trying to get
into Cuba to revive an underground, and refugees were killed trying to
get out of East Germany into West Berlin.

Kennedy remained obsessed with Berlin, expecting Khrushchev to
tighten the screws, although he had failed to sign his separate peace
treaty with East Germany. Kennedy told Sorensen, "If we solve the
Berlin problem without war, Cuba will look pretty small. And if there is
a war, Cuba won't matter much, either."

The media's attention span, usually brief, was kept alive in Berlin by
spectacular escape stories. The year 1961 had closed with a student,
Dieter Wohlfahrt, 19, bleeding to death at the barbed wire barricade

while the Wall still was being built, unassisted by nearby British troops. General Clay warned the U.S. commandant, Major General Albert Watson II, that the same thing would happen on the American sector border one day, and he should be prepared to send in a squad of unarmed U.S. soldiers to the rescue.

In April 1962, an unknown East German soldier attempted to escape at Dreilinden, the combined Allied entry point to the city, and was shot and apparently bled to death. Clay again advised Watson to be prepared for such an incident on his territory. Clay had gone home when it happened: Peter Fechter, 18, a construction worker, was shot at the Wall on August 17, 1962, 150 yards from the U.S. post at Checkpoint Charlie. The lieutenant in charge called Watson for instructions, and Watson made an attempt to telephone Kennedy in Washington. He did not get through to the President, and Fechter agonized for an hour in sight of a crowd of West Berliners before Vopos carred off his body.

West Berliners for the first time turned against their own police, trying to reach the Wall to stone Vopos. A large-scale riot erupted on the west side of the Wall near Checkpoint Charlie on August 20, and for the first time the shout, "Ami go home!" was heard in West Berlin.

Fidel Castro's prestige had skyrocketed after the Bay of Pigs, and Cubans who opposed his revolution all but abandoned the interior underground. In other respects his revolution was in trouble. In January 1962, the Organization of American States suspended Cuba for attempting to export communism. By summer 1962, more than 200,000 Cubans had left the island since 1959, and 50,000 more would leave before the missile crisis cut off Pan American's regular flights. When PanAm resumed flights in 1965, another 200,000 would leave by 1970.

Castro ran a Mao-style permanent revolution, with pre-revolution Communists such as Blas Roca and Aníbal Escalante having edged out Castro's M26-7 comrades, then falling into disfavor when Escalante was banished to Prague for a year for trying to build his own empire. In May 1962, Castro ordered Soviet Ambassador Sergei Kudratsev out of Cuba, but the next month Castro reversed course, praising Soviet technicians and "the glorious Communist Party of the Soviet Union, led by the great and dearly loved friend of Cuba, Nikita Khrushchev."

Cuba's agriculture had collapsed, and the population was ordered to volunteer to cut sugar cane. Food was rationed; stores were empty, and there had been no trade with the United States since the Bay of Pigs. The CIA secretly was at war with Cuba in Operation Mongoose.

Castro was convinced that Kennedy was planning another invasion, and so was exile leader Miró Cardona, who came away from a meeting with Kennedy believing that the President was considering an invasion force of six divisions, about 90 times the size of the Bay of Pigs brigade. Castro did not execute the Bay of Pigs survivors as threatened, and even allowed a few to be ransomed privately. Richard Goodwin had passed a message to him through Brazilian President Joao Goulart that if the invaders were shot, public opinion would be so aroused that an invasion would be inevitable. Castro's anxiety over a new invasion was reinforced by Aleksei Adzhubei, Khrushchev's son-in-law and editor of *Izvestia*, who said he got that impression in an interview with Kennedy, whom he had seen in November 1961 and January 1962. The Cuban exile group Alpha 66, working with Mongoose, staged sabotage raids on Cuba that were roundly condemned in a *New York Times* editorial, presumably by Herbert Matthews.[1]

In early July, Raúl turned up in Moscow on a mission seeking more arms, accounting for Castro's kissing and making up with the Soviets. Che Guevara followed Raúl to Moscow in August. Between their Moscow trips, Castro spoke to thousands in Santiago on July 26, the anniversary of his first revolt, saying that Cubans had only to fear an invasion by the United States; no exile invasion could succeed. As he spoke a Soviet ship unloaded new weapons in Cuba.

On August 10, CIA Director John A. McCone sent a memo to Kennedy saying he believed that installations for launching offensive missiles were being built in Cuba. His aides tried to dissuade him, pointing out that such rumors had been around since before the Bay of Pigs, and that the Soviets were not equipped for that kind of long-range venture. McCone, however, believed a tip from Philippe Thiraud de Vosjoly, intelligence chief at the French Embassy in Washington.[2]

At a National Security Council meeting a week later, McCone elaborated on his belief that the Soviet Union was installing missiles in Cuba. Both McNamara and Rusk disputed him. The Soviets had not put offensive weapons into Eastern Europe, and they believed that the arms buildup was defensive. McCone pressed his case with newer evidence at a National Security Council meeting on August 22, at which Kennedy was present, and again the next day, once more in Kennedy's presence. McCone said the arms buildup in Cuba was massive and definitely included surface-to-air missiles (SAMs).

Realizing that the arms buildup would not long remain secret, the administration assigned Roger Hilsman, head of State Department Intelligence and Research, to brief reporters off the record on August 24. Hilsman said that between July 26 and August 8, eight ships had unloaded defensive Soviet ordnance in Cuba, including communications vans, radar vans, mobile generators, crates that could contain surface-to-air missiles which the Soviets already had supplied to Iraq and Indonesia. Hilsman said there were also several PT boats with 15-mile-range missiles and about 3,000 to 3,500 Soviet personnel on the island, none in uniform. His briefing was essentially reassuring.

McCone gave up trying to enlist McNamara and Rusk and went ahead with his honeymoon plans to go to Cape Ferrat, France, with his bride, Theiline McGee Pigott. Before leaving, McCone told Kennedy on August 27, "The only construction I can put on the material going into Cuba is that the Russians are preparing to introduce offensive missiles. I question the value of SAMs except as a means of making possible the introduction of offensive missiles."[3]

The next day Kennedy was asked at a news conference about a speech by Senator Homer Capehart of Indiana, who had said that Soviet troops, not technicians, were landing in Cuba, and that the United States should invade the island.

"We have no evidence of troops," Kennedy said. "I am not in favor of invading Cuba at this time." Pressed by reporters, he added, ". . . an action like that, which can be very casually suggested, could lead to very serious consequences for many people." Kennedy said that the United States had responsibilities in many sensitive spots around the world, "including West Berlin."

A reporter began to ask about a State Department briefing that had indicated "these are military technicians and other people who are probably going to operate missiles similar to the Nike missile. Is this in accord with. . . ."

Kennedy broke in, "Well, I can't, I don't know who told you that at the State Department—they're going to operate Nike missiles—because that information we do not have at this time. There certainly are technicians there. There may be military technicians. . . but in the sense that troops, the word troops is generally used, as it's generally understood, we do not have evidence that there are Russian troops there."

The next day, August 29, a U-2 flight with a CIA pilot returned from Cuba with photos showing two SAM missile sites in operational condition and large construction sites.

That day, while the U-2 still was over Cuba, Senator Kenneth Keating spoke on the Senate floor, saying that as many as 1,500 Soviet troops had landed in Cuba with war material. Two days later, Keating said that the Soviet arms buildup was "deliberately designed" to enable the Soviets to build missile sites on Cuba, a formulation similar to McCone's confidential warning to Kennedy.

The *Times* was not reporting Keating's specific warnings, although he was a New York Republican. Rather, it was reporting more generalized warnings by other Republicans and Senator Thomas Dodd, a Democrat. A *Times* editorial commented, "The sudden influx of Soviet bloc material and technicians into Cuba has again brought thoughtless demands to send American marines to take over the island or blockade it. Senator Tower of Texas has been clamoring for an invasion of Cuba for a long time. . . . If there is going to be nuclear war, it will not come from Cuba. . . ."[4]

Keating pressed the issue. On September 4, he was interviewed on NBC television, spoke on the Senate floor and held a news conference. Keating said he had been conservative in his estimate of 1,500 Soviet troops; there were "close to 5,000 Soviet men in uniform" in Cuba, equipped with armored cars, munitions and electronic gear. Keating said that more than ten ships were en route to Cuba with Soviet military supplies, including one ship each from East Germany, West Germany, Italy, Greece and Norway, and four to six flying the Liberian flag, plus several British ships headed for the Soviet Union to pick up cargo on charter for Cuba. Two sizeable Russian military camps had been built outside of Havana, including one at a former boys' reformatory, he reported.

While Keating was at the television studio, the White House called NBC to say that Kennedy would refute his statement as inaccurate, Keating was told. Pierre Salinger then issued a statement taking exception to the word "troops" and the expression "men in Soviet uniform." On the Senate floor Keating replied that quibbling over "troops" was a play on words.

That night Kennedy issued a statement saying that various sources had established

> . . . without doubt that the Soviets have provided the Cuban government with a number of anti-aircraft missiles with a slant range of twenty-five miles which are similar to early models of our Nike. . . . The number of Soviet military technicians now known to be in Cuba or en route—approximately 3,500—is consistent with assistance in setting up and learning to use this equipment. . . . There is no evidence of any organized combat force in Cuba from any Soviet bloc country, of military bases provided to Russia. . . of the presence of offensive ground-to-ground missiles. . . . Were it to be otherwise the gravest issues would arise.

Kennedy concluded, "The United States. . . will make sure that, while increased Cuban armaments will be a heavy burden to the unhappy people of Cuba themselves, they will be nothing more."

In Havana, Castro called Kennedy's statement "insolent."

Keating was in demand by the media, but not by the *Times*, which buried his remarks. A *Times* editorial said,

> The open and defiant military, as well as economic, buildup of the Castro regime by the Soviet bloc has elicited from President Kennedy a statement that at least clarifies the situation. The information available to Mr. Kennedy—no organized combat force, no Soviet military bases, no offensive capacity—is certainly better and more accurate information than outsiders, Senators included, can have. . . .[5]

(Matthews' editorials can be identified by irrelevant references to *economic* aid, Soviet *bloc* assistance, Cuba's *open* defiance and other anti-buzz words.)

Before issuing his statement on September 4, Kennedy received a message from Khrushchev promising that the Soviets would do nothing to cause trouble that could affect the 1962 congressional elections in November. Khrushchev remembered Harriman's solicitation before the 1960 election and offered the soothing message gratuitously. Since the Vienna summit, Kennedy and Khrushchev regularly exchanged messages through a channel that excluded the rest of the U.S. government, Bobby Kennedy picking up Khrushchev's notes from Soviet Ambassador Anatoly Dobrynin, an arrangement that increased the distrust of De Gaulle and Adenauer.

Also on that day Rusk wrote a warning cable to Khrushchev, "stiffened" by Bobby Kennedy, according to Arthur Schlesinger, saying that while the United States had "no hard evidence of significant offensive capability either in Cuban hands or under Soviet direction," the "gravest issues would arise" if it should be otherwise.[6] Schlesinger did not explain what was stiff about that formulation.

The Kennedy brothers' fury at Keating was boundless, out of proportion to the provocation. Kennedy's entourage—Schlesinger, Hilsman, Sorensen, Salinger, Harriman—missed no opportunity to attack Keating's character, intelligence and motives. Keating began to ask visiting reporters to step into the hallway, telling Victor Lasky that Bobby had bugged his office without a court order.[7]

Keating, a liberal Republican, was not an appropriate right-wing target for the Kennedys. At the outbreak of World War II, he had been a successful attorney, 41 years old, yet he went to war as a colonel in the China-Burma-India theater, won the Legion of Merit with Oakleaf Cluster, three battle stars and the Order of the British Empire as an aide to General Joseph W. Stilwell. He served seven terms in Congress before being elected to the Senate in 1958, was a civil rights advocate who supported social legislation and was popular in New York State.

Keating was, however, a critic of Kennedy's foreign policy. He had attacked Kennedy's handling of the Bay of Pigs and Berlin Wall and questioned what was going on in Vietnam and the Congo. He had pressed for a U.S.-led, allied boycott of Castro, but none of this explained the virulence of the Kennedys' reaction to him. The Washington press corps assumed the Kennedy rancor was normal election-year hostility, although Keating was not running.

The Kennedys' anger at Keating had another cause. He was pointing a spotlight on Cuba, where the Kennedys had been conducting large scale sabotage for a year—Operation Mongoose—and were engaged in secret attempts to assassinate Castro. In March and April 1962, two attempts to poison Castro failed when CIA contacts lost their opportunities or their nerve. In June a three-man hit team arranged by the CIA in cooperation with the Mafia infiltrated Cuba without success. On August 10, the day McCone first informed Kennedy that he suspected Soviet missiles on Cuba, McNamara was reported to the Senate Intelligence Committee to have suggested to a high-level meeting in the cabinet room that Castro be assassinated. (McNamara did not remember making the proposal.) On August 13, Brigadier General Edward Lansdale sent a memo from his Defense Department office to CIA official William Harvey ordering a stepup of CIA action in Mongoose, including "liquidation of leaders," and was told by Harvey he was stupid to put that in writing. In September, as Keating turned the spotlight on Cuba, the CIA was sending another three-man hit team into Cuba.[8]

McCone, stopping over in Paris on his honeymoon, lunched on September 6 with Roswell Gilpatric, Deputy Secretary of Defense, complaining that he could not get his conclusions across in Washington. McCone was receiving through the CIA station in Paris update reports on Cuba, and he sent telegrams to his deputy, Lieutenant General Marshall S. Carter, urging that the President be informed of the likelihood of missiles, adding warnings that Ilyushin-28 medium bombers also were being assembled on Cuba. Carter did not forward McCone's telegrams of September 7, 10, 13, 16 and 19.[9]

The *Times*, while scarcely mentioning Keating's continuing statements, retained its proprietary interest in Cuba and sent Tad Szulc to Miami to scout the Cuban exile community and the large CIA establishment there. Szulc reported that there were about 4,000 Soviet and other Communist-bloc military in Cuba, organized in compact units with their own transport, supplies and arms, functioning separately from Cuban forces. His sources described the Soviets as "service troops" or "housekeeping troops," and said that the arms buildup "appeared not to have any offensive capability, particularly because they lack transport to take them outside Cuba on military missions."[10] Szulc listed eight Soviet encampments, including the Torrens Boys' Reformatory near Havana, without noting that this confirmed Keating's report of some days earlier.

Szulc's series ended after three days under the reassuring headline, "Threat of Russian Buildup is Held More Political Than Military."[11] The series concluded that "the function of the estimated 4,000 officers and men appears to be logistic."

On September 7, Kennedy asked Congress for standby authority to call up 150,000 reserves. Administration officials off the record and the *Times* stressed that Berlin was the reason for the precaution. *Times* headlines said:

BERLIN IS BELIEVED
A MAJOR FACTOR
Link to Soviet's Shipments
of Weapons to Castro
Termed Secondary.

Much of the media believed that Cuba, not Berlin, was the reason for Kennedy's request. Two days later the *Times* conceded in an editorial that:

> Moscow's announcement of massive military and economic aid to Cuba represents a watershed in Hemispheric history. It was a power move in the cold war by the Soviet Union, as if a pawn had been advanced...Cuba now cannot be invaded—if such a folly were to be contemplated in present circumstances— without killing Russians. The added dangers of an invasion are clear...we have again and again been caught by surprise through a miscalculation of the strength of the Cuban regime and the unlimited determination of Fidel Castro. There is no greater error in war than to underrate one's enemies....[12]

As that editorial was written for what exiled Cubans were calling *The New York Tass*,[13] the CIA monitored the arrival in Havana on September 8 of the Soviet lumber freighter *Omsk,* noting its oversized hatches. The lumber freighter *Poltova* arrived on September 15. Both carried IRBMs or MRBMs. They were unloaded at night by Soviet personnel. Cubans living near the dock areas had been evacuated and the docks fenced off.

Keating finally made the *Times*, although in an AP story on Page 6, with a series of radio and television interviews broadcast September 9. Keating warned that a "horse trade" with the Soviet Union involving

Cuba and Berlin would be a betrayal. He said that the President himself had spoken on television of Berlin and Cuba in the same breath, and that the United States "must make it clear to everyone that no such deal is in the cards."

Keating said, "In brass tacks language, it would mean that Premier Khrushchev has told President Kennedy, 'You lay off on Berlin. We'll lay off on Cuba. But if you press us in Berlin, then we will put the screws on you in Cuba.' "

Both the President and Rusk angrily replied that Keating was meddling dangerously in foreign policy. Rusk asked reporters to quote informed sources to the effect that the Soviets might assume that Keating was sending up a trial balloon for the administration, a non sequitur.

Khrushchev replied to the Rusk-Bobby Kennedy telegram of September 4 in threatening terms on September 11. Khrushchev wrote that the arms sent to Cuba were defensive, and he warned, "Our nuclear weapons are so powerful in their explosive force, and the Soviet Union has such powerful rockets to carry these nuclear warheads that there is no need to search for sites for them beyond the boundaries of the Soviet Union." He accused the United States of preparing for aggression against Cuba and said, "If the aggressors unleash war, our armed forces must be ready to strike a crushing retaliatory blow at the aggressor."

Now the *Times* came alive with a three-column headline on Page 1:

SOVIET SAYS U.S. ATTACK
ON CUBA WOULD MEAN WAR;
PROPOSES DELAY ON BERLIN

WASHINGTON CALM	KENNEDY ASSAILED
Administration Terms	Moscow Asserts Bid
Warning by Soviets	To Call Reserves Is
Propaganda Move	Aggressive Step.

Kennedy was pressed at each of his news conferences about the Soviet weapons buildup in Cuba, and he reassured reporters again two days after Khrushchev's note that the arms shipments to Cuba did not constitute a serious threat. He added, ". . . if Cuba should ever become an offensive military base of significant capacity for the Soviet Union, then this country will do whatever must be done to protect its own security and that of its allies."

In Los Angeles, Richard Nixon, who was running his calamitous campaign for governor of California against Edmund (Pat) Brown, recalled on September 18 his 1960 campaign suggestion in the debates with Kennedy that the United States should "quarantine" Cuba to prevent an arms buildup there.

By this time, the intelligence services "had received more than 200 agent reports that there were offensive missiles being installed on Cuba," according to Air Force Major General George Keegan.[14] The CIA discounted the reports. Ray Cline, deputy chief of intelligence at CIA, told Elie Abel that a technically trained Cuban refugee being debriefed at the CIA processing center at Opa Locka, Florida, drew a sketch of the base-end of a 60-foot missile he had seen being transported, and it matched the Soviet intermediate-range missile. Another report said that Castro's pilot, drinking in a bar, had boasted that Cuba was invulnerable, now that it had atomic weapons. Cline dated the reports September 21.[15] Keegan said there was plenty of evidence before that.

George Ball, who had replaced the dovish Chester Bowles as Under Secretary of State in November 1961, testified before the House Select Committee on Export Control on October 3, 1962, that the Cuban arms buildup represented no danger. Using data assembled by Hilsman, which Hilsman said had been cleared with McCone, Ball told the committee that 85 shiploads of defense materials had arrived in Cuba, where there were now 4,500 Soviet technicians. There were 15 SAM missile sites established, with a total of 25 predicted, and four coastal-defense missile sites, along with 16 PT boats with missiles. There were about 60 older type MiG fighters in Cuba and at least one new MiG-21.

"Our intelligence is very good and very hard," Ball said. "All indications are that this equipment is basically of a defensive capability, and that it does not offer any offensive capabilities to Cuba as against the United States or the other nations of the Western Hemisphere."

The next day McCone, back from Europe, attended a special meeting of the National Security Council. He found that western Cuba—the area where he believed missiles were being based—had not been photographed for more than a month. Each U-2 flight required Kennedy's authorization, on recommendation of a committee headed by McGeorge Bundy, and Kennedy had avoided western Cuba because there were several SAM sites there. The committee had feared a U-2 might be shot down. McCone insisted on U-2 surveillance.

Ten days elapsed before a U-2 flight was authorized because the U.S. intelligence organization was undergoing a shakeup. Kennedy and McNamara had decided on a new attempt to consolidate intelligence under the new Defense Intelligence Agency to end the parochial bickering between the services and to settle disputes over the National Intelligence Estimates.

Air Force Intelligence, the most modern and global of the services, consistently had reported Soviet missile capability far greater than CIA estimates, and now was being almost dismantled. In compensation, and because of the failure of Gary Powers' U-2 mission over the Soviet Union in May 1960, McNamara insisted that Richard Bissell's U-2s be detached from the CIA and assigned to the Defense Department, to be piloted by men from the Strategic Air Command. Although the Kennedy insider historians reported that the U-2 flights over Cuba were delayed in part by Hurricane Emma, the main reason for the delay was the time required to check out SAC pilots with the U-2. A U-2 finally flew over western Cuba on October 14, carrying Air Force Majors Rudolph Anderson, Jr. and Richard S. Heyser. They returned with clear photos of offensive missile sites.

Keating, meanwhile, had declared in a Senate speech on October 10 that he had received confirmation that six IRBM launching pads were under construction in Cuba, that they could "hurl missiles into the heartland of America," and could strike Washington, D.C., the Panama Canal and Mexico City.

As the U-2 flew home with conclusive photos, Edward P. Morgan and John Scali interviewed McGeorge Bundy on ABC television. Morgan asked, referring to SAM sites, "Isn't it possible. . .that these could be converted into offensive weapons virtually overnight, and if so, what would we do?"

Bundy replied: "Well, I don't myself think that there is any present, I know there is no present evidence, and I think there is no present likelihood that the Cubans and the Cuban government and the Soviet government would, in combination, attempt to install a major offensive capability. . .and I believe most of the American people do not share the views of a few who have acted as if suddenly this kind of support created a mortal threat to us. It does not."

The U-2 photos were developed and evaluated by the CIA on the afternoon of October 15, a Monday. Bundy and Gilpatric, taking every precaution of secrecy, informed Rusk, Hilsman, Vice President Johnson, Ball and U. Alexis Johnson, but not the President. Bundy wanted Kennedy to get a good night's sleep before facing the crisis.[16] Bundy took the photos to Kennedy at 8:45 a.m. October 16 as the President had breakfast in bed.

The Soviet-Cuban plan provided for first-phase installation of 40 launching pads at four locations. At Remedios and Guarajay, there would be two battalions each of 1,900-mile range IRBMs, totalling 16 IRBM pads. It never was determined that the 16 IRBMs arrived in Cuba. They were the missiles described by Oleg Penkovskiy as the mass-produced R-12, which had proved reliable enough to test using a

16-megaton hydrogen bomb.[17] At San Cristóbal and Sagua la Grande, three battalions were to be stationed with 1,100-mile range MRBMs, altogether 24 reusable MRBM pads, with 42 missiles on hand and six en route, making a planned total of 64 large missiles in readiness.

The offensive launching pads would be ringed with 24 batteries of 25-mile range SAM missiles, each battery consisting of six to eight replaceable missiles aimed around the azimuth, and 22 longer range SAM batteries were ranged around the island. Castro also had received 100 MiGs, with more en route, a number of Komer class PT boats with ship-to-ship missiles, cruise missiles akin to the U.S. Matador and 20 Ilyushin-28 two-engined bombers. There were not 4,500 Soviet technicians, but 20,000 Soviet troops in four battle groups, equipped with tactical nuclear weapons similar to the U.S. Honest John, a formidable force that could act as Castro's Praetorian Guard. "There were 13 Soviet generals in Cuba," according to General Keegan. The buildup was to be completed by November 27.

Kennedy's reluctance to accept indications that the Soviets had put nuclear missiles on Cuba was conditioned by anxiety that Operation Mongoose and attempts to murder Castro might be revealed, and by something else: the Soviet nuclear threat was more formidable than the administration wished known. The missile gap was real.

The warning of a missile gap was launched in December 1958 by the improbable Roger Hilsman,[18] a World War II hero who then was research director at the Library of Congress. At a Washington meeting of the American Political Science Association, Hilsman said that the Rand Corporation, under contract to the Air Force, had concluded (in 1958) that the Soviets could deploy 300 ICBMs within the next 18 months, while the United States did not yet have an operational ICBM.[19]

The public was ready to believe in a missile gap a year after Sputnik-1 was launched on October 4, 1957, and the American answer, the Navy's Vanguard, collapsed on the launching pad in December 1957. The Eisenhower administration undertook a crash program to build the Minuteman ICBM.

Aside from being grateful for the missile gap issue in the 1960 campaign, Kennedy admired Hilsman as a veteran of guerrilla warfare. Before Kennedy was inaugurated, he asked Eisenhower to name Hilsman head of State Department intelligence, and Hilsman became the first New Frontiersman in office, before the President himself.

The controversy over the missile gap was between the Air Force, which said it was genuine, and the CIA, which said it was not. The first National Intelligence Estimate written by the CIA after Kennedy took office said there was no missile gap. It was one if the first news items put out by Secretary of Defense McNamara, and it caused some hilarity in the media, in view of the campaign rhetoric.

The announcement of no missile gap also made a goat of Hilsman. He was required to recant, while saying that his concern had been expressed sincerely, and that earlier under the Republicans there *was too* a missile gap. Once in office, the Kennedy administration did not need a missile gap, and Hilsman took it like a good soldier.

Hilsman had been right the first time. There was a missile gap, quantitatively, and it persisted. The rocket that launched Sputnik-1 was the SS-6, "designed to carry the big bang," according to General Keegan, former head of Air Force intelligence. Keegan said that by 1957 the Soviets had the three largest ICBM factories in the world in full production. "The CIA said it wasn't produced, but I've seen photographs of 6,000 of them, all over the Soviet Union," Keegan said. The Soviets produced so many SS-6s that it became the basic space booster, and "they still fire a lot of junk into space with them to impress the Third World."

The SS-6 is a big rocket, obsolete because it is liquid-fueled and not accurate enough to hit a missile site (and neither was Polaris 1). But it is a genuine ICBM, with enough reliability to menace such large targets as cities. Keegan said that at least 300 were deployed on soft sites at the time of the missile crisis.

When the Soviets in August 1961 broke the informal moratorium on nuclear testing and began exploding huge weapons in the atmosphere, the Kennedy administration assigned Gilpatric to calm public anxiety. In a speech in November 1961, Gilpatric said there was a missile gap, all right, but it was on the U.S. side. The Soviets did not have a reliable ICBM, he said, while the United States had "dozens," plus six Polaris submarines with 16 missiles each.

The Kennedy administration was relieved to hear from the Soviet internal defector Penkovskiy that "We Soviets simply do not have (ICBMs) that are accurate enough. . . . Right now (1961) we have a certain number of missiles with nuclear warheads capable of reaching the United States or South America, but these are single missiles, not in mass production, and they are far from perfect."[20]

In 1960 the communications revolution had struck the American intelligence community, as it would hit newspaper offices a few years later. The intelligence services were inundated with technical data, and Keegan was put in charge of a $200 million computer program to sort through it. One aim was to see if computers could pick out a synthesis of vital items. "We found out a computer can't do that," Keegan said. "But in the process we found out something else: the Soviets were preparing for war."

In 1961, along with the Berlin Wall and the resumption of nuclear testing, the Soviets conducted a staggering array of military maneuvers. Instead of the normal week-long annual exercise, the Soviets ran three of them in June and August and unprecedented maneuvers involving the total Soviet military force in October 1961,[21] expanding the Soviet budget by one-third to pay for them and the Berlin buildup.

The intelligence services monitored Marshal Rödion Malinovski's speeches, his talk of a revolution in nuclear weaponry, his weeding out of older officers. Khrushchev was remarking that he would not attack the United States, but "go in through the back door."

The Joint Chiefs set up an elaborate war game to try to discover why the Soviets were spending themselves into bankruptcy, and whether they had found an Achilles heel in American defenses. Tacticians for weeks moved red and blue teams on ten-foot-high maps in the underground war room, repeating global exercises over and over. They concluded that the Soviets had found a weakness: there were no plans for delegating Presidential nuclear authority. If nuclear weapons struck Washington and seven or eight command control centers, there would be no one with authority to execute the release of American nuclear missiles. The United States could be neutralized by a handful of medium-range missiles in Cuba, much more accurate than ICBMs, evading the NORAD early warning system, reducing reaction time to two or three minutes.

One result of the study was that tanker aircraft were converted into a fleet of communications aircraft, and one "Looking Glass" plane was kept flying at all times with a general and staff aboard, authorized to order nuclear strikes. "And it's still up there," Keegan said 18 years later.

As the missile crisis became apparent in October 1962, Ambassador Thompson sent a message direct to General Thomas S. Powers, head of the Strategic Air Command, saying that he had received information that "all combat forces in the Soviet Union are to be on a full combat footing by November 27." That was the date the intelligence services computed that the Cuban missile complex would be in place.

With the photographic evidence in his hands on the morning of October 16, Kennedy gave McGeorge Bundy a list of persons he wanted to see in the Cabinet Room at 11:45. The Executive Committee, called Excom by the media, would be in more or less continuous session throughout the crisis, meeting in George Ball's conference room at the State Department. It included Vice President Johnson, Rusk, Ball, Assistant Secretary of State for Latin America Edwin Martin, Deputy Under Secretary of State U. Alexis Johnson, Llewellyn Thompson, McNamara, his deputy Gilpatric, Assistant Defense Secretary Paul Nitze, General Maxwell Taylor (just shifted from Kennedy's staff to be Chairman of the JCS), CIA Deputy Director Carter (to be replaced after the first day by McCone, who was out of town when the photos were developed), Bobby Kennedy, Treasury Secretary Douglas Dillon, Bundy, Sorensen and Kennedy's aide Kenneth O'Donnell. Later, Dean Acheson and Adlai Stevenson sat in, as did retired Robert Lovett and USIA Deputy Director Donald Wilson.

Excom bypassed the National Security Council and was a political consensus group, with only two military men, Taylor and sometimes Carter of CIA. Unlike the Bay of Pigs emergency staff, there would be no back-talk from 30-Knot Burke, who had been replaced on the JCS by Admiral George W. Anderson, and Anderson would not be present. (After running the missile crisis blockade faultlessly, Anderson would be dropped from the JCS after a two-year term, fired by McNamara.)

In the burst of publicity when the missile crisis was resolved, the Excom group spawned the expressions "hawks" and "doves," but Excom essentially was a dovecote; only Nitze and the visitor Acheson were hawks. Kennedy seldom visited Excom, leaving his picked men to sort out options.

McNamara proposed doing nothing. His celebrated remark, "A missile is a missile. It makes no difference whether you are killed by a missile fired from the Soviet Union or from Cuba" was an admission that the Soviets did have ICBMs after all. The remark so delighted Hilsman that he used it, in revenge, on the dust jacket of his book, *To Move a Nation*. Hilsman was in a lasting feud with McNamara.

Bobby Kennedy, who opposed the talk of an air strike from the beginning—"Now I know how Tojo felt when he was planning Pearl Harbor"—also leaned toward doing nothing, as did Sorensen, who later wrote that before the U-2 photos arrived, Kennedy "refused to give in to the war hawks in the Congress and press (and a few in the Pentagon) who wanted to drag this country into a needless, irresponsible war without allies against a tiny nation which had not yet proved to be a serious threat to this country."[22] Ball also argued strongly against an air strike.

Acheson, not a member of the administration, and the Joint Chiefs, who were absent except for their new chairman Taylor, believed that the Soviets had offered an opportunity to invade Cuba and repulse communism from the Hemisphere. Acheson told Bobby Kennedy his repeated comparisons to Pearl Harbor were absurd. The Monroe Doctrine for decades had been a warning that the United States would not tolerate an agressive European power in the Americas, and the President had given sufficient warning in news conferences on September 4 and September 13.[23]

The Pentagon argued for an invasion. There were 45,000 Marines available on sea maneuvers near Puerto Rico. The Army's 82nd and 101st Airborne Divisions were alerted, 14,000 reservists were recalled to crew transport planes, and eventually the Army assembled 100,000 troops in Florida to be ready for contingencies. An air strike would be less effective than an invasion, and it would require 500 bombing sorties to take out all 40 offensive missile pads, 46 SAM batteries and the MiGs and Ilyushins, certainly killing some of the 13 Soviet generals. An invasion would accomplish much more at no more political cost.

Kennedy received Gromyko on the evening of October 18. The Soviet foreign minister told him that a small nation like Cuba, receiving defensive weapons, posed no threat to the United States, but that the United States was in a precarious political position in Berlin. After the meeting with Gromyko, Kennedy made his decision: a naval blockade of Cuba. Excom argued on, until Bobby vetoed an air strike as violating American ethics and tradition. McNamara said that a naval blockade would leave options open for a later air strike and subsequent invasion if it proved necessary.

By the time Kennedy met Gromyko, the Washington press corps was aroused and probing, and the British Embassy, headed by Kennedy's friend Ormsby-Gore, suspected that a serious crisis was in progress. The Soviets were monitoring both the reporters and the British, and their radar followed the stepped-up U-2 flights. It seems clear from the messages Kennedy and Khrushchev exchanged via Dobrynin that the Soviets understood that Kennedy knew missiles were on Cuba. Kennedy's reluctance to act between late July, when large arms shipments began reaching Cuba, and October 18 had encouraged the Soviets to press ahead. Acheson bowed out of Excom meetings and went home October 19. The Joint Chiefs sent a last appeal to Kennedy for an air strike or invasion and were turned down.

To decoy both the media and the Soviets, Kennedy left on an election tour in support of congressional candidates in Ohio and Illinois on Friday, October 19. He returned to Washington the next day, Salinger telling reporters that he had a feverish cold.

Excom gave Kennedy two final options on Saturday, naval blockade or air strike, knowing that the decision had been made. Stevenson, brought into the group late, suggested United Nations inspection to make sure the missiles were gone, and also proposed giving up Guantánamo naval base and Jupiter missiles in Turkey, where there also might be UN inspection.[24]

On Sunday Kennedy called in key congressmen, some being flown into Washington from districts without major airports on Air Force jet fighters, to tell them that he intended to quarantine Cuba, using Nixon's word rather than "blockade." Senators Earl Russell of Georgia and William Fulbright of Arkansas both said it was a half measure, the dove Fulbright surprisingly advising an invasion to get it over with. Fulbright later said he believed that a naval blockade meant direct U.S.-Soviet confrontation, but that the Soviet technicians could stand aside if the United States invaded Cuba. Russell later said he "begged on my knees" for an invasion instead of a blockade.

Kennedy also called in Ormsby-Gore and discussed options with him, allowing Ormsby-Gore to feel that he had influenced the decision for a naval quarantine. Ormsby-Gore called Kennedy the next day to propose that the blockade arc be moved from 800 miles to 500 miles from Cuba, to give ships more time to turn back. His suggestion was adopted over the objection of Admiral Anderson, who didn't want his ships within range of Castro's air force.

Dean Acheson flew to Paris to inform De Gaulle and show him the aerial photos. De Gaulle, struck by the sharp photos from 14 miles high, commented, "C'est formidable," and added, "If there is war, I will be with you. But there will be no war."

The European ally most directly affected by the missile crisis, Adenauer, was briefed last, on Monday night, October 22. Like De Gaulle, he suggested that a quarantine was not a sufficiently forceful response.

A year later Marguerite Higgins, interviewing Adenauer shortly before Kennedy's death, suggested that Kennedy had made up for his indecision over the Berlin Wall by his performance during the Cuban missile crisis. Adenauer's response was characteristically pithy: "Was Cuba really a success?"[25]

Whether Cuba was a political success or not, it was a triumph of public relations and news management. Throughout the growing crisis, the Kennedy team had been hypersensitive to media requirements, beginning with the efforts to denigrate Keating. When U-2 photographic proof arrived on October 14, part of the delay in getting them to Kennedy was to avoid attracting the media's attention. Kennedy's election tour was a decoy trip ended by a decoy cold. Kennedy personally telephoned the publishers of the *Times* and *Washington Post* after hearing they had stories that a showdown was due and got both stories killed or modified. Reston had showed his story to the White House for clearance and already had softened it. McNamara telephoned the publisher of the *New York Herald-Tribune* and got its report killed.[26]

With news reports of the impending quarantine killed or made vague, the stage was set for the dramatic surprise announcement that Kennedy would make in a manner so challenging to the Soviets that their backdown would represent humiliation. As Kennedy prepared to speak his dramatic lines, 90 B-52s carrying hydrogen bombs took off, most of them over the North Atlantic; the rest of the 550-plane B-52 fleet loaded nuclear bombs, along with 800 B-47s and 70 B-58s, and 100 Atlas missiles, 50 Titans and 12 Minutemen went on Defense Condition Two alert, one stage short of war. Florida and Louisiana swarmed with Army and Marines.

Kennedy spoke on three television networks Monday evening, October 22 with a ringing denunciation of Soviet deception. He announced the naval quarantine of Cuba "as an initial step." He said the Soviets had placed offensive missiles on Cuba capable of striking Washington, D.C., the Panama Canal, Cape Canaveral and Mexico City. He recounted his exchanges with Soviet leaders, punctuating each of their replies with, "That statement was false." Kennedy called for a United Nations Security Council meeting and appealed to Khrushchev to "halt and eliminate this clandestine, reckless and provocative threat to world peace...abandon this course of world domination...move the world back from the abyss of destruction."

The Soviets did not show contrition but took the offensive as Stevenson raised the U.S. charges in the Security Council. Tass transmitted a long statement charging Kennedy with piracy and violations of international law, and a Soviet diplomat, Mikhail Polonik, said in the UN corridors, "This might be our last conversation. New York will be blown up tomorrow by Soviet nuclear weapons."

In Cuba, two MRBMs were ready to fire. Castro called a general mobilization and announced that Cuba refused Kennedy's demand for inspection. If the Americans sent Marines to inspect, "there will be 25,000 dead *gringos*," Castro said, using a pejorative common in Mexico but not in Cuba.

On Wednesday, 16 destroyers, three cruisers, an anti-submarine aircraft carrier and six utility ships of the Second Fleet drew the blockade line, an arc 500 miles north of Cuba, as 25 cargo ships in the Atlantic approached it.

British philosopher Bertrand Russell sent telegrams to Kennedy: "Your action desperate...no conceivable justification. We will not have mass murder...end this madness."

Kennedy replied: "I think your attention might be directed to the burglars rather than to those who caught the burglars."

Russell also telegraphed Khrushchev: "May I humbly appeal for your further help in lowering the temperature. . . . Your continued forebearance is our great hope."

Khrushchev replied to Russell suggesting a summit conference.

UN Secretary-General U Thant sent Kennedy and Khrushchev cables calling for "voluntary suspension of all arms shipments to Cuba" and for "voluntary suspension of the quarantine measures."

In the Pentagon war room, Navy men plotting on a wall map recorded some ships headed toward Cuba changing course. After a half dozen course changes, Rusk said to Bundy: "We're eyeball to eyeball, and I think the other fellow just blinked." Rusk repeated the remark later to ABC correspondent Scali: "Remember that we were eyeball to eyeball, and they blinked first."

That day Stevenson had his grand scene in the Security Council. "Do you, Ambassador (Valerian) Zorin, deny that the USSR has placed and is placing medium and intermediate-range missiles and sites on Cuba? Yes or no? Don't wait for the translation. Yes or no?"

Zorin, more amused than irritated, replied, "I am not in an American courtroom."

"You are in the court of world opinion," Stevenson declared. "You have denied they exist, and I want to know if I understand you correctly. I am prepared to wait for my answer until hell freezes over! And I am also prepared to present the evidence in this room, now!"

Enlargements of the aerial photos were wheeled into the council chamber, and Stevenson pointed out the missile sites with a pointer. He had been given the *coup-de-grace* stunt in the carefully prepared public relations campaign, and he made the most of it. Never again would the media be caught off guard during such elaborate preparations.

On Thursday, October 25, Walter Lippmann proposed in his syndicated column a "horse trade" previously proposed in private by Stevenson and in public by *The Times* of London: "The Soviet military base in Cuba is defenseless, and the (U.S.) base in Turkey is all but obsolete. The two bases could be dismantled without altering the world balance of power. . . . " Because Lippmann was close to the Kennedy administration, Khrushchev was to seize on the proposal.

But not all the Cuba-bound ships were turning away. The 12 that did turn around apparently had been those carrying offensive weaponry. On Friday, October 26, the U.S. Destroyer *Joseph P. Kennedy, Jr.,* named for the President's bomber-pilot brother, ordered the Panamanian freighter *Marcula* to heave to and be boarded. The encounter was carefully planned; the *Marcula* was known to be carrying inoffensive cargo under charter. It was boarded without incident and allowed to sail on. Kennedy ordered Admiral Anderson to avoid any other boardings. McNamara had nervously supervised Anderson's planning, and Anderson's mild remarks that the Navy was expert at blockades later cost him his position on the Joint Chiefs.

Other ships were running the blockade, and construction on the missile basis continued on a crash basis.

On Friday, ABC reporter Scali received a telephone call from Alexander S. Fomin of the Soviet Embassy, a KGB colonel and head of Soviet intelligence in the United States. They met, and Fomin asked Scali to sound out his government contacts on a proposal to ship out the missiles under UN supervision, a pledge by Castro not to accept offensive missiles in the future, and a U.S. pledge not to invade Cuba. Scali reported the proposal to Hilsman and Rusk, who told him it had real possibilities and might be worked out on an urgent basis with U Thant. Scali met Fomin again and entered his own demand that the Soviets guarantee not to put offensive weapons on Cuba.

As Scali met Fomin, a long telegram from Khrushchev arrived in Washington. It was part of the Kennedy media orchestration that it came to be described as incoherent and pleading; rather, it was discursive as Khrushchev described his experiences when Russia was devastated by Germany in two wars. Khrushchev argued that missiles could not be offensive without a backup army for invasion and occupation. It contained roughly the same proposal that Fomin had given Scali.

The next day, Moscow radio broadcasted a different message from Khrushchev. It added a demand for a swap of missile bases, saying that Cuba was 90 miles from the United States, but that "Turkey lies next to us." Khrushchev assured Kennedy in the message that the missile sites in Cuba were in Soviet, not Cuban, hands, the first direct admission that the sites existed.

That day Major Anderson, the SAC pilot who had photographed the missile bases on October 14, was shot down by a SAM missile. Castro later claimed he fired the missile himself, while inspecting a SAM command post and being instructed on how it functioned.

Excom approved a Joint Chiefs' recommendation that the missile site that killed Anderson be taken out with a single bombing attack. The Joint Chiefs believed the Soviets had fired the first shot as a test, and it could not go unanswered. Kennedy vetoed the attack.

At Bobby's suggestion, Kennedy decided to answer the first Khrushchev message, ignoring the second and thereby avoiding putting on the record at that stage the issue of missiles in Turkey. At the same time Gilpatric was assigned to write a scenario for removing missiles from Turkey and Italy.

As Anderson was shot down, Keating was saying that the weapons quarantine was not enough. He urged a complete blockade "to encourage Cuba's ultimate collapse." Keating said that Kennedy's ban apparently was limited to surface-to-surface missiles, bomber aircraft and related equipment. MiG fighter-bombers, torpedo boats, tanks and amphibious vessels were exempt from the ban.

The Khrushchev-Kennedy private channel through Dobrynin continued to function, and with Kennedy's approval Khrushchev sent Anastas Mikoyan to Havana to negotiate with Castro. Mikoyan reported back that Castro considered the Il-28 bombers to be gifts, which could not be returned. Khrushchev, Bobby and Mikoyan conducted a three-way exchange of messages.

Kennedy's reply to Khrushchev's first official message of Friday proposed (1) rendering inoperable the missiles under UN arrangements, (2) working out with the Acting Secretary-General of the UN an agreement to remove the missiles under UN supervision and (3) on the part of the United States, removal of the quarantine and assurances against the invasion of Cuba.

On Sunday, October 28, Moscow radio broadcast Khrushchev's answer to Kennedy's "acceptance" of Khrushchev's proposals:

> The Soviet government...has given a new order to dismantle the arms which you describe as offensive and to crate and return them to the Soviet Union....I regard with respect and trust the statement you made in your message of 27 October 1962, that there would be no attack, no invasion of Cuba, and not only on the part of the United States but also of other nations in the Western Hemisphere, as you said in your message. Then the motives which induced us to render assistance of such a kind to Cuba disappear.

Castro was not consulted. In Havana he smashed a mirror, cursing in rage. Meeting with Havana University students later, he said, "Khrushchev has no balls."[27]

In a low key, Kennedy acknowledged publicly Khrushchev's "statesmanlike decision." Negotiations dragged out, with U Thant joining Mikoyan in Cuba and Vasily Kuznetsov, who replaced Zorin at the UN, dealing fruitlessly with John J. McCloy. The crisis appeared over.

Rusk appeared on television on October 30 to announce that there was no thought of trading a Communist pullback in Cuba for Western concessions in Berlin, the statement that Keating had demanded that Kennedy make seven weeks earlier. "You cannot support freedom in one place by surrendering it in another," Rusk intoned. "We cannot connect in negotiations or in trade the problem of Cuba with the defense of freedom in other places." Much of the Washington press corps idolized Kennedy, and now they had something to jubilate. Michael J. O'Neill of the *New York Daily News,* on his way to taking over the newspaper, wrote, "Secretary of State Dean Rusk slammed the door hard tonight on any deal with Russia to trade a Communist pullback in Cuba for Western concessions in Berlin. . . ."[28]

To press his refusal of inspection, Castro added his own demands: U.S. withdrawl from Guantánamo, guarantees of an end of harassment from exiles and an end to surveillance overflights. In Castro's interpretation of the settlement, the United States was bound not to invade Cuba, ever, because the missiles were being removed, but Cuba was not bound to accept inspection because his proposals went unanswered and he was not a party to the negotiations. Castro's version of legality prevailed; subsequently, Presidents Johnson and Nixon reconfirmed the agreement not to invade Cuba so long as the Soviets placed no offensive weapons there.

The media pronounced the Cuban missile crisis over, although Keating and a few others remained unsatisfied that inspection had been dropped. Keating said that the United States did not know what had been left on Cuba, and there could be missiles and nuclear warheads hidden in caves, as well as nuclear armament for the newer MiG fighter-bombers.[29]

The *Times* conceded that Castro's refusal to admit UN inspectors was a snag, but not a fatal one. "A mitigating factor in the situation is that thus far the Russians appear to be carrying out the most important part of their bargain. Mr. Thant reports that he is 'reliably informed' that they are in fact dismantling their bases and are ready to ship their missiles back to the USSR. . . ."

Reston credited Kennedy with "saving the human race last week." His column defended government manipulation of the news. Reston noted that there were media complaints that officials had encouraged a number of false reports during the crisis, and that Arthur Sylvester, assistant secretary of defense, had said that lying is part of the government's arsenal. "The reflex action of the press," Reston wrote, "is to howl like a scalded dog every time it catches the government tinkering with the truth, but it can scarcely apply normal procedures to the actions of the first American government ever engaged in facing up to a nuclear war. And it is palpable nonsense to talk about these distortions as being 'unprecedented'. . . . As long as the officials merely didn't tell the whole truth, very few of us complained, but as soon as Sylvester told the truth, the editors fell on him like a fumble."

A *Times* editorial that day rejoiced that the Soviets had been caught managing the news, and now everybody in the Soviet Union would know that their newspaper lied. *Pravda's* commentators Yuri Zhukov and Victor Mayevsky had been in the United States, and they had assured their readers in Russia that no Americans believed Kennedy's fantastic tale of missiles, but shortly thereafter the Soviet press was full of admissions that the missiles were in Cuba after all. So *Pravda* was exposed, the *Times* exulted, and nobody would believe it any more. "And in *Pravda's* offices, we may suspect, there were some who wondered if it might not have been wiser to tell the truth from the beginning rather than 'manage' the news," the editorial said.[30] Weird.

Two years after the missile crisis, with Kennedy dead almost a year, another election rolled around. The Kennedy team had not forgotten Keating, the man who had, to them, soiled an almost perfect triumph. Who could run against the popular Keating?

New Yorkers liked their Senators, Keating and Jacob Javits, but Keating had a small problem in the spring of 1964. Odds were mounting that Barry Goldwater would be the Republican candidate, and he was likely to poll near zero in New York State, where the *Times* and the liberal establishment had given him a Neanderthal image. Adlai Stevenson had New York residence, and he was the likely choice to oppose Keating until President Johnson ruled Bobby Kennedy out as a vice presidential candidate.

Keating was scheduled to nominate Nelson Rockefeller at the Republican Convention and had disputed Goldwater on occasion. He differed with Goldwater's advocacy of giving command decision over tactical nuclear weapons to military theater commanders, and Goldwater opposed civil rights legislation that Keating had sponsored. As Keating declined to endorse Goldwater, the New York State Conservative Party renounced him, meaning the Republican vote would be split.

Bobby had declared himself out of the New York race in June, because he did not live in New York, but with Goldwater's nomination in July, inviting a Republican debacle, Bobby quickly seized the Democratic and Liberal nominations for New York Senator.

The battle between Keating and Bobby Kennedy was a national event, although the conclusion was foregone. Bobby's campaign was certified as dirty by the state Fair Campaign Practices Committee—but after the election was over.

The missile crisis was not an issue. It was fixed in history as a Kennedy triumph, with the dramatic quotations still in mind: "Eyeball to eyeball;" "A missile is a missile;" "This is the night I should go to the theater;" "His finest hour." Keating brought it up only once during the campaign and got a negative reaction. He said in Watertown on September 9, 1964: ". . . government press agentry insisted on calling Soviet combat troops 'technicians' and constantly minimized the extend of the Communist buildup. . . . There were artifical distinctions between 'offensive' and 'defensive' weapons, and there were denials about the arrivals and placement of missiles. . . . There is a similar pattern of misinformation in Vietnam." Keating proposed a "freedom of information bill."

Keating ran on his record of supporting aid to education, housing, unemployment, health, Medicare, anti-poverty programs and foreign aid. Bobby simply charged that Keating had not supported those programs. Keating protested to the Fair Campaign Practices Committee that Bobby was falsely saying Keating had opposed federal aid to education since 1947 and was "using the same techniques" on other Keating voting records.

The committee sent Bobby a confidential letter warning that his description of Keating's position on the nuclear test ban issue was "not only false and distorted, but also appears to be either a deliberate and cynical misrepresentation or the result of incredible carelessness."

The *New York Herald-Tribune* printed part of the letter, and the committee hastened to apologize to Bobby for the breach of confidence, nullifying the effect of the committee's criticism.

Keating was reduced to charging that Bobby was "a Back Bay carpetbagger who lives in Virginia and votes in Massachusetts," who was "looking for a power base for his future operations. He apparently has decided that New York can do more for him that he can do for the nation as Attorney General or for his home state of Massachusetts. . . ."

Bobby called Keating's voting record a fraud and mentioned his dead brother's name in every speech, often along with his other dead brother, Joe.

General Clay, Arthur Burns and seven Nobel Prize winners organized committees for Keating, and the *Herald-Tribune* endorsed him as "a model of principle," but the newspaper Keating had counted on, the *New York Daily News,* ran out on him. Four times the *News* ran editorials attacking Keating for not endorsing Goldwater, saying there was no choice between him and Bobby, and finally endorsed the Conservative Party's Professor Henry Paolucci, taking votes from Keating.

Keating twice paid for 30 minutes of television time to debate Bobby, and ended up debating an empty chair. When they finally met on Barry Gray's radio show, Keating was asked about Bobby's charge that he had accepted money from jailed Teamsters Union President Jimmy Hoffa. Keating replied, "So far as I know, Hoffa has not contributed anything to my campaign." Bobby said, "I believe you have received a $1,000 contribution from Hoffa," offering no substantiation. He had made the same charge against Hubert Humphrey in the crucial John F. Kennedy campaign in West Virginia in 1960, but the media had forgotten it.

The Kennedy team and the *Times* joined in Bobby's campaign. Hilsman, just booted from the Johnson administration and a professor at Columbia University, wrote an article for the *Times* suggesting that Keating's missile warnings in 1962 were responsible for the death of the pilot Anderson:

> The charge that Keating was more interested in personal publicity than his country's welfare may be extreme. But until the Senator comes forward with a better explanation than he has so far supplied, one of two possible conclusions is inescapable: either Senator Keating was peddling someone's rumors for some purpose of his own, despite the highly dangerous international situation, or, alternatively, he had information that the United States government did not have that could have guided the U-2 to the missile sites before October 14, and at less risk to the pilot.[31]

Keating repeatedly had said in 1962 that "all the information I had was either furnished or confirmed by government sources." If McCone, the most conspicuous Republican in the Kennedy administration, had been a source, Keating could not reveal it.

Bobby, 38, defeated Keating, 64, by 800,000 votes, not so wide a margin as it appears. Johnson swamped Goldwater in New York State by 2,600,000 votes, an unprecedented debacle.

Keating was defeated at an age too late for a comeback, but the Kennedy entourage was not finished with him. All of the Kennedy insider historians put Keating into the basic source books and public libraries as a blackguard. Schlesinger quoted at length Hilsman's scurrilous letter to the *Times* in *A Thousand Days,* adding that Keating recklessly distributed "wild exile reports." Hilsman wrote in *To Move a Nation* that Keating and Goldwater had created public pressures that "foreclosed some of the policy alternatives" (including McNamara's alternative to do nothing.) Sorensen wrote in *Kennedy* that Keating "inflamed the domestic political scene," and "talked of Soviet troops and then of offensive missile bases at a time when no credible, verifiable proof existed of either."

It appears likely that, without Keating's pressure, the President would not have gone on record before the missiles were confirmed that the United States would not tolerate them. If the President had not made such public statements, it is more likely that the McNamara option would have been adopted. Keating literally forced Kennedy to take action when the missile photographs were produced, and he never was forgiven for it.

The Keating episode is instructive because he became the lightning rod for the fanaticism of the keepers of the Kennedy myth, who, with the media's help, were successful for decades in imposing "Kennedy values" on the conduct of foreign policy.

A loose string left over from the missile crisis was the existence of 60 Jupiter and Thor missiles in England, 30 in Italy and 15 in Turkey.

The withdrawal of the 15 Jupiters from Turkey without consulation had foreseeable but unpredicted consequences. The Turks, without friends in Europe, regarded the missiles as symbols of their modernity and their badge of membership in the Western Alliance. The Jupiters were as important to the Turks as Skybolt was to the British in 1962. When the missiles were pulled out in a U.S.-Soviet deal over their heads, the Turks began turning away from the United States and toward accommodation with the Soviets, particularly on the part of Bulent Ecevit's Republican Peoples Party. After improving relations with the Soviets, the Turks invaded Cyprus in 1974, following the overthrow of President Makarios, which had been encouraged by the Greek junta. Turks occupied 40% of the island, but they did not immediately put settlers into Famagusta, the port and resort center. When they did begin to settle Turks in Famagusta in August 1977, the first thing they did was to change the name of the main boulevard from "J. F. Kennedy Avenue" to "Sanjar Pasha Kadese."[32]

The Cuban missile crisis still is in overtime, with a final score not yet recorded. Soviet troops and large amounts of weaponry still are on the island. Castro was better off after the crisis than before it, and during the late 1970s he could dispatch his armed forces to far-off adventures, but the United States could not. The crisis helped Kennedy, but it may not have helped the United States. Khrushchev was a loser, but the Soviet Union may not have been; it was inspired to build a blue-water navy by the maximum humiliation inflicted by White House news management.

In the memoirs Khrushchev dictated in the village of Petrovo-Dalyene before his death in 1968, he said, ". . . now that the climax of tension has passed, and we have exchanged commitments with the American government, it will be very difficult for the Americans to interfere. . . ." He was sure that Latin America would soon be Communist. "Lyndon Johnson assured us that he would keep Kennedy's promise not to invade Cuba."[33]

Kennedy had not, however, made a commitment not to have Castro murdered, and more assassination attempts were mounted, some continuing past John F. Kennedy's death.

Chapter VI
Skybolt

*"American policy is friendly to the neutrals, neutral
to the enemy and hostile to its friends."*

—Allied Diplomat to Marguerite Higgins in 1963

A month after the Cuban missile crisis, while euphoria was growing in Washington, President Kennedy inadvertently scuttled the government of Harold Macmillan, his best friend among world leaders.

The media liked to believe that Macmillan resigned over the Profumo security scandal, the unfortunate friendship of his Secretary for War John Profumo with Christine Keeler, who also was friendly with a Soviet naval attaché through Stephen Ward, a socialite later widely publicized as a security risk. Macmillan himself blamed most of his troubles on De Gaulle, and he continued to treasure his friendship with Kennedy. But Macmillan was at least half aware that it was Kennedy's cancellation of Skybolt that did him in.

In March 1960 Eisenhower and Prime Minister Macmillan met at Camp David and reached an agreement on Skybolt that resolved a British dilemma. It also made up for some of the damage Eisenhower had done at Suez in 1956, when Britain had been stamped a third-rate power vulnerable to Soviet nuclear threats.

Eisenhower offered to sell the British, without warheads, either Polaris missiles or Skybolt, a 1,000-mile range, two-stage air-to-ground missile, and the British offered the use of its naval base at Holy Loch, Scotland, for the U.S. Navy's new Polaris-missile submarines, offers not directly tied but an understood tradeoff. The British chose Skybolt over Polaris—"not merely a verbal understanding but a formal and binding agreement,"[1] even though Skybolt still was in development.

As the Cuban missile crisis ended, the United States had about 650 B-52 bombers, more than 100 Atlas and Titan missiles, the solid-fuel Minuteman in production, Polaris submarines with about 150 missiles and a popular assumption that the missile gap was in Washington's favor. For the U.S. Air Force, Skybolt was a high priority item, its means of holding up its corner of the nuclear triad and an almost invincible weapon. Unlike Minuteman, it could not be targeted in advance by the Soviets. B-52s already had Hound Dogs, missiles with a 600-mile range, but they were not rockets. Essentially jet drones, the Hound Dogs would be vulnerable to the SAM missiles as Skybolt would not.

For the British, Skybolt meant renewed status as a nuclear power. Britain was losing nuclear credibility because its Vulcan bombers soon would be unable to penetrate Soviet air space with nuclear bombs. Skybolt would reinforce Britain's status as the only U.S. nuclear partner. Economically strapped, still in the process of dismantling the empire, the pound falling daily against the strengthening deutschmark, the British gratefully abandoned their own Blue Streak missile program, which was plagued with cost overruns.

A year after the Skybolt agreement, Camp David was host to a different kind of conference, an informal outing of bright, young recruits to the new Kennedy administration, inhaling their whiff of power. A bull session developed on the subject: what could they do to ensure that the President left his mark on hsitory? Their consensus was that the most fundamental issue was the prevention of nuclear proliferation. No means were available to deny nuclear weapons to Communist nations, so the logical place to start would be to deny them to allies, particularly to make sure that West Germany did not go nuclear, but also to wean Britain and France away from nuclear weapons.

During Kennedy's first year in office several of his White House aides, including Carl Kaysen, Jerome Wiesner and Budget Director David Bell, tried to persuade McNamara to drop Skybolt as expensive and redundant. They were backed by Charles Hitch, controller of the Pentagon, but McNamara was wary of stirring up the Air Force lobby in Congress. He restored Skybolt funds that had been tentatively cut from the 1962 budget.

The internal attack on Skybolt was renewed in 1962, opponents of the missile pointing to cost overruns and estimates that development would take another two years. By the fall of 1962, Maxwell Taylor had become chairman of the Joint Chiefs of Staff, and with the Navy pressing for Polaris funds, he took a neutral position.

In August 1962, McNamara was persuaded by Hitch and Harold Brown, his director for research, that Skybolt should be dropped, but to dampen the outcry from the Air Force, he released some production funds in September, bringing to about $400 million the amount spent on the project. The Air Force was aware of the dispute, but thought it was winning.

In September Britain's Defense Minister, Peter Thorneycroft, visited McNamara, who told him he was disturbed at Skybolt's rising cost and lagging schedule. Thorneycroft, like the Air Force, did not get the impression that Skybolt would be abandoned. McNamara declined to bite the bullet and reveal that Skybolt was going to be cancelled, although he told aides he expected that the news would leak to the media by about December 10.

After Thorneycroft's report to Macmillan, the prime minister recalled that a McNamara speech at the NATO meeting in Athens in May had been leaked to the media, although nominally it was secret. His speech had, "with vigor and clumsiness," strongly condemned any national nuclear forces except American forces. Macmillan suspected that a failure of Skybolt would be welcomed in some quarters of the Kennedy administration "as a means of forcing Britain out of the nuclear club."[2]

Through October, the Kennedy administration was absorbed by the Cuban missile crisis. In early November, as the Soviets backed away from confrontation over Cuba, Thorneycroft was notified in vague terms that the Defense Department was considering alternatives to Skybolt.

On November 7, Kennedy met with McNamara, McGeorge Bundy, Rusk and Paul Nitze, head of the Pentagon's "second State Department," to discuss Skybolt. Kennedy was committed to abandoning the missile, so the discussion centered on alternatives for Britain, perhaps selling them Polaris, the original alternative offered by Eisenhower. Kennedy suggested that his friend, British Ambassador Ormsby-Gore, be given the bad news, and McNamara volunteered to do it. Ormsby-Gore was shaken by the news the next day, although McNamara again equivocated by telling him that no decision would be made for three or four weeks.

Kennedy made the decision final on November 23 in a meeting with McNamara, Bundy and several aides. Rusk twice sent letters to McNamara warning against cutting down Britain, but the ambiguous letters were drafted by his aides, and Rusk revised them only superficially; they were letters to get off the hook. There were complications in whatever decision was made: France would be further estranged if Britain were favored with nuclear-tipped Polaris missiles; Kennedy wanted Britain in the European Economic Community, a prospect that seemed likely under Macmillan but unlikely if a Labor government came to power in Britain.

McNamara was in no hurry to face Thorneycroft, and set a meeting with him in London for December 11, the day before both were due to attend the NATO ministers' meeting in Paris. In the meantime, the media got into the act. In London, Lord Beaverbrook's *Daily Express* warned on Page 1 on November 29 that the State Department was trying to strike down Skybolt, the British independent deterrent. On December 7, *The New York Times* reported discretely below the fold on Page 1: "The Kennedy administration has decided that the Air Force does not need the Skybolt missile as a strategic weapon. The Air Force disagrees . . . "

The story had been leaked to the *Times'* Jack Raymond, beating McNamara's prediction by three days.

Raymond's story was a "good leak" in that it did no damage; its details and predictions were accurate and presented the cases of all sides; it informed of an important pending decision; it alerted the British that the matter was not to be brushed away; it was welcomed by the Air Force and probably by McNamara as a means of easing into the bad news he was so reluctant to give the British. Raymond was not easy to manipulate because he would bring his knowledge impartially to the bare bones of the leak. It was a different kind of leak from the directed, manipulating, erroneous and one-sided leak to a like-minded reporter that became common later in the 1960s.

McNamara arrived in London to a superheated British media reception, telling reporters before he met Thorneycroft that Skybolt was "a very expensive program and technically extremely complex. It is no secret that all five test flights attempted so far have failed."

The British media exploded with charges of "the greatest double-cross since the Last Supper."

The New York Times chimed in with an editorial siding with the British and the Air Force, although not strongly. Under the headline "Continue the Skybolt," the editorial said that British anxiety was understandable, and the cancellation could have serious political and military repercussions on the Macmillan government. The *Times* recommended a half measure: "continued development funds for the next fiscal year."[3]

In London, McNamara still did not flatly tell Thorneycroft that Skybolt was cancelled; it could still be discussed a week later when Macmillan and Kennedy would meet at Nassau in the Bahamas. Then McNamara flew to Paris, where the annual NATO ministers' meeting was about to start, and met with Rusk and a number of their aides. Rusk urged giving Britain Polaris, linked to NATO use only, to avoid a more serious break.

Macmillan earlier had scheduled a meeting with De Gaulle on the edge of the NATO meeting and flew to Rambouillet. In Paris, Thorneycroft, McNamara, Rusk, French Defense Minister Pierre Messmer and their aides scurried about, conferring in the absence of a clear U.S. policy line.

At Rambouillet, De Gaulle took the occasion to lecture Macmillan, reminding him that he had offered cooperation in missile development six months earlier at their last meeting, when they had decided on joint development of the supersonic commercial airliner Concorde. He warned Macmillan that Britain's special relationship with the United States conflicted with its application to join united Europe, and he remarked that Kennedy in two years had managed to let down all of the major NATO allies.

Macmillan quarreled with De Gaulle over stalling on Britain's entry to the Common Market, but he evaded the missile issue. He would learn in Nassau what Kennedy had in mind. He had not given up hope that Skybolt could be rescued, and if it were abandoned, he expected to receive Polaris to ease the pounding he was taking in the British press.

In Washington, State Department Under Secretary Ball, who had been involved with Skybolt only peripherally, now took an activist's role, urging that France should not be further antagonized by giving Polaris to the British, which might doom Britain's entry into the European Economic Community. Ball proposed that the British might continue Skybolt development at their own expense, no doubt knowing that Britain would not contract with the Douglas Corporation thousands of miles away, and he pushed hard for an alternative Multilateral Force, or MLF, an idea pressed by Henry Owen, deputy to Walt Rostow in the Policy Planning Council, and Robert Schaetzel, deputy to William Tyler, Assistant Secretary of State for European Affairs. Ball sided with those who saw nuclear nonproliferation as a priority, and he saw MLF as a route to return to the U.S attack on national nuclear forces.[4]

MLF originally had surfaced as an idea in the State Department of Christian Herter during the Eisenhower administration. Then, it was seen as a means of giving NATO nations a stake in nuclear strategy when they were reluctant to accept Thor and Jupiter IRBMs on their territories. As revised, MLF would absorb European funds and appetite for nukes, giving them a pseudo-role in nuclear affairs: surface ships with Polaris missiles would cruise with multinational crews and American skippers, precluding independent national nuclear forces. The ships also would be sitting ducks, easy to trail and target, unless an international navy were built to screen them. In sum, an expensive flim-flam.

Ball would fly with Kennedy to Nassau, where his boss Rusk would be absent.

Just before Macmillan met with De Gaulle, Kennedy was asked about Skybolt at a news conference. He suggested that Skybolt was so complex that "it has been really, in a sense, a kind of engineering that is beyond us." He repeated that five tests had been unsuccessful, but he added that no final decision would be made until he had met with Macmillan in Nassau.

Before leaving for Nassau, Kennedy taped a television interview with three network correspondents, George Herman of CBS, William H. Lawrence of ABC and Sander Vanocur of NBC. The content of the interview was mostly a summation of the Cuban missile crisis, and the *Times* headline on Page 1 said, "President Says Cuba Prevented a Soviet Accord."

The *Times* report of the television interview ran to several columns jumped to an inside page, and buried near the bottom of the story was the news: "The Skybolt missile is being cancelled because it would require $2,500,000,000 and other means of maintaining the nuclear deterrent are sufficient." The report quoted the President as saying, "There is just a limit to how much we need as well as how much we can afford to have a successful deterrent . . . . how many times do you have to hit a target with nuclear weapons?"[5] The *Times* had changed its mind about its editorial of a few days previous, and no longer considered the Skybolt decision news. Kennedy was, after all, the victor of the Cuban missile confrontation, and the *Times* simply turned off the negative Skybolt story.

Heading for Nassau, Macmillan learned of the television interview from American correspondents, and the British scrambled to get a text of it.

Kennedy met Macmillan in Nassau with Skybolt already publicly shot down. Ball pressed the President not to give the British complete Polaris missiles with warheads and to retain an option for the multilateral sea force that would give other NATO nations an illusion of nuclear participation.

Out of the Nassau meeting came an agreement that Britain could buy new Polaris A-3 missiles, still in development, without warheads, tied to NATO use after consultation, and a pledge by both nations to work for MLF. The State Department hastened to offer France a "similar" opportunity, and Ball visited Adenauer to say that Kennedy was serious about MLF.

Britain's media derided the deal. It was, instead of independent Skybolt, a costly, NATO-tied missile not yet built that would require new submarines to carry it.

All of Europe hooted at the "multilateral farce." Editorialists speculated on a British first mate on an MLF ship, perhaps a Danish helmsman, German engineer and French chef, although the chef's post surely would be disputed by the Italians, who would decline to be waiters in the officers' mess. In Washington, Ball was proud of his accomplishment, saying, "If the Secretary had gone and I'd stayed home, MLF would have been lost entirely."[6]

On January 14, 1963, De Gaulle "staged his drama,"[7] as it was called in Washington. At a press conference, he rejected Britain's entry into the European Economic Community until such time as the British could "transform themselves" into Europeans. He rejected the American offer to sell to France "Polaris missiles when we have neither the submarines to launch them nor the thermonuclear warheads to arm them."

Adenauer met De Gaulle in the period between the Nassau conference and De Gaulle's press conference reading Britain out of Europe. Adenauer summed up the Skybolt incident in his sparse language, writing in his memoirs that De Gaulle had offered Macmillan a common European attempt to replace Skybolt but that Macmillan "still owes a reply." Adenauer wrote:

> Macmillan then flew to the Bahamas and closed the Polaris agreement with Kennedy, with all the consequences this had for England's freedom of action. This was characteristic. England wanted the special relationship with America. That was its policy, to which it sacrificed whatever was necessary. One must be completely clear on this. Any time when the Americans thought dif-

ferently from the Europeans, the English would not think like Europeans but like Americans. This is a fact today, and it won't be otherwise tomorrow.[8]

Adenauer believed it would be even worse under the British Labor Party, where some members of the party were "really Communists."

No one was killed, wounded or scratched by the Skybolt fiasco, and the American media dropped the subject, although MLF stories hung around until President Johnson pulled the plug on the gaudy ghost fleet. To the American media, the British had simply been trying to get something for nothing. There was not much follow-up to Skybolt in the foreign affairs journals although, as Adenauer and De Gaulle indicated, the incident laid the basis for the fall of Macmillan's government, the succession of Harold Wilson's sterile Labor government and De Gaulle's subsequent expulsion of NATO headquarters from Paris and American troops from the Communications Zone in France.

The cost of removing American installations, ports and airfields from Com Z and reestablishing them elsewhere in Europe was estimated between $25 and $35 billion, the lesser figure ten times the projected cost of Skybolt. If Skybolt had been produced in 1963, it would have given the American nuclear deterrent a more flexible configuration and cheaper options for the future. Possibly by the end of the 1970s, a more accurate Skybolt-2 would have eased the dilemma faced by President Carter when he decided to cancel the B-1 bomber and MX missile, both to be reconsidered at astronomical prices by President Reagan.

When McNamara went to London in December 1962 and told the press that all five Skybolt tests had failed, Major General George Keegan picked up the newspapers and was flabbergasted.

> I had just come from watching the third successful test of Skybolt—sensational. And I read in the newspapers that we said it was a failure, too complicated, beyond our technology. So Macmillan's government fell, and it was a good government. De Gaulle defected from NATO, and it cost us $35 billion to dismantle Com Z. Then we withdrew our nuclear bombs from the Canadian air force, and the Diefenbaker government fell—not much of a government, but then . . . .[9]

Aside from international and defense considerations, Skybolt left the Kennedy administration with a residue of bitterness, suspicion and blame-assigning between departments and between the administration's Indians and their department chiefs. Kennedy was disturbed enough to assign, in March 1963, Richard E. Neustadt to interview participants in the Skybolt affair in Washington and London. Kennedy was looking for culprits, aside from himself and McNamara, and Neustadt found that the fault was spread through the White House staff, Bundy's staff, the State Department and Defense Department. With caveats to loyalty and good intentions, he did single out two State Department officials at the deputy assistant secretary rank whose names remained classified top secret 18 years after the events.

Neustadt reported to the President in his study, *Skybolt and Nassau:*

> Superficially, the finger points to personalities . . . two in particular . . . (who had) a blinkered view of policy, limited perceptivity, low tolerance for listening, unconcern for feedback and a tendency to shove . . . . They ranked objectives and assigned priorities by light of *their* official duties; *their* bureaucratic interests, *their* personal ideas.[10]

Neustadt cautioned that he doubted the answer lay in "cutting off their heads," and he had the temerity to remind the President that the two manipulators were following precepts found in Kennedy's speeches. The two men were not chiefs; they were high-ranking Indians who were "intent on Europe and on non-proliferations, comforting themselves with (Professor Robert) Bowie's happy thought that they could use the President as though he were a bludgeon to be wielded in support of their priorities."

Keegan, who studied the complete Skybolt report, said that "the people around Kennedy were making foreign policy, not the President. The idea was to keep nukes out of allies' hands, to manipulate the British out and to keep the West Germans out. Their idea was, "We will start by getting the British out, by reneging on Skybolt . . . . Dick Neustadt found a small group of brilliant kids restructuring world power relationships. Harold Brown was involved, and the McGeorge Bundy entourage."

In November 1962, during the Skybolt affair, a certificate of incorporation was filed for the Institute for Policy Studies, a new think tank, naming Marcus G. Raskin, Richard J. Barnet and David Riesman trustees. Since Raskin was leaving Bundy's National Security staff, and Barnet was leaving his post as deputy director for political research at the Disarmament Agency, it is tempting to think that they were among Neustadt's busy Indians. However Walt W. Rostow said that Raskin "lasted a very short time, indeed, on Bundy's staff, and he was fired for reasons that have nothing to do with Skybolt .... I don't know that anyone left the government over Skybolt."[11]

According to Barnet, he and Raskin decided to leave the Kennedy Administration after the first three months. On April 14, 1961, the day before Cuban exiles flying B-26 bombers took off from Nicaragua to strike at Castro's air force to raise the curtain on the Bay of Pigs invasion, members of the Arms Control and Disarmament Agency, White House Staff and State Department met to confer on the administration's disarmament priorities. Raskin and Barnet looked around at "the whole military-industrial establishment sitting there at one table," and as Barnet recounted, "Marc and I both grimaced at the same moment—and we knew we didn't belong there."[12]

Raskin, Barnet and Arthur Waskow, also a Kennedy administration whiz kid, began then planning for IPS, the radical think tank that would become the nerve center of the New Left. Finding funds and organizing the institute took about two years. Robert Borosage and Peter Weiss, executive director and chairman of the board of trustees respectively in 1981, said that IPS actually was founded in 1963, its founding trustees including Thurman Arnold, David F. Cavers, Freeman Dyson, Hans J. Morgenthau, Steven Muller and Gerard Piel.[13]

Raskin, 26 when he joined McGeorge Bundy's National Security staff, had come to Washington as a legislative assistant to Representative Robert Kastenmeier, a liberal Democrat from Wisconsin. Raskin had helped write the "Liberal Papers," a pie-in-the-sky project under the imprimatur of James Roosevelt that advocated total disarmament, dissolution of existing alliances and encouragement of revolutionary change in the developing world. The papers suggested that liberals join in an American version of the Fabian Society, a precurser of Britain's Labor Party.

Barnet was a Boston lawyer new to Washington when he joined the Kennedy administration.

Early funding for IPS came from well-known liberal foundations including the Ford Foundation, Milbank Foundation, the Commonwealth Fund, the Stern Family Fund and individuals. As IPS projects were perceived as radical, liberal funding fell off, and IPS leaned more on radical foundations, including the DJB Foundation, whose founder Daniel J. Bernstein had said that the chief enemy of mankind is "the injustice of governments, and of the United States government in particular," and the Samuel Rubin Foundation. Rubin's daughter Cora, later spokesman for visitors to Hanoi, married Peter Weiss, of the radical National Lawyers Guild, who would become influential in the Rubin Fund and chairman of the board at IPS.

Raskin and Barnet churned out books of policial philosophy critical of the American system and solicitous of the problems of the Soviet Union.

Raskin wanted to see "the national security state *dismantled*" (his italics).[14] He described the United States as an imperialist power that had colonized its citizens, dehumanizing them, a viewpoint similar to that of Herbert Marcuse, guru of the 1960s revolt, in his *One Dimensional Man.*[15] Like Mario Savio of the Berkeley Free Speech Movement (see Chapter XI), Raskin saw the university as "the fundamental shield and terrorizing instrument of the state," and he believed that "the American imperium is now viewed as the world's primary enemy by the poor and the young."

Barnet was convinced that the United States threatens the Soviet Union, not the other way around, and that the Soviet "threat" was a pretense of the U.S. military-industrial complex seeking high military budgets.[16] Barnet believed that, while the United States had "procedural freedoms" of speech, press and assembly, the Soviet Union had "substantive" freedoms of medical care, jobs and housing, and that Soviet citizens preferred their freedoms to ours.[17]

At the time of IPS' founding, Kennedy's buildup in Vietnam was practically unknown and of no concern to Raskin and Barnet. A major target of IPS at its founding was the corporation, especially the international corporation, which was seen as an especially invidious tool of colonization. During the founding of IPS, its directors picked up practical experience in business esoteria, alien to run-of-the-mill revolutionaries, such as incorporation procedures, legal responsibilities for subsidiaries or lack of them, tax law and rules of procedure for exemptions. IPS would turn corporate rules against the corporate system itself.

As a result of corporate expertise, there was a drawing together of New Left groupings at IPS headquarters at 1901 Q Street, N. W., in Washington and an endless spinoff of new organizations controlled by or allied with IPS through interlocking directorates. Raskin was a director of *Ramparts* in the 1960s, but the magazine was not economically viable. The Internal Revenue Service will not permit a publicly supported organization to devote a substantial part of its activity to propaganda, so *Ramparts* could not be tax-exempt. A new tax-exempt Foundation for National Progress could, however, distribute its publication to members, so *Mother Jones* became a successor to *Ramparts,* relying on IPS writers and echoing IPS themes, available to members of the Foundation for National Progress.

Another early IPS spinoff was Dispatch News Service, which would specialize in stories of American atrocities in Vietnam, winning a Pulitzer Prize for Seymour M. Hersh.

Eventually IPS would become a power in Washington, with its international subsidiary, the Transnational Institute, allied institutes on the West Coast, in Boston and in the South, direct ties to the Carter administration, regular contributors to *The New York Times* and access to prestigious publishers such as Random House.

In universities throughout the country there were plenty of leftist instructors, but since the brief McCarthy period there had been no center to coordinate them; IPS would assume that role. No longer would the CIA, FBI, defense industries and transnational corporations have the university campuses as their exclusive recruiting ground. During the 1960s, IPS would do its part in making some of the universities inaccessible to them.

IPS was born in the Kennedy administration out of the Bay of Pigs, Cuban missile crisis and Skybolt affair to become a rallying point for what had been considered a group of disarmament freaks near the lunatic fringe. The Washington press corps welcomed a new think tank, its members sure to be informed leakers all. The founding of IPS could not have been better timed, as the media was about to discover that we had become committed in Vietnam.

Chapter VII
Kennedy in Berlin

"The Prince need only be victorious and maintain his rule to ensure that the means whereby he does so will be universally regarded as honorable and praiseworthy. For the rabble is concerned only with appearances and with success, and the world consists of rabble."

—*Niccolò Machiavelli*

A week before President Kennedy went on television to announce the presence of Soviet missiles on Cuba and a U.S. Navy quarantine of the island, most editors knew from Senator Keating's warnings that a crisis involving Cuba and probably Berlin was brewing. Those with correspondents in Bonn sent them to West Berlin to be ready for what might come.

It was a welcome assignment. West Berlin, recovering from the initial shock of the Wall, was running on adrenalin, defiant and vibrantly alive. Berliners liked being in the eye of the world again, and there still was a thin chance that Ulbricht's regime might founder on the Wall. The Bonn government was pouring in subsidies to keep up morale, and Axel Springer was building a new publishing house smack against the Wall, its windows overlooking East Berlin.

No one in Germany believed that there was a danger of Soviet retaliation against West Berlin for whatever might happen in Cuba; the Soviets were not in an offensive stance. Although American military convoys and trains were stopped on the access routes to Berlin, and Soviet jets on "training flights" buzzed airliners in the air corridors occasionally, these were only harrassments, quickly over, never pressed to a test of strength. Marshal Konev, who had brought in an army of rapists in 1945, saying that he "detested, despised and yes, hated, Germans," and then returned to the city in 1961, was going back to the Soviet Union and retirement.

With newspapers' front pages devoted to Cuba, correspondents in West Berlin in October 1962 were on paid vacations, covering a nonstory, sending brief dispatches that Gromyko had dropped in on Ulbricht on his way home from telling Kennedy there were no missiles on Cuba, and that Adenauer visited the city before his scheduled trip to Washington. British and American correspondents, who hung out together, took nationalist views of the far-away Cuba crisis. The British did not see what the fuss was about. If there were missiles on Cuba, so what? If the United States didn't like it, there was no problem in crushing the Cubans, so close to the United States and so far from the Soviet Union.

The correspondents' Berlin idyll came to an end on the night of October 26, when police in Hamburg raided the offices of *Der Spiegel* magazine, arrested executives, sealed the offices and took away a truckload of documents.

There was instant outrage in West Germany, jealous of its press freedom after the Hitler era and military occupation, and in Britain, where the suspicion had not died that Adenauer was under the control of the Gestapo. In the United States, editors could barely get the raid on *Der Spiegel* into the papers on the day that the Cuban missile crisis was tentatively, but not really, settled.

The Spiegel affair, which brought down Adenauer's government and hastened the Chancellor's retirement, involved a personal vendetta, national security, political ideology and a coverup attempt by government officials that could have been a dress rehearsal for Watergate a decade later.

Rudolf Augstein was a 24-year-old editor when British occupation authorities in Hamburg abandoned their magazine, *Diese Woche,* because it was disrespectful of authority. Augstein held the staff together, scraped up financing, changed the name to *Der Spiegel* (The Mirror) and sectioned the magazine's format, after the model of *Time.* From its founding in 1947, the magazine gained readers steadily.

In 1955, on the occasion of the Paris accords under which West Germany joined NATO, Augstein wrote a widely remarked editorial, "Farewell to Our Brothers (in the East)," that elucidated Augstein's plea for West German disarmament and neutrality as a bait for reunification negotiations. Augstein believed, almost alone in the world, that a note from Stalin to the Bonn government in March 1950 might have been a genuine and negotiable offer for German reunification.

By 1956, Augstein was 30 and recognized as a publishing genius and political *enfant terrible,* strongly anti-Adenauer. That year, the Minister for Atomic Affairs, Franz Josef Strauss, 41, was promoted to Defense Minister, and Augstein invited the brilliant political comer to visit him in Hamburg. Augstein later told a BBC interviewer that they got along well enough in the meeting. Both had faced the Soviets on the eastern front, Augstein as a teenager; both were nationalists after their fashions, and both had been anti-Nazi. They were ready to part amicably at the Hamburg railroad station when Strauss missed his train. Back they went to Augstein's kitchen, where they sat awaiting the next southbound express.

The talk grew animated, and their differences emerged. Augstein, slight at 5'4" and aesthetic in his short-cropped Caesar hair styling, soft-spoken but with an arrogance often associated with Prussian intellectuals, faced the earthy Bavarian, Strauss, powerfully built with a huge chest and no neck. When Strauss spoke with vehemence, his voice carried a tremor, as though he could barely control his volcanic energy. When Strauss left, Augstein recalled thinking, "That man must not become Chancellor."

Strauss appeared on *Der Spiegel's* cover on January 2, 1957, with a long article that included Augstein's interview with him. The piece said Strauss was brilliant, courageous and vital, noting that he had been South Germany's bicycle-racing champion in 1934 and had set records in scholarship. It also concluded that he was power-hungry and a deceptive war-lover who sought to destroy what he had once called "the Soviet Reich." In the specious psychohistory mode, Augstein deduced that Strauss was disappointed that he had won only one medal in the war before being evacuated from the Russian front, an artillery lieutenant, with both feet frozen.

From the beginning of 1957, *Der Spiegel's* readers could count on a story about Strauss, either ridiculing or polemic, up to 13,000 words long, every week for the next six years. *Der Spiegel* monitored everything Strauss said, or was said to have said, and quoted it out of context to render such meanings as: Strauss reflects Nazi thinking; Strauss crudely insults pacifist professors; Strauss baits wartime émigrés like Willy Brandt; Strauss believes that conscientious objectors are cowards; Strauss creates panic and gives the Soviets reason to fear Germans; Strauss flirts with atomic war.

Strauss, who talked to the media bluntly or with Bavarian humor, made himself an easy target. He took legal action against a painter in Schwabing who displayed a portrait of Strauss as a butcher with bloody hands, making the painting a collector's item. He tangled with an officious policeman in front of Adenauer's chancellory, after instructing his chauffeur to drive to the gate on the wrong way of a 20-foot one-way approach, and then tried unsuccessfully to get the cop fired.

After several months of *Der Spiegel's* attacks had begun to coalesce the leftist press against him, Strauss gave the magazine another interview to dispel Augstein's charges that he was seeking atomic weapons in collusion with France. For page after page, Strauss denied in detail questions aimed at eliciting from him an admission that he sought nuclear arms. Strauss said he did want tactical nuclear weapons made available to the *Bundeswehr* under U.S. control, and he offered a million marks to anyone who could prove he had said he wanted control of nuclear arms. Augstein's accompanying editorial, "Franz Josef's Legend," implied that Strauss was lying and argued that if West Germany received nuclear weapons, East Germany would, too.

When Strauss became engaged to Marianne Ziecknagl, daughter of a brewer from Rott-am-Inn, *Der Spiegel* featured a story on the girls Strauss allegedly left behind. The marriage gave *Der Spiegel* two weeks of copy and pictures ridiculing the butcher's son and the brewer's daughter emerging from the church under an aisle of *Bundeswehr* officers' crossed swords. A photo showed the happy couple under an umbrella while the little flower girls were drenched with rain.

In April 1961, in the fifth year of the anti-Strauss campaign, *Der Spiegel* published an unsigned, 15-page polemic declaring:

> . . . in the Federal Republic a man has grown big who unceasingly feeds mistrust between the great nations and has demanded for the Federal Republic weapons that could unleash the 'suicide' of a Soviet attacker and with it the suicide of humanity. As sole pretender to the (chair) of the chancellor, this man can support himself on twin pillars of power, on the *Bundeswehr,* which he has

stamped to an instrument of his career, and on the Bavarian Christian Socialist Union, which three weeks ago unanimously voted him its chairman, or its 'chief.'

The face of this man, who, with a vocabulary like 'total distruction,' 'suicidal risk,' 'absolute deterrent,' 'criminal stupidity,' 'dynamic deterrent,' and who tosses the words like a juggler, everyone in the Federal Republic knows: the face contemporaries have described as 'like a stein of beer' *(Time)*, or . . . 'almost exactly what the French mean when they say boche.' (William S. Schlamm). . .

Strauss went to court to stop the harassment, on one occasion winning a temporary injunction. *Der Spiegel* appealed and published the verdict, saying, "the court has forbidden us to say the following things" and listing the items.

After five years on the chase, *Der Spiegel* had not found any actionable misconduct on the part of Strauss, when a friend and political associate, Passau publisher Johann Evangelist (Hans) Kapfinger, ran afoul the law. Kapfinger was accused of bedding a Yugoslav émigré woman to whom he had loaned money for a boutique.[1] While Kapfinger went through the court and media wringer, *Der Spiegel* prepared a huge takeout for its January 29, 1962, editions charging that Strauss, at Kapfinger's urging, had recommended to the U.S. Army an apartment designer named Lothar Schloss, who was connected to the Finanzbau A.G. (Fibag), to build apartments for a U.S. base. *Der Spiegel* charged that Kapfinger and Strauss were to share in the Fibag profits.

The Fibag affair caused judicial and parliamentary investigations, both of which cleared Strauss of *Der Spiegel's* charges of misusing influence. There were no kickbacks; the U.S. Army had decided not to build the housing, making it a non-affair. A Nürnberg court then forbid *Der Spiegel* to repeat that Strauss had violated his duties or had intended to share in Fibag profits, or to say that Strauss influenced other government agencies to give designer Schloss contracts worth $50,000. *Der Spiegel* repeated the charges anyway, partly by reprinting stories from other publications that had picked up the information originally from *Der Spiegel*.

Strauss went to court again to stop the repetitions, and *Der Spiegel* responded with a 16-page special section recapitulating the case and reproducing documents presented in court—which the investigations had called harmless—apparently on the theory that reproduced documents look stark and incriminating whatever they say.

The first Fibag story was timed to Kapfinger's trial on charges of extorting sexual companionship from Nada Illmann, for which he was sentenced to four months, suspended, and given a $1,250 fine. To underline the unrelated story's connection to Strauss, *Der Spiegel* headlined its report "The Bosom Buddy."

Der Spiegel's September 26, 1962, issue began a new saga, "Uncle Aloys."[2] Augstein's accompanying editorial explained that this new series on Strauss

> ...would not have appeared if Strauss had followed through his intention to leave the Defense Ministry and become Bavarian minister-president in Munich...there is nothing left for us to do but 'damage him professionally.'
>
> To those who charge that we are covering an important person with scandal, we answer, the way of thinking of the West German voting population and its majority government leave us no other choice. Democracy in this nation apparently can be brought to bloom only with a thick club. Strauss himself is only half guilty. The lack of criticism with which (the voters) place over the democracy the man they think to be strong drives a politician like Strauss to wantonness.

Augstein's sustained and unprecedented attack on Strauss was based entirely on personal and ideological animosity, risking the credibility of the magazine. The attack was succeeding because about four-fifths of *Der Spiegel's* content was first-class journalism, much of it exclusive and well-researched, although written in a convoluted style, some of it entertaining without malice. *Der Spiegel* appeared to be put together by about five editors, four of them master craftsmen and the fifth a hippy on LSD.

While Augstein was writing his "Uncle Aloys" editorial brandishing a club at West Germany's democracy, Conrad Ahlers, a senior editor, was working at a top secret document obtained by the magazine's Bonn bureau: the NATO evaluation of its 1962 fall military exercise, "Fallex-62."

The exercise was a maneuver without troops, projecting what might happen amid the chaos if the Soviets attacked with atomic strikes simultaneously at West Germany, England, Italy and Turkey. *Der Spiegel* published Ahlers' 12,000-word article on October 10, 1962, under the headline, "Conditionally Prepared for Defense."

The thrust of the article was that Defense Minister Strauss had failed; West Germany's armed forces were graded only "conditionally prepared" by the exercise referees, the lowest of four possible ratings. The referees' verdict was not a reflection on Strauss; NATO's criticism was that West Germany's forces could not meet their role well with their current equipment, deployment, size and mobility—mostly budgetary problcms. A secondary theme of the article was that posses-sion of tactical nuclear weapons could not help Strauss' *Bundeswebr,* Augstein's perennial theme.

Aside from its strained theses—similar to *The New York Times'* later manipulation of the Pentagon Papers—the article was authoritative and loaded with military secrets. It included a history of recent NATO tactical and strategic decisions, a manpower and weapons catalogue, NATO's estimate of Soviet attack plans and a discussion of the old NATO organizational scheme MC70 versus the new MC96 plan, pro-posed at thc cnd of the Eisenhower administration, which tentatively included Strauss' wish for medium-range nuclear missiles stationed in Germany under U.S. control—a deployment that would be a top U.S. priority in the early 1980s.

The article was loaded with specifics: Hamburg would not be de-fended; NATO expected a 14-day warning period preceding a Soviet attack to move aircraft to bases they do not normally use; troop trans-port timetables; NATO's planned tactical nuclear strikes on Baltic ports; the mining of Bavarian forests to free U.S. troops there for com-bat.

The article reported that Kennedy had rescinded the MC96 plan and fired NATO commander General Lauris Norstad for advocating tactical nuclear weapons for European troops, after first admonishing him, "Remember you're an American."

Adenauer in parliament called the publication "an abyss of treason."

Two weeks after publication of the Fallex-62 article, Augstein rushed into print at deadline an editorial signed with his pen name Jens Daniel—he also used the pen name Moritz Pfeil—attacking President Kennedy's decision to quarantine Cuba

Jens Daniel wrote:

> Whatever one can accuse Castro of, and he has grown wild, it is also incontrovertible that the U.S. supported the criminal Batista regime for 18 long years.
>
> Differentiating between 'bad' attack-rockets of the Soviets and 'good' defense-rockets of NATO in Italy and Turkey betrays a thought-provoking mixture of moral extremism and propagan-distic hypocrisy. When the U.S. may ally itself with Syngman Rhee and other monsters, why not Khrushchev with Castro? When a ring of medium-range rockets may be erected along the borders of the Soviet Union, why not a rocket base near the U.S.?...
>
> The Western world was ruled last week as they like to see it in Texas, from the saddle.

Police raided *Der Spiegel* at 10 p.m. on Octover 26, 1962, on orders of the federal prosecutor, technically acting on a citizen's complaint that the article on Fallex-62 was treason. No editor in Germany credited the explanation, even though two military officers also were arrested.[3] It seemed clear that Strauss' famous temper had gotten the better of him. Even Axel Springer's *Bild Zeitung,* an adversary of Augstein, rushed to *Der Spiegel's* defense, offering the use of its library.

Four days after the raid, Strauss told the *Frankfurter Abendpost,* "I may say that I and the leadership of the Defense Ministry had nothing to do with starting this action. On that night I had no idea about the kind, extent or aim of this action of the federal prosecutor's office." He told Nürnberg's *8-Uhr Blatt,* "I had nothing to do with the affair, in the truest sense of the word."

Strauss also denied in parliament that he had ordered the raid, but by November 8 he was forced to concede that he did "offer official help" when the federal prosecutor asked Spanish police to arrest Ahlers, who was on vacation in Spain with his wife. The West German military attaché in Madrid, Colonel Achim Oster, knew Ahlers from the time when both worked for the Atomic Energy Ministry, and he refused to seek Spanish police help without a direct order from the Defense Minister, so Strauss talked with Oster on the telephone. Ahlers and his wife were arrested, then flew back to West Germany voluntarily.

Strauss also had asked his deputy, Volkmar Hopf, to contact his opposite number in the Justice Ministry, Walter Strauss, with the effect of bypassing the Justice Minister, Wolfgang Stammberger, a Free Democrat who had voted against clearing Strauss of the corruption charges raised by *Der Spiegel.* Strauss said he bypassed Stammberger because he thought the Free Democrats, who were loosely allied with Augstein, would tip him off in advance of the raid. That proved Strauss knew of the raid in advance.

Stammberger resigned in indignation. Free Democratic leader Erich Mende threatened to bring down Adenauer's coalition unless Strauss were fired. In jail, Augstein studied the Bible and wrote of lessons he had learned from it. In an editorial written in jail, Augstein suggested that he was the successor to the hero of German press freedom, *Weltbühne* publisher Carl von Ossietzky, who was awarded the Nobel Peace Prize while in a Papenburg concentration camp under Hitler. Adenauer, in parliament, replied that Augstein was a self-made millionaire who had enriched himself by publishing state secrets. "I find that vulgar," Adenauer said.

Strauss, ready to yield and resign, rallied when his Christian Socialist Union won state elections in Bavaria, increasing its majority, on November 25, a vote of confidence in Strauss.[4] Strauss had campaigned day and night in Bavaria, but the victory did not help, and he resigned November 30, to study economics at Freiburg University and then to become minister-president of Bavaria.

When *Der Spiegel* was raided, *The New York Times* prudently played the story on Page 3, since treason was a serious charge, and because Cuba preempted Page 1. It made up for lost ground with extensive coverage in November, but in thousands of words the *Times* published, it never cited the items in the Fallex-62 article that had been stamped top secret or cosmic secret, and it never implied the extent of Augstein's six-year vendetta against Strauss, ignoring the atmospheric context. Like the Pentagon Papers case nine years later, the Spiegel affair was described purely in terms of an attack on press freedom, although the Fallex-62 document contained current military secrets.

Reports by Sydney Gruson, chief of the *Times* Bonn bureau, stressed demonstrations by students and intellectuals sweeping West Germany, their placards reading, "They attack *Der Spiegel,* but they mean democracy;" "My God, what is happening to Germany?" "Who will be pulled out of bed tomorrow?"

Gruson described *Der Spiegel* as a rather mischievous news magazine "that delighted in goading the government and puncturing inflated egos." He commented, "From what went on, a newcomer to West Germany might think that no one had ever leaked a secret to a newspaper before. The fact is that many have been, and deliberately, when it suited a minister's purpose."[5]

A *Times* portrait of Augstein said that "his friends, colleagues and employees describe him as a man modest in both his ambitions and habits, burning with zeal to protect the people against injustices that Authority is bound to impose." It added, "His critics say that he has a Napoleonic complex set by his failure to make his way in politics. He lusts for power, the critics add, and uses the pages of *Der Spiegel* to further his personal and political vendettas."[6] Gruson remarked that Strauss' original denials, now modified, "substantiated charges that Mr. Strauss was not a stickler for the rules of democracy."[7]

A description of *Der Spiegel* said it succeeded

> ...perhaps because it had a minimum (sic) of political philosophy of its own and concentrated on muckraking, picking into stories and incidents that the daily press left alone.... Because Mr. Augstein feuded bitterly with Chancellor Adenauer it was, in effect, anti-government. Its reputation was founded and consolidated on its coverage of internal German affairs. But in any editorial slant that came through its news columns, it reflected Mr. Augstein's bent for a more nationalist, neutralist foreign policy.[8]

A portrait of Strauss said that "almost everyone concedes that what was one of the most brilliant postwar political careers in West Germany is in ruins." It said that Strauss previously had shown "a lack of political sensibility and what even his friends considered an alarming amount of bullheadedness." Accepting *Der Spiegel's* complaint, the *Times* said, "The Defense Minister sought bases in Spain for the West German armed forces, apparently oblivious to the connection that everyone else immediately made to Hitler Germany's previous links to Spain." It claimed that Strauss' proposal for tactical nuclear weapons under U.S. control for the *Bundeswehr* was a prospect that "appalled many Germans almost as much as it did many foreigners."[9]

The next day a news analysis by Gruson congratulated at length West Germans for their "overwhelming outcry that brought down the government over its legal action against the news magazine."[10] A *Times* editorial also congratulated the Germans, with less enthusiasm, after Adenauer formed his last government. It said, "The crisis has shown that German democracy lives. But by and large, it is still in its adolescent stage. It is time for it to grow up."[11]

The *Times'* most telling contribution to world opinion on the Spiegel affair was, surprisingly, an analysis by Hanson W. Baldwin, an internationally respected military expert, concluding that no important secrets were revealed by the Fallex-62 article. Baldwin wrote that "to well-informed Americans the article appears to carry little information that was not generally known to the Russians or to other observers. . . . Both the figures enumerated and the weaknesses cited in *Der Spiegel* are entirely familiar to Western observers."[12]

Baldwin's article, widely cited, was a body blow to the case of Strauss and Adenauer. It was angrily disputed by government witnesses in preparations for Augstein's trial. Perhaps the Soviets knew that Hamburg would be declared an open city, so they would need few units on the north German plain, but most students of NATO did not. Germans were under the impression that U.S. Air Force units were stationed deliberately at bases hidden in the Eifel mountains like Bitburg and Hahn, away from population centers, only to be told by *Der Spiegel* that the Soviets had the bases targeted, and the jets would be moved to commercial airports of the cities.

Baldwin's exoneration of *Der Spiegel,* and Gruson's warnings in the *Times* that a Strauss victory in Bavaria's elections would doom Adenauer's government, inspired the Christian Socialists to run full-page advertisements in Bavarian newspapers the day before the state elections that attacked foreign critics of Strauss for blindly springing to Augstein's defense. The ads said that in the United States the Spiegel affair was being used "by the old co-existence idealists and fanatics to put pressure on their government to get it to jettison the interests of 'the eternal German troublemaker' in order to reach a settlement with Moscow."

The *Times* recognized that it was being addressed. Gruson reported that the advertisement "savagely attacked foreign critics of the handling of the Spiegel case in a tone and language that many people here found reminiscent of the early nineteen thirties when the Nazis were trying to get into power."[13] The *Times,* like Augstein, had found a way to call Strauss a Nazi.

The Christian Socialists' advertisement was not far-fetched nor in any way Nazi-like. The Spiegel affair, and the way it was being reported in the United States, *was* making it easier for President Kennedy to deal with Adenauer, the eternal German troublemaker, in Kennedy's efforts to call off the cold war with the Soviets.

Adenauer, who had lost his majority a month after the Wall was erected, was made a lame duck by the Spiegel affair. He was conferring in Washington with Kennedy, by now his open adversary on Germany policy, at the time of the Bavarian elections, telephoning to Bonn to learn if he still had a government. Adenauer was able to form a new government, after Strauss resigned, only by agreeing to Ludwig Erhard as his successor and promising to retire by October 1963. Ironically, in view of Free Democrat Augstein's efforts to find a corruption case against Strauss, the Free Democrat who dumped Adenauer, Erich Mende, later became a salesman for Investors Overseas Services, the Robert Vesco-Bernard Cornfeld multimillion-dollar swindle, and vanished from the political scene.

Kennedy and Adenauer had been at loggerheads throughout 1962, barely keeping up the appearances of an alliance

Early in his administration, Kennedy had a talk with Adenauer's ambassador, Professor Wilhelm Grewe, who was West Germany's leading authority on international law. In their talk, Kennedy probed the possibility of East and West Germany increasing contacts on such matters as technological exchange and trade. West Germany already had a carefully constructed trade and credit arrangement with East Germany, designed to encourage East Germany's dependence on Bonn.

Grewe, who had gotten along well with the Eisenhower administration, was slightly alarmed at the implications of a new course that Kennedy was suggesting. Grewe had helped write the Paris accords that gave West Germany sovereignty, by which Adenauer at some risk had rearmed and joined NATO in May 1955. Kennedy's talk suggested to

Grewe that Bonn could be asked to accept the nation's division as permanent. He reminded Kennedy that American statesmen, unfamiliar with China, had decided that Chinese Communists were agrarian reformers, and had urged a coalition of Chinese Nationalists and Communists with disastrous results. Grewe had stepped on a Democratic Party corn, the who-lost-China dispute.

Kennedy, furious, felt that Grewe was calling him naive. His aides said they never had seen the President so angry. That Grewe's suspicions were correct gave Kennedy real cause for anger.

Grewe also reported to Adenauer remarks by policy makers in the Kennedy administration, including Kennedy's own remark that "The East Germans have had 15 years to decide whether they want to migrate to West Germany."

By April 1962, Grewe was almost isolated in Washington. He was taking part in continuing meetings with State Department Under Secretary Foy Kohler and the Ambassadors of Great Britain and France. The United States was pushing a package to defuse the Berlin conflict that would include a U.S.-Soviet agreement to prevent the spread of nuclear weapons—which would sink MC96 and Strauss' bid for U.S.-controlled tactical nukes—a nonaggression declaration by NATO and the Warsaw Pact, a commission of mixed East and West Germans to promote contacts between the two Germanys, and an international commission of Western, Communist and neutral nations to settle disputes over the use of access routes to West Berlin. The United States was negotiating alone with the Soviets on the plan, confirmation that Washington was reconciled to two Germanys, and Adenauer was detemined to fight it.

Rusk was ready to broach the plan to Soviet Ambassador Anatoly Dobrynin when it was leaked to the West German press, causing embarrassing headlines in West Germany. Kohler summoned Grewe to his office, dressed him down and blamed him for the leaks. When Grewe emerged, he was beleaguered by Washington reporters and television cameras. He responded to a question by making specific his warning hint at the time of the Berlin Wall: abandonment of German reunification would throw into doubt West Germany's membership in NATO. Grewe knew; he had written the accords.

The Kennedy administration broke off the four-power planning talks, and instruction went out to excommunicate Grewe. His calls were ignored by the administration's leading figures.

During a visit to West Berlin in May 1962, Adenauer denounced the American plan. He said that the proposed access commission would place the burden of casting the deciding votes on members from neutral nations, who would be caught between representatives of the Western and Communist countries, an untenable position for them.

Adenauer increasingly was leaning on his relationship with De Gaulle, siding with France regularly on Common Market issues, to the point that Kennedy was being asked at his press conferences about De Gaulle's influence over Europe and the extent of the Paris-Bonn axis. De Gaulle's "third force" independent Europe was, in fact, becoming Adenauer's fallback position in case relations with the United States worsened.

Back in Bonn from his Berlin trip, Adenauer let it be known in a background briefing for American correspondents that he felt Kennedy was steadily downgrading Germany's interests since he had met Khrushchev in Vienna, that Washington was sledge-hammering any German protests by publicly denouncing the Germans as whiners, and that he resented the excommunication of Grewe, a man who had tried to represent his country's interests.

Kennedy's answer to Adenauer was a State Department request that he recall Grewe; his usefulness was at an end. It was perhaps the only time an American President so unceremoniously kicked out the ambassador of a friendly country. Arthur Schlesinger, Jr. reported, without context, that ". . . Wilhelm Grewe so bored the White House with pedantic and long-winded recitals that word finally was passed to his government that his recall would improve communications. . . ."[14]

Grewe was given a public farewell in the Rose Garden. Kennedy shook his hand and said into the television cameras, "I'm sorry to see the ambassador go."

Adenauer capitulated publicly in an interview in *Die Welt,* two days after De Gaulle had called for an independent Europe free of Anglo-Saxons. "We must under no circumstances release the United States from the North American Treaty Organization," Adenauer said. "There are no longer any big powers left in Europe. The United States, the Soviet Union and tomorrow, if not already today, Red China—these are the only big powers. Europe's influence must nonetheless be maintained, but this should not mean the setting up of a defense organization separated from the United States."[15]

In February 1962, Frances Gary Powers, the U-2 spy shot down over the Soviet Union in May 1960, was exchanged for Soviet *rezident* spy Colonel Rudolf Abel at the Glienicker Bridge between East and West Berlin, after secret negotiations by attorney James B. Donovan, who also negotiated the ransoming of the Bay of Pigs prisoners.[16] Most of the media reported that Frederic L. Pryor, a young economist held for six months in East Berlin, was released through Checkpoint Charlie at the same time as a bonus.

Communist negotiators don't give bonuses. Pryor was released primarily through the efforts of Berthold Beitz, general manager for Krupp, who had been enlisted by a business associate, Millard Pryor, Frederic's father, of Ann Arbor, Michigan.[17]

Through the Pryor incident, Kennedy's attention was drawn to Beitz, who had wide connections in the East bloc, partly through his acquaintance with Polish Communists. During World War II, Beitz, an oil company executive in occupied Poland, had rescued a man who later became a member of the Polish Communist Party Central Committee. Beitz regularly reported to Adenauer's Foreign Ministry on his East bloc visits and dealings, and was annoyed that the Chancellor accepted his information without accepting his advice to build up trade with the East.

After the Cuban missile crisis, with the ruined Soviet game plan that might have held the United States in check while the Soviets practiced extortion on Western Europe, the Soviets embarked on an export drive instead, offering a wide range of barter deals contingent on Western credit. Beitz visited the Soviet Union in May 1963 and met with Khrushchev, who gave him an expensive shotgun. Beitz laid the groundwork on that trip to set up the first major Western firm's offices in Moscow.

Two months before Beitz's visit with Khrushchev, Adenauer had taken extraordinary measures to block a West German-Soviet oil pipeline deal that the Hösch A. G. said would be worth about $9 billion by 1980, when it was due to be completed. Three Ruhr firms had signed contracts the previous October for $50 million worth of pipe, a first installment. The Soviet offer was complex: the 40-inch pipe would have to be made partly of Soviet iron, and it would have involved a consortium of banks to provide credit backed by the Bonn government—to be repaid eventually in oil, requiring creation of a West German governmental energy company to handle the oil distribution. The NATO Council recomended against the deal and added oil pipeline over 19 inches in diameter to its list of embargoed strategic exports. There were several political overtones. The deal would help the Soviets bring oil to East Germany for that country's prosperity and military use; the deal could institutionalize West German-Soviet energy trade; it might make Bonn dependent on a Soviet energy source, and to Adenauer, it might encourage the United States to loosen its own trade restrictions with the Soviets, as the *Times* was advising Kennedy to do in editorials.

The Free Democrats intended to desert Adenauer's coalition on the pipeline issue, voting with the Social Democrats to lift a government decree implementing the NATO recommendation, under a deadline imposed by parliamentary rules to act on such decrees. Adenauer noticed that about ten Free Democrats and Social Democrats were absent, and for the only time in his 14 year tenure as Chancellor resorted to the parliamentary device of pulling the Christian Democrats and Christian Socialists out of the chamber until the deadline expired, defeating the motion and retaining his ban on the pipeline deal.

United States policy on the pipeline deal was equivocal. Publicly it was opposed, and Brewster Morris, chargé d'affaires at the U.S. Embassy, tried to talk Free Democratic leader Mende out of abandoning Adenauer on the issue. But Kennedy was in the process of revising U.S. policy toward Soviet trade.

In the aftermath of the Cuban missile crisis, Kennedy had reverted to his original intentions when he first approached Khrushchev in Vienna: he would again offer to end the cold war through more cooperation with the Soviet Union on a two-superpowers basis.

In the summer of 1963 Adenauer was on his way out. Willy Brandt was consciously patterning his image and his campaign style after Kennedy's. West Berlin appeared calm. Kennedy needed to mend some fences in West Germany, the country that remained the major stumbling block to ending the cold war.

Kennedy was a new man after the Cuban missile crisis, and Washington a revitalized city, but the President had some trepidation about the kind of welcome he might receive in West Germany. Before going there he laid out his program in a speech at the American University in Washington on June 10, 1963. It was intended to be a turning point in world relations, and the British liberal daily, *The Guardian,* commented, "His passage warning the American people 'not to fall into the same trap as the Soviets, not to see only a distorted and desperate view of the other side, not to see conflict as inevitable,' should rank (it) among the great state papers of American history." The Soviet media published the full text.

Kennedy's speech, a plea for an end to the cold war and institutions to buttress a lasting peace, expressed both disappointment in the Soviet leadership and respect and sympathy for the people of the Soviet Union, who had suffered 20 million dead in World War II and might again be devastated in the first 24 hours of a new war. In announcing a new attempt at conciliation with the Soviets, Kennedy pledged that "the United States will make no deal with the Soviet Union at the expense of other nations and other peoples, not merely because they are our partners, but because their interests and ours converge."

Accepting as a goal the Soviet slogan of "general and complete disarmament," Kennedy announced two moves: the United States would again unilaterally end nuclear tests in the atmosphere until other nations conducted such tests, and he, Khrushchev and Macmillan had agreed to start new negotiations in Moscow, not Geneva, toward a comprehensive nuclear test ban treaty.

Kennedy pledged, "The United States, as the world knows, will never start a war. We do not want war. We do not now expect a war. This generation of Americans has had enough—more than enough—of war and hate and oppression. We shall be prepared if others wish it . . . but we shall also do our part to build a world of peace where the weak are safe and the strong are just. . . . "

The American University speech lacked one element: there was no suggestion of what kind of offer could be made to induce the Soviets to accept practical coexistence. Kennedy saved that element for his trip to Germany. It was to be a loosening of American, and thereby Western, restrictions on commerce with the Soviet Union, as editorially advocated by the *Times*.

The advance party preparing the ground for Kennedy in West Germany was led by Pierre Salinger, the President's press chief. Salinger arrived on a sunny afternoon in May at the American Embassy Club in Plittersdorf, a middle-class restaurant and bar that had become one of the small capital's social meeting places. He joined correspondents at the bar and was asked almost immediately, "Why did the President kick Ambassador Grewe out of Washington?"

Salinger shifted the long cigar in his mouth and said curtly, "Because he was a shit."

He turned away, then turned back, removed the cigar and said, "He was shooting off his mouth in public, sabotaging everything we were doing."

Behind the bar the two German bartenders, Rudi and Hubert, brothers who spoke perfect English and followed politics closely, polished glasses, masking their faces. That night the word was all over town that Salinger had called Grewe in public a *Scheisskerl*. Ten years later Salinger expressed shock at the expletives on the Nixon tapes.

Shortly after Salinger left, the concrete bandstand in the club restaurant was destroyed by jackhammers to make room for more tables and so that Kennedy would not appear to be on a dias above the other guests. The club was outfitted with new Kelly-green, wall-to-wall carpeting, a full banquet service of porcelain trimmed in Irish green, a full array of glassware and decorated silverware. After Kennedy's visit the club gave off a green sheen.

At Kennedy's banquet, seated at his table within conversational range was Berthold Beitz, the country's leading champion of trade with the East. Beitz knew East German Premier Willi Stoph and had friendly relations with Polish Foreign Minister Adam Rapacki, who was allowed to float foreign policy trial balloons for the Soviet Union. Beitz agreed with Soviet Minister of Trade Nikolai Patolichev that there were "oceans of trade" to be had in the Soviet Union.

A week before Kennedy's arrival, Beitz had offered correspondents in Bonn an excursion by Rhine steamer to Essen, where he was asked over drinks on the terrace of the Villa Hügel if he had ambitions to be foreign minister. Beitz had answered, "I think it would be untenable to be the German foreign minister without having the firm owner behind you."

At Kennedy's arrival at Bonn-Cologne airport, Adenauer's welcome had been rather blunt.

"Your visit, Mr. Kennedy, is a political act," Adenauer said. He recalled that Kennedy had pledged in his American University speech that "the United States will make no deal with the Soviet Union at the expense of other nations or other peoples," adding that there was no better way to demonstrate such determination than by visiting West Germany, the other nations of Western Europe, and Berlin. That said, Adenauer welcomed Kennedy "from the bottom of my heart."

Kennedy appeared amused at Adenauer's nerve. He replied that the unity forged in time of danger "must now be maintained in time of peace. . . it must find the way to a new peace." He had come, Kennedy said, "to pay tribute to a great European statesman, an architect of unity, champion of liberty, friend of the American people, Chancellor Adenauer."

At a dinner toast that evening, Adenauer continued to needle: "It was the United States—at first Mr. Acheson and then Mr. Truman, then Mr. Dulles and President Eisenhower—who helped us Germans, a conquered people, when we were completely down." He hoped that the "gratitude toward America" that Kennedy had "seen in the eyes of the crowds will help you to make decisions with that clarity and that forcefulness that statesmen require."

Adenauer's barbs, hints of Kennedy's indecision and lack of forcefulness, bounced off harmlessly. His time was over. In Wiesbaden Kennedy invited Adenauer's successor-to-be, Ludwig Erhard, "the rubber lion," to ride with him standing in the presidential limousine. Erhard blushed with pleasure, transported by the crowd's cheers.

Adenauer's little airport speech could have been annoying, and Kennedy took the trouble to defuse it at a press conference at the Foreign

Ministry that was televised live by satellite to the United States, a communications innovation. Kennedy set the tone for the press conference by rigging the first question.[18]

Normally, presidential news conferences are occasions for correspondents to demonstrate that they are hard-nosed, and an easy-pitch question that the President can bat out of the park is taboo. But for the first question at Kennedy's press conference of June 24, 1963, the presidential finger pointed to a handsome young woman raising her hand.[19] She asked:

"Mr. President, would you please tell us of what importance you attach to the relationship between your country and Germany at the present time, and what you think the German role should be in the European development of the future?"

Kennedy replied that the German-American relationship was "more vital today" than ever, with Germany "in the front lines of the struggle" as "a powerful country which has made an astonishing comeback." Germany had demonstrated "a great influence in Europe . . . directed towards liberal progressive, international monetary and trade policies," and he was confident that the two countries would work "in the closest relationship. . . ."

Later in the press conference, sure enough, a German reporter asked, "At the airport yesterday there seemed to be a note of difference of emphasis between your remarks and those of Chancellor Adenauer. He seemed to be more concerned with your concern to defend Europe, while you were concerned with new approaches to peace. Has this difference manifested itself in your private talks with the Chancellor?"

Kennedy replied, "No, I thought that the Chancellor was quoting—some of his remarks were a quotation of a speech which I gave at the American University two weeks ago. . . ."

Kennedy's tour was a smashing success, huge crowds greeting him everywhere. Erhard later called Kennedy, "This radiant personality"—and he was. He stood out in mob scenes the way Arletty stood out in the crowds in "Children of Paradise," as though an invisible spotlight were on him, tall, holding his injured back erect at a slight angle, laughing and radiating youthful vigor. In Frankfurt's Pauls Church, birthplace of German democracy in 1848, Kennedy pledged, "We will risk our cities to defend yours, because we need your freedom to defend ours." Adenauer never believed it. It was not reasonable, he wrote in his memoirs, that the United States would accept nuclear destruction of its cities to protect Germany or Western Europe.

Flying to Berlin, the climax of his triumphant tour, Kennedy knew what he was going to say at the Free University, an institution sponsored largely by American foundations. He would give the key—and least-noticed—speech of his Germany visit. Standing on West Berlin soil, Kennedy would offer the Soviets an inducement to end the cold war.

Kennedy had another Berlin speech to make, at Schöneberg Rathaus, the city hall, which could be less serious, a crowd-pleaser. Kennedy had something of a block regarding foreign languages. He wanted to throw in some German phrases, and on the plane he practiced saying, *"Ich bin ein Berliner."*

"If you want it to come out in Berlin dialect, make it, *'Ik bean ein Bearliner,'* " one of the experts offered.

Kennedy tried it: *"Ik bean ein Bearliner."*

Another phrase: "Let them come to Berlin!" Was it, *"Lassen sie nach Berlin kommen,"* or *"Lasst sie nach Berlin kommen"*? Either one would do.

Mayor Brandt and the trade unions had organized Kennedy's reception. Factories and schools were closed, and the whole city turned out. In front of city hall a dense crowd of 120,000 packed the square. On the fringes of the crowd a few sober young men carried placards: "When Does Wall Fall?" "Why So Hard in Cuba and So Soft in Berlin?" "Clay for President!" "Stand Firm, Mr. President," "We Demand Germany's Reunification." There were friendly signs, "Tell Your People Our Thanks," "Your Visit Is More Than a Thousand Words." "Against Strategy of Annihilation, for Strategy of Peace. Welcome Mr. President—Socialist Youth of Berlin," and "Where's Jackie?"

At city hall, Kennedy's crowd-pleaser speech rocked along, drowned out by cheers when he mentioned General Clay, gaining momentum. Kennedy said that 2,000 years ago, the proudest boast was "Civis Romanus sum," but "today, in the world of freedom, the proudest boast is (pause) 'Ik bean ein Beeleener!" Kennedy had dropped an "r" and muffed the pronunciation but the translator repeated his phrase. He chuckled and thanked the interpreter for "translating my German," but the full-throated roar of the crowd was like nothing Kennedy had ever heard.

Kennedy plunged ahead, propelled by the roar of the crowd, and in his enthusiasm he ad-libbed a line (here put in italics) that dismayed his policy advisers:

> There are many people in the world who really don't understand, or say they don't, what is the great issue between the free world and the Communist world. Let them come to Berlin! There are some who say that communism is the wave of the future. Let

them come to Berlin! *There are some who say, in Europe and elsewhere, we can work with the Communists. Let them come to Berlin!* [20] And there are even a few who say it's true, communism is an evil system, but it permits us to make economic progress. *Lasst sie nach Berlin kommen!*—let them come to Berlin!"

He ended the speech repeating *Ich bin ein Berliner,* this time close to the Berlin dialect.

At the end of the city hall balcony, Dean Rusk turned away and all but held his head in his hands. The President had just said exactly the opposite of what he had come to say. He had said that you couldn't do business with the Soviets, and he had come to say at the Free University that you could. The Soviets had been diplomatically alerted to watch for the Free University speech, and Kennedy now was told that he should soften it even more, although the prepared texts already had been distributed to correspondents.

When Kennedy got to the university, most of the Washington press corps did not get out of the bus to listen to that last speech. They had a striking color story to work on before the plane took off for Ireland, and they already had the speech text. Many were typing on the bus as Kennedy spoke, handing off to runners copy on the sensational welcome Berlin had given Kennedy.

Outdoors, under the sun, before an audience of young people, Kennedy ad-libbed much of his Free University speech, discussing the future of the city in terms of the university's motto, "Truth, Justice, Liberty."

Kennedy said most of the things he was expected to say, reconfirming a commitment to German reunification, which brought the first spontaneous applause. He spoke throughout the speech of change and of the danger of accepting the status quo, or of accepting (cold war) slogans.

Truth, Kennedy said, "requires us to face the facts as they are, not to involve ourselves in self-deception. . . . Let us deal with the realities as they actually are, not as they might have been and not as we wish they were."

Justice, Kennedy said, requires doing whatever could be done during the transition period to free reunification to "improve the lot and maintain the hopes of those on the other side." Here he read carefully from his text, replacing only two words: "It is important that the people in the quiet streets to the East be kept in touch with Western society, through all the contacts and communications that can be established, through all the trade that Western security permits." He had changed "barren confines to the East" to "quiet streets." He had delivered the message to the Soviets he had come to deliver: "through all the trade that Western security permits."

Liberty, Kennedy said, required "a united Berlin, in a united Germany, united by self-determination and living in peace." But it was a goal that "may be obtainable most readily in the context of a reconstitution of the larger Europe on both sides of the harsh line that now divides it."

Kennedy hinted at a kind of Marshall Plan for Eastern Europe, including the Soviet Union, recalling that George C. Marshall had proposed aid for "the commonly accepted geography of Europe—west of Asia," but that the Communists had rejected it.

The President said that the

> ...people of the Soviet Union, even after 45 years of party dictatorship, feel the forces of historical evolution. The harsh precepts of Stalin are officially recognized as bankrupt....And where the possibilities of reconciliation appear, we in the West will make it clear that we are not hostile to any people or system, provided they choose their own destiny without interfering with the free choice of others.

So that leftist students would not take him too literally, Kennedy ad-libbed, "I'm not impressed with opportunities for popular fronts around the world—no democrat can ride that tiger. I do believe in the necessity for great powers working together to preserve the human race, or otherwise we can all be destroyed."

From the university, Kennedy left for the airport and Ireland, telling companions, "We'll never have another day like this one as long as we live." Kennedy said he would leave a note for his successor, "to be opened at a time of some discouragement," and in it he would write three words: "Go to Germany."

Shortly after Kennedy's arrival in Bonn, East Germany had announced that Khrushchev was coming to East Berlin. Khrushchev arrived to thin crowds two days after Kennedy's departure from Berlin. The usual factory groups and school classes were marched out along his welcoming route, but many drifted away before his arrival. Other Soviet bloc leaders arrived to help Ulbricht celebrate his 70th birthday, and an informal Warsaw Pact summit met for a few hours.

If Khrushchev was annoyed at the poor popular turnout, he did not show it. Kennedy's speech at the Free University had pleased him. On July 2, Khrushchev, speaking to 8,000 Communist functionaries, announced that the Soviet Union was willing to sign a limited nuclear test ban treaty, barring tests in the atmosphere, outer space and under water. He said the Soviets never would permit inspection by outsiders, but with underground tests left out of the treaty, the question of inspection should not arise. He added that the treaty "must be augmented with a nonaggression pact."

New negotiations for a test ban treaty were scheduled in Moscow for two weeks after Khrushchev spoke, and the limited nuclear test ban treaty along Khrushchev's lines was quickly concluded, to be hailed as one of Kennedy's major achievements. Over the years the American demand for a large number of permanent inspection stations in the Soviet Union had been whittled down to an argument in early 1963 over whether the Soviets might permit two or three visits a year to suspected test sites. The treaty Kennedy approved gave up the principle of inspection, and the terms under which it was concluded were the same that the Eisenhower administration had rejected in March 1960, except that no new moratorium on underground tests was involved.[21] Meanwhile the Soviets had established a permanent edge in large-scale warheads.

Like the Berlin Wall, the Spiegel affair and Kennedy's change in American policy toward Germany were watershed events affecting the course of Germany's future. Kennedy's visit to Germany completed a switch in United States backing from the cautious conservatives under Adenauer to the adventurous Social Democrats under Willy Brandt.

Adenauer's lame-duck government moved to accommodate Kennedy's Free University proposal to release the brakes on East-West trade, although not to the extent of immediately reconsidering the massive pipeline deal. Not until 1966 did Bonn ask NATO to end the embargo on large-diameter pipe exports to the Soviet Union, which was done in November 1966. By that time the realities of what the Soviets could offer in commercial exchanges had proved disappointing, and Beitz was in difficulties over the long-term credits that Krupp had arranged for the sale of whole factories to the East bloc and to developing countries. In March 1967 Krupp's cash-flow position, tangled in $600 million worth of long-term credit arrangements with more than 200 banks, required the Bonn government to bail out the firm. Beitz lost his free hand to an executive council named by the Bonn government and major bankers.

Kennedy's change in policy proved more profound politically than economically. When Kennedy left Berlin, some Germans thought that he understood the supplication implied in the welcome he had received, and had left Germany with a new appreciation of the imperative of German reunification. He had arrived barely mentioning reunification, but ended his tour stressing it in both his city hall and Free University speeches. At the Free University he had ad-libbed praise of nationalism as a spur to freedom, and praising nationalism in Germany was not what he had come to do.

Not long after Kennedy's visit, West Berlin police cracked down on refugee helpers, previously regarded as heroes who often received quiet police help. By 1964 they were being described as gangsters and extortionists, because some were charging fees to cover bribes and increasingly expensive escape procedures. The escape helpers also were a monkey wrench in the works of the East-West understanding now required by American policy.

A month after Kennedy's visit to Berlin, Brandt went to a symposium at the Evangelical Academy in Tutzing, where his companion and adviser, Egon Bahr, proposed a new policy toward East Germany that he called *"Wandlung durch Annährung"*—change through rapprochement. The theory was that East Germany's Communists could be mellowed and made more amenable through a West German policy of contacts, conciliation and cooperation, the basis of Brandt's *Ostpolitik*.

Bahr made a number of secret visits to the Soviet Union and to East Germany, and Brandt, while still mayor of West Berlin, had several secret meetings with Pyotr Abrassimov, Soviet Ambassador to East Germany, after dropping tentative plans to meet with Khrushchev in East Berlin as too provocative. In March 1970, five months after becoming Chancellor, Brandt met with East German Premier Willi Stoph in Erfurt, East Germany, then in Kassel, West Germany, before flying to Moscow in August of that year to conclude a treaty with the Soviet Union that fixed the two Germanys as separate nations. Bahr frequently said that his original inspiration for *Ostpolitik* came from Kennedy's book, *The Strategy of Peace*.[22]

The Spiegel affair, too, played out over several years. When Augstein was released from investigative confinement, he embarked on a speaking and debating tour, establishing a 20-page insert on yellow paper in *Der Spiegel* to record his speeches and debates. Augstein laid claim to the title, leader of German youth, and the yellow-page inserts were marked with notation: (applause) or (heavy applause) after his remarks.

The *Times'* defense of Augstein established a bond between the newspaper and *Der Spiegel*, and Augstein later contributed to the *Times'* Op-Ed page. In early 1965 a treason trial for Augstein appeared imminent, and the *Times'* new bureau chief in Bonn, Arthur Olsen, contributed a long resumé of the affair, "The Man Who Holds the Mirror to Germany." *Der Spiegel* was "recognized as a significant political force; a voice in the wilderness that commands attention, if not respect, at the least a devil's advocate in the public life of the Bonn Republic, at best the real Opposition to the complacent political establishment in Bonn." Augstein was "essentially an intellectual and a critic. . .not a likely leader for the reform movement he prescribes to restore spirit and purpose to the German Federal Republic. In that hypothetical peaceful democratic revolution, he is more of a Tom Paine."

West Germany's Tom Paine was receiving similar support from *Le Monde* in Paris and some British publications. In May 1965, treason charges against Augstein were dropped by the Federal Constitutional Court in Karlsruhe. The court then turned to Augstein's suit that his arrest was illegal. One justice, disqualified himself, and the court split 4-4, dismissing Augstein's suit, ruling that sufficient evidence existed to justify the raid and arrests.

Conrad Ahlers, who had been arrested in Spain through the intervention of Strauss, became government spokesman in Chancellor Brandt's first government, and wrote in *Christ und Welt* that, on reflection, Strauss had been justified in suspecting treason. Strauss meanwhile had been Finance Minister in Chancellor Kurt Kiesinger's grand coalition.[23]

Strauss' libel suit against Augstein crawled through the courts at a slow pace. In a Munich court in April 1965, a parade of witnesses testified to being falsely quoted in articles attacking Strauss. Strauss' attorney said he was willing to forego damages if Augstein would print retractions and pay court costs.

Augstein rose in court to say he wouldn't enter into "any rotten compromises. I want to know if I am right when I say my accuser is a minister guilty of corruption."

Augstein's attorneys then presented a 72-page brief summing up charges against Strauss and adding some new ones: that Lockheed Aircraft Corporation had put Strauss and actress Jayne Mansfield together at an intimate supper in Beverly Hills, that the German Consul in San Francisco had paid for a black prostitute for Strauss, and that the owner of the Wienerwald Restaurant in the Waldorf-Astoria in New York had provided Strauss with a call girl. An avalanche of new lawsuits threatened over the unproven charges.

Augstein's defense was that if Strauss had not actually profited from corruption, he was nonetheless depraved, and depravity was the same thing as corruption, so Augstein insisted on his right to call Strauss "corrupt."

Augstein's attorney Otto Gritschneider told the court: "Strauss doesn't believe that the law applies to him. That is the general line of our accusations. . . . We don't mean the private individual Strauss, but only the political personality with his effect on the state. For him, only the laws of his own power and his style of power apply. A state that Strauss would form if he could would be a corrupt state. That must be prevented."

West Germany treated libel as a criminal matter, and compensation awards were small. The court award to Strauss for massive and systematic libel was a major award—25,000 marks plus 90% of court costs, and an injunction to *Der Spiegel* not to repeat falsehoods. Augstein said he would not pay it, and another court subsequently doubled it. Augstein again failed to pay, and the court doubled it again. Eventually Augstein kept criticism of Strauss within normal bounds.

Augstein had expended enormous time, effort and money, risking jail and the credibility vital to his magazine, with his unsubstantiated charges, to prevent Strauss from becoming Chancellor, and he had won. With the young, Augstein's credibility was enhanced, not damaged, and West German university students carried *Der Spiegel* conspicuously outside their books as a badge of rebellion in the late 1960s and 1970s.

Der Spiegel became the chronicler of the student rebellion of the late 1960s, praising the riot against Shah Mohammad Reza Pahlavi in West Berlin in 1967 that resulted in the death of student Benno Ohnesorg and the resignations of Mayor Heinrich Albertz and Police President Erich Dünsing. It made an international figure of Rudi Dutschke, ideologist of the *Sozialistische Deutsche Studentenbund*. Dutschke and SDS accepted Augstein's promotion and financial support, while publicly spurning Augstein as a granddad afraid of dirtying his hands with real revolution. *Der Spiegel* took on a tone of anxiously soliciting young revolutionaries. It published a cover story on Dutschke, "the only young German leader with charisma," and provided archive photos to the *Berliner Extra Dienst*, an anti-establishment newspaper edited by a former *Spiegel* editor.

In 1968 *Der Spiegel* began a campaign against publisher Axel Springer, whose publications, especially *Bild Zeitung* and *Die Welt*, were dealing harshly with young revolutionaries. *Der Spiegel* ran lengthy attacks on Springer, along with promotions of student radicals, in every issue between January 1 and April 8.

On April 11, 1968, Josef Bachmann, 23, an immigrant from East Germany who admired Hitler, shot and seriously wounded Dutschke, also from East Germany, with a modified starter's pistol. A Berlin mob, mostly students led by attorney Horst Mahler, attacked the Springer publishing house next to the Berlin Wall with Molotov cocktails, causing extensive damage and destroying two police motorcycles with firebombs. Springer plants in Hamburg and smaller cities also were attacked. *Der Spiegel's* national edition of April 15, for the first time that year, omitted any mention of Springer, SDS or Dutschke. Only in the limited edition reaching Berlin was there a one-page insert reporting that Dutschke was shot. In Paris, Daniel Cohn-Bendit, an associate of Dutschke, led rioting that President De Gaulle cited when he later retired abruptly.[24]

Riots in West Berlin against the Shah and against Springer created the backdrop for the founding of the Red Army Faction in 1970 by Ulrike Meinhof and attorney Mahler. At the Free University that year, an exodus of professors began after students attacked conservative professors with paint, eggs and fists. In May 1970, Rolf Kreibich, 31, an instructor from radical student ranks, was elected president of the university, and professors left in squads.

History Professor Hans Herzfeld said, "I tried to save what was left, but I can't continue. Scientific work is no longer possible at the university." He said the new university law adopted by the West Berlin legislature, giving custodial personnel a vote, was "grotesque." Students received lectures on "Leninism today" from Soviet reserve Major General Igor Tulpanov, 67, who had been the colonel in charge of the political section of the Soviet military administration in East Berlin just after the war, under General Ivan Serov and Colonel Vladimir Semyonov. Tulpanov had been credited with ending free instruction at Humboldt University in East Berlin, the act that caused the creation of the Free University.

Not long after Tulpanov was a guest lecturer, a riot at the Free University caused a good deal of destruction, and rioters tore down the university's great circular emblem. They were photographed standing like big game hunters over the emblem, each with a foot on it and its slogan, "Truth, Justice, Liberty."

Chapter VIII
Kennedy and Diem

"For twenty centuries, the sum total of evil in the world has not diminished. No second coming, neither divine nor revolutionary, has accomplished it."

—*Albert Camus, L'Homme Revolté*

For more than a decade, as Congressman and Senator, Kennedy held a consistent view of Vietnam. The country could not achieve peace without communism unless the Vietnamese were assured of complete independence, and it would be "futile and self-destructive. . . to pour money, material and men into the jungles without at least a remote prospect of victory."[1] Kennedy sometimes altered the conditions under which the United States might legitimately intervene, but he held to a general course toward an independent Vietnam. When he became President he sent a proconsul to dominate South Vietnam and began a military buildup that would become massive after his death.

While still a Congressman, Kennedy became acquainted with Ngo Dinh Diem, a fellow Catholic and a Vietnamese nationalist, who was living in exile at Maryknoll seminaries in Ossining, New York, and Lakewood, New Jersey, whom he met in the company of China-born Senator Mike Mansfield of Montana. Kennedy regularly followed *The New York Times* reports on Vietnam in the 1950s, and as a Senator he repeatedly cited the newspaper in his speeches to the effect that American money was propping up the French there.

During a congressional junket to Saigon in 1951, Kennedy had a long, illuminating discussion with Edmund Gullion, U.S. chargé d'affaires. At an embassy briefing, Representative Kennedy asked why the Vietnamese should be expected to fight to keep their country French. General Jean de Lattre de Tassigny, who at the time was credited with turning around the war against the Vietminh, registered a formal complaint against Kennedy's interference in the affairs of a friendly country.

Kennedy returned from his 1951 Far East trip to report that the United States had allied itself with a colonial regime that had no real support from the people. Not one to leave a French general unanswered, he said in the House, "The task is. . . to build a strong native non-Communist sentiment within these areas and rely on that as a spearhead of defense rather than on the legions of General de Tassigny."

Kennedy's intervention also irritated General de Gaulle, then out of power. In April 1945, just before Hitler committed suicide in his Berlin bunker, De Gaulle had requested American transport to move French reinforcements, idle in Africa and Madagascar, to Indochina, where he expected a French-Japanese clash. De Gaulle wanted France in on the kill when the Japanese were defeated, but transport was scarce, and years later when writing his memoirs, De Gaulle still was angry that President Truman had refused his request "on any number of pretexts."[2]

At the end of World War II, French troops in Indochina—about 12,000 Europeans and around 38,000 Vietnamese—lived in uneasy coexistence with the Japanese occupiers under a mutual defense accord between Tokyo and Vichy. With the end of Vichy, De Gaulle expected an attack, and he was willing to fight the Japanese if he could devise tactics that were not suicidal. "French blood spilled on the soil of Indochina would constitute an imposing claim," he wrote. He was bitter that, when a French column later managed to evade Japanese attackers in Hanoi and contacted the Americans, "even the American aviation based in China. . . did not lend them assistance."[3]

Just as Anthony Eden would suspect that U.S. behavior during the Suez crisis was aimed at supplanting British influence, so was De Gaulle confirmed in his suspicion that the United States was ready to supplant French influence in Indochina when Truman recognized the sovereign nation of Vietnam and sent a small Military Assistance Advisory Group there in July 1950. President Eisenhower, who gave the French military equipment, aided the French beleaguered at Dien Bien Phu with only 200 Air Force technicians and 10 B-26 bombers, refusing strikes from a U.S. aircraft carrier and a French request for Marines, in part because Britain's Eden refused to join in.

Under Eisenhower, Senator Kennedy proposed an amendment to the Mutual Security Act that would have tied U.S. aid to measures encouraging freedom and independence for the countries of Indochina, "including the intensification of the military training of the Vietnamese." The amendment was not adopted.

In a Senate speech on June 30, 1953, Kennedy, in part inspired by his acquaintance Diem, said that the government of Emperor Bao Dai "lacks popular support. The degree of military, civil, political and economic control maintained by the French goes well beyond that which is necessary to fight a war. . . . I strongly believe that the French cannot succeed in Vietnam without giving concessions necessary to make the native army a reliable and crusading force."

Vice President Nixon was asked to comment on Kennedy's speech and replied that anything other than victory by the French and Bao Dai was unthinkable.

As the French position in Indochina deteriorated in early 1954, the Eisenhower administration blew hot and cold. On January 14, Dulles spoke of "massive retaliation" against Communist encroachments, drawing media fire for the provocative phrase. On February 10, Eisenhower said he could "conceive of no greater tragedy than for the United States to become involved in an all-out war in Indochina." But he commented on April 7 that "the loss of Indochina will cause the fall of Southeast Asia like a set of dominos."

The day before Eisenhower gave expression to the domino theory, with the French about to lose Dien Bien Phu, Kennedy spoke in the Senate. Kennedy said that the Communists would win, either if the nation was partitioned or if a coalition were formed with Ho Chi Minh, so the French had to be supported, with reluctance. Kennedy favored a policy of "united action" by many nations and guarantees of political independence for the nearby associated states. Kennedy in 1954 believed that the French were the villains, that Ho Chi Minh was widely popular, but he favored joint intervention—not solo—if the end was to be an independent, non-Communist Vietnam.

On May 8, 1954, the French fortress complex at Dien Bien Phu fell to the Vietminh's General Vo Nguyen Giap. Dulles cabled Colonel

Edward G. Lansdale, who was in Manila advising Philippine President Ramon Magsaysay in his battle with the Hukbong Magpaplaya ng Bayan, or Peoples Liberation Army, to fly to Saigon immediately. Dulles had alerted Lansdale in February that he would be sent to Saigon if a French collapse occured.

Lansdale had served in the area with the OSS during World War II, and he had advised the French, as a CIA operative, the year before. He arrived in Saigon as Vietnam entered into the chaos following the French-Bao Dai defeat. That same night the Vietminh blew up ammunition dumps at Saigon airport. Lansdale was joined on July 1 by Major Lucien Conein, who also had worked with the French.

Diem, long a candidate for national leadership, returned from France, where he had continued his exile. Lansdale was on hand to watch his arrival and thought that Diem had missed a chance to greet crowds and make use of his popularity. Diem had accepted the offer of Bao Dai to become premier on conditions that amounted to Bao Dai's abdication. He had refused the premiership from Bao Dai in 1951, going into exile rather than serve the French. Diem found no government in operation, rival militias warring on each other and on the French, whose intentions were uncertain. He formed a government of desperation, and Lansdale became an adviser based on spontaneous personal rapport.

Two weeks after Diem took over what would become South Vietnam, the Geneva conference on June 21 produced an armistice between the French and Vietminh, providing for two temporary zones in Vietnam, all-Vietnam elections in a year, small limits for foreign military advisers and provisions for negotiations between the various belligerents in Vietnam, Laos and Cambodia. The French pulled out of the north, leaving anti-Communist Catholics there without protection, and a million of them fled to the south, some on a French airlift and others on American naval vessels. About 90,000 Vietnamese went north on rusty Polish merchant ships, while an estimated 10,000 Communist cadres remained underground in the south.

In 1954, Ho Chi Minh in the north and Diem in the south faced similar caldrons of conflicting interests: strong religious sects, bandit gangs the size of armies, large Chinese and Cambodian minorities, French business interests, hill tribesmen who filed their teeth to points, political factions that had collaborated with the Japanese or the French or both. Ho's forces, organized on Leninist lines, could employ unrestrained intimidation in a closed society with few foreign observers. Diem had only an embryo political party, a small army forming around Christian militias and plenty of kibitzers.

In the north, General Giap, who became Ho's interior minister, crushed one by one the armed nationalist and bandit organizations. Opposition members of the National Assembly vanished. Moral Intervention squads went into villages to capture and flay the mayor or "leave his head dangling from a bamboo pole in the middle of the village, warning that anyone who takes it down will suffer the same fate." The squads would "burst into a village meeting, call out the names of five boys. . .and gun them down after reading a 'death sentence'."[4] In November 1956, Ho executed at least 50,000 resisting peasants and sent 100,000 more to forced labor, according to French sources.[5]

In the south, Diem also cracked down on opposition as soon as he was able to do so, although without the mass executions or raw intimidation. His secret police eventually would round up 50,000 to 100,000 political suspects for varying periods of time, in the process picking up most of the Communist stay-behind cadres.

Diem, whose reputation was of independence and stubbornness, knew the Communists well. Ho had held him prisoner under near-starvation conditions for four months in 1945 and then offered him a cabinet post in a front government. Diem asked him only one question in their interview: "Why did you kill my brother (Ngo Dinh Khoi)?" When Ho said it was a mistake and could not have been avoided in the turmoil, Diem walked out, and Ho let him go. The fastidious Mme. Nhu, imprisoned by Ho with her baby, also barely survived four months living in the same garments.[6]

The prevalence of Western reporters and diplomats in South Vietnam might have restrained cruder forms of intimidation, but it did not interfere with traditional Oriental means of consolidating a government. Bernard Fall reported that Lansdale bought off the opposition, buying the Cao Dai General Nguyen Thanh Phoung for $3.6 million, and a Hoa Hao sect warlord, Tran Van Soai, for $3 million.[7] Lansdale did not confirm it, but he wrote that the warlords were in financial trouble, their troops unpaid, and that several sects joined the South Vietnamese army and received back pay. He wrote that the Cao Dai sect's leader Trinh Minh The, who received a $2 million bribe according to Fall, was a patriot.[8] However it was done, Diem's troops defeated the Binh Xuyen gangster sect, which controlled the police, and its Hoa Hao allies, in the battle of Saigon in 1955.

In 1956, as South Vietnam began to resemble a nation with a government, Diem refused to permit the all-Vietnam elections called for by the Geneva agreements, on the ground that South Vietnam had not signed accords negotiated by foreigners. The Eisenhower administration did not push for elections, Eisenhower believing that the results would have been dictated by Communist intimidation.

Diem did not believe that Western democracy would work in Vietnam. In a speech in the National Assembly on April 7, 1950, he had stressed that the country should reject both fascism and communism, but it couldn't imitate Western democracy, either, because it "brought relative freedom to a minority, at the same time that it diminished the effectiveness of the state." Diem believed that emerging nations required centralized power, and he relied on his Can Lao party, mostly Catholics, who were the educational and technological elite of Vietnam. Fall called the party, which kept its membership and organizational structure secret, "a state within a state," and wrote that Diem was a mandarin and autocrat guided by "personalism, something like human dignity," a philosophy of the 1930s developed by the French Catholic Emmanuel Mounier.[9]

During the American election campaign of 1960, Communist infiltration from the north increasingly alarmed the small U.S. establishment in South Vietnam. Elbridge Durbrow, Eisenhower's Ambassador, warned in September that Diem's regime was "in quite serious danger" both from the Viet Cong infiltrators and from a slump in Diem's popularity among Saigon intellectuals. He proposed to Secretary of State Herter that he have a heart-to-heart talk with Diem aimed at easing what he saw as Diem's too-authoritarian rule. Durbrow wrote that he would propose to Diem either disbanding his Can Lao party or making its membership public. He would also propose that the opposition be given a larger role in parliament, that public officials be required to publish their financial situations to counter talk of corruption, that control of the press be moderated, and that Diem's brother, Ngo Dinh Nhu, be sent to a diplomatic post out of the country, along with his wife and Tran Kim Tuyen, head of the secret police. Durbrow wrote that Diem was "the best available Vietnamese leader," but ". . . if Diem's position continues to deteriorate as a result of failure to adopt proper political, psychological, economic and security measures, it may become necessary for the U.S. government to begin consideration of alternative courses of action and leaders in order to achieve our objective."[10]

Two months after Durbrow's attempt to twist Diem's arm, and three days after Kennedy was elected President, South Vietnamese paratroops attempting a coup shot up Diem's bedroom in the Presidential Palace. Diem padded around the palace grounds in his slippers, exhorting his guards to fight. Diem was captured, but he managed to talk the paratroops into negotiations while a signal went out to relief troops. The coup was crushed, and Diem believed that Durbrow at least had known of it.

Shortly after Diem survived "the young officers' coup," Lansdale, now an Air Force Brigadier General, went to South Vietnam on a last mission for the Eisenhower administration. He returned and wrote his report on January 17, submitting it to the Defense Department during the changeover to the Kennedy administration. Lansdale recommended that "Ambassador Durbrow should be transferred in the immediate future...I doubt that he himself realized how tired he has become...the recognized government of Vietnam does not look on him as a friend."[11] Lansdale said that Diem suspected Durbrow of at least condoning the November 11 coup attempt.

At Diem's arrival in Saigon in 1954 no one had expected his government to survive, but he had made remarkable progress until 1959, when Ho completed his consolidation in the north and turned his attention to South Vietnam, Laos and Cambodia.

Ho's infiltrators moved methodically into Laos to build the Ho Chi Minh trail down the side of South Vietnam and into Cambodia, toward Saigon, much as a contractor builds a foundation before erecting a house. The North Vietnamese presence in Laos tipped the political balance there, encouraging a wild-card military leader, Kong Le, to upset a de facto truce by siding with the Communist Pathet Lao, proteges of Ho (see Chapter IX).

Two days after Lansdale submitted his report and one day before Kennedy was to be inaugurated, Kennedy met with Eisenhower and the secretaries of state, defense and treasury of both administrations. Eisenhower told Kennedy that it was imperative that Laos should be defended, with unilateral intervention as the last resort, because there was no chance of an arrangement with Kong Le, and the fall of Laos to the Communists would endanger all of Southeast Asia.

The Laos crisis, worse than he had thought, was thrust on Kennedy before his inauguration. He was not inclined to take Eisenhower's advice, which sounded to him like the "military firemen's" ventures he had condemned in Senate speeches. Kennedy believed he had a remedy for the brushfire wars in Indochina: more sophisticated counterinsurgency. He had told the Senate a year before that "nuclear power cannot protect uncommitted countries against a Communist takeover using local or guerrilla forces...we need forces of an entirely different kind to keep the peace against limited aggression." Before Kennedy was two weeks in office he ordered McNamara to place more emphasis on the development of counter-insurgency forces, and he gave back the Green Berets to the Army's Special Forces. A green beret joined Kennedy's plastic-encased coconut message as an Oval Office desk ornament.[12]

The report submitted by Lansdale just before Kennedy's inauguration dovetailed with Kennedy's ideas, and Lansdale was summoned to see Kennedy in the first days of the new administration.

Lansdale's report, written with informal eloquence, pole-axed the new President, who told Lansdale he would be sent to Saigon as Durbrow's replacement. The suggestion that Lansdale become Ambassador was quickly vetoed. Roger Hilsman reported that the Pentagon did the vetoing, because Lansdale, as an ex-CIA agent, was too political, and that on three occasions the State Department tried to get Lansdale sent to Vietnam.[13] That does not entirely jibe with the various versions of the Pentagon Papers, which indicate that State was horrified at the idea of Lansdale joining the department at that rank. Lansdale's former adversaries, the French colonialists, had given him a worldwide reputation as an adventurer and gunslinger, a characterization picked up by Graham Greene in his novel, *The Quiet American.*

Lansdale's report proposed backing a counter-insurgency effort in Vietnam, suggesting that the United States needed "a hard core of experienced Americans who know and really like Asians, dedicated people who are willing to risk their lives for the ideals of freedom and who will try to influence (the Vietnamese)...with the warm friendships and affection which our close alliance deserves..." He opposed sending troops; the Huks had been defeated in the Philippines without U.S. forces.

Lansdale warned against overthrowing Diem:

> ...the only Vietnamese with executive ability and the determination to be an effective president...(if a coup should succeed) I believe that a number of highly selfish and mediocre people would be squabbling among themselves while the Communists took over....
>
> President Diem and I are friends. Also, he is a man who put other Vietnamese friends of mine in jail or exiled them. It is hardly a blind friendship...(but) Diem is human and does not like the idea of people trying to kill him out of hatred...he has now had nearly 7 years of venomous attack by the Communists who know that he is a major obstacle which must be destroyed before they can win....

Lansdale wrote that misguided Americans attempting to impose a particular form of democracy had taught the Saigon opposition the wrong lesson: they had learned to be carping rather than to form an alternative program. He proposed making a genuine ally of Diem rather than pressuring him for purely American goals: the theme of Kennedy's speeches in Congress. When the *Times* omitted the Lansdale report from its version of the Pentagon Papers, it omitted criticism of itself. David Halberstam, in *The Best and the Brightest*, dismissed the report as Lansdale recommending Lansdale.

It was Kennedy's instinct to send Lansdale to Vietnam, but threats of resignations by high official turned the President around. The ease with which Kennedy was dissuaded from sending the most experienced American to the scene of the problem confirmed Adenauer's observation that Kennedy was susceptible to too many advisers. Diem asked at least four times that Lansdale be sent to him in some kind of capacity, and each White House refusal increased Diem's doubt and suspicion. Lansdale was taken off Vietnam entirely and assigned instead to planning Operation Mongoose sabotage attacks on Cuba, an area he did not know. He was not stationed in Vietnam again until 1965, two years after Diem's murder, during the troop buildup he had advised against.

During his first week in office, Kennedy studied another long-prepared counter-insurgency plan completed during the Eisenhower administration. He decided to retain Ambassador Durbrow for the time being. In March, a month before the Bay of Pigs, he instructed the Defense Department to launch "guerrilla operations against Vietminh territory as soon as possible." He accepted a Joint Chiefs' recommendation to raise the U.S.-paid South Vietnamese army from 150,000 to 170,000 men and the Civil Guard from 32,000 to 68,000. But in Saigon, Durbrow continued to hold up the funds for new troops as a means of pressuring Diem into reforms.

Three days before the Bay of Pigs invasion, Kennedy's deputy assistant for national security, Walt Rostow, recommended gearing up the Vietnam operation to coincide with Kennedy's appointment of Ambassador Frederick (Fritz) Nolting to replace Durbrow. Rostow proposed briefing Nolting "on the priority you attach to the Vietnam problem," sending Vice President Johnson to Saigon, sending a military hardware team to Vietnam to study new gadgets and techniques for clandestine warfare and introducing "a substantial number of Special Forces types." Rostow placed priority on appointing "a first-rate backup man in Washington," a place to put Lansdale, but State would help knock Lansdale out of the Washington action entirely.

In Vietnam, Diem was re-elected president for another five years on April 9 with 89% of the vote. American correspondents in Saigon derided the election as either fixed or because of Diem's control of patronage.[14]

Lansdale submitted an evaluation of Diem on April 25, writing:

> .... Diem's 60 years have been full of sharp tests of his moral courage, of devotion to a highly principled ideal of patriotism... the truth has been hidden by decades of 'character assassination' by Communists and French colonialists.... brother Nhu is a whole complex subject in himself, as is Madame Nhu in herself. Both have been defamed maliciously.... Diem (is) our toughest ally against communism in Southeast Asia... a 60-year-old bachelor who gave up romance with his childhood sweetheart to devote his life to his country.... He is a person of immense moral courage and demonstrated physical courage. He is intensely honest.....[15]

Lansdale also wrote a first-draft report for Kennedy's interdepartmental Presidential Task Force on Vietnam in April. It never reached the President, the State Department taking over the report and rewriting it to put Vietnam policy under the State Department rather than the Defense Department.

Lansdale's report began: "After a meeting in Hanoi on 13 May 1959, the Central Committee of the North Vietnamese Communist Party publicly announced its intention to 'smash' the government of President Diem.... Following this decision the Viet Cong have significantly increased their program of sabotage and assassination...."[16]

Here we will jump forward ten years into a different political environment. Reports and memoranda like Lansdale's were not known to the media when they were written in 1961 and Vietnam was a backwater story. By 1971, when the *Times* came into possession of what it called the Pentagon Papers, Kennedy and Diem both were seven years dead; Vietnam was a media obsession that had forced one President to resign and threatened to unseat another, and the Senate was proposing to withdraw from Vietnam if North Vietnam would release American prisoners of war.

By 1971, the *Times* had been committed for six years to ending American involvement in Vietnam, and its editors seized the opportunity offered by its exclusive possession of the 4,000 documents of the Pentagon Papers to manipulate the history of the Vietnam war to press the case for withdrawal (see Chapter XVI). One of the striking examples of the *Times'* manipulation of the Pentagon study was its treatment of Lansdale's role. The *Times* version of the Pentagon Papers omitted Lansdale's prophetic documents of 1961, which are indispensable to understanding the options that were offered to Kennedy. The media, public and courts accepted the *Times'* interpretation of the Pentagon study, tending to excuse Kennedy's decisions since all of the advice apparently offered him was unfortunate.

Lansdale appears in the *Times* version of the Pentagon study at length in his Graham Greene incarnation of 1954 through a document (anonymous but perhaps written by Lansdale) reporting on his Saigon Military Mission in 1954-1955. The *Times* singled out a minor point in it to stress that Lansdale's team had contaminated the fuel supply of the Hanoi bus company in 1954, giving the reader the impression that this attempt to cripple transport was trivial, adventurous and juvenile. Indeed, Halberstam in *The Best and the Brightest* ridiculed Lansdale for "putting sugar in gas tanks."[17]

Lansdale's 1961 reports at the moment that the United States was becoming involved in Vietnam, omitted by the *Times*, also were discarded by Kennedy. Although Lansdale began his draft of the April 1961 report with the most important point, that the Central Committee decision of May 13, 1959, began the infiltration drive into the south, *Times* reporter Fox Butterfield buried this decision deep in his report on the Pentagon study: "The decision that had been made privately by the Politburo was ratified by the Central Committee at its 15th meeting in May 1959. All available evidence suggests that this was 'the point of departure for D.R.V. intervention,' the (Pentagon study) narrative says." Butterfield added his own observation further downplaying the event: "Scholars and journalists who have studied the origins of the insurgency, but who have not had access to American intelligence reports, have not attached such significance to that 15th session." Butterfield was attempting to prove that "the war began largely as a rebellion in the South against the increasingly oppressive and corrupt regime of Ngo Dinh Diem," and the American "official" version that the Communists were bent on taking over the country from the beginning is treated almost parenthetically: " 'It is equally clear that North Vietnamese Communists operated some form of subordinate apparatus in the South in the years 1954-1960,' the Pentagon study says."

On April 26, 1961, Lansdale was ordered to Vietnam as operations officer of the Presidential Task Force, to leave Deputy Defense Secretary Gilpatric as director and backstop man in Washington. Lansdale never went. McNamara was called into Kennedy's office. He returned and changed the orders in his own handwriting to read that Lansdale would go to Vietnam "when requested by the Ambassador (still Durbrow)."[18]

At that point the Laos crisis flared up. The Pathet Lao and Kong Le seized the strategic Plain of Jars. The moment of decision had come on Eisenhower's recommendation. On April 19, the Joint Chiefs sent out tentative orders for landing 5,000 men plus air elements at Danang, Vietnam, and another 5,000 in Thailand, both groups to threaten a move on Laos. At a National Security Council meeting on April 29, Admiral Burke said, "If you give ground it will be harder to stand next time. If we give up Laos, we will have to put forces into Vietnam and Thailand. It's better to hold now than later." The Pentagon Papers indicate that Rusk stopped the dispatch of troops, advising Kennedy to send "no combat troops to Vietnam at this time."

Gilpatric and Lansdale had asked an urgent meeting on May 1 to approve the Task Force draft report that Lansdale had written. Under Secretary of State Ball asked a day's delay. On May 3, the State Department presented a redraft of the Task Force report. It eliminated a special role in Vietnam for Lansdale, and it shifted the chairmanship of the Task Force from Gilpatric to Ball in the State Department.

Lansdale submitted a memo to his Defense Department superiors:

> My strong recommendation is that Defense stay completely out of the Task Force as now proposed by State. . . . Having a Defense officer, myself or someone else, placed in a position of only partial influence and no responsibility would only provide State with a scapegoat to share the blame when we have a flop. . . . The U.S. past performance and theory of action, which State apparently desires to continue, simply offers no sound basis for winning, as desired by President Kennedy.[19]

Lansdale further commented to Gilpatric on Ball's report: "The elected president of Vietnam is ignored in this statement as the base to build on in countering the Communists. This will have the U.S. pitted against Diem as first priority, the Communists as second."

The Task force was established under Ball, and then it became almost inoperative. Kennedy countermanded the order to send 10,000 men to threaten the Communists in Laos, and instead approved sending 100 extra men to the U.S. Military Advisory Assistance group in Saigon, going beyond the 685-man limit frozen by the Geneva agreements. The United States had not signed the agreements, but had said it would observe them.

On May 11, Kennedy approved sending 400 Special Forces troops covertly, attached to CIA, and he ordered the new Ambassador, Nolting, to work out an arrangement with Diem for their use. Several government groups had made studies and submitted widely varying proposals for sending troops. Gilpatric and Lansdale had advised sending 3,200 military instructors to train two new Vietnamese divisions.

As the 400 Green Berets were on their way, Vice President Johnson talked with Diem in Saigon and raised the possibility of sending troops, along with the possibility of a bilateral mutual defense treaty. Diem did not want either.

Johnson reported to Kennedy: "... Asian leaders at this time do not want American troops involved in Southeast Asia other than in training missions... recently colonial people would not look with favor upon governments which invited or accepted the return this soon of Western troops."

During the Vienna summit meeting with Khrushchev, Kennedy reached an agreement to neutralize Laos. W. Averell Harriman, the coexistence advocate who had solicited Khrushchev to stay out of the 1960 election campaign, was standing by in Geneva attempting to negotiate neutrality for Laos. To Diem, the negotiations simply meant delay. North Vietnamese infiltrators would have an unchallenged route to within a few dozen miles from Pleiku, where they would be in a position to attempt to cut South Vietnam in half.[20]

Harriman's negotiations would continue for a year, when 15 nations, including the Soviet Union, agreed to withdraw military forces and end paramilitary aid. The CIA had been supplying Meo tribesmen with weapons, which were then cut off. The North Vietnamese, however, did not leave, the CIA reporting that 7,000 of them remained in Laos. They would be built up to 70,000 by 1972.

In view of the North Vietnamese violations of the agreement, the United States responded by resuming clandestine supply of arms to the Meo. Eventually 200 to 300 CIA operatives worked with 36,000 Meo tribesmen, but Harriman, from Washington, controlled each military item and each mission. The result was that the war in north Laos spread to the south, where the CIA had no Meo.[21]

Diem, anticipating that the Laos negotiation would turn out the way it did, on June 9 changed his mind about U.S. troops, writing Kennedy to request funding for another 100,000-man increase in his army and "a considerable buildup of selected elements of the American armed forces." Diem cited "perils following events in Laos," and "an enormous accumulation of Russian war material in North Vietnam." He also felt threatened from Cambodia, charging that Prince Sihanouk "takes refuge in Communist servitude under the guise of a neutralist."

The White House, where Kennedy had just returned shaken by the meeting with Khrushchev, did not reply to Diem until August. Then Kennedy authorized a 30,000 increase in Vietnam's army and postponed a decision on sending more U.S. advisers.

In late September, as the situation in Laos deteriorated despite the ongoing negotiations, Diem met with Nolting and surprised the Ambassador with a request for the bilateral defense treaty he had turned down when Johnson suggested it in May. He believed Laos was falling to the Communists, and Viet Cong infiltrators now controlled much of the delta in South Vietnam.

A new batch of proposals for intervention were prepared for the National Security Council meeting of October 11. The Joint Chiefs recommended a major increase in the U.S. draft (because of the Berlin crisis) and the dispatch of 40,000 troops to Vietnam quickly, with perhaps 128,000 to follow. Acting Assistant Secretary of Defense William Bundy wrote in a note to McNamara: "It *is* now or never if we are to arrest the gains being made by the Viet Cong....An early and hard-hitting operation has a good chance (70% would be my guess) of *arresting* things....But if we let, say a month, go by before we move, the odds will slide...."

Kennedy decided to first send his military adviser, General Taylor, to Vietnam, accompanied by Rostow, Lansdale and Sterling Cottrell of State. Kennedy also sent covertly 12 Air Force Jungle Jim patrols with planes designed for guerrilla warfare, to serve under the military advisory group.

Before the Taylor mission arrived in Vietnam, Diem asked Nolting for fighter-bombers, civilian pilots for helicopters and U.S. combat-trainer units, his first direct request for Americans in combat roles.

As Taylor's team left the United States, the *Times* published a report on the mission's objectives, which the Rand analysts of the Pentagon Papers concluded was leaked by Kennedy himself. The *Times* reported that the question of sending U.S. troops "in the indefinite future" was at "the bottom of the list" of items that Taylor would discuss with Diem. The *Times'* authority was such that the rest of the media dropped the question of U.S. troops for Vietnam. Diem also dropped his tentative request for troops.

Although Diem did not ask Taylor for U.S. soldiers, Taylor's final report recommended an aid package that would include sending 8,000 to 10,000 U.S. troops to the delta in the guise of flood-control engineers. The proposals went through another revision in a joint Taylor-Rusk effort.

During the intensive decision-making in Washington in November 1961, as the Berlin crisis boiled, Kennedy's Ambassador to India, his old Harvard tutor Professor John Kenneth Galbraith, stopped over in Saigon on his first visit to Vietnam. Galbraith sent a cable to Kennedy from Saigon via CIA communications ("more secure and faster"), followed by a long letter.

Galbraith's cable of November 20, 1961, said:

> I have just completed three intensive days in Saigon which, with CINPAC talks gives me a much better feeling for this tangled situation. . . there is scarcely the slightest chance that the administrative and political reforms now being pressed on Diem will result in real change. . . . He will promise but he will not perform because it is most unlikely that he can perform. . . . In the absence of fundamental reform, the help we are now proposing will not save the situation. . . . As I will argue there is no solution that does not involve a change of government. To say there is no alternative is nonsence (sic) for there never has seemed to be where one man has dominated the scene. So while we must play out the ineffective and hopeless course on which we are launched for a little while, we must look ahead very soon to a new government. On this more later. . . . [22]

Galbraith's follow-up analysis on November 21 from New Delhi said, with Galbraith's customary arch self-confidence:

> From my stay there, talks at CINCPAC and Bangkok, previous reading of the traffic and experience of the region, I feel reasonably sure of my ground.
>
> The Viet Cong insurrection is still growing in effect. . . . In the absence of knowledge of the admixture of terror and economic and moral evangelism we had best assume that it is employing both. We must not forever be misguided by those who misunderstand the dynamics of revolution and imagine that because the Communists do not appeal to us they are abhorrent to everyone.
>
> In our enthusiasm to prove outside intervention before world opinion we have unquestionably exaggerated the role of material assistance (to the Viet Cong). . . . That leaders and radio guidance come in we know. But the amount of ammunition and weaponry that a man can carry on his back for several hundred kilometers over jungle trails was not increased appreciably by Marx. No major conflict can depend on such logistic support.
>
> A maximum of 18,000 lightly armed men are involved in the insurrection. . . . Ten thousand is more probable. . . .

Galbraith argued that whatever Diem's merits or demerits ("a heavy theological dispute"):

It is agreed that administratively Diem is exceedingly bad. . . .

The SVN army numbers 170,000 and with paramilitary units of the civil guard and home defense forces a quarter of a million. Were this well deployed on behalf of an effective government it should be obvious that the Viet Cong would have no chance of success or takeover. Washington is currently having an intellectual orgasm on the unbeatability of guerrilla war. Were guerrillas effective in the ratio of one to fifteen or twenty-five, it is obvious that no government would be safe. . . .

The key inescapable point, then, is the ineffectuality, abetted debatably by the unpopularity, of the Diem government. This is the strategic factor.

. . . It is politically naive to expect (Diem to reform). He senses that he cannot let power go because he would be thrown out. . . . He probably senses that his greatest danger is from the army. . . .

Ambassador Nolting. . . though acting loyally, is not happy about the pressures on Diem. He believes rather that we should lend him our prestige and power while working more gradually for reform. This policy in my analysis would merely confirm Diem in his inadequacy, a risk which Nolting concedes. It follows from my reasoning that the only solution is to drop Diem.

. . . Without doubt Diem was a significant figure in his day. But he has run his course. He cannot be rehabilitated. Incidentally, this view is held independently by the senior political councillor of our embassy, the man who has been longest in Vietnam.

. . . In my view, dropping Diem will be neither difficult nor dangerous. The Viet Cong are in a position to cause trouble widely over the country. That is far from meaning that they are able, with their small number, to take over and control the country. . . .

We should not be alarmed by the army as an alternative.

You will be aware of my general reluctance to move in troops. On the other hand, I would note that it is those of us who have worked in the political vineyard and who have committed our hearts most strongly to the political fortunes of the New Frontier who worry most about its bright promise being sunk under the rice fields. . . . [23]

Thus, Galbraith became the first on-the-record Kennedy administration official to urge that Diem be deposed. In the *Times* version of the Pentagon Papers, stress is laid on the tentative and conditional suggestions of Durbrow to scout for an alternative to Diem, although Durbrow was an inherited Ambassador with no weight in the new administration. The *Times'* analysis written by Hedrick Smith implies that dissatisfaction with Diem grew slowly over two years, not that his ouster was proposed by an influential aide in Kennedy's first year. Galbraith is not mentioned.

Sixteen years later, Galbraith recalled his report to Kennedy in an interview with BBC radio, but he apparently forgot that he had sent two reports, on consecutive days, the main thrust of both being that Diem had to go.

As Galbraith recalled in the BBC interview, his main concern was to prevent American troops being sent to Vietnam. He explained to BBC interviewer Michael Charlton that he had picked up the top-secret Taylor-Rostow report recommending flood-relief troops from Rostow's desk, and "I was outraged by the thing. The idea of military involvement there horrified me...." So he had spoken to Kennedy, who suggested that he stop by Vietnam on his way to India and take a look.

Asked by Charlton what was the essence of his report, Galbraith replied, "Become militarily involved there." He said he did not think he had recommended pulling out the small military mission, "that we should continue any work of rural salvation and assistance that seemed useful, but that for us to be involved in succession to the French would be quite wrong....''[24]

Since Galbraith did not mention the subject of dumping Diem to the BBC—the main thrust of both his cables—he did not explain how deposing a leader would differ from French tutelage in Vietnam.

Five months after Galbraith's messages, the situation in South Vietnam had improved again, with morale boosted by the incoming American aid and a formal strategic hamlet program under way.

At that point, Galbraith sent Kennedy another memorandum with a long list of suggestions, most of which had been implemented or were being discussed. They began: "...keep door open to a political solution, involve other countries, reduce commitment to the present government of South Vietnam...."

Galbraith suggested that Harriman talk with the Soviets about Vietnam and went on, "...our long-run position cannot involve an unconditional commitment to Diem.... We cannot ourselves replace Diem. But we should be clear in our mind that almost any non-Communist change would probably be beneficial and this should be the guiding rule for our diplomatic representation in the area...."

Kennedy sent Galbraith's memo to McNamara (probably along with his earlier messages) for the Defense Department's evaluation.

Given Kennedy's pixyish sense of humor, it is not inconceivable that he sent the memo to McNamara to watch the explosion when the Joint

Chiefs read the instructions of the wise old guerrilla fighter from the jungles of Harvard and the Office of Price Administration. Exactly what they needed was a fatuous windbag who had spent "three intensive days" in Saigon and believed the Viet Cong represented a local, unsupplied insurrection.

But it probably wasn't a joke. The evidence is that Kennedy took Galbraith's messages seriously. The Rand analysts treated them solemnly.

The explosion at the Pentagon came instanter. The Joint Chiefs sent their boss McNamara a cold letter noting that both the President of the United States and the Secretary of Defense had publicly confirmed the intention of the United States to support Diem, the elected president. General Lyman Lemnitzer signed one of the harshest letters the Joint Chiefs ever dared send their civilian boss.

The State Department denied complicity in Galbraith's intervention, saying that the memo had not gone through channels. Harriman dismissed it as "a private communication." But Galbraith's advice eventually was adopted.

Kennedy had taken office pretty much determined to go into Vietnam with unconventional forces, but one thing after another delayed the move: the Bay of Pigs, the Berlin Wall, the Soviets breaking the moratorium on atmospheric nuclear testing, debates and careful studies by the military and the diplomats, interdepartmental warfare over how to go about it.

The State Department usurped military decisions and then postponed making the decisions. Rivalry was intense between the Joint Chiefs and the CIA, especially after Kennedy denied the military the satisfaction of bailing out the CIA at the Bay of Pigs. The CIA was in the process of dismantling the military intelligence services—the eyes and ears of the JCS—and, as General Keegan commented, the Joint Chiefs suspected that the CIA, like State, was "corrupted by proximity to the levers of power."

Lansdale's skills and programs fitted like a glove President Kennedy's public pronouncements on the subjects of combatting communism, counter-insurgency and goals in Southeast Asia. The President's speeches and press conference answers on these subjects are included in an annex to the Senator Gravel Edition of the Pentagon Papers, and some read as though they had been written by Lansdale. Yet Kennedy rejected Lansdale and accepted a mixed bag of advice from McNamara, Rusk, Ball, Galbraith, Hilsman, etc.—the antipodes of Lansdale. There were two Kennedys, the eloquent public image and the real one.

Diem, knowing from his experience of living in the United States during the Korean war the indifference with which most Americans regarded Asia, continually wondered when the Americans would run out and leave him to the combined power of the North Vietnamese, the Chinese and the Soviets.

To the media, Vietnam was a backwater in 1961, 1962 and the first half of 1963—until the Buddhist crisis. The unsettled Laos situation still outranked Vietnam in news value. But the major media kept Saigon staffed because it had been a great news story in 1954 and surely would be one again. The most experienced reporters could not be wasted there, with the Berlin Wall, the Cuban missile crisis, the British government ready to fall, De Gaulle throwing NATO out of France, the nuclear non-proliferation treaty, China threatening India after occupying Tibet, Arab revolts in Iraq, Yemen and Syria, coups in South America. So the media sent promising and energetic young correspondents to Saigon—who would come to regard the word "young" as the highest form of insult. Saigon had American officials, an overlay of French civilization, good communications, and it was deemed an important country. Laos had none of this, so Saigon became again press headquarters for Southeast Asia.

In 1963, few Americans knew anything about Vietnam and few Vietnamese knew anything about America. There were few books on Vietnam in U.S. libraries, and they were mostly written by the French, who had their own axes to grind. Nobody spoke the language.

Correspondents in Saigon struggled with their editors over all manner of Oriental-Occidental mixups. When the Ngo family became headline names during the Buddhist crisis, there was a period of sorting out in newsrooms where they were not well known. There was Ngo Dinh Diem, the president. Ngo Dinh Nhu was his brother, who did what, exactly? Ngo was the family name, so why wasn't Mme. Nhu called Mme. Ngo? Was she Diem's sister, or his sister-in-law? Harried editors told their rewrite men, "Don't ask me, look it up in the *Times*."

Both the Saigon correspondents and State Department researchers suffered from a dangerous little bit of knowledge. They knew the answers to the simple questions and were impatient with dunderheads who did not. They knew that language itself, even in proper translation, was a problem. "Mandarin" was a laudatory term in Vietnam, but pejorative in the United States, and the correspondents used the word to effect against Diem. Conversely, Mme. Nhu noticed that flamboyant journalists' language had effect, so she spoke in shocking images. She thought that was how Americans made themselves understood.

The American correspondents in Saigon had more than their editors' neglect to frustrate them. The clandestine nature of the Kennedy military buildup through 1962 and 1963 poisoned the atmosphere between officials and reporters. The correspondents saw and reported the buildup, but the story went unnoticed at home. There were no big headlines, no congressional inquiries into a covert American involvement in the war. Kennedy's skillful public relations, and a Washington press corps hypnotized by him, squashed the correspondents' story. Editors and the American public took the military buildup as a natural phenomenon, like snow in winter.

Most reporters know that the U.S. Army will dissemble when it can because secrecy is an integral part of warfare, and they also know the Army is clumsy and vulnerable in its dissembling. The U.S. military mission in Saigon and the Embassy had been forced to lie more than usual: while Washington and Saigon spokesmen still were denying an American combat role, the reporters were seeing American-piloted helicopters shot down in the still-small-scale guerrilla war. They blamed the military spokesmen and the Embassy for the deception.

In an effort to patch up press relations, the State Department hired a genuine foreign correspondent as the Embassy's spokesman. Not only was John Mecklin, late of *Time*, an experienced correspondent, he also was a friend of Lansdale's and had reported the 1955 battle of Saigon that made Diem a secure president.

Mecklin had been reporting the Berlin Wall crisis in 1961 when his problems with *Time* multiplied. Newsmagazine correspondents, like tabloid correspondents, operate under a special category of pressures and frustrations. Their copy is almost always rewritten after a team of researchers has had at it, and the finished story often bears no resemblance to what was cabled. Newsmagazines skip good stories early in the week to concentrate on a crucial weekly deadline, and everything happens six hours after that deadline. In Germany, Mecklin's marriage was breaking up, and in a period of distress he punched out a young UPI reporter for no reason that anyone at the party could divine.

Caught in Saigon between a devious and divided government in Washington and his natural friends, the reporters, Mecklin eventually sided with the reporters. He criticized their arrogance, but he believed they were more straightforward than some of the American officials.[25]

Today, reading the books of the Saigon correspondents, class of '63, a reader is struck by the impression that Vietnam was the only story in the world in 1963, while in fact it ranked, even with Diem's death, far behind President Kennedy's assassination, the civil rights marches and even the debate over the nuclear test ban treaty. But the correspondents' books reached the bookstores in 1965, as Johnson escalated the Vietnam war and Vietnam *was* the only story.

During 1962, press reporting from Saigon began to become a story in itself. *Time* magazine complained in 1962 that the correspondents tended to "color it gloomy," and that was before Vietnam made any headlines. A few reporters challenged the opinions of the Saigon press corps, and a press dispute developed that will be called here the Halberstam-Higgins war, after the main protagonists.

Of all the wars going on in Vietnam in 1963—the ARVN vs. the Viet Cong, Diem vs. the Buddhists, the State Department vs. the Defense Department vs. the CIA, the Vietnamese intellectuals in Paris vs. Vietnamese officers—it probably was the American press war that ultimately determined the fate of South Vietnam. It was a war for the hearts and minds of the American editors and peasantry, and the decision on the winners was made in 1963, to be held tenaciously until 1975, when South Vietnam fell.

Chapter IX
The Halberstam-Higgins War

"A man who makes a mistake and does not correct it makes another mistake."

—*Confucius*

David Halberstam arrived in Saigon as *The New York Times* correspondent in September 1962 after ten months in the Congo, where he had won a New York Newspaper Guild award for foreign reporting. He was 28, and he had done everything right; he had been graduated from Harvard, and he first went to work for a Mississippi newspaper, then on to four years at the *Nashville Tennessean,* ideal seasoning for a Boston-educated New Yorker.

Marked as an unusual talent when he joined the Washington bureau of the *Times,* he was there only briefly before being sent to the Congo for his baptism of fire.

In the Congo he was, for a time, the lone American special correspondent among wire service and network men. He made a friend of Horst Faas, the Associated Press' prize-winning photographer, who would later share a villa with him in Saigon. From British correspondents in Africa, Halberstam picked up worldly skepticism and practical lessons that can be learned only in the field, such as securing alternative communications and pigeoning out dispatches with airline pilots or travelers.

The U.S. ambassador to the Congo, Edmund Gullion, who as a chargé in Saigon had helped make Vietnam intriguing to Kennedy, told Halberstam tales of Southeast Asia.

Halberstam asked the *Times* for the Saigon assignment, and there he replaced the fabled Homer Bigart, who had just coined the resident correspondents' slogan, "Sink or swim with Ngo Dinh Diem."

After the Congo story, with its discomforts and what seemed to Americans to be its peripheral significance, the color and complexity of Vietnam and the civilized amenities of Saigon captivated Halberstam. He would say it was a correspondent's dream.

Halberstam arrived after the clandestine Kennedy military buildup had been going on for nine months. The Vietnamese military had two new divisions, naval patrol craft, new transport aircraft, new guns and armored personnel carriers. Americans were serving in the field as advisers and flying transport helicopters, armed helicopters and fighter-bombers.

He arrived at a moment of anger among resident correspondents over the expulsion of *Newsweek's* François Tully, a veteran who had fought the Japanese in Indochina with the French army, taken his discharge in 1947 and had lived in Saigon for 17 years.

Six months earlier, the Vietnamese government had tried to expel the *Times'* Bigart but had backed down under American government protests. Six correspondents protested Tully's expulsion to President Kennedy, and were themselves warned by the Vietnamese assistant defense minister that their negative reporting made them candidates for expulsion. The six Americans, all scornful of French colonialism, did not accept that in Vietnamese eyes their protest to Kennedy was colonialist. Tully was told to expedite his departure in view of his colleagues' "attempt to create a law of their own in sovereign South Vietnam."[1]

The correspondents blamed Madame Nhu, the "Dragon Lady," for Tully's expulsion. *Newsweek* noted that Tully's "brutally frank reports about the way the war against the Viet Cong was waged have long irritated the government."

Also coinciding with Halberstam's arrival, Admiral Harry Felt told the AP's Malcolm Browne at a press conference, "Why don't you get on the team?" The remark became another press corps slogan.

Halberstam, Harvard class of '55, was pleased to find United Press International's Neil Sheehan, Harvard class of '58. Halberstam began working out of the AP office, but he quarreled with Browne, criticizing his dispatches as not aggressive enough, and moved out, into Sheehan's UPI cubbyhole office in spite of the crowding.[2]

Halberstam immediately detested Mme. Nhu, whom he found vain and power-mad. He found it embarrassing that Diem "paid homage to himself" on national day, October 26, as the founder of South Vietnam. He agreed with Sheehan that Diem and the Nhus were an obstacle to winning the war, and that Diem had "little instinct for his people" from whom "the Nhus had cut him off."[3]

On trips to the field, Halberstam discovered Lieutenant Colonel John Paul Vann, who criticized the passivity of Vietnamese officers, and he adopted a pessimistic view of how the war was going. He gave no credence to General Paul Harkins, head of the U.S. military mission, whom he saw as an orthodox and unimaginative officer, or to Ambassador Nolting, who appeared to Halberstam to be blinded by his loyalty to Diem.

Halberstam broke with CIA station chief John Richardson when Richardson tried to tell him that Diem's brother Nhu was a patriot. When Halberstam said that Nhu was anti-American, Richardson replied that was part of his patriotism, given Vietnam's recent colonial status. Halberstam concluded that he could not understand Richardson because the two of them operated within different frames of reference. That was accurate, and it usually takes an American correspondent longer than a year or two to begin to lose his strictly American frame of reference.

In 1962, Halberstam, like the others, was not being published much. The Cuban missile crisis preempted newspaper space until December. Even the Congo he had left behind was getting more space in the papers than Vietnam in the first months of Halberstam's Vietnam tour, which was to last only 18 months. After three months of legwork, making contacts and forming convictions, Halberstam was struck another blow; the newspaper strike in December closed all New York City newspapers for 114 days. He kept filing for the *Times* national edition and syndicate wire, but his central audience was gone.

In January, during the strike, the first big story broke: the United States lost five helicopters in a battle at Ap Bac, and the Viet Cong got away. In a chase after the battle, a Viet Cong group was captured the next day, but Halberstam doubted that it was the group that downed the helicopters. The correspondents' reports of a devastating defeat brought Admiral Felt back to Saigon, where General Harkins assured him the battle had been a victory for the government. Felt and Sheehan had an angry exchange at the airport, Felt telling Sheehan, "You ought to talk to some of the people who've got the facts," and Sheehan rejoined, "You're right, Admiral, and that's why I went down there every day."

Halberstam and Sheehan had become close, and with others, including Browne and Charles Mohr of *Time* magazine, formed a group of like-minded resident correspondents. An Army officer who served in Saigon at the time, later transferred to West Germany, told me at U.S. Army European Command headquarters in Heldelberg, "I know newspapermen pal around together and exchange tips, hell, that's natural. But these guys sat together, sometimes in front of you in a Saigon cafe, and general-staffed their stories. Every story that went out supported the other stories. The reports were as alike as *Pravda, Isvestia* and *Trud.*"

In *The Making of a Quagmire,* Halberstam was candid about the close *Times*-UPI cooperation. He noted repeatedly, "Neil Sheehan and I wrote. . . ." "By this time, Sheehan, Perry, Turner, Rao, Am and myself had created a small but first-class intelligence network. . . ." "Neil and I compared notes. . . ." "Back at the office, Neil and I swapped notes and began writing. . . ."

Together, the stories of Sheehan and Halberstam blanketed nearly all American dailies, radio stations and television clients with the same viewpoint through the UPI wire and *Times* syndicate. They were reinforced by AP stories in a similar vein, and further backed up when Mohr could get his copy past the recalcitrant editors at *Time. Newsweek* remained hostile to Diem after Tully's expulsion.

The small American press corps in Saigon was pessimistic about the country's future, but some veterans were not discouraged to the degree that the young Turks were. Keyes Beech of the *Chicago Daily News* liked their drive and aggressiveness, but thought that the Saigon group sometimes went overboard.

Special correspondents who disagreed with the group filed their dispatches, but the effect was faint against the blanket point of view that got home first in the two wire services and the *Times.* Editorials and editorial cartoons in American newspapers reflected a "Diem must go" consensus that became rabid when the Buddhist crisis descended on South Vietnam in the summer of 1963.

While the crisis was building, Halberstam was engaged with Sheehan and Mert Perry of *Time* on a joint project to document what they believed was a serious deterioration of the military situation in the delta. The *Times* carried Halberstam's long analysis after a delay on August 15, 1963, at the height of the Buddhist crisis. It warned of ominous signs that the war was being lost, of a Viet Cong buildup in the delta and of an on-going Communist offensive.

Halberstam's story directly contradicted the reports that Washington was receiving from General Harkins, the CIA's Richardson and Nolting. Secretary of State Rusk denied Halberstam's report at a Washington press conference, saying that sabotage, propaganda and large-scale Communist attacks all were declining, and the South Vietnamese government's strategic hamlet program, under the direction of Nhu, was moving forward. In Saigon, Major General Richard Stilwell, the mission's operations officer, briefed correspondents, denouncing the story and Halberstam by name.

President Kennedy received *Times* publisher Arthur Ochs Sulzberger and asked if he had thought of transferring Halberstam. Kennedy was widely quoted as asking, "Who elected David Halberstam to run the foreign policy of the United States?"

The war-deterioration story was, however, secondary to the Buddhist storm that gathered through May, June, July and exploded in August, 1963. Its beginnings caught the Saigon correspondents unprepared, and few of them, as Halberstam noted, had ever been in a pagoda, or knew anything about Buddhism or its Vietnamese particulars. They saw it as a religious conflict, transposing it into Occidental terms, something like the conflict between Catholics and Protestants in Northern Ireland, to which it bore no relation.

The old imperial city of Hué in the north of South Vietnam was a Ngo family stronghold. Diem's brother Ngo Dinh Thuc was Archbishop of Hué, and his brother Ngo Dinh Can, patron of the Oriental city, was called by the correspondents the unofficial governor of the district.

In early May, Diem attended a celebration in Hué for his brother Thuc on the 25th anniversary of his being named Archbishop. Diem, who was trying to encourage nationalism, noted that Vatican flags were flying in the city along with the South Vietnamese flag. On May 6, Saigon sent out a circular reminding of an existing ordinance that religious flags, of all religions, were to be displayed by churches and pagodas only.

By that time, Hué was already bedecked with Buddhist flags for the May 8 celebration of Buddha's 2,525th birthday. Vietnam's interior minister, Bui Van Luong, visited Hué on May 6, saw the Buddhist flags flying, and told local authorities not to apply the circular until after the Buddhist celebration. Hué's police got the circular before the advice, and took down some of the flags. Luong later told a United Nations investigating team that he also visited the Tu Dam pagoda to assure Buddhist leaders there that the flag regulation would not be enforced.

Thich (the venerable) Tri Quang, an enigmatic Buddhist leader in Hué who had come from North Vietnam, told some of his followers to obey the circular and take down their flags. Then he prepared a reception for Hué city officials when they went to the Tu Dam pagoda on Buddha's birthday: banners lettered with strident anti-government slogans. During the religious ceremony, Thich Tri Quang took over the microphone and delivered a vitriolic speech, laced with anti-Diem slogans, charging a discriminatory ban on Buddhist flags. His speech was recorded, and the Buddhist leader that evening sent a crowd from the pagoda to the Hué radio station, then arrived himself carrying the tape recording and demanding that it be broadcast.

The radio station director locked himself in the little station against the increasingly unruly crowd and telephoned the province chief, who arrived and debated with Thich Tri Quang. Then the province chief, Nguyen Van Dang, a Buddhist, summoned armored cars. Major Dang Sy arrived with troops to disperse the crowd. A riot broke out, and firemen turned hoses on the crowd. The province chief later testified that he took Thich Tri Quang into the station and broadcast appeals to the firemen to turn off the hoses when two loud explosions shook the building and he heard broken glass, gunshots and exploding grenades.

None of the Saigon reporters knew this background when they were told on May 8 by the Diem government that the Viet Cong had murdered nine Buddhists in Hué with plastic explosives.

Halberstam received a call from the Vietnamese director of information and did not believe the government's story. He did not attend the government's press conference because he was just leaving for a brief vacation in Hong Kong.

News dispatches that went out of Saigon said that government troops had fired on protesting Buddhists in Hué and killed nine persons. Diem's version, that a Viet Cong bomb had killed the demonstrators, was mentioned and simultaneously discredited. The Buddhist crisis had begun.

The reports alarmed Washington. The stories from Saigon said that 70% to 80% of the country's population was Buddhist, so it appeared that a religious clash would turn the majority of the country and the army against Diem. Ambassador Nolting urged Diem to settle the incident quickly by paying indemnity for the victims, admitting the army's guilt for the killings and calling together an investigative commission. Diem agreed to pay indemnity, but he refused to admit the army's guilt, declaring that it was not true. Despite his reputation for integrity, Diem was not believed in Washington.

Nolting left for a scheduled home leave in June, and in his absence from Saigon the State Department switched from kid-gloves treatment of Diem back to the hard line of former Ambassador Durbrow. William Truehart, chargé d'affaires in Saigon, was instructed to warn Diem not to take reprisals in Hué, or the United States could not support him. Diem agreed to call an investigative commission, but he continued to deny government guilt for the killings.

Thich Tri Quang, meanwhile, moved from Hué to Saigon and took over the Xa Loi pagoda. He staged a series of well-organized Buddhist demonstrations, while American officials wrung their hands over the intransigent Diem, who clung to the Viet Cong bomb story.

On June 11, a Buddhist monk, Thich Quang Duc, 77, got out of a car in a Saigon square, sat in the lotus position and was doused with gasoline by two monks. Quang Duc then lit a match and was engulfed in flames. Malcolm Browne and a Vietnamese photographer had been tipped in advance that something newsworthy would happen, and both took photographs that were front-paged around the world, touching off imitation immolations in points as widespread as Brazil and the United States.[4]

Halberstam raced to the scene, shocked as the monk burned and a young Buddhist priest intoned over a microphone, "A Buddhist priest becomes a martyr." It was said that Thich Quang Duc's heart did not burn, and it was borne on a pillow to the Xa Loi pagoda, where it was enshrined.

Mme. Nhu was interviewed by NBC television shortly after the spectacular death of the monk, and she told the world, using an expression her daughter had picked up listening to Americans discussing the event at the Post Exchange, that Buddhist leaders "have done nothing but barbecue a monk, and, at that, not even with self-sufficient means, since they had to import gasoline."

Nolting still was on leave. His deputy Truehart met with Diem, who declined to disavow Mme. Nhu.

The immolation of Thich Quang Duc brought a new player on scene. In Washington, Marguerite Higgins, chief of the *New York*

Herald-Tribune bureau, received marching orders from her editors. She was to fly to Saigon and concentrate for six weeks on an analysis series to straighten out the picture. She was not to distract herself by filing day-to-day spot news, but to dig into the story in depth and explain how Diem had changed from a hero into a monster, find out how the war really was going and discover if the U.S. Embassy and military mission were staffed with high-ranking idiots.

Higgins arrived in Saigon looking, as she sometimes did, deceptively innocent and helpless. She went first to the Xa Loi pagoda, which she knew, and was surprised to find the familiar place of meditation, usually silent except for soft bells, a bustling propaganda center. The young monk spokesman, Thich Duc Nhiep, asked her, "Ah, Miss Higgins, you are from New York, how is the play?"

She did not immediately understand, thinking he was speaking of a drama. No, he meant newspaper play. The monks were busy studying U.S. Information Agency digests of American press stories on the Buddhist crisis.

She had hardly left the pagoda when she was summoned back by Thich Tri Quang, who was not usually available to journalists, and with whom Halberstam never spoke. In an exchange, sometimes acrimonious, lasting more than two hours, the monk asked Higgins to warn President Kennedy not to appear to be associated with Diem's actions. There would be more self-immolations, "not just one or two, but ten, twenty, maybe fifty," and they would blacken Kennedy's reputation as well as Diem's.[5]

Higgins came away from the interview convinced that Thich Tri Quang's actions were entirely political and would not stop until the government fell or Tri Quang was defeated, and that he might be a Communist provocateur following a sophisticated scenario. While the monk later was reported punished by the Communists, Higgins learned through French contacts that he had been arrested twice by the French for meetings with Ho Chi Minh, that his brother worked in Ho's interior ministry, and that he had been a disciple of Thich Tri Do, leader of Hanoi's Buddhist puppet organization.

Higgins had almost magical entrée. In her tour of South Vietnam, she had long interviews with Diem, his brother Nhu, the heavily attacked presidential counselor, and Mme. Nhu. She had long talks with Richardson and the British counter-insurgency expert Robert Thompson, who was soon to be knighted. She covered the length of South Vietnam, from Hué and Danang in the north to Can Tho and Bac Lieu in the south, with stopovers in a dozen combat areas including those near Cambodia and at the bottom of Laos, the end of the Ho Chi Minh trail.

She did not file breaking news, so the climax of the Buddhist crisis—the pagoda raids—occurred as she left South Vietnam, and she was not heard from on what the media took to be the big story.

While Higgins was in the field interviewing peasants, priests, captured Viet Cong, ARVN officers and soldiers, American advisers, and village mayors, the Saigon press corps was pinned down in the capital by the burgeoning Buddhist crisis, coupled now with coup rumors. Back in New York, Higgins' newspaper was using wire service reports that she would attempt to refute on her return.

On the Fourth of July, 1963, President Kennedy was sitting on top of the world. After the humiliation of the Bay of Pigs and the Berlin Wall, and the nerve-wracking confrontation of the Cuban missile crisis, suddenly everything was coming up roses. Kennedy had just returned from West Germany, where he had accomplished all he had set out to do and more. The troublesome Adenauer had been sidelined; the media had not yet caught on that Kennedy had called off the cold war in Berlin, but Khrushchev's response was positive, and a limited nuclear test ban treaty appeared in the bag. Running the world was not so difficult after all, once you got the hang of it.

South Vietnam remained troublesome. The small-scale war there was going well, contrary to reports by the Saigon press corps, and Ho Chi Minh was hinting at negotiations toward a truce. The problem was Kennedy's old acquaintance Diem, whose stubbornness and defiance was giving the United States—and Kennedy—a black eye in the world media.

Diem at 62 was as intractable as old Adenauer and old Arthur Krock, the *Times* man who had been a Kennedy mentor since childhood and whom Kennedy now rejected. It was easy to get rid of such honorable men; they were not whistle-blowers.

Kennedy had decided to remove Diem, and in June he had changed American policy to an iron-fisted approach. Diem had defied him, and so had his sister-in-law, Mme. Nhu, who was not Kennedy's kind of woman.

Kennedy called on the Fourth of July an extraordinary meeting. The timing was characteristic; it feinted out of position the hounds of the press while Washington was deserted except for tourists, and when news bureaus were skeleton-staffed. Kennedy often made decisive moves while the media was lulled: he was vacationing in Glen Ora when the Bay of Pigs invasion was launched; he had been out of reach on his yacht when the Berlin Wall went up; he staged a campaign tour at the height of the Cuban missile crisis. On the Fourth of July, he could go to his office to collect the mail and catch up on accumulated traffic without attracting attention. On June 27, while in Ireland, he had announced that Henry Cabot Lodge would replace Nolting as ambassador to Saigon.

Rather than beat down objections over Diem's removal that might come from McNamara, Rusk, McCone, General Taylor and Vice President Johnson at a National Security Council meeting, Kennedy called a meeting of anti-Diem, second-echelon State Department and White House men. Together they would present the heavyweight cabinet members with a *fait accompli.*

At 11 a.m. on July 4, Kennedy met in the Oval Office with Under Secretaries of State Ball and Harriman, Assistant Secretary for Far Eastern Affairs Hilsman and National Security adviser McGeorge Bundy, and Bundy's deputy for Southeast Asia Michael V. Forrestal. Together with Lodge, the participants would constitute the Washington coup group.

Lodge had run for vice president with Nixon in 1960, and if Vietnam should go sour, as the *Times* was reporting it was doing, it wouldn't hurt to have a prominent Republican involved—a conclusion reached later by Rand analyists of the Pentagon Papers. Lodge had been the incumbent Massachusetts Senator whom Kennedy had defeated in 1952, and in a political sense, Kennedy was confident that he had Lodge's number.

Nolting had cut short his vacation as Buddhist demonstrations made news in early July and had reported to Washington, urging the administration not to overthrow Diem.

On July 5, Nolting met with Under Secretary Ball, who asked what would happen if there were a change in government. "The Ambassador replied that. . .in his view, if a revolution occured in Vietnam which grew out of the Buddhist situation, the country would be split between *feuding factions* [my italics] and the Americans would have to withdraw, and the country might be lost to the Communists."[6]

Ball's question reflected the key issue discussed at the Oval Office the day before. Then, Hilsman, who wrote up notes of the meeting in a memo, said that "Everyone agreed that the chances of chaos in the wake of a coup are considerably less than they were a year ago. An encouraging sign relative to this point is that the war between the Vietnamese forces and the Viet Cong has been pursued throughout the Buddhist crisis without noticeable let-up."[7]

Forrestal had "reported on General Krulak's views that even if there were chaos in Saigon, the military units in the field would continue to confront the Communists."

As reported in Hilsman's memo, Forrestal's comment implied that Krulak had nothing against a coup, since it would not impair the war effort. It is one of several misrepresentations of Krulak's position under which the general finally was buried.

When the *Times* published the Pentagon Papers in 1971, the unusual composition of the July 4 meeting was not stressed. No one was there from the Pentagon or the CIA, nor was Rusk present. It was the Diem-must-go school, with no dissenters.

The American press corps in Saigon was unaware that the President discussed a coup on the Fourth of July, but they were getting reflections from the United States that a coup might come; they thought the reflections came from their own reporting of coup rumors.

Newsweek reported in its July 15 issue that "one Western official" had said, "Diem cannot win the war because he had lost the people." The report carried weight because Benjamin Bradlee, *Newsweek's* Washington bureau chief, was an intimate of Kennedy.

Newsweek continued:

Coup? The fact that Lodge will not arrive until September... has led some critics to speculate that the United States is not exactly pressing hard for quick action, or is, perhaps, hoping that the Vietnamese themselves will have solved the problem by then—possibly by a military coup of which rumors abound.

Later, in the September 9 issue, *Newsweek* again used the "Coup?" lead-in:

Coup?... There is no guarantee that if the U.S. engineers a military coup against the family, as it is plainly hoping to do, that the new regime will prosecute the war vigorously and with the same sense of purpose that, in the early years at least, had inspired Diem and his tightly knit family.... Yet plainly something has to be done, and quickly, before the Nhus can consolidate their power and hand President Kennedy, facing the prospect of an election year, a humiliating defeat.

When Kennedy discussed a coup on July 4, the Buddhist crisis had not yet reached its climax. The pagoda raids, which the Saigon press corps would call the turning point in American policy, were six weeks away. The Pentagon Papers analysts concluded that the turning point occured during Nolting's vacation in June.

In Saigon, Diem and the Nhus read the American media reports of a possible coup just as the Buddhist monks and Hanoi did. Nhu called in generals at least twice to warn them to tighten up against a coup.

Diem, even with Nolting's support, never had felt secure under the protection of the Kennedy administration. The Americans persistently saw the country in Occidental, especially American, terms, and were assuming an overlord position, attempting to impose American values on a Oriental society that Diem knew well. He knew he had been "on trial" with the Americans, and when Lodge was named as Nolting's successor, it confirmed Diem in his belief that the United States would run out on him. Mme. Nhu commented, "They have sent us a proconsul."

During the talk of coups, Marguerite Higgins came into Saigon from the field with a few words for reporters at the Caravelle Hotel bar. Attractive and looking less than 42, she still was old enough to be the mother of some of the correspondents. Like a hangdog class of boys caught throwing spitballs, several heard her comments that their reporting was careless, sloppy, misleading and biased. To begin with, the war was going well in the countryside. The Buddhists were not a majority in the country, but a minority of perhaps 15%.[8] Thich Tri Quang was a political provocateur, and he represented only a minority of the minority Buddhists. The correspondents were misrepresenting everything the Ngo family did or said because they could not put it into the country's context.

The correspondents did not contradict Higgins; instead, they seethed.

Higgins had covered the last year of World War II in Germany and sometimes had been ahead of the troops. She had seen the liberation of Buchenwald and Dachau concentration camps, and after the war had been a bureau chief in Berlin during a riotous era of Soviet threats and Communist kidnappings. She had been the *Herald-Tribune's* bureau chief in Tokyo in 1950 when the Korean war broke out, and she had gone immediately to South Korea. When Major General Edwin Walker ordered her out, saying it was no place for a woman, she went over his head to General Douglas MacArthur, and stayed to win the 1954 Pulitzer Prize. She had written *War in Korea,* a best-seller. Before that war was over, she had gone to Vietnam to cover the fall of Dien Bien Phu. She had many friends in Saigon, which she was visiting for the seventh time, and nobody in town had credentials approaching hers.

But Higgins was not filing daily stories, and events were racing past her. She had some strikes against her; she had married Lieutenant General William F. Hall, U.S. Air Force, and was suspected of being a captive of the dissembling military. As the most publicized of the heroines of World War II, she epitomized the generation that had overshadowed the new generation of reporters.

Contrary to the public notion, news people do not enjoy intramural fights. Higgins did not attack the Saigon group in her copy, which she knew would be a mug's game, but she was appalled by the quality of reporting out of Saigon. Eventually she was moved to say, "Reporters here would like to see us lose the war to prove that they are right."

When Higgins' series finally appeared, and the *Times* cabled Halberstam about her stories, he replied, any more questions about "THAT WOMAN'S COPY AND I RESIGN, REPEAT RESIGN."⁹

Nolting flew back to Saigon in July for one last month, attempting to persuade Diem to accept a degree of guidance from Washington and perhaps to send the Nhus abroad. Diem asked him how President Kennedy would react if he were asked to exile Bobby and Ethel.

On August 7, Higgins spent five hours with Diem, who at one point asked her, "What am I to think of the American government, Miss Higgins? Am I merely a puppet on Washington's string? Or, as I had hoped, are we partners in a common cause? . . . Almost daily I hear broadcasts over Voice of America or of inspired articles in the American press discussing whether Washington is going to retain my services or throw me out. . . ."¹⁰

When Higgins asked him about plots, he answered carefully: "I do not think Ambassador Nolting is plotting against me. I do not think Richardson is plotting against me. I know there are American officials who are preparing the way in the event the decision is taken to try and get rid of me. . . ."

Diem warned against America's siding with those Vietnamese in the city who wanted an American protectorate. "Such intrigues go against the deep longing of the Vietnamese people to be truly free of foreign rule."

Of the Buddhists, Diem repeated that religious strife was alien to the country, and "I have kept my side of the bargain. But if I must keep silent, why don't the Americans tell the truth, that this so-called Buddhist affair has nothing to do with religion but is a fight to topple my government?"

The United States was saying something else. On August 14, Roger Hilsman, in a broadcast over the Voice of America, said that the Buddhist crisis "was beginning to affect the war effort."

A week later, Higgins arrived in New York, still angry at the provocative VOA broadcast, and called Hilsman in Washington. "The Embassy says the Buddhist crisis is having no effect on the war," she said, "But your VOA broadcast said there is. What did you base it on, *The New York Times?*"

"Partly that," she quoted Hilsman as saying, "The *Times* and other press dispatches out of Saigon."[11]

On August 19 and 20, as Higgins left Saigon, Halberstam, Sheehan, Mert Perry and other correspondents received tips that a government crackdown on the pagodas was imminent.

Halberstam was told on August 19 by a Vietnamese source that Nhu would raid the pagodas using his American-trained special forces under Colonel Le Quang Tung. He also was told that Nhu had met with the generals, ordering tighter precautions against a coup and telling them to "raze the city with artillery" if a coup occured.[12] Halberstam filed what he believed to be verbatim notes of Nhu's meeting with the generals.

The next day Halberstam visited the Xa Loi pagoda with Perry. Monks at the pagoda said they knew about the impending raid and showed no alarm. That evening Halberstam was alerted by Sheehan that truckloads of troops were moving toward the pagodas. Sheehan reached the U.S. Operations Mission, near Xa Loi pagoda, but Halberstam was held a block away by police.

The raid was, Halberstam wrote, "a horror spectacle," with a monk thrown off a balcony, screams as the troops smashed up the pagoda, Buddhists carried out. . . . "it was impossible for me to tell how many were killed. . .the true toll never was known."[13]

Communications had been blacked out for the raid, but Sheehan, according to Halberstam, talked a U.S. Army communications man into sending out 150 words on the raid that gave him a world beat. Halberstam's own report, which went out too late to make the *Times* that day, said that the raids bore the stamp of Ngo Dinh Nhu. He wrote later: "I felt that I never had made a safer *assumption.*" (My italics.)

The day after the raids, Diem broadcast a decree of martial law, citing an increased war threat and sabotage of his policy of conciliation with the Buddhists "by political speculators who have taken advantage of religion."

Halberstam, Sheehan and others scoured the city trying to piece together whether the masses of troops in the city meant that a coup had occured. That day the *Times* printed Halberstam's "stamp of Nhu" report.

To Halberstam, all the evidence pointed to Nhu as responsible for the pagoda raids, but he was out on a limb with the "stamp of Nhu" because he had no hard evidence. He talked to CIA chief Richardson and was dumbfounded when Richardson said that the CIA had not known that the raids were coming. "An American intelligence friend" told Halberstam that the CIA *had* known the raids were coming, and that the raids were the work of Nhu and Colonel Tung: "It didn't have a damn thing to do with the army."[14]

Halberstam's anonymous intelligence friend, the only confirmation for the Nhu-did-it story, was unusual in 1963, when CIA men had not yet begun to contradict their station chiefs.

Richardson, who was relieved from his Saigon post one day after Halberstam reported a conflict between him and the subsequent Ambassador, Lodge,[15] never had spoken for publication when I contacted him in 1979. Sixteen years after the events, he did not express rancor.

"After the pagoda raid, Halberstam and I met by chance in the hallway of the Embassy for an exchange that lasted five minutes or less," Richardson said. "He asked me if the CIA station had known beforehand of the planned raid. It was a no-win question for me, but I told him the truth, namely that we hadn't. His subsequent story correctly stated that CIA has been caught once again unawares."

Richardson did not know where Halberstam got the Nhu-did-it story.

"I was quite well acquainted with Nhu, and it seemed to me he deferred in a disciplined way to Diem's authority and leadership," Richardson said. "My guess would have to be that Diem made the decision whether it was left to Nhu to give the order or not."

In 1979, as in 1963, Richardson felt that the pagoda raids, and U.S. reaction to them, marked the crucial turning point in U.S.-Vietnamese relations, and he believed throughout that the raids were greatly overplayed by the American media.

"As I recall, not a single person was killed in the pagoda raid, nor do I remember anyone being seriously injured," Richardson said. "One U.S. public safety officer was reported to have been horrified as he witnessed a Vietnamese special forces officer kick a couple of Buddhist nuns in the rear as he bundled them on one of the trucks, but some of our own police around the nation don't do much better. Of course, all this occured before the race and student riots of the 1960s, and couple of burnings too, in our country, so Americans didn't have these experiences to compare with."

Richardson said, "If Nhu and Madame Nhu were urging a harder line on the Buddhists—as I think they were—I can't fault them from their point of view. In my opinion, then as now, the Buddhists were not seeking only redress of religious rights but the overthrow of the Diem government. They would not have been conciliated by concessions any more that the Shah's opposition was to be by the concessions in Iran in 1978."

Richardson said he believed that Halberstam and Sheehan were "young, crusading reporters who were out to get Nhu and quite possibly Diem and his government. I remember a cocktail party conversation once with Sheehan. I told him that we had carefully and continually canvassed alternative leadership possibilities and had found none. Did he want us to take a flying leap in the dark in the midst of a guerrilla war? His answer was, 'Yes.' "

On August 22 Halberstam filed the most sensational story of his career: "Highly reliable sources said here today that the decision to attack the Buddhist pagodas and declare martial law was planned and executed by Ngo Dinh Nhu, the president's brother, without the knowledge of the army."

Halberstam reported that the raid in Saigon was carried out by secret police and special forces partly dressed in uniforms of various branches of the Vietnamese army under the direction of "Colonel Le Quang Tung, a man personally loyal to Mr. Nhu."

Washington had been jolted by the pagoda raids, which violated an agreement Diem had reached with the Buddhists on June 16. An additional shock was that during the raids telephone connections were cut to the U.S. Embasssy and homes of senior American officials in Saigon. Harriman and Forrestal drafted a stiff public statement deploring the raids as "a direct violation by the Vietnamese government of assurances that it was pursuing a policy of reconciliation with the Buddhists." The CIA reported that, after General Tran Van Don had signed the martial law decree, the military appeared to have assumed control.

When Halberstam's Nhu-did-it-alone story arrived at the *Times,* diplomatic correspondent Tad Szulc was reporting a different version from Washington: "The United States government believes that a group of Vietnamese army commanders convinced President Ngo Dinh Diem that he should order a crackdown on the Buddhists and declare martial law. . . ." That is, the generals did it.

The *Times* did the honorable thing and printed both stories side by side under the headline:

Two Versions of the Crisis in Vietnam;
One Lays Plot to Nhu, Other to Army.[16]

Szulc's story, from State Department sources, said that five or six army commanders had called on Diem August 18 to warn that the situation was getting out of hand in the dispute with the Buddhists. The generals contended that a section of the Buddhist leadership opposed any conciliation, and that resolute military action was called for. The generals recalled that such action had put down the civil war with the Cao Dai and Hoa Hao religious sects in 1955.

Both Halberstam's and Szulc's stories sounded plausible. A great deal hinged on the outcome of which story would be accepted as the truth: the credibility of the Saigon press corps would be proved or broken by the decision, and, as it turned out, Diem, Nhu and Can would live or die by the verdict.

James Reston believed Halberstam's version. He cabled the beleaguered correspondent, "KEEP GOING BECAUSE WE'RE ONLY GETTING PROPAGANDA THIS END."

That day Halberstam reported growing anti-American sentiment in Saigon, and diplomatic sources saying that at least 100 priests, students and Boy Scouts had been killed or wounded in Hué, where government troops had demolished a giant statue of Buddha.

The U.S. media erupted with anti-Diem, anti-Nhu and anti-Mme. Nhu articles, editorials and columnists' commentaries.

The *Times*, in an unsigned portrait of Nhu on August 20—editions also carrying Halberstam's quotation of Nhu's alleged orders to raze the city—had quoted an "observer" as saying that Nhu is "a kind of Oriental Richelieu," and it noted he was "devious." It reported that Nhu controlled the secret police and the Revolutionary Labor Party, "many of whose members inform on their neighbors." The article quoted "a recently returned U.S. correspondent" as saying of Diem, Nhu and Mme. Nhu, "There has been no family like it since the Borgias."

Time magazine in its issue of August 12 also quoted the nameless correspondent, "There has been no family like it since the Borgias." The *Herald-Tribune* also quoted the anonymous phrasemaker on August 23: "There has been no family like it since the Borgias." *Newsweek* was late on the resurrection-of-the-Borgias scoop, and not until its issue of September 2 did *Newsweek* find the correspondent saying, "There has been no family like it since the Borgias." Catching up, *Newsweek* added that Nhu "is an arrogant, anti-American intellectual," who, in addition, had "a low, rasping voice." Mme. Nhu was "an acid-tongued termagant."

Editorial cartoonists joined in the attack. One of the milder cartoons, by Bill Mauldin, showed Diem steering a junk onto the rocks, its sail a U.S. flag. A pennant from the mast proclaimed, "U.S. prestige."

On August 24, four days after Halberstam first reported that the pagoda raids bore the stamp of Nhu, an unprecedented event occured in

Washington. The State Department admitted to reporters that its first briefings blaming the generals had been wrong; the Pentagon had been wrong; the CIA had been wrong. Halberstam and the Saigon press corps had known more: Nhu had done it. The free and unfettered American press had triumphed.

Times correspondent Hedrick Smith (not Szulc, who now looked a bit gullible for accepting the State Department's word) reported from Washington under the headline, "U.S. REASSESSING CRISIS IN VIET-NAM," the turnabout at the State Department:

"Officials here are moving to the conclusion that Ngo Dinh Nhu, brother of President Ngo Dinh Diem, brought about this week's crack-down on Buddhists in South Vietnam and is now the most powerful individual in the country."

Smith's report said:

> Embassy reports and other information from Saigon indicate that top Vietnamese generals did approve plans for martial law, but not for the raids on Buddhist pagodas, shootings and widespread arrests carried out by the Special Forces under Mr. Nhu's control. . . . If the disenchanted generals unite, they would repre-sent a grave threat to the president and Mr. Nhu.

Halberstam that day reported that the military governor of Saigon, Brigadier General Ton That Dinh (a Diem man) had closed the Univer-sity of Saigon and secondary schools. The report said, "It was reliably reported today that Major General Tran Van Don, who has been named acting chairman of the Joint General Staffs, is telling friends that he had no knowledge of the attacks on the pagodas and that he was a virtual prisoner when they took place. . . . "

The *Times* cabled the State Department's backdown to Halberstam: "STATE DEPARTMENT NOW COMING AROUND TO YOUR VIEW WHAT HAPPENED AND WHO DID IT AT PAGODAS STOP CHEERS CHEERS AND MORE CHEERS."

Halberstam yelled for Sheehan, and other reporters came too. In his book, Halberstam reported:

> Charlie Mohr said, 'You guys are the first reporters I've ever known who scooped the State Department by four days.'
>   Holding up the cables proudly, I said to Charlie, 'Well, that's the end of the press controversy out here. We've finally broken through. Now they'll understand.'[17]

Higgins was not appearing in the *Herald-Tribune*, which was run-ning wire service stories backing up her adversaries. She was writing her series and racing around Washington trying to fill in the holes.

Her six-part series began on August 26, and it was no longer a bomb-shell. It did not contain the main news story, the pagoda raids. It did not attack the Saigon group of correspondents; it only reported a completely different assessment of the war, of the Diem government and of the Buddhist political agitation. It reported that the war was going well, that Buddhist agitators with few followers were bent on over-throwing the government, that the furor in Saigon was mostly in print and bore no relationship to the calm in the countryside.

In an article on Buddhism and her interview with Thich Tri Quang, she wrote: "What did the Buddhists want? Diem's head, and not on a silver platter, but wrapped in an American flag."

Higgins' articles caused no ripples and drew no reader mail. She appeared to be an apologist for General Harkins, Ambassador Nolting and the Ngo family. Diem inadvertently reinforced her apologist image: he would not speak with Truehart, who, he said, had given asylum in the Embassy to a Communist agent, Thich Tri Quang, and instead of cabling President Kennedy with assurances that there had been no coup and that he remained in charge, he cabled that message to Higgins.

There would be further skirmishes and mopping up, but the Halberstam-Higgins war was over, with Higgins routed. Few in the media supported her observations. One who did was columnist Joseph Alsop, who was experienced in Asia, and he was attacked by an unlikely coalition of media commentators and Washington officials including Harriman and Hilsman. Alsop saw his credibility decline and his long Asian experience rendered useless.

Lodge had arrived in Saigon August 22 as Halberstam was filing his Nhu-did-it dispatch. Lodge arrived as a proconsul, carrying a letter from Kennedy putting all U.S. agencies there under his control, including the military mission and the CIA. He talked first with Buddhists, including Thich Tri Quang, who was in asylum in the Embassy, and did not seek out Diem. He later informed the State Department it was his policy to let Diem come to him.

A week later, the English-language *Times of Vietnam* published a wild-sounding story charging that the CIA was engaged in a coup plot with the blessing of high officials in the State Department, with the aim of establishing a puppet government. The State Department called the report "nonsense," and the CIA in Washington said it was "absolutely false."

The Vietnamese newspaper's report proved to be accurate in its main elements. The celebrated Cable of August 24 had given Lodge direct orders to proceed with a coup, and Lucien Conein would sit with the Vietnamese generals as it was carried out.

August 24 was a Saturday, and anyone who could get out of steaming Washington did so. President Kennedy, McCone, Rusk, McNamara and his deputy Gilpatric all were out of town. It was two days after Halberstam had published a plausible, detailed account of how Nhu had planned the pagoda raids in gesture of defiance of the United States.

Two events happened that day: Harriman, Hilsman, Forrestal and Ball drafted the Cable of August 24, which Ball would sign as Acting Secretary of State, and State Department officials conceded to reporters that it had been Nhu, not the generals, who raided the pagodas. The cable to Lodge instructed him to contact these same generals—now exonerated—for a coup.

The next day the Voice of America carried a broadcast in Vietnamese saying:

> Current information makes it clear that these attacks on the pagodas. . . were carried out by the police, supported by small groups of special forces not under the command of the Vietnamese armed forces. . . . High American officials blame police, headed by President Diem's brother Ngo Dinh Nhu, for anti-Buddhist actions in the Vietnam Republic. The officials say Vietnam military are not, repeat, not responsible for last week's attacks against pagodas and the mass arrest of monks and students. . . . The officials indicate that the U.S. may sharply reduce its aid to Vietnam unless President Diem gets rid of secret police officials responsible for the attacks. . . .

The VOA broadcast was repeated the next day in English.

Among those shaken by the inflammatory broadcasts were several Congressmen and Higgins, who knew exactly what was happening but could not get across a story of American duplicity.

She called VOA chief Edward R. Murrow, who instructed his spokesman Lowell Bennett to inform the media that the State Department had authorized, and in fact initiated the broadcasts. Hilsman had briefed Stewart Hensley, UPI's authoritative correspondent, giving him the U.S. position off the record. Then Hilsman called VOA to tell them that the information coming over their UPI ticker was authentic, even though no source was given, and VOA took it as an instruction to use the material.

The Cable of August 24 has in it, beside the fatal orders to Lodge, these phrases: "It is not clear that *whether* military proposed martial law or *whether* Nhu tricked them into it. . . ." and "We recognize the necessity of removing taint on the military for pagoda raids and *placing blame squarely on Nhu.* You are authorized to *have such statements made in Saigon* as you consider desireable to achieve this objective. . . ."[18] (My italics.)

But that means that the sudden switchback by the State Department was dictated by the political necessity of "removing taint on the military. . .and placing blame squarely on Nhu" "whether" he did it or not. The generals had to be absolved because they would be the next government of South Vietnam.

That, in turn, means that the Saigon press corps had not really been proven right, yet their public vindication set the tone for all of the anti-military, anti-U.S.-establishment reporting from Vietnam through 11 more years of war.

Malcolm Browne, who flew back to Saigon from his post in Yugo-slavia in 1975 as South Vietnam's end was near, did not want to talk about Vietnam when I spoke to him about it in 1978, "especially in view of the terrible way it ended there." Browne took part in negotiations with Communists at the end and was, like everyone, double-crossed. He and his Vietnamese wife were evacuated at the last minute. They still were trying, in 1978, to maintain contact with relatives there.

Still, I asked if Halberstam could have been set up with the Nhu-did-it story.

"Well, Nhu did do it," Browne said. "There never was any doubt about that. I think he even told me he did it a few weeks later." Browne said he talked with Nhu at a rally of Nhu's youth movement, and Nhu spoke "about the necessity of the pagoda raids," which Browne took to be confirmation that he had ordered them.

"Nhu did have some qualities," Browne said. "But he did the pagoda raids. I think he felt he had an authorization from Richardson, the station chief there." Browne said the raids were serious, even though "only ten or 12 people were killed all that summer," because "the Buddhists *are* a majority, maybe not all of them very religious. . . ."

Even if the order for the raids came from Nhu, there is no evidence that he "planned and executed them without the knowledge of the military." In view of Thich Tri Quang's subsequent agitation, there was apparent justification for the raids in wartime—raids intended to find and arrest him—but he escaped to asylum in the U.S. Embassy.

What is certain is that the State Department confirmed Halberstam's Nhu-did-it story without regard to whether it was true or not, and with evidence in State's hands against it.

During the Nixon administration's court fight against publication of the Pentagon Papers in 1971, the *Chicago Sun-Times* published on June 22, 1971, two memos it said Hilsman wrote to Rusk in that period of turmoil. One warned that Diem and Nhu might be opening "neutralization negotiations" with Hanoi, and the U.S. should let it be known "unequivocally that we shall hit (North Vietnam) with all that is necessary to force it to desist." In view of Diem's earlier defiance of Ho, it is surprising that Hilsman believed he was seeking negotiations.

The *Sun-Times* reported Hilsman's memo of August 30, 1963, urging that all of Diem's family be brought "under the control of the coup group," and said: "We should warn the coup group to press any military advantage it gains to its logical conclusion, without stopping to negotiate." The memo said that if Diem should make a last stand at the palace, the coup group should be encouraged "to fight the battle to the end and to destroy the palace if necessary to gain victory."

The memo advised, "Unconditional surrender should be the terms for the Ngo family. Diem should be treated as the generals wish."

The day after the *Sun-Times* report in 1971, Hilsman, then a Columbia University professor, held a press conference in New York to say that the first memo discussed contingency plans in the wake of what he said were Nhu's raids on the pagodas, and the second memo expressed "my personal feelings about what we should do." The memos do not appear in any versions of the Pentagon Papers.

By September 23, 1963, Maggie Higgins in Washington had gotten a piece of the story of the secret Cable of August 24. She reported, "A diplomatic cable that backfired in South Vietnam is the fuel stoking a white-hot Pentagon-State Department feud involving high Kennedy administration officials."[19]

She reported that Hilsman had prepared the cable, "a kind of invitation to the Vietnamese army to get rid of President Diem and his brother and sister-in-law, the highly publicized Ngo Dinh Nhus," and that Harriman had approved it while Defense Secretary McNamara was out of town and was not consulted. She had some details wrong; she had been told that Ambassador Lodge opposed the coup and put a brake on it. But when Higgins got mistaken information, she would correct it.

In fact, Lodge, only three days in Vietnam, had replied on August 25 advising against making any last-chance, futile appeal to Diem—it would only warn Nhu—and recommending that the approach to the generals be immediate. Contact was arranged through Conein—and the generals turned down the coup! They believed that too many troops were loyal to Diem, and they were not sure that the United States was in earnest.

In a series of cables to Washington, Lodge pushed for a quick coup: "We are launched on a course from which there is no respectable turning back: the overthrow of the Diem government."

On October 2, Higgins reported that the Cable of August 24 was more than a State-Defense dispute: the Hilsman-Harriman cable went out "while every key administration official was out of town, including President Kennedy, Mr. McNamara, Mr. Rusk and Central Intelligence Agency head John McCone."[20]

Her new information had shaken her faith in Lodge. She reported that Lodge had replied on August 25 that General Harkins would have the CIA check with the Vietnamese generals.

"But before the CIA could go into discrete action," Higgins reported, "the Voice of America had broadcast to the world on the night of August 25 what everyone inside Vietnam took to be a public invitation to the Vietnamese military to take over power inside the country. The broadcast was based on a background briefing given by Mr. Hilsman to two news agencies.

"What the CIA check learned was that the Vietnamese military officers, for all their anti-Diem talk, were not ready for revolt...."

Higgins' reports were cannonballs, but they were propelled by a half charge. The *Herald-Tribune* was dying, wounded by the 1962-63 strike that had cut its circulation to 600,000. Kennedy had cancelled 200 White House subscriptions to the newspaper, charging a pro-Republican bias in news selection. In 1966 the *Herald-Tribune* would go under, leaving no challenger in the area to the *Times*.

Lodge acknowledged on August 31 that the coup would not work. He proposed a program for getting Mme. Nhu and Archbishop Thuc to leave the country, to confine Nhu's functions to the strategic hamlet program, to appoint a prime minister and to release arrested Buddhists and students.[21] On the same day, a National Security Council meeting, with Rusk as chairman in Kennedy's absence, considered Lodge's proposals.

At the August 31 NSC meeting, Hilsman was on the defensive, with Kennedy absent. He was questioned by Nolting, McNamara and Taylor. Paul M. Kattenburg of State accused General Harkins of not pressing the generals for a coup, but Rusk defended Harkins, saying, "It would be better for us to start on the firm basis of two things—that we will not pull out of Vietnam until the war is won, and that we will not run a coup." McNamara agreed.[22]

Vice President Johnson, silent through the meeting, was asked to comment by Rusk. Johnson said he saw no alternative to Diem, and "we should stop playing cops and robbers."

VOA chief Murrow attended the meeting, commenting that the condemnation of the Diem regime was now worldwide. The observation was accurate: the VOA, the U.S. media, the State Department, Hanoi and the world resources of the Soviet system all were following the same line.

Following the meeting, Hilsman wrote a memo to Rusk on September 16, advising against moving to a "reconciliation track" in dealing with Diem. He wrote, "It will not be possible to switch from a 'reconcilation track' to a 'pressures and persuasion track' if the former does not work—except in the event that Diem and Nhu provide us with another dramatic act of repression as an excuse."[23] Hilsman repeated that Nhu was running the country.

In the awkward situation, with a coup authorized but no generals to carry it out, Kennedy scheduled a new visit to Vietnam by McNamara and Taylor. Lodge objected to their intrusion, and the President sent him a personal cable on September 18, saying that it would be made clear that "the visit is not designed to bring comfort to Diem."[24]

Walter Cronkite interviewed Kennedy on CBS on September 2. The President said, "I don't think that unless a greater effort is made by the government to win popular support that the war can be won out there. . . . With changes in policy and perhaps in personnel, I think (the government could regain the support of the people)." This was the President himself, not an indirect Hilsman statement over VOA, speaking to the world at large, and the remark was almost universally interpreted as a green light for a military coup. Aid to Colonel Tung's special forces already had been reduced quietly, which the Vietnamese generals took as the evidence they had required that the United States was in earnest.

McNamara and Taylor returned from their mission on October 2, to report that "the military campaign has made great progress and continues to progress." Their long and detailed report contained the obligatory browbeating of Nhu, but it also conceded that Diem needed him, and that Diem ran the country. The report mentioned the coup in a few words to oppose it: "We believe this course of action should not be undertaken at this time." If, as Hilsman and Arthur Schlesinger, Jr. contended later, Kennedy sent them to be convinced of the necessity of dumping Diem, they returned unconvinced.

On October 3, as Higgins reported details of the Cable of August 24,

Halberstam topped her with a story of more immediacy, if less history, from Saigon:

> Ambassador Henry Cabot Lodge and the head of Central Intelligence Agency operations in Saigon do not agree on United States policy in Vietnam.
>
> The Ambassador would be happier with a new CIA chief. (The present CIA chief in Saigon is believed to be John Richardson.)
>
> Informants here say Mr. Lodge had told Washington he wants a new chief, and that the CIA is fighting back hard. . . .
>
> Part of the present struggle over the CIA chief is believed to have a parallel in a struggle by Mr. Lodge against Major General Paul Harkins to establish himself as the real as well as the nominal head of the American mission here. . . . [25]

The next day, the *Times'* Max Frankel reported from Washington: "President Kennedy was reported today to have recalled 'for consultations' the head of Central Intelligence Agency operations in South Vietnam, presumably to end his policy dispute with Ambassador Henry Cabot Lodge." Frankel quoted sources familiar with State Department operations. [26]

That day McNamara was reporting to the Senate Armed Services committee. Higgins reported that McNamara testified U.S. agencies were working together well in Saigon, and that he found "no evidence of insubordination by the Central Intelligence Agency." [27]

The uproar was such that Kennedy moved to calm it, praising Richardson by name at a news conference. A subsequent investigation in Congress determined that Richardson had followed orders obediently and loyally. When the Pentagon Papers were published eight years later, a number of Richardson cables were included in the *Senator Gravel Edition* (not in the *Times* version) that indicated he was following orders to the extent of appearing to swing over to the anti-Diem line.

With Richardson gone, General Harkins was the last Diem supporter in Saigon among key Americans, and Lodge had cut him out of the cable traffic. When Harkins learned from a Pentagon cable that the coup plan still was alive, Kennedy, Harriman and Hilsman felt that the Defense Department was going behind their backs in communicating the information to its representative in Saigon. Harkins learned on October 30 that renewed efforts toward a coup were about to be effected. In a quick reply to General Taylor, he pleaded:

> In my contacts here I have seen no one with the strength of character of Diem, at least in fighting Communists. Certainly there are

no generals qualified to take over in my opinion. . . . After all, rightly or wrongly, we have backed Diem for eight long hard years. To me it seems incongruous now to get him down, kick him around and get rid of him. . . . Leaders of underdeveloped countries will take a dim view of our assistance if they too were led to believe the same fate lies in store for them.[28]

That same day Lodge and Kennedy adviser McGeorge Bundy exchanged a flurry of cables, Lodge urging that the coup be permitted to proceed. A Lodge cable noted at the end that Harkins did not concur.

The Saigon press corps had been waiting for a coup since August. In September, Halberstam and Sheehan dug into the story of Colonel Tung's special forces, which had been financed by the United States.

Money for Tung's forces already had been trimmed, and in Washington Senator Frank Church (D-Idaho), with Kennedy's approval, had introduced a resolution on September 12 condemning Diem for repressing Buddhists and calling for an aid cutoff unless Diem reformed.

In October, Halberstam and Sheehan wrote their findings about U.S. financial support of Tung and the partial cutoff. They pigeoned the stories out to Manila to be cabled there, with the request that their bylines not be used. Halberstam reported in his book that they had been warned Tung would take revenge, so they moved into the villa of information officer Mecklin, who by now was on the correspondents' side in the Diem controversy. On October 19 Tung was notified that his troops would receive further U.S. support only if they left Saigon, where they were protecting Diem, and engage the Viet Cong.

Time bureau chief Mohr had answered a request from his editors for a piece on the press controversy, but when he sent it, the article was not used. Instead, *Time* ran a press-section piece on September 20 that Halberstam charged had been dictated by editor Otto Fuerbringer. The *Time* piece said the correspondents:

. . . tend to band together in an unofficial club. . . . the country is completely alien to their experience. . . . None of them speak the language with any fluency. . . . The reporters have tended to reach unanimous agreement on almost everything they have seen. But such agreement is suspect because it is so obviously inbred.

A few weeks ago a correspondent flew out from the U.S. to Saigon for a first hand look and, ignoring the assessments of the resident correspondents, reached independent conclusions. Club members were furious. (The newcomer's interpretation of the Buddhist crisis) was greeted in the Caravelle bar by simmering indignation.

Mohr and Mert Perry demanded a retraction of equal length, and then both resigned from *Time*.

Their resignations packed a punch, even if the effect would wear off. A basic rule of journalism (it's my rule, too) is that the correspondent is always right and the editor at home is always wrong. Every rule has an exception, and it was not clear if this was the exception. *Time* was in an uproar, even though correspondents' copy is routinely rewritten there.

Time's editors sued for peace, running another press-section piece on October 11, regretting Mohr's resignation and partially apologizing for roughing up the Saigon group. It featured a combat-scene group photo of Halberstam, Sheehan and Browne, and it noted that Halberstam, along with Grant Wolfkill and John Sharkey of NBC, had been beaten by police who seized their cameras.

The new *Time* piece heaped praise on Halberstam, quoting a White House adviser as suggesting that "The *Times'* Halberstam is a more trustworthy source of information than all the official cables available in Washington." It noted that James Reston had said, "Halberstam is brilliant," and Louis Lyons, curator of Nieman fellowships at Harvard, called him "absolutely prophetic."

Time's apology was not entirely abject. It noted that Browne and Sheehan had been in heated arguments with their home offices over their coverage, and that AP had told Browne to take a month off and cool down. It asked whether the correspondents "have given their readers an unduly pessimistic view of the progress of the war and the quality of the Diem government?"

But it noted that Lodge had said, "The regular press corps here is appealing, brave and tremendously hard-working."

Mme. Nhu, meanwhile, had reached the United States on a tour she hoped would help explain the Diem government's position. Her hard-hitting language, which she thought to be the way one got through to Americans, backfired when it came from a foreigner. At Harvard, a

crowd of 17,000 persons hissed her when she criticized American behavior in Vietnam, and 500 students outside the auditorium picketed,
threw eggs and rattled the windows as she spoke.

An editorial cartoon showed her on television, finger raised in a lecturing pose, while a viewer winced and held his head, muttering,
"From morning 'til night." Bill Mauldin's cartoon showed her with a
rope, pulling down a giant statue of Buddha.

Higgins was in Germany as the Saigon coup moved toward its denouement. On the day of the coup, she arrived in Washington with the
first interview Adenauer had given since his retirement. Adenauer had
told her that America showed itself "much too afraid" at the time the
Berlin Wall went up. He said that "for 60 hours the mayor of Berlin
could not get any response out of Washington . . . the Americans even
tried to tell us it was a good thing because the flow of refugees was
stopped . . . It was a tremendous success for Moscow. . . . You cannot
imagine the despair of the German people."[29]

Higgins had left the *Herald-Tribune* for *Newsday*, where she would
have the freedom of a columnist. Her column picked up 62 subscribers, a narrow base from which she would continue to do battle
against the victors of Saigon.

Halberstam was tipped off that a coup was under way with a cryptic
message sent to him and Sheehan from a source he did not name:
"Please buy me a bottle of whiskey at the PX." He sent a coded message to Sheehan, who had obeyed reluctantly his editors' orders to
take a rest in Japan. On November 1 the troops of General Tran Van
Don and General Duong Van (Big) Minh attacked the Presidential Palace. Diem and Nhu, anticipating the coup attempt, were not there, but
in the home of a Chinese friend in the Cholon district.

At 4:30 p.m. on November 1, Diem telephoned Lodge. He said:
"Some units have made a rebellion and I want to know what is the attitude of the United States?"

Lodge: "I do not feel well enough informed to be able to tell you. I
have heard the shooting, but am not acquainted with all the facts. Also,
it is 4:30 a.m. in Washington, and the U.S. government cannot possibly
have a view."

Diem: "But you must have some general ideas. After all, I am a chief
of state. I have tried to do my duty. I want to do now what duty and
good sense requires. I believe in duty above all."

Lodge: "You have certainly done your duty. As I told you only this
morning, I admire your courage and your great contribution to your

country. No one can take away from you the credit for all you have done. Now I am worried about your physical safety. I have a report that those in charge of the current activity offer you and your brother safe conduct out of the country if you resign. Have you heard this?"

Diem: "No. (pause) You have my telephone number."

Lodge: "Yes. If I can do anything for your personal safety, please call me."

Diem: "I am trying to re-establish order."[30]

Neither the military governor of Saigon, General Dinh, nor the delta commander, General Cao, responded to Diem's calls. When the palace battle had gone on for 14 hours, Diem and Nhu surrendered on the basis of Lodge's and the generals' guarantees of safe conduct. They were murdered in an armored car. Colonel Tung surrendered and was taken into a garden and shot in the head.

The American press corps in Saigon reported jubilant crowds in the streets. European correspondents in Saigon reported that the crowds were thin and under organized direction.

There was no official U.S. expression of regret.[31] Mme. Nhu, who had been ostracized in Washington, where Kennedy did not permit his wife to see her, was in Los Angeles, the last stop on her tour to win hearts and minds. She called Maggie Higgins in Washington, and Higgins contacted the State Department to get her children out of Vietnam.[32]

Mme. Nhu received a call in Los Angeles from attorney Richard Nixon in New York, who said he was heartsick at the reports. Nixon had been in Paris the week before the coup, where he told reporters that "the choice is not between President Diem and somebody better, it is between Diem and somebody infinitely worse." He discussed with Mme. Nhu Diem's brother Can, who had been refused asylum in Hué and was flown on a U.S. military plane to Saigon, where Vietnamese officers arrested him and returned him to Hué for trial. Nixon later wrote that Diem's assassination was "a sordid episode in American history."

Nixon inquired in Washington without effect. At the Vatican, Archbishop Thuc asked Pope Paul VI to help his brother, and the Pope contacted Lodge in Saigon. Lodge went to Hué to speak with Thich Tri Quang, his recent guest in the Embassy, about clemency, but the monk refused. Can was tried and executed. So was Major Dang Sy, who had tried to quell the riot at the Hué radio station the preceding May.

Diem had not been a dictator or even much of an intimidator. He had invited United Nations investigators. His secret police were more akin to Western plain-clothes men than to totalitarian secret police, and they had not even been able to intimidate Thich Tri Quang. Diem had resisted intimidation throughout his life.

Those who overthrew Diem from the United States would say that it all had been unnecessary, that Diem had been too unyielding.[33] But once the U.S. media was united against what it thought was the Borgia family, Diem was beyond help. Banishing his brother and sister-in-law would not have helped, but would have brought on a coup by nationalists among the generals who would have seen Diem as weak. Appeasing Thich Tri Quang was not possible short of turning the government over to him. Kennedy had decided in June that Diem had to go and had begun withdrawing Diem supporters from the U.S. Embassy before the Buddhist crisis became acute.

Halberstam was thought to be in danger from Diem loyalists, and with Diem's death he vanished from the pages of the *Times* for a time. Diem's obituary, under headlines including, "MANY TERMED HIM A WEAK ALLY" and "His Anti-Communism Was Regarded as Insufficient to Offset Drawbacks," was written by Robert Trumbull, chief of the *Times* Southeast Asia bureau, from Hong Kong.

A year after Diem died, Keyes Beech of the *Chicago Daily News* stopped at the bar of the Hotel Royal in Phnom Penh with Dennis Bloodworth of *The Observer* of London for a drink or two. Beech, who would stay on until the end in 1975 and become the dean of Saigon reporters, had respected Diem. Beech said he was "the only true Vietnamese nationalist of stature in South Vietnam," but his reports were not seen in the New York media center.

Also drinking at the Hotel Royale bar was Wilfred Burchett, the pro-Communist Australian, accredited to *L'Humanité* in Paris and widely published in Communist newspapers throughout the world. Burchett had worked for London newspapers including *The Times* before switching to the Communist side. He had reported the Korean war from North Korea and was charged by American prisoners with joining in interrogations and intimidation. Australia had lifted his passport, and Burchett traveled on a Cuban passport given him by Fidel Castro, while maintaining apartments in Moscow and Phnom Penh. Burchett, perhaps the only Westerner who has written for both *Pravda* and *The New York Times* Op-Ed page, had for years described Diem as a despot, weakling and tool of American imperialism, but recently he had seen his attacks on Diem equaled or surpassed by Halberstam, Sheehan and even Robert Shaplen of *The New Yorker*.

"Burchett was loaded," Beech said, "or he wouldn't have been so expansive. I forget why I was sober enough to remember all this. Among other things, he told me the Chinese had one of our Sidewinders, a dud fired by a Chinese Nationalist plane at a Chinese MiG during the Quemoy flareup in 1958.''

Burchett said he was in South Vietnam with the National Liberation Front when Diem was assassinated, and they thought it was a hoax. When Nguyen Huu Tho, head of the NLF, was convinced that Diem was dead, Burchett quoted him as saying, ''The Americans have managed to do what we couldn't do for nine years.''

Beech filed that story, and this time the wire services picked up his dispatch. He quoted Burchett as saying that the assassination of Diem was a wholly unexpected gift to the Communists that marked the turning point in the war.

Burchett had said: ''Diem was a national leader, and you never will be able to replace him—never.''[34]

Sixteen years later, Beech reflected that Burchett had proved right: ''Diem never was replaced.''[35]

Chapter X
The Alibi Books

"I don't care about meeting the chief editor; I want to meet the feuilleton editor."

—*19th Century French Politicians' Cliché*

When President Kennedy was murdered in Dallas on November 22, 1963, the world was a more insecure place that it had been three years earlier.

Castro was unchallenged in Cuba, allied with the Soviet Union and an example for imitators in Central America and the Caribbean. Nasser's army was seizing towns in Yemen and threatening Saudi Arabia. Laos, the priority problem at the beginning of 1961, had been "neutralized" and was beyond help. In Indonesia, where a diplomatic mission by Robert Kennedy had hastened the exodus of the Dutch, Sukarno was leaning on the Indonesian Communist Party and about to ally himself with China.

Germany's division had been accepted, leaving West Berlin a vulnerable financial burden. Adenauer and Macmillan resigned a month before Kennedy's death, signals that Social Democratic and Labor governments would come to power, bringing with them an anti-NATO bias in their left wings. NATO languished in neglect, its headquarters soon to be expelled from France. De Gaulle was telling allies that the United States could not be counted on in an emergency, and in September he had said, "France sympathizes with the tribulations of the Vietnamese people" and would offer "cordial cooperation with all Vietnam in ridding it of foreign influence."

Losers littered the scene in the West, but there were some winners. In the spring of 1964, Halberstam shared the Pulitzer Prize with Malcolm W. Browne of AP. James Reston had "gone to bat" for him before the Pulitzer committee, Halberstam noted, although he thought that Neil Sheehan should have won the prize. Halberstam also won the Overseas Press Club's George Polk award for courageous reporting and the Louis Lyons award from Harvard's Nieman Foundation. Sheehan won the Sigma Delta Chi award, giving the Saigon press group a clean sweep of major awards. Eight years later Sheehan would win the Sigma Delta Chi and George Polk awards, among others, for the *Times* series on the Pentagon Papers.

The *Times* hired Browne and Charles Mohr and dispatched Halberstam to Warsaw. The *Times* later took on Sheehan at Halberstam's urging, and would round out what became its anti-war team with Seymour M. Hersh, who exposed the My Lai atrocity without having been to Vietnam.

Maggie Higgins, a loser, had left *The New York Herald-Tribune* a month before Kennedy's death to write a syndicated column. She learned in Hong Kong of Kennedy's death and cabled a reaction story that reflected her grief. Kennedy had been a friend, and although she had begun to uncover the story behind the coup that killed Diem, she had not thought to implicate the President.

The day before Kennedy died, Higgins had been in Phnom Penh, listening to a two-hour speech by Prince Sihanouk. He ended it by asking the crowd: "Are we going to take foreign aid from the United States that gives us aid with one hand and stabs us in the back with the other?" The crowd chanted back, "Never! Never!"

Higgins quoted a diplomat in Phnom Penh: "Since November 1, the prince has convinced himself that what the United States did to Diem in Vietnam might one day be tried against him, if he crossed Washington's will." The United States had been sending Sihanouk about $30 million a year. Sihanouk renounced it, and the number of official Americans in Cambodia dropped from 300 to 20 as Sihanouk turned increasingly toward China.

In the aftershock of Kennedy's assassination, Americans spared little attention for what was happening in Vietnam and Cambodia, but Higgins doggedly kept on tracking down the origins of Diem's death and the accompanying debacle in Southeast Asia. It was a valiant effort that would cost her life, but now the effort was doomed. It could not be done without blackening the name of the martyred President, too much for the nation to take.

Kennedy's aides and advisers were more aware than most of the condition of the world in 1964. All administrations leave historical memoirs, but the books of the Kennedy administration's heralds came out urgently and in quantity, along with books by the Saigon press corps. There was much to be explained, and all of the alibi books were praised by *The New York Times Book Review*, certification that made it incumbent on schools and public libraries to make them available permanently.

The book review is one of the most powerful weapons of a strong publication in periods when journalism is the continuation of war by other means. The *Times'* lock on book reviews is one of its keys to power, the others being its large foreign staff and the *Times*-government interchangeable men. *Times* book reviews are "the daily literary fix of millions" (Eliot Fremont-Smith), and the weekly *Book Review* is also sold by separate subscription. Often more people read the *Times* book review than read the book, so that the reviewer's opinion has more weight than the author's.

In the esoteric field of foreign affairs, other reviewers waited for the *Times* before judging a book, just as many newspapers, like the *New York Daily News*, accepted the *Times'* judgment on daily foreign events. A *Times* book review reaches an influential audience: intelligent, susceptible to becoming engaged, varied enough to include those not already persuaded. Major book publishers are in the *Times* circulation area, and are inclined to refuse a manuscript that they know will not be reviewed by the *Times*.

The Kennedy era alibi books offer an insight into the leverage of *Times* book reviews, where the editors also had the newspaper's credibility to defend.

Reviewing the Book Reviews

The Making of a Quagmire, David Halberstam, Random House, New York, 1965.
The Best and the Brightest, David Halberstam, Random House, 1972.

The *Times* reviewed *The Making of a Quagmire* twice, once in the daily by Eliot Fremont-Smith (April 19, 1965) and once by Halberstam's friend from Saigon, Professor Bernard Fall, in the Sunday *Book Review* (May 16, 1965).

The Fremont-Smith review was coupled with mention of Malcolm Browne's *The New Face of War* (Bobbs Merrill, Indianapolis), which had a preface by Henry Cabot Lodge, and it noted that the Browne and Halberstam books confirmed each other.

Fall's review was coupled with a discussion of John Mecklin's *Mission in Torment* (Doubleday, New York), and the books reinforced each other even though Halberstam was a reporter and Mecklin an official on the other side of the desk, apparently a double confirmation of authenticity.

Both reviews stressed Halberstam's love and affection for the Vietnamese people, with the implication that those in Saigon who had disagreed with him had none. Fall went out of his way to cite Halberstam's condemnations of Ambassador Nolting, General Harkins and Admiral Felt, and to add Mecklin's scorn for McNamara, Rusk and General Taylor. Fall did not mention the names of Hilsman, Harriman, Thich Tri Quang or Ngo Dinh Nhu, and neither reviewer mentioned the scoop that made Halberstam's name a household word, his Nhu-did-it report on the pagoda raids. Fall touched on the press war in one line, mentioning that Halberstam smarted under ". . . the glib charges of a passing female colleague, of a syndicated columnist and of a *Time* rewrite."[1]

Both reviews were advertising copy and were sophisticated enough to sell a lot of soap.

A dissenting review:

Halberstam at first reading is an engaging writer, and *The Making of a Quagmire* starts off as a "good read." It is a tale of correspondents' derring-do, first in the Congo: Halberstam, caught in a crossfire between United Nations and Congolese troops, learns from a laconic Fleet Street reporter that the snipers must be Indian UN troops; neither the Swedes nor the Congolese could come that close. In Vietnam, Halberstam is amusingly self-deprecating: when he steps off his first helicopter into a rice paddy wearing his Abercrombie & Fitch jungle gear, he sinks straight down to his neck. A reader likes Halberstam.

But after this promising opening, no more clowning. The stakes soon become enormous, and a reader may feel he already has seen the movie. Halberstam discovered that the country was run by a dictatorial president who paid homage to himself and had little instinct for his people. Diem once had been a decent sort, but his sinister brother Nhu

and his sister-in-law Madame Nhu, whose pointed fingernails dug cruelly into the upholstery as she talked of Buddhists, had cut Diem off
from the people. Halberstam did not see her exercising her claws on
the upholstery, but heard at second hand of such a television film shot.

Halberstam reports unsubstantiated gossip from "palace sources."
Mme. Nhu called Diem a coward and hurled a tureen of soup across
the table at him; Nhu reportedly used opium and heroin.

The ruling family was losing the war by refusing to permit the army
to fight, and it had the effrontery to expel critical correspondents.
(Halberstam eventually was expelled himself, but from Poland, by
President Jozef Cyrankiewicz, with no fuss, no muss.) The family had
cowed the U.S. Ambassador, the head of the American military mission
and the CIA station chief, all of whom were sending misinformation to
Washington.

On his first combat trip in October 1962, Halberstam met Lieutenant
Colonel John Paul Vann, adviser to the commander of the Vietnamese
Seventh Division, Colonel Huyhn Van Cao, a vain man and Diem's protege. Because Vann's headquarters were in the Mekong delta only 25
miles from Saigon, he became the officer most correspondents saw
first in the field. Vann felt that Diem's refusal to accept casualties hobbled the troops' aggressiveness, and Cao and other commanders
would not follow up strikes or fight at night. Vann later left the Army in
anger, his briefing unheard by the Joint Chiefs of Staff in Washington.
Halberstam blamed Marine Corps General Victor Krulak, who became
a personal enemy, for blocking Vann's report to the JCS. Vann returned
to Vietnam as an armed AID official and was killed in a helicopter crash
in 1972.

Halberstam had been eight months in Vietnam when the Buddhist
crisis broke in May 1963 in Hué, where no correspondents saw it
happen.

"In the beginning it was primarily religious, with limited objectives;
in the end it was primarily a political movement clearly trying to
bring down the government, to which all dissident elements in the
country had rallied," Halberstam wrote. Many disagreed that it ever
was religious, and the dissident elements that rallied to it were the
correspondents.

In August, Halberstam was approached to take part in a coup against
Diem.

"One day in August an important Vietnamese whom I trusted said
he wanted me to have lunch with him and one of his friends. . . . I was
told that my two companions were part of the young officers'
coup . . . they told me they wanted me to cover the story from the
inside."

Halberstam was to be "kidnapped" so he would have an alibi if the coup should fail, and was given a military radio. "I left them to consider the proposal for a while, talked with Sheehan, decided that journalistically it was worth the risk for such a story, and agreed. . . ."

The coup did not materialize, but Halberstam's willingness to participate no doubt circulated through Saigon's intelligence circles. He might as well have advertised in the local newspapers: "Disinformation accepted."

Halberstam went into detail on his major story, that Nhu ordered and organized the pagoda raids, and into the State Department's vindication of his world beat four days later, but offers no confirmation that his "assumption" was accurate.

He discussed the Cable of August 24, writing in 1965, after Higgins had described it accurately in the *Herald-Tribune,* but his description bears little resemblance to the cable as produced in the Pentagon Papers six years later:

> . . . the State Department reportedly instructed Lodge to tell the generals that their question about action in the event of Nhu dealing with Hanoi was of course hypothetical, but that the United States was always interested in supporting anti-Communist governments. This message received broad support: by Roswell Gilpatric. . . by Richard Helms. . . by Rusk and George Ball and by the President at the White House. When Mike Forrestal, head of the Vietnam Task Force who drafted the cable, called General Krulak at the Pentagon about Taylor's position, Krulak verbally gave Taylor's approval. . . .

No description could be more misleading or full of errors of detail.

By 1965, Halberstam and Hilsman were allies, and Hilsman also would write of suspicions that Nhu intended to deal with Hanoi. Maggie Higgins would deny that Krulak approved the cable, and Hilsman's version appeared to bear her out.

For all the self-confidence Halberstam displayed in *Quagmire,* defensive notes crept in: ". . . when the Pulitzer Prize for foreign reporting was awarded to Mal Browne and me in the spring of 1964, it had a very special meaning for me; the Supreme Court within our own profession had upheld the right of a reporter to follow his conscience even in a delicate situation such as this." Halberstam wrote, rightly, that other major newspapers did not meet their obligations in the period: "If some of us had more jounalistic power than was merited, it had been granted us purely by default."

There is a striking omission in *Quagmire*. Although the Buddhist revolt is at the center of the story; Thich Tri Quang, given asylum by

Truehart in the U.S. Embassy and protected there for 10 weeks by Lodge, is mentioned only once, when he is identified as the Buddhist leader of Hué—*Othello* without Iago.

There is a fundamental discrepancy between *Quagmire* in 1965 and *The Best and the Brightest* in 1972. Halberstam first wrote that none of the correspondents questioned the necessity of the United States to be in Vietnam:

> What about withdrawal? Few Americans who have served in Vietnam can stomach the idea. It means that those Vietnamese who committed themselves fully to the United States will suffer the most under a Communist government, while we lucky few with blue passports will remain unharmed; it means a drab, lifeless and controlled society[2] for a people who deserve better. Withdrawal means that the United States prestige will be lowered throughout the world. . .the enemies of the West will be encouraged to try insurgencies like the one in Vietnam. . . .

But in 1972 he wrote: ". . .affected primarily by two men, my friend Neil Sheehan and my colleague Bernard Fall. . .in the fall of 1963 I had come to the conclusion that it was doomed and that we were on the wrong side of history."

In *Quagmire,* Halberstam recalled an incident that shook the correspondents' community in the Congo. Two reporters saw from a distance what they thought was Secretary-General Dag Hammarskjold disembarking from a plane and reported his arrival. But Hammarskjold's plane had crashed; he was dead. The mistake was easy to make, and Halberstam shuddered at the thought that he might have made it if he had been there, aborting his career.

In recounting the incident was Halberstam trying to tell us something? He had seen little, at a distance, of the raid on the Xa Loi pagoda, described it graphically, suggested deaths where there had been none. In Washington a group of conspirators read his "stamp of Nhu" report, and the next day in Saigon someone told Halberstam that Nhu had done it, and it had nothing to do with the army. The dispatch lit a fuse that set off a chain of explosions that lasted until 1975, but it did not end Halberstam's career, it propelled him to fame.

The *Times* made *The Best and the Brightest* its cover review in the Sunday *Book Review*: "Halberstams' most important and impressive book." Reviewer Victor S. Navasky had some small reservations: Halberstam had "only partly answered the vastly ambitious questions he set for himself," and he had adopted the New Journalism in assuming he knew what thoughts passed through Lyndon Johnson's mind. But Navasky concluded that Halberstam's judgment must be sound because "he has been there, and he has been back." (Halberstam visited South Vietnam briefly for *Harper's* magazine in 1967.)

A dissenting review:

The Best and the Brightest started as a series of profiles Halberstam wrote for *Harper's* and *Esquire* on McNamara, General William Westmoreland, McGeorge Bundy, William P. Bundy, General Taylor and George Ball (the very brightest). It turned into the Vietnam book again; one alibi did not suffice. The first half of the book is a reprise of *Quagmire,* now with Washington counterparts to the Saigon players. The second half is a catalog of Johnson administration failures presented to reinforce the theme that the war was unwinnable.

By 1972 Halberstam was defending positions like those of Harriman, Hilsman, Forrestal and Ball, outcasts of the Johnson administration. He was ready to publish in 1971, when the Pentagon Papers appeared, requiring revisions, and Halberstam was irritated that Sheehan had not tipped him to the existence of the Pentagon Papers.

The Cable of August 24 was in print, and now Halberstam interpreted it this way:

> With the Vietnamese military pressuring the Americans to absolve the army from responsibility for the (pagoda) crackdown, the Voice of America soon began broadcasting honest assessments, placing the blame on the Nhus. In addition, Lodge received a cable from Washington saying that the Nhus must go. . . . It was, in effect, the go-ahead signal for a coup. . . . The cable had been drafted by Harriman, Forrestal, Hilsman and George Ball on Saturday, August 24, at the President's suggestion.

(Originally Halberstam had been told Forrestal drafted it; now Hilsman enters, but third in the list.)

Halberstam also had learned of Lansdale's report of January 17, 1961 (ignored by the *Times*), which came out this way:

> Lansdale wrote a lengthy and very pessimistic report critical of both the Americans and Diem, but particularly of the former. This was important, because Lansdale was one of the men who had invented Diem, and you do not knock your own invention, but more significant, it was indicative of the Lansdale approach and that of other Good Americans, those sympathetic to Asians. . . . He recommended a new antibureaucratic team in the Lansdale mode. . . . What Lansdale was recommending was, of course, Lansdale.

Halberstam's admiration had grown for Harriman, Ball and Lodge, whose arranging of the coup was "shrewd, forceful and tough." His attitude had hardened toward those of another persuasion. Lansdale had committed mindless and petty sabotage in 1954. Walt Rostow was "an anti-Red tiger." McNamara was, "there is no kinder word for it, a fool." Harkins was "a man of no real reputation of his own" and "a man of compelling mediocrity. He had mastered one thing, which was how to play the Army game, how to get along, how not to make a superior uncomfortable." Halberstam did not report that Harkins was General George C. Patton's right-hand man in World War II, and had been chief of staff of the 8th Army in Korea. Harkins' last message in defense of Diem must have made all of his superiors uncomfortable, including the President.

Nolting, Halberstam's original target, who had been so fiercely attacked by Harriman in Washington discussions that President Kennedy stepped in, "left government to become an international representative of the Morgan bank (and to write various newspapers a commemorative letter on the annual occasion of Diem's death, a date which in the country Nolting professed to love had become a national holiday)." Actually, until South Vietnam fell in 1975, crowds coming out annually for memorial services for Diem increased year by year.

A Thousand Days, Arthur Schlesinger, Jr., Houghton Mifflin, Boston, 1965.

It was not surprising that the *Times* headlined one of its three reviews of *A Thousand Days*, "A Magnificent History."[3] Schlesinger was almost the same as a ranking staff member of the *Times,* his by-line having appeared in the *Book Review* and Op-Ed page more often than many *Times* staffers of equally long tenure. The book was a *tour de force*, 1,087 crammed pages completed in 14 months, indispensible to historians for its chronology and dialogues if not for its insights.

When Schlesinger's book came out in 1965, there was an unfortunate prelude to the *Times* reviews. *Life* was publishing trimmed installments of the book, and newspaper commentators accused Schlesinger of "writing for personal profit and political revenge" and to promote the candidacy of his friend, Bobby Kennedy. Schlesinger was attacked on television by Vice President Hubert Humphrey for denigrating President Johnson. Schlesinger deleted from the book a scene in which Kennedy wept in Jackie's arms after the Bay of Pigs, a scene called offensive after *Life* published it.

Before reviewing the book, the *Times* defused the situation with a long magazine piece on the *Life* controversy by William V. Shannon, one of the *Times*-government interchangeable men who was then a member of the editorial board and later Ambassador to Ireland. Shannon's warm and intimate treatment of Schlesinger set the stage for the reviews, was a pre-publication review in itself, and offered plugs from famous persons: Yale historian John M. Blum saying, "Schlesinger is a superb historian...one of the three or four best men working on things American." It noted that Schlesinger's best friend was the ever-popular Galbraith.

Next up to bat was the daily reviewer, Fremont-Smith: "...this is the book we all have been waiting for...at once a masterly literary achievement and a work of major historical significance....Mr. Schlesinger demonstrated how great history is conceived and written."[4]

The Sunday *Book Review* critic was historian and presidential biographer James MacGregor Burns, who found the book "remarkable... astounding...exciting," an achievement that "caught both the sweep and ferment of the thousand days."[5] Personalities were presented in "diamond-sharp vignettes." Without getting into the book's substance, Burns concluded, "A great President has found—perhaps he deliberately chose—a great historian."

A dissenting review:

Arthur Schlesinger, Jr.'s appointment as President Kennedy's special adviser in 1961 caused Reuben Maury, the *Daily News* editorialist, to write: "Junior is an Egghead to end all Eggheads. We shudder to think what might turn up in the President's speeches."

White House intellectual, sober-faced jester in a court that could appreciate an intellectual pratfall, lunching weekly with the President, inquisitive and bright, Schlesinger produced more a eulogy than a chronicle, but he revealed a full bookload of gossip.

The flaw in *A Thousand Days* is that it purports to be the inside story, but it is not. Either Schlesinger overestimated the degree of intimacy the Kennedy brothers allowed him, or he misjudged them, because the book does not reflect issues that later turned out to have occupied the Kennedys' minds, such as the attempts to kill Castro and Kennedy's real reaction to meeting Khrushchev in Vienna. There is a body of opinion that holds Schlesinger is too brilliant to be as naive as he pretends to be. He was, in any case, too talky to be trusted with seeing sensitive cable traffic.

Schlesinger did have influence in one area, but he plays down his role as an important adviser on Cuba. He agonizes over his failure to oppose forcefully the Bay of Pigs venture. He wrote that there never was any plan for U.S. air cover, so no air cover was "withdrawn," a charge that never was made; the charge was that Kennedy cancelled planned exile air strikes.

He appears to take seriously Nikita Khrushchev's alleged anxiety, expressed to Walter Lippmann, that West Germany would acquire nuclear weapons and "invade East Germany," the last thing on any German's mind. He denigrates Adenauer's reaction to the Wall: "He did not at the time propose any form of direct action against the Wall...and referred vaguely to a NATO embargo of the Communist bloc...." He dismisses the Grewe incident in a manner as high-handed as Salinger's.

Why Schlesinger could not be an insider was illustrated by his relations with "my friend Kornienko," a Soviet diplomat-operative. His descriptions of meetings with Kornienko are in discord with reports published elsewhere that Schlesinger, as an OSS agent in Paris, was the alert anti-Communist who spotted the Soviet agent and pacifist Noel Field, who even fooled Allen Dulles.

As the Bay of Pigs invasion cranked up, and a Cabinet go-ahead was expected on April 12, 1961, Schlesinger recalled:

> The meeting of April 12 was preceded by a strange incident whose significance even today remains undecipherable to me. I received a call from Georgi Kornienko, the counsellor of the Soviet Embassy, for an immediate appointment. Soon a sharp-eyed, moon-faced man appeared, speaking fluent but somewhat informal English...he said courteously that he did not fully understand the policy of the United States toward Latin America, and especially toward Cuba....I came to know Kornienko better in time, and we used to lunch together at regular intervals until he returned to Moscow at the end of 1963. These luncheons were never very productive.

Later, Schlesinger noted, "On July 5,[6] I received a visit from my friend Kornienko....(he) expressed himself as puzzled by the American attitude toward Berlin....Finally, he said, 'the real trouble is that you don't believe we are sincere when we say that we honestly wish to keep things as they are in West Berlin within the new context....'"

On the basis of his talk with his friend Kornienko, Schlesinger wrote a memo to try to steer the President off the hard line on Berlin that Acheson was pressing. Schlesinger's paper included the questions, "Where do we want to come out if we win the test of wills? German reunification, for example; what is our real objective toward this traditional objective?" Thus the harmless bystander played a role in writing off reunification at the suggestion of a Soviet agent.

On the Cable of August 24, Schlesinger reported that Kennedy saw the draft at Hyannis Port "without knowing that Rusk, McNamara and McCone had not okayed it"—as though Kennedy were the employee and they the bosses. Schlesinger quoted Lodge as saying that the coup was like a rock rolling downhill. It could have been stopped only by aggressive American intervention against the Vietnamese army on behalf of Diem and Nhu. No one in the administration, however naive, could have believed that in 1965.

Schlesinger relied on Halberstam, Hilsman, Lodge and the President for his version of Vietnam in 1963, and he had all the details wrong from the May riot in Hué ("Diem's troops fired indiscriminately into the crowd, leaving a moaning mass of dead and wounded") to the denouement: "It is important to state clearly that the coup of November 1, 1963, was entirely planned and carried out by the Vietnamese. Neither the American Embassy nor the CIA were involved in instigation or execution."

Kennedy, Theodore C. Sorensen, Harper and Row, New York, 1965.

Sorensen was the first Kennedy man to resign in the Johnson administration and the first to publish a serious history, beating Schlesinger by a month, but he got relatively short shrift in the *Times* reviews. He was not a *Times* man, and perhaps the book review editors did not want to preempt the Schlesinger reviews.

The *Times* daily reviewer, Charles Poore, called *Kennedy* "one of the fundamental source books of our time," and a "tremendously impressive portrait of John F. Kennedy," but he stressed personal anecdotes and did not go overboard on the book's significance.[7] James MacGregor Burns, a friend of Schlesinger who had *A Thousand Days* coming up for review, gave *Kennedy* a good ride in the Sunday *Book Review*, but picked a number of nits. "Sorensen writes from so central a vantage point in Kennedy's inner circle that he knows a great deal— but his perspective is stunted.... He judges friend and foe with all the subjectivity that Kennedy would have, but without the authenticity and perhaps the generosity...."[8]

My review:

Sorensen was so different from the rest of Kennedy's team that his individuality commands respect. Younger than the others, not an Ivy Leaguer, a Nebraskan who had not been outside the country when he went to work for Kennedy in 1953, a liberal whose political future would be blocked because he registered with his draft board as a conscientious objector at the time of the Korean war, he nevertheless was more an insider than Schlesinger was.

Sorenson's book defends Kennedy with a to-the-bitter-end tenacity, rather than with the killer instinct toward apostates shown by Schlesinger and Hilsman. Like the others, he provides much detail on the Cuban missile crisis and slights less favorable episodes like the Berlin Wall. Unlike Schlesinger and Hilsman, he was in the room when many crisis decisions were being made, and the President trusted him, next to Bobby, on missions requiring a personal envoy.

Sorensen comes closer to leveling with the reader on Khrushchev's successful bullying of Kennedy at Vienna, although not close enough to be called candid. Knowing too much inhibited Sorensen. When Sorensen replaced a key line in Kennedy's Berlin speech at city hall with an elypsis, it was characteristic of the book. What the author brushed under the rug would have been a real contribution to history, because Sorensen knew what Schlesinger apparently did not know.

To Move a Nation, Roger Hilsman, Doubleday, New York, 1967.

If a novelist or a team of Hollywood writers invented Roger Hilsman, nobody would believe the character. He was a World War II hero, like Kennedy mentioned in dispatches. His last exploit, in the confused days of Japan's surrender, was known to the nation through a *Readers Digest* inspirational story:[9] Hilsman helped rescue his father from a Japanese prison camp in Mukden, Manchuria.

A West Pointer, Hilsman joined Major General Frank D. Merrill's Maruaders in Burma in the summer of 1944 and fought the Japanese occupiers for 25 days before being seriously wounded by four bullets. Freed from further combat duty, he returned anyway and led a band of 300 Burmese guerrillas who tied up about 3,000 Japanese troops.

Throughout the war he had sought information about his father, Colonel Roger Hilsman, who had been captured in the Philippines. When Japan announced on August 10 that it would surrender following the atomic bombing of Hiroshima and Nagasaki, but before Japan accepted final terms on August 14, an OSS rescue mission was organized to parachute into Mukden, where high-ranking prisoners were believed held. It was not certain that Japanese forces there would observe the ceasefire ordered by Emperor Hirohito. Hilsman caught a ride on a flight to Hsian, China, and missed the takeoff of the OSS team. He flagged another ride on a B-24 to Mukden and was ready to jump when the pilot saw two Soviet planes on the landing strip, indicating that the Soviets, who had just joined the Pacific war, had taken over. Hilsman landed and found his father dressed in a uniform that he had kept clean and wrapped in paper for his rescue after three and a half years.

Hilsman had found out that he was not afraid. His record also made him invulnerable when he tangled later with Kennedy administration military leaders; none of the generals or admirals could intimidate him.

Hilsman's public launching of the "missile gap" in December 1958 brought him into early controversy with Kennedy's Defense Secretary, and the Kennedy administration began with Hilsman and McNamara at odds, and Hilsman attesting to what he knew was not a proven truth.

By the time that Hilsman became a member of the Washington coup group that would destroy Diem, he had been a celebrity, the herald of the missile gap and the goat. His loyalty was to an administration and to a man. He did not get along with his boss, Rusk, who said he "went out of channels," a euphemism for Hilsman's direct dealings with Kennedy that left Rusk in the dark. When Johnson became President, Hilsman was the first of the coup group to be eased out.

The *Times* reviewed *To Move a Nation* twice. Fremont-Smith said the book "should become a standard work. Intelligent, lucid, blunt, vastly revealing. . . an endlessly fascinating book. . . intelligence integrity, sensitivity, good-will and conviction also count for something. . . ."[10] Historian Walter Johnson, in the Sunday *Book Review*, gave Hilsman high marks for "many wise and perceptual comments on the politics of policy-making."[11]

A dissenting review:

Hilsman's good will, mentioned by Fremont-Smith, eventually cost him most of his Washington friends, some muttering about integrity. Hilsman apparently regarded working in Washington as a form of guerrilla warfare, with the heads of departments akin to Oriental warlords disputing control of the lush valley. The first two chapters of the book are an indictment of Rusk: Kennedy wanted the State Department to lead the others, but Rusk refused to take charge and instead stalled and dithered. If anything went wrong in the administration's conduct of foreign affairs, it was Rusk's fault, not Kennedy's. Hilsman quoted others to cut up Rusk: "The members of a Cabinet are a President's natural enemies," said Vice President Charles G. Dawes; "President Kennedy's favorite quotation from Dante was that the hottest corner of hell was reserved for those who preserve their neutrality in times of moral crisis," said Bobby Kennedy; "How do you fire a Secretary of State who doesn't do anything, good or bad?" said Kennedy himself.

Hilsman also savaged McNamara, citing McNamara's missile-is-a-missile remark and then spelling it out: "The clear implication of

McNamara's position was that the United States should do nothing."

He was highly suspicious of John McCone when Kennedy brought him aboard: "a rich, Irish Catholic Republican, militantly anti-Communist," but he finally concluded that McCone had "a rough and ready sense of decency." Hilsman's friend Halberstam used almost the same description of McCone, omitting the decency and adding "almost reactionary" and "a possible war profiteer."

Hilsman continued to attack Keating, three years after he lost his Senate seat to Bobby Kennedy. All this does violence to the caveat in Hilsman's prefatory note: "...although there is at least one hero in this story, there are no villains at all."

To Move a Nation, The Politics of Foreign Policy in the Administration of John F. Kennedy, is presented as a scholarly study, sponsored by the Washington Center of Foreign Policy Research and Columbia's Institute of War and Peace Studies. It examines the Congo crisis, China's attack on India, Indonesia, Malaysia, Laos—but, curiously, nothing at all on the Berlin Wall and a scant five, uninformative pages on the Bay of Pigs. The Cuban missile crisis is a Kennedy triumph and a Soviet catastrophe.

Two of the subjects, Laos and Indochina, give insight into Hilsman's liberal bent.

His description of Laos, where the Eisenhower administration had backed various horses, is lucid because Hilsman had been there. The country's strongmen were neutralist Prince Souvanna Phouma; his half brother Prince Souphanouvong, who led or was the figurehead of the Pathet Lao (created by the North Vietnamese Communists), and anti-Communist General Phoumi Nosavan. The 1960-1961 crisis occurred when Kong Le took part of the Royal Laotian Army over to the Pathet Lao as the United States turned more to Phoumi and away from Souvanna Phouma, who eloquently cursed American infidelity. Kennedy rejected the Joint Chiefs' advice to go into Laos with a large force or not at all, and then agreed with Khrushchev at Vienna to neutralize the country. Despite Khrushchev's promise, the Geneva negotiations to neutralize Laos dragged on 15 months, during which time Harriman bullied Phoumi into a compromise that never was honored by the North Vietnamese. But Hilsman believed that his friend Harriman was successful, and he noted that while Harriman was negotiating, Kennedy promoted Harriman to be Assistant Secretary of State for Far Eastern Affairs, the post Hilsman later would take over. Hilsman judged that, as a limited goal, the Laos deal was "a victory—of sorts."

In Indonesia, Hilsman appeared to like Sukarno, the lusty lifelong revolutionary who first made an amalgam of nationalism, Marxism and

Islam. He was pleased that Sukarno appeared to like and respect Kennedy after Kennedy invited him to Washington.

Sukarno already had Chinese and Soviet backing for Indonesia's annexation of West New Guinea (West Irian) from the Netherlands, which wanted it made a United Nations trusteeship. Kennedy sent Bobby to Indonesia where, in effect, the United States joined the club backing Sukarno. Indonesia got West Irian in a handoff from the United Nations, and Holland got refugees who turned terrorist.

Although Sukarno had built up the Indonesian Communist Party to balance his anti-Communist army, and although he had threatened to attack the Americans in Vietnam in a pincers movement with China, adding that he would "chew up Malaysia and spit it out" for joining SEATO, Hilsman believed that the sexy little rascal was only joshing. Hilsman was proud of Harriman (The Crocodile) for snapping back at a television interviewer who called Sukarno a Communist, "He's not a Communist, he's a nationalist!"

Strangely, none of this was altered in the 1967 edition of Hilsman's book, although Sukarno had been deposed for two years, leaving the economy—which Kennedy had praised for its success in 1961—a shambles in 1965.

The Laos and Indonesia sections gave a classic picture of liberal priorities and accommodations: the anti-Communist Phoumi was bullied into submission through withholding aid, insulted as an opportunist and destroyed; the pro-Communist adversary Sukarno was aided and complimented on his ruinous administration. And always, failures are successes.

Then comes Vietnam, and the book's *raison d'etre*, the climactic Chapter 31, entitled, "The Cable of August 24," that damning message discovered by Maggie Higgins in 1963. Hilsman wrote that the cable said, "If Diem remained obdurate, the United States would have to face the possibility that the regime would not be preserved." In a footnote, Hilsman wrote that the cable's "basically accurate version" appeared in *A Thousand Days*, and that "partial and sometimes distorted versions appear in Mecklin, *Mission in Torment*, and Higgins, *Our Vietnam Nightmare*." Hilsman could not know that within four years the Pentagon Papers would reveal just the opposite.

Hilsman wrestled with another Higgins story: the Voice of America broadcasts that invited a revolt against Diem. He wrote: "Lodge had also agreed with the plan to arrange for a Voice of America broadcast that would remove the taint from the Vietnamese army." Hilsman was to brief AP, UPI and *The New York Times*, but in the rush he could only reach Hensley of UPI. The Voice was supposed to check the UPI story against a "press guidance" telegram, but by mistake included Hensley's speculation "that the U.S. may sharply reduce its aid to Vietnam unless President Diem gets rid of secret police officials responsible for these attacks (on the pagodas)." Hilsman wrote that Rusk cabled Lodge apologizing for the "failure of the machinery," and that the Voice carried a State Department denial that a decision had been made to cut aid.

Hilsman explained Halberstam's report that General Krulak okayed the cable for the Pentagon in a way that leaves it cloudier than ever:

> Krulak located General Maxwell Taylor in a restaurant, and Taylor cleared the August 24 cable for the military side of the Defense Department. Although Taylor did not know it at the time he cleared the cable, Forrestal had already released it. General Krulak had telephoned that he had located Taylor, and that everything was all right—from which Forrestal had assumed that Krulak had already obtained Taylor's approval, which he did not actually get for another hour and a half. But it made no difference, Taylor approved the cable without question.

Taylor later raised hell, and Hilsman's account was a tortuous way of saying that Krulak did not approve the cable.

Hilsman said he resigned from the Johnson administration in January 1964 in opposition to Johnson's Vietnam policy, although Johnson had no policy then and resisted escalating the war for another year. Hilsman wrote that it was clear Johnson was listening to those who would seek a military solution, and Hilsman had concluded that a military solution could not be found.

At Columbia University, Hilsman became an active anti-war lobbyist. In 1970 he reported that President Nixon was rebuffing a Communist peace offer on terms that many Americans would find acceptable. Hilsman wrote that Nixon was planning only a gradual reduction of troops before the 1972 elections and intended to continue the war, not end it. He called Vietnamization of the war less successful than reported, if not a fraud, and insisted on the basis of his private contacts with North Vietnamese diplomats that the Hanoi peace signals were genuine.[12]

When the *Times* published the Pentagon Papers in 1971, Hilsman was one of the first casualties. Even though the *Times* interpretation made Lodge the most forceful advocate of a coup against Diem, the Cable was out, and Hilsman's circumlocutions were bared.

Hilsman called a press conference in New York to say that his bloodthirsty memos—printed in the *Chicago Sun-Times* before they were mentioned in the *Times*—represented a contingency suggestion and his own personal feelings. He stressed that Kennedy had "no detailed knowledge of the time or place" of the coup.

By 1977, when he was interviewed on BBC's Third Program, Hilsman added another suggestion. It was Rusk who had inserted the critical and fatal paragraph into the Cable, although Hilsman said of the Cable, "I drafted it."

Hilsman explained to interviewer Michael Charlton:

> . . . I drafted a telegram which said we will instruct the Voice of America to say it was the Special Forces and not the army; and if there is a coup, we will examine the new government on its own merit. Rusk then added the paragraphs saying that if there were an interim period of indecision we would endeavor to supply any anti-Communist forces through other channels than Saigon port.
>
> Hilsman: . . . what happened was that it went by secured communications to President Kennedy at Hyannis Port, and to Secretary Rusk who was at the UN. It came back from Kennedy with no change, but it came back from Rusk. . . .
>
> Charlton: Just let me stop you right there. In other words, Kennedy made no alterations to the telegram as you drafted it?
>
> Hilsman: No.
>
> Charlton: And he had seen it and approved it in that form?
>
> Hilsman: That's right, yes. It came back from Rusk though with an additional paragraph, about which some of us had some reservations, but which said: If there is an interim period in which two factions are struggling we will endeavor to support all anti-Communist factions through other ports than Saigon.
>
> Charlton: And that was the crucial extra paragraph.
>
> Hilsman: That was the crucial extra paragraph.
>
> Charlton: And Rusk was wholly and personally responsible for that extra addition?
>
> Hilsman: Yes.
>
> Charlton: What happened then?
>
> Hilsman: Averell Harriman and I went out and tried to find the Acting Secretary, who was George Ball, who was on a golf course in the rain. We came back to his house and we got on the telephone, or George Ball got on the telephone.[13]

BBC asked Rusk about it.

> Charlton: My information is that a crucial paragraph in that telegram which went out from the State Department was added by you?
>
> Rusk: Oh, I don't think so. I was out of town. It was discussed with me on the telephone.

Charlton: Yes, but did you add anything to it as a result of that discussion?

Rusk: I don't recall that I did.

Charlton: The crucial paragraph I am talking about which was subsequently interpreted as giving the green light to the generals to go ahead and make a coup involved the State Department making it clear that American aid support would be supplied through alternative ports, or ports other than Saigon. That paragraph was added by you. Is that true?

Rusk: It might have been added by the State Department, but I just don't recall that paragraph at all. Certainly not, I don't recall myself as author of it.

Charlton: But you approved it?

Rusk: I didn't have a text in front of me. It was cleared with me on the phone in rather general terms because we were on an open telephone line.[14]

The Cable of August 24, as published in the Pentagon Papers, contains no reference to ports other than Saigon.

By 1967, when Hilsman's book came out, the United States was in revolt against the war, especially in universities. Those who had been anti-Diem in 1963 for not pursuing the war vigorously were now anti-war and considered that the war had been hopeless from the beginning. Since Diem always had been doomed by the hopeless war, they were guilty of nothing. Now they all were on the same side, Hilsman, Harriman, Forrestal, Ball, Halberstam, Sheehan and the *Times*. Their wagons were drawn in a circle to defend against marauding Indians, and both Hilsman's and Schlesinger's books praised the courageous young correspondents of the Saigon press corps. Hilsman's book cited Schlesinger's book with praise. Schlesinger's praise of Hilsman was quoted on Hilsman's book jacket. The *Times* praised them all, closing the circle of mutual admiration and mortaring in the building blocks of history reposing in the nation's libraries. The most dangerous marauding Indian, Maggie Higgins, was dead.

Our Vietnam Nightmare, Marguerite Higgins, Harper & Row, New York, 1965.

Higgins had no hand in killing Diem, and she felt no personal guilt or threat of exposure. She did feel compulsion to straighten out a piece of history before it became set in concrete.

Her book never was reviewed by the *Times*.

It contained in essence the accurate version of events in 1963, from the pagoda raids to Diem's murder, which would become the sensational heart of the Pentagon Papers in 1971, when few would recall that she had been right from the beginning.

While Schlesinger was writing a wide sweep of instant history touching many bases in flight, Higgins was doing legwork focused on six months of 1963 in Vietnam and Washington. Her book did not attack the Saigon press corps, but it rechecked the stories that spurred Diem's overthrow.

Higgins had tried to report to the *Herald-Tribune* that Buddhists were about 15% of the population in South Vietnam, usually were non-political and did not constitute an automatic majority against Diem, but in 1964 she found Rusk still telling a press conference that Buddhists were 80% of the population. So her book began with a treatise on religious statistics and Vietnamese Buddhism, striving to show that Buddhists were not persecuted, that political violence and suicide violated the religion's tenets, and that Tri Quang was a revolutionary politician rather than a monk, with a small, well-organized following.

After Diem's death, South Vietnam went through five governments in 14 months. Higgins described how Tri Quang used choreographed riots and bonze-burnings to bring down each one that showed any promise of fighting the Viet Cong, including General Nguyen Khanh's Buddhist-dominated government. Tri Quang forced the release of arrested Communist agents and purged the administrations of Diemist officials, that is, anyone of competence.

In Hué, she re-examined the May 8, 1963, flag riot that touched off the Buddhist crisis. She concluded, painstakingly gathering evidence, that it had followed a scenario, and that Viet Cong plastic bombs killed eight (not nine) victims while Tri Quang was safe inside the radio station, as Diem had said in denying government guilt. She found that the condemned Major Dang Sy, a Catholic, had ordered his troops to use Mark III concussion grenades, which are nonlethal and could not have caused the blast damage the victims suffered. She cited the United Nations investigators' report that no one was killed at the Xa Loi pagoda. The UN investigators had looked up by name priests reported killed and found them alive and well. She noted that the Buddhist riots, before and after Diem fell, regularly numbered about 3,000 persons—the same persons.

Tracking down Halberstam's Nhu-did-it scoop, Higgins got a statement from General Tran Van Khiem, chief of staff in 1963, on how the pagoda raid decision was reached:

> On August 20, all the key generals were called to the Presidential Palace for a discussion of the situation caused by the demonstrations in the city. Ngo Dinh Nhu, the president's brother, put the

question of what to do up for discussion. The first to take the floor was General Tran Van Don (acting commander of the Vietnamese forces and a Buddhist). The general said that continued disorders could not be tolerated. These disorders deeply undermined the peoples' faith in the power of the government to keep the situation under control. The ringleaders of the disorders had to be rounded up. . . . The pagodas could not be privileged sanctuaries for subversion. It was not possible to give one group the privilege of breaking laws (demonstrations were illegal). Soldiers in battle had the right to expect a certain discipline on the home front. . . .

Khiem said that following a discussion among the generals, they decided unanimously to send a written petition containing all their individual signatures to President Diem asking permission to proceed with the plan ". . . (it was) done within hours. General Don had given a similar account to American officials in Saigon, which was sent to Washington and accounted for the first State Department announcement that the army had raided the pagodas."

Then, as the Cable of August 24 went out ordering Lodge to prepare a coup, the State Department made its unprecedented switch: "Current information makes it clear that these attacks on the pagodas. . .were carried out by the police, supported by small groups of Special Forces troops not under the command of the Vietnamese armed forces."

Higgins dug into that in Washington. "The game was to clean up their (the generals') image," an official told her, so that when the generals took over they could be pictured as a virtuous lot, innocent of the pagoda raids that caused such panic in some parts of the Kennedy administration.

Diem countered the State Department's "deceit," Higgins reported, by asking the generals to sign a document attesting to the truth, and they did.

Higgins recapitulated the Cable of August 24 as she had first reported it in 1963 and tracked down the circumstances of how it was authorized, an account close to the later description by the Pentagon Papers analysts.

She reported:

The Acting Secretary of Defense, Roswell Gilpatric, who was at his farm on the outskirts of Washington, also had the cable described to him over the telephone in a startling bit of byplay by other actors in the unfolding drama.

To 'clear' the cable with the Defense Department, Mike Forrestal. . .first placed a call to Vice Admiral Herbert D. Riley, director of the Joint Chiefs. . . . Admiral Riley did not pretend to be a specialist on Vietnam and sensed that the cable might contain international dynamite. So he tracked down General Krulak. . . who also was at the Chevy Chase Country Club (the locker room). General Krulak, who until that moment had heard nothing about the telegram, also felt a sense of alarm and told Forrestal at the White House that he would come down immediately and read it over. Once at the White House, and gravely concerned about the content of the message, Krulak insisted that Forrestal call Under Secretary Gilpatric at his country place.

Mr. Gilpatric said he was frankly surprised that such an important set of instructions should be rushed out on a weekend, but he did not feel he ought to veto the telegram since Forrestal told him flatly that it had 'the approval of the President.'

In McCone's absence, the cable was described, again cryptically, to Richard Helms, deputy director of the CIA, who also did not feel disposed to veto something 'approved by the President.'

If my facts are correct, and I have done a lot of detailed checking, the manner in which this cable was sent raises a lot of questions. Is this really the way to run a war, let alone formulate national policy?

Higgins added, "There are knowledgeable Americans who believe that Lodge had been given instructions for 'radical surgery' against the Diem regime before leaving Washington."

She also interviewed the successful coup generals. The leader, General Duong Van (Big) Minh told her, "Diem could not be allowed to live" because of his support in the countryside.

Higgins went into Hilsman's suspicion that Nhu was threatening to deal with Hanoi through a Polish diplomat. She looked up the diplomat, Dr. Mieczyslaw Manelli, Polish member of the International Control Commission, who told her he had seen Nhu on September 7 for an hour at a reception, along with other diplomats. Nhu had told him that South Vietnam was not interested in a ceasefire, which Hanoi had hinted at in a July broadcast. The Italian Ambassador, who had been present, confirmed Manelli's statement. Manelli said he had "told American officials the truth many times."[15]

Did Nhu take opium and heroin? Checking with his associates, and after a lengthy interview with Nhu in August 1963, Higgins concluded that it was not possible.

Had Nhu cut Diem off from the people? Nolting, in a letter to Higgins in 1965 wrote:

Diem was an indefatigable traveler. He was out of Saigon two, three days out of every week. . . . In addition to army headquarters and outposts, he visited the remotest villages and districts, Camau, Montagnard villages and training camps, off-shore islands, 17th parallel, etc. . . . he was intensely interested in local rural problems—health conditions, schools, water supply, roads, canals, seeds, fertilizer, crop diversification, land ownership, land rents, housing, etc. . . . He was not a good orator before big crowds, but extremely effective with groups of peasants and villagers, informing, inquiring, genuinely interested and sympathetic. . . . He was anything but aloof as depicted. . . . our usual schedule was to leave Saigon at 5 a.m. . . . I am sure there was real rapport and mutual respect between President Diem and the large majority of rural people. . . . He used to spend his 1½-day Christmas holiday, the only days he took off, in the remotest military outpost he could find, with the troops. . . .

And last, was Diem losing the war in the summer of 1963, when Hanoi was broadcasting ceasefire feelers? Higgins had reported in August 1963 that the war was going well, and she had been condemned as a military sycophant for her trouble in touring the boondocks. Everything in the Pentagon Papers supported her. The war turned against the south after Diem's death.

Higgins' book contains an angry high point. When the coup occurred, Mme. Nhu called her from Beverly Hills but did not reach her. Higgins, returning late from a Saturday night party, called her back at the Beverly Wilshire Hotel.

Le Thuy, the Nhus' 19-year-old daughter, answered.

'Mother is upset,' said Le Thuy, as if this were a source of surprise to her. 'She wants to talk to you about the children.'

In Saigon, I had met Madame Nhu's four-year-old daughter in the Presidential Palace. I knew there were also two boys, Quyen, 11 and Trac, 15.

But when Madame Nhu came on the line, she spoke first of her husband and brother in-law.

'Do you really believe they are dead?'

'I'm afraid so.'

'I could spit on the world,' Madame Nhu said bitterly.

Silence. What was there to say?

'Are they going to kill my children too?' she asked.

'It's the last thing President Kennedy would want,' I said in some agitation. . . .

'Then why doesn't the United States government do something to help me get them out?' said Madame Nhu, who by now was quite plainly speaking through sobs, a broken warrior if there ever was one.

'I'll put the question to the State Department officer in charge of Vietnam,' I promised.

'Hurry,' said Madame Nhu. 'Please hurry and ask about Can.'

Can is Diem's brother who was in control of Central Vietnam.

It was 2 a.m. I roused Assistant Secretary Hilsman out of a sound sleep.

'Congratulations, Roger,' I said. 'How does it feel to have blood on your hands?

'Oh, come on, now Maggie,' said Roger. 'Revolutions are rough, and people get hurt.'

Hilsman did get the children out, and they rejoined Mme. Nhu in Rome. She would not stay in the United States, "a country that has stabbed me in the back." Hilsman had told Higgins that Can could have asylum, but Can was executed instead.

Hanoi began stepping up infiltration into the south immediately after its experts had analyzed the Voice of America broadcasts calling for Diem's overthrow. After Diem's death, infiltration became a flood, and Johnson did not respond to it.

Higgins summed up:

> In 1963 Vietnam was able to export 300,000 tons of rice. Supplies flowed smoothly from the farmers in the countryside to the wharves of Saigon. In 1965 Vietnam had to import rice because the roads into the city had been cut . . . . In the summer of 1963 the average number of Viet Cong attacks was two to three hundred a week. Few were larger than company or battalion size. The heaviest weapon usually was the machinegun. In the summer of 1965 the Viet Cong were often making six hundred attacks a week, many by two or three regiments at a time, and weapons included mortars, flame-throwers, recoilless rifles and artillery. . . .

After Diem's death Higgins went back to Vietnam three times for exhaustive tours. On a visit late in 1965, she contracted a jungle fluke, a parasite that attacks the liver and other organs, and she died in Walter Reed Hospital in Washington, at 45, on January 3, 1966.

The *Times* gave Higgins a large, two-column obituary, unstinting in its praise of her reporting in World War II and in Korea. It never mentioned that she had reported from Vietnam.

Chapter XI
The Revolution Begins and the Six Day War

"Many of these extremists are highly intelligent and very verbal. Unfortunately, their claim to act out of high motives, and their often attacking real evils, has misled many well-meaning people to overlook that their true motif is hate, not desire for a better world.""

—Dr. Bruno Bettelheim

Lyndon Johnson's term as Vice President of the United States was more dreary than most. Without him, Kennedy would not have won the Southern states necessary to make him the first Catholic President, but in Kennedy's administration there was no role for Johnson. Kennedy's Ivy League entourage considered the Texan an unmannered galoot, as did the sophisticated Eastern media.[2] Unlike Nixon, who had thrived amid the frustrations of the vice presidency, Johnson, his advice ignored, grew increasingly morose.

Foreign policy did not interest Johnson, and he undertook his missions to Berlin and to the Far East dragging his feet. His assignments, heading the President's Committee on Equal Employment Opportunities and chairing the National Aeronautics and Space Council, kept him out of the public eye and did not absorb his energies. Unused to idleness, Johnson surreptitiously built up his family fortune, accumulating Texas radio and television stations in the name of his wife Claudia, or Lady Bird.

The murder of President Kennedy in Dallas on November 22, 1963, two cars ahead of Johnson's car, hurled Johnson out of his decline. Dazed and overwhelmed, he nevertheless arrived in Washington on Air Force One, with Kennedy's widow and casket, his long-restrained energy unleashed.

Johnson immediately set up the Warren Commission, bullied Supreme Court Justice Earl Warren into heading it, and called the Cabinet together to ask Kennedy's men to stay on, "not just for a while, but as long as I was President."[3] He made good on his offer after his landslide victory over Barry Goldwater a year later, and Johnson insisted that he never fired a Kennedy man. The *Times* was among the media leaders who congratulated Johnson for keeping the Kennedy team, but working without his own men weakened Johnson's presidency. When Nixon lunched at the White House with Johnson during the 1968 transition, Nixon asked him why he kept the Kennedy men after winning in 1964. "Yes, you won by—what was it, 61, 62 percent? That would have been the time for you to clean house," Nixon said.[4]

If Johnson fired no one, he made life uncomfortable for those who had been his tormentors, and he eased out most of the members of the White House coup group against Diem. Theodore Sorensen resigned on January 16, 1964; Arthur Schlesinger, Jr. left on January 29. Roger Hilsman, who had been promoted to Assistant Secretary of State for Far Eastern Affairs in August, left on February 26 to accept a chair at Columbia University, telling a press conference that he had not been fired. (Columbia later refused to accept Henry Kissinger.) Michael Forrestal was shifted to the State Department, cut out of Vietnam traffic and eventually resigned. George Ball stayed on until 1967, when he served briefly as United Nations Ambassador before resigning.

Johnson was President longer than Kennedy, and was in office effectively longer than Nixon, but his presidency had the feel of an interregnum. He was an accidental President, a Southern Christian identified with his region, something of an enigma to the industrial Northeast, which was surprised and suspicious that he turned out to be a liberal on domestic issues. Aware that his past could not stand intense media investigation, Johnson had not been sure that he wanted to run for President. In 1948 he had gone to the Senate, to be positioned as a potential President, by the margin of 87 votes in a fixed Texas Democratic primary, and his manner of collecting radio and television stations also could not stand close scrutiny. As President in 1964 he hesitated to run until his wife pointed out that, even if he did not run, the media would ask, "What skeletons in the closet—what fear of disclosure" made him decide to retire?"[5] After Johnson's death, witnesses in Duval County surfaced to say that, indeed, the 1948 primary had turned on cemetery ballots.

In the Senate, Johnson had become a persuasive, tough, canny *Gauleiter* who could reckon interests, cajole and twist arms. As President he would be essentially a domestic leader. Although he had learned something about foreign affairs in the Senate and had no inclination to "crawl back into isolationism of the 19th century," he would regard international crises as distractions from a President's real business at home.[6]

Domestic affairs immediately seized his attention and energy. Johnson presided over a simmering, diffused revolt that the population at large never acknowledged as a true revolution, so it never was resolved, adding to the sense of interregnum.

The United States is too large for a revolution to become apparent through the seizure of the capital and television stations, so the revolution of the late 1960s never was certified as such. It began as a racial conflict, the result of the North's failure to assimilate the black migration from the South after World War II and the lagging of the South behind the rest of the nation.

The black revolt had been stirring in the Eisenhower administration with boycotts and sit-ins in the South and the division of blacks into separatist sects in the North. A sit-in at a Woolworth's lunch counter in Greensboro, South Carolina, on February 1, 1960, made national news. During the 1960 campaign, Kennedy had raised black hopes for change when Bobby Kennedy intervened to get the Reverend Martin Luther King, Jr. released from jail, but once in office, Kennedy took no action on civil rights for more than two years. By 1963, Black Muslims were pressing their own program of racial segregation, the writer James Baldwin was promising *The Fire Next Time*, Students for a Democratic Society had begun propaganda visits to the South, and in King, a civil rights activist since 1956, the Southern Christian Leadership Conference had found a charismatic leader.

In February 1963, Kennedy finally sent a message to Congress calling for comprehensive civil rights legislation, but his proposals were not yet organized into legislative bills. In late March, Republicans, including New York Senators Keating and Javits, submitted a package of civil rights bills that was praised by the *Times* editorially[7] and by James Reston, while Javits and the *Times* joined in criticizing Kennedy's stalling in the face of Southern Democratic congressional opposition.

In May, with King and 283 others facing trial for civil disobedience, police with dogs suppressed a major demonstration in Birmingham, Alabama, arresting about 500 marchers. For several days police routed demonstrators. A motel and King's home were bombed by white supremacists on May 11, touching off rioting. A sniper ambushed and killed Medgar Evers, field secretary for the National Association for the Advancement of Colored People, in Jackson, Mississippi, June 12, and a riot followed his funeral.

The outbreak of violence in Mississippi and Alabama got the Kennedy administration moving, and the President proposed extensive civil rights legislation on June 19, but civil rights organizers said they would not hold off a demonstration they were planning for Washington. The march on Washington in late August brought 200,000 to hear King deliver his "I have a dream" speech launching the civil rights movement as a national crusade. But in September, a Birmingham church was bombed, killing four black girls, and two persons were killed in rioting that brought out the National Guard. Four days after the church bombing, Kennedy appointed a Presidential commission to try to restore communications between blacks and whites, but two months later he would be dead.

In one of Johnson's first acts as President, he addressed Congress five days after Kennedy's death, rising to eloquence in a plea to "end all teaching and preaching of hate and evil—and violence." Johnson moved Congressmen as he never had been able to do before, making civil rights legislation a tribute to Kennedy's "dream of equal rights for all Americans" to prove that "John F. Kennedy did not live, and die, in vain."

Seizing on the national sense of guilt, shock, disillusion, and the Congress' subdued sense of national crisis, Johnson rammed through the Civil Rights Act of 1964 and launched his War on Poverty while congressional obstructionists were paralyzed by the feeling of cataclysm caused by Kennedy's assassination. But before Johnson signed the Civil Rights Act in July, demonstrations, sit-ins and boycotts were proliferating throughout the South, and a major riot in Jacksonville, Florida, lasted three days with hundreds arrested. Three civil rights workers, northern whites Michael Schwerner and Andrew Goodman, and black James Chaney, were murdered in Mississippi June 21, 1964, their bodies buried and found only two months later. In Stockholm, King accepted the Nobel Peace Prize.

Two weeks after the Civil Rights Act was signed into law, a major riot erupted in Harlem when an off-duty policeman shot a teenager. The rioting lasted four days and spread to the Bedford-Stuyvesant district of Brooklyn. The Harlem riot toll was one dead, 202 arrested, 117 stores wrecked and looted. In Brooklyn police counted 22 injured, 276 arrested, 556 stores looted. Major riots followed in Rochester, New York, and Jersey City, Elizabeth and Paterson, New Jersey, rioters using Molotov cocktails. South Chicago and North Philadelphia erupted. The exodus of middle-class whites from the cities to the suburbs swelled to a tide. Harlem, once a colorful center of New York's pluralistic culture and a tourist lure, segregated itself and became off-limits to whites.

Within a month after the first major urban riots of 1964, a new element of revolution emerged at the University of California at Berkeley.[8] Mario Savio's Free Speech Movement was not directly tied to the black revolt, nor was it related to Vietnam, where Kennedy's surreptitious troop buildup still was unrecognized in late 1964. For many of the participants, the Free Speech Movement was more related to the panty-raid fad of the 1950s than to serious politics, although the leaders were serious enough. In October, Berkeley saw a three-day fun-demonstration over the suspension of eight Marxist students for political activity on campus. By November campus protests were a daily ritual.

Savio became something of a national figure when the *Times*, a continent away from Berkeley, took note of him.[9] The *Oakland Tribune*, owned by conservative Republican Senator William F. Knowland, urged the university to get rid of its radicals, as it had done off and on since 1948, and the battle lines were drawn.

Savio had taken a summer "freedom ride" to Mississippi with the Student Non-Violent Coordinating Committee, but his priority concern was not so much civil rights as the military-industrial complex and the university's part in training researchers for it. A native New Yorker who had first studied at Manhattan and Queens Colleges, he was allied at Berkeley with a number of "revolutionary socialists" including Bettina Aptheker, 20, also a New Yorker, who was a member of the Communist-front W. E. B. DuBois Club and daughter of Herbert Aptheker, director of the American Institute of Marxist Studies and a long-time member of the Communist Party leadership.

In early December, about 1,000 students, including members of SDS from other states, seized the administration building of the university in Berkeley, while Joan Baez entertained with civil rights songs. California Governor Edmund (Pat) Brown ordered removal of the sit-in strikers, and about 800 were arrested, the Berkeley cops patting some of the coeds on the fannies but not using violence.

The New York Times had been in the forefront of the civil rights movement, both its reporters and its editors taking serious risks to advance the causes of voter registration and elimination of discrimination.[10] Now the *Times'* sympathy for revolutionary causes expanded to include the Free Speech Movement, taking the police raid seriously, even tragically. The *Times* editorialized:

> The tragic aspect of the dispute is that it probably never would have arisen if the university had not felt it necessary last September to forbid political recruitment or fund solicitation for off-campus activities on a 25-foot strip of bricked-over land at the edge of the campus. Unquestionably there is merit to the complaint of Dr. Clark Kerr, the university's able president, that the students have displayed irrationality and intransigence. Unquestionably, too, part of the trouble has been fomented by left wingers from outside the student body. But it is also plain that there has been a breakdown of communication between the administration and large elements of the university community.[11]

New Yorkers tend to view the West Coast as a foreign country, a rather primitive one, so it is not surprising that the *Times* would offer cavalier advice to Berkeley, just as it does to Cuba or Haiti. But the *Times'* international stature, and its virtual endorsement of the students' strike, elevated the Free Speech Movement even beyond a national issue: in West Berlin the APO (Opposition Outside Parliament) and in Amsterdam the Provos, took the Free Speech Movement as a model for sit-ins and student strikes.

Shortly after the *Times* editorial pat on the head, Savio, Aptheker and others visited SDS at the University of Michigan and journeyed on to New York, where Savio spoke at the Overseas Press Club. Now an international figure, within academic circles at least, Savio addressed student rallies at Columbia University and Queens College, urging students to demand their rights through strikes and civil disobedience. His movement, vague as it was, along with SDS and SNCC, later would become core organizations of the anti-war movement when Johnson and McNamara escalated the Vietnam war.

The black revolution continued to gain momentum as Johnson forced through the Voting Rights Act of 1965. A week after Johnson signed the bill, the arrest in August of a drunk-driving suspect in Watts, a suburb of Los Angeles, touched off a week of rioting, firebombing and for the first time gunfire against police by about 200 armed blacks. Watts was left in ruins, with 33 dead, 762 injured and 2,255 under arrest, while ambushes continued in nearby communities, killing a policeman in Long Beach.

In the *Times*, columnist Tom Wicker sympathized with the rioters a continent away and chided the police. Wicker cited Johnson's warning that "another nation" of blacks was being created. and wrote: "The problem is that, having created the other nation, the white man cannot live with it—as the riots also indicate—except by harsh repression and force. That is the way of South Africa, not of the land of the free and the home of the brave."[12] Wicker drew a connection, which did not then really exist, between the anti-war demonstrations in Washington and the Los Angeles riots.

Senator Kennedy, now called Robert in the media instead of Bobby, following his election, contradicted the retired Eisenhower, who had said the violence was symptomatic of a general increase in violence. Kennedy declared that the blacks "feel the law is their enemy." Watts was followed by riots in Chicago and Natchez, where the National Guard was called out.

By 1966, the cities were braced for what was being called "the long, hot summer," a season of black rioting that was coming to be accepted as a natural phenomenon. Watts erupted again in the spring, leaving two dead. In July, 5,000 rioted for three days in Chicago. There was widespread looting in Cleveland and riots in Troy, Brooklyn and Amityville, New York; South Bend, Indiana; Jacksonville, Florida; San Francisco and Oakland; Atlanta; Benton Harbor, Michigan; Waukegan, Illinois; Milwaukee and Wauwatosa, Wisconsin; Dayton, Ohio.

While Johnson concentrated his energy on trying to put out racial fires and launch his war on poverty, foreign policy demands for decision crowded in on him from around the globe, most of them to result in piles of paper at the State Department, White House and CIA. All of the problems that had been present at the beginning of the Kennedy administration still were there, along with some new ones, but none were so urgent as the albatross of Vietnam.

When Johnson became President, Kennedy had sent without publicity 16,500 troops to Vietnam; two or three thousand more were in the pipeline, and tentative plans called for an escalation to about 23,000 by the end of 1965. Although North Vietnam poured infiltrators into South Vietnam after Diem's death, Johnson resisted proposals by the Joint Chiefs, then under General Taylor, to "put aside self-imposed restrictions," assume direction of the war and win it by carrying it to North Vietnam through bombing, commitment of U.S. troop units and large-scale commando raids on the North.

McNamara visited Vietnam in December 1963, less than a month after Kennedy's death, and reported to Johnson that the situation was "very disturbing." Ambassador Lodge was operating as a loner, without coordinating information with General Harkins; North Vietnamese infiltration had stepped up, giving the Viet Cong control of populated areas in key provinces; Big Minh suspected that the United States might try to neutralize South Vietnam like Laos "because of editorials in *The New York Times* and mention by Walter Lippmann and others."[13]

McNamara recommended no substantial increase in U.S. resources and personnel, but rather South Vietnamese covert actions against Laos and North Vietnam. Minh soon fell to a coup by General Nguyen Khanh, beginning a musical chairs round of coups, all of the governments attacked by the small but vocal Buddhist political group of Thich Tri Quang.

Johnson insisted on learning every detail of events in Vietnam, usually following the advice of McNamara in the end. The Joint Chiefs he inherited from Kennedy no longer included an outspoken Admiral Burke or a General LeMay, so that "McNamara's war" was the result of committee management by White House and Defense Department civilians, State having retired from the scene.

The war was conducted with the worst possible strategy from a military, political and economic point of view: attempted intimidation of the North through stages, variously called "graduated response" and "progressive squeeze-and-talk."

That Johnson resisted increasing U.S. involvement in Vietnam is evident in the Pentagon Papers; he had advised Kennedy from the beginning not to send troops, and he brought back Diem's reply that no troops were wanted. It was apparent in Johnson's isolation of CIA Director McCone, already isolated for having called the Cuban missile crisis too soon. McCone, more strongly than the Joint Chiefs, urged Johnson to accept the JCS advice for large-scale troop deployment, or to win the war through heavy bombing, or get out, but not to make incremental troop increases. When McNamara and McCone visited Vietnam together in March 1964, McCone disagreed with McNamara's recommendations as "too little and too late." McCone found it hard to get to Johnson after his Vietnam recommendations. He was eased out and replaced by Admiral William F. Raborn, Jr.

While Johnson avoided sending troops, he invested heavily in building up South Vietnam, not only its military forces but also its economy in an extension of his war on poverty. Part of the South Vietnamese military effort went into trying to stop coastal infiltration. The Soviets responded by building up the North Vietnamese navy with a fleet of torpedo boats.

North Vietnamese PT boats, new to the war, attacked the destroyer *Maddox* on August 2, 1964, and the *Maddox* again and the *C. Turner Joy* on August 4. Johnson presented to Congress a resolution prepared for such a contingency, now hastily revised, that would "approve and support the President, as Commander-in-Chief, to take all necessary measures to repel any armed attack against the forces of the United States and to prevent further aggression."

The Gulf of Tonkin resolution, passed August 7 by a vote of 88 to 2 in the Senate and 416 to 0 in the House, endorsed actions already taken by Johnson: reprisal strikes by fighter bombers from the carriers *Constellation* and *Ticonderoga* against four North Vietnamese torpedo boat bases and an oil storage depot. Johnson had announced on television on August 4 that he was sending another attack carrier group to the Western Pacific, had moved interceptor and fighter-bomber aircraft into South Vietnam and had alerted selected Army and Marine Corps units for movement, so Congress understood that it was authorizing an expansion of the war.

In view of Johnson's television announcements, the Gulf of Tonkin resolution was above board and normal procedure. When the *Times* published the Pentagon Papers, the resolution was treated as a sinister plot calculated in advance to seize the PT boat pretext to widen the war. This was an opinion long held by Marcus Raskin, one of Neil Sheehan's benefactors in the Pentagon Papers scoop, who claimed insider knowledge of the plot although he had left the government 18 months before the Gulf of Tonkin incident.[14] George Ball, much later, backed up this view, saying, "I think there was a feeling that if the destroyer got into some trouble, that would provide the provocation we needed. . . I doubt whether you could call it a conspiracy. I find that rather too strong a word. I think it was a tactical opportunity they were looking for."[15]

McGeorge Bundy, on the other hand, said later, "Let me say at the outset that, contrary to some of the interpretations that people in *The New York Times* placed at the time of the publication of the Pentagon Papers, the Tonkin Gulf incident was totally unexpected and unpremeditated on the part of the Johnson administration."

As Bundy and Johnson both noted, Johnson's election was coming up, and he did not want a Vietnam disturbance in August 1964. There was no escalation for six months after the resolution was passed. Nevertheless, it became a given "fact" of the anti-war movement that the

Tonkin Gulf resolution was a deception of Congress after publication of the Pentagon Papers, partly because its sponsor, Senator William Fulbright, said he had been conned, partly because the *Times* called it a deception, partly because Daniel Ellsberg said it was a deception.

Ellsberg, the Marine lieutenant of the Suez crisis of 1956, came to Washington just as Congress passed the Tonkin Gulf resolution, summoned from the Rand Corporation in Santa Monica to join the Defense Department near the top as an adviser to Assistant Secretary of Defense for Security Affairs John T. McNaughton. A hawk when he joined the government, Ellsberg would later give the Pentagon Papers to Senator Fulbright, expecting him to deduce from them that he had been duped into his role as sponsor of the resolution and that he would make the collection of documents public.

As Ellsberg arrived in Washington in August 1964, he passed, like a ship in the night, his future collaborator, Anthony Russo, who already was taking a radical's view of the war. Russo joined Rand in California as Ellsberg left.

Russo was a bright, alienated young man from the South, where he had grown up "a half-breed Italian loose amongst a swarm of plantation WASPs." Russo had earned a master's degree in engineering but then had quit the NASA Langley Space Laboratory in Hampton, Virginia, because it was "clearly a front for military research."

Russo won a fellowship to the Woodrow Wilson School of Public and International Affairs, where he studied under Professor Oskar Morgenstern and Professor Richard Falk, one of the original anti-war activists. Russo went to Rand in California knowing that it had been primarily an Air Force think tank, as a sort of impostor:

> I think I felt that I could be a kind of anthropologist observing the natives in the village of the Pentagon. And, of course, the Rand Corporation was where the action was, covering all bases from the thermonuclear aspect of things to research in Vietnam. I had the naive notion that, if reason could be brought to bear in a process that looked deeply questionable to me, then perhaps some good could be done. I was caught up in the myth of working from within. Professor Richard Falk was less sanguine about this whole affair than I was. My friends were similarly skeptical. I was alone in thinking the belly of the whale might be an interesting place to work.[16]

Thus the flip-talking rebel, already believing that the Viet Cong were patriots, joined the think tank that helped plan war options. He would not meet Ellsberg for a year, when both were in Vietnam.

Early in 1965 Communist Vietnamese units struck the American base at Pleiku, using recoilless rifles and weaponry heavier than those the Viet Cong usually employed. On February 7, 49 U.S. fighter-bombers struck the North Vietnamese army barracks and staging area at Dong Hoi, just across the Demilitarized Zone, the first air strike into North Vietnam.[17]

The *Times* published its first outright anti-war editorial:

> The Vietnamese situation has reached a new stage. The war will not be the same since the Viet Cong attacks on Pleiku and the reprisals against North Vietnam which continued yesterday. . . . President Johnson has in the past denied that the United States has any intention of carrying the war to North Vietnam. Yet he considered it necessary in the past few days to help the South Vietnamese raid North Vietnam twice. . . since Peking and Moscow are committed to help Hanoi, the dangers of the future are only too obvious.[18]

The next day's editorial said:

> Those who profit by the American presence want the United States to stay. Those who feel frustrated by American power— nationalists, Communists, Buddhists and probably the majority of the peasantry, who simply ask to be left alone—want America to go. The motives (of the administration) are exemplary and every American can be proud of them, but the crucial questions are: Can it be done? Is the price too high? Was the military decision in the Kennedy administration mistaken? Are the dangers of escalation too great? Is this a good battleground of the cold war on which to fight? Is the United States losing more than it is gaining?. . . Is this war necessary?[19]

The first American bombing had a side effect of opening North Vietnam to American visitors, although not to those who might be critical. A number of American individuals and groups slipped into North Vietnam in 1965, among them a group that included Yale Professor Staughton Lynd, a Marxist and pacifist, Herbert Aptheker, Communist teacher, and Tom Hayden, a founder of SDS and a member of SNCC.

When it appeared that the trio would not be prosecuted under the Logan Act, prohibiting private persons from dealing with a foreign government, and would not lose their passports, the *Times* had the passport of Assistant Managing Editor Harrison E. Salisbury validated for travel to North Vietnam.[20] Salisbury wrote to "a Communist friend who might be able to obtain a visa to North Vietnam."[21]

Salisbury's first dispatch from Hanoi, printed on Christmas Day, 1966, challenged the Johnson administration's claims that the city's residential areas were not hit by bombing of the rail yard, a truck park south of Hanoi, the Paul Doumer Bridge and oil storage tanks outside the city. Salisbury reported that all of the targets were in built-up, inhabited areas, and "Christmas Eve found residents in several parts of Hanoi still picking over the wreckage of homes said to have been damaged in the United States raids of December 13 and 14." He reported, "Contrary to the impression given by United States communiques, on-the-spot inspection indicates that American bombing has been inflicting considerable civilian casualties in Hanoi and its environs for some time past." He cited the village of Phuxa, a suburb "possibly four miles from the city center," where 24 Vietnamese were said to have been killed and 23 wounded, while the attacking pilot was shot down.

Hanson Baldwin, the last relative hawk on the *Times,* reported that the Defense Department was making every effort to pinpoint bombing on military targets, while acknowledging that it was impossible to avoid civilian casualties completely. The *Times* headline read:

CIVILIANS' AREAS
HIT, U.S. ADMITS.[22]

The *Times* editorialized:

Washington has denied that recent attacks on military targets in the Hanoi area came within the city limits or amounted to 'bombing Hanoi.' But the fact that this is a distinction without a difference has now been made evident by Mr. Salisbury's report from the scene.

He found that significant damage to civilian areas within the city occurred during the December 13-14 attacks. Whether this resulted from pilot errors or from North Vietnamese antiaircraft shells and missiles falling back on the city, or from a combination of the two, does not leave the civilians any less dead.

Salisbury, who toured with Wilfred Burchett[23] as a guide, supplied a photograph taken in Hanoi that could not be said to show bomb damage as distinguished from dilapidation, but the photo did have an anxious-looking, appealing Vietnamese child in the foreground looking into the camera. Salisbury's further dispatches described waitresses at his hotel taking up rifles to fire at planes overhead (but nothing about bombs dropping), and praise of North Vietnamese unity and determination. His last dispatch reported that Ho Chi Minh expected Hanoi to be destroyed, so officials were working on blueprints of a new city to be built on its site.

Salisbury expected a Pulitzer for his Hanoi trip, to go with the one he had won in Moscow in 1955. He reported in *Without Fear or Favor* that he lost out by one vote, but that Turner Catledge considered the Hanoi dispatches a high point of his term as managing editor.

The Salisbury dispatches made him anathema to Washington, where administration figures referred to "the *Hanoi Times*" and Dean Rusk telephoned Arthur Sulzberger to ask if Salisbury had gone to Hanoi with instructions to report as he did, but they made Salisbury a hero to the anti-war movement. Walter Lippmann wrote that those charging Salisbury had made himself a tool of enemy propaganda were stooping to self-deceiving nonsense. Salisbury was in demand again on television talk shows and embarked on a speaking tour across the nation, starting at Columbia University to a standing ovation. To the anti-war movement, Salisbury and the *Times* had caught the Johnson administration in another lie, and the U.S. was bombing Vietnamese civilians indiscriminately.

President Johnson's obsession with Vietnam almost excluded his making policy in other foreign areas, which he left to Rusk. The Western European nations gave Johnson no aid or comfort in Vietnam, and he reciprocated by considering NATO and the European Community problems for which Europeans were responsible. Johnson believed that both NATO and the European Community were in disarray because of De Gaulle, and nothing could be done about the obstinate Frenchman. Johnson met De Gaulle for the first time on the occasion of Kennedy's state funeral, and regarded him as deceptive and anti-American.[24]

Aside from Vietnam, Johnson took decisive action in foreign policy only once, during the turmoil in the Dominican Republic in April 1965. Early in Kennedy's administration the long-time *caudillo,* Leónidas Trujillo, had been assassinated in a coup.[25] Johnson had been on hand to meet the first freely elected Dominican president in many years, Juan Bosch, when he was inaugurated in 1962, and had not been impressed. When a military junta overthrew Bosch in September 1963, Kennedy's Defense Department made contingency plans for sending in the Marines if it should prove necessary, and Kennedy cut off economic aid. Some aid was restored when a provisional civilian government was established under Donald Reid y Cabral. In April 1965, a mixed army-civilian revolt broke out, with first indications it was backed by Communists and supporters of Bosch.

Johnson later described Bosch as "an intelligent, pleasant man with an attractive personality, and he was full of ideals," but off the record he thought Bosch naive and ineffective. He was ready to believe advisers who thought that if Bosch returned to power he would be a figurehead, probably briefly, for Communists of three Dominican factions, pro-Soviet, pro-Mao and pro-Castro. Johnson remarked that having Bosch return as president "would be like having Arthur Schlesinger, Jr. president of the Dominican Republic."

The Dominican crisis blew up suddenly. Johnson stressed in his memoirs the gruelling and careful considerations of alternatives by the usual ad hoc groups, but actually his action was precipitous. He sent in 2,000 Marines and part of the 82nd Airborne Division on the pretext of evacuating Americans, while appealing to the Organization of American States for authorization to do so. The troops served as a buffer between rebels and mainstream anti-Communist Dominican army forces, and Johnson was left with the dilemma of how to get the troops out.

While conferring with his new CIA chief, Admiral Raborn, Johnson heard a suggestion from Raborn's deputy Ray Cline that the best possibility for a Dominican president might be former President Joaquin Balaguer, who was in exile in New York. Johnson took another quick decision: "That's it. That's our policy. Get this guy in office down there!"[26] Balaguer duly defeated Bosch in the elections.

Johnson took some heat for his Dominican snap judgments, but his intervention limited bloodshed and probably did as much good as harm. Contrary to forecasts of the liberal media, the intervention did not deepen hostility in Latin America.

In other parts of the world, Johnson was less lucky. His open hostility to De Gaulle climaxed in a De Gaulle press conference on February 21, 1966, in which the French president announced that he was not leaving NATO, but was withdrawing French military participation. NATO headquarters would have to leave Paris, and the bases of the U.S. Communications Zone through France would be dismantled.

De Gaulle was not alone in feeling that, except for the Vietnam obsession and an occasional local foray such as the Dominican venture, the United States was in retreat around the world.

Six months after DeGaulle's renunciation of NATO, Moshe Dayan, who had directed Israel's 1956 Sinai campaign, visited South Vietnam as a correspondent on special assignment for the *Washington Post*. As a VIP guest, he went out with the lst Cavalry (Airmobile) Division and saw a neighboring company ambushed by the Viet Cong, taking casualties of 25 dead and about 50 wounded. Dayan later saw the aftermath of an attack by three battalions of Viet Cong, about 1,000 men, on a company of about 130 South Koreans that left 237 Viet Cong killed by supporting U.S. air and firepower. He walked among the dead Viet Cong, not unmoved.

Dayan left South Vietnam bemused. American tactics, he thought, were dictated by domestic political demand for minimum casualties, and the tactics left the initiative to the enemy, which was relatively poorly armed in 1966. Israel was poorly armed, too, and had virtually no U.S. weapons. Dayan had seen a good part of the 1,700 helicopters the U.S. Army had in Vietnam, more than all the helicraft in Western Europe, with Chinook and heavy crane helicopters depositing in the battlefield 155-mm guns, bulldozers and command-communications caravans. Dayan, who had more reason than Johnson to dislike De Gaulle, had to agree with De Gaulle that the Americans did not know what they were doing.

Less than a year later the Six Day War exploded, a watershed event that would determine for a long time the future of the Middle East, and the United States had virtually no influence in it.

A prelude to the Six Day War occurred on April 7, 1967, when some of the 1,500 Syrian gun emplacements on the Golan Heights shelled three Israeli kibutzim in northern Israel. Israel's French-built Mirages and Mystères bombed the gun emplacements that had done the shelling, and then shot down six Syrian MiGs that came out to challenge them.

In a speech in Cairo on May Day, Nasser offered Syria any planes and pilots it requested from his Soviet-built air force of 419 warplanes.

On May 12, a Soviet intelligence officer in Cairo informed Nasser that Soviet satellite surveillance had confirmed Syria's charge that Israel was massing troops on the Syrian border for an attack. The next day, Soviet President Nikolai Podgorny told Nasser's aide Anwar Sadat, who was visiting Moscow, that Israel was preparing to attack Syria, and Sadat telephoned the report to Nasser. Nasser moved two divisions of Egyptian troops into the Sinai, joining one already there, as the Arab media reported an impending Israeli attack on Syria. Israel ordered partial mobilization of the reservists who made up the bulk of its army.

Israeli Prime Minister Levi Eshkol invited the Soviet Ambassador in Tel Aviv to visit the northern border with him to see that there were no troops there, and the Ambassador declined. Eshkol did not believe that

Egypt would attack; its performance in Yemen had not been impressive.

At the United Nations, Egypt informed Secretary-General U Thant that hostilities might break out and that UN Emergency Force troops maintaining the truce since 1956 should leave the Sinai, but should stay at their posts in Gaza and at Sharm el-Sheikh at the entrance to the Gulf of Aqaba. On the advice of his deputy, Ralph Bunche, U Thant informed Egypt that the UNEF was indivisible, and part could not be removed while another part stayed on duty.

Nasser formally demanded on May 17 that all UNEF forces leave, and U Thant complied immediately on the ground that all parties had to agree to their stationing. Nasser had continued the Sinai buildup, and by May 20 there were 80,000 Egyptian troops with 900 tanks in the Sinai.

By May 20 the governments of the United States, Britain, France and the Soviet Union, along with most Middle East correspondents, knew that Nasser was forcing a showdown and there would be, almost inevitably, another war, even though Eshkol's government had few hawks in it.[27]

On paper, Israel's military position did not look good. It had half the aircraft of Egypt and its allies. Although the air force was the most modern part of the Israeli Defense Forces, with two dozen new French jets and a handful of French Nord Atlas transports along with a few A-4 Skyhawk ground-support planes from the United States, most of its planes were veterans of the 1956 war. The army's firepower was low, its heaviest artillery the obsolete British 25-pounder. Israel's armor was a motley collection, including tanks and half-tracks of British and Soviet manufacture captured in 1956, some solid British Centurion tanks and a handful of American Pattons, and new French AMX-30 light tanks that had proved to be vulnerable in desert warfare.

Before the 1956 campaign, Israel had acquired from the French some of the little American Sherman tanks left behind in Europe after World War II, and Israeli mechanics experimented with the hulks. Before the 1967 war, Israel acquired Shermans in considerable numbers from West Germany, which had used them to train border police before joining NATO. Adenauer, agreeing that West Germany owed compensation to surviving Jews, allowed Defense Minister Strauss to give the Shermans to Defense Minister Shimon Peres in part payment. Israelis installed new diesel engines in the Shermans and mounted new turrets on them with French 75 guns to create a tank, small but rugged, that became the workhorse of Israeli armor.

Israel had no self-propelled guns, so some of the Sherman chassis were used as mounts for 105-mm guns. The recoil from the gun would knock over the light tank chassis unless fired almost straight ahead, so the Israelis mounted A-frames at the rear of the improvised self-propelled guns. A crew would aim the contraption in the general direction of the target, drop the A-frame to dig into the earth and steady the chassis against recoil, refine the aim and let fly.

Compensating for the inferior weaponry, Israel had a corps of superior officers headed by Yitzhak Rabin, the chief of staff, highly motivated citizen soldiers and excellent intelligence. Veteran British and French officers and reporters who had seen the 1956 war did not doubt that Israel could win a war, and the CIA told Johnson, and he relayed to Foreign Minister Abba Eban, "If the UAR attacks, you will whip hell out of them." That was not, however, the issue to Israelis. The issue was how many casualties the small nation could take while whipping hell out of them. Heavy casualties would stop immigration into Israel, as fatal as losing the war.

The Kennedy administration had continued the Dulles policy of 1956, selling no arms to Israel. On the eve of the Six Day War, the only American weapons the Israelis had acquired from Johnson were a few Hawk missiles, which never would be fired, a squadron of subsonic Skyhawks and a handful of Patton tanks, sold evenhandedly to Israel, Syria and Jordan. At Nasser's buildup in the Sinai, Israel asked the United States to sell it some weapons, and was told by Rusk and McNamara that no arms could go through the pipeline in time to help in the current crisis. Israel received a small shipment of machine gun bullets.

On May 22, Nasser visited his troops to announce that his forces had taken over the former UNEF position at Sharm el-Sheikh, and "under no circumstances will we allow the Israeli flag to pass through the Gulf of Aqaba." Israel ordered full mobilization, and the Johnson administration came to life with a proposal for a multinational task force to escort Israeli shipping through the Straits of Tiran. Johnson insisted, however, that the force had to be multinational, and he wanted the ships of De Gaulle in the "Red Sea Regatta."

Eshkol made plans for an Israeli preemptive strike for May 26, but Johnson's warnings caused a postponement. Johnson met with Abba Eban that day and told him, "Israel will not be alone unless it decides to go it alone." Eshkol postponed the attack a second time. By then, only the Dutch and Australians had agreed to join Johnson's Red Sea Regatta, with the British in tentative agreement. Johnson also cautioned Eban that he would need congressional approval for the naval escort, which could not be rushed.

In Israel, the press and public in demonstrations demanded that Dayan, out of the army for ten years and a bystander as an opposition member of parliament, be brought into the army or government. On June 1, after a wrangle in the Cabinet, a unity government was formed naming Dayan Defense Minister and bringing into the Cabinet the minority opposition figure and old Irgun chief, Menachem Begin.

In Moscow, Gromyko called in the Israeli Ambassador and warned that Israel would face serious consequences if it made a preemptive strike. On June 3, France informed Israel that it was holding up delivery of arms already paid for, De Gaulle explaining that he did not want to give Israel the means to start a war.

Israel's new Cabinet was in emergency session on June 4 when a message from Johnson informed Eshkol that De Gaulle had refused to join the naval task force and again warned Israel not to launch an attack. Johnson's message stressed the importance of "who fires the first shot," and Dayan considered the message "negative and discouraging." It appeared to mean that Nasser's blockade of Tiran was not considered an act of war, and that the United States would blame whoever fired first.[28] Any delay meant that Israel might have to sustain the first blow, lengthening the war and increasing casualties.

King Hussein, until then in a state of hostility with Nasser, flew to Cairo and signed a defense pact putting his Arab Legion under Egyptian command, as in 1956. Ahmed Shukairy, the loquacious attorney Nasser had put in charge of the Palestine Liberation Organization, broadcast over the PLO radio in Cairo a call to "drive the Israelis into the sea." Hussein returned to Amman with Shukairy, who told correspondents there that he expected Jordan to attack Israel.

On June 5 at 7 a.m. Israel sent 183 warplanes, almost all of its air force, against 11 Egyptian military airfields, destroying 197 Egyptian planes in an hour and a half. The Israeli planes returned, refueled, and 164 of them took off again at 9:30 a.m. on a second strike at 14 Egyptian military airfields, destroying 107 more Egyptian planes. Nasser had lost 304 of his 419 planes, and Israel had undisputed control of the air.

As the planes took off, Israel sent a message to King Hussein through General Odd Bull, the Norwegian UNEF commander, asking him to stay out of the war. Hussein replied through Odd Bull that his air force would give the reply. Hussein meanwhile telephoned Nasser—his conversation monitored by Israeli intelligence—and Nasser assured him that Egyptian troops were routing the Israelis. At 11 a.m. Jordanian artillery shelled Israel's Lod airport and West Jerusalem, apparently aiming at parliament, which stayed in session.

A third wave of Israeli air attacks destroyed all 28 of Hussein's aircraft, 53 of Syria's 112 aircraft and ten Iraqi aircraft that had been sent to Jordan.

Three hours after the first Israeli air strike, the hot line in the Pentagon was activated by Moscow for the first time. The hot line had been installed in August 1963, but never had been used except for tests and to exchange New Years' greetings. Kosygin was calling Johnson to demand that he stop Israel, or 10 Soviet warships that had entered the Mediterranean from the Black Sea would do so. Johnson agreed to do everything he could for a ceasefire, but Johnson also ordered the 6th Fleet to break the precautionary 100-mile limit and move to 50 miles from Israel's coast. Johnson expected the Soviets to monitor the movement and probably hang back, as they did. The silent gesture was the last help Johnson would give the Israelis until wrangling began at the United Nations after the war was decided.

Within four days, Israel had seized the Gaza Strip in two days of fighting, seized Jerusalem and driven through Jericho to the Allenby Bridge to occupy the West Bank, and crossed the Sinai to reach Kantara East on the Suez Canal. On June 8, two Israeli jets and a PT boat by mistake rocketed and torpedoed the U.S. military spy ship *Liberty* a few miles off the Sinai coast, even though it flew the American flag. This was the trigger-happy Middle East, where deception is the rule rather than the exception, and the Israelis expected Egyptian and Soviet vessels in the area with antennae aimed at the coast. The *Liberty* was all but destroyed, with 34 killed and 74 wounded Americans, to Israel's dismay.

The Johnson administration's efforts had been directed at ending the war from the start, through warnings to Israel and action at the United Nations. Israel accepted a ceasefire ordered by the Security Council, but Egypt did not. Suddenly Egypt accepted the ceasefire on June 8, as everyone in Israel knew that the next target would be the 1,500 Syrian guns on the Golan Heights.

Almost all of Israel's limited military force and equipment was in the south, much of the material across the Sinai, and the men and equipment could not be brought quickly to the Syrian border. Israel had perhaps 50 to 100 of its own tanks and half-tracks for the initial reckless assault up the mined escarpment of the Golan Heights. The second, larger, wave of attack was made in captured Jordanian tanks, armored cars and trucks, many of them still carrying portraits of King Hussein on their radiators. The impossible assault, driving miles uphill through winding roadbeds of shifting sand into the teeth of Syrian bunkers, concrete fortresses and dug-in Patton tanks used as additional artillery, took two days. Few outsiders saw it, because Israel closed the roads north to correspondents at 4 a.m. Those who saw the attack would never forget it. No one could have done it if the Syrian leadership had not panicked and pulled back most of the Syrian forces to defend Damascus. Israeli forces reached Kuneitra, on a line predetermined by Dayan, on June 10, and found the city deserted.

Rusk called Abba Eban "in near panic" to ask where the Israeli troops, 40 miles from Damascus, were headed.[29] He demanded that Israel accept the Security Council's ceasefire, and Israel complied, its mission accomplished against U.S. advice.

The *Times* saw the Six Day War coming on with foreboding. The *Times* is an American institution, not a Jewish one, and Israel had been a thorn in its side even before the nation was created.

Gay Talese, a *Times* insider, reported:

> Throughout his lifetime to the year of his death . . . George Ochs-Oaks overwhelmingly opposed the Zionists and all other advocates of a Jewish State in Palestine, and this view was also endorsed by Adolph Ochs (founder of the *Times* and brother of George) and for years it was part of the editorial policy of *The New York Times*. When Arthur Hays Sulzberger became publisher of the *Times* he made speeches and statements urging Jews not to agitate for a Jewish Palestine state, and in 1939 Sulzberger was among a group of influential Jews who urged President Roosevelt not to appoint Felix Frankfurter to the Supreme Court because they believed it would intensify anti-Semitism in America, a notion that Roosevelt resented and ignored.[30]

When Hitler came to power, the Ochses and Sulzbergers got their distant relatives out of Germany, but Adolph Ochs refused to open the subject of the plight of the Jews in Germany for discussion in the *Times'* letters column "because of the volume of mail that would pour in and because under the *Times'* rules he would have to devote equal space to the other side." Instead, he sent his managing editor Frederick Birchall to Germany to report on Hitler and the Jews.[31]

Times opposition to the creation of Israel was vocal when President Truman issued a statement on October 4, 1946, advocating that 100,000 European Jews, survivors of concentration camps, be permitted to immigrate to Palestine, while at the same time calling for a change in U.S. immigration laws to permit surviving Jews to come to the United States. The *Times* condemned in an editorial Truman's interference in Britain's negotiations on Palestine, and the next day noted in a news story that *The Times* of London had picked up the editorial. Then the *Times* put an extraordinary headline on a lengthy commentary:

Truman's Palestine View
Flouted Foreign Advisers
Swayed by Political Aides, President Is Held
to Act Counter to U.S. Policy.

The headline was mystifying, because under the Constitution the President makes foreign policy, and advisers are there for him to flout. The commentator, James Reston, gave birth in the article to the "powerful Jewish lobby," writing that there was no doubt that Truman had been influenced by "one of the most powerful lobbies ever organized in Washington."[32] (The powerful lobby was not able to get Jewish survivors admitted to the United States then, was not able to get arms credits for Israel for 20 years, and lost all of its battles against selling sophisticated arms to Saudi Arabia, but Reston's creation became dogma in the American media.)

Truman had said, "In the light of the terrible ordeal which the Jewish people of Europe endured during the recent war and the crisis now existing, I cannot believe that a program of immediate action along the lines suggested above could not be worked out."

Reston dismissed Truman's concern, writing, "It is generally conceded in the capital that the plight of the Jews in Europe is only one aspect of the melancholy story of the displaced persons of Europe, of whom the Jews are a minority."

Once Israel was established as a state, the *Times* took a strictly evenhanded approach to the Israel-Arab dispute, a tightrope act that, given the *Times'* close association with the State Department, teetered toward the charismatic Nasser.

In 1956, the Suez crisis caught everyone unprepared. The *Times* prudently delayed comment on John Foster Dulles' actions, and by the absence of commentary implied approval of Dulles' moves against Britain, France and Israel. Finally, in an editorial the *Times* blamed the Suez mess mostly on the British, French and Israelis, secondarily on Nasser and the Soviets, concluding that "it seems clear that much more has been lost than gained (by the assault on Suez). . .a renewed conviction of the Arab-Asisan world that imperialism and colonialism are still alive. . .the Russian position strengthened, the Western position (including that of the United States) weakened, Nasser as great or greater a menace than ever and the United Nations flouted."[33]

Reston's comment that day included a careful swipe at Israel: "In the Middle East we have seen a new dictator goad the Israelis to the point where they connived at military aggression, flouted the United Nations which created that state in the first place and scorned the repeated appeals of President Eisenhower."

Eleven years later, the Six Day War posed more of a problem than ever because leading Israelis had become well-known and attractive world figures. The *Times* urged a Security Council resolution to force Nasser to revoke his Gulf of Aqaba blockade, conceding that Nasser would ignore it, and pressed for Johnson's international naval force as a second step. At the same time it sent Reston, even-handedly, to Cairo first, then Israel. From Cairo, Reston reported that Nasser did not want a war, that Arabs understood Western sympathy for the Jews after the holocaust, but that Israel was regarded as a U.S. base and a barrier dividing the Arab nation physically, and it could never be accepted until Israelis divorced themselves from Western beliefs.[34]

Reston barely made it to Tel Aviv on the last flight via Athens as the war broke out and the *Times* called for an immediate ceasefire. The next day he reported that the Israelis considered the war won.[35] In both a column and a news story, he stressed that the victory, already won, did not mean peace, that Israel would have to invite Palestinian refugees to return, and that "probably only the United States and the Soviet Union, working together, can lead the nations away from this disastrous course." Tom Wicker led his column, on the third day of the war, "Israel has resorted to violence and won its victory. . . . Yet victory is not necessarily settlement."[36] On that day the *Times* declared the war over in an editorial headlined, "The Four-Day War."

Reston was back in Washington before the Israelis had captured the Golan Heights, writing again that the United States and Soviet Union would have to get together on the Middle East, although his column had some sensible remarks as well: "Moscow has lost because it backed the wrong horse. Washington has been saved because the Israelis didn't follow its advice. Nasser lost because he swallowed his own bologna. And even Israel is in danger of losing because it is now tempted to think that military power will save a small nation in the midst of a vast and hostile Arab world."[37] Editorially, the *Times* appealed to Premier Alexei Kosygin, visiting the United Nations, to cooperate with Johnson, and to Israel not to annex Jerusalem. Israel ignored its advice and annexed Jerusalem on June 28. The *Times* deplored the action in its leading editorial June 29.

Times coverage and commentary on the Six Day War was thorough and gloomy throughout, contrasting sharply with the euphoria of the rest of the media and in Washington. Most Americans, including Johnson, sympathized and identified with the beleaguered Israelis and counted their success a victory for democracy and comity. No Arab prisoners were lynched, executed or even seriously roughed up. No cities were bombed. Barriers and anti-sniping walls came down in Jeru-

salem, where Arab and Israeli populations mingled in the first days after the war, and no one was barred from a religious shrine. It occurred
to almost no Americans that Israel had saved itself alone, without the
help of American weapons, against disastrous American advice and in
the face of American obstruction.

Americans accepted Israel's victory as a natural gift, a lift in morale
when Americans needed it to counter the discouraging Vietnam war
and simmering revolt at home, just as the spoils of war were accepted
as America's due. The Israelis gave the United States the first intact, operative SAM missiles the Americans had seen up close, along with their
control centers—vital information for the Vietnam war. Aberdeen
Proving Ground filled up with Soviet tanks, armored cars, small arms,
cannon of all calibres and ranges, barrage rockets and launchers—a
wide variety of ordnance to be tested for everything from metallurgy
to its manufacturing techniques, along with operation and maintenance manuals. General Keegan said that the intelligence value of the
Israeli gifts was incalculable.

Victory made the Israelis potentially valuable allies for the first time,
and turned some of the Vietnam doves in Congress into hawks on the
Middle East. The Johnson administration made a contribution in the
United Nations to the terms of the armistice, Security Council resolution 242, giving Israel a basis to hope for a negotiated settlement with
its neighbors.

Few Americans pondered the Six Day War because the revolution at
home again seized their attention.

The black revolt in the United States joined with the anti-war revolt
in 1965 after the Reverend King declared that the Vietnam war ob-
structed the realization of civil rights, making official a tentative alliance. Anti-war activists seized on reports that the Johnson build-up in
Vietnam resulted in black infantry soldiers doing more than their share
of fighting. For a time, the two revolts, black and anti-war, reinforced
each other. The alliance broke down because the black revolt was
spontaneous and reckless, and the anti-war revolt was intellectual and
manipulated.

On the heels of the Six Day War an insurrection erupted in Newark,
where the arrest of a taxi driver touched off a four-day rampage that
left 24 dead, 1,200 injured and 1,216 jailed. It was followed immediately by warfare employing tanks and machine guns against rioters in
Detroit, where looting lasted from July into August and destroyed
whole sections of the city.

Johnson, operating from an Oval Office that was turned into a war room, sent into Detroit 4,700 Army paratroopers and tanks to back up 1,500 National Guardsmen. The Detroit riots left 43 dead, uncounted injuries and 3,365 prisoners with little precedent on how to deal with such numbers, and more than 1,000 businesses destroyed by fire-bombs and looters. On August 14 SNCC issued a newsletter attacking Zionism and charging Israeli atrocities against Arabs, and black rioters in some cities singled out Jewish businesses for looting.

The long hot summer proceeded with riots or racial clashes sweeping through Albany, Nyack, Peekskill, Mount Vernon, New Rochelle, Rochester, Syracuse, Oyster Bay, Wyandanch, New City, Johnstown, Newburgh, Ithaca, Poughkeepsie and Buffalo, New York; New Britain, New Haven, Hartford and Waterbury, Connecticut; Trenton, Englewood, Elizabeth, Plainfield, Passaic, New Brunswick, Jersey City and Atlantic City, New Jersey; Philadelphia, Pittsburgh, Chester and Erie, Pennsylvania; Cairo, Aurora, Peoria, Rockford and Waukegan, Illinois; Youngstown, Columbus, Des Moines, Lorain and Toledo, Ohio; Albion, Flint, Grand Rapids, Jackson, Kalamazoo, Saganaw and Lansing, Michigan; Gary and South Bend, Indiana; Minneapolis, Minnesota; Wichita and Great Bend, Kansas; Providence, Rhode Island; Kansas City, Missouri; Omaha, Nebraska; Milwaukee, Wisconsin; Los Angeles, Long Beach, Fresno, San Bernadino, San Francisco, Oakland and Sacramento, California; Phoenix, Arizona; Portland, Oregon; Boston, Massachusetts; and Washington, D.C. Blacks with rifles walked into the state legislature at Sacramento, and 14 rioters were shot dead in Buffalo.

The *Times* saw some legitimation in the riots, noting that in Newark, a predominantly black and poor population still was governed by whites "who, many Negroes are convinced, do not want to share that power equitably with black men."[38] But, by 1967, the *Times'* first preoccupation was not the civil rights cause it championed, or the danger presented by Israel, but the anti-war revolt. It missed no opportunity to portray the Vietnam war as immoral and the Johnson administration as devious, even though Johnson was behaving as the *Times* suggested in regard to the Middle East and civil rights. *Times* columns, editorials and news columns attacked Johnson's conduct of the war.

On the day the Six Day War broke out, the *Times* reported that Roger Hilsman charged the Johnson administration had not started bombing of North Vietnam in retaliation for the infiltration of regular North Vietnamese troops into South Vietnam as it claimed, but "to try to bring Hanoi to its knees." Appearing on *CBS's* Face the Nation, Hilsman challenged the explanation of his old boss, Dean Rusk, and said he did not think the war could be won politically. In the same story, the

Times quoted George Ball, recently out of the Johnson administration, as saying, "I happen to think that the bombing of the North is not useful, that the political cost is too high and the risks too great, and that the overriding military advantage has not been demonstrated."[39] Almost four years after Diem's assassination, the *Times* still promoted the Washington coup group.

Times editorials thundered against the bombings, and its columnists were unanimous that the Vietnam war never could be won. Tom Wicker, on the eve of the Six Day War, wrote:

> Last week American forces suffered 2,929 combat casualties, the highest weekly toll so far; 313 of these were battle deaths, making a total of 1,177 killed in the last four weeks . . . the opposing forces are not only strong and effective but have been able to take a major combat initiative. General Westmoreland's headquarters reported this week that so far in the war, 1,398 planes and 888 helicopters have been lost. . . . The war is now costing the United States an estimated $24 billion a year and big new troop increments would run up the bill again. . . . No wonder no one is talking these days about a coonskin on the wall. Whose skin, in fact, is being hung on whose wall?[40]

In the spring of 1967, Raskin and Waskow of the Institute for Policy Studies, in concert with the anti-draft movement that was proliferating in organizations across the United States,[41] wrote the "Call to Resist Illegitimate Authority," which was published in the *New York Review of Books*. It charged that the war was illegal, and that the United States was committing acts in Vietnam that had been declared crimes against humanity at the Nürnberg trials after World War II. It urged readers to permit their signatures on the document to be made public and to send a contribution to RESIST, the anti-draft organization headed by Professor Noam Chomsky, the revolutionary linguist at the Massachusetts Institute of Technology. Raskin became the first defendant to be acquitted in the trial of the Boston Five: Dr. Benjamin Spock, the Reverend William Sloan Coffin, Jr., Mitchell Goodman, Michael Ferber and Raskin, on charges of conspiracy to counsel and aid draft resisters.

Chomsky's RESIST was in competition with a New York-based group sponsoring the Mobilization Committee, although some intellectuals belonged to both groups. The committee—Mitchell Goodman, Henry Braun, Denise Leverton, Chomsky, Coffin and Dwight Macdonald—had plans for a real revolutionary demonstration. They recalled that Norman Mailer had been effective in drawing media attention in the nation's first political street demonstration in many decades, on behalf of Fidel Castro, at the time of the Bay of Pigs invasion. Goodman was appointed to solicit Mailer to lead a march on the Pentagon in Washington.[42]

The march was a significant act of revolution, since no one knew how it might come out, especially if the demonstrators, badly led and undisciplined, managed to get inside the Pentagon. Mailer, receiving Goodman's call, would write that he "felt one little bubble of fear tilt somewhere around the solar plexus." He was kidding, of course, or, as he put it elsewhere in his report, "lying like a psychopath." What he felt tilting was a bubble of excitement, maybe, but not fear, as there was only a fun-chance that he might be injured or incarcerated, given his prominence and the batteries of lawyers available to him. Fear was something else, what one felt in Newark or Detroit, or going up the Golan Heights.

Mailer's armies of the night did not penetrate the Pentagon, and they were released after brief detention, but the attack on the Pentagon had a lasting effect in an unexpected area. The financial and critical success of his book, accompanied by praise from the *Times*, *The New Republic* and even *Time* magazine, suggesting that Mailer was the nation's best journalist, was an important stimulant to the New Journalism, which had been called purple prose when it had been the Old Journalism. In the book, which Mailer called a novel to signify its imaginary content, Mailer found witness Harvey Mayes of Hunter College to report soldiers beating a girl:

> She twisted her body so we could see her face. But there was no face there; all we saw were some raw skin and blood. We couldn't see even if she was crying—her eyes had filled with blood pouring down her head. She vomited, and that too was blood. Then they rushed her away.[43]

Apparently these are Mailer's words, as they are quoting someone but not put in quotation marks, that is, not a real quote.

All of the Washington press corps was on hand for the assault on the Pentagon, watching every minute, and none saw any serious violence. Like Halberstam's pagoda raid, the most colorful parts were in the mind of the writer reprocessing someone else's report. Straight news reporters could not compete with the practiced mix of sex, sadism and blood of the imaginative novelist. Two months earlier, real faces of rioters, police and National Guardsmen had dissolved in blood in Detroit and Newark, and henceforth straight reporters were on notice to jazz it up, find the blood.

Although the media did not consider the march on the Pentagon, bloodless, a serious act of revolution, some of the participants did. Arthur Waskow, one of the original founders of the Institute for Policy Studies, wrote in the magazine *Liberation*, "The Pentagon siege can be treated as a tactical event to be analyzed and criticized as one possible model for future physical confrontations. This is a necessary process: There will be more occasions for physical confrontations and they ought to be much better planned than the Pentagon was. Can we do better at the Democratic Convention in Chicago?"[44]

The revolution did do better in Chicago, and *Liberation's* editor David Dellinger would be in the front lines.

Dellinger had gone to Hanoi with Tom Hayden of SDS on Hayden's second trip, along with Nick Egleston, an SDS leader. Dellinger urged the North Vietnamese officials to give more visas to American reporters and other groups, and the North Vietnamese responded by suggesting a meeting in Prague, between themselves, Viet Cong officials and Americans interested in helping. Dellinger promised to arrange a meeting.

While in the Far East, Dellinger also met Wilfred Burchett in Phnom Penh, with instant rapport. Dellinger was quickly on a first-name basis with Burchett, and later told the House Committee on Un-American Activities, "I consider him to be a very honest journalist and very helpful."[45]

Dellinger also visited Paris and met National Liberation Front officers, including Xuan Thuy, Mme. Binh and Colonel Ha Van Lau. Back home, he sent out discrete letters inviting anti-war leaders to the Prague conference in August. Those invited were told to reserve five pounds of luggage weight for literature to be given to the North Vietnamese to take home, and Dellinger later told the House committee that he had in mind sending copies of *Liberation,* the Communist publication *Guardian* and selections from *The New York Times.*

Altogether 40 American leftists went to the conference, which was moved to Bratislava from Prague, in September 1967, among them Dellinger, Hayden, Rennie Davis—all later defendants in the Chicago conspiracy trial—and an assortment of Quakers, black militants and Marxists. The purpose of the conference, Dellinger wrote, was "to create solidarity and mutual understanding between revolutionaries from Vietnam and their American supporters who are trying to change the United States."

One of the participants, Stephen S. Schwarzschild, wrote in *Dissent* that the conference produced no hard news and nothing new at all, because the Vietnamese (including Mme. Binh and some North Vietnamese of fairly high rank) balked communication by rigidly repeating primitive propaganda. Dellinger, however, excused the Vietnamese their doctrinaire position because they were "intensely involved in the defense of their homeland and have suffered incalculable casualties."

Dellinger returned to Czechoslovakia with Robert Greenblatt in June 1968, while Soviet troops were maneuvering there and the nation's fate hung in the balance, for a conference with Tran Van Anh and Pham Van Chuong.

It was a perfectly natural thing, Dellinger told the Senate committee, in the spirit of keeping communications private, that he and Greenblatt arranged with the Vietnamese to use a simple code in their cable messages, in which, for example, "Harry" would mean Hungary, and "Peter" would mean Poland. Dellinger also visited Havana twice in 1968, once in January, when he had his passport validated by the State Department for the trip as a reporter, and once in November for an operation in a Havana hospital, after the shambles of the Chicago Democratic Convention, and while Richard Nixon was being elected President.

Chapter XII
The Prague Spring
and Chicago Summer

"This stage of intellectualism has, in every nation, been the precursor of collapse, for it produced an antipathy to war and to military service. This development may well be hailed as an improvement, for war is hateful and brutal. But it always results in the destruction of the civilization concerned."[1]

—Sir John Glubb

At the time of President Kennedy's murder, he was an idol in Czechoslovakia, especially of the young, but also to some of the Communist functionaries and to the public at large. His drive for detente with the Soviet Union made his poised charm eligible for exhibition on Czech television and in the press, and he became the first Western politician so displayed as Czechoslovakia emerged from 15 years of isolation.

Czechoslovakia tentatively opened its doors to the West in the early 1960s because the nation was bankrupt. A curtain-raising event occured in October 1962, when President Antonín Novotný had Prague's giant statue of Stalin pulled down, six years after de-Stalinization in the Soviet Union, a gesture to tidy up golden Prague for cash-carrying visitors.

At the end of World War II the country had been in an advantageous position in central Europe, uniquely untouched by the war, its industrial plant intact. It was also on good terms with its liberator, one of two nations, the other being Bulgaria, to give the Red Army a genuine welcome.

By 1963 Communist mismanagement and Soviet exploitation had wrecked the economy. The Skoda works, its facilities expanded and preempted for the military, produced 60,000 cars in 1963, compared with Volkswagen's million. The Tatra still was built by hand, but as a company car for the Communist Party. New steel mills at Košice bought high-priced ore from the Soviet Union, then sold back the steel cheaply or put it into tanks delivered to bankrupt Egypt at Soviet direction. Shops were full of a combination radio-television-record player with a small TV screen, unsalable at any price. A small cassette recorder was produced, but it didn't work. At great cost low-power motorcycles were produced that stalled on a slight grade, so they were sold for a few dollars each on the flatlands of The Netherlands. There were skis available in shops "because there is no snow in Cuba."

Food shortages in January 1963 caused some panic, and in February visa requirements were eased as a display of confidence. Czechs could visit Hungary and Yugoslavia without exit visas, and Western tourists could enter with pickup visas, a generous exchange rate of 28 crowns to a dollar—later lowered to 16—and a promise of no police harassment. A Western consortium produced a Western movie, with the Czechoslovakian army playing cavalrymen and Indians at bargain prices.

A student disturbance on May Day, 1963, was called a riot, then settled by negotiation. The Prague government opened the Viola Club for young people, and the Redouta, a jazz bar. The kids at the Viola, in blue jeans, ducktail haircuts and sandals, heard Russian protest poets protesting how Hollywood had treated Marilyn Monroe, and explained to visitors, "We're like beatniks," although they knew they were not the real thing, with adult supervision and a return to work in the morning.

In 1964 the Viola got a look at the genuine article when Allen Ginsberg arrived to be crowned King of the May. The annual May Day poetry reading turned into a riot, and 12 youths were sentenced to three to 14 months. Ginsberg was deported after police "found in the street" his notes, said to implicate Party members in unwholesome sexual shenanigans.

In April 1963, the Slovak Writers' Union met in Bratislava and heard poet Laco Novomeský and novelist Ladislav Mňačko denounce Stalinism and national cowardice during the purge trials of the 1950s. The opening gun had been fired in the intellectual revolt. A month later the Slovak Journalists' Union adopted a resolution calling for "accepting the consequences of the personality cult," a veiled demand for the resignation of Novotný, president and Party leader.

In Prague, Czech writers echoed the unrest, at the same time chagrined that backward Slovaks had been first. They were not able to break censorship, however, until Novomeský found a way.

In the summer of 1964 Novomeský tried to organize a 20th anniversary reunion of veterans of the August 1944 Slovak uprising against the Nazis. Little was known then about the revolt, even in Czechoslovakia, because the Czechs of Prague had suppressed reports of it. The Slovak uprising had involved some Soviet advisers, parachuted in, and some foreign volunteers including a number of (non-Communist) French escapees from Nazi forced labor who had found refuge in Budapest. The Slovak guerrilla harrassment of German troops evacuating from Romania had contributed to the war effort by tying up the German troops who crushed it, as the four-day Prague uprising during the German evacuation of the city in May 1945 had not contributed.

Novotný forbid Novomeský's 1964 reunion. It was almost the perfect issue to underline the basis of everything that happens politically in Czechoslovakia, the antagonism between Czechs and Slovaks, also under communism.

A 1000 years ago, at the time of the incipient Moravian Empire, perhaps Czechs and Slovaks had been the same people. But Moravian King Svatopluk had scarcely got his empire started when Magyars arrived to settle what is now Hungary, and the Moravian Empire was extinguished after perhaps 30 years of existence. The tribes who became Czechs fell under the domination of German kings; the Slovaks under Hungarian kings. Golden Prague acquired Charles University 600 years ago and the cultural benefits of German prosperity, while Slovaks and Hungarians spent centuries trying to hold back the Turks. In the process the Slovaks picked up the Hungarian direct and candid way of speaking and more of a willingness to fight.

The Czechoslovakia created after World War II was democratic, progressive, nonviolent, well-organized and, under Czech direction, pacifist, but it did not have an historical identity. The question, "To whom or what should I be loyal?" puzzled Czechoslovaks, as would be demonstrated again in the Prague Spring.

Although Novomeský had to postpone his Slovak uprising reunion, he received a consolation prize. Novotný called him to Prague and presented to him the Klement Gottwald Prize for his literary work. Gottwald had been in charge when Novomeský went to prison for more than four years, while his chief in the uprising, Gustav Husák, went to prison for more than nine years.

Back in Bratislava with the Gottwald Prize, Novomeský, as the national poet, simply defied the censors, and the magazine he dominated, *Kulturný Život,* already daring in a Communist country, went to war against the controlled Prague press, joined by several other Bratislava publications. With censorship slack in Slovakia, Czech intellectuals scurried to catch up with the Slovaks, and a Byzantine series of political changes and mini-purges occured in the Communist Party.[2]

When the Six Day War broke out in the Middle East, Ladislav Mňačko slipped out of the country to cover it as a correspondent, and Czechoslovaks railed at the official pro-Arab, anti-Jewish propaganda. The 4th Writers' Congress convened in Prague as the war ended, after Novotný had prevented the convention for seven years. In the preceeding three years of creeping liberalism, 1,360 of the writers had taken trips abroad, some of them selling their work for hard currency, and the union had been official host to 1,200 foreign writers. Czechoslovakia was in a cultural boom, selling abroad its movies and novels, with an atmosphere in artistic circles so open that several East German writers took up residence in Prague, along with several French and American writers.

Reporters were barred from the writers' congress, a major political event, and Andreas Kohlschütter of the *Neue Züricher Zeitung* was arrested twice and held for 29 hours for receiving notes on speeches from writers attending.

Jiří Hendrych, the Presidium member who led the Communist Party delegation to the congress, walked out in fury when author Ludvík Vaculík spoke. Vaculík said the Party had turned the population into "an amorphous, malleable mass easily ruled by any dictator," and that citizens without rights had degenerated to a moral and political level that was lower than that of prewar Czechoslovakia.

Novotný expelled three writers from the Party: Vaculík, Ivan Klima and Antonín J. Liehm. Jan Procházka was dropped as a candidate member of the Central Committee. Hendrych took the magazine *Literární Noviny* away from the writers' union and put it under the Ministry for Culture and Information. Writer Jan Beneš was sentenced to five years for subversion in informing foreign journalists of events at the congress.

Party seizure of the writers' magazine did not work. The public boycotted it, and the writers founded *Literární Listy*, which, although censored, paid for itself.

In October the Journalists' Union held its congress in its well-disciplined tradition and condemned the writers.

At the end of October 1967 the Party Central Committee met to act against the revolutionary threat. It was in session on October 31 when university students at the Strahev dormitories staged a protest march, ostensibly against failures of electricity and water at their living quarters. Police with clubs broke up the demonstration by 2,500 marchers, although their protest, organized by Law Faculty professors at Charles University, was a model of decorum.

Students met at the Philosophy School with representatives of the Party and government, with Professor Eduard Goldstücker as mediator. Jailed for four years in the purge that caught Husák and Novomeský, Goldstücker would be an important player in the Prague Spring. The students' demand that police wear numbered badges was met; their victory legitimatized their protest.

The Party Presidium, or politburo, began meeting in marathon sessions, wrangling over how Novotný was running things. In December Novotný sought help from Soviet Ambassador Stepan Chervonenko, and Brezhnev arrived to rescue Novotný on December 8. The Presidium was divided on Novotný's future; four demanded that he resign, while six spoke for his staying on. The dissidents had no agreed successor for him. Brezhnev decided that the dispute was an internal party matter. He left telling the disputants, "Settle it among yourselves," a vote of no-confidence in Novotný.

The Presidium called the Central Committee into session in late December. Novotný was attacked for calling in Brezhnev without consulting them.

Czech army units were holding unusual winter maneuvers in the Prague area, and Novotný had the deputy defense minister, Colonel General Vladimir Janko, give orders for two divisions to move into the city. Lieutenant General Václav Prchlík heard of the order and informed the anti-Novotný Communist group that a coup was impending. Czech journalists later said that Presidium member Alexander Dubček sent personal envoys to the army units asking them not to cooperate with Novotný. The tanks did not roll, either because Novotný called off the coup or in response to Dubček.

In the Central Committee plenum, Novotný denied attempting a coup, and he denied a report that he had given Miroslav Mamula, the Party Secretariat's security enforcer, a list of 1,030 prominent Communist politicians, writers and professors for mass arrest.

The Central Committee met again in early January 1968 for the showdown. A majority had coalesced around the mild-mannered and little-known Slovak, Dubček, the candidate of reformers who felt they could dominate him.

One of the reformers was Josef Smrkovský, who was not a beginner at manipulation. During World War II, Smrkovský was an underground leader who directed the brief Prague uprising in early May 1945. While it was going on, emissaries from General George Patton arrived in Prague from Pilsen, where Patton's Third Army had advanced. Against Winston Churchill's urgent advice, Eisenhower had told Patton not to advance further, but Patton, who had taken Messina in Sicily against orders and gotten away with it, apparently believed he could take Prague if the city invited him to do so. Although Prague radio broadcasts called for help, Smrkovský, as deputy chief of the national committee that organized the uprising, met Patton's envoys on May 7 and told them that the Czechs wanted to be liberated by their fellow Slavs, the Red Army. Patton's army did not move unopposed into Prague on May 8, as it could have done, and Marshal Konev's forces entered Prague on May 9, putting Czechoslovakia into the sphere of Soviet liberation.

During the *putsch* of February 1948, when Communists in the coalition government of President Eduard Beneš felt the power they had won in 1946 elections slipping away from them in public discontent, Smrkovský again played a fateful role. He issued orders arming the Peoples Militia, the move that forced Beneš to sign a new cabinet list dictated by the Czech Communists and Soviet Ambassador Valerian Zorin, and the iron curtain rang down.

Twenty years later the Central Committee pushed through a resolution for its first secret ballot, a choice between Novotný and Dubček. Dubček was voted in and Novotný out by a vote said to have been about 70 to 40.

In January 1968, Czechoslovaks accepted the change at the top without reaction. Novotný was feared and disliked, but he remained the country's president, and Dubček was an unknown quantity who appeared to be a Soviet 100-percenter. Dubček's father, Steve Dubček, had immigrated to the United States before World War I, had been a Wobbly, and had returned to Slovakia just before Alexander was born in 1921. The family, with 300 others, had gone to help build a new Soviet Union in Central Asia. Dubček grew up in the Soviet Union from 1925 to 1939, returned to be an obedient Communist, was wounded in the Slovak uprising, and had been selected to attend the Moscow party college between 1955 and 1958.

In East Germany, the suspicious Walter Ulbricht took alarm when Novotný was deposed, but other neighboring Communists thought the January 1968 reshuffle in Prague was routine. In Budapest, Sándor Barcs, the personable head of MTI news agency and Hungary's Communist press lord, was telling Western reporters, "Nothing's going to happen in Czechoslovakia. You know the Czechs; they don't make trouble. You ought to watch the Poles. Gomulka is getting senile. Their politburo is split, each man for himself, and something has to happen there."

But something was happening in Czechoslovakia. Major General Jan Šejna, a Novotný protégé, close collaborator with the KGB and with Mamula, and a high-living friend of Novotný's son Antonín Novotný, Jr., defected to the United States. Šejna's defection gave the reform Communists an ideal stick with which to beat Novotný: his crony was "jeopardizing the security of the nations," and the Soviets could only approve a media campaign against him. Šejna had been implicated in Novotný's aborted military *putsch*. Shortly after the defection, the putschist General Janko committed suicide when he was summoned to the Central Committee building. The vice chairman of the Prague Supreme Court, Josef Breštanský, hanged himself in the woods near Prague when the Bratislava youth newspaper *Smena* charged him with terror sentences in 1955.

Novotný, still president and trying to save what was left, purged high government offices, at the same time that the Central Committee was demoting hard-liners in the Party. Among those fired were Interior Minister Josef Kudrna, chief prosecutor Jan Bartuška, ideologist Jiří Hendrych, the "mini-Beria" Mamula, trade unions president Miroslav Pastyřík and Vladimír Koucký, the Party's international liaison man.

Goldstücker was elected president of the Writer's Union. The army staff joined in demands that Novotný resign the presidency. Novotný amnestied the punished writer Jan Beneš on March 22 and resigned the presidency the same day.

A secret event had happened in February that made all the changes possible; media censorship had been practically lifted by a new Party directive to censors. Prudently, the Czechoslovak media did not report the event.

Censorship had been direct and effective, except for the slip-ups in Bratislava. A censor sat in every publications' newsroom, the last man to see copy before it went to a printer, who would not set the type without the censor's stamp. A 1948 directive from the Party Secretariat to the censors made every item touching on ideology a matter of national security, with the censors liable for breaches. The new directive, which writers credited to Josef Špaček, who was unofficially handling the duties of Hendrych, told censors they could not withhold their stamps unless the story actually violated national security matters such as defense secrets.

The media tried its wings with caution. There were no sensationalized stories. The rash of resignations, suicides and firings were reported laconically and briefly. There were demands for rehabilitation of the regime's victims of the 1950s and compensation for survivors, but no demands to prosecute their persecutors. Nevertheless the volume of news burgeoned, and newspaper circulation climbed five times normal. The whole nation watched the 7 p.m. newscasts. At Radio Free Europe in Munich, where the Czech desk for years had picked over Prague's newspapers for something worth passing on to news editors, an inundation of Czech and Slovak newspaper, television, radio and Četeka news agency copy buried the translators.

Hardline Communists were in panic. Drahomír Kolder declared, "We can't permit the press, radio and television to become a forum for views contradicting the whole policy of the Socialist movement."

The public watched skeptically, without cheers. The media conducted a lively dispute over Novotný's successor as president, but to the man on the street it still was a Party quarrel over the next dictator. Smrkovský was a Party reform candidate; he had done four years in prison under Gottwald. General Ludvík Svoboda, the old commander of the Czech Legion who had arrived with the Red Army, was a Hero of the Soviet Union, and then had been banished to a collective farm, was another reform candidate. Slovak Communists wanted Gustav Husák, leader of the Slovak uprising. Young Communists wanted Čestmir Císař; some of them called him their Kennedy.

Prague writers said the decision had been made; the politicians had settled on Svoboda, still a name with the Soviets.

Was Husák out because he was, like Dubček, a Slovak? "Not only that," a writer at *Literární Listy* said. "We don't want Husák. He's a good man, but he is too hard for us. He's bullheaded, and when he gets something in his head, nothing can dissuade him. He is too tough, and we are afraid of that quality of his." In quoting conversations with Czechoslovaks, the rule of identifying sources will be broken. Some sources remained in Czechoslovakia or may be able to return there on visits.

The day after Novotný resigned, the Warsaw Pact held a secret summit meeting in Dresden, East Germany; Dubček, Premier-designate Oldřich Černík and a delegation of hardliners Josef Lenárt, Kolder and Vasil Bilak met with Brezhnev, Ulbricht, Gomulka, Kádár and Zhivkov

(Romania's Nicolae Ceauşescu was not invited). Ulbricht and Gomulka warned Dubček to get his house in order. The Czechoslovak media did not report the meeting was in progress, only reporting its bristling communique after Dubček had returned.

The belated news reports implied that the Czechoslovaks had toed the line at Dresden, and Czechs remarked to each other, "I told you it wouldn't last."

In East Berlin, politburo member Kurt Hager addressed a congress of Communist philosophers on the Dresden meeting, which he called "a cold shower on the strategists of West Germany." He charged that West Germany had infiltrated Czechoslovakia "with the aim of subverting the Socialist countries from within, of dividing them, and especially of isolating the DDR."

Hager recalled that Smrkovský had served a prison term in the 1950s for being a "West German agent," and in that he went too far. The Czechoslovak press attacked Hager furiously. *Prace*, the trade union newspaper that had become the country's most complete daily, called East Germany's *Neues Deutschland* the "mouthpiece of the East German Central Committee," a most un-Communist sort of language.

At this point Svoboda was elected president, with 282 of 289 National Assembly votes, while a dour Novotný looked on.

Svoboda's election turned into a quiet spring festival, and lined up outside Hradčany Castle to salute him was a troop of Prague Boy Scouts, the first seen in the country in two decades. Their mothers had made them partial uniforms. Bishop František Tomášek issued his first pastoral letter. The Party published proposals for the rehabilitation of Vladimir Clementis, Rudolf Slánský and others, and reversed the 1967 ouster of writers from their union.

Maybe it was the perfect weather, or perhaps the Hager controversy—in which the Czechoslovak media dared challenge the dangerous East Germans to defend purely national, not Communist, interests. Maybe it was the Boy Scouts. But this was the Prague Spring; at the beginning of April Czechoslovakia turned a corner somehow and was marching off at the oblique, everyone in step, in a new direction.

One night in April, the Prague radio newscast ended with a financial note: "In Prague today the black market rate for the dollar is 35 to one." There couldn't be any doubt after that. May Day saw thousands march in a celebration of liberation; not a rowdy to be found and not all that much drinking, just streets full of people expressing friendliness to each other, warmth and happiness, laughing and a few crying.

Czechoslovakia was a thoroughly Communist country at the beginning of 1968 despite the slack liberalization after 1963. In the elections of 1946 the Communists had won 46% of the vote, although they needed the Social Democrats of the disguised Communist Zdeněk Fierlinger[3] to dominate the government. After the February 1948 *putsch* and apparent murder of Foreign Minister Jan Masaryk, the Czechs did not recoil from the Communists; they rushed to join the Party in the second half of 1948, especially intellectuals and professionals, giving Czechoslovakia the highest proportion of the population party members in the world, one out of every three adults.

In spite of this national vote of confidence in communism and the Soviet Union, pliable and cooperative Czechoslovakia was made the most victimized country in the anti-Tito purges of Eastern Europe in the early 1950s, on the direct orders of Stalin, Beria and Mikoyan. Klement Gottwald was once cheered as loudly as Dubček would be, but under his aegis a whole top echelon of Communists was tried and executed or committed suicide, beginning with Foreign Minister Vladimir Clementis and Interior Minister Rudolf Slánský. Hundreds went to prison for long sentences, including many of the leading Communists of the Prague Spring. At least 25,000 Czechs and several thousand Slovaks served prison sentences or forced labor in the uranium mines, and hundreds of thousands lost their jobs in the terror of 1949 to 1954.

Some of the early victims had been priests and conservative businessmen who had not fled the country. The nation remained tightly closed for a decade, almost a mystery country.

One result of the terror of the 1950s was that throughout the erratic liberalization that crept over the country after 1963, through all the reorganizations, boom in the arts, media freedom and reshuffle at the top, all the actors on stage were Communists, with the exception of a handful of writers and professors who got along well with the better class of Communists. All of the organizations and forums were Communist, and at least two-thirds of the population never was heard from in 1968.

Czechoslovakia had been, as George Bailey wrote in *The Reporter* in the early 1960s, a kakistocracy, a government of the worst. In late 1967 and early 1968, the leadership, cultural and political, had changed hands from menacing, ugly and despised Communists to more handsome and better mannered Communists, in the hope of taking the nation out of organized cronyism into the decentralized economic program of Professor Ota Šik. Anyone under 30 did not remember anything except Communist rule, and after two decades of ruthless suppression, there could exist no forum, newspaper or system of leadership selection for the majority of non-Communists. So the new leaders were called "popular." They were the best of the worst.

In the spring of 1968 that began to change when former political prisoners formed a network of K231 clubs, named after the paragraph of the Penal Code under which most of them had been sentenced. Some older citizens, once entrepeneurs and professionals, formed KAN, clubs of Politically Engaged Persons Without Party Affiliations, and 5,000 persons, mostly young, jammed into the first announced meeting of the Prague chapter.

These embryo political parties, daring under the Soviet threat to intervene in Czechoslovakia, never selected more than tentative leaders, and neither group had access to any publications, all of which were now run by Communists cheered in the West as reformers. Communist editors, whether reform or orthodox, excluded spokesmen of K231 and KAN from their pages.

In May the reform Communist leaders announced there would be Warsaw Pact maneuvers held in Czechoslovakia. The word circulated, but it was not immediately printed or broadcast, that the Soviets had demanded to station troops in Czechoslovakia as in Hungary, East Germany and Poland.

The new regime lied with more grace than the old one, with an appearance of candor. The new Defense Minister, General Martin Dzúr, announced the maneuvers but said they were only staff exercises. When the maneuvers began in June, there was no hard-news announcement of where they were, when they began or how large they were. The media reported that there were no East German troops, only East German staff officers present. The Soviets were said to be represented by only two regiments. Soviet Defense Minister Marshal Andrei Grechko was on hand at the beginning, but the Warsaw Pact commander, Marshal Ivan Yakubovsky, ran the exercise.

Through June Soviet troops in large numbers moved through the country, familiarizing themselves with roads, bridge tolerances and overpass clearances. Warsaw Pact political leaders dropped in to look over Dubček and his team, Kosygin taking the occasion to vacation at Karlový Vary. West German political figures visited Prague for the first time, including Free Democratic Party leader Walter Scheel and Federal Bank President Karl Blessing. Prague swarmed with Western tourists, filling the hotels, the overflow bunking in private homes.

The end of the maneuvers was announced for June 30, but the Soviet troops did not leave. The government denied that Yakubovsky had said they would remain into August, but the troops did remain.

Literární Listy published "2,000 Words," an appeal to retire dogmatic Communists by Ludvík Vaculík, which became the manifesto of the reform movement. Smrkovský denounced it as dangerous, but using mild language, in a reply, "1,000 Words."

Soviet, East German and Polish publications continued a drumbeat of warnings to the Czechoslovak reformers. Letters of warning arrived from the Soviet, East German, Polish, Hungarian and Bulgarian politburos, but the Czechoslovak Party Presidium did not publish them.

Dubček was summoned to a Warsaw Pact meeting in Budapest, and the Czech media did not announce it as flat news, rather, the press backed into the story by commenting that if Dubček were to go to a summit in Budapest he would face a kangaroo court. Public optimism of the spring had become fatalism by July.

Western correspondents regularly visited *Literární Listy*, where the writers' talk was informative and candid, even though the Communist Party kept a representative in the office monitoring what was said. At this juncture correspondents asked, "Is it true that the Party won't let Dubček go to a summit, and there's nothing the Soviets can do about it?"

"Dubček can't go to a summit," a writer said. "If he left our soil now, it would increase restlessness and tension, so he can't go."

He spoke blandly and fatalistically: "The liberalization isn't going to succeed, because the Soviets are not going to let us do it. We're fighting now to retain the gains we've made. KAN came around and wanted us to publish their program. We turned them down, and we asked them not to publish it anywhere else, either. We advised them to go at things slowly, and first get admitted to the National Front. Nothing like an opposition party can be tolerated any more, and without an opposition, liberalization won't work in this country."

He continued: "You saw that K231 was attacked in *Rudé Právo* (the Party newspaper) today. They've been told that if there is to be any prosecution of judges, prosecutors or secret police, it will be orderly and calm or not at all. They are almost out of business. The same thing would happen to KAN if it speaks out now."

Is KAN important?

"It is potentially important. If we don't have an opposition of some kind, we will slip back into the old system with new faces. But we have to drop that, for the time being, or the Soviets will intervene. I don't think the Soviets want to, but the East German troops are still there on the border. The orders have gone out to army units not to resist. It would be pretty useless in any case. We wouldn't get any help."

The same writer, during a stroll outdoors where he could not be overheard, said, "I joined the Party to destroy it." How many of the reform Communists were secret anti-Communist saboteurs could not be known, but probably there were not many. His position was both heroic and equivocal, since he enjoyed the privileges accorded to Party writers while exercising the authority to prevent publication of KAN's program. His advice to KAN was well-intentioned, but it denied to KAN's leaders the hero's role he preempted for himself.

The Warsaw Pact leaders convened in Warsaw instead of in Budapest, without Dubček. Hungary's Kádár saw Dubček secretly on his way to the summit.

The Communist bloc leaders, pressed by Ulbricht, Gomulka and the Ukraine's Pyotr Shelest, issued a menacing letter:

> . . . The Reaction publicly announced its political platform under the title '2,000 Words,' which included an open appeal for struggle against the Communist Party and constitutional power, for strikes and disorder. This is essentially a platform for counter-revolution. . . . a situation has emerged which is utterly unacceptable to the Socialist countries. . . . Can't you see that your Party is losing control?

The letter demanded, "All political organizations active against Socialism must be stopped. The Party must get the mass media under control. . . . The Party must unite itself on the principle of Marxism-Leninism and democratic centralism."

Brezhnev sent Dubček an ultimatum to come to Moscow, Kiev or Lvov. Dubček declined, and asked the Soviets to come to a meeting in Prague, or to Košice, near the Ukranian border.

On July 22 news reports from Moscow said that the entire Soviet politburo had left Moscow for the meeting with Dubček. The Moscow reports were premature, but they created some alarm. The Czechoslovak Party Presidium quickly fired General Prchlík, who had exposed Novotný's coup plans and who had been attacked by name in the Soviet press for advocating a change in Warsaw Pact command structure. That day 31 Czech students returned from the Bulgarian border, where they had been beaten up and refused entry to attend the World Youth Conference in Sofia.

The Soviet politburo's train finally did leave Moscow and turned out to be headed for Čierna-nad-Tisou, a railroad switchyard on the Ukranian border. On the Czech side of the border, railroad workers ran a train onto a siding carrying a long banner on its side reading, "Settle it among yourselves," Brezhnev's remark to Novotný the preceding December.

Author Pavel Kohout published in *Literární Listy* a "Citizens' Appeal to the Presidium," exhorting the Czechoslovak Presidium members by name to stand firm. A young sociologist, Vladimir Vlastatý, set up a counter in a downtown arcade and collected 10,000 signatures on Kohout's appeal in a few hours. The next day signature counters manned by students appeared throughout the city, and thousands stood in lines to sign the appeal.

In Čierna, Brezhnev fell ill for a day, and Dubček visited him on the Soviet train. The talks dragged on four days.

President Svoboda announced on August 1 that the talks were over, speaking of "cooperation" in a tone so solemn that it touched off panic. Before Svoboda spoke, Prague students had marched to the radio station to demand that their appeal for a rally be broadcast. Negotiating through the closed grillwork with radio officials, they listened to Svoboda on transistor radios. Kneeling on the sidewalk, they painted signs on butcher papers, dipping their fingers into the paint, "To the Old Town Square, 9 p.m.," and stopped passing streetcars to tape signs on their sides.

Radio officials appeared to tell the students they had permission to broadcast the rally appeal on the city's public address system; it could be heard in Prague but not outside the city, where it might alarm outsiders. The appeal was broadcast on the system installed by the Nazis to announce war victories at the beginning of World War II.

About 10,000 persons gathered in darkness at the Old Town Square, raising chants, "Tell us the truth!" "Where is Dubček?" "Long live Tito!" "Long live Romania!" They swarmed over the monument to Jan Hus. A police car nosed into the square and then withdrew to howls of protest. Another car approached, bathed in floodlights of a television crew walking backwards before it. Smrkovský, the Party's crowd pacifier, walked in the lights. An improvised public address system did not work, so he entered a building on the square and reappeared at the balcony.

"Tell us the truth!" the crowd roared.

"I won't tell you anything unless you keep order," Smrkovský said. "It has been a long and difficult negotiation. I will go home and get some sleep. I could use it." The crowd quieted.

Smrkovský said they could be satisfied with the results. The renaissance was a Czechoslovak matter. A meeting of one day would be held in Bratislava to avoid a schism and ensure cooperation with the Socialist nations.

The next day Brezhnev arrived in Bratislava on his special train, cheered by the Slovaks. Dubček kissed him on both cheeks, although he did not kiss Ulbricht or Gomulka. At Ulbricht's appearance the Slovak crowd turned silent.

Dubček appeared on television with his unruffled air. He declared, "We kept our promise to you. We have the same convictions we took to the talks, to continue resolutely on our road. . . . I can tell you sincerely we can be quite satisfied with the results and the spirit of the talks. . . . The nation's sovereignty was not threatened."

There was no conference in Bratislava. The summit leaders rested at a trade union recreation center, closed off on a hillside. At noon on August 3, the combined politburos of the Warsaw Pact nations, minus Romania, arrived in a long convoy of black limousines at the top of Mount Slavin and marched at a funereal pace to the monument to 6,000 Soviet soldiers who died driving the Germans from the southern part of the country. Brezhnev wiped a tear from his cheek with his handkerchief. The Bratislava conference was a demonstration that Soviet soldiers had died to liberate Czechoslovakia.

By evening the leaders had signed the ten-page Bratislava Declaration, and simultaneously the Defense Ministry in Prague announced that the last of Soviet maneuver troops had left the country. Foreign Minister Jiří Hájek joined a group of Western correspondents to interpret the Declaration, assuring them that the Czechoslovaks had won all their points.

The document was a long catalog of pledges in Party Chinese, binding the Czechoslovaks to democratic centralism and to "educate the masses in the ideological spirit of Socialism and the relentless struggle against all anti-Socialist forces."

In Prague, students organized demonstrations to demand what the wooly Declaration meant. They beleaguered the radio station until 4 a.m. Dubček, Smrkovský, Josef Špaček, Čestmir Císař, all the reform leaders followed by the students, gave interviews insisting that the confrontation was over. The crisis atmosphere faded away.[4]

Czechoslovakia in 1968 was *The New York Times'* kind of story. The *Times* had a phalanx of correspondents in Prague throughout the year, usually three or four, headed by the veteran Tad Szulc, until he broke his leg putting out an accidental fire in the U.S. Embassy, then for a time Henry Kamm, a future Pulitzer Prize winner, who retained some caution and skepticism. *Times* correspondents in Moscow, Warsaw, Belgrade and Bonn contributed to the story and were available for forays to Budapest, East Berlin and Bucharest. At that period the *Times* had 42 foreign correspondents, and about a quarter of them worked on the Prague story.

As an advocate of detente and an ardent opponent of the Vietnam war, the *Times* was accorded more than usual entrée to Communist sources and interviews. Events in Czechoslovakia in the first eight months of 1968 confirmed the conviction of *Times* editors that Communists are people, capable of feeling, heroism and decency, and that communism's evolution into something better was inevitable, even though it had been thrown off the track for a time by Stalinism.

The *Times* took an intense interest in the fate of the Czechoslovaks, and its hundreds of thousands of words on the events dominated the thinking of the American media on the subject. No media institution in the world could have matched the troops and firepower the *Times* threw into the Czechoslovak crisis. It would be an exaggeration to say that the fate of the Czechoslovaks was as much in the hands of Abe Rosenthal, John Oakes and the *Times* commentators as it was in the hands of Brezhnev, Gomulka, Ulbricht and Shelest, but it is no exaggeration to say that Americans would have known little of the events if it had not been for the *Times*. The rest of the American media was absorbed by the revolution at home until jostled by the *Times* coverage of Czechoslovakia. My newspaper, the *Daily News*, would not send me to Czechoslovakia until well into the spring.

The *Times* did a real service with its extensive coverage, which amounts to a book in the *Times Index* of 1968 that is indispensible to historians.

With all of this, the reporting and commentary, filtered through the New York editors and headline writers, came up wrong as an assessment of what was likely to happen and why it would happen in Czechoslovakia. The *Times* so ached to see the liberal Communists succeed in Czechoslovakia that it generated, along with its salutary interest, a deceptive optimism that pervaded the American media much as *Times* pessimism on Vietnam had done in 1963. Nowhere does the *Times* peculiar ideology emerge more clearly than in its handling of the Prague Spring and the Warsaw Pact invasion.

On the day that Novotný lost the Party leadership, the story shared Page 1 with the federal grand jury indictment of pediatrician Dr. Benjamin Spock on charges of conspiracy to aid draft dodgers, along with the Reverend William Sloane Coffin, Jr., Mitchell Goodman, Michael Ferber and Marcus G. Raskin, "the Boston Five." The *Times* was full of heroes resisting authority that day, and a long profile praised Dubček as a brave man twice wounded in the Slovak uprising in terms reminiscent of Herbert Matthews' praise of Fidel Castro when Castro had been as unknown as Dubček.[5]

By mid-March the *Times* editorialized under the headline, "Evolution in Czechoslovakia," that the United States should grant Czechoslovakia most-favored-nation tariff treatment to encourage liberalism, showing an enthusiasm that Czechoslovakian citizens had not yet displayed.[6]

As Svoboda became president and Novotný went into obscurity, Harry Schwartz, a member of the editorial board, recapitulated Czechoslovakia's recent history, apparently taking at face value the assurance of a Czech reformer that in 1948 the Czechs had not swung to the party out of opportunism but had genuinely believed that they could build a communism superior to that of the Soviets.[7]

News stories and editorials in May repeatedly sounded the theme of a power struggle in the Kremlin between sound Communists, like Kosygin, and a "Stalinist faction." An editorial expressed hope that Kosygin's visit to Prague would permit him to sway the Stalinists on his return to Moscow.[8] Szulc wrote of Dubček and the "fiery intellectuals and students that stand behind him" while cautioning that the Communists might be de-Communizing themselves.[9] Peter Grose, from Washington, speculated that the Soviets might permit the Czechs to trade with the West, establish relations with West Germany and even change the rules of Soviet dominance in Comecom and the Warsaw Pact, but they could not repudiate their alliance or give up the Communist monopoly of power.

In June the *Times* was forced to worry editorially that the Soviet, Polish and East German troops might "throttle the still infant Czechoslovak effort to create a fusion of communism and democracy," but the notion appeared so outrageous that the *Times* could not countenance it.

In July Henry Kamm sent unvarnished dispatches on the Soviet campaign of intimidation while Dubček was refusing to go to a Warsaw Pact meeting, but the *Times* also stressed the pressures on the Soviets. It published over three newspaper pages a 10,000-word essay by Professor Andrei Sakharov, circulated clandestinely in Moscow, urging that the Soviets *support* the bold initiative of the Czechoslovak reformers and calling for a new policy of cooperation with the United States.[10] The Sakharov manifesto, repeating the convergency theory that suited *Times* ideology, had no influence on the Soviet leadership, and, for that matter, most Americans were no more interested in converging with the Soviet Union than they were being converted to Islam by the sword.

Throughout the confrontation at Čierna the *Times* found reasons for optimism. Schwartz reported from Bucharest that Moscow had made a serious blunder in threatening the Czechs; it was losing support in the Communist world.[11] An editorial expressed relief that the Soviets had yielded to Czech demands to meet on Czechoslovakian soil, and again offered Sakharov's solution: the Soviets should embrace the Czech reforms.[12]

From Washington, Reston commented that Johnson had done nothing as the Soviets bullied the Czechs, but asked:

> What could Lyndon Johnson say today that would rally the community of nations against Soviet interference in Prague? Who would listen to complaints from Washington about using pressure on a client state in defense of national interests—at a time when Mr. Johnson had just summoned President Thieu of South Vietnam to Honolulu (to force his acceptance of talks with the Viet Communists)? The two situations are not, of course, similar in our eyes, but in the eyes of much of the rest of the world American intervention in South Vietnam seems much more brutal than Soviet intervention in Czechoslovakia.[13]

At the same time that Reston compared U.S. efforts to aid an ally while also bullying him with the Soviet bullying of Czechoslovakia, the *Times* editorially endorsed Johnson's doing nothing about Czechoslovakia.

> With the war of nerves against Prague mounting in intensity, it is essential for the West to avoid providing any fuel for the Soviet propaganda machine. Pretexts used for propaganda could be used tomorrow to 'justify' Soviet military intervention. . . . Moscow's dilemma is intense. . . use of force would split the world Communist movement, frustrate *détente* with the West and injure the climate the Soviet Union needs for its own more moderate internal reforms. Moscow's interest lies in accommodation with Prague, but will Russia's leaders have the wisdom to see it?[14]

The *Times* was seconded by its London correspondent, who was busy covering the Vietnam war and the Prague Spring from there. Anthony Lewis quoted the usual unnamed diplomatic sources to advise: "The West can help most by remaining quiet and calm." Lewis explained that the situation was different from the 1938 sellout of Czechoslovakia at Munich, and the expert opinion was that the Soviet leaders "do no want to take the risk of seeing a Communist country in the heart of Europe become non-Communist."[15]

Once again the *Times* pressed the theme that Washington should only stand by, saying in an editorial that the Czechs did not want help. "They seek to settle the conflict as a 'family affair.' It is their best chance."[16]

As the Čierna meeting ended columnist Tom Wicker also advised U.S. silence. He wrote that what the Soviets:

> ...must see is an increasing military threat through what is essentially a long military corridor from West Germany to Soviet soil.... it is hard to see how the United States could come vigorously to the aid of the Czechs—even if they wanted to, and even if Vietnam and other requirements did not make it exceedingly difficult to find the resources for any conceivable response.[17]

The *Times* accepted the assurance of Dubček and Smrkovský that the Čierna meeting went well, editorializing that "one probability emerges. The Soviet Union is not about to invade Czechoslovakia.... The evidence suggests that the courage and unity of the people of Czechoslovakia have paid off in these negotiations. The lesson will not be lost on the other peoples of Eastern Europe."

Henry Kamm was cautious and skeptical of the Bratislava agreement, but *Times* headline writers wrote over his story: "PRAGUE VICTORY APPEARS SECURE AS PARLEY ENDS."[18] The next day, as the Republican National Convention opened in Miami, preempting Page 1 space, the *Times* repeated, "DUBČEK CONFIRMS A PRAGUE VICTORY IN 6-NATION TALKS."

Relieved and with new confidence, the *Times* trumpeted the Czechs' victory in an editorial that also explained how it happened, "Face Saving at Bratislava." It said:

> The suppressionist elements in the Kremlin leadership and their neolithic allies in Eastern Europe have suffered a massive defeat. Behind the monumental collection of face-saving clichés in the Bratislava statement lies the plain fact that the crude Soviet effort to intimidate Alexander Dubček and his associates has backfired, with damage to Moscow's prestige.

Moscow's leaders had been divided, the *Times* explained, and

> ...the almost unanimous disapproval of Moscow's bully-boy tactics by Western Europe's Communist parties as well as by the Romanians and the Yugoslavs exerted a healthy influence on the Kremlin hotheads. But most important was the unity and imperturbabilty of the people of Czechoslovakia. They did not panic, and their support for Dubček was so nearly universal that Moscow could find no reputable Czech or Slovak politician to play the role that János Kádár played in Hungary twelve years ago.... The consequences are likely to be profound....[19]

In fact, the face-saving clichés in the declaration were stern orders.[20]

After Bratislava, a mild wave of corruption rolled over Prague, and tourists complained that hotel employees were stealing their socks from the laundry. Tuzex girls in the lobbies of hotels and in the bars, so-called because they required payment in Tuzex coupons good in hard-currency shops, received new competition. The regular girls were assumed to receive retainers from the STB, but the new girls were less likely to have secret police connections. German businessmen said that several fortunes had been deposited in Swiss banks by Czech officials who had purchasing authority, remarking, "The virtues of the free enterprise system are returning." A few Czechoslovaks made plans to emigrate. Larger numbers took their first vacations in Western nations, some in their antique cars.

Tito visited Prague for an enthusiastic public welcome. Ulbricht visited too, receiving no public attention. Yakubovsky turned up on the East German border again, along with Marshal Pyotr Koshevoi, commander of Soviet forces in East Germany, and the East German defense minister, General Karl-Heinz Hoffmann. A Czech journalist said, "The Soviets won't move in. They don't want to elect Richard Nixon President, do they?"

Slovak Communists prepared for their separate Party Congress, scheduled for August 26, when they planned to get rid of Vasil Bilak and elect Gustav Husák head of their party. Prague scheduled the 14th Czechoslovak Party Congress for September 9, when the reform Communists planned to eliminate the 40 Central Committee members who were the most Moscow-true.

Hungary's Kádár took an unannounced vacation in the Crimea. He received a go-ahead at a meeting with Brezhnev to approach Dubček one more time, and Kádár met Dubček secretly at Komárno, Slovakia, on August 17. There is no reliable account of the meeting. When the invasion came three days later, Kádár, sensitive to his earlier reputation for treachery, vanished from public view until mid-October.

On the evening of August 20, two unscheduled Soviet passenger aircraft asked permission to land at Ruzyne airport in Prague. The first unloaded civilians, all men of military age, who lounged in the waiting room ostensibly waiting for minor repairs. The second plane parked on the tarmac. At 11 p.m., as armored columns raced over the borders into Czechoslovakia, the civilians seized the airport and control tower along with a handful of Czech STB men under Lieutenant Colonel Viliam Šalgovič, a deputy interior minister. The parked Soviet communications plane guided in an armada of Soviet Antonov-12 transports carrying airborne troops and squat little tanks. Radar in West German registered chaff. By 2 a.m. all of Czechoslovakia's major airports had been seized.

The Party Presidium had been meeting at the Central Committee building on the bank of the Vltava to study a new ultimatum from Brezhnev. At 11 p.m. the switchboard lit up with calls from the eastern and northern borders, reporting tanks and armored cars of the Soviets and their allies clattering into the country. The Presidium dispersed, Dubček remaining in his office with Smrkovský and František Kriegel, waiting for arrest. Limousines of the Soviet Embassy arrived full of airborne troops, who entered and tore telephone wires from the walls but did not pronounce an arrest. STB Colonel Bohumil Molnař had trouble finding men willing to accept the mission, but finally a party of Soviet troops and STB men arrived, one of the Czechs pronouncing Dubček, Smrkovský and Kriegel arrested in the name of the revolutionary people.

None of the editors or technicians at Četeka would dispatch an appeal for Warsaw Pact aid written by Soviet Ambassador Chervanenko and a small group of collaborators in the government. Postal Minister Karel Hoffmann issued orders to close the country's telephone lines, but telephone workers left telex relays in place to the Alcron Hotel and other locations where Western reporters worked. *Rudé Právo* editors refused to print the appeal for Soviet aid ordered by their boss, Oldřich Švestka.

In downtown Prague, crowds came out by dawn, whistling, shrieking, shaking their fists at Soviet tanks wheeling and rearing on Wenceslas Square at youths throwing bottles and stones. A Czech threw a flaming flag on a tank, and the tank and Soviet troops sprayed the statue of St. Wenceslas with bullets. Girls climbed on the tanks and stuffed sweaters into the cannon barrels. Youths threw crates of garbage at the tanks and chalked swastikas on the turrets. No one threw a Molotov cocktail or lethal object.

At the office of television chief Jiří Pelikan, Soviet troops shot up the installation and defecated on Pelikan's desk next to a copy of *Pravda* with his name underlined in its harsh commentary. Czech collaborators Švestka, Bilak and Alois Indra met at the Soviet Embassy with General Ivan Pavlovsky, commander of the invasion. Several others of the collaboration regime balked at meeting so early, waiting to see what would happen first.

There was no fighting and no bullets were fired at the Soviets. At the radio station on Vinohradska street, a truck carrying unarmed Czech youths waving a large flag careened around the corner and was destroyed by Soviet gunfire that killed four youths. Soviet troops methodically shot up the radio station, starting by spraying bullets across the top floor windows, then moving down floor by floor. Tanks smashed parked cars flat. Czech youths leaped on a tank with a burning mattress, and down the street a Soviet ammunition trailer blew up. Up the street from the radio station Soviet troops poured gunfire into a building, and tank shells razed it.Czechs on the scene denied that shots had come from the building.

In downtown Prague, Soviet troops shot a young man, Milan Kadec, carrying a Czechoslovak flag. On the Old Town Square a barricade was thrown up, using a streetcar and automobiles. Marie Charouskova, a young woman, was shot in the back running for a streetcar.

In Bratislava four demonstrating youths were shot. Ostrava radio reported several killed there. Czechs threw paving stones at tanks, but not at soldiers. They threw burning rags but not Molotov cocktails. There were no authenticated reports of a bullet being fired at the Soviets. No Soviet casualty was claimed as a result of attack, and when Soviet soldiers were injured in accidents with their heavy equipment, Czechs stood in line to volunteer blood.

About 170 members of the National Assembly gathered at their office building on Gorki Street. Surrounding Soviet troops told them they could leave the building, but they would not be permitted to reenter it. They all stayed there six days. A Soviet officer entered and was ordered out by General Bohumir Lomský, who was wearing his uniform with medals appropriate to a former deputy commander of the Warsaw Pact. Once feared as a Novotný man, he had thrown in with the reformers.

The country's only contingency plans for invasion had been made by radio and television men. Brno and Plzeň television were broadcasting, and in Prague radio men fanned out through the city to 20 clandestine transmitters, broadcasting about ten minutes each in relays.

At the airport, Dubček, Oldřich Černik and Bohumil Šimon, a candidate Presidium member, were loaded onto one plane, Smrkovský, Kriegel and Špaček on another. The planes took off for landings in Poland and then the Ukraine, arriving in Moscow a day later. For the last leg of the trip, the captives, some of them roughed up, were given clean shirts.

President Svoboda flew to Moscow with Kolder, Indra, Defense Minister Dzúr and Gustav Husák, acknowledged by tacit consent to be the Slovak Communist leader, although the Slovak Party Congress was aborted. Moscow television showed Svoboda and Podgorny embracing, but in fact the old general pushed away the Soviet president's embrace. Moscow television had used an old film.

The clandestine radio broadcast an appeal for the 14th Party Congress, scheduled for September 9, to meet immediately in Prague instead. Earlier in the summer 1,543 delegates had been elected in local Party meetings, and nearly all of them were believed to back the reformers. The delegates slipped into town with only vague ideas of where to go for information. Some caught a radio broadcast giving the Congress location, but the Peoples Militia, once feared by reformers, had elected new leaders, and it became an organizer and protector of the 14th Party Congress. Militia members found about 1,100 of the delegates and directed them to the ČKD factory at the edge of town, where they entered as workers reporting for a shift. While they elected a new Central Committee and a new Presidium of reformers, workers in other factories mined a national Party Congress to throw Soviet intruders off the scent.

The Soviets could not make arrests stick. Prisoners turned over to the STB were freed again. Wenceslas Square was a graffiti exhibition, including the monument to the saint, where an honor guard of young people stood at attention holding flags amid flowers and candles dedicated to those killed in the demonstrations. Their death notices with their photographs were cupped in flowers. St. Wenceslas was draped in black.

Soviet soldiers lay on their tanks, smoking moodily, occasionally gesturing with guns when someone spoke to them. Each night at 10 the Soviets opened up with automatic weapons and an occasional bass-toned anti-tank gun, aimed in the air, a sign of curfew—"Yakubovsky's Prague Concerto." Czechs grew used to the gunfire and went out anyway. Each night the Soviets tore down posters and signs, to find them replaced by morning: "Lenin, awake! Brezhnev's gone crazy." "The Tashkent Circus is playing Prague. Please don't feed or pet the animals." "Ivan come home; Natasha has a sex problem." "Parade today of Soviet technological accomplishments and fashionable uniforms." "Collaborators meet tonight at the Lucerna Bar. Identifying sign will be turned-up coat collars."

Among the poems, cartoons, news bulletins and notices posted through the city was a wanted list of traitors: Alois Indra, Drahomír Kolder, Vasil Bilak, Karel Mestek, Miloš Jakeš, Vilém Nový, Jan Piller, Josef Lenárt, Viliam Šalgovič, Paulovský, Rytr, Molnař, Kozuch, Rupé, Rezek, Klima, Bokr, Milat, including those so obscure their first names were not known to the accusers. About half the graffiti was aimed at

East Germans, sons of the Nazi invaders of 1938, although East German troops remained in the north of the country and did not reach Prague.

In Wenceslas Square, a Polish army captain with his soldier driver parked their jeep in front of the Jalta Hotel, the captain exploding in anger when a Czech passerby told them it was illegal to park there. Andy Borowiec of the *Washington Star* was delighted with the spectacle, and asked the captain in Polish how it felt to invade his brother Slavs. The captain, only about five feet, four inches tall, but who looked like he was hewn from rock, snapped out a curse and said, "They asked for it. They were the ones who invited the Russians here in the first place. Now let them live with their friends."

In Moscow, the Soviets separated Kriegel, veteran of the Spanish civil war and once Mao's physician, from the others during negotiations. At Čierna Kriegel also had been excluded from the talks as "that Galician Jew." During negotiations Husák disagreed with the reformers on one point: he said the 14th Party Congress had been illegal, because it was overweighted with Czechs and had few Slovaks. Dubček fainted during negotiations, and Svoboda threatened suicide. At the end of it, Brezhnev was said to have gestured at the Soviet collaborators Kolder, Indra and Bilak, saying to the others, "Do what you want with them." Indra collapsed with a heart attack, from which he recovered.

On the morning of August 27, an elderly man walked up Stepanska Street from Wenceslas Square, calling out in the manner of a town crier what he had heard on the radio: "Our leaders are at Hradčany Castle! Everyone to the castle!"

They had arrived at the airport almost unseen, but Smrkovský said into a radio reporter's recorder at the airport, "I kneel in the dust before the behavior of the Czechoslovak people. I greatly deplore what you have had to go through this past week. We have all returned, yes, Kriegel too." The author of "1,000 Words," who had said the people were too easily manipulated to be trusted with full democracy, had been saved by the people's nonviolent protest.

The popular reaction to their return was the key to my judgment of the progressive Communists' revolution. Only a few hundred heeded the town crier's call and the radio's directions to go to Hradčany Castle. Some Czechs said it had been Dubček's duty to kill himself in Moscow. A few thousand went to the National Assembly building later to hear Smrkovský's report, but they chanted "Long live the ČSR," the initials of the republic before communism. They did not chant, "Long live the ČSSR." A man in the crowd said, to general approval, "Communism is dead in the hearts of these people."

Husák spoke on the radio, denouncing the 14th Party Congress. He was chosen by the Soviets to run Czechoslovakia. Most of the writer spark plugs of the spring were in hiding, although the seized *Literární Listy* appeared from the underground as *Listy.* One woman writer talked on a stroll where she could not be overheard. "None of your friends can see you. They are afraid of physical destruction. In Moscow the Soviets threatened 'worse than Hungary.' Husák has turned traitor. I'm sorry, I can't stay any longer."

For about two and a half weeks, the *Times'* confidence that the Bratislava Declaration had freed Czechoslovakia had appeared to be confirmed. David Binder reported from Bonn that Ulbricht had been forced to offer normalized relations to West Germany, and that signs pointed to "a major switch in Soviet policy on West Germany—away from total hostility and toward conciliation."[21] A *Times* editorial, "Shock Waves After Bratislava," said, "The defeat Moscow and its allies suffered in their recent confrontation with Prague inevitably forced a rethinking of attitudes on many issues. . . ." It cited an alleged East German thaw, and foresaw a new Czechoslovak-Yugoslav axis.[22] Binder reported that Ulbricht was in grave danger, and that the Berlin Wall might not be as solid as it looked.[23]

On the eve of the invasion, a *Times* editorial expressed concern over "New Tension in Prague," and warned the Czechoslovak reformers that they should not give in to Moscow's demands to reimpose censorship. Now it reported, two weeks late, the real meaning of the face-saving clichés in the Bratislava Declaration: "Indeed, the Kremlin may even be threatening to interpret the Bratislava Declaration as a warrant for forceful intervention if censorship is not reimposed."[24]

The invasion devastated the *Times* editors and editorialists, grinding *Times* ideology under tank treads. Readers may not have noticed, because, after the shock and a slight change of gears, the *Times* continued on course: it was a defeat for the Soviets. "Has Moscow Lost More than it Won?" asked a headline.[25] Noting the demonstration in Moscow's Pushkin Square led by Pavel Litvinov, it asked in another headline, "Will Prague Spawn Tomorrow's Soviet Revolutionaries?" Harry Schwartz wrote that in London, cellist Mstislav Rostropovich "played a Dvorak concerto and then left the stage with tears in his eyes."[26]

Now, with the damage done, the *Times* reversed its advice to Washington to do nothing, commenting, "Americans would do well to assess soberly this nation's responsibility for last month's rape of

Czechoslovakia. From Mr. Dubček's triumph last January until the Soviet invasion, Washington did almost nothing to show serious goodwill toward the liberal regime....It is not a pretty chapter in American diplomacy."[27]

Less than a month after the invasion, the new liberal Central Committee and Presidium elected by the clandestine 14th Party Congress were declared illegal, and a new Congress elected a new Presidium. The *Times* was relieved, because it contained a surprising number of well-known reformers. Western relief must have amused the Soviets, who put their men at the levers of power.

The reform Communists and some of the once-daring writers rejoined the kakistocracy. A few, including Kriegel and Hájek, were fired. Some emigrated. None was executed. A majority went back to secure jobs, servicing the Communist system. Laco Novomeský, author of the prelude to the Prague Spring, denounced the reformers as naive and supported his colleague Husák. Smrkovský, reduced in stature, stayed on. Dubček was reduced in stages to ambassador, then to a clerk's job in Bratislava. Kamil Winter, television news editor, was one of the few to say bitterly on BBC that the Czechoslovaks should have fought and died, to leave something for survivors to build on. Czechoslovakia slid back into its long night.

In Western Europe the media treated the Prague Spring as the most important development since the Hungarian revolution 12 years earlier. In the United States most of the media did not take interest until the threat of Soviet intervention surfaced in June, and it was not a leading story until the Čierna and Bratislava summits. As in Vietnam in 1963, when Halberstam, Sheehan and Browne set the tone, so did the abdication of the rest of the media in 1968 allow the thorough *Times* coverage to promote the Dubček-Smrkovský faction of the Communist Party to potential saviors of freedom and democracy.

Johnson, who was a lame duck President when the invasion occured, barely mentioned it in his memoirs, only to say that it prevented his arranging a summit in Moscow to launch negotiations to control strategic nuclear arms. Johnson apppeared to resent that the Czechs had delayed Strategic Arms Limitation Talks into the administration that succeeded his. In Johnson's declarations of neutrality during the crisis, the United States in effect encouraged the Soviets to take the decision to invade.

For American editors, the Czechs had not fought, *basta*. No more story. During the intermittent American media coverage, the myth had been established that the Czechs wanted progressive communism. But a large part of the truth was the Czechoslovaks would not fight for Dubček and Smrkovský. Czechoslovaks had not been out of the night long enough to have an alternative worth fighting for. During World War II, the Royal Air Force said that its Czechoslovak pilots could fight, and fought as well, if not so brashly, as its Polish pilots, and Czechs under Svoboda fought well alongside the Red Army against Hitler. Brezhnev delayed invading Czechoslovakia for months until he was sure there would be no resistance either from the Czechs or from the West.

The election year 1968 left the first high-water marks of the revolution in the United States. Assassins killed Martin Luther King, Jr. and Robert Kennedy. Robert McNamara resigned, admitting his personal defeat, and turned the Defense Department over to Clark Clifford. President Johnson, under siege and unable to speak in public except at military bases, announced his impending abdication. Riots in Chicago made impossible the orderly democratic selection of a candidate to succeed him.

It was a suitable year to compare the rival ideologies in the United States, and it seemed to me that the anti-Communists, or counter-revolutionaries, were more trustworthy and less dogmatic than the revolutionaries, or anti-anti-Communists. The anti-Communists welcomed the Prague Spring and hoped that reform communism would work, even though it contradicted their rule that communism cannot be reformed. As a member of the dwindling anti-Communists, I assured *The Reporter* magazine, "If you're wondering what to believe from Czechoslovakia, you might as well believe it all until it proves wrong." I quoted a Bratislava editor, "Things have never gone this far in any Communist country. Cross your fingers for us." A month later, *The Reporter*, a victim of the revolution, went under.

The revolution, however, wanted it all: proof in Czechoslovakia that communism is capable of reform and proof in Vietnam that the Communists are invincible; both goals pursued with unswerving dogmatism.

In the first months of the year, as Dubček was unseating Novotný in Czechoslovakia, a watershed event occured in Vietnam. Communist forces launched all-out attacks throughout South Vietnam during the Tet holiday ceasefire, while half the South Vietnamese forces were on leave.The attacks were preceded by the siege of U.S. Marines at Khe Sanh beginning January 20 and North Korea's seizure of the U.S. intelligence ship *Pueblo* three days later. The offensive began January 29 with assaults on American and South Vietnamese garrisons in northern South Vietnam and erupted spectacularly in Saigon January 31 with kamikaze assaults by teams of Vietnamese sappers against the U.S. Embassy and the Presidential Palace. They climaxed in the temporary capture of Hué and a Communist massacre of civilian officials there.

The American military had warned that a Communist build-up had occured and an offensive was likely, including a year-end warning by General Earle Wheeler, chairman of the Joint Chiefs of Staff, and a mid-January television interview of General William Westmoreland.

When the attacks came, on a greater scale than expected, the U.S. military compared them with the last-gasp Battle of the Bulge waged by Germany in World War II and insisted that the offensive had been a disaster for the Vietnamese Communists, who had wasted their best cadres. The media responded with derision.

The press corps in Saigon, at a peak of 464 reporters including 179 Americans, jolted by the ferocity of the attacks and caught with an anti-war mind set, almost unanimously called the Communist offensive a debacle for the United States.[28]   Walter Cronkite, "the most trusted man in America," visited Vietnam for the second time and said on CBS television that the United States was mired in a stalemate and must negotiate, "not as victors."

Peter Braestrup, in his monumental, two volume, 1,446-page study *Big Story*,[29] documented the mass "aberration" of the American media, but no major publisher would print it. Eventually 2,500 copies were printed in Colorado, and few editors read it. A paperbook edition was long delayed.

Braestrup concluded, "In overall terms, the performance by the major American television and print news organizations in February and March constitutes an extreme case. Rarely has contemporary crisis-journalism turned out, in retrospect, to have veered so widely from reality."[30] Contrary to the media, the failed offensive crippled the Communists until late 1969 and hobbled them thereafter.

Braestrup, who quit the *Times* to become the *Washington Post's* bureau chief in Saigon for the period of the Tet offensive, did not browbeat the media, and he found examples of outstanding reporting on Tet, calling Charles Mohr of the *Times* the best consistent reporter. But he noted that "the *Times* and *Washington Post* in particular, published considerable 'analysis' and second-hand reportage, much of it clouded by error and hypothesis. . . written far from the scene."[31] He noted that Mohr, when he wrote a piece later in 1968 analyzing Tet as a setback for Hanoi, "received letters from *Times* readers expressing surprise and disbelief."[32] Braestrup found that, for the *Times*, "the enemy was almost infallible."[33]

The Saigon press corps got off on the wrong foot when the U.S. Embassy was attacked. Like Halberstam at the time of the pagoda raids in 1963, they were held back at a point where they could not see the attack by 19 Vietnamese sappers on the Embassy, and most reported erroneously that the Vietnamese had captured the U.S. chancery itself.

At Khe Sanh, where 5,500 Marines and 500 Vietnamese Rangers were beleaguered for 77 days, the media reported throughout doom predictions comparing the siege to Dien Bien Phu. Khe Sanh was, in contrast to Dien Bien Phu, a trap for the Communists, who were relatively bunched in targets in the jungle hills, where bombs, artillery and napalm could be effective against them. The Marines lost 206 killed and 852 wounded during the long siege. Westmoreland estimated that the North Vietnamese lost 10,000 to 15,000 men, conceding that it was an educated guess.[34] Although the North Vietnamese attempted to remove their casualties, Marines later found 1,603 bodies at the perimeter of the fortress complex, a small percentage of those killed. Yet the media would not concede a Marine victory at Khe Sanh.

Similarly, the media noted at first that 200 civilians were murdered by Communists at Hué, then raised the estimate to 400. The follow-up was reported as a footnote and no longer news; diligent search by South Vietnamese officials found by mid-1971 that 4,756 officials apparently had been massacred and hidden in mass graves; 2,810 bodies were found, and 1,946 remained missing.[35]

The American media reported Tet as Armageddon, that the Communists had won a major psychological victory and had proved that South Vietnam never could be secure.

During the Tet offensive, Daniel Ellsberg was back in Washington, recalled from Rand again to help contribute to decision-making in the new crisis period and to help produce options for the new Secretary of Defense, Clifford.

While Ellsberg was in Washington, the *Times* produced a major exclusive that swept the ground from under Westmoreland's claim that Tet was a Communist setback. On March 10, 1968, a three-column Page 1 headline said:

WESTMORELAND REQUESTS 206,000 MORE MEN,
STIRRING DEBATE IN ADMINISTRATION
FORCE NOW 510,000
Some in Defense and State Departments Oppose Increase.

The bombshell exclusive, by Neil Sheehan and Hedrick Smith, had been held up for the large-circulation Sunday newspaper, and the second paragraph had been revised at the request of New York editors to stress Westmoreland's "plea" for a 40% increase in his forces "to regain the initiative" from the enemy.[36]

Braestrup pointed out that the scoop was seriously flawed and out of date. The Joint Chiefs had made pre-Tet request for more troops because of heavy North Vietnamese infiltration. On February 28, Westmoreland renewed it in the hope that Johnson would adopt a more aggressive strategy and would permit an incursion into Laos, the linchpin of Indochina that Eisenhower had warned Kennedy about in 1960. The Westmoreland troop request was to pursue an opportunity, not to "regain the initiative." The *Times* never corrected the story, Braestrup noted.

Ellsberg had leaked the story to Senator Robert Kennedy, whose staff had leaked it to Sheehan and Smith of the *Times*. Ellsberg later confirmed that he was the leaker, telling columnist Jack Anderson that when he saw the story in the *Times,* he thought, "Wow, that's the greatest leak that ever was."[37]

Spurred by that success, Ellsberg obtained from CIA analyst Samuel A. Adams documents that appeared to show that the military had underestimated Communist strength in South Vietman by about half, and looked up Sheehan and Smith, who took him to their bureau chief, Tom Wicker. Sheehan broke the story of the allegedly mistaken estimates in the *Times* on March 19, 20 and 21, probably contributing to Johnson's decision to recall Westmoreland and make him chairman of the Joint Chiefs.[38]

Johnson asked the FBI to find the leaker, and agent W. Donald Stewart reported to J. Edgar Hoover on March 19 that it was Ellsberg. Stewart, who wanted to prosecute Ellsberg and Sheehan under the espionage act, was told by an aide to Clifford that the Secretary of Defense did not want his good relations with the media disturbed, and when the CIA was informed of that decision, the CIA said it had no interest in pursuing the case. By that fluke, Ellsberg escaped unexposed, Anderson reported for United Features Syndicate.

At the same time that Ellsberg was leaking secret cables to Sheehan, he wrote an interpretation of the Tet offensive for Morton Halperin's office for international security affairs at the Defense Department, an estimate that proved entirely mistaken but which received wide circulation in the government.

Ellsberg wrote:

> In terms of our earliest, most ambitious objectives. . .or even, most of our less ambitious goals—I think that the war is over; those aims are lost. I expect the Tet offensive—and those events I

am quite sure will follow in the next two months—to have decisive impact on the course of the war, decisively foreclosing most evolutions favorable to us.... By that time things are going to get much worse; and then, they will not get better.... The Tet offensive and what is shortly to come do not mark a 'setback' to pacification; it is the death of pacification, as it has been conceived.... If Khe Sanh has not already been attacked by then, it will probably be in even greater danger than now, with tension increasing.... I am forced to predict not only that the 'blue' areas will contract in the next few months and the 'red' zone expand... but that the new red on the map will *never go back*. Not without, say, 400,000 more U.S. troops.[39]

In 1971 columnists Rowland Evans and Robert Novak reported Ellsberg's "spectacular misinterpretations" of Tet 1968, commenting bitterly that "those who correctly interpreted Tet as a calamitous Communist setback are in disgrace" (in 1971).[40]

Repercussions in Congress and in the media from the distorted troop-request story and the reports of doom over Tet were at a height for the New Hampshire primary on March 12. Senator Eugene McCarthy won 42% of the Democratic vote in New Hampshire, a public repudiation of Johnson, who was not a listed candidate. On March 16 Robert Kennedy, who had assailed Johnson's policies on February 8 and urged a negotiated pullout, announced his candidacy. On March 31, Johnson went on television to announce a partial bombing halt, willingness to negotiate with Hanoi and, with a tear running down his cheek, that he would not run for re-election.

Three days later Johnson could announce that Hanoi had agreed to peace negotiations—in principle—but disagreements over a site and preconditions would drag on for another six months.

For Ellsberg, the act of leaking to Kennedy and then to Sheehan marked a break point. From Washington he went to a conference on "Revolution in a Changing World" at Princeton, Russo's alma mater. There he met Eqbal Ahmad, a radical Pakistani scholar and outspoken anti-Zionist, and Janaki Tschannerl, an Indian girl who introduced him to Ghandian nonviolence. She persuaded him that Martin Luther King, Jr. was the hope of the United States, with his understanding of nonviolent resistance to governmental authority.

Just as Ellsberg turned his attention to King, and the day after Johnson's announcement that Hanoi was willing to talk peace, King was murdered by James Earl Ray in Memphis, Tennessee, where he had been leading protests that began as a garbage strike. Rioting broke out in 150 American cities. Johnson called troops into Washington, D.C.

on the day the siege of Khe Sanh was lifted. Nationwide, the riots left 30 dead, thousands injured and required calling out 34,000 National Guardsmen and 20,000 Army troops. The war at home threatened to become as bloody as in Vietnam.

On April 11, six days after King's death, Rudi Dutschke, the charismic student leader from East Germany, was shot and wounded in West Berlin, touching off destructive riots aimed especially at the printing plants of conservative publisher Axel Springer. Attorney Horst Mahler, who would become a founder of the terrorist Red Army Faction (or Baader-Meinhof gang), led thousands of young people in a Molotov-cocktail assault on Springer's West Berlin plant overlooking the Wall.

In Paris, Dutschke's friend Dani the Red Cohn-Bendit led student riots that reached the Sorbonne on May 3 and expanded into a May general strike that paralyzed French industry and would eventually contribute to President De Gaulle's decision to resign.

A bemused Tad Szulc noted that, in the midst of the Prague Spring, Kosygin was taking the waters in Karlový Vary and the Czechs were radiant, but Paris was burning.

The violent European student rioting, a product of imitating American anti-war rebels, reflected back to the United States, and on April 23 Mark Rudd led SDS students taking over Hamilton Hall at Columbia University in a protest against plans to build a gymnasium in Harlem Park that would deprive blacks of recreation space. Blacks joined the SDS takeover, carrying guns, and when Rudd opposed a shoot out with police, the blacks ordered him out of the building. Rudd's student troops took over another Columbia building instead.

In the macho battle for revolutionary leadership, the whites had backed down at Columbia, and Rudd's nerve was in question.[41] He was facing expulsion when he spoke at a rally May 21, calling for a second takeover of Hamilton Hall by SDS, with a slogan from a poem by LeRoi Jones, "Up against the wall, motherfuckers!" Police raided the campus a second time May 22, and the violence of rioting at Columbia became a model for college revolts nationwide. Some of those in the May 22 melee would be professional rioters at the Democratic Convention in Chicago.

Following a pattern of revolutions, the student anti-draft and anti-war campaigns, developing since 1964, were deep in a struggle for leadership in 1968, the main contenders being the Progressive Labor Party and SDS, especially in its New Left faction. The alliance with black militants, who originally had inspired the revolt, continued to be given lip service, but cooperation deteriorated as the white revolutionaries battled for power. SDS, strong at Columbia, the University of

Michigan, Berkeley, Kent State and the University of Chicago, included such spinoffs as the Youth International (Yippie) Party of Jerry Rubin, who had been a member of the Congress of Racial Equality and had visited Cuba via Czechoslovakia with a Progressive Labor delegation in 1964 before upstaging Mario Savio as a member of the Free Speech Movement by running for mayor of Berkeley in 1967.

In June 1968, SDS held a six-day convention at Michigan State University in East Lansing. Rudd failed to be elected to the national leadership, which went to Mike Clonsky of California and Bernardine Dohrn of Chicago, but Rudd's troops joined in plans for a massive demonstration at the Democratic Convention in August.

Violence at the Democratic Convention had been promised earlier when a number of radical and anti-war groups met in March at a YMCA camp at Lake Villa, a Chicago suburb, to form a broad front for protests.

The Lake Villa conference, called by the National Mobilization to End the War in Vietnam, was a follow-up to the march on the Pentagon in 1967. National Mobilization's head was David Dellinger, editor of Liberation News Service, an aging revolutionary at 53, who had asked Rubin to be project director of the Pentagon march. Tentative leaders for the Chicago Convention demonstrations were elected: Dellinger, Rennie Davis of Chicago and Vernon Grizzard, a Boston draft-resistance leader. Later, Tom Hayden was added to the list of leaders. Two weeks after the Lake Villa meeting, Martin Luther King, Jr. was murdered, and Dick Gregory of CORE promised 5,000 marchers would be in Chicago for the convention.

The media, especially the *Times*, gave extensive coverage to preparations for the demonstrations. Both the Chicago police and the FBI had infiltrated radical groups and were well aware of demonstration plans. For several years the media had assigned young reporters—the only ones with entrée to the "don't trust anyone over 30" generation—to the youth revolt in its various manifestations from civil rights through political revolt to the drug and acid rock culture. The *Times* reporter at the Chicago Convention who had the most impact at his newspaper was J. Anthony Lukas, who had just won a Pulitzer Prize for his sympathetic investigation of the life of Linda Fitzpatrick, a wealthy girl from Greenwich, Connecticut, who was murdered while on drugs in Greenwich Village.

On the eve of the convention, Lukas reported that, while it would be rash to predict how many demonstrators would appear, the figure of 50,000 appeared conservative, and organizers' estimates went up to "a seemingly inflated 'over a million,'" Among them would be "10,000 to 15,000 Yippies, hippies and other free souls...."[42]

As it turned out, only a fraction of the estimated demonstrators turned up in Chicago, but they were more determinedly violent than expected. Everyone knew there would be a violent clash. The 11,900 Chicago police earlier had used excessive force, demonstratively, breaking up a peace demonstration on April 17. The Illinois National Guard, 5,600 of them called up August 20 at the mayor's request, ran riot control exercises, guardsmen playing rioter roles. The media assigned teams to the expected riots. Mayor Richard Daley had intelligence reports that radicals planned to assassinate three Democratic candidates: Hubert Humphrey, Eugene McCarthy and George McGovern. The Yippies of Rubin and Abbie Hoffman threatened to dump LSD into the city's water supply.

The disruption of the Democratic Convention, although later called a police riot by a special commission, was doggedly continued by its organizers through the convention's four days. It successfully suspended the democratic process by preventing rational debate in the International Amphitheater, and left the Democrats, who had nominated Humphrey and Senator Edmund Muskie, so divided that the main challenger, McCarthy, refused to endorse the ticket.

The *Times* blamed the debacle wholly on Mayor Daley, not on the organized rioters. *Times* reporter Steven V. Roberts commented that there had been two conventions, one in the Amphitheater and one in the streets, the latter representing candidates McCarthy, McGovern or Teddy Kennedy, although the demonstrators, including Tom Hayden, had said they wanted no part of working within the Democratic Party.[45]

Neil Sheehan, commenting from Texas, where Johnson sat out the convention, wrote that Chicago had shown the limits of Johnson's power, and that Johnson's discredited Vietnam policy had "shared deeply in the Mayor's discredit." Columnist Tom Wicker wrote:

> After Mayor Daley's brute policemen clubbed down American youngsters in the streets, Vice President Humphrey expressed no outrage over this excessive and unjustified resort to raw force but observed piously in his acceptance speech that 'violence breeds violence and it cannot be condoned whatever the source'. . . . These were not snipers, looters or terrorists. . . . No plastic bombs or Molotov cocktails were thrown. . . . The marchers were political dissidents, many of them radical, most of them idealistic, demonstratedly brave, concerned for their country and their fellow men. . . . They did not threaten law and order. . . these were our children in the streets, and the Chicago police beat them up.[44]

The *Times'* fury at Daley and the Chicago police, rubbing off on Humphrey, abated rather quickly, because a greater catastrophe had occurred earlier in August. In Miami the Republicans had nominated on the first ballot the *Times' bête noire* since the Hiss case in 1948. Unprecedented violence in the United States and uncertain leadership in the Vietnam war for seven years had brought back Richard Nixon, resurrected from the ruins of his 1962 defeat for the California governor's chair.

A *Times* editorial changed tone to express pleasure that Humphrey had "come around" to saying that the Chicago police might have overreacted, the *Times'* position. "There is need now for the leaders of both parties to reach out and make contact with a considerable number of young people, some of them Yippies, most of them not, who feel alienated from the political process." It said that Chicago's "club-happy police force" posed grave dangers to "those values all Americans cherish."

Humphrey was quickly rehabilitated in the *Times;* Nixon would face him for the presidency, and the *Times'* anger had threatened to damage the only man between Nixon and the White House.

Chapter XIII

The Counter-Revolution and the Cambodia Incursion

> *First citizen: "What he hath done famously he did it to that end; though soft-conscienced men can be content to say it was for his country, he did it to please his mother, and to be partly proud."*
> *Second citizen: "What he cannot help in his nature you account a vice in him. You must in no way say he is covetous."*
> *First citizen: "If I must not, I need not be barren of accusations; he hath faults, with surplus, to tire in repetition."*
>
> —*Shakespeare, Coriolanus*

When Richard Nixon was elected President on November 5, 1968, everyone knew him. After his election defeats of 1960 and 1962 and his political obituary on ABC television, he was the all-American loser, everyone's ne'er-do-well Uncle Dick, come to tell the family picnic a long joke and then flubb the punch line. The tense body carriage and cramped style of an introvert in an extrovert's game had been familiar for more than two decades.

No one had been more investigated, poked at, pried around and made to account for every penny. His anti-communism, an affront to the revolution, was well known since the Hiss case, and so were Nixon's views, including changes that had occurred in them along the way. The electorate was not sold a bill of goods.

Nixon was elected to do a job that had proved to be beyond his competitors: to end the Vietnam war without catastrophe and to quell the various revolutions—black, youth, drug, permissive and ideological—before they got out of hand. Few were enthusiastic about him, but the public judged Nixon qualified to pull the nation out of an eight-year decline.

Nixon's stamina was established; he was still there after 21 years of media pounding. He was not a liar; all politicians dissimulate on occasion, but Nixon's overstressed earnestness, enthusiastic hyperbole or transparent evasion on such occasions amounted more to confession than to deception.

He was not venal; although the media derided the bathos of his 1952 "Checkers" speech, some recalled that it was the first full disclosure of a national candidate's personal finances, and Nixon had left office after 14 years in the House, Senate and vice presidency with a puny net worth of $48,000. Before he lost to Kennedy in 1960, he had not been interested in money, an attitude relatively common in the West but incomprehensible in New York City, and was surprised that his advice could be sold for money.

He was not afraid; if the Eastern media scorned his 1959 kitchen debate with Khrushchev as showboating, some realized that Moscow had an intimidating atmosphere in the first year that it admitted tourists, and by 1968 the public knew that Kennedy had not stood up well to intimidation in his private debate in Vienna with Khrushchev.

Although the *Times* and much of the media called Nixon's 1958 South American tour a diplomatic disaster, no catastrophe followed from it, and some recalled that Nixon and his wife won an ovation from Congress for escaping assassination with grace and standing under a hail of spittle through the playing of the Venezuelan anthem at Caraças airport. Nixon's professed sympathy for refugees was genuine enough, as the Hungarians knew, and the Nixon family's two servants were refugees from Cuba.

As a Quaker backslider who had renounced his religion's distinctive tenet to join the Navy and serve in the Pacific, Nixon had an insight into the psychology of pacifism, a key to his recognition of Priscilla and Alger Hiss, Whittaker Chambers, Noel Field and a number of Quaker-allied personalities who had served the Soviet Union in the name of pacifism.

While the media attributed to him a dog-in-the-manger attitude toward rivals, and the Kennedy clan had attached a "no class" label on him, the public was not convinced. Nixon had not undercut Kennedy or Johnson while they were in office, rather, offered his support or silence in periods of crisis. Urged to criticize Kennedy by German reporters in West Berlin, Nixon declined without innuendo, saying, as he often did, that he did not have all the facts available to the President. Johnson thanked Nixon for his backing on Vietnam.

Part of the public suspected that if Nixon had won in 1960, there would not have been a Bay of Pigs fiasco, perhaps not a Berlin Wall, and no excruciating slow squeeze over years in Vietnam. Regularly described by the *Times* as indecisive, contradictory and without vision, Nixon was seen by his supporters as decisive, determined and unlike Kennedy, not a man of half-measures.

Nixon's election was a public repudiation of the New York-based media. Edith Efron, in a two-year statistical evaluation of prime time television transcripts during the seven-week period of the 1968 campaign, found a massive bias against Nixon on the three networks, the basic dispensers of campaign news. Network commentary resulted in "portrayal of Mr. Humphrey as a quasi-saint. . .portrayal of Mr. Nixon as corruption incarnate," she reported.[1]

From studying the taped commentaries, she found that each network made the gesture of a positive statement about Nixon and then loosed a flood of unsubstantiated vilification.

She found that ABC said that Nixon had "fine powers as a debater and extraordinary political astuteness," but on the negative side the network

> . . .said or implied that Mr. Nixon is: an unkind automaton; overconfident; intellectually intimidated by reporters; coldbloodedly intent on marketing himself; a man who is lamentably lacking in qualities of mind and spirit; a man who lacks principles and clear vision, who lacks compassion and does not understand the epic forces that govern the world; that he is massaging the prejudices of the whites against the young, the poor and the black; that he is unattractive to the young and cannot communicate with them; that he is a liar; a posturer; a pseudo-statesman and a pseudo-philosopher; that he is morally unprincipled; a racist; that he is divisive, is trying to set Americans against each other in mutual

fear and suspicion; that he is an obstacle to peace because of his anti-Communist background; that he is a mechanical, robotic man, calculating, posturing and without emotion; a man who talks in generalities, a poseur; a man who inspires no confidence or enthusiasm; a man who is not big enough for the role of President; an untrustworthy man; a man from whom one shouldn't buy a used car; a cheerleader at his own rally; a man who is weak and fearful before hecklers; restless; a man who will not keep his campaign promises; a man who experiences nagging fears; a man whose speeches are like freeze-dried pieces of bland pap; whose oratory is uninspired and slick; a man who is in extreme conflict from holding in the desire to go for his enemy's jugular; a man whose nature it is to go after an enemy with a club or meat axe, a man with the psychology of a murderer.

On CBS, it was said that Nixon was "a man of great dimensions," but commentary also

> . . . said or implied that Mr. Nixon is: a boring anti-climactic presence at his own rallies; overconfident; that he is unyoung, unhandsome and unsexy; that his own followers do not like him; that he is a man with a rancorous streak; a liar, a man who lacks ability, character or principles; a man who is a danger to his country; a hard-core anti-Communist in the past; a man who is appealing to the race prejudices of young and old; a racist; cynical; irresponsible; an anti-Semite; a hypocrite; devoid of principles; a man who appeals to failures and malcontents; inhuman; a computing machine who is programmed by a programmer; a man who deliberately misleads Americans; a man who appeals to fear and hatred; who fabricates strawmen; who stands for nothing; a game-player; a wrecker; an egotist; nonhuman; untrustworthy; an obstacle to peace; emotionally false; playing the hero; a man whose followers are indifferent to him; an anti-Communist who impugned the patriotism of opponents; a man who makes contradictory campaign promises; a man whose supporters are not convinced by him; a man who makes vicious and false accusations without taking responsibility for his words, a square who believes in heroes.

On NBC, it was said that Nixon was calm and serene in the face of hecklers, but it was also

> . . . said or implied that Mr. Nixon: traveled the low road of anti-communism; lacks perception and compassion; does not understand the epic forces that govern the world; that he is tricky Dick, given to attacking liberals as Communist sympathizers; inconsistent; cynical, shallow and shockingly irresponsible; malicious,

posturing as a winner; a man who used commercial gimmickry and fakery to win his support; a man who utters bromides; a man whose followers are bored with him and don't like him, who only cheer him because his writers know how to write applause lines; a cruelly mocking man, a liar, a hypocrite, a name-caller, a man who appeals to fear and hate in the electorate; a man who fails to talk seriously to the public; a racist WASP who wants to hold Negroes down economically; a hater of Negroes; a man whose audiences don't like him and are only responding to theatrical gimmicks; an opponent of racial and economic justice; a venal militarist.

The above characterizations, each supported by tape recordings of network commentary, may have been in part the considered opinions of the networks' commentators, but the similarities in all three networks suggest they were a product of the pack journalism that had proliferated since the Halberstam-Higgins war in Vietnam in 1963 and reached a tentative high point in the almost unanimously mistaken evaluations of Tet 1968.

Efron concluded that ABC-TV, CBS-TV and NBC-TV "together broadcast the quantitative equivalent of a *New York Times* lead editorial against him every day—for five days a week for the seven weeks of the campaign period. And every editorial technique was employed on the three networks to render the pro-Nixon side less 'forceful' than the anti-Nixon side. . . ."[2]

The unanimous opinion of the New York-based networks was at odds with newspaper publishers nationwide. *Editor and Publisher* reported that 634 dailies endorsed Nixon, 146 endorsed Humphrey, 12 endorsed George Wallace, and 250 were uncommitted. The circulation of newspapers endorsing Nixon was 34.6 million, compared with 9.5 million for those endorsing Humphrey. The nation's press still had diversity, and the collective opinion of its publishers was almost the opposite of the networks.

There is no doubt that the network editors and commentators were influenced in some degree by the *Times* and *Washington Post,* the commentators' daily reading. The *Times* fought Nixon's candidacy through the summer and took the unusual step of endorsing formally a rival candidate for nomination, Nelson Rockefeller, citing his exemplary experience.[3] The *Washington Post's* bellwether cartoonist Herbert Block was so virulently anti-Nixon that his cartoons regularly drew reader complaints.

When Nixon was nominated at Miami, the *Times,* after a drumbeat of charges that he had taken no positions, editorially attacked his pro-

Israel policy as too hard a position. Nixon had told B'nai B'rith, "As long as the threat of Arab attack remains direct and imminent, 'sufficient power' means the balance must be tipped in Israel's favor. . . . I support a policy that would give Israel a technological military margin to more than offset her hostile neighbors' numerical superiority."

The *Times* commented:

> The American commitment to Israel's survival is clear and unequivocal, but American policy had been based on the belief that preservation of an approximate arms parity offers the best chance of avoiding another Middle East war. . .does Mr. Nixon believe Moscow is unlikely to react to a definite American commitment to give Israel a 'technological military margin' over its hostile neighbors?

The *Times'* fear was misplaced; just as the Soviets had introduced sophisticated weapons into the Middle East in 1955, it was at that moment pouring modern weaponry into Egypt and Syria[4] without regard to potential Nixon actions. Nixon's campaign promise won him few Jewish votes, but he kept it.

In the late summer and early fall, it became more awkward to attack Nixon. All opinion polls showed him leading Humphrey by wide margins, especially after the debacle of the Democratic Convention. The *Times* disparaged the polls, reporting that the uncertainties of 1968 were such that polls were "more likely to be wrong in 1968 than at any time since 1948," when the *Chicago Tribune* had relied on polls and early returns to give the election to Thomas E. Dewey.

As election day neared, the polls showed Humphrey closing the gap, partly because Eugene McCarthy relented and gave a late endorsement, conditional on Humphrey recognizing the Viet Cong, partly because of rumors that Johnson might succeed in getting peace negotiations started with North Vietnam. Contrary to *Times* editorial opinion, the leaders of North Vietnam cared very much who won, and did not want to see Nixon elected.

Now the *Times* took the gloves off in a series of endorsements of Humphrey that amounted to a declaration of war on Nixon. The first *Times* endorsement filled the entire editorial space, and it meant, the *Times* said, "a favorable judgment on the personality and character of one man and an adverse judgment on his rival. Mr. Humphrey is a warm, generous, idealistic, open man. Mr. Nixon has gradually risen above the personal abuse and the narrow partisanship of his early campaigns, but he remains slick and evasive on some of the seminal issues."[5]

The editorial found Humphrey superior and Nixon inferior in every department. Humphrey would work for arms control, while Nixon "has resurrected the 'missile gap' argument misused by President Kennedy and insists he will not enter into arms negotiations with the Soviet Union until sometime in the future when this country has reached new and unspecified superiority in nuclear strength." Humphrey would heal black-white relations; Nixon promised "more energetic use of police measures." Humphrey would work for peace in Vietnam; Nixon would try for victory. The sole argument for Nixon, the *Times* said, was that he "might produce a period of calm and consolidation. But this presupposes that he is a popular and widely trusted figure like General Eisenhower, which he manifestly is not, as his divisive and partisan record over the years makes clear. . . ."

That particular editorial managed to be mistaken on every count. Two days before Nixon's inauguration, Defense Secretary Clark Clifford confirmed a massive Soviet ICBM build-up over the preceding two and a half years, justifying Nixon's concern, and despite the build-up, Nixon negotiated the first Strategic Arms Limitation Treaty. Black-white hostility was not exacerbated under Nixon. Nixon pulled U.S. troops out of Vietnam and did not insist on victory. Nixon's term did see the revolution in the United States abate—until Watergate.

In the last days of the campaign, Nixon watched stoically as the rumors of Johnson's peace negotiations came true. He had been tipped off early by Henry Kissinger that Johnson was close to a breakthrough in his Paris preliminary talks on stopping the bombing permanently and making the talks serious peace negotiations. Kissinger, an occasional adviser to both the Kennedy and Johnson administrations, had been introduced to the Nixon team by his patron, Nelson Rockefeller. Through John Mitchell, Nixon's campaign lieutenant, Kissinger warned Nixon not to make any Vietnam proposals that might boomerang if peace talks were announced. It was helpful advice. On October 28, eight days before the election, Johnson received a message from Kosygin that Johnson interpreted as a Soviet guarantee of North Vietnam's good will if negotiations were to start.

Johnson announced the breakthrough to peace talks on October 31, along with a conditional bombing halt, and Nixon, at a rally that night at Madison Square Garden, could only say, "Neither I nor my vice president candidate (gesturing at Spiro Agnew) will say anything that might destroy the chance to have peace." Nixon was sure that it was an election ploy to aid Humphrey, and in fact real peace talks did not materialize in the remainder of Johnson's term.

Nixon credited Johnson with a legitimate attempt to save something of his record in Vietnam, but he also boiled at the timing of the announcement to the moment that it would most help Humphrey. The peace-talks coup lost some of its effectiveness three days before the election when South Vietnamese President Thieu said that South Vietnam would not take part in Johnson's talks. Johnson had the FBI bug the South Vietnamese Embassy in Washington and Nixon supporters to see if Nixon had a hand in it.

Johnson's announcement of a peace-talks breakthrough called for another *Times* endorsement of Humphrey and an unprecedented blast at Nixon under the Grey Lady's rules of etiquette. After praising Humphrey's record, the editorial said:

> It is difficult to evaluate fairly the record of Richard M. Nixon because that is so brief and thin. He served only four years in the House and two years in the Senate during which time he was preoccupied almost exclusively with communism as a domestic danger. Only 39 when he was chosen as General Eisenhower's running mate in 1952, he spent the last 16 years divorced from major public responsibility, the first half of them in the frustrating office of Vice President and the second half as a private citizen. His record on the great issues is virtually nil.[6]

The voters disagreed. They concluded, in concert with such foreigners as Adenauer and De Gaulle, that Nixon knew how the world works. Nixon won over Humphrey by 31,770,237 votes to 31,270,533, a small plurality of less than a half million votes. George Wallace polled a high 9,906,141 votes, partly racist votes but also sternly law-and-order votes that might have gone to Nixon in a two-man race.

It had been the *Times'* rule to congratulate the winner of an election, enthusiastically in Kennedy's case, and to commiserate with the loser, but the rule did not apply to Nixon. An editorial noted that Nixon had achieved a mere plurality, faced a Democrat-controlled House and Senate, and would have to enlist bipartisan cooperation. Grudgingly, it said, "This newspaper did not support Mr. Nixon, but we have always recognized that he is an intelligent, able man who is essentially a moderate, responsible conservative on most issues. His long years in national politics have given him the political skills which are a necessary part of a successful President's equipment." It noted that Nixon's campaign left few personal wounds or bipartisan animosities because "his wide lead in the public opinion polls" earlier had enabled him to run a responsible campaign, implying that had it been otherwise, his campaign would have been vicious.[7]

An inside-page banner headline said of Nixon's plurality: "Victory Margin Probably Smaller than Kennedy's in '60" although figures were available then to show it was four times larger.

A profile of Nixon stressed that he had many faces and played many roles, the "smooth world traveler," "the triumphant if aging ballplayer," "the cautious politician," "briefly, the healer and sage," "the professional tactician," but his program remained unknown. It said that many voters wondered, "What does he want the presidency for other than to be President?" and was he the "new Nixon" or the "old Nixon"?

Reston's commentary said Nixon

> ...does not enjoy the power of hero worship, the national respect and trust that enabled President Eisenhower to govern with a Democratic Congress...he has won the presidency not so much on his own personal strength as on the reaction of a frustrated people against a tired administration that had staggered and blundered into grievous difficulties both at home and abroad.

Reston said that Nixon "starts with no clear mandate from the people, no great fund of personal popularity, and an opposition in Congress that contains many elders of both houses who have regarded him with suspicion and even personal hostility ever since he was in the House of Representatives a generation ago."

Tom Wicker did not accept the election and wistfully hoped for a computer breakdown that might change the vote result in California. He took some solace from Nixon's loss in Texas, "the big prize in the South." Wicker believed that Humphrey might have won if he had accepted the dove plank on Vietnam in the Democratic platform.

Of the *Times* commentators, only C. L. Sulzberger, who often was out of step with the New York office, noted that "No American President at the moment of taking office has known the world so extensively as Richard Nixon," and that in his travels Nixon "did his homework thoroughly," winning the "respect of statesmen of different ideologies."

Most newspapers run a world-reaction story on a presidential election, and the *Times*' lengthy reaction report blatantly reversed the order of significant comment. It said,

> World reaction on the election of Richard M. Nixon as President appeared to be divided yesterday between fears that he may prove too militant in his dealing with Communistic governments and anxieties that he would lead the United States back into isolation and reduction of foreign aid....His outspoken anti-

communism caused concern in liberal circles in Europe.

Buried deep in the story was the notation that De Gaulle had supported Nixon, and deeper still that "some South Vietnamese officials" welcomed Nixon's election. The headline said, "Anxiety Noted in Reaction Abroad...."[8]

Nixon entered the White House with the Kennedy-Johnson albatross of Vietnam around his neck and on clear notice that he could expect no quarter from the *Times*. Moving into the White House, Nixon's staff found that Lyndon Johnson had made the mansion into a fortress. In the basement was a bomb-proof shelter and command post with television monitoring screens and stocks to hold out against mob assault. In the Oval Office Johnson had installed a tape-recording system, actuated by a toggle switch on the desk by Johnson's chair. Nixon had the Army Signal Corps remove the system, but he would change his mind a year later.

With the elections over, the media pressed Nixon to reveal his "secret plan" to end the Vietnam war. Nixon said he never had claimed a secret plan, and recalled that he told the Associated Press on March 14, 1968, that "If I had a gimmick I would tell Lyndon Johnson." He did intend to withdraw American troops, but only after stepping up training of South Vietnamese troops and equipping them. He had long contemplated mining Haiphong harbor, where most Soviet military supplies entered North Vietnam, and he thought that diplomatic resources had been neglected. He did not intend to quit Vietnam, bug out, as he expressed it, and all of the Asian leaders he had met on his travels had urged that the United States remain involved in Vietnam. De Gaulle had advised him in 1963 that China could not be permanently isolated, and so had Adenauer in 1967. Nixon contemplated a discrete approach to China, but he kept it to himself. Shortly after Nixon took office in 1969, Canada and Italy exchanged diplomatic relations with China, and there was no grumbling or comment from Washington.

The media watched attentively as the Nixon administration took up the Paris peace talks, where Nixon named Henry Cabot Lodge to replace W. Averell Harriman, partly because of Lodge's relatively good relations with the anti-war media.

Johnson's election eve breakthrough in the Paris peace talks was an agreement to shift into real negotiations. The discussions from March to October had been on the basis, we will stop the bombing if you will enter negotiations under a partial truce. The "breakthrough" included a number of understandings which the North Vietnamese did not specifically endorse but "assented to by silence." One of the understood conditions was that the North Vietnamese would not attack South Vietnam's cities, as in the assaults on Saigon and Hué during Tet 1968. However, negotiations did not start immediately after the October breakthrough because South Vietnam balked and Hanoi insisted on the National Liberation Front having the same status at the negotiations as South Vietnam.

Nixon assumed office with no real negotiations started and the media advising him to be ready to react to a 1969 Tet offensive. Nixon told Kissinger he would rather take the initiative than wait to react, and he turned his attention to the sanctuaries in Cambodia, some of which overlapped into South Vietnam. The United States believed there were about 200,000 North Vietnamese in 15 areas of the Cambodian border. Actually, there were more than 300,000 North Vietnamese in the enclaves at the period, and few if any Cambodians, since the border area had experienced hot pursuit and artillery shelling for many years.

In the last half of 1968, the war had been in a lull; the cost of Tet 1968 was clear in the inability of the Communists to mount a major assault. In February 1969, with Nixon less than a month in office and picking up the Paris peace talks, Hanoi launched its Tet 1969 offensive, pale by comparison with 1968, concentrated on American installations. In the first week, 336 Americans were killed, 453 in the second, 351 in the third, while South Vietnam lost more than 500 military men each week. On February 9, General Creighton Abrams reported that photo reconnaissance and other information had pinpointed the headquarters of North Vietnam's Central Office for South Vietnam (COSVN) in the Fishhook, a bulge of Cambodian territory into Vietnam. Abrams asked for a B-52 strike at COSVN, and Ambassador Ellsworth Bunker seconded the recommendation.

Nixon on February 23 ordered the Fishhook sanctuary bombed secretly, then reversed the order to reconsider the timing of a strike in relation to the peace talks, and to ponder Defense Secretary Melvin Laird's advice that air strikes could not be kept secret long.

When the Viet Cong rocketed Saigon March 15—considered a breach of the "gentlemen's agreement" at the peace talks—Nixon ordered the B-52 strike on the Cambodian sanctuaries on March 17. There was no complaint, no reaction at all, from Phnom Penh, Hanoi or Peking.

Nixon ordered further strikes without enemy protest. The early strikes surely contributed to the North Vietnamese decision to permit the NLF to offer a ten-point peace plan at the Paris talks. The plan was unacceptable to the Nixon administration, but it was the first real Communist gesture toward negotiation. The *Times* editorialized, "The National Liberation Front's offer of a ten-point peace plan at Paris yesterday represents a potentially significant step toward a Vietnam settlement." The editorial noted that the Front omitted the usual insistence that its plan was the only one possible, hinting at real negotiations. "After months of posturing and propaganda, that is progress," the *Times* said.[9]

On the same day, dropped into the bottom of Page 1 was a fateful story leaked to William Beecher of the *Times* Washington bureau. It said:

> American B-52 bombers in recent weeks have raided several Viet Cong and North Vietnamese supply dumps and base camps in Cambodia for the first time, according to Nixon administration sources, but Cambodia has not made any protest.
>
> In fact, Cambodian authorities have increasingly been cooperating with American and South Vietnamese military men at the border, often giving them information on Viet Cong and North Vietnamese movements into South Vietnam. . . .

It was the wrong leak at the wrong time. Not only did it open the Nixon administration to attack for the secret bombing of a neutral nation, but it jeopardized Prince Sihanouk, who was remaining neutral by giving way to both sides, allowing North Vietnam to ship in military supplies through his port, Sihanoukville, and also remaining silent on the bombings.

At a press conference Sihanouk was asked about Beecher's story. He said, "I have not protested the bombings of Viet Cong camps because I have not heard of the bombings. I was not in the know, because in certain areas of Cambodia there are no Cambodians. I have not been informed about that at all, because I have not lost any houses, any countrymen, nothing, nothing. Nobody was caught in those barrages—nobody, no Cambodians."[10]

Nixon and Kissinger were, in Nixon's word, enraged at the Beecher leak, because the bombing of Cambodian sanctuaries was working well and saving American lives. Kissinger contacted J. Edgar Hoover, and the FBI wiretapped 18 individuals, including four newspapermen and others in the State Department, Pentagon and on Kissinger's National Security Council staff—the first step toward Watergate.

The secret bombings coincided with a secret exchange of letters between Nixon and Ho Chi Minh through the French intermediary Jean Sainteny that led to a new breakthrough in the Paris talks. By August, Kissinger was meeting secretly with Xuan Thuy in Sainteny's Paris apartment, the beginning of three years of secret diplomacy aimed at ending the war.

Nixon appealed in a television address to the "great silent majority of my fellow Americans" for unity, receiving a flood of supportive letters and telephone calls. The anti-war movement's response was a New Mobe demonstration by a quarter of a million people in Washington November 15 that saw scattered violence throughout the capital.

Sir Robert Thompson, who was consulted by Nixon, has said that the sanctuary bombing program produced remarkable results. He told BBC that Tet 1968

> . . . had in fact destroyed most of the Viet Cong regular and regional units inside South Vietnam. In other words, they had nothing, or very little, left to defend their rural base areas with. This enabled the South Vietnamese to regain control in the countryside very rapidly, which is what happened between 1969 and 1970. I've never been so staggered in my life at the speed with which control was regained in the countryside.[11]

The Beecher leak was the kind of news story that is of great importance to politicians in Washington, Moscow, Peking, Hanoi, Phnom Penh and Saigon, but not the kind of story that excites the average news consumer. If the United States was bombing Cambodia's border areas, and the ruling prince didn't care, the story was not worth heated editorial comment or a daily follow-up, and the *Times* did not press the story. Nixon ordered a second strike on the Cambodian sanctuaries in April, then periodic strikes through August—the "Menu" strikes that involved more than 3,000 B-52 sorties, each tearing out a mile-long strip of jungle.

The air strikes, reverting to secrecy despite the leak, further slowed the war in South Vietnam; there was less for correspondents to report, and they looked for peripheral stories.

To the *Times,* a major story was the atrocity at My Lai-4, a hamlet destroyed by First Lieutenant William Calley, Jr.'s Company C, First Battalion, 11th Brigade, 20th Infantry Division, during the Communist offensive of Tet 1968.

My Lai-4 was a satellite hamlet of the larger village of Songmy on the South Vietnamese coast. The Songmy complex, its dense population appearing in pink on Army maps, was known as Pinkville. My Lai-4 was believed to be the haven of the 48th Viet Cong battalion when Calley's 100 men went in following an artillery barrage during the American media hysteria at the height of Tet on March 16, 1968. The village was wiped out in what became the major American atrocity story of the Vietnam war.

More than a year after the event, a Vietnam veteran, Ronald L. Ridenhour, who had not been at My Lai, heard from former buddies of atrocities committed at My Lai, wrote an anguished letter and sent 30 copies of it to Congressmen and Pentagon officials. In September 1969, the Army filed court-martial charges against Calley and was investigating 36 others.[12]

Before Calley was charged with the murders of civilians at My Lai, Seymour M. Hersh, a former member of the Associated Press Washington bureau, was tipped off in Washington of the inquiry. He contacted Ridenhour and began a survey of soldiers who had been involved in the attack on My Lai, compiling a dossier of first and second-hand accounts. His reports were distributed by Dispatch News Service, a subsidiary of the radical left Institute for Policy Studies of Marcus Raskin and Richard Barnet, which was waging a campaign in Congress to coalesce Congressmen against the war. Ridenhour later returned to Vietnam as a reporter for Dispatch News Service.

Hersh won the 1969 Pulitzer Prize for international reporting for his discovery of My Lai, and wrote two books on the atrocity, all without ever having seen Vietnam.

Reed Irvine, of Accuracy in Media, has pointed out that the *Times* index of 1969 contains three and a half pages of fine print references to My Lai stories, while it has only minor references to the Communist massacre of an estimated 4,800 persons, dead and presumed dead, in Hué at the same period. The *Times* hired Hersh as a special investigative reporter, editor Abe Rosenthal calling him "the hottest piece of journalistic property in the United States."

Hersh was not a stranger to the *Times* when he broke the My Lai story. In 1968 he had been a press spokesman for Senator Eugene McCarthy's campaign for the Democratic presidential nomination. While at the AP, he had submitted a report 17,000 words long warning that the U.S. military was developing deadly bacteriological warfare agents, including a "doomsday bug" that would be immune to antibiotics. When the AP editors cut the story to 1,700 words—still long for a wire service story—Hersh resigned. He then placed his story in a 4,000-word version in the *Times Magazine*.[13]

Hersh's story said that Russia, China and Poland were working on bacteriological warfare, and the leading research center was in England, but "perhaps the biggest culprit—in terms of perpetuating a

C.B.W. arms race—has been the U.S. military." Hersh cited U.S. training schools for officers from 35 nations and American bacteriological capabilities. His alarming report drew reader mail, both denouncing it as misleading and praising it.[14]

Less than two months after Hersh's article in the *Times Magazine,* Nixon ordered the destruction of U.S. germ warfare stocks and an end to the biological warfare program, just at the time when Hersh was being widely cited on My Lai.

As the My Lai story sent war correspondents to the ruins of the village in the fall of 1969, the anti-war movement, both peaceful and violent, was gearing up for demonstration spectaculars, spurred on, rather than slowed, by the death in Hanoi of Ho Chi Minh in September. Weathermen practiced brawling with clubs and chains in Detroit and Oakland, California, in preparation for the Days of Rage. The Weathermen staged a four-day rampage in Chicago in October, ostensibly to protest the trial of the seven men charged with conspiring to riot at the Chicago Democratic Convention. The Days of Rage riots were followed immediately by Moratorium demonstrations, which were greeted by laudatory *Times* editorials, columns and a four-column, Page 1 headline stressing the Moratorium's peaceful nature:

> VIETNAM MORATORIUM OBSERVED
> NATIONWIDE BY FOES OF WAR;
> RALLIES HERE CROWDED, ORDERLY.[15]

At the Moratorium rally of a quarter million persons in Washington, the main speaker was Richard Barnet of the Institute for Policy Studies. In New York City, a counter-rally of thousands of Nixon supporters was hastily organized around hard-hat construction workers.

Shortly after the Days of Rage and the Moratorium, another Timesman got a visa to North Vietnam, following in Salisbury's footsteps. Fox Butterfield, the *Times* expert on Asia, accompanied by his grandfather, the Cleveland industrialist Cyrus Eaton (who once had received a troika of horses from Khrushchev for his service to East-West cooperation), arrived to find that, "In Hanoi, Leaders and the Public Seem Confident."[16]

Butterfield reported the North Vietnamese were so "determined, natural and relaxed," that he could find no evidence that U.S. bombing had affected morale. He met with Premier Pham Van Dong, Le Duc Tho and leaders of the Vietnam Committee for Solidarity with the American people, and reported that among visitors to Hanoi was Cora Weiss, of the New Mobilization to End the War in Vietnam, negotiating for the disclosure of the names of 200 of the several hundred American prisoners. Butterfield's rosy report on conditions and morale in Hanoi so directly clashed with other reports, including a *U.S. News and World Report* account by French journalist and former Hanoi resident Pierre Darcourt, that Efron reprinted the two accounts as a study in bias, Appendix A., in her book, *The News Twisters.*

Nixon's decisions in the first year of his presidency were taken in an atmosphere that would not have been tranquil even without the Vietnam war, although most of the media accorded him the usual 100-day honeymoon. Student protests unrelated to the war had made battlegrounds of universities including Harvard, Cornell and City College of New York, where open admission was the issue and black and white students fought pitched battles for turf. Internationally the dollar was under attack, and West Germany was forced to float the mark, the first devaluation of the dollar from outside. In the Middle East, Nasser had embarked on the War of Attrition along the Suez Canal, in which Egypt would accept large-scale casualties while inflicting casualties on Israel almost comparable to those of the Six Day War.

Prince Norodom Sihanouk, onetime king and once the near-unanimous electoral choice of Cambodia for premier, feared North and South Vietnam about equally. In 1947, the year Sihanouk became king at 18 while opposing French colonialism but not fighting it, there was a large scale infiltration into Cambodia by Ho Chi Minh's Viet Minh troops and cadres in the name of "anti-colonialist solidarity."

Ho had founded the Indochinese Communist Party in Hong Kong in 1930, despite its name almost entirely Vietnamese, although many Western scholars were unaware of it until the latest of open breaks between the Khmer Rouge and North Vietnamese Communists ruined Cambodia in 1975. For a time after the Geneva agreements of 1954, the North Vietnamese Communists vacated Cambodia as required under the Geneva accords—to build up the Viet Minh in South Vietnam, violating the accords.

During the Kennedy build-up in South Vietnam, Sihanouk tilted his neutralism slightly toward the Americans (he liked American jazz and played the clarinet), while at the same time accommodating the Viet Minh and allowing them to be supplied secretly through the port of Kampon Son, later Sihanoukville. He maintained good relations with the Soviet Union and with China, and was friendly with Wilfred Burchett, the Communist journalist in the employ of the KGB, who maintained an apartment in Phnom Penh beginning in late 1963. Sihanouk collaborated with Burchett on his book, *My War With the CIA*.[17]

Although Diem had been one of Sihanouk's enemies, Sihanouk was shocked by his murder under U.S. auspices. He renounced U.S. aid and accused the CIA of fostering rebellion in Cambodia by supporting the Khmer Sarai, an old anti-Communist faction in Cambodian politics, based in 1963 in Thailand and South Vietnam.

With the Johnson administration's escalation of the war in 1965, Sihanouk broke relations with the United States and turned increasingly to China and to France. His country of 6.5 million in 1969, bordered by 16 million South Vietnamese, 20 million North Vietnamese and 33 million Thais, was in a position of helplessness comparable to Czechoslovakia's. He was aware that throughout the Johnson administration, the Joint Chiefs had contemplated air strikes against the Vietnamese sanctuaries in Cambodia, so his decision not to react to the Nixon air strikes had been thought out in advance. Despite the *Times'* revelation of the secret bombings in May, Sihanouk restored diplomatic relations with the United States in July.

In January 1970, Sihanouk and his wife Monique flew to France for a two-month vacation at a clinic in Grasse, leaving the country in charge of Premier Lon Nol and Sihanouk's cousin, Prince Sirik Matak, both anti-Communists. The Pentagon had estimated after Tet 1968 that it would take North Vietnam two years to recover and resume large-scale infiltration, and the schedule proved accurate. North Vietnam began heavy infiltration into South Vietnam and Cambodia at the time Sihanouk left the country.[18]

Sihanouk was about to return home when about 20,000 Cambodian demonstrators, presumably organized by Lon Nol, sacked the embassies of North Vietnam and the Viet Cong in Phnom Penh on March 11. More demonstrations in Phnom Penh followed, and the government announced a call-up of 10,000 men to reinforce its 35,000-man army. On March 13, the Cambodian government, sans Sihanouk, ordered all Communist Vietnamese forces to leave Cambodia within 48 hours.

While Sihanouk was in Moscow en route home, he learned from Kosygin that the legislature had deposed him and named the long-time anti-Communist Lon Nol chief of state. Sihanouk flew to China and a meeting April 24 in a village south of Canton with North Vietnam's Pham Van Dong, the Pathet Lao's Prince Souphanouvong and the head of the Viet Cong's National Liberation Front, Nguyen Huu Tho. The meeting was Sihanouk's first step toward becoming nominal head of the Khmer Rouge, long-time adversaries whose name had been bestowed by him. Available evidence supports the reports of Nixon in *RN* and Kissinger in *White House Years* that Lon Nol's coup caught the

Americans by surprise, and that it was not engineered by the CIA. Nixon believed that Sihanouk might be able to return despite the coup.

Part of the large North Vietnamese forces facing South Vietnam in the border enclaves wheeled to face the small Cambodian army, launching 29 attacks in three weeks in an advance toward Phnom Penh. Cambodians meanwhile were killing Vietnamese who remained near Phnom Penh, their bodies floating down the Mekong into South Vietnam.

Nixon had reduced U.S. troop strength in South Vietnam from 549,000 to 434,000, and on April 20 he surprised the anti-war movement by announcing that another 150,000 troops would come home by the end of 1970. At the same time, he ordered the CIA to re-establish a station and communications in Phnom Penh if the capital did not fall to the North Vietnamese and to find ways of getting some arms to Lon Nol's army.

Nixon was aware that any U.S. move into Cambodia would revive the anti-war movement, but the Communist advance on Phnom Penh, combined with two inviting targets of Communist concentration on Cambodia's border constituted a unique opportunity. On April 26 he made his decision to "go for broke."[19] The South Vietnamese army would move into the Parrot's Beak, a protrusion of Cambodia into South Vietnam 33 miles from Saigon, and U.S. troops would invade the Fishhook, another sanctuary jutting into South Vietnam 50 miles from the capital.

On April 29, the South Vietnamese government announced its attack on the Parrot's Beak, preempting almost half of the *Times'* Page 1. A four-column headline said:

> U.S. AIDS SAIGON PUSH IN CAMBODIA
> WITH PLANES, ARTILLERY, ADVISERS;
> MOVE STIRS OPPOSITION IN SENATE.

Subheads said: "RISING PERIL SEEN; Nixon to Speak on TV Tonight—Action is Termed Limited;" "SENATORS ANGRY; Some Seek to Cut Off Funds for Widened Military Action;" "Big Allied Sweep Aimed at Enemy Sanctuaries."

John W. Finney led his story on Senate reaction with John Stennis of Mississippi and Robert Griffin of Michigan praising the action, but the *Times* headline writers reached lower into his story to stress the anxieties of Mike Mansfield of Montana, George Aiken of Vermont, Mark Hatfield of Oregon and George McGovern of South Dakota.

An angry editorial commented,

President Nixon, who was elected on a pledge to bring peace in Vietnam, has instead escalated the war into Cambodia in a rash move that has the gravest implications for the United States....If the current American-supported South Vietnamese invasion of Cambodia is necessary to protect American and other 'free world forces' in South Vietnam, how long will it be before we are told that American forces must move into Cambodia to protect the American advisers and the 'free world forces' that are now there?[20]

The *Times* did not have to wait more than a few hours.

Nixon went on television on April 30 to announce the combined U.S.-South Vietnamese incursion into the Fishhook, stressing that it was not an invasion and that troops would be withdrawn. He said,

We stopped the bombing of North Vietnam. We have cut air operations by over 20%. We've announced the withdrawal of over 250,000 of our men. We've offered to withdraw all of our men if they will withdraw theirs. We've offered to negotiate all issues with only one condition, and that is that the future of South Vietnam be determined, not by North Vietnam, and not by the United States, but by the people of South Vietnam themselves. The answer of the enemy has been intransigence at the conference table, belligerence at Hanoi, massive military aggression in Cambodia and stepped up attacks....

Nixon said the action was necessary even if it made him a one-term President.

Nixon's speech included an oratorical phrase that caught on and obscured the speech's content, much as his remark about Checkers had obscured his disclosure of personal finances that was the point of his 1952 speech. He said, "Small nations all over the world find themselves under attack from within and without. If, when the chips are down, the world's most powerful nation—the United States of America—acts like a pitiful helpless giant, the forces of totalitarianism and anarchy will threaten free nations and free institutions throughout the world."

The "pitiful helpless giant" speech brought out the banner type at the *Times:*

NIXON SENDS COMBAT FORCES TO CAMBODIA
TO DRIVE COMMUNIST FORCES FROM STAGING ZONE.

The *Times* editorial, "Military Hallucination—Again," stormed:

Time and bitter experience has exhausted the credulity of the

American people and Congress. Presidential assurances can no longer be accepted in an area where actions. . . speak louder than words. . . . If reports from Phnom Penh that the attack was launched without consultation with the Cambodian government are true, the strike is a clear breach of Cambodian neutrality, the Geneva Accords and the principles of international law which the administration has repeatedly cited in connection with the long-known and equally illegal Communist Vietnamese presence on Cambodian soil. . . . Fortunately Mr. Nixon's tough approach has produced strong opposition in both houses of Congress. . . .[21]

On May Day Nixon went to the Pentagon for a briefing by the Joint Chiefs on the Cambodia incursion. He told officers there, "I want to take out all of those sanctuaries. Make whatever plans are necessary and then just do it. Knock them all out so that they can't be used against us again, ever."[22] The media-spurred storm in Congress, and the threat of legislation proposed by Senators John S. Cooper of Kentucky and Frank Church of Idaho to withhold funds for attacks on the sanctuaries, forced Nixon to cancel his order.

Leaving the Pentagon, Nixon was surrounded by reporters and a supportive crowd. Speaking of soldiers in the incursion, Nixon said,

I have seen them; they're the greatest. You see these bums, you know, blowing up the campuses. Listen, the boys that are on the college campuses today are the luckiest people in the world, going to the greatest universities, and there they are burning up the books, storming around about this issue, you name it. Get rid of this war and there will be another one. Then out there, we have kids who are doing their duty. . . . They stand tall, and they are proud.

The *Times* headlined, "Nixon Puts 'Bums' Label on Some Radical Students," as demonstrations and riots closed down dozens of American universities. At Kent State, Ohio, a mob burned down the ROTC building on May 2, and Governor James A. Rhodes called out the National Guard.

A *Times* editorial, "Cambodian Quagmire," said Nixon's "shocking decision to send American troops into Cambodia immediately raises the question, can they get out?" It cited the "pitiful helpless giant" phrase as evidence that Nixon's motives were not what he said they were, but a demonstration of machismo and "jingoistic language."[23]

Columnist Anthony Lewis, in London, leaped to the defense of the rioting students, writing that the same President who asked students to respect great institutions such as universities "orders a massive armed attack in a foreign country without going through the procedures laid down by the Constitution for making war or even asking Congress for less formal support." Nixon gave the students every reason to be cynical, wrote Lewis.[24]

Columnist Tom Wicker charged, "The invasion of Cambodia ordered by President Nixon makes it clear that he does not have and never has had a 'plan to end the war' "—the quotation marks implying that Nixon had made such a claim. Repeating several times in quotation marks the phrase "plan to end the war," Wicker wrote, "whatever his motives and his policy, Mr. Nixon relied heavily in his appearances before the nation on deception, demagogery and chauvinism." Wicker repeated a charge he had made before the election, that Nixon exaggerated in charging that there had been "slaughter and savagery" following the Communist victory in North Vietnam in 1954, and he echoed that Nixon's "pitiful helpless giant" phrase was "pure jingoism."[25]

Reston, in his commentary, found "A Confused Capital" following the Cambodia incursion. Sounding a favorite theme, Reston warned that it would bring the Brezhnev hawks to ascendency in Moscow over the moderates like Kosygin: ". . . lately Leonid I. Brezhnev, with the support of the Soviet armed services, had apparently prevailed over Premier Alexei N. Kosygin, and is now taking a much bolder line in the Middle East." This could not, however, be attributed to the Cambodia incursion, as Israel had charged before the South Vietnamese move into the Parrot's Beak that Soviet pilots were flying MiGs for Egypt in the War of Attrition.

On May 4, about 600 students at Kent State University surrounded a company of Ohio National Guard, some of the students throwing rocks the size of baseballs. Guardsmen opened fire, killing four students and wounding 11.[26] Sharing Page 1 with the *Times* report, another story said "37 COLLEGE CHIEFS URGE NIXON TO MOVE FOR PROMPT PEACE." The *Times* reported that university presidents had written Nixon warning that the American invasion of Cambodia had generated "severe and widespread apprehension on our campuses." It added that in Washington, the leaders of the National Student Association and the former Vietnam Moratorium Committee called for an indefinite nationwide university strike. Within days, 400 colleges were closed.

Four of Kissinger's staff aides resigned—Anthony Lake, William Watts, Roger Morris and Larry Lynn. A group of Harvard professors, including Richard Neustadt, Adam Yarmolinsky, Francis Bator and Thomas Schelling, visited Kissinger in Washington to break relations with him.

In New York, more than 50 publishers and editors of the country's most prestigous book publishing firms met to form the "Action Committee of Publishers for Peace," a first indication that books supporting Nixon's Vietnam policy would not find publishers among the major houses of the Northeast. The *Times* quoted the committee chairman, Christopher Cerf, 26 (son of the legendary Bennett Cerf, who taught a generation of Americans something of the outside world through his Modern Library), as saying, "We intend to use all our resources and skills to help make the Nixon administration aware of this new ground swell for peace."[27] Christopher Cerf was as good as his word. His Random House already had published *The Vietnam Reader,* books by Richard Barnet of IPS and Seymour Hersh's My Lai books, and would become the prestige publisher of the anti-war movement.[28]

We were now close to realizing Andrei Sakharov's convergence theory. In the Soviet Union only one point of view was permitted by the government, dissenters reduced to distributing carbon sheets of their self-published thoughts. In the United States, wide distribution of ideas was to be restricted to one point of view by a cartel of like-minded major publishers and book reviewers. Although Sir Robert Thompson was the world's best-known authority on counter-insurgency, his warning would be suppressed by the *Times* and his book, *Peace Is Not at Hand,*[29] would not find an American publisher because it was disrespectful of *The New York Times.*

The *Times,* editorializing daily since the Parrot's Beak incursion, urged Congress on May 5 to restrain a willful President and suggested that a drop in the Dow-Jones Industrial Average of 19.05 points was caused by the incursion: "Another 1929?"[30]

As anti-war fever rose, Reston's columns turned harsher: Nixon was "not 'determined' over anything. One day he is persuaded that peace is within our grasp, the next he is convinced by his military advisers that his whole command may be in danger unless he expands the war." Reston saw "tragic consequences" in Nixon's "wild contradictions."[31]

An editorial the same day found Nixon's statement on the Kent State tragedy "deplorably unfeeling. . . nor does it show any compassion or even understanding." The next day's editorial made Nixon responsible for Kent State: "The fury that grips college youth is fed by a conviction that the administration itself had contributed to the repressive mood that made the Ohio National Guardsmen overquick on the trigger."

Wicker echoed the editorials: "It was obtuse and heartless for President Nixon to say of the dead at Kent State only that 'when dissent turns to violence it invites tragedy'" (which was not all that Nixon said). Wicker charged that Agnew deliberately aimed at class warfare for political purposes: "It was indecent for Spiro Agnew to call this awful event 'predictable and avoidable'. . . . Mr. Agnew's sustained and inflammatory assault on some young Americans could have had no other purpose, and no other result, than to set generation against generation and class against class for the calculated political purposes of the Nixon administration."[32]

On the morning of May 9, Nixon, the insomniac, got into his limousine with his physician, Dr. Walter Tkach, and his valet, Manolo Sánchez, and drove to the Lincoln Memorial, where a group of students held an anti-war vigil. Nixon spoke to about eight surprised students, asking where they had come from. He attempted to explain what he had tried to say in his television speech: "I know that probably most of you think I'm a S.O.B., but I want you to know that I understand just how you feel. . . . I was just as close to being a pacifist as anybody could be." Nixon recalled he had been excited at Neville Chamberlain's statement about peace in our time, when he was just out of law school and ready to be married. Before World War II, he had thought that "the prospect of going into service was almost unbearable," and he had "thought Churchill was a madman." He said,

> In retrospect, I now realize I was wrong. I think now that Chamberlain was a good man, but that Churchill was a wiser man, and that we in the world are better off than we would be, because Churchill had not only the wisdom but the courage to carry out policies that he believed were right, even though there was a time when both in England and all over the world he was extremely unpopular because of his 'anti-peace' stand.

Nixon advised the group to see the world, describing his own early eagerness to see South America, talking of the cities of Europe, Prague and Moscow, answering questions. The group grew to about 30, one of them saying, "I hope you realize that we are willing to die for what we believe in," and another adding, "We are not interested in what Prague looks like. We are interested in what kind of life we build in the United States." Nixon said he talked about Prague because "the world is going to get much smaller. We are going to be living in all parts of the world, and it is vitally important that you know and appreciate and understand the people everywhere, wherever they are, and particularly understand the people in your own country."

Dr. Tkach took a picture of Nixon and a demonstrator with the demonstrator's camera, and Nixon left, telling the group, "I just hope your opposition doesn't turn into a blind hatred of the country, but remember this is a great country, with all of its faults. If you have any doubt about it, go down to the passport office. You won't see many people lining up to get out of the country. Abroad, you will see a number lining up to get in."

No reporters were present at the Lincoln Memorial between 4:30 and 7 a.m., but Nixon met Garnett D. Horner, of the *Washington Star,* when he returned to the White House from breakfast at the Mayflower Hotel and told him about it. Robert B. Semple, Jr. of the *Times* picked up on the story to provide "a revealing glimpse of a man who has been under exceptional strain for the last few weeks. . .who is said to have enjoyed few restful nights since he decided, on the evening of April 27, to send American troops into Cambodia." Semple found a witness, Joan Pelietier, 20, from Syracuse University, who apparently joined the group late and heard little of what was said. Semple quoted her as saying, "Here we came from a university that's completely uptight, on strike, and when we told him where we were from, he talked about the football team, and when somebody said he was from California, he talked about surfing."[33]

The media commentators zoomed in on the *Times'* report, not the *Washington Star's,* deriding Nixon's gauche insensitivity in talking about football and surfing to the young rebels.

At the *Times* Washington bureau, Max Frankel perceived that Nixon faced a "minority" revolution—all revolutions start as minorities—but he was more worried that the revolt would bring on heavy-handed repression, the ever-present *Times* fear of fascism.

Under the headline, "Nixon: He Faces a Divided, Anguished Nation," Frankel wrote on Page 1 of the *Week in Review* that Nixon was "bidding frantically for peace with a rebellious minority that challenged not only his policies but also his qualities of leadership and understanding of his people." Frankel wrote that the Cambodia and Kent State crises "sent tremors of fear through the White House that revolt and repression might be nearer than anyone had dared to imagine. They brought home, at least to most of the President's advisers, the realization that the national security was endangered by much, much more than the Viet Cong or the Communists."[34]

Here was the basis of what would become Watergate: Nixon's attempt to curb a revolution, and the media's portrayal of his actions as calculated repression. Frankel challenged Nixon's credibility in his television appearance after Kent State, writing that Nixon contended that he was not surprised by the reaction. . .

only by the misunderstanding of his motives. He moved into

Cambodia to hasten the end of the war, he insisted, and thus he really shared the objectives of his critics. Nervous, bland but in no sense apologetic and obviously resenting the need to justify himself in living color, the President urged that while the action was hot the rhetoric remain cool, cited his own tolerance of dissent as an example of the 'safety valves' that are at work to protect American society from revolution or repression. . . .

Wicker's next column again challenged Nixon's statement that there had been a bloodbath in North Vietnam in 1954 and revived the Halberstam-era charge that only Diem's South Vietnam committed atrocities. Under the headline, "Mr. Nixon's Scary Dreams," Wicker wrote that Nixon should stick to facts: ". . . the record disclosed no evidence that such an atrocity (in the North) had occurred," and investigations showed that "there was no bloodbath in North Vietnam in 1954," Wicker cited International Control Commission figures that only 19 complaints were received on political reprisals and only one involving murder in North Vietnam in the two years after the armistice, while in South Vietnam 214 complaints were lodged against Diem, and by 1957, when Diem "summarily barred the I.C.C. from any further investigations, 1,047 complaints were still pending against him." Wicker wrote, "So the only events resembling mass political reprisals after the 1954 armistice occurred in the South, not the North. What did happen in North Vietnam was a harshly repressed peasant revolt in 1955 and 1956 against a severe land reform program. It had nothing to do with Ho Chi Minh's takeover. . . ." Wicker even excused the Communists' massacre at Hué in taking issue with Nixon's charge that at least 3,000 were executed, Wicker wrote, "But D. G. Porter and L. R. Ackland, writing in the *Christian Century* of November 5, 1969, have reported their findings, after careful research, that most of these wicked executions took place in the heat of battle and as 'the revenge of an army in retreat' and were not the deliberate policy of Hanoi."[35]

Western Europe took its cue on what to think of the Cambodia incursion from the *International Herald-Tribune,* published in Paris by the *Times* and *Washington Post.* With the combined resources and correspondents of the two newspapers plus the *Post's* syndicate ally the *Los Angeles Times,* the *IHT,* concise and picking the best material, was on some days the world's best newspaper. To Europeans it *is* the United States, delivered every morning to the desks of every chancery on the continent.

In the week encompassing the Cambodia incursion and the Kent State riot, the *International Herald-Tribune* suspended the normal practices of journalism, its front page black with doomsday headlines and imprecations against Nixon, the opinions of columnists Reston, Lewis and others on Page 1 under news headlines. France always had opposed American involvement in Vietnam. Now the *IHT,* America to its readers, gave license to all the left-wing opposition to the war in West Germany and other nations, while effectively silencing any remaining supporters of Johnson's or Nixon's Vietnam policies. Anti-war demonstrations were organized throughout Europe, encouraged rather than discouraged by West Germany's new government under Chancellor Willy Brandt.

The 60-day incursion into Cambodian border areas was, like Tet 1968, a major military victory turned into defeat by the media. Anti-war Senators and the international clamor prevented Nixon from any follow-up and allowed Hanoi to regroup. The incursion crippled Communist military actions for another year, and even Theodore H. White, no friend of Nixon, called it a year later, "one of the most successful operations of the long Vietnam war."[36] The incursion killed 11,349 enemy troops, captured 2,328, destroyed 60% of Communist supply caches in Cambodia and captured 22,892 rifles, 15 million rounds of ammunition plus larger weapons and 435 vehicles that were turned over to Lon Nol's hard-pressed army.

The invaders did not find COSVN, the North Vietnamese headquarters that had been in the Fishhook but had moved out at the time of Lon Nol's coup, and the media announced that the invasion had failed in its objective. But the number of American combat deaths dropped precipitiously, by the end of the summer reaching the lowest levels in three years.

When Nixon moved into the White House, speechwriters who took up quarters there included Ray Price, Pat Buchanan, William Safire and Tom Charles Huston, the youngest at 28.

Huston, a conservative intellectual and former head of Young Americans for Freedom, was an outspoken counter-revolutionary, angry at the license permitted demonstration organizers and commuters to Hanoi via Havana and Prague. Haldeman made Huston his monitor within the formal intelligence agencies of subversives, demonstration organizers and saboteurs.

In July, Huston suggested that the Internal Revenue Service, accustomed to receiving orders from Kennedy and Johnson to audit the returns of some adversaries such as steel industry executives, should look into the ideological organizations involved in the anti-war movement, some of which enjoyed tax-exempt status.

On July 24, 13 IRS agents were convened to discuss 77 organizations that might be a threat to national security. Huston wanted to know where their funding came from, whether they had legitimate tax exemptions and whether their contributors also were claiming charitable deductions.

In the process, Huston discovered that the IRS, like the State and Justice Departments, was heavily salted with Kennedy-era Democrats more eager to pursue rich Republicans than scruffy revolutionaries or even Soviet illegals. The media later made a martyr of CBS correspondent Daniel Schorr because the IRS audited him and the FBI began a full field investigation of him—an investigation quickly dropped when Schorr said he had not considered accepting a government job and did not want to be investigated—but the media's horror was spurious; all of Dan's friends and enemies in the media enjoyed seeing his cockiness tested, if only for a few hours.[37]

Huston then was sent for a tour of duty with the Defense Intelligence Agency. He learned there that there was little or no coordination between the various intelligence agencies, largely because J. Edgar Hoover ran the FBI like a fiefdom. Shortly after Nixon took office, Hoover abolished the Liaison Section with the CIA because the CIA would not identify an FBI agent who had passed on information to them without Hoover's express permission.[38]

What Huston had yet to learn was that the FBI was in a state of internal warfare. The legendary Hoover, a friend of Nixon, was 74 when Nixon took office and losing his grip. Associate Director Clyde Tolson, who ran the bureau with Hoover, was aging rapidly, partly disabled by a series of slight strokes and often absent. Bitter rivalry within the second rank of the FBI leadership, especially between W. Mark Felt and William C. Sullivan, reached a state of feud; when Hoover fired Sullivan, Sullivan challenged the bigger Felt to a fist fight. Dissention within the FBI dated back to 1965, when Hoover had feuded with Attorney General Robert Kennedy, and in upstaging Kennedy had ordered such deep cutbacks in national security wiretapping that the FBI's No. 3 man, Alan H. Belmont, retired, disheartened.

During the uproar over Kent State, when legions of anti-war demonstrators camped in Washington parks and Ellsberg testified before Fulbright's Senate Foreign Relations Committee, some White House staffers were braced for a physical assault on the White House perhaps led by an intrepid Norman Mailer or Abbie Hoffman, backed this time by Weathermen throwing bombs.

At that point Nixon's exasperation with the intelligence services boiled up. The FBI could tell him nothing of the demonstrators' plans, or of their connections to Soviets and Cubans in New York. He thoroughly distrusted the CIA, with its Ivy League liberalism and protective stance toward the Eastern establishment and the Kennedys, and Kissinger was sending back CIA reports with scrawled notations, "inadequate." Federal prosecutors, who were consumers of FBI produce, appeared to be siding with New Left defendants against the police, and courts produced acquittal after acquittal in riot cases. Middle-rank government employees were joining demonstrations and anti-war teach-ins, and when 250 State Department employees signed a manifesto condemning the invasion of Cambodia, Nixon could neither fire nor monitor them.

A month after Kent State, on June 5, Nixon summoned to the White House the heads of the intelligence community for a dressing down. Hoover, Helms, General Donald Bennett of DIA, Admiral Noel Gayler of the National Security Agency, were giving him no intelligence on possible revolutionaries or saboteurs in the government. Nixon was convinced that the anti-war movement had more organization than the agencies had found, more financing, more connections to the international terrorist groups that were surfacing from the Middle East to the Caribbean with offshoots in Germany and Ireland. Angry, caustic, demanding to know who was calling the shots in the anti-war movement, Nixon ordered them to form an Interagency Committee on Intelligence under Hoover, with Huston representing the White House, to produce a counter-revolutionary intelligence program.

The target of the meeting was Hoover, who returned to FBI headquarters furious at having been dressed down in front of the other intelligence chiefs. He unloaded the committee on FBI Assistant Director William C. Sullivan, who welcomed the assignment. Although Sullivan characterized himself as a liberal Democrat, he had long complained that Hoover, trying to preserve his image after 40 years of service, had "put the Domestic Intelligence Division of the FBI out of business," even refusing a CIA request for surveillance of two known Soviet agents posing as businessmen in New York.

Huston gave to Sullivan a long litany of administration complaints. Sullivan wrote later:

> Huston was right and we both knew it. Because his criticism was cogent and factual, I agreed with him. . . . In fact, I had outlined the same problem in a classified personal letter to Richard

Helms... before I heard from Tom Charles Huston, but Helms felt that there was nothing either of us could do about it so long as Hoover was in control.... To me, Huston looked like manna from heaven.[39]

Sullivan's subcommittee put together a 60-page report, essentially removing restraints on domestic intelligence that had been imposed by Johnson in 1966 and subsequently by Hoover's unilateral decisions.

Hoover objected to the plan in a series of meetings with Sullivan, then agreed to register his objections in footnotes to the plan, which he assigned Sullivan to write for him.

Huston meanwhile warned Haldeman by memorandum, passed on to the President, that Hoover would not go along unless Nixon called him in for a stroking session. He wrote, "At some point Hoover has to be told who is President." Nixon, having chewed out his old colleague Hoover once, declined to face him again.

Sullivan noted:

All the plan amounted to, apart from an analysis of the intelligence problems facing us, was a recommendation to reinstitute the programs and policies which Hoover himself had initiated, encouraged and approved years ago and which the FBI had carried out under his direction for so many years. It was the few secondary provisions that upset Hoover. The provisions for better interagency coordination were anathema to him; he believed that he and the FBI operated best independently and unilaterally.... The thought of someone... looking over Hoover's shoulder and checking his work was out of the question.[40]

Sullivan added that "during my thirty years with Hoover, I never once heard the director say that he was against any FBI program on constitutional grounds or because it would be illegal."

All four intelligence chiefs signed the final report, which the media would call the Huston Plan when it was revealed to press orchestration in the heated atmosphere of the Sam Ervin show by John Dean three years later.[41] Sullivan, responsible for writing the draft, commented, "In fact, the plan wasn't Huston's at all—it summed up the thinking of the subcommittee as a whole... everyone who heard about it in my division was elated. They were as eager as I was to get back in business against the Soviet agents who were operating so freely within our borders."[42]

A directive implementing the report went out to intelligence agencies on July 23, with orders to report progress by September 1, the be-

ginning of the new university term. Hoover went to Attorney General
Mitchell to repeat his objections. Mitchell consulted with the CIA, then
advised Nixon to drop the project. Haldeman ordered all of the agencies to return their copies of the directive, and the Huston Plan was
aborted during the period that Daniel Ellsberg was distributing copies
of the Pentagon Papers around the capital.

Theodore H. White, who later was one of the first to try to make
sense of the labyrinthine complexities of Watergate, wrote in *Breach
of Faith* that Huston was put in charge of a super-police, and that the
Huston Plan was Nixon's initial heresy, "a breach in the guarantees that
America's Constitution holds for its citizens." Still, puzzled, White
softened the charge: "The Constitution is not an easy document to interpret; it is full of contradictions; Nixon had been caught in one of
those contradictions, as had many Presidents before him."[43] To White,
the Huston Plan's proposals were "mind boggling. . . . Of Huston, it
can be said that he was true and loyal to what he felt was right, and a
menace to the Republic."

White's condemnation is more than overdrawn—the writer-White
winning out over the reporter-White. He was writing in 1974, when
peer pressure in American journalism was almost unanimous to call
Watergate a Presidential plot to take over the country and impose a fascist system. Nixon was not Hitler; Huston was not Heinrich Müller;
Sullivan, who created the report and saw the country being damaged
when it was aborted, did not have a Gestapo mentality, and the program fell far short of domestic intelligence measures of World War II,
which the nation survived without too much trouble.

To Sullivan, whose men wrote most of the report, Huston was "a
man of integrity and character," and he regretted Huston's resignation
from the White House staff, which would later leave legal affairs in the
hands of another young man, John Dean III.

The Huston Plan was four days old when John Dean, 31, a bright
and eager protégé of Mitchell at the Justice Department, joined the
White House as legal counsel. John Ehrlichman was leaving that post
to become the President's adviser on domestic affairs. Dean reported
to his new office on July 27, 1970, while Haldeman still was trying to
get compliance on the Huston Plan from Hoover. Hoover's bridges
were burned to Huston, whom he called "that hippie" and addressed
as "Mr. Hutchinson" or "Mr. Hoffman," and the Hoover problem was
tossed to the new man, Dean.

Huston, assigned to Dean's staff, would not permit Dean to see the
intelligence program until he had security clearance. Two CIA men arrived to administer to Dean an oath, and he received clearance for

TOP SECRET/Comint. Dean received the Huston Plan, his first classified government document. He turned to his old boss, Mitchell, and was relieved to hear that Mitchell already had decided to kill the project. Mitchell and Dean proposed, instead of the Huston Plan, an interagency Intelligence Evaluation Committee, which they hoped would bring Hoover on board again.

Dean had not been investigated by the FBI for his security clearance, and he thought the oath-taking ceremony silly. Immediately he began squirreling away classified documents in a brown envelope in his home.[44]

Three years later, when the media was obsessed by Watergate to the exclusion of all other news, and the nation's attention was riveted on the televised Ervin Committee hearings, three top secret memos on the Huston Plan leaked to the *Times,* which headlined over four columns on Page 1:

> DOCUMENTS SHOW NIXON APPROVED
> PARTLY 'ILLEGAL' '70 SECURITY PLAN.

The story, by John M. Crewdson, said:

> President Nixon approved a plan for expanded domestic intelligence gathering in July, 1970, after being cautioned that parts of it were 'clearly illegal,' and involved 'serious risks' to his administration if the operations were ever discovered, according to White House documents.
>
> The program, which Mr. Nixon described in part last month, was approved by him through H. R. Haldeman, after Tom Charles Huston, a staff assistant to the President, told Mr. Haldeman, 'We don't want the President linked to this thing, with his signature on paper . . . all hell would break loose if this thing leaks out.'
>
> In a statement issued May 22, Mr. Nixon said that he had rescinded his approval of the '1970 intelligence plan' five days after he ordered it put into operation. He attributed the switch to 'reconsideration. . . prompted by the opposition of Director Hoover.'[45]

Inside, the *Times* reproduced three top secret memos over a full newspaper page.

The part of the plan that Huston's memo to Haldeman pointed out was illegal concerned burglaries of foreign embassies and targets like the Weathermen and Black Panthers, the Panthers already having been the target of FBI burglaries.

Times publication brought forth the cries of "Gestapo!" that so influenced Teddy White, but examined today, the memos look like what William Sullivan said they were, notes on a necessary intelligence effort at a time when South Vietnam still existed, and not exceeding the FBI's efforts under Hoover in the past.

Dean reported that when Huston joined his staff, he warned Dean "with rabid conviction" that the nation "would surely crumble from within if the government failed to deal with the revolutionaries and anarchists who were bent on destroying it." Dean did not believe a revolution was occurring, and he wrote of Huston, "In fact, none of the dire predictions in his report came true."[46]

Dean's *insouciance* over the revolution is understandable, in that he acknowledges in his book the help of David Obst, friend of Daniel Ellsberg, agent for Seymour Hersh and former editor of Dispatch News Service, an offshoot of the Institute for Policy Studies.

Huston resigned from the Nixon administration in 1971 and returned to law practice, still predicting that the unchecked revolution would win. Huston's predictions came true, and the revolution sent Dean to jail, although he never realized it.

Shortly after Huston left Washington, Hoover forced Sullivan to retire from the FBI in an acrimonious exchange of letters, and a year later Hoover died. During the Watergate ordeal, Sullivan was outraged at Dean's testimony before the Ervin Committee, in which he said Dean twisted his account of their talks, but Sullivan never was permitted to appear before the committee to refute the testimony. Sullivan believed that because Hoover aborted the Huston Plan, the White House fell back on its own resources and set up the unprofessional plumbers.

Chapter XIV
Revolt in Jordan

"A revolution is not a garden party."

—*Mao Tse-tung*

As Prince Sihanouk fell to a coup and Nixon made war on North Vietnamese sanctuaries in Cambodia in the spring of 1970, the Middle East, all but ignored by the Kennedy and Johnson administrations, was boiling up both along the Suez Canal and in Jordan.

For a brief period after the Six Day War in 1967 there had appeared to be a chance for peace in the Middle East. Israel's victory had been quick and complete. Majority opinion in Israel favored evacuating the West Bank, Gaza Strip, Sinai and part of the Golan Heights in exchange for a peace treaty, keeping three conquests: Sharm el-Sheikh, the Golan slopes and Jerusalem. But the Arab position was unique in that they did not have to speak with their conquerors.

Immediately after the Six Day War, a large delegation of Soviet officers headed by the Red Army chief of staff arrived in Egypt to evaluate the causes of the debacle and to begin a massive re-supply and training program. Two months later the Soviets invited Syrian Defense Minister

Hafez Assad to Moscow, offering him the same terms Egypt had accepted: a military buildup conditional on Syria's accepting supervision by Soviet experts. At the end of August, an Arab summit in Khartoum wrote off any peace negotiations, decreeing no contact with Israel. The summit decided that Nasser would allow the Suez Canal to remain closed indefinitely, punishing the West, the canal revenues to be made up by the oil-rich states.

In his first weeks in office, Nixon held a National Security Council meeting on the Middle East and assigned its problems to Secretary of State William Rogers and Assistant Secretary for Near East Affairs Joseph Sisco. Kissinger, ruled out of the Middle East because of his Jewish origin, would be occupied with Vietnam. In office three months, Nixon met Jordan's King Hussein in Washington and sought his help in re-establishing diplomatic relations with Egypt and other Middle East nations that had broken relations in 1967. Nixon held out the prospect of U.S. arms supplies to Jordan.

By 1969 Nasser, surfeited with Soviet weaponry but not organized for an offensive, turned the continuing border clashes along the Suez Canal into heavy artillery attacks on Israeli posts, willing to accept high Egyptian casualties to inflict casualties that might sap Israel's small population. In the first half of the 17-month War of Attrition, Israel retaliated with deep-penetration air raids that destroyed Egypt's oil refineries.

In January 1970, Nasser made a secret trip to Moscow. As a result, the Soviets took over entirely Egypt's air defense system, stepping up the installation of radar facilities and SAM missile sites. In April, three squadrons of Soviet pilots flying modern MiG jets went operational in Egypt; they were discovered when Israeli jets shot down five of them over Egyptian territory. The discovery forced Israel to cease penetration raids; it could not take on the Soviet Union.

Rogers, meanwhile, at the end of 1969, proposed a peace initiative to settle the 1967 war, essentially an Israeli withdrawal from territories occupied in 1967 in exchange for guarantees from Arab nations to recognize Israel's territorial integrity. Israel refused a peace without a treaty and without negotiating with its adversaries, bitterly recalling Nixon's campaign promises to tilt toward Israel.

Nixon, pressuring Israel to permit an American opening to Egypt and the Arabs through the Rogers Plan, suspended the delivery of 25 Phantom jets and 100 Skyhawks to Israel in March 1970, one month before the arrival of Soviet pilots in Egypt. Sisco went to Israel to confer with Dayan, finding him more conciliatory than Prime Minister Golda Meir; Dayan was willing to listen to the proposition that the Soviets were more dangerous to the Middle East than the Egyptians were. Criticism of Nixon's pressure on Israel continued in the United States, including in the Senate. Meir wrote Nixon expressing her fear of betrayal.

While attempting to ward off the furor raised by the Cambodia incursion, Nixon showed his irritation at the "unyielding and short-sighted pro-Israel attitude prevalent in large and influential segments of the American Jewish community, the media and intellectual and cultural circles."

Angry at being called anti-Israel or anti-Semitic, Nixon wrote a note to Kissinger saying it was ironic that dove Senators were ostensibly coming to Israel's rescue. What the Israelis must realize, he wrote:

> . . . is that these people are very weak reeds. They will give Israel a lot of lip service, but they are peace at any price people. When the chips are down, they will cut and run, not only as they are presently cutting and running in Vietnam, but also when any conflict in the Middle East stares them in the face. On the other hand, their real friends (to their great surprise) are people like Goldwater, Buckley, RN et al., who are considered to be hawks on Vietnam but who, in the broader aspects, are basically not cut-and-run people.[1]

Nixon's memo to Kissinger said:

> We are *for* Israel because Israel in our view is the only state in the Mideast which is *pro*-freedom and an effective opponent to Soviet expansion. . . Mrs. Meir, Rabin, et al., must trust RN completely. He does not want to see Israel go down the drain and makes an absolute commitment that he will see to it that Israel always has 'an edge.'

But Nixon stressed that Israelis must understand that he must carry the 60% silent majority in the United States to be of any use to them, and it did not help to be opposed by the Jewish community, 95% of which had voted against him.

> We are going to stand up in Vietnam and in NATO and in the Mideast, but it is a question of all or none. This is cold turkey, and it is time that our friends in Israel understood this. We are going to be in power for at least the next three years and this is going to be the policy of this country. Unless they understand it and act as if they understand it now, they are going down the tubes.[2]

Through the summer of 1970 Israeli jets pounded Egyptian radar and SAM sites close to the canal, but SAM missiles knocked down five

Israeli planes. In June, Rogers proposed an interim plan for separating forces at the Canal, and in August both sides accepted a 90-day ceasefire in the War of Attrition. Nasser's Egypt immediately broke the ceasefire terms, moving up SAM missile sites close to the canal. Nixon, by this time with one eye on Jordan's turmoil, called it a Soviet breach of faith and renewed deliveries of Phantom jets to Israel.

In May, Nasser had confirmed that Soviet pilots were helping out, and Kosygin acknowledged that the Soviets were giving Israel's Arab enemies "extensive aid." Nixon's withholding the Phantoms to encourage negotiation had backfired.

The War of Attrition, fought with artillery and aircraft, had no role for two of Nasser's creations, the Palestine Liberation Organization and the Palestine Liberation Army, both of which moved out of Egypt in 1969. The PLA moved to Syria, leaving a small contingent in Egypt, and became part of the Syrian armed forces. The PLA was Soviet-equipped, its leaders in an interlocking directorate with one of the PLO's factions, As Saiqa, the leader of which was Zuheir Mohsen, a Syrian officer.

Yasser Arafat's Al Fatah, Nasser's favorite faction, moved its headquarters to Amman, Jordan, on the route to Kuwait, where Fatah's first cells had been founded in 1958. Also headquartered in Amman was the Popular Front for the Liberation of Palestine of Dr. George Habash, a relatively new PLO faction. Habash originally had been a Nasser protégé, but his movement experienced several defections, its splitoffs including the Popular Democratic Front for the Liberation of Palestine under Naif Hawatmeh—an Iraqi and Soviet favorite—and the Popular Front-General Command of Ahmed Jebril.

By 1970, the year after Arafat won leadership of the PLO and had begun his attempt to unite the various factions' guerrilla armies in a Unified Command, the PLO was seen by Arab politicians as the militant, coming vehicle of Arab political expression. The PLO had potentially unlimited financing from Saudi Arabia, the Gulf States and Iraq, Libya and Algeria, all soon to be among the world's richest per-capita nations. The factions represented national interests of sponsor nations: Fatah for Egypt, Saiqa for Syria, the Arab Liberation Front for Iraq, the Popular Front-General Command for Libya, although alliances shifted like the desert sands. The PLO and its factions also found sponsors outside the Muslim world, the Popular Democratic Front and Fatah with the Soviet Union, Habash's Popular Front with China and North Korea.

Leadership of the PLO by 1970 was a valuable prize to the men who were striving for it, by now all professional revolutionaries who had won some wealth and status through their profession. In his *White House Years,* Kissinger confessed that he never did understand what the Jordanian revolt of 1970 was all about, although surely he knew that its main element was the struggle over who would lead the PLO.

Jordan's King Hussein was a different kind of man from Cambodia's Prince Sihanouk, but he found himself in the middle of forces comparable with those that brought down Sihanouk, with Israel in the role of South Vietnam, Hussein's Bedouin officers and troops in the role of anti-Communist Cambodians under Lon Nol, the PLO factions like the Khmer Rouge clients of hostile neighbors, and the Chinese and Soviets hoping to influence the outcome from outside.

Jordan's population in 1970 was roughly half Bedouin and half Palestinian Arabs. The Palestinians, more urban and enterprising, had rebuilt Amman and had run much of its commerce since the establishment of Israel as a nation. Jordan was in effect a Palestinian state with a Bedouin king, Sandhurst-educated and in 1970 still pro-Western. Hussein ran a moderate government, with Palestinian Arabs in the legislature and at all levels of government including prime minister. He had been more generous than any other Arab leader to refugees of the Six Day War and to the PLO leadership in terms of equality and social acceptance. His police and security forces were relatively free of the charges of brutality leveled at his Arab neighbors.

Until 1968, Hussein's army had helped PLO guerrilla raiders into Israel, but Israeli reprisals fell on the soldiers' forts, not on the guerrilla fortresses within refugee camps, and Hussein attempted to restrain guerrilla attacks into Israel, just as the Saudis and others attempted to restrain guerrilla attacks from Lebanon, the Arab world's banking and communications center.

Hussein's generosity and moderation represented softness to the PLO revolutionaries, to whom confrontation was their reason for existence. In Jordan, they were developing into a state within a state, following their own rules, setting up roadblocks and collecting extortion, careening through the cities in battered black Mercedes sedans, with their weapons, bent on mysterious urgent business.

In February 1970, Hussein attempted to bring the guerrillas under Jordanian law and banned the carrying of weapons in public. Arafat ordered 5,000 guerrillas alerted, including those of the Popular Front, who were just joining the Unified Command. Guerrillas attacked the king's motorcade on the airport road, Hussein escaping assassination, and clashes at police stations left eight guerrillas and seven soldiers dead. Hussein suspended the ban on carrying weapons, and then negotiated with PLO leaders for their self-policing of the ban, which never was enforced.

In April, Assistant Secretary Sisco, touring the Middle East to win support for the Rogers Plan, dropped Amman from his schedule after anti-American demonstrations by PLO factions. Hussein, his position weakened by the implication that he could not keep order, demanded that the United States recall Ambassador Harrison Symmes, who had advised Sisco not to visit Amman.

In early June, guerrillas kidnapped U.S. Embassy counsellor Morris Draper, releasing him the next day, and on June 9 Hussein escaped a second ambush, leaping from his car near Suweilih to return fire while his bodyguard was killed. His army in retaliation shot up a jeepload of Popular Democratic Front guerrillas. Hussein's officers, angry at the ambushes and skirmishing, demanded that he bring the PLO under control, and Western correspondents began arriving in Amman for the first phase of Jordan's revolt. Major Robert P. Perry, the U.S. Embassy's assistant Army attaché, who was a Yale graduate and student of Arabic, opened his front door to guerrillas and was shot dead through the still-closed screen door. Guerrillas seized half of Amman in general warfare.

Habash's Popular Front guerrillas seized the Philadelphia Hotel in downtown Amman next to their headquarters, holding 22 guests hostage. Then the Popular Front raced up the hills to capture the Intercontinental Hotel perched on a ravine overlooking the city, seizing hostages there, mostly Western correspondents, 15 of them British, 14 American, five West German, four Canadian and several French. Two of the Americans, William Touhy of the *Los Angeles Times* and Jesse Lewis of the *Washington Post,* escaped to the airport and Beirut.

Negotiating with Arafat, Hussein reached a ceasefire with a promise that the national assembly would investigate grievances, but Habash refused to accept the ceasefire, threatening to blow up the two hotels with his hostages. Saiqa joined in refusing to recognize the ceasefire. Hussein capitulated to the demand of the Popular Front and Saiqa, and fired his uncle, army commander Major General Sherif Nasser Ben Jamil, and hardline division commander Major General Zaid Ben Shaker.

In Beirut, with its wide variety of newspapers, Hussein's capitulation to Habash was a media sensation, and a mob of 3,000 burned down the Jordanian Embassy, ostensibly because Hussein's troops had fired on refugee camps, but more likely because he had shown weakness. The Lebanese army stood a half block away and watched the embassy burn, its first and fatal capitulation to PLO guerrillas. Habash was the hero of Beirut.

Habash visited the Intercontinental on June 12 to address his hostages. He delivered an emotional speech, asking how they would feel living in a refugee camp, waiting in vain for a water wagon to come. "Believe me, and I am not joking," he said in his perfect English, "we were determined to blow up the hotels with the hostages in them if we were smashed in the camps." His hostage audience applauded his speech, and several rushed up to shake his hand when he said they were free to go. The Red Crescent said that the June mini-war left 200 dead and 500 wounded.[3]

The *Times* published a strange editorial on the Jordanian unrest, appearing to believe that the "Palestinian Peril" was a threat to Moscow as well as to the West:

> The rise of guerrilla power in the more moderate Arab states is not only bad news for Washington and Tel Aviv, it should also evoke serious concern in Cairo and Moscow. If the guerrillas gain complete freedom of action along the Jordanian and Lebanese frontiers with Israel they will be in a position to sabotage the negotiated settlement that the Egyptians and the Russians still say they prefer. . . . To prevail, any agreements must offer to the mass of the displaced Palestinians—from whom the guerrillas draw their strength—a reasonably attractive alternative to the all-or-nothing struggle described by the guerrilla fanatics. . . .[4]

When the showdown came in September, Nasser was entirely on the side of the guerrilla fanatics and against Hussein.

On the day that the *Times* discussed the Palestinian peril, Nixon and Kissinger discussed Hussein's problem and gave the issue to the Special Action Group for contingency planning, a group composed of Kissinger, Under Secretary Elliot Richardson and Deputy Defense Secretary David Packard. Their plans made in June would, in part, be put into effect in September.

The *Times* published a portrait of Habash under the headline, "Marxist Leader of Commandos." It said:

> Dr. George Habash, the principal beneficiary of the days of bloodshed and terror, is fast becoming the voice of the new Arab revolution. It was he who continued the fighting after the better-known commando leader—Yasser Arafat of Al Fatah—had agreed to a ceasefire, and it is he who will claim credit for the concessions the Palestinians won from King Hussein.

The profile appeared to be admiring in describing Habash's "unflinching militancy," "iron purpose" and his oratory: ". . . all revolutions throughout history have been ones of the exploited against the exploiters, the oppressed against the oppressor and the poor against those who have been the cause of his poverty, wretchedness and misery...revolutionaries must be Marxist," it quoted Habash as saying. The *Times* commented, "Some believe that he could long ago have replaced Mr. Arafat as the over-all commando leader but for his Marxism, his refusal to get involved in bureaucracy, and the fact that he is a Christian in a largely Muslim movement."[5]

Just as the *Times'* earlier enthusiasm for Fidel Castro had a profound effect in Cuba in 1959, so did the *Times'* admiring portrait reinforce Beirut's echo to Habash's hostage coup. Young recruits in the refugee camps went to the Popular Front, not to Fatah, and Arafat's leadership was thrown into question. There was talk of a switch-alliance between Fatah and the Jordanian army to suppress the Popular Front.

As Amman subsided into an uneasy quiet that summer, Rogers' efforts to start negotiations toward a Middle East settlement appeared to make headway. In July, Nasser agreed to a tentative, 90-day ceasefire in the War of Attrition, and Israel agreed to its terms after Nixon publicly pledged that the United States would do nothing to endanger Israel's security. While PLO spokesmen denounced the negotiations, no eruption occurred immediately; too much was happening on the intramural PLO front.

Of the various PLO factions, Arafat's Fatah was the only one that had tried consistently to keep a door open to Western nations by disassociating itself (publicly but not privately) from international terrorism, although not from terrorism directed against Israel. Habash's Popular Front was actively recruiting international terrorists, as was Hawatmeh's Popular Democratic Front, but once the foreign recruits were in the Middle East, they were passed around to all factions without discrimination. After September, Fatah would organize its own terrorist squads, first Black September under Mohammed Daoud Oudeh (Abu Daoud), then Black June, a breakaway group of Mazen Sabry Al-Banna (Abu Nidal).

Among the 1970 recruits to Habash and Hawatmeh were the Venezuelan Communist Ilyich Ramirez Sánchez (Carlos), who ended his studies at Moscow's Patrice Lumumba University that year, and the founding members of the West German Red Army Faction, or Baader-Meinhof gang.

In June, a group of the Germans arrived in Beirut from East Berlin on the East German airline Interflug—Ulrike Meinhof secretly was a member of East Germany's Socialist Unity Party—accompanied by the French leftist journalist Michele Rey and their guide, Said Dudin. The party included Horst Mahler, Petra Schelm, Brigitte Asdonk, Heinrich

Jansen, Hans Jürgen Bäcker, Manfred Grashof and Wolfgang Thoms. A few days later, they were joined by Ulrike Meinhof, Andreas Baader and Gudrun Ensslin. The trio had stopped by Milan to pick up funds from Italian publisher Giacomo Feltrinelli, who later blew himself up in a bombing.[6]

The Germans were met by Ingrid Siepman, girl friend of Dieter Kunzelmann, who had been with Fritz Teufel among the first recruits of the PLO. Also in training that year with the Popular Front were members of Devjenc of Turkey, the Irani National Front, the National Front for the Liberation of Eritrea, the Japanese Red Army, Uruguay's Tupamáros and the Dutch Red Help. They were there to meet Dr. Wadia Haddad, Habash's second in command.[7]

Haddad was the original mastermind of PLO-connected international terrorism. He had been a founder of the Arab Nationalist Movement, an abortive organization that preceded the PLO, and like Habash was a Christian Arab educated in medicine at the American University in Beirut. Haddad ran terrorist "operations" and maintained close contact with the breakaway Ahmed Jebril, head of the Popular Front-General Command, who claimed credit for planting a bomb on a Swissair plane that crashed after takeoff in February 1970, killing all 48 persons aboard, including Israelis.

Haddad had grandiose plans to press Habash's advantage over Arafat: he would hijack four airliners simultaneously, using international recruits in some of the hijackings. Habash would be, for public relations purposes, off stage; he would be reported visiting North Korea.

On September 1, Hussein escaped the third assassination attempt of the year, one that may have been staged by Habash to bring Western correspondents back to Amman. New skirmishing between the PLO and the army began, and on September 6 a Pan American Boeing 747 was hijacked to Cairo, the first jumbo jet hijacked, where it was evacuated and blown up. Simultaneously a Transworld Airlines 707 was hijacked to a desert landing strip near Amman, where it landed next to a hijacked Swissair DC-10. A fourth attempt on an El Al plane failed as security guards killed one hijacker and captured Leila Khalid of the Popular Front, along with Nicaraguan Patrick Arguelo and West German Gabriella Tidman Kricher. The hijackers were in custody in London when, three days later, a British Overseas Airways VC-10 was hijacked to the desert near Amman, its passengers to serve as exchange hostages for the London captives. Altogether 414 hostages were held on the three planes in the desert.

The *Times* evidently believed that the hijackings were a protest against the Suez ceasefire, which had gone into effect August 7, an unusual interpretation. A news analysis from Washington by Max Frankel said:

> In the judgment of some of the best-informed officials here, the Palestinian guerrillas have now shown themselves able to wreck any Middle Eastern settlement that might be negotiated without them. That estimate acknowledges a significant political success by the Arab guerrillas in the airline hijackings last week and anticipates further terrorist actions from them...the United States knows next to nothing about them, politically or physically, and it concedes that it sees no means of giving them a place in the negotiations or a stake in the outcome. . . . [8]

The analysis sounded the perennial *Times* theme of giving terrorists, or the Soviets, something to negotiate for, even when they refused negotiation.

In Amman, the holders of the hostages, who had blown up the three airliners on September 12, were not talking about Middle East negotiations, but about using the hostages to ransom PLO terrorists held in several countries. The Popular Front spokesman, Bassam Sherif, then a handsome, brusk, dynamic young man of flamboyant arrogance, announced that 54 of the hostages were being retained, crew members and Israelis, including some with dual American nationality. They were in secret locations, and "any stupid attempt to free them by force will only endanger their lives." The Popular Front had a list of demands, but the key one was freedom for a number of PLO prisoners held by Israel, Germany and Switzerland, plus some Algerians, a Swiss and the El Al hijackers held in London. [9]

Arafat, however, was not taking the repeated Habash coups lying down. He had plans too. With Syrian help he would seize a part, if not all, of Jordan.

On September 16, Joe Alex Morris, Jr., of the *Los Angeles Times* and David Hirst, of the *Manchester Guardian,* both experienced Middle East correspondents, heard rumors that something was happening in north Jordan. They allowed me to tag along. To drive north required a Fatah pass through PLO roadblocks, and fortunately Morris recently had interviewed at the sandbagged Fatah headquarters in Jebel Hussein refugee camp one Abu Omar, who had authority to issue passes. Abu Omar balked at me: "The *Daily News!* I know that Zionist rag. I used to go to Columbia." I argued that the paper was run by Irish Catholics and employed the only Arab by-liners in New York, Jimmy Jemail, a

Lebanese, and Issa Karashi, an Egyptian, and Abu Omar relented and wrote out the pass in Arabic. He remarked owlishly, "Remember, we'll check everything you write. I'm writing that this one is a Zionist agent, and they should do with him what they want." When I sent my dispatch later, I noted his remark to my editor, resulting in one of the few stories that was printed as I had written it.

Driving north, we picked up two policemen who invited themselves aboard at a roadblock, but who got out when we reached guerrilla territory, courteously warning us that there was trouble up ahead. Once past the PLO roadblocks manned by youths with Kalashnikovs, we found in Irbid Fatah headquarters the local Fatah leader, Abu Sami.

Abu Sami's story of what was happening, a fanciful one, was that water carriers from a refugee camp had been ambushed at a spring outside Irbid by King Hussein's troops. The PLO had taken their bodies to town and displayed them on ice in front of the City Hall. The guerrillas had risen in wrath, and now the district governor and all the police were holed up in the police station. The Jordanian army had withdrawn beyond tank-gun range from the city. There were 12,000 Iraqi troops in the area, in sympathy with the PLO.

Abu Sami said that Abu Hassan, Arafat's chief of intelligence, was asleep in the Fatah cellar, after arriving to take charge, and perhaps we could see him later.

At the police station, a fortress around a courtyard, the surrounding streets were deserted, doors and windows shuttered. Inside the police station the atmosphere was tense but nonchalant.

The district governor, Ahmed Hindawi, said he expected the situation to return to normal within 24 hours. But over the obligatory coffee an officer remarked that food was running short, although local boys sold them bread through the barred windows at night. Beleaguered, they were at the mercy of any heavy guns the PLO chose to bring in.

When we returned to Fatah headquarters, Abu Hassan was awake, still tired, unshaven, perspiring as one does when sleeping in the daytime in the Middle East. He looked older than the 29-year-old swinger who already was a hero to the youth of Beirut and called by Arafat, "my own son." This was Ali Hassan Salameh, who would later marry Georgina Rizak, the Lebanese Miss Universe, and mastermind a number of assassinations, including the massacre of Israeli Olympics athletes in Munich in 1972.[10]

Abu Hassan's story of the Irbid events was more persuasive than Abu Sami's. He was the chief political commissar of Asifah, the fighting arm of Fatah, and he announced, "We are in a civil war." There had been some fighting in Irbid: the local leader of the king's militia, Kamel Abdel Kader, had resisted, "and we shot him down." A revolutionary court had sentenced in absentia nine officers for ordering firing at Palestinians. One of them was a close friend of Hussein, Brigadier Bajet Mhaisen, who had just arrived from his previous post as military attaché in London. The sentences, Abu Hassan said, meant that the nine officers were fair game "to be shot on sight by any guerrilla or citizen."

Hussein, he said, had been given an ultimatum the night before: form a pro-PLO "government of national authority," or north Jordan would secede. That evening, he said, a 300-man congress would meet in Irbid to "elect a council, a revolutionary central committee of North Jordan."

Central Committee was a Leninist term, would the council be "something like what the Russians call a soviet?"

Abu Hassan smiled tolerently, saying, "I don't use that word. Yes, I am a Marxist, and I admire Mao. But Marxism-Leninism is only a method of analyzing."

Irbid was being patrolled by carloads of Fatah, Popular Democratic Front, Arab Liberation Front, Saiqa and other guerrilla groups—but no Popular Front. Arafat had shut Habash out of the start of the civil war. Habash's guerrillas would be tied up fighting in Amman, and not on the Central Committee of North Jordan, the first sovereign Palestinian state.

We typed our stories on our knees in the swaying car racing back to Amman airport, where we pigeoned the copy out to Beirut with a businessman boarding a Royal Jordanian Airlines plane.

It was still light, so we stopped at a supermarket to stock up for the war that appeared inevitable the next morning. The owner, a Palestinian, was pulling down the steel shutters, but not soon enough to shut us out, and with us a quartet of guerrillas carrying Kalashnikovs entered the store. The guerrillas did not pay when they left with armloads of groceries, and the disconsolate owner did not ask them to pay.

At 5 a.m. on September 17, Amman awoke to artillery and small arms fire erupting throughout the city; a blazing firefight at short range was going on in the ravine under my balcony. On the street side of the Intercontinental, guests had a close-up view of a gangland style gunfight with pistols and Tommy guns in the still-skeletal building under construction across the street. Jebel Hussein, the Fatah-controlled refugee camp, and the Popular Front-controlled Jebel Wadhat camp were under artillery fire.

The *Times* was at hand with editorial advice:

The showdown between King Hussein and the Palestinian guerrillas in Jordan is a dangerous but inevitable development....If
the guerrillas win they will at least be forced into a position of responsibility where they can more easily be held accountable for
their intransigency and reckless criminality both by their own
subjects and by the international community....Any overt
American or other Western attempt to intervene militarily would
only serve the guerrilla goals of radicalizing and rallying the Arab
world against the West. Western military intervention cannot
save Hussein nor the 54 hijack hostages.... [11]

The next day the *Times* gave equal space to two Page 1 stories of dis-
tinctly unequal worth: Nixon saying privately that he would be in-
clined to intervene if Iraq or Syria should join the fighting, and the
Soviet news agency Tass also lamenting the bloodshed and calling for
Iraq and Syria to stay out, both nations being Soviet arms clients who
would have to stay out if Tass said so sternly. As events turned out,
Nixon meant what he said; Tass did not. In Washington the Special
Actions Group met in repeated sessions.

By coincidence, Israeli Prime Minister Golda Meir arrived in the
United States just before heavy fighting broke out in Jordan. Her visit
had been long planned, after U.S.-Israeli relations had reached a low
point in March as Nixon suspended delivery of the promised Phantom
jets.

Meir was to see Nixon on Israel's new concern: Egypt was cheating
on the six-week-old ceasefire and building up SAM missile bases along
the Suez Canal—cheating that Israel had expected but the United
States had downplayed. The Nixon administration responded by leaking the news that the U.S. would release the Phantom jets to Israel. In a
commentary, the *Times'* Terence Smith noted that the Jordan crisis had
wiped away the "extravagant optimism" that Nixon had displayed
over the Suez ceasefire agreement. [12]

As the *Times* stressed Nixon's discomfort, 250 Syrian tanks, their
markings painted over with PLA insignia, rolled across the border into
north Jordan. Nixon pressed Meir to alert Israel's Defense Force and be
prepared to join the U.S. Sixth Fleet and other contingency units of
American troops to rescue Hussein. He sent another strong note to the
Soviet Union warning that the United States would react to outside interference in Jordan.

Israel's leaders did not particularly want to rescue Hussein. Israelis
had been in frequent contact with Hussein, and his responses always
had been noncommittal or negative. A sizeable minority in Israel believed that Jordan, a Palestinian state ruled by an alien, British-imposed

monarch, might be as well off in the long run if Hussein fell and the PLO took over. Golda Meir, moreover, was irritated at Nixon's attempt through the Rogers Plan to win the confidence of Nasser and the unstable Syrian regime, where power was being contested between Premier Nureddin Attassi and the defense minister, Hafez Assad.

In the wrangling of September 21-22, Meir gave in to Nixon on the Jordanian situation, and issued a limited call-up of troops, promising air strikes if Syrian armor advanced on Amman. Nixon moved the Sixth Fleet, alerted Army units and notified the Soviets of his intention to intervene if necessary.

The *Times* issued repeated warnings against intervention. An editorial said, "The greatest danger, of course, is an evolution of events in Jordan that would bring about a Soviet-American confrontation. But even short of that crisis, unilateral American intervention could result in an explosion of Arab nationalism. . . . "[13]

At the Intercontinental Hotel in Amman, where virtually all rooms facing the street and 30% of those overlooking the ravine had been hit by small arms fire, and Swedish cameraman Ohle Ohlesson had been hit in the thigh on the first day of the war, guests were ordered into the basement by Jordanian officers "for their own protection." Lying on the floor of the hotel's basement nightclub, we heard unpleasant news on David Hirst's transistor. Habash's Popular Front had said it would "kill all Americans without exception" if the United States should intervene. Apparently the hostages were meant, but the besieged hotel guests would become hostages if the guerrillas won. BBC also said that units of the U.S. 8th Infantry Division in West Germany had been put on alert, and an advance party had gone to Turkey, presumably to scout a staging area for intervention in Jordon.

It should be confessed that, like most persons in a siege or hostage situation, I was not eager to be rescued by firepower, and in a lamentable lapse, I would have been inclined to agree with the pusillanimous *Times* editorials at that moment. "I don't believe this," I told Hirst. "Nixon can't intervene here; he's still up to his neck in outrage over the invasion of Cambodia. He can't get into another war here; everybody would land on him."

So much for those of us of little faith. To general astonishment, the Syrian tanks did not advance. The Syrian air force, three times the size of Jordan's, stayed grounded, because if it had flown, Israel's air force would have shot it down. The Iraqi troops did not move. In fighting with Hussein's army, Syrian armor retreated back across the border.

On September 22, a bus convoy escorted by Jordanian armed jeeps and an armored car moved nearly all of the reporters, businessmen and diplomats from the Intercontinental Hotel to the airport, where we waited overnight for an evacuation Red Cross plane.

That night, the darkened airport saw some embarrassing journalism. The television correspondents and crews had large stores of precious film collected over a week with no way of getting it out. The television correspondents, mostly Vietnam-era men accustomed to traveling from one brushfire war to another, already had done their stand-ups before the cameras, a couple of them on the relatively safe balcony of my room, but at the airport all of the television and radio correspondents felt compelled to record their last commentaries and voice-overs for film shows, to be ready for dispatch on arrival in Beirut.

All of the publicly rehearsed and recorded reports, done in the darkness of the airport waiting room, appeared to be tales of blood and slaughter featuring the correspondents' personal adventures. Most of them used imaginary casualty estimates and implied that the Jordanian army, their protectors, had used ruthless tactics, although Hussein correctly protested that his troops had used restraint in trying to keep casualties down.[14] No report that I heard gave any suggestion of what the war was about or what the implications of the war might be, other than grave predictions of doom. It was dismally parochial reporting that would reach every home in the United States. The revolt in Jordan was an ideal opportunity to learn something about the PLO and to evaluate forces and prospects in the Middle East, but few American correspondents took advantage of it, and none that I know of in the electronic media.

The next morning we flew out, leaving the smoking city still under sporadic fire. In Beirut, I filed my obligatory war diary, kept during the siege, and the next day went to the U.S. Embassy to ask for a briefing by a Middle East expert. I drew a State Department counsellor who told me, "Hussein might survive this, but he could not possibly survive American military aid, which would mark him as a tool of imperialism and Zionism to almost all Arabs. Hussein is now identified with the worst disaster in Jordan's history. If he wins, he will have to be guarded 24 hours a day. He'll be forever known as the butcher of Amman."

This advice did not sound logical to me, and I ventured that, after all, Hussein appeared to have won, and winning is better than losing. It did not seem likely to me that most of the Jordanians I had seen wanted the PLO to win. Still, I filed the diplomat's advice, the most misleading story I ever wrote, although I deleted the catchy "butcher of Amman" quote which seemed to go too far, and my story appeared in the *Daily News* under the headline "Hussein Will Never Live the Carnage Down."[15] Most newspapers, including the *Times,*[16] published similar "butcher of Amman" stories, and all of us proved dead wrong. From the experience, I adopted the rule that if an official insists on anonymity, he is either being misleading or covering up that he does not know. I also acquired a healthy distrust of Middle East experts.

The stories of Hussein's ruthlessness, which were false, did a great deal to obscure what had happened and to denigrate the effect of the low-keyed American-Israeli threat to intervene. Neither Nixon nor the Israelis trumpeted their part in the outcome, and Nixon at the time and later gave credit for Hussein's victory to "the superb fighting by Hussein's troops."[17]

What really had happened was that Jordanians, including Palestinians, had stood by Hussein, but that would not have saved him from a full Syrian assault aided by the 12,000 Iraqi troops. One person had saved Hussein's crown, Nixon. Not Kissinger, who was unsure what the war was about; not the reluctant Golda Meir; not Nasser, who railed against Hussein's attempt to "liquidate the Palestinian resistence" and in whose Embassy in Amman Arafat had taken refuge; only Nixon, but there were no cheers for the feat in the American media. Nixon had "almost gotten the United States into another war."[18]

There was no excuse for my own erroneous contribution to pack journalism. I had spoken with Arafat, Habash, Bassam Sherif, Abu Hassan, Abu Sami and their Lebanese journalist supporters, and it never had appeared reasonable that anything like a majority of Jordanians-Palestinians would voluntarily choose to be ruled by them. The supermarket owner and the nearby pharmacist in Amman, both Palestinians, had their businesses shot to pieces, and both appeared to have resented paying tribute to PLO guerrillas.

There also was a telling incident during the siege of the Intercontinental. The French reporters had been the most mischievous of the besieged group of 114 media people. On the first morning of the war the French had contributed their part to wrecking the kitchen, making their own breakfasts while hotel employees still were huddled in the basement. A French television crew was accused of stealing beer from other correspondents' bathtub coolers after water was shut off, and of the ultimate crime of using toilets that could not flush in other correspondents' rooms.

Eric Rouleau, internationally known Arabist from *Le Monde,* early in the siege demonstrated his expertise by recognizing the Palestinian accent of one of the soldiers guarding inside the hotel. He asked the

Palestinian how it felt to shoot at his brothers. The solder was non-committal, wandered off, and returned with his officers searching for Rouleau. Rouleau hid out from room to room while French correspondents sent out an SOS via a Jordanian officer. On September 20, the day the correspondents got out of the hotel briefly for a quick walk to the British Embassy two blocks away—and scuttled back when a Jordanian soldier was hit by a sniper in front of the hotel to cries of "Allah akhbar!" and furious shooting by his comrades—two small buses pulled up to the hotel with a Jordanian armed escort.

The French ambassador had arranged for the evacuation of the French correspondents to Aqaba. From there, they hoped to get out and file their stories, perhaps through Eilat, a few thousand yards away. The French correspondents all piled into the buses, along with one ringer, a French-speaking BBC correspondent, and drove off. Two days later they returned, on evacuation day, refused entry by the Israelis, who were receiving a hostile press in France. The French went to the end of the evacuation list, which had been organized by the correspondents' elected chief, Michael Adams, a former *Manchester Guardian* reporter who was in Amman trying to arrange the release of the airliner hostages, and his major domo, *Newsweek's* Arnaud de Borchgrave. The lesson of the incident was that Rouleau had erred in assuming that Palestinian soldiers in Hussein's army were disloyal.[19]

The *Times* correspondent in Amman, Eric Pace, did some of the best reporting on the war, but his reports were overshadowed by *Times* editorials and house-written commentaries. Pace was the first to telephone that the war had broken out, lying on the floor behind the reception desk in the glass-littered lobby, making his call a pool dispatch available to all news organizations with representatives in the hotel. Pace stayed behind in Amman when the rest of us pulled out. During the June crisis, he had chased Arafat around the Intercontinental, as I trailed along, asking Arafat's comments on the murder of Perry and the rapes of two American Embassy women. Arafat expressed chagrin that Perry was "unfortunately caught in a crossfire between guerrillas and two tanks"—demonstrably untrue, and said, smiling ingratiatingly, that the culprits who had raped the American women had been caught by Fatah and executed forthwith. "They were not our men," Arafat said, smiling at our mutual understanding that none of this was true. Pace filled that story, but the *Times* attributed the statements to a spokesman.

When Hussein had put down the revolt, the *Times* published a house-written accolade to Arafat under the headline "Stuff of Arab Legends," that ignored his defeat in calling Arafat "a hero to millions in the Arab world." The portrait said:

> For multitudes disillusioned by the failures of established Arab leaders in their conflict with Israel, active hope centers on the soft-spoken Mr. Arafat. . . . These days his leadership among the guerrilla organizations is unchallenged. His decision to stay on in Amman to head the outnumbered guerrillas in the bitter fighting against King Hussein's army has elevated him to a new level of esteem. . . . Unlike other Arab leaders, who often seemed to offer nothing but rhetoric, Mr. Arafat offered action. . . .[20]

Hussein hoped to end the revolt without having to subdue the guerrillas in north Jordan by force. He accepted Nasser's mediation even though Nasser condemned him and had given Arafat refuge in the Egyptian Embassy at the end of the fighting in Amman. Hussein boldly flew to Cairo. On September 27, Hussein and Arafat signed an agreement dictated by Arab summit leaders that the guerrillas did not intend to keep.

The next day Nasser, seeing off Arab League summit leaders at Cairo airport, was felled by a massive heart attack. Egypt plunged into a paroxysm of grief, and correspondents poured into Cairo. After Nasser's tumultuous funeral, I returned to Jordan and to Irbid, still in rebel hands, where Joe Morris, a PLO guerrilla named Mohammed and I managed to get arrested by the Jordanian army when we rounded a turn in the road into an army roadblock. We were taken to an army headquarters, Morris indignant that the truckload of soldiers ahead of our car kept rifles trained on us.

To the British-educated colonel stuck with our case, I pleaded that my newspaper, the largest in America, was an unshakable friend of King Hussein, which made me suspect to the guerrillas; if Mohammed were not released with us, my usefulness would be at an end. The colonel, after telephone calls to his brigade headquarters, released us all, keeping Mohammed's Kalashnikov. On the drive into Irbid, the Jordanian sergeant who had led our capture leaned back from the front seat, telling Mohammed they had planned to flay him alive, but instead decided to release him in a gesture of magnanimity. He hoped Mohammed's friends would draw the proper conclusions from the army's generosity. Mohammed was not consoled by being freed, lamenting that he would spend the rest of his life paying for the lost, well-worn Kalashnikov, for which the Russians were requiring Fatah to pay $180 each.

As we left Irbid, the PLO guerrillas were beginning to evacuate the area, moving into Syria. We thought the revolt was over, but it would linger on in north Jordan until 1971.

At the end of 1970 Nixon was in his customary paradoxical position. He had won an important military and strategic victory in the Cambodia incursion, drastically reducing American casualties and allowing the withdrawal of more U.S. troops from Vietnam, and he had laid the groundwork for U.S. leverage in the Middle East, but almost no one in the American media credited him with success in either endeavor.

The anti-war movement's anger was such that on October 29 Nixon's motorcade was attacked by a rock-throwing mob of about 1,000 persons in San Jose, California, an incident dismissed by much of the media as perhaps faked, but which William Safire, a witness, called "the most serious attack on a national leader in American history."[21]

No one appeared to notice that Nixon's stock had gone up in the Middle East. Relations with Israel had been terrible when Nixon enlisted the Israelis to help rescue Hussein, and now, suddenly, relations were excellent; he had won the Israelis' respect for acting in Jordan. Nixon now owed a debt to Israel for its assumption of risk over Jordan, but he had a callable I.O.U. from King Hussein. Hussein owed his throne to Nixon, and his participation in Middle East peace plans only awaited a favorable constellation of progress with Egypt and Syria, progress that was temporarily delayed but prospectively enhanced over the long run by the death of Nasser.

Entering 1971, Nixon was ahead of schedule with his foreign policy strategies, yet his popularity was sinking under attacks by anti-war demonstrators and a flood of anti-war books (see next chapter) by the political cartel of the Eastern book publishing industry. Yet even the anti-war movement was about to wane, as it had done for a time in 1969, unless a catalyst could be found as a focus of attention. The catalyst was in the offing; the Pentagon Papers were about to be published.

Chapter XV
The Pentagon Papers

"... but man, proud man! Dress'd in a little brief authority, most ignorant of what he's most assured, his glassy essence, like an angry ape, plays such fantastic tricks before high heaven, as make the angels weep."

—Shakespeare, Measure for Measure

The generation of students that went to American colleges in the 1950s was remarkable for its political passivity. Sprinkled into most classrooms were men studying under the GI Bill. Most of them had not seen combat, but some had been on Guadalcanal or on the beaches of Normandy, and they were a few years older than the average student, more mature and disciplined. They represented the awesome cataclysm of World War II, and where they walked, they dominated. The younger students had seen the fighting on newsreels and thought, as Butch Cassidy said to the Sundance Kid of the Indian railroad agent tracking them over rock, "Look what he's doing; I couldn't do that. Could you do that?" After 1952, the President of the United States was the former Supreme Allied Commander in Europe, and for the next three decades all American Presidents would be veterans of World War II.

The nasty little war going on in Korea in the early 1950s had none of the scope or grandeur of World War II, although it killed, through combat and disease, millions of Koreans and Chinese. Bloody and incomprehensible, the Korean War was marked by Communist fanaticism, false confessions tortured out of American prisoners, a death rate of almost 60% among captured Allies, organized Communist intimidation and revolt among those captured by the Allies. To the frustration of the South Korean leadership and the American military—where casualties were relatively light[1]—it ended unsatisfactorily with a return to the status ante-bellum.

With good reason, the college students of the early 1950s were subdued. They advocated no causes. They relieved their predominant conservatism by swallowing goldfish and staging panty raids on sororities. Underneath, something simmered: the generation gap.

Daniel Ellsberg, the gifted son of a Detroit engineer, spent most of the decade at Harvard University. Born in the Depression year of 1931, Ellsberg, until the age of 15, was required to practice the piano "four hours a day, twelve hours on Saturdays," and was forbidden rough recreation that could injure his hands.[2] Then his mother died in an automobile accident in which Ellsberg and his father, the driver, were injured, and Ellsberg was freed from the piano. He was attending the exclusive Cranbrook prep school in Bloomfield Hills, Michigan, on a scholarship, and the next year he was graduated first in his class. At Harvard, also on a scholarship, he was active on the *Crimson*, the newspaper, and president of the *Advocate*, the literary journal. He was graduated in 1952, a youthful 21, third in a class of 1,147, with a B.A. in economics. He also won a year at Cambridge, England, and then returned to Harvard for post-graduate work.

Everyone agreed that he was destined to become a man of influence, and Ellsberg did become one of the rare individuals who changed things. "A man *can* make a difference," he would say.

While at Harvard in 1954, Ellsberg married Carol Cummings, a Radcliffe girl whose father was a Marine brigadier general. Squalid and disheartening revelations were emerging from the recent war in Korea. The surviving American prisoners had just come home, and the world was learning that almost all of them had broken under torture and deprivation and signed false confessions. It was a new low point for the prestige of the American military, but Ellsberg defied the prevailing mood, enlisted for two years in the Marine Corps in April 1954 and was sent to Officers Candidate School. When his hitch was up in 1956, Poland was rioting and near revolt, and the new president of Egypt, Nasser, was threatening to disrupt the Middle East with the seizure of the Suez Canal.

Ellsberg had done well in the Marine Corps, an eager young officer. He extended his tour of duty, hoping to see combat, the missing ingredient that would bring him abreast of the World War II generation. The autumn of 1956 found him aboard a troopship in the Mediterranean when the Hungary and Suez crises erupted almost simultaneously. Ellsberg was ordered to make a contingency plan for an assault on Haifa.

No pretense of psychoanalyzing Ellsberg will be made here, but it was a curious turn of fate. Ellsberg's parents, of Russian Jewish origin, had become Christian Scientists, and he had no particular sense of Jewish identity, much less divided loyalty. Still, like other 100% Americans, he must have wondered, well-educated and politically aware as he was, what the United States was doing on Nasser's side, opposing its allies Britain and France and the friendly young nation of Israel. Israel was eight years old, 11 years away from the Holocaust, and it had fought the British and assorted Arab armies to a standstill. It was fired with the determination to go down like the defenders of Masada rather than submit to anyone's domination.

Laconically, parenthetically, Ellsberg wrote of the incident, "As our troopship steamed toward the southeastern corner of the Mediterranean at the outset of the crisis, I was assigned—as battalion operations officer—to draw up an amphibious landing plan for Haifa, while my partner made one for Alexandria. It would have gone worse for our battalion, we supposed, if we had to use mine."[3]

That's all Ellsberg wrote of the incident. As things turned out, his ship only evacuated Americans from Alexandria, and he did not see combat. In February 1957, he was discharged as a first lieutenant and returned to Harvard as a member of the elite Society of Fellows to complete studies for his Ph.D.

In 1959 Ellsberg was chosen to deliver the Lowell Lectures, an educational ceremony that later would be routinely taped for Public Television. His lecture on "The Theory and Practice of Blackmail" described Adolf Hitler's intimidation of Austria and Czechoslovakia based on documents of the Nuremberg War Crimes Trials. He had studied the endless volumes of trial documentation, and it left a lasting impression. It is possible that his interest in the trials was connected with his near brush with fighting Israelis. But if he seldom referred to the Haifa incident, he would later refer often to the War Crimes Trials, professing to believe in 1969 that he might be prosecuted as a war criminal for his hawkish advice as a Defense Department policy maker. He would write that his study of the War Crimes Trials showed him "what a documentary record of an aggressive war looks like. It looks like the Pentagon Papers."[4] It is difficult to see a similarity in the two sets of documents.[5]

After almost a decade at Harvard, off and on, Ellsberg was well known to the faculty that would decamp en masse to Washington with President Kennedy. Henry Kissinger, who would be left behind by the exodus, invited Ellsberg to address his celebrated seminars. Professor Walt Rostow would recommend that the Kennedy administration hire Ellsberg. At Harvard Law School, Ellsberg's name was known to Professor John McNaughton and to the dean, Archibald Cox. If Ellsberg still had been at Harvard in 1961, instead of moving to the Rand Corporation in Santa Monica, he might have reached Washington three years earlier than he did.

While at Harvard in 1958, Ellsberg became a Rand consultant, analyzing Air Force intelligence estimates that indicated a massive Soviet missile buildup. The report he worked on was the one leaked to Roger Hilsman, then at the Library of Congress, who announced its conclusions, creating the "missile gap" campaign issue. Ellsberg wrote an enigmatic line in his book, "The missile gap predictions were disproven by intelligence in the fall of 1961, not earlier, as often supposed."[6]

In 1964 Ellsberg was summoned from Rand to join the Defense Department near the top as an adviser to Assistant Secretary of Defense for Security Affairs John T. McNaughton.

Only 39 at the time, McNaughton was one of the most promising of Kennedy's Harvard recruits. Tall, handsome, a decorated four-year Navy veteran of World War II and a Rhodes scholar, he had the trust of Defense Secretary McNamara. He joined the Kennedy administration as a deputy assistant defense secretary in security, the section dealing with the arms race and nuclear proliferation. President Johnson promoted him to head the section, and McNaughton's role expanded to providing some of the Vietnam war planning.

Ellsberg arrived in Washington as Congress passed the Gulf of Tonkin resolution on August 7, 1964, and it would be months before Johnson used the resolution to commit more U.S. power to the war in Vietnam.

Diem had been dead almost a year, and Ellsberg knew little about Vietnam. He was not yet aware that with Diem's death "the political control structure extending from Saigon down into the hamlets disappeared," and North Vietnam had poured reinforcements into the south.[7] That is, Ellsberg did not know that things had gone to hell after Diem died.

The American-favored coup government of General Duong Van

(Big) Minh had lasted three months before a coup by General Nguyen Khanh replaced it. McNamara and William Bundy had been frank in public statements that the situation was deteriorating, but the Johnson-Goldwater election campaigns were heating up, and Johnson was speaking appropriately in terms of restraint. Maxwell Taylor had replaced Henry Cabot Lodge as Ambassador in Saigon and was sending messages expressing doubt that Khanh's government would last very long.

Taylor advocated on August 18, as Ellsberg joined the government, an orchestrated bombing campaign against North Vietnamese military targets and infiltration routes, to begin about January 1, 1965. Earlier contingency plans for air strikes against North Vietnam, to escalate within 30 days to full-scale bombing aimed at punishing North Vietnam, "raising the level of pain," had been submitted to Johnson in May by William Bundy, McNaughton and William H. Sullivan, but for nine months no bombing of the North was undertaken. Ellsberg saw the documents as he began learning about Vietnam and saw nothing evil in them at the time, but six years later his new wife would read them and say, "This is the language of torturers." Ellsberg would decide they were "bloody-minded, genocidal, conspiratorial, anti-democratic documents," realizing that "these people I had associated with in Washington were torturers, managers of torture."[8]

That awakening would take time. Ellsberg was a hawk in 1964, when he found his new boss McNaughton, who had just received his promotion and new responsibilities, anticipating the worst in Vietnam. On September 3, McNaughton forwarded a new plan of action for Vietnam with a wide range of proposals and options. It started off, "The situation in South Vietnam is deteriorating," which was not a surprise to those who had opposed the coup against Diem. McNaughton's proposals ranged from creating a Navy base at Danang[9] to significantly enlarging "the U.S. role in the pacification program inside South Vietnam—e.g., large numbers of U.S. Special Forces, divisions of regular combat troops, U.S. air, etc., to 'interlard' with or take over functions of geographical areas from the South Vietnamese armed forces...." The memo also suggested that, failing a reversal of the downward trend, "the alternative objective is to emerge from the situation with as good an image as possible in U.S., allied and enemy eyes." It included the remark, "If worst comes to worst and South Vietnam disintegrates or their behavior becomes abominable, to 'disown' South Vietnam, hopefully leaving the image of a 'patient who died despite the extraordinary efforts of a good doctor.' "[10]

Ellsberg later wrote and commented often that he was struck by the contrast between official optimism about the war and the pessimism of his doom-oriented office, but actually, as noted, there was no public optimism at the period. McNamara was consistently gloomy in public. Ellsberg went to work handling papers that he called "full of discrepancies and contradictions."

Early in his work, Ellsberg said, McNaughton gave him a project so secret that he was not to consult with anyone on it. Ellsberg was to define, "What are the better and worse ways to lose the war in Vietnam?"[11]

Ellsberg said McNaughton warned him before he started that he should understand "that you could be signing the death warrant to your career in even working on such a task. . . . Many people have had their careers ruined for less than this." Ellsberg said that was a reference to the McCarthy period in the 1950s and charges that the Democrats had lost China.

As Ellsberg settled into Washington work, enthusiastic and near the levers of power, the man to whom he would give the Pentagon Papers, Neil Sheehan, was hired by the *Times,* joining Halberstam, Malcolm Browne and Charles Mohr of the anti-Diem days. Harrison Salisbury reported that Abe Rosenthal was reluctant to take on Sheehan, but Reston and Halberstam pushed hard for his hiring. Sheehan went through a trying period in late 1964. Already an award-winning, nationally known foreign correspondent, he was put on run-over-dog stories on the *Times* city side while waiting for a foreign assignment. Through Gay Talese, a friend of Halberstam, Sheehan met Susan Black, and when he was sent to Jakarta on temporary assignment, he called her to join him there for an exotic wedding. From Indonesia, the Sheehans went on to Vietnam.

Beyond a buildup of naval power, President Johnson had been reluctant to commit more military forces to Vietnam to meet the escalating infiltration and chaotic political situation left by Diem's death. American troops in Vietnam had a defensive and support mission until April 1965, when Johnson authorized Marines at Danang to undertake offensive missions.

In June 1965, General Westmoreland was authorized the first combat troop units—44 battalions, about 175,000 men—and in late July he asked for 24 more battalions to stop the deterioration that McNaughton had stressed nine months earlier.

As the first combat troop units began pouring into Vietnam in the Johnson administration's "slow squeeze" build-up, Ellsberg, estranged from his first wife, volunteered in July 1955 to go to Vietnam for the State Department's AID program. He joined the staff of Major General

Edward Lansdale, who had been denied a role in Vietnam by the State Department during the Kennedy administration. Ellsberg's service in Vietnam coincided with the Johnson build-up, until late summer 1967—the period of intense Americanization of the war, with all of its overtones of colonialization, PX culture and media cynicism about the American role in Vietnam.

Ellsberg landed in Saigon around the time that Sheehan arrived with his bride for Sheehan's second Vietnam tour. Like Halberstam before him, Ellsberg discovered that Sheehan had been at Harvard when he was a graduate student there. Ellsberg, as an armed State Department civilian, often worked in the field with Colonel John Paul Vann, who had resigned from the Army and headed an AID field team. Sheehan was close to Vann, a sought-after source for correspondents. After Vann was killed in a helicopter accident in 1972, Sheehan took a leave from the *Times* to write his biography. A year after arriving for his second tour, Sheehan left Vietnam—Ellsberg attending his farewell party—to return to the United States and the Washington bureau of the *Times*.

Ellsberg apparently admired Lansdale, who was even more of a legend than Vann. He noted in his book that Lansdale "hoped to concentrate on encouraging political development, but (he was) assigned by Ambassador Lodge the thankless task of coordinating U.S. civilian activities directed toward 'pacification.' " (Lodge had returned to Vietnam on Taylor's retirement in 1965.)

One of Ellsberg's first contacts in Vietnam was Anthony Russo, the intellectual hippy field analyst who had joined the Rand Corporation as Ellsberg had left it for Washington. Russo had gone to Rand already radicalized, and his revulsion from the war was being intensified as he supervised Vietnamese interrogators of prisoners taken by the government.

At the time of Ellsberg's arrival, Saigon was filling up with correspondents. Diem's death had been covered by a handful of reporters, but the aftermath drew about 60 correspondents in 1964 and then hundreds after U.S. combat troops arrived in force in 1965. Some of the correspondents were anti-war and anti-administration, reflecting the mind set established in the Diem era and the precedent of Halberstam's spectacular career. Some non-professional reporters received accreditation as correspondents, among them radio reporter Patricia Marx, an engaged pacifist and daughter of toy tycoon Louis Marx, who was not a pacifist.

Ellsberg, the hawk, and Patricia Marx, the dove, conducted a modern, rocky romance that resulted in marriage several years later in the

United States. Both became close to Tran Ngoc Chau, who headed operations for South Vietnam's rural development ministry, and who would be sentenced to ten years in prison in 1970 for contacts with his brother, a Viet Cong agent.

In October 1966, Ellsberg flew to Washington to draw attention to a report that progress in pacification was bogged down. He flew back to Saigon with Kissinger, still a Harvard professor and an occasional consultant for the Johnson administration, who was being held at arm's length by Johnson's security adviser Walt W. Rostow. (McGeorge Bundy had been transferred to State.) Kissinger told friends he learned a great deal from Ellsberg, who still was a hawk despite the ministrations of Russo and Patricia Marx.

In the spring of 1966 Johnson decided tentatively to bomb North Vietnam's oil depots at Haiphong, but a final go-ahead was delayed for the project—long advocated by the Joint Chiefs—because a number of peace initiatives were under way through U Thant, Charles de Gaulle, Harold Wilson and others. On June 29, 1966, air strikes began against the North's oil facilities, by which time the oil supplies were well dispersed.

Late that year, Harrison Salisbury of the *Times* was admitted into North Vietnam, and his reports stressed civilian victims of the air attacks. Don Luce, of International Volunteer Service, discovered that the South Vietnamese held prisoners in "tiger cages"—cells built by the French in the colonial era that had bars and entree at the top instead of on the side. Morley Safer of CBS filmed a Marine igniting a thatched hut with a Zippo lighter in an act of apparent vandalism.[12] Ellsberg had come to Vietnam at a time when the war was receiving a dismal press.

By May 1967, Ellsberg was disturbed enough about the war to write a memorandum to Secretary McNamara urging a documentary study on how the United States got into the war and what kept it involved. He had come to believe that the U.S. role in Vietnam "was not outrageous or criminal, but I strongly believed that it must be ended."[13] He never received a reply from McNamara, but he believed that he was the legitimate father of the Pentagon Papers.

At about that time, McNaughton suggested to McNamara a study similar to the one Richard Neustadt had done on the Skybolt fiasco for President Kennedy. McNamara had just met with 20 Harvard professors at the Kennedy Center at Cambridge, Massachusetts, and he talked over the project with Senator Robert Kennedy, who urged him to order the study. McNamara authorized the study on June 17, 1967.

Johnson had just promoted McNaughton to become Secretary of the

Navy when he was killed on July 19, 1967, along with his wife Sarah and his son Theodore, 11, as a Piedmont Airways plane they had boarded at Asheville, North Carolina, collided with a private plane with the loss of 82 lives in both planes.

Ellsberg returned to the United States just after McNaughton's death, following a bout with hepatitis in a military hospital in Thailand.

Ellsberg resigned from the government that same month and returned to Rand in Santa Monica. Turning against the war, mourning his key friend and supporter in the administration, Ellsberg was adrift and directionless. He said he suffered at the time a feeling of "acute powerlessness." Now he was a combat veteran; never again would he feel constrained to hold his tongue when men spoke who had been under fire, but he was out of the arena of action.

In Washington, overall authority for the new Vietnam study devolved on the new Assistant Secretary of Defense for Security Affairs, Paul Warnke, who already was known as the Defense Department's dove. Warnke's deputy, Morton Halperin, then 28, would deal directly with the project, and its director and principal author was to be Leslie Gelb, then 30, a *Times*-government interchangeable man. "For that time, I was classified as a dove," Gelb said.[14]

The Pentagon Papers, then, were born in an unlikely spot, a dove cote in the Defense Department.

McNamara had brought to Washington the terse, one-paragraph memo, and it is unlikely that he envisioned a 47-volume study running to 7,000 pages that would take weeks to read. He wanted the effort to be encyclopedic in scope, but also "an index of useful, handy information." According to Gelb, McNamara started the project off with a list of 100 questions "mostly about current events. . .how did we know how many Vietnamese Communists we were really killing; how did we know when a hamlet was pacified?" Some were historical: "Was Ho Chi Minh really an Asian Tito? Were there occasions in the past when we could have extricated ourselves without any loss of credibility?"[15] Gelb's account implies that McNamara was preoccupied with extrication, as Ellsberg's account implies that extrication had been uppermost in McNaughton's mind from the beginning.

Gelb requisitioned historical files from the State and Defense Departments, from the CIA and other agencies, but he received few from the White House. As he began work he concluded that the historical context needed more consideration. He drew up a list of about 30 studies and suggested they be undertaken.

Gelb and Halperin had difficulty getting qualified historians to work on the studies—about 36 analysts took part—and among those who declined were Kissinger and Colonel Alexander Haig. One who eagerly accepted Gelb's call to work on the studies was Ellsberg, adrift in Santa Monica and needing a focus for his energy. Ellsberg was called to Washington in September 1967 to work on a study dealing with Kennedy's 1961 decision making. While he worked, Norman Mailer led the armies of the night against the Pentagon, emerging a media hero.

Ellsberg delivered a book-length draft analysis of his study assignment and then returned to Rand. The various analysts and authors in the project did not agree on interpretation, as was natural, and Colonel Paul F. Gorman, who had held a command in Vietnam, was one of two colonels who objected to Ellsberg's participation in the study. Ellsberg returned to Rand in California not authorized to see the other studies or the final version of his own.

While Ellsberg was in Washington in the fall of 1967, he spoke before a group of CBS editors, urging that the United States force a return to civilian government in South Vietnam and then require that the new government negotiate with the National Liberation Front. Another speaker at the seminar was Senator Robert Kennedy, who sent Frank Mankiewicz to ask Ellsberg to meet with the Senator.

At his first meeting with Kennedy, Ellsberg was impressed with the Senator's concern for the Vietnamese people, and also with the informal way Kennedy changed his shirt during their conversation. The following spring, during the Tet 1968 offensive, Ellsberg saw Kennedy again. He declined an offer to quit Rand and go to work full-time for the Senator because he had just entered psychoanalysis with Dr. Lewis Fielding in Beverly Hills. At that meeting he leaked to Kennedy the story of the Army's 206,000-man troop request that was published in distorted version in the *Times*.

Ellsberg and Kennedy met several times in the spring of 1968, and now that Kennedy had a good shot at becoming the next President, Ellsberg might have regretted that he had not taken the full time job with him. Kennedy's February 8 attack on Johnson's Vietnam policies had echoed Ellsberg's speech of the preceding autumn, indicating that the two men were on the same wavelength. While not full time, Ellsberg did write a draft speech for Kennedy during the primary campaign in California. After delivering the speech to the Ambassador Hotel in Los Angeles, Ellsberg went on to Chicago with Russo to attend a conference at the Adlai Stevenson Institute. There Ellsberg again ran into Eqbal Ahmad and met Hanoi-visitor Tom Hayden, getting an introduction to SDS, the Progressive Labor Party and the struggle for leadership of the New Left. Hayden's SDS in two months' time would spearhead the attack on the Democratic National Convention.

While in Chicago, Ellsberg watched late California primary returns, then went to bed. The next morning he watched television reruns of the assassination of Kennedy by Sirhan Sirhan, breaking into sobs. Both King and Kennedy were murdered just after becoming idols of Ellsberg.

Back in Los Angeles, Ellsberg answered an advertisement in the anti-establishment *Los Angeles Free Press* and attended his first orgy.[16] He used the name "Andrew Hunt," and on later excursions the name "Don Hunter." It would later cost Ellsberg some of his support among anti-war activists, not because of the orgies, but because he used false names. He told Barry Farrell:

> The use of a pseudonym? Obvious reasons. Going to a nudist camp, working for Rand, having a security clearance. Rand wouldn't have been too pleased. I didn't know most of the people on those scenes, and I didn't know what they were into or what their backgrounds were, and I just didn't want my real name to be found in their address books. If they were to get in trouble one way or another, it seemed the prudent thing for me to do. I still would do it. A lot of those people were into group sex, and nobody was quite clear as to what the legal status of group sex was. They thought it was legal, but they weren't 100 percent sure.

At one of the scenes, Sandstone resort, Ellsberg met Gay Talese, who was researching hedonism, and since Ellsberg's cover had been blown by *Harper's*, Talese later mentioned the "Don Hunter" episode in his book, *Thy Neighbor's Wife.*

That autumn Ellsberg met Kissinger again. Kissinger, preparing for a call no matter which candidate became President, Humphrey or Nixon, was scouting Rand for Vietnam analysts.

Around Christmas 1968, Ellsberg and two other Rand men were called to the Pierre Hotel in New York, where President-elect Nixon had set up his transition headquaters. Kissinger, knowing that Ellsberg was increasingly dovish but evidently unaware that Ellsberg had been leaking secret documents to the *Times* and was becoming an anti-war activist, asked him to prepare Vietnam options for the incoming administration. Ellsberg did so, convinced that Nixon would not choose the option of getting out. He said that Kissinger struck out the option of immediate withdrawal.

The transition periods between Democratic and Republican administrations are traumatic times in Washington. In December 1968, the Johnson administration was dispersing, his appointees looking for the best employment chances. McNamara proposed to Johnson that the Vietnam study be scanned for declassification and published. Johnson declined. Paul Warnke signed on with the Brookings Institution, to be followed by Leslie Gelb, who would later move to the Carnegie Institute for International Peace. Morton Halperin, surprisingly, was taken on by Kissinger to join the new National Security Council staff.

The chief doves of Defense Department security—Warnke, Halperin and Gelb—regarded Warnke's copy of the Vietnam study as their common property. Halperin telephoned Harry Rowen, president of Rand, to ask him to store their set of the volumes outside the normal Rand security system but in a top-secret safe, as each page was stamped "top secret" and "sensitive," where it would be available to them.

Rowen received on December 18, 1968, a memorandum written on the stationery of Warnke's Office of the Assistant Secretary of Defense, signed by Warnke, Halperin and Gelb. It said that access by others to that copy of the papers must be approved by two of the three signatories, and such access would be approved for employees recommended by Rand, provided that Rand give notification first. A second document gave Ellsberg access to the papers. In December, Ellsberg carried eight volumes to Rand when he returned to Santa Monica, and the following March 4 he carried another batch of ten volumes to Rand after signing a sworn statement in Washington that he would guard them as a courier.

Shortly after Nixon was sworn in as President on January 20, Ellsberg did another job for Kissinger. He moved into the Executive Office Building and spent the month of February helping Winston Lord and Halperin draft National Security Council Memorandum No. 1, made up of answers to detailed questionaires on Vietnam practices and options that had been submitted to the Defense Department, State Department, CIA and the U.S. Embassy in Saigon. Then Ellsberg went back to Santa Monica.

On May 9, William Beecher broke the story of the secret bombing of Cambodia in the *Times*, the leak that drove Kissinger up the wall. The *Times* contended that it was not a leak at all, but information that had come from its own men in the field in Vietnam, a claim that is not plausible because the story contained too many Washington-sourced details. It led to 18 FBI wiretaps, including one on Halperin that picked up 15 calls made by his house guest, Ellsberg, that were noted but not recorded.[17]

At about the time of the Cambodia-bombing story, Ellsberg pressed

Gelb to get the Pentagon Papers declassified and published. Gelb told him to see McNamara, who had become president of the World Bank. Ellsberg and Halperin both pressed Gelb and Warnke to make all of the papers available to Ellsberg, but Gelb testified later at Ellsberg's trial that he and Warnke at first refused.

Ellsberg meanwhile was consolidating his acquaintences with pacifist and radical left opponents of the war, attending in August a conference of the War Resisters League at Haverford College, where the featured leader was West Germany's Pastor Martin Niemöller, the aging former U-boat hero of World War I Germany, who had become an international pacifist legend.

Through part of the summer Ellsberg studied the Pentagon Papers, but apparently he did not have a complete set. On October 6, 1969, Gelb wrote to Rowen at Rand, giving authorization to move a complete set of the study from Rand-Washington to Rand-Santa Monica "for use by Mr. Ellsberg." Now Ellsberg had all 47 volumes at his disposal, and by the end of October he had finished his study of them.

In Santa Monica, eight persons had read part or all of the papers, dividing in their evaluation of what the papers meant. Russo said later that at Rand there was a chasm that "came about because of the ruling-class split." He likened it to an earthquake fault running through the organization.

Six staff members at Rand wrote a letter to the *The New York Times*, just before Gelb authorized the full set for Ellsberg's use, urging that the United States withdraw its troops from Vietnam within one year. Instead of printing the letter in its letters column, the *Times* sent a correspondent to Santa Monica to write a story summarizing the proposals of the Rand experts.[18] The *Times* story singled out Ellsberg as the most influential of the signers, as he had spent two years in Vietnam for the State Department, and it noted another signer, Melvin Gurtov, had published regularly on Vietnam for two years. Other signers were Oleg Hoffding, Arnold L. Horelick, Konrad Kellen and Paul F. Langer. The *Times* did not publish their whole letter, so the *Washington Post* subsequently did. Now Ellsberg was on the public record in New York and Washington as an active opponent of the war.

At his 1973 trial in Los Angeles, Ellsberg said that he began copying the papers, all of them, on September 30, 1969, on a Xerox machine at the advertising agency of Lynda Sinay, then 26, with the help of Russo, Sinay, Ellsberg's son Robert, then 13, and daughter Mary, 10. At the trial, the recently married Lynda Sinay Resnick testified that she had cut off the labels "secret" and "sensitive" from the papers as they were copied, and that on occasion others were present, including Ellsberg's girl friend at the time, Kimberly Rosenberg, and Vu Van Thai, former South Vietnamese Ambassador to Washington.[19] She estimated that the copying took ten days to two weeks. It was the beginning of a copying cottage industry, as the papers were copied and recopied and stashed around the country over the following months.

Ellsberg had been moved to take the responsibility and the risk of going to jail "for the rest of my life," he said, because:

> . . . friends in the administration revealed to me the outlines of future policy. President Nixon, I was informed, had in effect made his choice from among the options that I and others at Rand had helped draft at the end of 1968; and his choice was *not* . . . the option of extrication, a definite end to our involvement. Once more an administration planned to postpone failure; to buy time by maintaining indefinitely American troops at reduced levels in Vietnam, and by continuing to impose American bombing, Indochinese casualties, and the threat of worse.[20]

For a long time Ellsberg did not identify any of the friends in the administration who had given him that view of Nixon's intentions. In the euphoria after his mistrial, and when all charges against him had been dismissed, Ellsberg told *Rolling Stone* magazine that one of his informants was Halperin. "In September '69 I learned from Halperin that the policy had not gone as he (Halperin) had hoped in June; that Nixon and Kissinger had chosen one of the options we had laid out earlier—not the excluded option for unilateral withdrawal—but the option to win the war."[21]

Ellsberg said,:

> . . . Mort and several others, in particular John Vann who had very close contacts with the Department of the Army, first told me one part was being deceptively presented (to the public): Total withdrawal was not in mind, but a slow reduction of troops, as slow as Nixon could get away with, politically, down to a large residual force that would stay indefinitely.

Halperin, who had been gradually cut out of decision making after the FBI tap on his phone started in May, resigned from the government just before speaking with Ellsberg in September.

In September Halperin also told Ellsberg that Nixon's conciliatory speech in May, after the Cambodia incursion, which Halperin had helped draft, contained a hidden threat which Kissinger had drawn to the attention of Soviet Ambassador Anatoloy Dobrynin: "No one has anything to gain by waiting." Halperin also, in September, drew Ellsberg's attention to the Beecher story on the secret bombing of Cambodia, as evidence that Nixon and Kissinger actually intended to step up the war.

Ellsberg said he started copying the Pentagon documents on September 30 thinking:

> What I lacked then was documentary evidence of what I had just been told by Halperin, Vann and three or four others who are still with the government. . . . But I did have something unusual. I had the Pentagon Papers. . . . If I could show that at least once in the past an administration had acted in a conspiratorial fashion, people should at least consider the possiblity that it was happening again.

As subsequent events showed, Halperin had given Ellsberg mistaken advice. Nixon did pull out all of the troops, although anti-war activists could say that the *Times* publication of the Pentagon Papers forced him to do so. When Ellsberg copied the Pentagon Papers, Nixon already had reduced troop strength, and at the time of *Times* publication in 1971, troops had been cut from the Johnson peak of 541,000 to about 250,000. In May 1972, when Ellsberg's book was published, there were 69,000 American troops left in Vietnam, and Nixon told Senate Majority Leader Mike Mansfield that all of them would be out in four months. That timetable was delayed by another abortive North Vietnamese offensive, but the troops all were out ten months later. The effect of *Times* publication of the Pentagon Papers might equally have been to lengthen the timetable by the encouragement that publication gave to Hanoi. The Pentagon Papers, then, were published for a questionable motive. It took the Pentagon Papers plus Watergate to force the United States to abandon Vietnam entirely.

As soon as he had copies, presumably in mid-October, Ellsberg flew to Washington and on November 6 gave a selection of the papers dealing with the Tonkin Gulf resolution to Senator William Fulbright, chairman of the Foreign Relations Committee, who had complained of being duped into sponsoring the resolution. Ellsberg reported that Fulbright was delighted to get the documents, but he held off making them public because Nixon was withdrawing troops from Vietnam. By March 1970, Ellsberg had given Fulbright most of the study. Fulbright wrote to Defense Secretary Melvin Laird three times—on November 8, 1969, January 19 and July 10, 1970—saying that he knew of the study and asking that it be released (officially) to the committee. Laird declined, citing national security. As the study failed to surface in the committee hearings, Ellsberg offered copies of parts of it to Senator George McGovern, Senator Charles Mathias and later to Representative Paul N. (Pete) McCloskey of California.

In Ellsberg's accounts of giving the Pentagon Papers to Congressmen, and his reasons for it, he never mentioned one other direction he took to make the papers public as a means to ending the war.

At the same time he gave the papers to Fulbright, about November 1969, he also gave a section of the study dealing with the Kennedy administration's period of direct involvement in Vietnam—the part of the study that included the assassination of Diem and eventually made the best copy for newspapers—to Marcus Raskin, Richard Barnet and Ralph L. Stavins of the radical left Institute for Policy Studies in Washington.[22]

Although IPS had friends on Capitol Hill in 1969, among them Representatives John Conyers of Michigan, Bella Abzug of New York, James Abourezk of South Dakota and Anthony Moffett of New York—the last two defenders of the Palestine Liberation Organization—many Congressmen were leary of IPS at the time.

Ellsberg "made the papers available, through intermediaries, to scholars of the Institute for Policy Studies, a radical-left think tank in Washington," Sanford J. Ungar reported in the *Washington Post*. "For about a year the institute would make free use of the Pentagon Papers without any controversy. They were not hidden away in any particularly secretive manner, visitors remember having no trouble seeing them."[23]

Through 1970, IPS was in possession of more organized knowledge of American policy history in Vietnam than anyone outside the government, knowledge that bestowed power. IPS organized seminars and teach-ins to spread its information among its clientele, while Stavins, Raskin and Barnet worked on a book manuscript based on the papers.

IPS Fellows interviewing past and present government officials, knowing from the Pentagon Papers what questions to ask, began to get high marks as people who had done their homework. The Institute gained prestige. It could have scooped the *Times* and published the Pentagon Papers first, but its leaders chose to wait almost two years and publish instead *Washington Plans an Aggressive War*,[24] a polemic warning that American officials and military officers might face war crimes trials.

"I was not interested in the Pentagon Papers as such," Raskin said. "I was interested in American policy." Questioned in 1980, he could not recall details of how the Pentagon Papers changed hands a decade before. It is likely that Raskin, Barnet and Stavins believed, as did Ellsberg, that revealing secret documents might be a criminal offense.

Given their radical reputations and their connections to international radical groups, that assumption might have been right. The *Times'* meat could have been their poison, although their sets of the Pentagon Papers were identical. If IPS had published the Pentagon Papers, would Supreme Court Justice Hugo L. Black have commended IPS for its "courageous reporting," as he congratulated the *Times*? Would IPS have won the Pulitzer?

While IPS found its uses for the Pentagon Papers without publishing them, Ellsberg on April 15, 1970, severed connections with Rand after a call from his ex-wife, Carol Cummings Ellsberg, who warned him that the FBI was investigating him. She had learned from the children that they had helped him copy secret documents, as had her mother. Ellsberg's former mother-in-law had notified the FBI. The FBI checked at Rand, and was told that the Defense Department was looking into the matter. The FBI bowed out.

Ellsberg resigned from Rand and took a position as a senior research fellow at the Center for International Studies at the Massachusetts Institute of Technology in Cambridge, where his friend Professor Noam Chomsky was a hero to anti-war students.

A month after moving to Boston, Ellsberg testified on May 13, 1970, before Fulbright's Foreign Relations Committee. In his book, he said that testimony was the reason why he resigned from Rand: he was determined to appear before the committee and had no intention of clearing his testimony with the Defense Department, as would be required of Rand employees.[25] He did not mention in his book the FBI visit to Rand on April 17.

Ellsberg took his case to the influential Senate forum while furor raged over the killing of four students at Kent State. As strikes closed 400 universities across the nation and tear gas lingered from a demonstration of 200,000 persons in Washington, Ellsberg told the committee, "The striking difference between the two sides (in Vietnam) is that those who back the Communist side do not on the whole regard it as a lesser evil, but as a cause worth dying for."

He quoted to the committee, "a friend of mine, Morton Halperin," as saying that Presidents typically make decisions based on domestic considerations, but clothe the decisions in public "with a language of national security and strategy . . . ."

Ellsberg appeared to be saying that Nixon had ordered the incursion into Cambodia for domestic reasons, a non sequitur, considering that the anti-war revolt had been growing in the country for five years.

During the Diem era, Ellsberg had been involved with Soviet affairs, and not with Vietnam, but he nevertheless explained "Diemism, and

Diemism without Diem" to the committee:

> And perhaps I should describe Diemism more fully. It implies a narrow political base for the regime; exclusion of all other groups such as the Buddhists, the students, unions, the Hoa Hao and Cao Dai, from any participation in power, and the use of divide-and-rule tactics on them, an authoritarian police-state regime, suppression of free speech, suppression of political activity, total unwillingness to negotiate with or tolerate the existence of activity of the Communists and extreme reliance on the Americans. This constitutes the context which is called 'Diemism'.

Ellsberg made clear in his book that he did not regret Diem's death, embellishing his remarks to the committee:

> The Nixon administration took another view of Diemism, and since it was on (Nixon's) mind predicated on support of Thieu and his repressive measures. . . it almost surely presumes a huge American presence as well.
>
> That, in turn, I might say, reflects another attitude, a nostalgic attitude, for the earlier days of Diem, which could be similarly paraphrased, 'Diem would have won if only we had assassinated David Halberstam instead. . .'[26]

During the committee hearing Fulbright referred to the Pentagon study, saying it should not be kept secret. Fulbright again referred to the study on the Senate floor, saying on August 7, "I hope that the first enterprising reporter who obtains a copy of this history will share it with the committee."

In November 1970, Ellsberg visited Kissinger to ask if he had read the McNamara study, the Pentagon Papers. Kissinger had his hands full in the fall of 1970. He was absorbed in the attempt to get Vietnam negotiations moving; there had been the Jordanian civil war and the death of Nasser; the election of Salvador Allende's minority government in Chile; a sub rosa Soviet attempt to establish a base for nuclear submarines at Cienfuegos Bay in Cuba, and almost as Ellsberg and Kissinger were talking, the stoning of Nixon's car by a mob in San Jose. Kissinger was familiar with main points of the McNamara study, but he had little time that could be used profitably pondering the 47 volumes.

As Ellsberg talked with Kissinger, Halperin was writing in the *Times*: "President Nixon's Vietnamization policy, far from getting us out of Vietnam, will at best lead to an indefinite presence in Vietnam of thousands of American troops. It could well drive the President to massive escalation, the mining of Haiphong harbor and saturation bombing of North Vietnam."[27] Mining of Haiphong harbor had been an option pushed by the Joint Chiefs since 1965, and Halperin's report was a tip-off it was under consideration.

Ellsberg later told an interviewer:

> I'd say the blackest time in that period (late 1969) was the week-end I knew he (Nixon) was going to mine Haiphong. I'd been waiting for that for three years at that point. The policy, I'd been told by various people, who included Mort Halperin, who had just left the White House, and several others, the policy had been one involving threatening to mine Haiphong to the Russians, to Hanoi, and readiness to carry it out, a willingness, and it would fail. Mining of Haiphong didn't matter so much in itself, that was a minor crisis, but that would be the cover for the unrestricted bombing of North Vietnam, just flatten it.[28]

Unrestricted bombing never materialized.

Ellsberg's opinion of Kissinger was lower than his evaluation of Nixon. He told *Rolling Stone* later,

> . . .the man who, with his boss, has dropped more bombs than any human being in history, bugging and lying as necessary, is perceived as a peacemaker, as a lovable wit, a charming fellow, as anything but the murderous creep that he is. . . . On Vietnam, Kissinger's effect has been not only disastrous but criminal in every respect. The judgments involved were stupid, blind, arrogant and criminal, and the murderous implications of the policy were all realized. We're talking about men who loosed four million tons of bombs on Indochina.[29]

Although Ellsberg lapsed into invective after his acquittal in 1973 at the height of Watergate, he still controlled his rage in February and March 1971, when South Vietnamese troops undertook their second offensive, driving into southern Laos under U.S. air cover to try to cut the Ho Chi Minh trail. Ellsberg wrote in measured and scholarly language in *The New York Review of Books* that the invasions of Cambodia and Laos could not succeed and could only create "two, three, many Vietnams in Southest Asia," as though Nixon were compelled by Che Guevara's curse.[30] The Laos incursion did not achieve all of its objectives, although it relieved pressure on South Vietnam for a year, and North Vietnamese troops did turn on the Laotian and Cambodian armies, making Ellsberg's predictions in part accurate. South Vietnam said it lost 1,350 men and suffered 4,271 wounded, a 28% casualty toll for the Laos incursion, and killed 13,812 North Vietnamese soldiers, destroyed or captured 100 tanks, 300 vehicles, 176,000 tons of ammunition, 6,500 weapons and 65 million gallons of gasoline—statistics that were doubted by the American media.

Ellsberg revised his article later for inclusion in his book as the section retitled, "Murder in Laos."

While Ellsberg was copying the Pentagon Papers, and distributing them to Congressmen and to IPS, Neil Sheehan had not been doing as well as expected at the Washington bureau of the *Times*. He was not a favorite of the bureau chief, Max Frankel, and he had hardly gotten his teeth into a good story since 1968, when Ellsberg was giving him secret cables.

At about the time of Ellsberg's last civil conversation with Kissinger, Sheehan received a routine assignment from Roger Jellinek of the *Times Book Review* to review Mark Lane's *Conversations With Americans*. Lane had burst on the book scene with *Rush to Judgment*, challenging the Warren Commission's report that a single assassin had killed President Kennedy. While many did not believe the full story of the assassination had been told, Lane's assassination book did more to establish his reputation as a sloppy polemicist than it did to build his reputation as a reporter.

Sheehan thought that Lane's new book was scurrilous, although it opposed the war as he did, and it is a wonder that the *Times* thought it should be reviewed at all, let alone twice. Still, Sheehan took the assignment seriously and spent time on it, mostly to point out errors and to amend to the review his own thoughts on Vietnam. In the review, he suggested that American officials responsible for Vietnam war decisions should face war crimes trials.

At IPS, Raskin and Barnet saw Sheehan's review sounding their theme, and recognized that it also chimed with Ellsberg's thought. They pointed out the review to Ellsberg and urged that he give Sheehan the Pentagon Papers.[31]

Sheehan, meanwhile, had received a second assignment from Jellinek at the *Book Review*.[32] Mark Sacharoff, an assistant professor of English at Temple University, had submitted a list of 33 books, all condemning the Vietnam war, and suggested that an article be built around the outpouring of anti-war sentiment that was being encouraged by the Action Committee of Publishers for Peace. Dan Schwartz, Sunday editor of the *Times*, turned down the idea for the *Times Magazine*, regarding the selection as one-sided. The anti-war authors included Noam Chomsky, Seymour Hersh (two books), Mark Lane, David Dellinger and Representative (Father) Robert F. Drinan of Massachusetts, who would try to impeach Nixon on his own and later would be ordered out of politics by Pope John Paul II. Over Schwartz' objections, Jellinek gave the assignment to Sheehan to "review" the 33 books, a dream assignment for a polemicist.

Raskin and Barnet contacted Sheehan through an IPS offshoot, a tentative Commission to Investigate the War Crimes of Americans in Vietnam, which included some Army officers. The commission called Sheehan to congratulate him on his review of the Lane book. Sheehan then met with Raskin and Barnet, and at Raskin's further urging, Ellsberg called Sheehan to discuss war crimes.

In February 1971 Sheehan showed Ellsberg a draft of his review article, a very long polemic against American conduct of the war. At the end of February, Ellsberg visited Washington to take part in a panel discussion of Vietnam at the National War College. On that occasion, Ellsberg had a long talk with Raskin, who again urged him to see if Sheehan could get the Pentagon Papers published at the *Times*.

Ellsberg earlier had realized that the *Times* was the most powerful vehicle for the Pentagon Papers, and he had asked several newspapermen, including Ben Bagdikian, how to get through to *Times* editors, even though Bagdikian was a *Washington Post* editor. He had asked the same question of Edwin Diamond, a former reporter who was lecturing at MIT.

The *Times* represented power, and Ellsberg wrote in his book that in Vietnam "*the President was part of the problem*," and every President would postpone getting out of Vietnam until the next election, so the solution was to "bring *power* on the executive branch from outside."[33] (Ellsberg's italics.)

Ellsberg called Sheehan on February 28, and they laid down ground rules for an approach to the editors of the *Times*. Ellsberg asked that the whole study be published, aware that he was asking the impossible, but seeking as full a publication as possible. He also knew that in editing, summarizing, rewriting and through omission, a newspaper could manipulate the papers to say anything.

Sheehan already had been primed by IPS. He had seen some of the documents in the possession of Raskin, Barnet and Stavins, although he had not seen the complete study.

In the absence of bureau chief Frankel, the key man at the *Times* Washington bureau was Reston. Sheehan told Reston the story: He could get the top secret archives of the Vietnam War, but on condition that it all be published, in book form if not in the newspaper, and he warned that some of Reston's friends in the government might be compromised by publication. Reston called New York and reported that Sheehan was on to "the biggest story of the century."[34] Later that day

Reston gave Sheehan authorization to proceed.

On Frankel's return from out of town, he balked at the idea of such massive exposure of classified information until Sheehan produced sample documents he had obtained from IPS. Frankel took the papers to New York and showed them to Abe Rosenthal and James Greenfield, the foreign editor and a *Times*-government interchangeable man. No one, according to Harrison Salisbury, ever asked Sheehan his sources,[35] but Frankel was aware that IPS had the documents, and he was worried that IPS might release them first.

With a go-ahead from his newspaper, Sheehan traveled with Ellsberg to Boston, where Ellsberg showed Sheehan the set of documents and allowed him to examine them, but not to remove them. Ellsberg gave Sheehan a key to the apartment where the Pentagon Papers were stored, leaving Sheehan in some doubt as to whether Ellsberg had given him clear use of the papers.

At about the same time Ellsberg gave a broad description of the study to Tom Oliphant of the *Boston Globe*. Oliphant looked up Halperin and Gelb, and then published a story headlined, "Only Three Have Read Secret Indochina Report: All Urge Swift Pullout."[36] The story did not cite from documents, and it did not cause a stir.

On March 19, Sheehan and his wife "stole" the Pentagon Papers (in Salisbury's word) from the Boston apartment and Xeroxed them over a period of three days with the aid of a *Times* staffer who provided $1,500 in *Times* funds.[37] The "theft" was academic; in May, Ellsberg gave Sheehan another set of the papers that had been hidden in New York.

In New York, as a *Times* team worked on the Pentagon Papers, the *Village Voice* reported echos of "a fierce internal debate" that had raged at the *Times Book Review:* the whole issue of the powerful publication, a key intellectual organ of the Eastern establishment, had been given over to one man, Neil Sheehan, who was not even a regular book reviewer.[38] Some editors thought that the political tirade Sheehan had published would ruin his reputation.[39]

Sheehan's unprecedented mass review of 33 books was published on March 28, 1971, taking up most of the *Book Review* under the headline, "Should We Have War Crimes Trials?"

Editor John Leonard sent out 100 advance copies and received plugs for the huge review from columnist Nicholas Von Hoffman of the *Washington Post* and Mike Wallace of CBS.[40]

What the disgruntled editors and reviewers at the *Book Review* did not know, but what a few insiders at the *Times* did know, was that Sheehan had received the Pentagon Papers. His review was orchestration for a major coup yet to come.

Sheehan's long article was more an editorial than a review, mentioning the 33 books only in passing. He found that Mark Lane's "purported interviews" in *Conversations With Americans* were not entirely to be blamed on Lane, but were the kind of "scurrilous attack" invited by American policy in Vietnam.

Sheehan's message was American war guilt. American cruelty and American resort force "has failed."

Sheehan wrote, "If you credit as factual only a fraction of the information assembled (in the 33 books) about what happened in Vietnam, and if you apply the laws of war to American conduct there, then leaders of the United States for the last six years at least, including the incumbent President, Richard Nixon, may be guilty of war crimes." President Kennedy, who had committed the United States to intervention in Vietnam and plotted the coup against Diem, was exonerated by Sheehan's timetable; he had died seven years previously.

The United States, Sheehan wrote, was an occupying power.

> Air power, and artillery as a corollary weapon, were directed by an occupying power, the United States, at the civilian population in the rural areas of the country under occupation. The targets of the bombs and shells were the noncombattants themselves, because it was believed that their existence was important to the enemy. Air power became a distinct weapon of terror to empty the countryside.

The timing of Sheehan's review was impeccable. The next day a court martial at Fort Benning, Georgia, found First Lieutenant William Calley guilty of the premeditated murder of at least 22 unarmed Vietnamese civilians at My Lai, a verdict that caused flags to be flown at half mast across the United States and draft boards to resign en masse. A featured author in Sheehan's review was Seymour Hersh, who had exposed the My Lai atrocity through interviews with soldiers who had returned to the United States. Sheehan's review condemned the Army for dismissing charges against Major General Samuel W. Koster, the division commander over Calley.

When Sheehan's review appeared in print, he already was in New York, leading the team working on 43 of the 47 volumes of the Pentagon Papers. The *Times* editorial board met with expanded members and voted to publish with only one dissent, magazine editor Schwartz. Veteran foreign correspondent C. L. Sulzberger also registered dissent from afar. Lawyers had been consulted. Louis Loeb, 72, the *Times'* chief attorney from Lord, Day and Lord, opposed publication and broke his 40-year association with the *Times*. Attorney James Goodale stepped into the breach, approved publication and would later fight for it.

Suites were engaged on the 11th and 15th floors of the New York Hilton. Loads of reference books were trucked in, along with a truckload of loose Xerox copies that made up the 7,000 pages of the Pentagon Papers.

Ellsberg had held out four volumes of recent diplomatic exchanges that still could have a bearing on Vietnam peace negotiations, but they did not remain secret long. Columnist Jack Anderson published their pertinent parts after the *Times* broke the Pentagon Papers story.

At the *Times* building on West 43rd and Broadway, an executive office of the paper's book publishing division was sealed off with temporary walls as a composing room, where the 42 newspaper pages of the series were set in type.

Foreign Editor Greenfield, who had been a spokesman for the State Department, took charge at the Hilton of a staff of more than ten persons working on the mass of documents. The team at the Hilton was ordered not to show their faces at the *Times*. Counting reporters, management personnel and printers, only about 75 persons at the *Times* knew what the secret project was, but most editors and reporters knew that something big was in the wind.

The *Times* editors decided not to merely trim and condense the various studies included in the Pentagon Papers to fit the available space, but to boil down and interpret them under the by-lines of its own men. That meant that the authors of the *Times* articles had an input into interpretation beyond mere selection.

Greenfield told BBC years later, when Michael Charlton challenged him on whether the *Times'* version was "highly contentious and distorted,"

> Let me tell you that when we first began writing the papers, when Mr. Neil Sheehan and Mr. Hedrick Smith wrote their first versions, we scrapped them because they had both been in Vietnam, they could not resist their own comments. We scrapped the first version, and believe me as an editor there was blood all over the floor, because when you have somebody rewrite a seventeen-thousand-word piece from the beginning to end you are in trouble already, and we were all cooped up in several hotel rooms, never leaving them practically, so it was a very difficult thing.
>
> But the fact is we said, no, we want every paragraph, as I said,

to come out of the Papers, so that a footnote can be made and so forth. Those pieces never have been challenged because they all referred back to the original documents. . . .[41]

In fact, the *Times* articles were challenged repeatedly, although not immediately by the rest of the media because only the *Times* had seen the whole study. A few, including columnist Joe Alsop, instantly challenged the *Times* version of the Pentagon Papers as manipulated, but not many editors had the background to challenge genuine documents. Most individuals who challenged the objectivity of the *Times'* version, including Maxwell Taylor, Walt Rostow and Roger Hilsman, were persons involved in the subject matter, and they could be discounted as alibi-seekers for their roles in decision making. (See next chapter for challenges.)

The ranking editors at the *Times* understood that publication of the Pentagon Papers, in a version written by their own men, irrevocably made the *Times* an anti-war activist publication. Thereafter, if the war should be won by South Vietnam and the United States, the *Times* would be lined up in the queue of losers. For the *Times* to win and retain its credibility, the United States had to lose the war or withdraw. Publication therefore was a direct attack on the Nixon administration, which could not be allowed to win or draw in the war.

Salisbury understood what was at stake. He wrote: "One can imagine the Watergate break-in without the Pentagon Papers affair; one cannot imagine the Watergate exposé, the whole debacle of the Nixon presidency, without the Pentagon Papers."[42]

Salisbury was uneasy about publication.

I felt, perhaps more strongly than some, that there was real danger of the Nixon administration seizing upon the Pentagon Papers and trying to use the issue to destroy *The New York Times.* . . . In a memo to the publisher I cited the parallels of Nixon's use of documents in the Hiss case and the earlier use of documents in the Amerasia case. 'I think we should be sophisticated enough to recognize that not everyone in Washington wishes us well '

Salisbury wrote.[43]

Ellsberg, too, regarded publication as an assault on the Nixon administration. In 1973 he would say, "I think the Pentagon Papers will have had a cause and effect. Not alone, of course, but a very strong effect, contributing effect on, in the first instance, getting Richard Nixon and his gang out of office."[44]

On May 9, West Germany told its Common Market partners it would float the Deutschmark, cutting it loose from the dollar. It was, in effect, a unilateral devaluation of the dollar from outside, made necessary by Germany's determination to avoid a ruinous inflation. It was also the signal of impending economic storm, an urgent focus of attention for the Nixon administration.

As the clandestine *Times* team compiled its Pentagon Papers version in the Hilton, most or all of the documents also were being studied in Moscow.[45] Some time during Ellsberg's 20-month effort to get the Pentagon Papers published in the United States, the Soviet Union received a set of the papers. It could have come from a number of sources, since it was open season on the papers after Warnke's copy was deposited at Rand in Santa Monica.

In 1974, Dimitri Simes, a recent emigré from the Soviet Union, confirmed that the papers were known before *Times* publication at the KGB-supervised Institute of World Economy and International Relations and the Institute for the U.S.A. and Canada, two official Soviet academic organizations. Simes, who had worked at the institutes in 1971, told Herb Romerstein, a staff member of the House Intelligence Committee, that when the *Times* published the papers, they naturally were studied at the institutes. He said that colleagues at the institutes told him that the *Times* articles contained nothing sensational; the contents already were known, and "summaries" of the documents already had been circulated at the institutes.

When I spoke to Simes in 1980, he had become an authority on the Soviet Union at Johns Hopkins University, a champion of detente, a candidate-member of the liberal Eastern establishment about to appear on the *Times* Op-Ed page and on Public Television, and the Pentagon Papers episode was something of an embarrassment. He stressed that he had not personally seen the documents or the summaries; he only knew that the documents evidently had been in the Soviet Union before *Times* publication, but he could not elaborate further. He appeared to regret that he ever had brought the matter up.

One indication that the Pentagon papers were in the hands of the Soviets early was the publication by July 22, 1971—quick action following *Times* publications—of *The Stages of War and Duplicity,* the official Soviet Union book on the Pentagon Papers, rushed into print by Moscow's Publishing House of Political Literature in what the preface said were "a great number of copies."

The Moscow version of the Pentagon Papers quoted copiously from the *Times* series, and since it could not appear to praise a free press, explained awkwardly that Big Business had switched sides in the war, because it had become more costly than profitable.

The Moscow book also contained a curious quotation from Richard Barnet within a comment of its own:

> It is scarcely accidental that the biggest share of the war profit pie went to the corporations closest to Washington politicians who were most active in escalating the 'dirty war.' Richard Barnet, co-director of the Institute for Policy Studies in Washington, wrote: '. . . Freshman Congressman Lyndon B. Johnson obtained a major defense contract for his principal financial backers, the Brown and Root construction firm. The same firm thirty years later was called upon to turn South Vietnam into a succession of military bases at considerable profit. In the Johnson years, Texas moved ahead to become the third-ranking state in military contracts. Between 1962 and 1967 the value of prime contracts awarded to Texas firms increased by 350 percent.'

The Soviet book quoted "R. Barnet, *The Economy of Death*, New York, 1969, pp. 122-123.[46]

In Cuba, Fidel Castro's *Granma* was delighted to find Senator Wayne Morse paraphrasing Castro, on the occasion of the Gulf of Tonkin resolution, saying, "History will not absolve us." *Granma* commented, "Nixon must be worried by the turmoil that has been unleashed (by *Times* publication of the Pentagon Papers), which has directly and indirectly implicated all those having anything to do with the criminal genocide in Indochina."[47]

Shortly after the *Times* published its first installments of the Pentagon Papers, during the period the *Times* was under injunction and before it had completed publication of its series, the Soviet Embassy in Washington received a second copy of the papers. (See next chapter.) That delivery, known and reported briefly in the American media, would have the curious effect of aiding, not endangering, Ellsberg's legal defense by causing a long delay in Ellsberg's trial.

All that was in the future in early June 1971, and Ellsberg claimed that he did not know that in New York the presses were about to roll on one of the most significant publishing events in American history.

Chapter XVI
The Media Joins
the Revolution

"Treason doth never prosper; what's the reason?
For if it prosper, none dare call it treason."

—*Sir John Harrington*

On the night of June 2, 1971, Henry Kissinger hurried into the Lincoln Room at the White House, out of breath, to give Nixon exhilarating news. A message had arrived through the Pakistani Embassy diplomatic pouch from Chou En-lai containing a formal invitation from Mao Tse-tung for the President to visit China. It was the culmination of an effort to break China's isolation that had been going on secretly through Romanian, Pakistani and other channels since early February 1969. In April 1971 Nixon had ended the long trade embargo of China in response to China's invitation to a U.S. table tennis team, and an initial, tentative reply from Chou to the Nixon administration had followed. Nixon found a bottle of cognac and poured a drink for Kissinger and himself. In the next days they laid out a plan and timetable that would take Kissinger to China secretly to prepare the ground for Nixon's visit.

Ten days after Mao's invitation, on June 12, Nixon had his best day at the White House. He gave his daughter Tricia to Edward Cox at their wedding in the Rose Garden, where everything was coming up roses.

That evening at 9 p.m. the *Times* introduced its scoop on Page 1, avoiding sensation, with a mild headline in small type discretely centered over four columns:

Vietnam Archive; Pentagon Study Traces

3 Decades of Growing U.S. Involvement.[1]

Neil Sheehan's story, with a 10-point lead, said that the *Times* had come into possession of a 3,000-page analysis accompanied by 4,000 documents—altogether 2.5 million words—that had been commissioned by McNamara. It said the authors of the study reached broad conclusions and specific findings, listing what it said were the analysts' conclusions in tendentious language, for example, "The Johnson administration, though the President was reluctant and hesitant to take the final decisions, intensified the covert warfare against North Vietnam and began planning in the spring of 1964 to wage overt war, a full year before it publicly revealed the depth of its involvement and its fear of defeat." The main article that day would attempt to prove this conclusion, which was Sheehan's, not the analysts'.

An accompanying Page 1 story by Hedrick Smith said that 30 to 40 government officials, civilian and military, had worked on the study for a year. It reported that the study was undertaken after Assistant Secretary McNaughton had written to McNamara: "A feeling is widely and strongly held that the 'Establishment' is out of its mind."

Inside the paper, the stories jumped to six full newspaper pages of analysis and documents on the period February to August 1964, including the Tonkin Gulf resolution, in a 17,000-word main article by Sheehan under the headline, "The Covert War."

The main article began:

> The Pentagon papers disclose that in this phase the United States had been mounting clandestine military attacks against North Vietnam and planning to obtain a congressional resolution that the administration regarded as the equivalent of a declaration of war. *The papers make clear that these far-reaching measures were not improvised in the heat of the Tonkin crisis.*

(My italics of a particularly tendentious description of contingency planning, which is at odds with the analysts' denial that the Tonkin crisis was premeditated.)

The Pentagon study was, as its supervisor-editor Leslie Gelb said later, "not history, but inputs to history." Its authors strove for objectivity, but its overall slant was that of its supervisors, Warnke, Halperin and Gelb. In its documents, studies and summary analyses, material could be found to make a case for a number of viewpoints, depending on who was summarizing and interpreting it. Ellsberg, in his *Papers on the War*, wrote that the *Times* version was useless to historians, who should use the *Senator Gravel Edition*, which has fewer serious omissions. The more complete Defense Department edition, *United States-Vietnam Relations, 1945-1967*, was little read, and the *Times* labeled it—the original—biased![2]

If the *Times* had assigned to the series reporters more tolerant of military men, say, Hanson Baldwin or Drew Middleton, the interpretation would have been entirely different. Here is a sample viewpoint that can be fully supported by the study, given a bit of selective quoting from it: "The 7,000-page Pentagon study shows that throughout the long Vietnam conflict the Joint Chiefs of Staff consistently were vetoed by dilettante civilian strategists, then called upon to rescue a deteriorating situation, then vetoed again." Such a thesis would be slanted and not entirely correct, but possibly closer to an accurate interpretation than the *Times* presented.

As noted earlier, the *Times* systematically excluded from its Pentagon Papers documents that damaged its friends (e.g., John Kenneth Galbraith), or might exalt those the *Times* considered dubious (e.g., Edward Lansdale) or made Hanoi appear the aggressor. (See Chapters VIII and IX.)

It is said that a bartender can fiddle a bar to cheat the customers 42 different ways, from the thick-glass 1/2-ounce jigger to pouring cheap Scotch from an expensive bottle. From the beginning article the *Times* fiddled the Pentagon Papers; let me count the ways, some of them:

First, to begin the series with the Tonkin Gulf episode was illogical journalistically and historically, but politically expedient. By normal news logic, the most newsworthy part of the study was that dealing with the assassination of Diem, although it had previously been reported in detail by Marguerite Higgins and quashed by the *Times*. The Tonkin Gulf episode was, however the part of the series which, properly manipulated, would be most effective with Congress, which at that time was debating legislative amendments to prevent Nixon from continuing the war. As expected, Congress was outraged, and nine days after the *Times* series started, during the *Times'* brief martyrdom under injunction, the Senate passed an amendment by Mike Mansfield that would have demanded a troop pull-out in nine months if American POWs were freed. The House killed the amendment, but the Senate action constituted a breakthrough in sentiment. The *Times* version omitted the Pentagon analysts' conclusion that the Johnson administration had tried to avoid the Tonkin Gulf clash.

Second, by throwing the reader into the beginning of the Johnson administration, out of historical context, it was possible to show Johnson making contingency plans without mentioning that the death of Diem had spurred a rapid Communist infiltration into the South; indeed, Sheehan's long article skips over the Communist build-up, giving the impression that contingency scenarios were motivated by Washington's aggressive instincts and not as a response to anything.

Third, publisher Arthur Ochs (Punch) Sulzberger was "let down" by the first draft of Sheehan's initial article and sent it back to be rewritten.[3] Sulzberger may not have been entirely joking when, after heated debate on the legality of printing the documents, he gave the go-ahead for the project saying, "Gentlemen, I've decided to print the documents and not the story." The implication is the *Times* slanting was conscious, not unconscious.

When the *Times* published Quadrangle and Bantam book editions of its *The Pentagon Papers* with impressive speed a few weeks after newspaper publication, the approach was more logical. In the book version, the chapters were lined up in historical sequence, and Sheehan's initial article became Chapter 5. The second sentence of what had been the newspaper lead of the first article, the sentence earlier italicized, "The Papers make clear that these far-reaching measures were not improvised in the heat of the Tonkin crisis," the sentence that could not be supported and would goad Congress, was deleted. In the book, it served no purpose.

These manipulations were subtle. They could not be recognized by anyone who had not read the study, and no one in the news business had, except the *Times* men, who had spent three months at it. Some manipulations would not become apparent, such as crucial omissions, until the Senator Gravel and Defense Department versions were published. Still, the rest of the media should have been skeptical of a series introduced by the *Times'* most engaged anti-war reporter, Sheehan, who had just called for war crimes trials. Instead the media, sluggishly at first, accepted without question the *Times'* protestations that its version was objective and authentic *The Pentagon Papers*.

Choosing to start with the Tonkin Gulf episode had one disadvantage for the *Times*. It pilloried the Johnson administration, and some dull-witted readers might therefore interpret it as favorable to the Nixon administration. James Reston refuted that notion. In his column he stopped short of saying the papers were stolen, but he stressed that the *Times* was not playing ball with Nixon: the papers had "not been released or leaked by the Nixon administration."

History is not the long suit of Americans, even *Times* readers, and on the first day of publication there was no reaction. Television news ignored it, and *Times* editors' telephones did not ring with inquiries. Editors called their counterparts on another newspaper and asked them to cable congratulations to Sulzberger, who had gone to Europe, to reassure him that the series was important, and their colleagues complied with the request.[4]

In Washington, Kissinger took alarm instantly. The *Times* series was a double threat: it was an all-out political assault on any kind of further conduct of the war, so it could take the conduct of foreign policy out of the administration's hands, and if left unchallenged, it was an invitation to a further hemorrhage of government secrets. A direct threat to national security was less imposing but still substantial. Defense Secretary Laird skimmed the study and reported that 95% of the material should have been declassified, but the other 5% was sensitive. It might leave the administration in the position of being "a little bit pregnant." The whole study could enable hostile intelligence agencies to draw up a chronology to relate to other events and gauge Washington's methodology and timing requirements. The study would embarrass some allies, make them less willing to work with a fishbowl government and if unchecked might bare the government's ongoing projects that depended on secrecy. It certainly would encourage North Vietnam to continue the struggle.

The *Washington Post*, which worked closely with the *Times*, was alerted to the *Times* scoop just before publication, and its editors recognized that it would make news. Editor Ben Bradlee threw a team into a matching effort: veterans Chalmers Roberts, Murray Marder, Don Oberdorfer and Michael Getler. The *Post* was reduced to scurrying around trying to find a copy of the study, reporting that the White House did not have one and Kissinger denied knowledge of it, while Roberts and Marder rewrote the *Times*, repeating its distortions, a humiliating exercise. Their story started, "The Johnson administration planned for major American military action against North Vietnam nearly five months before the 1964 Tonkin Gulf incident, according to documents made public yesterday by the *New York Times*."[5]

While the reporters worked, Bradlee received a call from Marcus

Raskin of IPS, a friend of Bradlee's first wife. He was "hush-hush and secret," but wanted to have breakfast with Bradlee the next morning, Monday, the 14th.

At breakfast, Raskin, Barnet and Stavins offered Bradlee for serialization the manuscript of their book based on the Pentagon study, *Washington Plans an Aggressive War.* The IPS group said they no longer had their source material, but might be able to get it back, depending on how the *Post* handled their book. Roberts that day took a look at the manuscript and told Bradlee to forget it. It was "just atrocious. . . . It was infuriating because they kept paraphrasing things, or they'd take one sentence out of quotes, and you never knew what the rest said. It smelled like they'd grabbed out what they wanted to prove their own case. . . . I told Ben I wouldn't touch it with a ten-foot pole."[6]

That day the *Times* continued the series on Page 1, again jumping to six pages inside, under the headline, "Vietnam Archive: A Consensus to Bomb Developed before '64 Election, Study Says."[7] The story, again by Sheehan, centered on the Johnson administration meetings in September to November 1964 that set the course of the administration's "slow-squeeze" policy and controlled bombing. By adopting this sequence of story telling, the *Times* salvaged the reputation of an old ally, George Ball. Discussing the Security Council meeting of November 24, the report said, "In the account of this meeting, Mr. Ball makes his first appearance in the Pentagon history as the administration's dissenter on Vietnam. Ball advocated limited bombing only as reprisal against Communist offensives, while seeking Soviet backing for negotiations."

For two decades Ball represented positions in harmony with *Times* editorials: against the use of force against Castro, against reprisals for the Berlin Wall, for negotiation and cooperation with the Soviet Union, against Diem, in a consistent pattern of solicitation of the Soviet Union and disregard of allies' interests.

In defending its publication of the Pentagon Papers while under injunction, the *Times*, in an editorial filling the whole space, excused only one government official:

> It seems to have been accepted without question by virtually everyone in the top ranks, except Under Secretary of State George Ball, that the interests of the United States did lie, at any cost and overriding any risk, in military victory for the South Vietnamese government even to the point of major American participation in a war on the land mass of Southeast Asia.[8]

If the series had been presented chronologically in the *Times,* or if it had begun with the coup against Diem, Ball could not have been singled out for praise or as official justification for publication. His "first appearance" in the Pentagon study would have been as a prime mover in the coup group that caused Diem's murder and the ensuing American moral commitment to stay in Vietnam.

On the first day of publication Attorney General John Mitchell, acting on Laird's formal complaint, asked the *Times* to refrain from publishing more to avoid "irreparable injury to the defense interests of the United States." The *Times*, amid passionate internal debates, refused. Assistant Attorney General Robert Mardian telephoned Harding Bancroft, executive vice president of the *Times*, to say that the government would seek a court injunction. Mitchell and Mardian not only would lose; they would go to jail in the Watergate affair.

A *Times* editorial demonstrated that, although the Pentagon Papers concerned earlier administrations, the target was Nixon:

> . . . the President seems clearly to believe that the United States had not redeemed a pledge on which he has previously insisted as a condition for withdrawal 'that we give the South Vietnamese a reasonable chance to defend themselves against Communist aggression.' Many millions of Americans, including this newspaper, believe on the contrary that the United States long ago more than fulfilled whatever obligation it may have had in this respect. . . .[9]

The lines were drawn. The *Times* faced Nixon in direct challenge: call off the war or else.

Nixon recognized the challenge. He had seen Sheehan's book-review suggestion that he might be tried as a war criminal, and he later wrote that "the *Times'* decision to publish was clearly the product of the paper's anti-war policy rather than a consistent attachment to principle." He noted that the *Times* earlier had attacked a leaker of a different persuasion, Otto Otepka, an anti-Communist who had fought to keep leftists out of the State Department by leaking security investigations to Congressmen.[10]

While the *Times* and its supporters isolated the issue as freedom of the press, the internationally minded, a minority in the United States, recognized the stakes in the power struggle. Henry Brandon, reporting from Washington to *The Times* of London, said:

> What used to be undeclared war between the Press and the American government has now become a declared war between, on the one hand, *The New York Times* and now the *Washington Post*, and, on the other, the Nixon administration. . . . Daniel Ellsberg, if he is the culprit, now belongs to the New Left which first hoped that Senator Eugene McCarthy would help it to power. It is

now using *The New York Times* (which of course sees the publication in a different light) to get at the liberals who are still in control of the Democratic Party.

Like the *Washington Post* and the foreign media in general, *The Times* of London was busy boiling down the *Times'* version of the Pentagon Papers into more concise and stark stories to fit its limited space, in the process magnifying the *Times'* distortions of the study.[11] One of the London-based reporters so engaged was William Shawcross, being introduced to Indochina.

With the first three massive *Times* articles published, Judge Murray I. Gurfein of the U.S. District Court of New York issued a temporary injunction, ordering the *Times* to suspend publication but refusing the government's demand that the *Times* return the stolen study and documents. For the next 15 days the *Times'* lead story under massive headlines was itself and its fight against blind injustice. Headlines, editorials and columnists thundered against the "unprecedented example of censorship."[12]

Reston's column began, "For the first time in the history of the republic the Attorney General of the U.S. has tried to suppress documents he hasn't read about a war that hasn't been declared." From London, columnist Anthony Lewis reported that American allies had made no complaints against publication. The next day Murray Marder reported in the *Washington Post* that allies *had* complained, but the *Post's* cartoonist, Herbert Block, backed Reston, depicting Mitchell as an executioner. *Post* columnist David Broder, accepting the *Times* version of the papers unquestioningly, wrote, "One cannot read the Pentagon history of this tragedy without being overwhelmed by a sickening feeling of deception and betrayal."[13] Senator Frank Church charged the administration with "nothing less than censorship of the press."

The *Washington Post's* assistant managing editor, Ben Bagdikian, who had worked for a time at Rand and knew Ellsberg, recognized Ellsberg's thinking in the *Times* series and tried to contact him on Wednesday, June 16, as the *Times* angrily complied with the court ruling and did not publish its fourth article. After one of his contacts asked him to make calls from a public booth to avoid tracing, Bagdikian reached Ellsberg and flew to Boston to get a copy of the papers, returning to deliver them to Bradlee's home. Now the *Washington Post* team could write its own series, but without benefit of the long study the *Times* had enjoyed. The *Post* decided not to print whole documents, but to cite from them, and on the whole the *Post* series, after the initial copying from the *Times*, was less biased. But the *Post* series never could be *The Pentagon Papers*, a creature firmly fixed in the public mind as a legitimate offspring of the *Times*.

The White House and FBI immediately had prime suspects for the leak of the Pentagon Papers to the *Times*. Morton Halperin was a suspect; his telephone had been tapped by the FBI from May 1969, after the leak of the Cambodian bombings to Beecher, and the tap continued for a year after his resignation from Kissinger's staff to join the staff of Senator Edmund Muskie in September of that year, a circumstance that would later be called crass political espionage by the media.[14] The prime suspect was Ellsberg, who had gone underground and would later say he moved between five different sanctuaries. In Los Angeles, police quickly picked up Anthony Russo, who charged he was beaten by police on two occasions.

In North Vietnam the Pentagon Papers were a dominating theme on Hanoi radio. In South Vietnam, they were denounced and banned from the press, raising a cry of censorship from the American correspondents. In Paris, the Viet Cong representative at the peace talks, Mme. Nguyen Thi Binh, told a news conference on June 16 that the papers "confirm a truth we often have expressed at this table, to wit, that the American administration, with the goal of establishing a neo-colonial regime in Vietnam, conceived a plan for unleashing war and spreading it stage by stage." North Vietnam's spokesman in Paris, Nguyen Than Le, said the publications were "further proof of U.S. aggression."

In New York a former *Times* reporter, Sidney Zion, telephoned Barry Gray, host of a radio talk show on WMCA, offering a scoop: he could identify the leaker. Gray revised his show, and Zion appeared to name Ellsberg, stressing that he approved of Ellsberg's brave action. The *Times* sent reporter Murray Shumach to the studio, but he did not report on the show. At the end of the broadcast, Shumach gave Zion a message from *Times* metropolitan editor Arthur Gelb, brother of Leslie: he was "never to set foot in the *Times* again."[15]

The following evening the *Times* mentioned Ellsberg's name for the first time in connection with the papers, reporting on Page 15 that the FBI was looking for him. The *Times* reported that Zion had been denounced by Warren Hinckle III, former executive editor of *Ramparts*, and Thomas Humber, two editors who had worked with Zion on the defunct muckraking magazine *Scanlon's*, who said, "Sidney Zion's reprehensible act is that of a publicity-seeking scavenger."[16] Hinckle and Humber told the *New York Post*, "We are frightened to have ever been associated with such a man." Contacted in 1978, Zion would no longer talk about the episode, remarking, "They put me out of commission for about five years."[17]

While the *Times* was enjoined from printing its series, it reprinted stories from other newspapers. The press was in full revolt and was being systematically supplied by a nationwide Ellsberg network, editors of the *Boston Globe* and Knight chain accepting documents from unknown donors at rendezvous points. The government acted against the *Washington Post* and *Boston Globe* before realizing that the dike had broken, and it took no action to stop publication at the *Chicago Sun-Times, Los Angeles Times, Christian Science Monitor, St. Louis Post-Dispatch* and Knight-Ridder chain.

The FBI could not find Ellsberg, who was being interviewed by *Newsweek*, CBS and others. On prime time June 23, Walter Cronkite interviewed Ellsberg in a private home, in the fashion of clandestine interviews with Soviet dissidents.

Cronkite commented, "It's a black history as it's been drawn so far. Are there any heroes in it?"

Ellsberg said he had heard of a man named Bernard who had refused to fire at civilians at My Lai. "He's a hero."

Ellsberg concluded, ". . .Americans bear major responsibility, as I read this history, for every death in combat in Indochina in the last 25 years, and that's one to two million people."

Cronkite did not specify what he found black about the three articles on the Johnson administration. Apparently he believed the *Times'* implication that Congress had been deluded and the Johnson administration aggressively bent on war.

On June 22 Representative McCloskey received a call from the FBI to ask about the *Times* report on June 18 that he had the papers, a query delayed four days. McCloskey, who planned to challenge Nixon for the Republican nomination in the 1972 elections, did not want a private meeting. When McCloskey arrived at his office he cheerfully invited two FBI visitors into a room that had been set up as an NBC television studio, lights in place, crammed with reporters. The agents did not enter, but retreated.

The *Times* was delighted with McCloskey's caper and gave it a four-column headline on an inside page.

By June 24 the *Times* had worked through the underbrush of the lower courts with astonishing speed and appealed to the Supreme Court for relief. The Supreme Court's acceptance of the case on an emergency basis—no lives would have been threatened by a more orderly and measured consideration of the injunction—was an admission that the media revolt was out of hand and could not be controlled by the judicial system. The next day a warrant for the arrest of Ellsberg was issued.

Beating Ellsberg's arrest warrant by hours, the *Times* set in type Ellsberg's article, "The Quagmire Myth," which filled half the Op-ed page. Ellsberg argued that American Presidents had not stumbled into quicksand but had consistently decided against odds and options offered by qualified advisers. He tended to excuse Kennedy and blame "the right wing of the Republican Party (which) tattooed on the skins of politicians and bureaucrats alike some vivid impressions of what could happen to a liberal administration that chanced to be in office on the day a red flag rose over Saigon."[18] The *Times* noted that the piece was excerpted from an article Ellsberg had written for *Public Policy*, the Kennedy Institute quarterly.

After issuing statements for three days that he would surrender, Ellsberg appeared for arrest in Boston on June 28, accompanied by his wife Patricia, and was released on $50,000 bail.

Fifteen days after the *Times* was enjoined, the Supreme Court ruled six to three on June 30 that the government could not block news articles prior to publication, and the *Times* trumpeted its victory in a three-deck banner headline over eight columns. The decision on the narrow ground of prior restraint was preordained when the court accepted the case; no justice favored prior restraint, and the court was in any case rendered powerless by media civil disobedience. Technically, the decision did not rule 'out prosecution of the *Times* after publication, but in the real world the victory could not be countermanded. To have confirmed the injunction would have fanned revolutionary activity, perhaps to a showdown, and might have tied up the Justice Department indefinitely in pursuing the media in courts throughout the nation.

Justice Hugo L. Black's majority opinion was quoted as the frontispiece of the *Times'* Bantam version of *The Pentagon Papers*:

Only a free and unrestrained press can effectively expose deception in government. And paramount among the responsibilities of a free press is the duty to prevent any part of the government from deceiving the people and sending them off to distant lands to die of foreign fevers and foreign shot and shell. In my view, far from deserving condemnation for the courageous reporting, *The New York Times*, the *Washington Post* and other newspapers should be commended for serving the purpose that the Founding Fathers saw so clearly. . . .

Deception had indeed been done, but Black had not read the 47 volumes of the Pentagon study piled up in the courtroom.

Three dissenters, Chief Justice Warren Burger and Justices John Harlan and Harry F. Blackmun, called the decision precipitous, hasty, frenzied, frenetic, reached without examining evidence and under the pressure, as Harlan put it, "of some accident of immediate overwhelming interest which appeals to the feelings and distorts the judgment."

Burger said that the *Times* had "concealed for three to four months its possession of stolen property...secret government documents." He called the pressured proceedings "a parody of the judicial process."

Harlan said that the court had been "almost irresponsibly feverish," that the newspapers received the documents "with the knowledge that they had been feloniously acquired," and that "the potential consequences of erroneous decision are enormous."

Blackmun said that the *Times* "clandestinely devoted a period of three months examining the 47 volumes that came into its unauthorized possession...the case assumed a frenetic pace and character...." He warned that "if these newspapers proceed to publish...and there results therefrom 'the death of soldiers, the destruction of alliances, the greatly increased difficulty of negotiations with our enemies, the inability of our diplomats to negotiate,'...then the nation's people will know where the responsibility for these said consequences rests." Blackmun erred; it took time for the consequences to be realized, and the people did not notice.

The *Times'* triumph later would be accurately summarized by Harrison Salisbury: "The *Times* has come to fulfill a new function; it has become that Fourth Estate, that fourth coequal branch of government of which men like Thomas Carlyle spoke."[19] He added, accurately, "No other newspaper in America and no paper anywhere possessed comparable resources, esteem and influence. When the *Times* spoke, the chancelleries of Europe listened and the Kremlin took notice."[20]

The *Times'* victory was acknowledged universally. From Hamburg, Rudolf Augstein, publisher of *Der Spiegel*, returned the favor the *Times* had done him during the Spiegel affair, writing for the *Times* an article of fulsome praise to be distributed internationally. Augstein recalled that he had been jailed on charges of publishing 41 defense secrets "...and it was years before *Der Spiegel* could invalidate those absurd accusations." Augstein chose the word "invalidate" to refer to the West German Constitutional Court's decision, four to four, without mentioning it directly.[21]

Freed from restraint, the *Times* published in the same editions with the Supreme Court decision two long articles by Hedrick Smith filling 12 pages with the Kennedy administration's experiences in Vietnam. Now the series did have a dark and ignoble episode of the war. The 1963 coup against Diem had been the most newsworthy part of the Pentagon study, but the *Times* had been preëmpted by the *Chicago Sun-Times*. The *Sun-Times*, in far less space, had used the documents to confirm the earlier reporting of Marguerite Higgins, buttressed with documents which the *Times* did not have or did not use, including bloodthirsty memos by Roger Hilsman on the disposal of the Diem regime.[22]

With the Kennedy era quickly out of the way, the *Times* series resumed where it perhaps should have started, with articles by Fox Butterfield on the Truman and Eisenhower administrations' involvement. Public interest dropped.

Butterfield's second article, dealing with origins of the insurgency in South Vietnam, began: "The secret Pentagon study of the Vietnam war says the United States government's official view that the war was imposed on South Vietnam by aggression from Hanoi is 'not wholly compelling.'" *Times* editors liked that lead so well that the headline over eight columns on the jump-page said, "Vietnam Papers: Doubt Cast on View that the North Imposed War on the South."

This thesis, that the Viet Cong was a movement indigenous to the South, was a running theme of the New Left promoted by the Institute for Policy Studies since 1965, when it published *The Vietnam Reader* and *Ramparts Vietnam Primer.* It was expressed concisely in *Ramparts*, July 1965, in "A View from Phnom Penh," by Robert Scheer, who reported that the Viet Cong "fought almost entirely on their own, painstakingly securing arms and building up combat units with little more than moral support from Hanoi and Peking."

Possibly somewhere in the 7,000 pages of the Pentagon study there might be a fleeting reference to support Butterfield's lead and the *Times* headline, but it surely was not the thrust of the Pentagon study, and one recalls that Butterfield's report from Hanoi was a major exhibit in Efron's *The News Twisters.*

The *Times* series wound up with an article on Tet 1968 by E. W. Kenworthy that reinforced mistaken perceptions that Tet had been a calamity for the United States and repeated the Ellsberg-leaked version of the aborted troop request. It began, "Amid the shock and turmoil of the Tet offensive in February 1968, the Pentagon study of the Vietnam war discloses, the Joint Chiefs of Staff and General William C. Westmoreland sought to force President Lyndon B. Johnson a long way toward national mobilization in an effort to win victory in Vietnam."

The accusatory tone belied the substance of the article as Kenworthy over-reached.

"Camelot" was the only occasion in U.S. political history when feudalism was glorified, and publication of the Pentagon Papers brought back on stage the nobles, courtiers and court jesters of the period.

First to get the wind up was John Kenneth Galbraith, originator of the dump-Diem movement, who apparently wrote to the *Times* the moment he saw the first article. He thanked the *Times* for sharpening his sense of outrage, and he apologized for having campaigned for Johnson, the deceiver. In his patented, professorial prose, Galbraith wrote:

> What we have learned is that a small group of professionally assured, morally astigmatic and—a point to be emphasized—intellectually myopic men had undertaken deliberately to mislead Congress, the public and the people of the world at large as to their intentions and, so far as might be possible, as to their actions. They would largely have escaped criticism if the *Times*, in an action that belies much that is said about the modern institutionalized press, had not ripped away the protecting shroud. Whatever the plea, the primary effect of the present court action is to protect what is still undisclosed of this mendacity and duplicity. . . .[23]

Galbraith need not have worried; the *Times* did not intend to lift his shroud.

George Ball also surfaced quickly. After the *Times* discovered that he was the leading dissenter for peace, the *New York Post*, then such a faithful follower of the *Times* that it reprinted *Times* editorials on the papers case in their entirety, headlined, "Ball's Role as Dove Borne Out." Ball appeared on CBS's *Face the Nation*, introduced as the dissenter, on June 27, before *Times* publication of his role in the cable ordering the coup against Diem. Ball said that the Pentagon Papers should be published, but warned against searching for villains or heroes in them. Ball said that the papers might force more candor on the Nixon administration, adding that "they haven't got a great deal more time to get American troops out of this situation without a real blowup in the United States."

From Paris, Pierre Salinger, President Kennedy's spokesman, chimed in with an odd thought that revealed much about his political acumen: "The publication of these documents can only help Nixon. I would not be surprised if someone in the administration gave a helping hand."

The most beleaguered of the Camelot men was Roger Hilsman, to whom the *Times* gave almost half its Op-Ed page on June 28. The *Times* had Hilsman's role set in type, but not yet printed. The *Chicago Sun-Times* already had blown the whistle. Hilsman wrote that, although the material might mislead the public, the *Times* was performing "a public service of high order."

Hilsman said that publication did not endanger national security, although it might embarrass officials.

> On the other hand, publication can also protect people not just from embarrassment but from slander. I am an example. I left the government in disagreement over Johnson's Vietnam policy in 1964. [Aha! Hilsman was the leading dissenter. Ball left later.] In December 1970 and again in the last few days, apparently in an attempt to discredit a critic, a former aide to President Johnson made public documents that I had written which seemed to indicate that the United States had masterminded the coup against Diem in 1961 (sic).
>
> Publication of the whole record would prove that these documents were not related to the coup and that even though statements made by President Kennedy condemning Diem's policy toward the Buddhists undoubtedly encouraged the coup, the U.S. was not directly involved.

Hilsman warned that even when the *Times* published the Diem episode, the public might get "only a partial and subtly biased version, noting that the study authors "worked for McNamara" (Hilsman's enemy).

McGeorge Bundy, Theodore Sorensen and Arthur Schlesinger, Jr. strongly endorsed the *Times* publication, and all would appear in Los Angeles later at Ellsberg's trial to testify that national security was not involved.

Paul Warnke, whose office produced the Pentagon Papers, held a news conference that was suitably equivocal. The *Times* and *Washington Post* disagreed on what he said, the *Times* headlining, "Leader of War Study Sees No Security Threat so Far," and the *Post* headlining, "Warnke Opposes Publication of Report on Diplomacy." What Warnke had said was that publication of the volumes concerning ongoing diplomatic efforts could be damaging, that publication created "a mischievous precedent," and what worried him was "what it does to relations between people," but that he had seen no security breaches in material published so far. Warnke said, "Whoever released it violated a trust. Whoever released them had access to them on a privileged basis." He did not say it was Ellsberg, or that the released copy was his own.

Both former President Johnson and Robert McNamara refused to comment on the publication. Johnson told Nixon, "They just want to re-execute me." *Newsweek* quoted aides to Johnson in Texas who said he thought the publication represented "a dishonest, distorted and biased picture of his role," and that the circumstance of the leak "comes close to treason."[24] *Newsweek* said that Johnson suspected the late Senator Robert Kennedy, who had "pinned his hopes on Vietnam" for the 1968 nomination. Johnson's aides noted that Kennedy knew Ellsberg and had an input into the Pentagon Papers. According to Tom Braden of the *Los Angeles Times,* Robert Kennedy had urged McNamara to order the study.[25]

Walt Rostow, teaching in Texas, declined comment to the commercial media, but told the University of Texas newspaper *The Texan* that the *Times* was misleading the public. He said, ". . . the worst of it, in my judgment, is what *The New York Times* did in its first three articles. It proceeded from this limited evidence to draw conclusions which are in no way warranted by the evidence itself."[26]

Amid the acclaim for the *Times* and Ellsberg there were a few dissenting voices in the media. Columnist Joseph Alsop, treated as a renegade by the Eastern media, wrote after the first *Times* article: ". . . First, there is nothing very unexpected in the documents themselves. Second, they are now being interpreted in what has to be called a grossly mendacious manner." He called the "orgy of public hypocrisy . . . something that has to be seen to be believed." Alsop said that the *Times* headline, "A Consensus to Bomb Developed Before '64 Election," was a gross misrepresentation of the truth, and detailed the continuing argument over bombing during the period.[27]

Columnist Kenneth Crawford also charged that those professing shock at the first three *Times* articles were "either naive or hypocritical." He said that Gelb's statement that his team regarded the Vietnam war as a Greek tragedy demonstrated that the authors of the study had introduced their own prejudices.[28] Columnist Jerry Greene commented that there was something for everyone in the documents, and the first three articles were "shy on surprises, big on villains."[29]

Human Events commented that the papers showed that

> . . . it was John F. Kennedy's boys, the Bundy brothers, McNamara, et al., who stormed into the Vietnam jungle, then lost their nerve and failed to meet the challenge which they themselves

had articulated so well.... It was this collection of Cambridge Square albatrosses that clung to Johnson's neck, compounding the felony of his indecision with their own faint hearts. Then, anxious to re-establish their leftist credentials, they scrambled out of the mud bath, leaving Johnson and the nation in hip deep....[30]

Such voices were faint against the acclaim for the *Times*, and only Alsop and Rostow had the charge right: the Pentagon Papers were manipulated, false.

William F. Buckley, Jr., finding the exaggeration accompanying a political challenge amusing, concocted a hoax intended to needle Big Media. His *National Review* published a scoop, "The Secret Papers They Didn't Publish," pretending to document nuclear war plans, that was marked down by the publishing industry as the magazine's attempted suicide.

Among the comments there was a poignant note from the Communist *Daily World*, which was trumpeting the *Times'* exposures. The *World* ran a house ad:

> The *Daily World* has fearlessly exposed from the beginning the imperialist and racist war in Indochina and its destructive effects at home.... We shall continue. We will not be silent! But the noose of unpaid printers' bills, mailing and other charges is pulling tight. Our readers must loosen it! Rush your contribution today.

With Ellsberg's surrender, a Federal grand jury was constituted in Boston to investigate his transfer of the classified documents to the *Times* and another in Los Angeles that would return an indictment on his acquiring the government material from Rand.

Ellsberg was basking in the adulation of the Left and much of the media, moving rapidly, engaged in a constant round of interviews, television talk shows and speechmaking on the theme: "I did this clearly at my own jeopardy, and I am prepared to answer all the consequences.... Would you not go to prison to end the war?"[31]

Ellsberg's chances of going to prison were slim. If he were found guilty of something, by implication the *Times* and other media giants also would be guilty, and that could not happen. Ellsberg engaged a defense team that eventually grew to 35 attorneys. At first it included Senator Charles Goodell, a New York Republican appointed by Governor Nelson Rockefeller to serve out Robert Kennedy's term, but

Goodell's role would be limited to chairing Ellsberg's fund-raising committee after the Nixon administration disowned him and he failed to be elected in 1972, despite the *Times'* best efforts on his behalf. Ellsberg's team would be headed by Leonard Boudin, who had gotten Ellsberg's IPS friend Eqbal Ahmad separated from the Berrigan Brothers' trial and had defended Dr. Spock. Boudin's daughter Kathy, a Weather Underground leader, was being hunted at the time for a fatal bomb explosion in a Greenwich Village townhouse and later would be apprehended in a robbery-murder case. Russo, meanwhile, was jailed in contempt of court until October 1 for refusing to testify before a Los Angeles grand jury.

J. Anthony Lukas, the *Times'* expert on and sympathizer with rebellious youth, chronicled part of Ellsberg's whirlwind travels in the *Times Magazine,* following Ellsberg from a Norman Mailer party on Long Island to Washington, Los Angeles, Chicago, New York, Cambridge, New York again and Boston.

Along the trail Ellsberg picked up awards in Washington and Chicago, along with Ramsey Clark, Joan Baez, Benjamin Spock, Wayne Morse, George Wald, David Schoenbrun and others. He lunched with Eqbal Ahmad and Staughton Lynd, dined in Greenwich Village with Abbie Hoffman and Jerry Rubin, and conferred with Howard Zinn and Noam Chomsky—a glamour tour of revolutionary romance. At the high point of the tour in Chicago, Ellsberg and Russo took a dip with a couple of nude bunnies in the heated pool at Hugh Hefner's Playboy mansion—"all antiseptic. No real sex, not even any touching"—while his wife, amused, talked with Hefner, Clark, Morse and Pete McCloskey. The article was unabashed admiration for the superstar who had realized the American dream, from antiseptic bunnies to a brief breakdown in real tears for Randy Kehler, who had gone to prison for refusing the draft.[32]

The consuming demands on Ellsberg's time made it impossible for him to meet the deadline for his book. When the *Times* broke the Pentagon Papers, literary agent David Obst, who had been editor of IPS's Dispatch News Service and had represented Seymour Hersh and his My Lai books with Random House, sounded out publishers and met with Ellsberg to see if articles he had written could be made into a book. Ellsberg had told Obst, "See what you can get, but make it clear that the money will go to charity and that we control publicity for the book."

Dell Publishing won the heated competition with an offer of $150,000, placed in escrow for the American Friends Service Committee, Ellsberg's designated charity and the Quaker affiliate of the New

Left. Dell "planned to do it under a crash program,"[33] to take advantage of *Times* publication, which had been a major media event, but Ellsberg could not write a 20,000-word introduction within the deadline, and Dell dropped the project, retrieving its money. Simon and Schuster picked up the manuscript and announced that *The Stalemate Machine* would be ready in November 1971, but Ellsberg missed that deadline too. *Papers on the War* eventually came out in 1972, selling well, but a letdown because most of its contents had been publicized by then.[34]

The *Times*, however, had no problems publishing *The Pentagon Papers*, and Bantam announced, minutes after the Supreme Court decision freeing *Times* publication, that the book would be on the stands within a week. Esther Margolis, a Bantam vice president, announced that hard-cover bidders included British, German and Scandinavian publishers but American bidders did not get the book; the *Times* published it under its Chicago subsidiary, Quadrangle.

Ten days after the Supreme Court decision, Bantam had the book on sale, and within three days had sold out two printings, or 900,000 copies. By the end of 1971, 1,500,000 copies had been sold at $2.25 for a total sale of $3,375,000.[35] The *Times* offered the Quadrangle edition at $12.50 if ordered before November publication and $15 thereafter. Seven book clubs, including Book of the Month, chose it as an alternate selection, and almost all libraries across the nation bought multiple copies.

The *Times* collected a slew of awards for its series, from the Pulitzer Prize to a citation from Associated Press and awards from the Universities of Arizona and South Carolina.

The *Times'* annual report to the Securities and Exchange Commission does not reveal its profit from *The Pentagon Papers* because balances that year are obscured by acquisition of Cowles Publication properties. However, the *Times'* 1972 revenues jumped to $329,502,000 from $231,906,552 in 1970, and profits reached $13,602,000 in 1972 compared with $9,783,694 in 1970. That some of these gains derived from *The Pentagon Papers* was evident in the addition of 21 new clients to the New York Times News Service at expensive annual fees, making a total of 360 clients including 48 subscribers in foreign countries. In 1972 Quadrangle moved to New York and became the New York Times Book Company, Inc., the house *The Pentagon Papers* built.

During the period that the *Times* was under injunction, most or all of the Pentagon study was delivered to the Soviet Embassy in Washington. The FBI, which monitors the embassy, was aware of the delivery and later determined the circumstances, but that story did not leak, and the delivery man never was named.

Almost two years later, during Watergate fever and after charges against Ellsberg were dismissed, White House aide Egil Krogh, Jr. said in an affidavit that one factor that led him to authorize the break-in at the office of Ellsberg's psychiatrist was a report from the FBI that "the so-called Pentagon Papers were in the possession of the Soviet Embassy, Washington, D.C., prior to their publication." That would indicate two sets reached the Soviet Embassy, or that Krogh meant the Soviets had the papers before all of them were published. No one showed much curiosity.

The *Times* treated the affidavit as an affront, announcing it in a peculiar headline and lead paragraph:

KROGH DISPUTED
Justice Officials Deny
His Report About
Pentagon Papers.

The story, by John Crewdson, began, "Contrary to assertions in a sworn statement by former White House aide Egil Krogh, Jr., the Federal Bureau of Investigation had knowledge in late June, 1971, that the Soviet government did not possess the Pentagon papers 'before they were published' by the *New York Times*, according to Justice Department sources."[36] The implication was that Krogh was committing perjury.

The Crewdson story did not mention until paragraph 14, on the jump page, that the Soviet Embassy did get 6,000 pages of the study delivered during the period the *Times* was under injunction (confirming Krogh), and it noted that the issue of Ellsberg's distribution of the papers was never related to aiding and abetting an enemy of the United States during Ellsberg's trial (before it was aborted).

The choice of lead paragraph was (a) absurd, in that the FBI cannot guarantee knowledge that the Soviet Union does not have something, and (b) malicious, in that the meaning of Krogh's affidavit was twisted, to say nothing of (c) suspect, in quoting the usual anonymous sources. But this *Times* story was published when Watergate dominated the news to the exclusion of everything else, and any and all stories were being stretched to add to Watergate indictments.

While the *Times* was under injunction, the Pentagon Papers affair became a double media event: the media exposed and the media reported itself exposing, generating a high-intensity publicity glare. Huge *Times* headlines reported its court battles. When other newspapers got chunks of the papers, television crews interviewed the editors and filmed the presses running.

On the eve of the Supreme Court decision an interloper moved into the center of the media-generated spotlight, Senator Maurice (Mike) Gravel, Democrat of Alaska, not regularly a colleague of Senate doves.

Gravel was almost unknown to the public. He had been voted in an informal poll of congressional staff employees the "least effective" among Senators. He had come to the Senate in 1968 by defeating the club's oldest member, the legendary pacifist Ernest Gruening, 81, who had voted with Mark Hatfield of Oregon against the Tonkin Gulf resolution and had called U.S. involvement in Vietnam aggression, a charge Gravel had exploited in their primary contest.

In the summer of 1971 Gravel irritated liberals by voting with conservatives to keep loose filibuster rules. He intended to stage a one-man filibuster against extending the draft, shooting for Strom Thurmond's filibuster record of more than 24 hours straight. Life was imitating art, specifically the 1930s movie "Mr. Smith Goes to Washington," starring James Stewart. Like Stewart, Gravel was handsome and had a lock of hair that fell over his forehead during debate. The filibuster would not stop the draft, but it would make Gravel's name a household word, and newscasters would have to learn to pronounce Gra-VEL.

Gravel's filibuster plans already were announced when something better came along at the last moment, and the filibuster succeeded beyond his hopes. He was given the Pentagon Papers, became a media hero, and entered history books with the *Senator Gravel Edition.*

While in hiding, Ellsberg learned of Gravel's filibuster plans, and on June 18, during the period that the *Times* could not publish, Gravel received a telephone call from Ellsberg's intermediaries offering him the Pentagon Papers. Gravel had acquired some young, anti-war activist staffers, including Charles L. Fishman. Gravel took delivery of the papers shortly after midnight, June 24, when they were transferred to his car trunk from another car in downtown Washington, and hid them under the bed at his Maryland home. His staff camped out in his home for several days, sorting the papers and making copies to be turned over to the media later.

Gravel arranged with Senator Alan Cranston (D-California) to remain in the Senate to preside overnight, although Cranston tried to dissuade him from his venture. The new plan was for Gravel to read the Pentagon Papers into the *Congressional Record,* preëmpting the Supreme Court decision. He had determined that his congressional immunity would protect him from prosecution, provided that he confined his exposure of the papers to an official act.

Although Gravel had prepared by studying Senate rules to prevent adjournment, and had strapped a urinal bag to his leg and had taken an enema to ready himself for 30 hours on his feet, he was balked when leading Senators insisted on making a quorum call binding and not merely demonstrative. There was no quorum available in the next three hours, during which Gravel turned on Republican whip Robert Griffin of Michigan: "You motherfucker, as long as I'm a member of the Senate, I'll never forget this."[37]

Gravel angrily left the Senate chamber, walked down the hall and convened a meeting of his obscure subcommittee on Public Buildings and Grounds, inviting media representatives to take notes. Among those present were Senators Cranston and Harold H. Hughes (D Iowa), Representative John Dow (D-New York) and a brand-new Gravel employee keeping the record, Dr. Leonard Rodberg, a Fellow of the Institute for Policy Studies. After reading for three hours, Gravel broke down weeping, consigning the rest of his speech, the Pentagon Papers, to the subcommittee's record.

The media presented Gravel as a bold and independent mind. The *Times* profile noted the "compelling political ambition" of the "impetuous. . . darkly handsome Senator." Years later, evaluations of Gravel would be less kind.[38]

On August 18, government attorneys, busy fighting subpoena challenges in the Boston grand jury investigation of Ellsberg and the *Times,* learned from reading the *Washington Post* that Gravel, through his employee Rodberg, had turned the papers over to Beacon Press of Boston.

In *More* magazine, reporter Edwin Diamond, an acquaintance of Ellsberg, noted that Ralph Stavins, Marcus Raskin and Richard Barnet of IPS had based their book on the Pentagon documents, and wrote, "Since a member of Senator Gravel's staff—a physicist by training name Leonard Rodberg—is also a Fellow of the Institute, it would be possible to conclude that Gravel got his copy from Stavins-Raskin-Barnet rather than from Ellsberg."

What no reporter knew at the time was that Gravel had written to Robert G. Dunphy, Sergeant at Arms of the Senate, on June 29, the day of his reading, saying, "Dear Mr. Dunphy: Effective this date please add to my personal staff roll the name of Dr. Leonard Rodberg. Dr. Rodberg will serve as a special assistant to me, with full access to my office, performing duties I assign and under my direct supervision."[39]

Rodberg had worked as a scientific officer in the Disarmament Administration of the State Department, where he had Top Secret clearance, at the beginning of the Kennedy administration in 1961. He had moved in 1962 to the Arms Control and Disarmament Agency, where Barnet was deputy director for political research and already disaffected from government. Rodberg was made chief of the Policy Research Office of the Science and Technology Bureau in the disarmament agency, staying until 1966. He became a visiting Fellow at IPS in 1967 and a full-time resident Fellow in 1970. He contributed to a book commissioned by Senator Edward Kennedy opposing the antiballistic missile system and edited a study criticizing the U.S. military system and policy, *The Pentagon Watchers*.[40]

On July 8, Gravel flew with Rodberg and David Obst, literary agent for Ellsberg and Seymour Hersh, to New York to confer with Simon and Schuster. A deal was almost made to publish the papers, but it fell through when television news showed lines of customers buying the *Times*-Bantam version.

In November 1971, Beacon Press, owned by the Unitarian-Universalist Association, published the four-volume *Senator Gravel Edition*, after a number of Boston-area activists had helped edit it, including Noam Chomsky. Six commercial publishers had turned it down, saying the market was saturated.

When Rodberg was subpoened on August 24, 1971, government attorneys had not managed to get any significant witness to comply with a summons. Richard Falk, who had worked on the IPS book, resisted a subpoena, and Stavins, on the verge of being forced to testify under an offer of immunity, produced an affidavit by Rodberg saying that C. R. Wallace, an electronics specialist from The Spy Shop in Washington, had found "a sophisticated new type" of wiretap on the telephone in Stavins' IPS office. The government then withdrew its offer of immunity to Stavins, restoring his Fifth Amendment privilege, and he did not testify.

Now Gravel threw a monkey wrench into the government's investigation with telling effect. He protested that his official acts were "absolutely immune to judicial inquiry," and that his congressional immunity would be violated if his staff member, Rodberg, were forced to appear before the grand jury. Three subpoenas were issued for Rodberg, continuing into October, and successively Gravel blocked them with petitions. Federal District Judge W. Arthur Garrity, Jr. finally ruled on October 4, denying Rodberg's request to quash the subpoena and denying Rodberg's claim to a news reporter's First Amendment rights, but also issuing a protective order. The judge ruled that no witness before the grand jury could be questioned about Senator Gravel's conduct, and that Rodberg could not be questioned about his own actions on June 29, when he became an employee of Gravel, or on preparations for Gravel's meeting of his subcommittee.

Although the protective order hamstrung the government attorneys, Gravel appealed to the U.S. Court of Appeals and warned he would take the case to the Supreme Court. Further complaints by Gravel's and Rodberg's attorneys caused the court to summon the government attorneys for citation of contempt because they had tried to subpoena financial records of Beacon Press in violation of the judge's restrictive rules.

In Los Angeles, meanwhile, Ellsberg's attorneys protested that evidence was being gathered in Boston to use against him in Los Angeles. By October 18, several courts were involved in the dispute over proper testimony. On October 19, the Boston district court ordered the grand jury to suspend its inquiry after only one witness, an innocent bystander who knew Ellsberg, had been questioned.

The Los Angeles case then broke down when the government informed the court that the office of Ellsberg's attorney Boudin had been the subject of an unrelated national security wiretap, and conversations relating to Ellsberg may also have been overheard inadvertently. A mistrial was declared, and jury selection began over again.

On January 18, 1972, Boston Federal Judge Anthony Julian cancelled subpoenas of Stavins, Noam Chomsky and Richard Falk, and the Boston grand jury, the only one directing inquiry into Neil Sheehan and the *Times*, ground to a halt. It had heard no pertinent evidence, and it would not reconvene the following year, after Los Angeles Judge Matthew Byrne, Jr. dismissed with prejudice all charges against Ellsberg.

A strong odor hung over the suspension of proceedings in Boston, but the media never took an interest in the Rodberg case or in the public's right to know how the Pentagon Papers were disseminated or to whom. All of the forces of the establishment were lined up against the government, and perhaps the government's Justice Department was, too. In Congress, Senator Sam Ervin had become Gravel's chief defender, saying in a speech on November 29, 1971, that the Internal Security Division of the Justice Department was engaged in "a direct and broadscale attack on the rights of all Senators...."

The Institute for Policy Studies organized an informal congressional conference to discuss the Pentagon Papers over three days, July 27 to July 29, in the House's Rayburn Building. Backers of the conference included Democratic Representatives James G. Abourezk of South Dakota; Phillip Burton and Don Edwards of California; John Conyers, Jr. of Michigan; John G. Dow, Edward I. Koch, Benjamin Rosenthal, William Fitts Ryan and Bella Abzug of New York; Michael Harrington and Father Robert Drinan of Massachusetts; Bob Eckardt of Texas; Henry Helstoski of New Jersey; Robert Kastenmeier of Wisconsin; Abner J. Mikva of Illinois; Parren Mitchell of Maryland; John F. Seiberling of Ohio; and Donald Fraser of Minnesota, along with Senator William Fulbright and former Senator Gruening, then 85.

Conference participants included Tran Van Dinh of Temple University, once in Diem's cabinet; Cynthia Fredrick of Harvard; Melvin Gurtov of Rand; Doug Hostetter, a Mennonite who had gone to Hanoi in 1970 to negotiate a Peoples' Peace Treaty; Frank Kowalsky, a former colonel and Connecticut Representative; Ngo Vinh Long of Harvard; Don Luce of International Volunteer Service, who had discovered the tiger cages; David G. Marr of Cornell; Johnathan Mirsky of Dartmouth; the Right Reverend Paul J. Moore, Jr.; General Nguyen Chanh Thi, who led the 1960 coup against Diem; and Truong Dinh Hung David, whose father was in jail in South Vietnam.

With the witnesses assembled, stars of the three-day show were Ellsberg, Russo, Raskin, Halperin, Chomsky and Fred Branfman. The proceedings were published as a book, *Anatomy of an Undeclared War,* [41] "to meet a need. . .the people generally were not informed about the actual contents of the papers and their significance." Repetitious, providing no insights, wholly one-sided, drearily propagandistic, the conference was justly ignored by the media, except for a photograph of the participants in the *Times*. But a number of the participants would turn up later on a committee that would swamp the media, at the House Judiciary Committee hearings to impeach the President.

On July 1 Kissinger had time only for a glance at the triumphant headlines in the *Times* and *Washington Post* announcing the Supreme Court's decision. Later, he would write, "The publication of these documents was selective, one-sided and clearly intended as a weapon of political warfare," [42] but he had no time to give much concentration to the prospects opened by the court's fiat. He would fly that night into a complex adventure that depended on secrecy.

Kissinger, reporters were told, was going on a fact-finding mission to South Vietnam for a few days, then stop off for talks with officials in

Thailand, India and Pakistan on his way to see Ambassador David Bruce in Paris before returning home. The scenario called for Kissinger to become slightly ill in Pakistan on July 9, while he flew secretly to Peking, and then later to lose his media companions for a few hours in Paris while he conferred secretly with North Vietnam's Le Duc Tho on July 12.

Nixon, meanwhile, was wrestling with the Pentagon Papers from another aspect: the court-freed documents threatened to accelerate leaks. In his first reaction to publication, he had assigned John Ehrlichman to find out all he could about Ellsberg and his associates, whom he considered traitors, as the White House staff privately mimicked Kissinger's rage: "Ve vill destroy him!" Nixon assigned Haldeman to consider declassifying other documents of previous administrations to see if the political assault could be leveraged back against the attackers. Nixon was aware that Johnson, in his final days, had declassified selectively memos that incriminated Hilsman in the coup against Diem, although the media had paid little attention to them in 1968.

Nixon believed that a study of the Diem coup would show that Kennedy's directions had been more explicit than was revealed in the Pentagon study. There also had never been a full explanation of Kennedy's reasons for cancelling air strikes during the Bay of Pigs invasion, and Nixon was convinced that Johnson's 1968 election-eve bombing halt was a fraud, not really based on any breakthrough toward talks with the North Vietnamese.

Haldeman called Dr. Richard Allen, a conservative scholar, to ask his advice about declassifying all historical files of earlier administrations. Allen was enthusiastic but said he could not undertake the project because his conservative philosophy would invite charges of partisanship. The declassification assignment went to David Young, of Kissinger's staff. It languished partly because the CIA would not deliver a Bay of Pigs file, reluctant to have its role re-hashed. Nixon called in Richard Helms, who objected that he did not want anyone, particularly not Howard Hunt, rummaging in the CIA's dirty linen. Hunt, demoted during the Bay of Pigs enterprise, harbored live resentment against the former CIA deputy director, General Charles Cabell, and others, over the Bay of Pigs fiasco. Telling Nixon, "I have only one President at a time. I work for you," he promised to deliver CIA files on the Bay of Pigs, but when Helms produced the material Nixon found it incomplete.

The FBI's investigation of Ellsberg meanwhile was proving a fiasco. When J. Edgar Hoover learned that FBI agents had questioned Louis Marx, Ellsberg's father-in-law, who every Christmas gave Hoover toys to pass out to children, Hoover instantly demoted C. D. Brennan, assistant director of the Intelligence Division, and transferred him to Cincinnati. FBI Deputy Director William C. Sullivan went to bat for Brennan through Ehrlichman and Attorney General Mitchell, starting a break with Hoover that would lead to Sullivan's own dismissal.[43] Ellsberg inadvertently had cleaned out a top echelon of the FBI.

Aside from not being able to find Ellsberg or pinpoint significant accomplices, and bungling the initial investigation at Rand in 1969, the FBI had let evidence that might have been crucial slip through its fingers. The FBI had located a footlocker Ellsberg had stored at the Bekins Van and Storage Company in Los Angeles, but it was gone when agents got there, apparently picked up by David Obst, who indicated that the contents were needed for Ellsberg's book, the FBI reported to Nixon.[44] Two years later a local thief burglarized Ellsberg's Mill Valley, California, home, and the loot turned out to include secret documents that were not part of the Pentagon study. Ellsberg, by then invulnerable to the courts, retained the documents.

Ehrlichman, charged with investigating Ellsberg, passed on the assignment to Egil Krogh, described by Theodore H. White as "a man of immaculate personality, behavior and character," an Eagle Scout, who would be quite out of place and inept as a detective.

Krogh moved in with David Young, empowered to recruit a staff for what was originally both a declassification and investigative unit, responsible to Ehrlichman. Checking first with John Dean, Krogh hired G. Gordon Liddy, a former FBI and Treasury investigator with whom he had worked earlier on the White House task force on drug control. Charles Colson supplied Krogh with Howard Hunt, and Krogh, Young, Liddy and Hunt, assigned to plug leaks, moved into a basement room. Young hung out the jocular sign, "Plumbers."

As the Plumbers were being organized, William Beecher broke a new story in the *Times*: "U.S. Urges Soviet to Join in a Missiles Moratorium." Like Beecher's story on the Cambodia bombing leak, it was thorough, accurate and detailed, describing U.S. strategy, tactics and the fallback position in the Strategic Arms Limitations Talks with the Soviets in Helsinki. It revealed proposals that had not yet been made to the Soviets for limited anti-ballistic missile sites at the two nations' capitals and a cutoff date for making new ICBMs. It noted that, "strictly speaking, the American proposal allows the Russians to opt for equality. . . ."[45]

Nixon was reported to be livid. With the license of the Pentagon Papers decision, the *Times* now was announcing negotiating strategy. He demanded that Haldeman administer lie detector tests to "everyone in the State Department." Haldeman limited the tests to three officials.

Colson later said Nixon told him, "We've got a counter-government here, and we've got to fight it. I don't give a damn how it is done, do whatever has to be done to stop these leaks. . . . I don't want to be told it can't be done. This government cannot survive, it cannot function, if anyone can run out and leak whatever documents he wants to. . . . I want to know who is behind this. . . ."

Nixon ordered Colson to intensify the investigation of Ellsberg and his associates. He believed that Leslie Gelb or Morton Halperin had taken sensitive documents on current matters, as well as Pentagon study documents, to the Brookings Institution, and ordered Colson to get the documents out of Brookings: "Rifle the files if necessary." Nixon also called in Krogh and gave him "a heavy charge," ordering him to put his new unit onto "finding out all it could about Mr. Ellsberg's associates and his motives."

At this point, in July 1971, organizational breakdown began at the White House. Colson had hired Hunt, who now worked for Krogh. Haldeman had assigned Jack Caulfield, a former New York police officer, to Dean's still-low-ranking legal office, at a time when Dean was soliciting assignments in the manner of a born bureaucratic empire builder. Caulfield recruited Anthony Ulasewicz, a former detective. Preliminary organization of the Committee to Re-elect the President, CRP—later unanimously called CREEP by the media and even by Congress in official documents—was under way. At a review of the first re-election campaign plans in April 1971, Nixon had noted there was no provision for intelligence, and he wanted to know what violence-prone demonstrations organizations were planning, as well as what surprises his Democrat opponents might spring on him. The Pentagon Papers had added a new element of political warfare, and now Haldeman, Ehrlichman, Dean, Colson, Krogh and later Jeb Magruder of CRP had access to the security and investigative men Liddy, Hunt, Caulfield, Ulasewicz and James McCord.

On Colson's orders, Caulfield looked over the Brookings Institution and reported that the transferred documents were in a solid safe. Colson told him to fire-bomb the place if necessary, and send in Ulasewicz with the firemen to retrieve the documents. It did not happen, and Colson swore it was a joke.

Hunt, while working for Colson, had kept his job with Mullen and Company, a public relations firm run by Robert Bennett, which also worked for the CIA and had an account from Howard Hughes. Unknown to the White House, the CIA knew through Bennett's case officer much of what the White House was doing in intelligence work, and Bennett also offered through Hunt several proposals for Plumbers' projects, suggesting a witness to the Chappaquiddick affair and pointing out that documents on the strife-riven Hughes empire were in the safe of Hank Greenspun's newspaper in Las Vegas. Haldeman later concluded that the CIA might have been involved in Watergate, through Bennett, from the beginning.

Hunt also had kept up his Cuban contacts in Miami, particularly with Bernard Barker, a Bay of Pigs organizer who had become a banker and realtor. One of Hunt's Miami Cuban contacts, Eugenio Martínez, who had been captured at the Bay of Pigs and ransomed, remained on a CIA retainer, presumably giving the CIA a doublecheck look into Plumbers' activities.

Hunt had asked CIA colleagues to supply him with a psychiatric profile of Ellsberg, meeting opposition because Ellsberg was an American citizen and outside the CIA charter. When the White House pressed, the CIA came up with the normal response of bureaucrats, innocuous reports. The CIA reported that Ellsberg apparently had acted out of his own interpretation of patriotism.

Ehrlichman, through Krogh, ordered the Plumbers to try to get Ellsberg's discussions with his psychiatrist, and Hunt recruited Barker, Martínez and Felipe de Diego for the job. Liddy and Hunt flew to Los Angeles to case the offices of Dr. Lewis Fielding in Beverly Hills.

The idea of stealing Ellsberg's confessions to his psychiatrist, while repugnant, had a certain poetic justice. Ellsberg had stolen the Defense Department's confessions to its analysts when it was delving into its past to find the reasons for its behavior, and there was a tit-for-tat quality to the burglary. Nixon, in his memoirs, wrote, "I do not believe I was told about the break-in (of Dr. Fielding's office) at the time." But if he had been informed, he "would not have considered it unthinkable." ". . . I do not accept that it was as wrong or excessive as what Daniel Ellsberg did, and I still believe that it is a tragedy of circumstances that Bud Krogh and John Ehrlichman went to jail and Daniel Ellsberg went free."

Legally, the Liddy-Hunt expedition with three Cubans to burglarize the office of Dr. Fielding, an innocent party, was a straightforward crime, and a thoroughly botched one. Liddy posed for photographs by Hunt in front of the doctor's office, and Hunt had the CIA develop the film; prints naturally were retained by the CIA. When the burglars found nothing, they wrecked the place to make it appear the work of vandals. Liddy reported back to Krogh the failure of the mission, and Ehrlichman was aghast at the vandalism. He disbanded the Plumbers, but the curtain had been raised on Watergate.

Chapter XVII
Watergate Was
a Foreign Affair

"Nul ne peut regner innocemment."

—*Louis Antoine Saint-Just*

Publication of the Pentagon Papers in June 1971, hailed as a triumph of the free press, might have taken the conduct of foreign affairs out of Nixon's hands and made him a one-term President, if it had not been for his ace in the hole. While the *Times* fought injunction in the courts, Nixon's secret negotiations with China proceeded on track, and on July 9 Kissinger was secretly in Peking talking with Premier Chou En-lai.

With both the anti-war movement and Hanoi rejuvenated by the scent of victory over the beleaguered Nixon administration, and Congress on the verge of voting a compulsory pull-out timetable, Nixon appeared on television July 15 with what Kissinger called "the announcement that shook the world." Nixon reported that Kissinger had been meeting with Chou, and the President had received an invitation to become the first American President to visit China, "before May 1972." The announcement did shake Hanoi, where the Communist leadership increasingly would be forced to choose the Soviet Union over China.

If there had been no China opening, Congress surely would have emasculated the President in 1971; there would not have been a SALT-1 agreement; South Vietnam would have fallen in the 1972 North Vietnamese offensive; the United States would have been irrelevant to its allies, and there would have been no Israel after 1973 (see Chapter XIX).

Miraculously, the China negotiations had not leaked. The secret had been kept from Hanoi and from the Soviet Union, which had delayed repeatedly a Nixon-Brezhnev summit, leaving Nixon to stew in the anti-war juice, declining to offer him a public relations forum. Now an alarmed Politburo switched to active diplomacy in the Strategic Arms Limitation Talks and renewed invitations to a summit. On October 12 simultaneous announcements in Moscow and Washington said that Nixon would become the first President to visit the Soviet Union in the spring of 1972. That was topped by simultaneous announcements in Washington and Peking that Nixon would visit China first, in February 1972. Nixon had regained from the Soviets what chess players call a tempo, moving from a defensive position to the offensive, one move ahead.

As the summits were announced, Kissinger was meeting secretly in Paris with Le Duc Tho and Xuan Thuy. A dozen such secret meetings in the last three months of 1971 were based on a U.S. eight-point peace proposal made in October that was adamantly refused by the North Vietnamese, who were gearing up a new offensive for 1972.

For the new ARVN, the greatly expanded South Vietnamese army, the 1970 incursion into Cambodia's Parrot's Beak had been a military success, the first occasion under Vietnamization to strike at fixed objectives. The Laos incursion in early 1971 had ambiguous results; it relieved pressure on South Vietnam, and the North Vietnamese in late 1971 turned their offensives on Cambodia and Laos, cowing the small armed forces of both nations by the beginning of 1972.

The position of the American military in South Vietnam was, as always, paradoxical. In Nixon, the military leaders had a President who would follow their advice without fatal delays, but at the same time their troops were diminishing steadily, cut from a peak of 541,000 men to fewer than 200,000 at the beginning of 1972.

Nixon's response to the North Vietnamese build-up near the DMZ and the North Vietnamese attacks on Cambodian and Laotian capitals was to renew bombing in late 1971 of targets in southern North Vietnam, the first since Johnson's election-eve bombing halt in 1968. At the same time that the United States resumed bombing of North Vietnam, India, which had just signed a 20-year treaty of peace, friendship and cooperation with the Soviet Union, intervened in the revolutionary situation in East Pakistan, quickly defeating the Pakistani army and creating a new nation, Bangladesh. India's attack on Pakistan brought down the government of Yahya Khan, who had been Nixon's conduit to China, and put Pakistan in the hands of Zulfikar Ali Bhutto, who, ironically, had done much to provoke the East Pakistani uprising.

Two weeks before Nixon's trip to China, the *Times* published on Page 1 a discouraging evaluation of Vietnam peace prospects under the headline, "Hanoi Rules Out a Partial Accord."[1]

The story was an interview in Paris with Xuan Thuy, chief North Vietnamese negotiator, by Richard Barnet and Peter Weiss, respectively co-director and board chairman of the Institute for Policy Studies. The two radical leftists, on behalf of the North Vietnamese, publicly withdrew the Hanoi offer of summer 1971 to separate military and political considerations in negotiations for a settlement of the war. The 2,000-word article condemned the United States for permitting the unopposed re-election of President Thieu in South Vietnam in October. The two Americans quoted Xuan Thuy as saying, "Conditions are no longer favorable for ending the war by means of a complete military withdrawal alone." The United States must give a "credible sign" that it is prepared to disengage from South Vietnam politically as well.

On that day Hanoi also rejected formally in the peace talks Nixon's eight-point plan offered in October, calling it "deceptive." The Barnet-Weiss story, elevating the authors to the position of intermediary negotiators through the *Times'* prestige, was an entirely one-sided promotion of Hanoi and condemnation of the United States' negotiating position.

In mid-February, a week before Nixon's arrival in China, the United States intensively bombed the built-up North Vietnamese base areas north of the DMZ, and on February 24, two days before Nixon signed the Shanghai Communique with Chou, the North Vietnamese walked out of the Paris peace talks protesting the renewed bombing. The American bombing of North Vietnam had not derailed Nixon's invitation to China and had not deterred the Chinese from signing the Shanghai Communique.

At the end of March 1972, the North Vietnamese launched their first all-out conventional attack of the war across the DMZ, and followed it with a tank-led invasion from Laos into the central highlands of Quang

Tri province, repeating the classic drive to cut South Vietnam in two. A third prong of the 1972 spring offensive drove in late April from Cambodia toward Saigon through An Loc. It was the first North Vietnamese big push through conventional warfare, advancing tanks and modern Soviet artillery.

The United States Army in Vietnam now had been reduced to less than one-fifth its peak strength, and the remaining GIs had only to survive a few months longer and they would be out of it. The first near-mutiny occurred on April 12, when about 50 Americans at first refused to go on patrol around Phubei, then finally went, shouting anti-war slogans. Four days later the U.S. Air Force bombed near Haiphong and Hanoi for the first time since Johnson's 1968 bombing halt. The Soviet Union protested that four of its ships were damaged in Haiphong harbor.

The renewed bombing of the north, which included B-52s after April 10, revived anti-war activists in the United States, and Defense Secretary Laird was summoned by the Senate Foreign Relations Committee. Laird said on April 19 that he did not rule out the long-delayed mining of Haiphong harbor if the North Vietnamese did not call off their invasion of the South.

In late April a South Vietnamese regiment panicked in the central highlands, some soldiers clinging to helicopter skids to escape encirclement, and by early May, Quang Tri province was lost to the invading Communist army. As in Tet 1968, the American media called it doomsday.

On May Day, Representative McCloskey, now closely identified with Ellsberg, addressed a group, Lawyers Against the War, in New York, proposing a debate in Congress over whether impeachment proceedings should be brought against Nixon. McCloskey planned to challenge Nixon for the Republican nomination in August.

Two days later an enormous anti-war demonstration in Washington turned violent. A coalition of anti-war movements, familiarly called the Mayday Tribe by the *Times*, pledged to bring government operations to a halt.

The Nixon administration had prepared for the Mayday Tribe demonstration on a war footing, with Attorney General Richard Kleindienst in overall charge, bringing in federal troops, employing every intelligence group in the capital to pinpoint locations of each of the demonstrating organizations. Overhead in a helicopter, White House aides John Ehrlichman and John Dean looked down and filmed burning cars in Georgetown, rock-throwing battles and police chasing demonstrators with night sticks.

Rennie Davis, of the Chicago Seven, was arrested and held on

$25,000 bail, and the FBI picked up Abbie Hoffman, provisionally freed from his Chicago Seven conviction, charging him with crossing state lines to incite a riot.

The day before, J. Edgar Hoover had died, and the White House received reports that demonstrators would raise a Viet Cong flag at the Justice Department, center of mourning for the original G-man. Inspired by the construction workers' attack on anti-war demonstrators in New York City, Howard Hunt brought a handful of Cuban friends from Miami to Washington, where they flailed into demonstrators at the Justice Department. Daniel Ellsberg and Noam Chomsky were among those "clubbed and Maced," according to the *Times*.

Metropolitan Police grabbed the Cubans, presumably Felipe de Diego and Reinaldo Pico, but "a man in a gray suit," Howard Hunt, stepped in to tell police they were "anti-Communists and good men," and they were released. De Diego and Pico were not hired thugs; both had fought and been captured at the Bay of Pigs, had an abiding hatred of communism, and to them prison was not an abstraction. If they had swung on Ellsberg and Chomsky, doubtless President Thieu and General Ky would have done the same. Given an opportunity later, during the Watergate prosecutions, to send the Cubans to jail for the assaults, a court declined.

Ellsberg and Chomsky, neither seriously hurt, were arrested along with elderly Dr. Benjamin Spock, joining about 10,000 who were seized in the greatest mass arrest in the capital's history, some of the overflow being penned in the Robert Kennedy stadium. Most demonstrators were freed if they had $10 to forfeit, and later others were released if they would give a name and submit to fingerprinting and photography, with a judge's assurance that the records would not be turned over to the FBI and would be destroyed if the demonstrators were not rearrested. As in most prosecutions of anti-war demonstrators, the legal follow-up lapsed, and all of the demonstrators went free.

Senator Edward Kennedy charged that the Nixon administration had forced the Metropolitan Police to make the unprecedented mass arrests, a charge that the Metropolitan Police chief denied. The administration did urge other police departments to follow the lead of the D.C. police in putting down demonstrations.

Thousands of demonstrators stayed on in Washington for more than a week. As scattered disorders continued, Nixon announced on television on May 8 that U.S. planes were mining North Vietnamese ports, including Haiphong, and fighter-bombers struck targets in the Hanoi area.

In the House of Representatives a group of leftist Democrats introduced the first resolution to impeach Nixon, House Resolution 976, on May 10. Sponsors were Representatives John Conyers, Jr. of Michigan; Bella Abzug, William F. Ryan, Shirley Chisholm and Charles Rangel of New York; Ronald Dellums of California; Louis Stokes of Ohio and Parren Mitchell of Maryland, some of them earlier participants in the Institute for Policy Studies' congressional caucus on the Pentagon Papers. Their resolution was referred to the House Judiciary Committee, where no action was taken, although a number of the sponsors were members of the committee. Abzug also led a vigil of 19 congressmen joining demonstrators in a kind of asylum from the police.

At the end of the month the *Times* published an advertisement over two pages calling for Nixon's impeachment, paid for by the National Committee for Impeachment, which reproduced the House resolution charging Nixon with crimes against humanity.

The ad launching the impeachment movement listed its executive committee as Randolph Phillips, Richard A. Falk, Robert L. Bobrick, Elizabeth A. Most, Alfred Hassler and Ron Young; its honorary chairman was Ernest Gruening, who also had served as a sponsor for the IPS caucus on the Pentagon Papers.

The ad, with its Presidential seal and official-looking headline, "A Resolution to Impeach Richard Nixon as President of the United States," looked rather classy, so the *Times* reproduced it in photocopy to illustrate a news commentary by freelance writer Bernard M. Collier, although it was unusual for the *Times* to publish commentary from a freelancer. The commentary mentioned that the ad so angered *Times* pressmen that they demanded it not be run and delayed the first-edition press run for 15 minutes. It added that the next day an aide to Nixon appeared outside the newspaper and conveyed "the personal thanks of the President to the pressmen."

A caption under the four-column photocopy of the ad said: "A resolution, introduced in Congress May 10 and reproduced in an ad last week, above, has created a furor. Almost everybody agrees it has little chance this year. But if President Nixon is re-elected, says one observer, 'people will start to hear a hell of a lot more about impeachment.' "

This was before the bungled Watergate burglary, but the ubiquitous *Times* source—one observer—knew what he was talking about. Thus did the *Times*, editorializing surreptitiously in the guise of a news commentary by a freelancer, give notice that Nixon would be impeached, if re-elected, because he mined Haiphong harbor and threatened to win the war. To anyone looking for a foreign affairs motive for Watergate, here was the first smoking gun.

Columnist Anthony Lewis, meanwhile, had achieved a long-sought goal after years of reporting the Vietnam war from London; he got to Hanoi in the footsteps of Salisbury, while Salisbury himself was in Pyongyang, North Korea, to interview Kim Il Sung.

A foreign correspondent going to a new country for the first time usually can be assured of one of life's rewards. What is new is stimulating; things never are the way he had imagined them from previous reporting by others, and there is always something unexpected to learn. Lewis was cheated of the reward; things in Hanoi were exactly as he had expected them to be, and his dispatches read like reruns of Salisbury's dispatches of six years earlier. The same hotel chambermaids and waitresses grabbed the same helmets and rifles and took the same positions in the hotel garden looking for American planes; almost a carbon copy of Salisbury's 1966 report.[2]

Instead of a photograph of an appealing Oriental child in front of a dilapidated, and perhaps bombed, building, Lewis' first dispatch was accompanied by a photograph of Cuban surgeons operating on an eight-year-old boy reportedly injured by bombing in Namdinh City, south of Hanoi. Once again, though, bombing did not bother the sturdy North Vietnamese. As in Salisbury's dispatches, Lewis' reports did not actually reveal widespread damage, and Lewis did not report being bombed; there never would be carpet bombing of Hanoi.

Two weeks after the mining of Haiphong and targeted bombing of Hanoi, Nixon arrived in Moscow for talks with Leonid Brezhnev. Four days later, Nixon and Brezhnev signed the first preliminary strategic arms limitation agreements, a treaty limiting anti-ballistic missile systems, and a treaty limiting the number of launchers. While defective and limited, and accompanied by a three-year agreement to sell U.S. grain to the Soviet Union which proved disadvantageous to the United States, the agreements broke a log jam on arms negotiations that could have led to real progress by the end of Nixon's second term. Nixon also addressed the Soviet Union on television in a speech that even the *Times* called effective.

During Nixon's Moscow visit an episode occurred that surely was a high point in Nixon's life. As Kissinger described the occasion, Brezhnev "kidnapped the President of the United States" to his dacha about 40 miles from Moscow, leaving Secret Servicemen and others in Nixon's party scrambling to catch up. At the dacha the Soviets had planned an intimidation session.

Kissinger and his aides Winston Lord and John Negroponte arrived as witnesses in time to feel the air filled with electric confrontation. For three hours, Brezhnev, Kosygin and President Nikolai Podgorny in turn unleashed bullying diatribes against Nixon's criminal, ruthless and doomed aggression in Vietnam. Nixon listened stoically until Brezhnev warned, "There may come a critical moment for the North Vietnamese when they will not refuse to let in forces of other countries to act on their side." Nixon interrupted, "That threat doesn't frighten us a bit, but go ahead and make it."[3]

At 11 p.m., three hours after dinner should have begun, Nixon cut it short. He said he had withdrawn a half million soldiers from Vietnam, shown great restraint, but the North Vietnamese with their Soviet equipment had invaded South Vietnam, killed 30,000 South Vietnamese civilians, and they would not get away with it. His decision had been made in cold objectivity, although he wanted peace as much as the American people wanted it. Nixon advised the Soviets to get the North Vietnamese out of their intransigent stance. Kosygin told Nixon that a new peace proposal was needed, and Nixon replied coldly that the discussion had gone on long enough.

The meeting adjourned to dinner, where it suddenly became convivial, both sides joking and storytelling. Kosygin toasted the "good omen" that they could exchange thoughts freely. Kissinger believed the attacks had been a charade, to provide a transcript that could be sent to the North Vietnamese. Nixon had kept his tempo, staying a move ahead, and he knew that, with the usual cosmetic changes that come in last-ditch negotiations, he could stand on the SALT position that Kissinger was negotiating.

In private conversations with liberal friends later, Kissinger would ridicule Nixon's inflated ego and his satisfaction in retelling his stalwart role in the dacha confrontation. But both Kissinger and Nixon knew that a new element had entered U.S.-Soviet relations. All of the conflicting interests and mistrust remained, but the confrontation had stripped away pretense. For the first time American and Soviet leaders could speak to each other candidly, if warily. It had been a barroom brawl at the nuclear level, with a satisfactory outcome.

Nixon had now racked up a string of improbable actions that directly contradicted the advice of all of his critics. He had rescued King Hussein of Jordan without firing a shot at a time of turmoil in the United States when he should have been immobilized; he had renewed the bombing of North Vietnam even after publication of the Pentagon Papers; he had devalued the dollar in an election year, staving off growing chaos in world payments; he had opened a new era in Chinese-American relations, and he had mined Haiphong harbor without the Soviets cancelling his summit, to bring back an initial arms limitation agreement. The slight advantage of his tempo had grown to a stark advantage; he was at least one pawn up on the Soviets. To part of the media, it was baffling and infuriating. All of the things Nixon had done could not have been done by any of his prospective opponents in that election year, and the moves he made all had been called impossible.

At the end of May, as Nixon flew home from Moscow, a group of burglars directed by G. Gordon Liddy and E. Howard Hunt, Jr. from his Committee to Re-elect the President slipped into the Watergate office building in Washington, bugged two telephones in the offices of the Democratic National Committee and stole a number of documents. They were not detected, but the bug on the telephone of Democratic National Committee Chairman Larry O'Brien did not work, possibly because the Democrats' security men detected it and replaced it with a cheaper, low-powered transmitter that was found later in the phone by police. The burglars would return to fix it.

Nixon returned to Washington on June 1, speaking of a basis for a new relationship with the Soviet Union. Before the month was over he could announce that the Paris peace talks, which had been suspended in March after the North Vietnamese walkout, would resume. He had bombed the North Vietnamese back to the table, with a crucial assist by the South Vietnamese army.

At *The New York Times*, the doctrine that South Vietnam could not survive had appeared to be coming true during the first stages of the North Vietnamese offensive of 1972. The *Times Magazine* planned to publish two articles on how the unified Vietnam might look, one article positive, one negative. In London, Sir Robert Thompson received a request from the *Times* for a "2,500-word scenario on what will happen when North Vietnam takes over South Vietnam to include what you see as possible slaughter, but also to go beyond that to describe the kind of government that would be set up. . . . This would be used as companion piece for a more benign view of the probable outcome of the North's takeover."

Thompson, unconvinced that the South was losing, sent in August the requested article, "There Would Have Been a Bloodbath," remarking to the *Times* editors that the South Vietnamese army was gaining, and the question was "fast becoming hypothetical." Familiar with the *Times*, Thompson used no U.S. administration sources for his article, to avoid their being disparaged, but quoted almost entirely from Communist sources to buttress his bloodbath thesis and to underline that the Communists would, quoting Douglas Pike, "create a silence, and the world would call it peace."

On September 13, Thompson received payment for the article and a note from the *Times* apologizing that "we will not be publishing your article. We felt that your thinking, as exemplified in this piece, did not fully carry out our proposed thesis. . . ." Bitterly, Thompson noted that he never learned if the *Times* published a "more benign" prospectus "because I have the good fortune to live in an area where *The New York Times* is not available." Because he was worried at the "abysmal ignorance of the nature and course of the war and of what was happening" in media coverage, Thompson expanded the article into the book, *Peace Is Not at Hand*, published in London but not picked up by American publishers.

ARVN, humiliated through the North Vietnamese spring offensive, when two district capitals and a whole province were lost, had opened a counter attack in the central highlands in mid-May, at the time of the first impeachment move against Nixon. In June, they drove the North Vietnamese invaders back from Saigon into Cambodia, just after Nixon's talks in Moscow. In late August, a heavy U.S. air attack on five targets at Haiphong and a major army base 40 miles north of Hanoi destroyed 96 buildings in localized devastation on a World War II scale. By mid-September, ARVN had recaptured the Quang Tri Citadel, in effect winning the mini-war that the *Times* had declared lost. Coincident with the heavy bombing at the end of August, the White House announced that U.S. troop strength would be reduced to 27,000 men by the end of 1972, mostly maintenance men. Except for pilots, the U.S. combat role would be over.

Sir Robert Thompson, who was being consulted by Nixon, said later,

> Whatever the critics may have said about pacification and Vietnamization, the North Vietnamese and the Viet Cong understood that it was working. . . . We knew (the spring offensive) was coming. We didn't know exactly how much or exactly when and where. They put in twelve divisions. Now, naturally, when you do an initial attack with twelve divisions, you get some initial successes. Everyone thought the South Vietnamese were going to collapse, but even in the north, where the third division gave way, the North Vietnamese only made eighteen miles in three weeks, which isn't exactly an electric advance. . . the South Vietnamese held in the north; they held at Kontum and they held at
>
> An Loc. Now, the fact that they held on the ground made it possible for American air power then to inflict enormous casualties on the attacking forces, because here we were dealing with mass troops, and we were dealing with troops using T-54 tanks and all sorts of things that are targets for an air force. So the casualties in-

flicted on the North were twice what I had expected. . .if you
were going to keep T-54 tanks going, and if you were going to
keep 130-mm guns firing, you had to have trucks and trucks and
trucks. . .absolutely made for an air force to hit. The invasion
was smashed by American air power.[4]

On September 2, David Dellinger of Chicago Seven fame and Cora
Weiss, wife of IPS's Peter Weiss, announced they would fly to Hanoi
and bring back three American prisoners of war. It was the third occasion that Dellinger had been involved in such a gesture, each time freeing three men, always at a time when the fortunes of Hanoi were
sinking, to give the American anti-war movement credibility. It was expert public relations, worthy of the mind of Dellinger's friend Wilfred
Burchett, who was said to have suggested it to the North Vietnamese.

By October 21, 1972, North Vietnamese negotiators in Paris said
they were ready to accept a ceasefire, while still disputing provisions
for it. On October 26 Hanoi radio announced that agreement had been
reached on a nine-point peace program, and in Washington, Kissinger
told reporters, "Peace is at hand."

In South Vietnam, President Thieu, who already had broadcast to
his nation that the terms were unacceptable, declared in a National Day
speech on November 1 that the nine-point agreement "meant a surrender of the South Vietnamese people to the Communists." Nixon spoke
on television the next day, five days before the U.S. election, to say
that a Vietnamese ceasefire would be signed "only when the agreement is right." In Paris, Xuan Thuy, to hold off renewed bombing, said
the North Vietnamese would return to the table if the United States
were "serious," but he had no intention of improving the ceasefire
terms.

Thieu could not accept a ceasefire in place, leaving the North Vietnamese in South Vietnam, with both sides limited to replacing troops
on a one-for-one basis. He was proving not to be an American puppet.

What was precisely in the minds of Nixon and Kissinger never was
determined. Tad Szulc, writing in *Foreign Policy*, put most of the responsibility for accepting a defective ceasefire on Kissinger, reporting
that Kissinger had told him that Vietnam had to be settled at that time;
it was essentially a cruel sideshow to the larger objectives of American
foreign policy (detente and arms limitation). Szulc noted that General
Haig looked with alarm at Kissinger's negotiations.[5]

Professor Warren Nutter, Nixon's Assistant Secretary of Defense for
International Security Affairs, came to believe later that Nixon, too,
wanted a fig leaf for a pull-out, to cover a fundamental change in foreign policy posture geared to the elections.[6]

Robert Thompson, however, thought that "the rock was Nixon...Kissinger would have signed that initial agreement before the actual election in order to ensure the election....Nixon refused. He said it wasn't good enough, because the enforcement clauses were not there, or not sufficient enforcement clauses. In fact, the enforcement clauses never really got into the agreement."[7]

The reason the ceasefire remained defective was the mounting pressure of the Watergate investigations and congressional abandonment of Nixon.

Nixon won re-election by a landslide on November 7, George McGovern and his running mate, Sargent Shriver, carrying only Massachusetts and the District of Columbia, where the heavily Democratic government bureaucracy contributed to the 60% majority in the district, just the opposite from the national score. It was later determined in a study by S. Robert Lichter and Stanley Rothman that news media personnel in the higher income brackets—the Eastern establishment media elite—who would try Nixon in the press, voted 81% for McGovern and 19% for Nixon.[8]

Five days after the election, the U.S. Army turned over its headquarters at Longbinh to the South Vietnamese army, ending its role except for a small number of pilots and 19,000 GIs who remained temporarily to continue maintenance.

With the virtual end of U.S. military presence in South Vietnam, North Vietnam stepped up infiltration, returning to guerrilla warfare. On December 17, the U.S. Air Force heavily bombed north of the DMZ and again mined Haiphong harbor.

The war in Vietnam, close to being finished, had taken a quantum jump in technology. In June 1972, the U.S. for the first time had used laser-guided "smart bombs," destroying a hydroelectric plant and a new steel mill in North Vietnam. The smart bombs meant that targets like bridges, which had defied hundreds of fighter-bomber sorties, henceforth could be taken out with a single sortie. Hanoi, meanwhile, had received large numbers of more sophisticated SAM missiles, making high-altitude B-52s vulnerable for the first time. On December 18, Nixon announced an end to the bombing halt he had ordered in September when negotiations had promised to resume. He said the bombing would continue until a settlement was signed. For the first time, B-52s struck the Hanoi area, and in ten days of what the media called "the Christmas bombings," 16 B-52s were shot down as Soviet-directed North Vietnamese crews fired more than 1,200 SAM missiles.

Nixon announced a new bombing halt on December 30; the Paris peace talks would resume on January 8 with the reluctant South Vietnamese participating. Nixon had for the second time bombed the North Vietnamese back to the table. On January 23, Kissinger and Le Duc Tho initialed a settlement agreement, still with a ceasefire-in-place, and on January 27 the ceasefire was signed formally by four parties, William Rogers for the United States, Nguyen Duc Trinh for North Vietnam, Tran Van Lam for South Vietnam and Mme. Nguyen Thi Binh for the National Liberation Front. All American prisoners of war were to be released in 60 days. Kissinger visited Hanoi on February 10, and in March the last of 589 surviving American prisoners were released, just before the last GIs left South Vietnam on March 29.

It was an anticlimactic, foreboding end to the war, with both sides violating the ceasefire in minor incidents and Hanoi violating the infiltration ban from the beginning. South Vietnam remained precariously dependent on further U.S. material aid, on the implied threat of available U.S. air power and on the thin hope that Hanoi needed the U.S. economic aid provided for under the agreement. Nixon and Thieu held a two-day conference in early April, Thieu pledging never to ask for U.S. troops, both aware that there probably would be at least one more battlefield go-around.

The world greeted the provisional end of the Vietnam War with skepticism, Robert Thompson regretting that the Americans had not shown a little more stamina to reach the almost-attained Korean solution. When Thieu flew home from Washington, Nixon asked West German Chancellor Brandt to give Thieu's international standing a boost by seeing him en route, but when Thieu landed at Bonn-Cologne airport, he found that Brandt would not see him.

For years the American media had been saturated with Vietnam, but as the story appeared to dwindle in April 1973, the media already had forgotten it; absorbed in the new obsession, Watergate.

The rest of the world never could understand Watergate, not because only Americans were capable of understanding true democracy at work, but because it was so out of proportion to the momentous world events surrounding it. To the rest of the world, the parochial business of Watergate forced Nixon into the fatally flawed Vietnam settlement. Viewed from outside the United States, the two-year ordeal of Watergate was an orgy of self-serving politicians, who would turn out to be midgets when they took power, venting their wrath that Nixon had been nearing successful conclusion of the frustrating war that they had said could not be concluded. The Watergate prosecutions had nothing to do with preserving democracy, which was downgraded by both sides in the political warfare.

While Nixon could show some gains in dealing with Mao and Brezhnev, and the revolution at home appeared to be abating from its high point following the 1970 Cambodia incursion, Nixon's status had risen only with the electorate going into the 1972 election campaign; he was at loggerheads with the media and with the Washington bureaucracy.

The Justice Department, after a string of Attorneys General from Robert Kennedy to Ramsey Clark, was peopled with liberal Democrats. The Nixon administration found it almost impossible to prosecute violent anti-war demonstrators, while the Justice Department found it easy to prosecute corporations in antitrust suits, against administration policy. While Nixon complained to Attorney General Mitchell that his department was politicized against the administration, the *Times* took the offensive against Mitchell with charges that he was politicizing the department by pressing suits, against the will of department officials, in prosecutions of anti-war demonstrators. When Mitchell left Justice to become head of the Committee to Re-elect the President, the *Times* attacked both him and his successor, Richard Kleindienst, as unfit to serve.

Ellsberg, for a time the revolution's spearhead, had weapons at his disposal unavailable to Mao or Brezhnev, including a good deal of sympathy within the Justice Department and a media committed to defending the publication of the Pentagon Papers and therefore their agent of publication.

There never was much chance that Ellsberg could be convicted of anything. A typical media comment was that of Marquis Childs: "...no one can doubt that if Ellsberg and Russo are convicted on one or more of the 15 counts of the indictments and their convictions upheld by the Supreme Court, a shadow of secrecy and suppression will be felt at every level of government." The Supreme Court, although its ruling on the Pentagon Papers had been confined to barring prior restraint, would be in an awkward position ruling on any conviction of Ellsberg.

Accordingly, the trial of Ellsberg and Russo was delayed for a year and a half and mistrials were declared twice after interventions by the Justice Department.

At Ellsberg's first trial, after lengthy jury selection and technical challenges of the prosecutor's behavior, Judge William Matt Byrne, Jr. declared a mistrial in December 1972, when the Justice Department confirmed that two national security wiretaps could have prejudiced the trial. Ellsberg's attorneys also represented the new Marxist government of Salvador Allende in Chile, as well as having been forced to register as agents of the Cuban government (under protest), and the FBI had put a tap on the Chilean Embassy, which was in communication with attorney Boudin's office. A tap may also have been on the law office phone, and Ellsberg, Russo and 17 of their attorneys sued the government in a civil suit for almost $1 million in damages, a suit that dwindled away but cast a cloud over the second trial.

By the time Ellsberg's second trial got under way, the Ervin Committee was preparing a television trial of Watergate witnesses, and Ellsberg, in the light of Watergate publicity, was more a media hero than ever. His trial was attended regularly by a cheering section, and witnesses trouped to the stand to testify that he had revealed no vital secrets. Witnesses included Arthur Schlesinger, Jr., John Kenneth Galbraith, Theodore Sorensen, McGeorge Bundy, Robert Manning, Tom Hayden, retired Admiral Gene LaRocque—head of the (anti-Pentagon) Center for Defense Information and the McGovern campaign's military adviser; Representative McCloskey and Morton Halperin, who took on the role of Ellsberg's trial aide. Some government attorneys had wanted to make Halperin a co-defendant.

Testimony by Halperin, Gelb and Warnke was mutually contradictory over whether all had authorized Ellsberg to read the Pentagon documents, technically Warnke's copy. A furor arose over whether the government had tried to suppress the testimony of CIA-analyst Samuel Adams, whose report had been the original source of the "falsified" estimate of enemy strength in South Vietnam in the early Ellsberg leaks. While trial testimony of government witnesses pointed out that the issue of Adams' estimate was a dispute over whether to count Viet Cong noncombattant cadres, not a falsification, the point was lost on reporters at the trial.[9]

Nevertheless, some testimony incriminating Ellsberg was permitted at the trial. Ellsberg had signed eight pledges not to divulge secrets, including two while taking the papers to Rand as a courier that said, "I have requested and been granted custody of the following OSD Task Force Documents...Top Secret...I certify I will retain the above documents in my custody until returned to storage and that I will not reproduce or alter any part or parts thereof."

The first major government witness might have influenced the jury under normal circumstances. Lieutenant General William E. DePuy, who had been a division commander in Vietnam, said there was no doubt that documents Ellsberg had caused to be printed in the *Times* endangered national security.

DePuy said the Wheeler Report following Tet 1968, Ellsberg's original leak, was an unusual document:

> It is a report and an assessment, analysis, if you will, or a critique may be a better word, of the North Vietnamese and Viet Cong Tet

attack in some detail by the senior uniformed officer of the United States, based on his conversations with the high command in Vietnam. . . .

He analyzes and states the conditions of the Vietnamese forces, the weaknesses and strengths of the attack, the consequences of that attack, by so doing provides information which the high command in Hanoi and the North Vietnamese command in South Vietnam certainly would find interesting and useful to them, particularly if they had any intention of doing it again, and they did it again, in 1972.

DePuy quoted from the Wheeler Report, "(If the) enemy synchronizes an attack against the Khe Sanh/Hue-Quang Tri areas with an offensive in the highlands, while keeping the pressure on throughout the remainder of the country, MACV (Military Assistance Command Vietnam) will be hard pressed to meet adequately all threats."

DePuy said the Wheeler Report was more valuable to the North Vietnamese than their own intelligence because, "It is the difference between the value to us of a similar report written by General Giap, if we could get one, as opposed to an analysis by the Central Intelligence Agency reading the Hanoi newspapers and receiving and recording reports from American commanders."

The next government witness, Brigadier General Paul F. Gorman, who had served two tours in Vietnam, was on the Paris peace talks team and had worked on the Pentagon Papers, said the volumes contained material useful to foreign nations for both intelligence and counter-intelligence. The sections on the overthrow of Diem gave "a documented insight into American intelligence operations" and showed weakness in U.S.-South Vietnam relations that might be exploited.

Using a slide projector, Gorman reviewed several documents that appeared innocuous, then put together an intelligence analysis from them:

What this information would tell an analyst in 1969 (when Ellsberg copied the papers) is that for a period of six years, while the senior U.S. commander in the Pacific was looking at the possibility of having to put American forces into Southeast Asia by a plan numbered N. 32, throughout all of those six years a place called Danang was central to that planning, so central indeed that there were seven plans drawn up by his headquarters alone or for action in concert with our allies. . . .

This information would document the fact that Danang was, in 1965, a key location for American planning, particularly that American planning that had to do with the contingency of an overt invasion of South Vietnam by the North Vietnamese or by Chinese Communist forces...since the documents are numbered and named, he would have an item of information with which to trigger his intelligence....

Some intriguing testimony posed a question that never was answered as the trial ended abruptly. It suggested that Ellsberg, after receiving ten volumes of the papers on February 28, 1969, then picking up eight more on April 29, 1969, never did turn them into the Rand Corporation until May 20, 1970, when he suddenly dumped the 18 volumes on the desk of a colleague, Richard Moorsteen, after learning that the FBI was investigating him. The 18 volumes never had been checked in with Rand's officer in charge of classified documents. The documents officers, Jan Butler, neglected to log in the documents until December 29, 1970, so that when the FBI arrived, they were told that there were no such documents registered there.

Unresolved also was the question of where Ellsberg had been on the four days, April 29 to May 2, that he took to travel from Washington to Santa Monica with the eight volumes. Just before picking them up, he had attended the anti-war convention in Haverford, Pennsylvania, talking with anti-war activists, some of whom had been in contact with Communist officials in Prague and Havana. Two of the anti-war activists lived in Denver, where Ellsberg apparently stopped off while carrying the eight volumes.

In his trial testimony, Ellsberg said at first that he had left Washington on April 29 but was confused as to exactly where he went. A recess was called; Ellsberg presumably looked at his records to refresh his memory, and questioning resumed.

Under questioning by Special Prosecutor David R. Nissen, Ellsberg said:

> I apparently, clearly, left on the 29th, and that was not when I planned to leave, according to my trip report when I left Washington, so—when I left Los Angeles, and I can't make—we had a brief moment in the lunch recess to look at them (his ticket and itinerary), and I can't entirely resolve that. But the plan appears clear that I—ticket—that I left on the 29th, went through Denver, came back on the 30th to Los Angeles.

Nissen said, "I'm asking you, do you recall the trip, not what you might have looked at on the record."

Ellsberg said, "I do, of course, recall picking up the documents, and I recall spending—I now recall spending the night with John Vann (in Denver). Earlier I would not have placed that visit with John Vann on that date, but when I looked at the record I remembered it."

Nissen asked if Ellsberg had seen the two anti-war activists in Denver while he was visiting Vann. Ellsberg said he had not.

Nissen suggested that Ellsberg could not have seen Vann on that occasion, because Vann was not on leave, but in Vietnam. Now Ellsberg remembered. He had stopped off in Denver, but he had not stayed with Vann, and then went on to Los Angeles the next day.[10]

The *Times*, having been the major player in revealing the Pentagon Papers, might have been expected to make a show of objectivity by using Associated Press or United Press International reports of the trial, but instead sent reporter Martin Arnold to demolish the prosecution. Although Ellsberg tripped and stumbled in his testimony, he was a master of eloquence in the *Times*.

Arnold reported accurately that defense counsel Boudin set out to make General Gorman "if possible, not Mr. Chips, but Colonel Blimp, and at the same time destroy his basic premise" (that the Pentagon Papers were valuable to the enemy).

Arnold already had done his bit toward making Gorman a comical character:

> The general, a former combat leader in Vietnam and the top military man on the Defense Department task force that put together the Pentagon Papers, also served as a history professor at West Point. And his response to questions is delivered in a lecture-like manner—articulate, ordered, at great length, accompanied with skillful gestures of his hands to give meaning to his words. Today, for example, his answers were timed variously at six minutes, five minutes, seven minutes and five minutes. Yesterday he gave an answer so lengthy that he ended with the words, 'Thank you,' as a teacher might end a lecture on the class syllabus.[11]

Arnold awarded the debate points to Boudin, reporting that when Boudin said disdainfully, "America is leaking," " the jurors, as one, broke into loud laughter."[12]

There was, in fact, little point in reporters noting in their stories testimony damaging to Ellsberg. Eclipsed by the Ervin Committee's hearings on Watergate, the trial droned on, looking for a way to end, when the Watergate testimony provided it.

Chapter XVIII
Wallowing in Watergate

"Nightly and daily go they about me
Seeking how they may take me in the snare,
And by false witness seek to destroy me,
Make me a prisoner,
Then would they shout for joy!"

—*Psalmus Hungaricus*

Watergate, an apartment-hotel complex in Washington, lent its name to the media to signify an encyclopedic compendium of offenses and gauche behavior, real or disproven, committed by Nixon and his staff, ranging from abuse of power and obstruction of justice to opening aspirin bottles with one's teeth.

Space permits only a summary of the high points of Watergate. In the *New York Times Index of 1973,* "Watergate" covers 90 pages of fine print, equal to a normal book of more than 800 pages. Each index page lists about 38 stories, and during three months of the Ervin Committee hearings many thousands of words were printed each day of testimony and document texts, so that the average story that year probably exceeded 1,000 words. At a minimum estimate, the *Times* published three million words on Watergate in 1973, or 30 books of 100,000 words each. The *Index of 1974* did it all over again, 89 pages of fine print.

In early 1973, the last U.S. troops left Vietnam; it appeared that the war might be over, and the media revolution, like Hanoi, did not accept the outcome. As the *Times* had warned on June 4, 1972, two weeks before the word "Watergate" surfaced in the press, there would be "a hell of a lot of talk about impeachment" if Nixon won re-election in November 1972.

Several "Watergate" charges have been mentioned in earlier chapters: the national security wiretaps of 18 persons after the Cambodia bombing leak, failed attempts of IRS audits, the discarded Huston Plan and the Fielding burglary after the Pentagon Papers were published. Chronologically, well before the bungled Watergate burglary, the next charge was an alleged bribery attempt that was aborted.

The ITT Case

The United States balance of payments problem, resulting in devaluation of the dollar in Nixon's first term, reinforced Nixon's belief that decades of trust-busting had gone too far. American companies were being pushed out of world markets by government-sheltered monopolies in other countries. Nixon gave orders that companies were to be prosecuted and broken up only when they violated laws protecting fair competition, not simply for being big, a philosophy later adopted by the Reagan administration.

Three anti-trust suits were conducted against ITT, an international conglomerate, and a settlement divested ITT of some of its holdings. In one of the suits, a court dismissed the Justice Department's complaint, and Assistant Attorney General Richard McLaren appealed, another case of the bureaucracy overruling Nixon's orders. Nixon angrily telephoned Deputy Attorney General Richard Kleindienst and ordered him to withdraw the appeal and fire McLaren if necessary. Mitchell warned Nixon that Kleindienst might resign himself, and there would be hearings in a Democrat-controlled Congress, so Nixon desisted. Ehrlichman kept pressure on Justice Department officials, but McLaren persisted, and ITT was further divested of Avis Auto Rental and Levitt builders in a negotiated settlement. For ITT, it could have been worse.

After the ITT case was settled, columnist Jack Anderson reported on February 29, 1972, that ITT lobbyist Dita Beard, in a memo purportedly written to ITT Vice President W. R. Merriam, claimed to have arranged the ITT settlement in exchange for $400,000 and services to the GOP Convention in San Diego, where ITT owned Harbor Island

Hotel, a prospective site for GOP Convention headquarters. Mrs. Beard read Anderson's report and was promptly hospitalized in Denver with a heart attack.

The next day Anderson charged that Kleindienst, who had just become Attorney General as Mitchell moved to the Committee to Re-Elect the President, had lied about ITT during his Senate confirmation hearings. Kleindienst insisted that his hearings be reopened to clear his name, facing a hostile panel in an election year that included leading Democrats Teddy Kennedy and Birch Bayh. The *Times* editorialized that Kleindienst was a mediocre lawyer, a shady character, and should not be Attorney General anyway.

To Charles Colson of Nixon's staff, the Beard memo appeared full of error, a phoney. True, Nixon had wanted the convention in San Diego, believing it might swing California in a close race. ITT, for its own promotional reasons, had offered $400,000, later cut to $100,000, not to the GOP National Committee but to the San Diego Tourist Bureau for convention facilities. Colson, believing the Beard memo a forgery, sent Howard Hunt, disguised in an auburn wig he had borrowed from the CIA (to the media, a red wig), to interview Beard at her bedside. She denied writing the memo. John Dean meanwhile had borrowed the original memo from the Justice Department's L. Patrick Gray III, who had first given it to the FBI to be analyzed, then recalled it.

Two document analysts hired by ITT on the recommendation of the CIA-connected public relations man Robert Bennett examined copies of the document and called it a forgery, written on Beard's typewriter but seven months later than its date. FBI technicians, when they finally got the memo to study, could not brand it false. Mark Felt, who had been jumped over William C. Sullivan at the FBI before Sullivan was fired, began the first of a series of jousts with John Dean, who wanted the FBI report reworded to stress doubt of the document's authenticity, since the FBI could not lable it genuine. Felt believed the document was genuine,[1] whether Beard's claim was authentic or only making points with her boss, and Hoover was incensed when Felt told him Dean had used pressure, saying the request came "direct from the White House." Hoover, who would die in two months, released the FBI report, undercutting the ITT experts whose report had been backed by the White House, demonstrating FBI independence and contradicting the administration.

The Democratic National Committee, headed by Larry O'Brien, made hay of the ITT case in press and television interviews as the Kleindienst hearings dragged on painfully through April 1972.

The ITT conspiracy, if any, never worked out. The GOP decided in

May to move the convention to Miami because the ITT hotel in San Diego was vulnerabie to violent demonstrators, and later two Watergate special prosecutors could find no pay off in the ITT case. It had been an inconclusive event, but it intensified administration-media hostility and acerbated FBI-White House relations at the beginning of a campaign year. It did not help Pat Gray with the already demoralized FBI hierarchy when he was designated to succeed Hoover as FBI Director.

Gemstone

During the first campaign planning session in April 1971, Nixon ordered that political intelligence be included in the budget. He believed that better intelligence might have won for him in 1960 by preparing him for Kennedy's Cuba-speech coup and for rigged voting in Cook County. He almost had lost the 1968 election because he could not refute Johnson's dubious non-start of talks with the North Vietnamese and accompanying bombing halt a few days before the election, at a time when Johnson had been using the FBI for political intelligence on him, tracing Vice President Agnew's phone calls and bugging Anna Chennault to see if Nixon's team was making President Thieu obdurate.

Nixon had no qualms about political intelligence, so long as it would not be discovered. All major candidates had intelligence operations and security men to ward off others' intelligence. Hoover had told him that Robert Kennedy and Johnson both bugged Goldwater forces in 1964, and Johnson had used the FBI to bug Nixon's campaign plane in 1968, even though Johnson was not running.

After the preliminary April 1971 planning, John Dean, still a face in the crowd on the White House staff, proposed to Haldeman that Dean's legal office coordinate intelligence, but two months later the Pentagon Papers unleashed a number of loose cannon on intelligence projects. During the 1972 campaign, Haldeman, Ehrlichman and Nixon aides Dwight Chapin and Gordon Strachan, as well as CRP deputy chief Jeb Magruder all dabbled in campaign intelligence.

The first intelligence plan was proposed by Ehrlichman's ex-policeman, Jack Caulfield, now working for Dean's office, a plan he called Sandwedge, providing for buggings and burglaries on demand. Mitchell turned it down, commenting that Caulfield was not a lawyer. Dean then proposed that G.Gordon Liddy become CRP legal counsel, and the fervent counter-revolutionary was appointed on December 6, 1971, two and a half months after his bungled burglary of Dr. Fielding's office in Beverly Hills. Dean later said that Egil Krogh recommended

Liddy to him, and he also knew that Nixon had been impressed with a memo Liddy wrote on the pros and cons of Nixon's asking for Hoover's resignation.

Liddy, in his book *Will*,[2] said it was Dean who advised him that an elaborate campaign intelligence plan was called for, with a budget of perhaps $1 million. Liddy produced a plan he called Gemstone, complete with color charts professionally prepared by Hunt's CIA colleagues.

Liddy, Dean and Magruder presented Gemstone to Mitchell on January 27, 1972, and Mitchell was appalled. Liddy's plan was divided into operational areas: Diamond was a plan to drug and kidnap the Chicago Seven demonstration leaders if they showed up in San Diego and hold them a few days over the border in Mexico, since the FBI would not emulate De Gaulle, who regularly deported to Corsica violence-prone anti-Communists whenever Soviet leaders visited Paris. Ruby was a plan to plant spies in the Democratic candidate's campaign. Crystal and Opal were bugging operations, and Emerald was a chase plane to monitor bugs planted on the Democratic candidate's campaign plane. Sapphire would plant two blonde Miami prostitutes, acquaintances of Frank Sturgis, on a bugged houseboat moored by Democratic Convention headquarters in Miami. (John Dean's version implied a larger stable of prostitutes from a Baltimore whorehouse.) Quartz was a microwave telephone-interception operation. Turquoise would sabotage the Democratic Convention by turning off the air conditioning. Topaz was photo espionage, and Garnet, which caused Mitchell to explode when Liddy suggested it later, would have hired unwashed hippies wearing McGovern buttons to wait until television cameras were on them in McGovern's hotel room, and then urinate on the floor. (The room was scheduled to be Mitchell's when McGovern moved out of it.)

At the first presentation, Mitchell told Liddy he was more interested in protection against demonstrations and police cooperation, and sent him back to the drawing board. Liddy wrote that Mitchell told him, "And Gordon, burn those charts. Do it personally."

(One of the striking contradictions in reports by the Watergate defendants is Dean's version of the meeting: "I went over to Mitchell's desk. 'Unreal, and a little frightening,' I said in a low voice... 'Gordon, you ought to destroy those charts right away,' I said finally. 'I really think you ought to focus on demonstrations. That's our real problem area.' "[3] Everything Liddy reported Mitchell saying, Dean said he said.[4])

A week later Liddy returned with a revised plan, which Mitchell also rejected as risky and expensive. Gemstone, a fantasy plagiarized from *Mission Impossible,* was born dead, and Liddy eventually used $199,000 of a $250,000 budget, much of it mopping up errors. The media later would call it a plan to seize the country.

The Watergate Burglaries

Mitchell was resting at Key Biscayne from the consuming ITT case, interrupted with reports on his wife, Martha, who was ill with hysterical depression, when Magruder and Fred LaRue, Mitchell's right-hand man, a millionaire with no official title, visited him there with about 30 action memos on campaign plans. One of the memos was Liddy's latest revision of an intelligence plan, and again Mitchell demurred. Included in Liddy's plan was target Larry O'Brien, scourge of the ITT hearings, who was reported by Robert Bennett of the Mullen Company, the CIA-connected public relations firm, to have received an annual retainer of $180,000 from Howard Hughes through O'Brien's friend, Robert Maheu. The Hughes empire, then involved with the CIA in the *Glomar Explorer* deep-sea dredge, also was involved in massive litigation with the former director of its Las Vegas enterprises, Maheu. Bennett, on retainers from both Hughes and the CIA, had a personal interest in probing O'Brien. Nixon did too; in the 1962 California gubernatorial election, Democrats had made a scandal of a $205,000 unsecured loan that Hughes had made to Nixon's brother Donald.

Magruder later wrote that Mitchell, distraught and half paying attention, authorized budgeting $250,000 for Liddy's plan, but once again held it up. One item was a wiretap on O'Brien. Mitchell said to go ahead with that, and he would look again at the rest of the plan if the wiretap worked out. Liddy wrote that the objective was to find out what accusations O'Brien might be planning to spring on Nixon.

Haldeman's theory, worked out while he was in prison studying trial testimony, is that Nixon told Colson to get proof of O'Brien's retainer from Hughes and find out what he was doing to earn it; that Colson told Hunt to bug O'Brien's office at the Democratic National Committee, and that Hunt brought in Liddy, while Bennett and the CIA monitored the operation and perhaps through James McCord made sure that it failed.[5] McCord, in trial testimony, made it clear that his loyalty was to the CIA, not to a temporary President who, McCord believed, was trying in 1972 to emasculate the CIA as he had subdued the FBI after appointing Pat Gray to succeed Hoover.

Aside from the CIA's knowledge of the break-in, there was circumstantial evidence that others knew of it. John Stewart, director of communications for the Democratic National Committee, and O'Brien knew on April 26, 1972, that an attempt would be made by Cubans in Republican employ to bug O'Brien's office, that is, five weeks before the first Watergate break-in.

O'Brien was warned of sophisticated GOP bugging plans (apparently a whiff of Gemstone) when William Haddad, editor of the local *Manhattan Tribune*, wrote him about it March 23. Jack Anderson, who was in contact with Frank Sturgis, one of the burglars, and also with Haddad, also had hints of the coming break-in, although he did not write about it until more than a year later, in *Parade* magazine of July 22, 1973.

Stewart had gone to New York on April 26, before the break-ins, and conferred with Haddad, banker Ben Winter and a private investigator, Arthur James Woolston-Smith, who had been reporting activities of the Republican National Committee's New York public relations team, the November Group. The November Group had complained about interference on *its* telephone switchboard, requiring GOP security man McCord to sweep its office for bugs. The circumstantial evidence was offered to the Ervin Committee for inclusion in its final report by minority counsel Fred Thompson, but was rejected as "speculative."[6]

Altogether, there may have been a large audience on the night of June 16 when five men, led by McCord and monitored by Liddy, Hunt and Alfred Baldwin from across the street, slipped into the Watergate to be captured after midnight June 17, wearing rubber gloves and carrying cameras, bugging devices and a total of $2,300, most of it in one-hundred dollar bills numbered in sequence. Metropolitan Police detectives, on overtime pay, happened to be in the immediate vicinity. All of the burglars, McCord, Barker, Sturgis, Virgilio Gonzáles and Eugenio Martínez, once had been involved in the Bay of Pigs.

Nixon and Haldeman were in Key Biscayne, relaxing from the physical, emotional and intellectual strain of the Moscow confrontation. Mitchell and Jeb Magruder were in California. John Dean was in Manila, preparing to fly to San Francisco and Washington. Ehrlichman was in town, due to run the store at the White House. Magruder, who had given the Watergate go-ahead, received a phone call from Liddy and was in panic.

Campaign Finances

The course of modern campaign financing was set on October 28, 1958, in Robert Kennedy's home in Hyannis Port, where a meeting of 16 persons targeted ten state primaries for John F. Kennedy's campaign, seven of which would be undertaken. Assignments were made for a large-scale organization employing such professionals at the meeting as Larry O'Brien and pollster Louis Harris, although some amateurs like Archibald Cox, dean of Harvard Law School, also were present. Kennedy, flying in a private plane that ended the traditional whistle-stop campaign, overwhelmed Hubert Humphrey, barnstorming in a station wagon, in Wisconsin and West Virginia. Kennedy's tools were charm, organization, rapport with the media men accompanying him—and money. Kennedy told Ben Bradlee he spent $13 million to get elected in 1960 and still had a huge campaign deficit.[7] Two decades later, television advertising multiplied the bills, consuming millions in campaign funds.

In 1972, Nixon's campaign raised $60.2 million in contributions, a record, under Finance Committee Chairman and former Secretary of Commerce Maurice Stans. Stans did not have to exert himself much once Democratic primaries began to fall to George McGovern, who frightened businessmen.

A new, complex law, taking effect in mid-campaign on April 7, 1972, required that all major contributions be reported to the government's General Accounting Office. One of the law's ambiguities was whether pledges beating the April 7 deadline but delivered immediately afterward could legally remain anonymous. Stans computerized the accounting to avoid error and rejected more than 100 offers totalling $14 million from contributors who hinted at a quid pro quo, including an offer of $1 million from Michele Sindona, a banker then of good repute but jailed years later in the collapse of the Franklin National Bank.

Of the $60.2 million, about $700,000 was contributed by 19 corporations and $100,000 from an association, Associated Milk Producers Inc. (AMPI), violating the rule that they could contribute from employee-pooled funds but not from slush funds. There was no way for Stans' committee to know that the contributions were from slush funds, and some of the group made the same kind of contributions to Democrats that year.

For mundane reasons—if you gave the Republicans $25,000, then the Democrats would want the same—some companies habitually passed the money through banks in anonymous cashier's checks, or "laundered" their names from the contributions before April 7. In the case of Dwayne O. Andreas, a Minnesota businessman whose contribution triggered the investigation of campaign financing, he made his $25,000 contribution to Nixon's campaign through a local fundraiser, Kenneth Dahlberg, because he did not want to offend his friend Humphrey, but was alarmed at McGovern. The check laundered through Dahlberg's name was once again laundered by Liddy and Hunt through Bernard Barker's bank account in Florida. Andreas later was tried for a different challenged contribution to Humphrey and acquitted.

Eventually the 19 companies and some of their officers were fined, along with Armand Hammer and an employee of his for an illegal personal contribution of $54,000 in which false names were used. The companies were not fined for similar contributions to Democrats, but a few Democrats were caught in the Watergate net, largely because AMPI, normally a contributor to Democrats, handled its affairs sloppily. AMPI's former general manager, Harold S. Nelson, got a four-month prison sentence for illegal contributions to Senators Humphrey and Richard Clark, Representative James Abourezk, Oklahoma Governor David Hall and Kansas Governor Robert Docking, and Humphrey's 1970 Senate-campaign manager Jack Chestnut also got four months.

The Watergate-era media was not interested in Democrats, so AMPI's peccadillos were not news. The media zeroed in on two contributions made to Nixon men—Mitchell, Stans and Charles (Bebe) Rebozo—and an alleged Milk Fund bribe of John Connally. A Texas jury acquitted Connally of all charges.

After a lengthy trial at the height of Watergate fever in hostile New York City, a mostly-Democrat jury acquitted Stans and Mitchell of charges of illegally accepting $200,000 from Robert Vesco, president of International Controls Company, who also had contributed $50,000 on the record. The legal issues were whether pledged funds had been contributed on time and whether Mitchell and Stans had protected Vesco from investigation. Nine months after Vesco made the contribution to Stans, he was indicted by the Securities and Exchange Commission for allegedly looting Investors Overseas Services, which sold mutual funds to foreigners, of $224 million, and Stans sent back the $250,000 to Vesco, including the unchallenged $50,000. In the absence of evidence of illegality, neither Connally nor Mitchell-Stans would have been brought to trial, but Watergate fever demanded the prosecutions. In normal times, there would have been only embarrassment in the media for having accepted a contribution from someone who turned out to be a crook.

As finance chairman, Stans still faced charges on some of the 19 illegal company contributions, although no Democrats were charged for the same dealings. Having lost a year and $700,000 in legal expenses to win acquittal in the Vesco case, an almost broken Stans pleaded guilty to the last of a succession of Watergate special prosecutors, Henry Ruth, Jr., on five counts of non-willfully accepting contributions or late reporting, and was fined $1,000 on each count. Stans could not face another year in court, even though acquittal appeared likely.[8]

The other contribution that interested the media was $100,000 given to Nixon via Rebozo in 1969 and 1970 by Howard Hughes. Rebozo said the money was put in his safe and never spent, an awkward bundle of ambiguous legality that he returned to Hughes in June 1973. Prosecutors suspected that the money might have been spent and later replaced by Rebozo.

Watergate minority counsel Fred Thompson recounted how Rebozo was grilled five and six hours at a time by the special prosecutor's teams sent to Miami, investigated by five IRS agents, repeatedly called to Washington for grilling while investigators went through all of his business dealings for six years and questioned him on 400 telephone numbers he had called over that period. After a million dollars was spent on the investigation, nothing was found against Rebozo.

Herbert Kalmbach, Nixon's personal counsel and a close friend of Stans, who helped raise hush money for the Watergate burglars, served more than six months in prison after pleading guilty to promising an ambassadorship in 1970 for a contribution. Hugh Sloan, Jr., the young CRP treasurer who resigned after the Watergate burglaries, became the *Washington Post's* first source from Nixon's staff, and through Carl Bernstein and Bob Woodward volunteered to tell what he knew of the Watergate case to the special prosecutor. He was not prosecuted.

That was the extent of campaign financing corruption, grave or trivial depending on how one views the American campaign system, but probably not worth the millions of words of media charges, and many Democrats in Washington could look at Kalmbach and Stans and say, "There, but for the grace of God and the media, go I."

Dirty Tricks

From June to October 1972, the media identified Watergate in headlines with the words "Bug Case." The news stories involved the questions of who ordered and financed the bugging. On October 10, the case took on a new dimension with a *Washington Post* blockbuster story of about 3,000 words under the headline, "FBI Finds Nixon Aides Sabotaged Democrats." To the burglary-bugging was added political sabotage under the word Watergate, now signifying Nixon offenses.

Woodward had heard from his high-level secret informer, whom he called "Deep Throat," that at least 50 persons had been involved in widespread espionage and sabotage of Democratic primary candidates, and Bernstein had tracked down in California Donald Segretti, a young attorney and Vietnam veteran, who had been hired by Dwight Chapin to become an imitator of Dick Tuck, the long-time Democratic prankster who had plagued Nixon campaigns for years.[9]

The *Post* story's lead, "FBI agents have established that the Watergate bugging incident stemmed from a massive campaign of political spying and sabotage conducted on behalf of President Nixon's re-election and directed by officials of the White House and the Committee for the Re-election of the President," was not backed up by details in the story or subsequently. By no stretch of the imagination did Segretti constitute a massive campaign.

The media credited Woodward and Bernstein with a major scoop, and no one remarked that there had not been any claims of unusual sabotage from Democrats during the campaign, which was almost over when the scoop was published.

The story that launched "dirty tricks" as a major part of Watergate quoted at length three young attorneys who had been approached by Segretti to join in campaign sabotage but had declined to take part. It also quoted *Post* reporter Marilyn Berger as saying that White House aide Ken Clawson had told her he wrote a letter under a false name to the *Manchester Union Leader* saying that Senator Edwin Muskie condoned a racial slur by an aide on Americans of French-American descent as "Canucks." Clawson denied it. The story mentioned that Clawson had been a reporter at the *Washington Post* covering Mitchell's Justice Department, but it did not say that he quit the *Post* and joined the Nixon administration because he had opposed the *Post's* publication of the Pentagon Papers.

The dirty tricks that finally were uncovered by a massive media hunt were trivial and juvenile, except for two letters ascribing sexual peccadillos to Senators Humphrey and Henry Jackson. Haldeman later apologized to the Senators, being forgiven by Humphrey but not by Jackson.

Another *Post* story contained damaging factual errors: that the assaults on the Democrats were financed by "a secret, fluctuating $350,000-$700,000 campaign fund that was controlled by Attorney General John N. Mitchell while he headed the Justice Department," kept "in a safe in the office of the President's chief fund-raiser, former Secretary of Commerce Maurice Stans." There was a $350,000 fund, kept in a Washington bank.

In their book, Woodward and Bernstein reported that at Deep Throat's revelations, "Woodward was stunned. Fifty people directed by the White House and CRP to destroy the opposition, no holds barred?" Destroy? Segretti? In the same book, Bernstein interviewed Segretti, and found him "likeable, and his situation pathetic."[10]

Tax Evasion

As in the case of the new law on campaign financing in 1972, there had been a new tax law in 1970, with a deadline to meet. After July 25, 1970, official papers were no longer eligible for tax deductions as gifts. The stipulation was made so that future officials could not emulate Lyndon Johnson, who had taken large deductions for his papers. Johnson had advised Nixon to do the same, and Nixon had delivered his Vice Presidential papers to the National Archives before the deadline. The document deeding the papers to the government, however, was not delivered until after the deadline, and Watergate investigators found that it was back-dated to substantiate the tax deduction. White House aide Edward L. Morrow pleaded guilty to back-dating and received a seven-month sentence. Ralph G. Newman, a Chicago antiquarian book dealer and appraiser, was fined $10,000. Nixon was ordered to pay $476,431 in back taxes and penalties, all but wiping him out financially.

The tax story broke as the House Judiciary Committee was moving in for the kill in the spring of 1974, and the *Times* gave it an eight-column banner headline:

> NIXON TO PAY $432,787 IN BACK TAXES;
> CONGRESS PANEL STAFF AND I.R.S. FIND
> UNDERPAYMENTS IN 4 YEARS IN OFFICE.[11]

Theodore White remarked that "the *Times* proclaimed the news with a three-deck, front page headline of the same visual impact which had announced the Japanese attack on Pearl Harbor in 1941."[12]

John Doar, chief counsel of the House Judiciary Committee, struggled to make the technical tax violation and Nixon's improvements on his properties at San Clemente and Key Biscayne—required on security grounds—impeachable offenses, but they were voted down as insubstantial. Robert Abplanalp had spent $1 million of his own money to make his island retreat at Grand Cay, Bahamas, secure for Nixon's use.

Coarse Language on the Tapes

With the possible exception of Jimmy Carter, all recent Presidents have cursed the air blue in private. Nixon's problem was compounded by his earlier sanctimonious condemnation of Truman's swearing in public and the blunder of Press Secretary Ron Ziegler in substituting "expletive deleted" when the White House issued the first tape transcripts, causing much merriment. Although Kennedy's swearing was well known, the Kennedy men feigned horror at Nixon's language.

Newspapers that had an iron rule against printing profanity dropped the rule for Nixon's quotes.

So much was made of "Mafia language" in the White House that the sense of what Nixon was saying became deliberately twisted in the media. It was obvious that the quote, "I don't give a shit about the lira," meant, "I don't want to talk about that at this moment," but it was repeated in the press constantly (into 1982 in the case of the *Times*) as spurious evidence of Nixon's contempt for our Italian ally.

Much of the profanity was venting helpless frustration. Of McLaren, Nixon said, "I don't like the son of a bitch," but McLaren pushed the ITT case anyhow. When O'Brien's (and the *Washington Post's*) lawyer, Edward Bennett Williams, sued Mitchell over the Watergate break-in, Nixon ranted, ". . .this is war. . .I wouldn't want to be in Edward Bennett Williams' position after this election. None of these bastards. . . .We're going after him." Haldeman added, ". . .that is a guy we've got to ruin."

That sort of hyperbole was cited to justify John Dean, James Mc-Cord, Carl Bernstein and Bob Woodward in their advertising that they feared they would be assassinated. All are alive and well. None of Nixon's curses reached the vehemence of Senator Gravel's "motherfucker" threat on the Senate floor, known to the media but unreported except in Ungar's book.

The Coverup

If all the other charges that could be brought to bear on Nixon were minor or equivocal, his adversaries had him dead to rights on obstruction of justice, and everyone in Washington knew it almost from the beginning.

Jim Bishop, whose name was on one of Dean's enemies lists, wrote in his column four years after Nixon's resignation, "Immediately after Watergate there was a silence, as though a bleeding man had slipped into a shark pool. After that, it was a feeding frenzy. The press corps shredded the President and all his men. They were skeletonized."

Bishop added, "The Nixon student must find himself in agreement with two charges made by the President: (1) the press was his mortal enemy, and (2) he could not survive the chronic leak of secrets from inside his administration."[13]

From the beginning Nixon knew that, if he had not ordered the Watergate burglary, he had pressed several of his aides to get proof that Larry O'Brien, a charter member of Kennedy's Irish Mafia, was a crook. From that guilty stance, and not sensing early that the Presidency was at stake, he encouraged the coverup from the beginning, originally to save those he thought endangered—Colson and Mitchell—then the widening circle and himself.

It was said that Nixon could have survived if he had made a clean breast of it early enough. That would not have saved him. One confession would have opened the media floodgates just as the coverup did, because the Vietnam-primed media was his mortal enemy.

Repeatedly, both deliberately and inadvertently, Nixon had challenged the media's credibility, its heartbeat. Publication of the Pentagon Papers lined the media up against him unanimously; even newspapers that disliked the *Times* felt constrained to hail the *Times*, defender of their professional worth. Vice President Spiro Agnew had been assigned the task of refuting media bias, and with the help of Nixon's speechwriters Safire and Buchanan, he had beaten the media's commentators at their own game of invective, even to the light touch. The media, especially television, portrayed Agnew's sharp and sometimes amusing attacks as sinister threats to enforce conformity, attacks on the First Amendment, veiled threats to withdraw broadcasting licenses. It was indicative of media guilty conscience that a Vice President, in a notoriously feeble post, panicked television and had newspapers groping for comparisons with McCarthyism. What really hurt was that the public agreed with Agnew; the media *was* biased, *had* joined in packs to misinform about Vietnam and about Nixon programs.

Nixon's fatal affront to big media was his success in foreign affairs against the media's best advice. He had gotten American troops out of Vietnam, broken China's isolation, dealt with the Soviets on strategic arms when everyone had warned he could not do it that way. Before Watergate, the left fringe of Congress and the powerful *Times* both had threatened impeachment if he were re-elected. Confession over the burglary origin would not have ended the threat.

Haldeman believed that the President doomed himself just after the 1972 election when he asked for the resignations of all appointed officials, Cabinet and sub-Cabinet levels, in preparation for governmental reorganization, intending to find hard-nosed administrators who would reduce the bureaucracy and end its obstruction. He alienated all Washington, so the bureaucracy—e.g., Deep Throat and the voracious Justice Department attorneys—fought back, in Haldeman's theory. In that case, confession would not have helped, either.

The Watergate onion was peeled over a period of two years in three main stages: investigative reporting (mostly based on Deep Throat's leaks of FBI material) from June 1972 to spring 1973, the Sam Ervin show on television through the summer of 1973, and the impeachment hearings in 1974. For Nixon, it was two years of heavy shelling, for the public two years of disillusion that to many amounted to agony, but for the strange coalition of the far Left and the media, now entirely conformist, it was the best of times.

Some veteran reporters in Washington took little or no part in Watergate coverage, but it didn't matter; they were out. Editors thought they had become soft and complacent in Washington; young blood poured into the capital and rose swiftly, after the models of the tenacious Woodward and Bernstein of the *Washington Post*. University journalism schools introduced courses in investigative reporting. Well before the denouement of Watergate, Woodward and Bernstein finished their first book, with the help of, among others, the ubiquitous IPS-connected David Obst, who had helped Ellsberg, Gravel and Seymour Hersh, and would later help John Dean. Robert Redford and Dustin Hoffman already were scheduled to play them in the movie version of *All the President's Men*.

In terms of media shop talk, the first phase began with the *Post's* Bernstein and Woodward, local reporters not yet graduated to the status of national reporters, whipping the pants off *Times* veterans including the legendary Tad Szulc, and the *Times* bringing in a team of Woodstein look-alikes.

In the first reporting of the break-in, the *Post* put eight reporters on its detailed, 2,000-word story, with a sidebar on the security guard at the Watergate, Frank Wills, who discovered the burglary. The *Times* ran a less thorough, 700-word story on Page 30, without the by-line of Nathanial Sheppard, Jr., then an apprentice.

The next day Szulc, expert on the Bay of Pigs, zeroed in on Miami realtor Bernard Barker as the raider's probable leader and linked him to Nixon through Barker's Miami partner, Republican Party stalwart Miguel Suevez, a false start, but still implicating Nixon some old way. Szulc knew too much about the Bay of Pigs. That day Woodward and Bernstein led their story with a more significant nominee for raid leader, James McCord, identifying him as the security coordinator of CRP.

On Day 3, both the *Times'* Szulc and the *Post's* Woodward and Bernstein tied Howard Hunt to the break-in, Szulc emphasizing that Hunt had met previously in Miami with Cubans. Woodward had more; he had talked with Deep Throat, so the *Post* could top the *Times* again, reporting that Hunt was a White House consultant to Colson. The Bay of Pigs had Szulc on a false trail.

The rest of the media was left far behind. Everyone presumed that the burglary was connected to Nixon's organization, but everyone assumed it was at a low and irresponsible level, and if higher-ups were involved, it would be successfully covered up like past coverups by all administrations.

But on June 22, Bernstein connected Robert Bennett of the Mullen Company to Hunt, his employee, and discovered that Bennett earlier had raised funds for the Nixon campaign.

From Newport, California, Martha Mitchell telephoned Helen Thomas of United Press International, complaining that she was being held prisoner by thugs, her security guards, and that the campaign was a dirty one; she wanted her husband out of it. She did not explain that her outburst was triggered by news of the arrest of McCord, her former security guard, whom she liked. On July 1, Mitchell resigned as head of CRP, citing his wife's illness.

In New York, the *Times* editors were taken aback at the effrontery of the *Washington Post* in running away with the story while their 35-man bureau trailed behind. Bureau chief Max Frankel was touring the country doing election pieces. Tom Wicker pondered his column. Szulc, who would resign at the end of 1972 to write books, was irritated at being refused the title of diplomatic correspondent. Neil Sheehan was writing a book about John Vann. Washington bureau news editor Robert Phelps could get no production out of anyone except Walter Rubager, and New York did not follow up Robert Smith's initial discovery of Segretti because Smith (correctly) did not find a "massive campaign." Seymour Hersh, the bureau's heavy artillery, was engaged in his own project, and showed no desire to tangle with Woodward and Bernstein. New blood was unleashed on Watergate, including John Crewdson, Agis Salpukas, Wallace Turner, Nicholas Gage and Chris Lyndon. The bureau became young, but the *Times* could not catch the *Post*.

In July the *Times* got its first break. Rubager reported evidence from telephone logs that Barker had called a White House number repeatedly from Miami. Bernstein picked up that story the next day, but Rubager was on his way to Mexico City, where he reported that money found on the burglars came from four checks laundered in a bank there. Bernstein took off for Florida and ran down a fifth check, Dahlberg's. Together he and Woodward reported that the Government Accounting Office was auditing Maurice Stans' CRP funds, with special attention to the Kenneth Dahlberg $25,000 check, giving readers an erroneous impression that Dahlberg (for Dwayne Andreas) had made a special kind of clandestine contribution to a burglar's fund. (Which checks got to Liddy was accidental.)

Szulc, thrashing around for a story, reported that Hunt had fled to Europe, touching base in Spain. (Hunt was hiding with a friend in California.) A *Times* story by Robert F. Levey tied Liddy to Watergate.

Watergate still failed to ignite the public, and in August Nixon was re-nominated in Miami, winning all but one vote on the first ballot. The single vote went to Representative McCloskey, who attended the convention in the well-publicized company of Daniel Ellsberg, who still was waiting for his trial to begin.

At the end of August Woodward and Bernstein reported a garbled story: Liddy and Hunt had been inside the Watergate and barely escaped. Rubager topped that with an interview with Bernard Barker.

Through September, Woodward and Bernstein kept ahead, reporting Deep Throat's information that Magruder, Bart Porter and Liddy used secret funds for intelligence purposes, and that the Watergate grand jury investigating the burglary had called Mitchell and Kleindienst.

On October 10, Woodward and Bernstein broke the "massive sabotage campaign" of Donald Segretti. That day, the *Times*, itching to comment, swallowed its pride and quoted the *Post* in its editorial, headlined "A Sinister Affair." Segretti proved later to be not very sinister, but in rapid succession the *Post* team reported Muskie's belated complaint that his letterhead had been used for the fraudulent "sex letters" about Humphrey and Jackson, that Dwight Chapin had hired Segretti, and that Kalmbach had furnished funds to him. Segretti dominated the media for weeks.

Two weeks before the election, Woodward and Bernstein stumbled, bringing in Haldeman as one of five high-ranking Presidential associates allegedly authorized to approve payments from a secret campaign fund totalling $700,000, citing facts known to the FBI. They would concede in their book that major elements of the story were unsubstantiated, but the *Post* did not retract.

One other newspaper broke into the *Times-Post* monopoly when Jack Nelson of the *Los Angeles Times* published a vivid and detailed description of the Watergate break-in from a taped interview with Alfred Baldwin, the lookout across the street. Baldwin earlier had confessed to strangers who turned out to be Larry O'Brien's attorneys, and then to the grand jury.

Racing to catch up on that story, under pressure from editor Bradlee, Woodward and Bernstein learned from Democratic investigators that Baldwin had named Nixon aides who had signed memos in connection with the break-in. Improving on the *Los Angeles Times* story, the *Post* reporters named Robert Odle, William Timmons and Glenn Sedam as accomplices. They were wrong. The memos Baldwin had reported had nothing to do with Watergate. Woodward and Bernstein apologized in their book for marking the three men with the Watergate stigma, but their careers were in shreds.

Watergate still did not explode, and Nixon was re-elected President with a 61% majority, carrying every state except Massachusetts and the District of Columbia, home of the *Washington Post.*

Jeb Magruder, who had been in charge of the Liddy-Hunt team, was wary of Liddy, who had once told him, "Take your arm off my shoulder or I'll tear it off and beat you to death with it." He had immediately told Dean that he ordered the break-in because of pressure to do something from Colson and Strachan. His position made him one of the first to be called to testify before the Watergate grand jury in July and August. Magruder said that, on pledges of Mitchell and Dean that he would be provided for if convicted, he appeared twice before the Watergate prosecutors with a cover story: Liddy had been paid for legitimate security work, and had taken off on his own![4] Magruder was knee-deep in perjury, but he had held off the investigation until after the election.

The grand jury investigation, the Democratic National Committee's $1 million civil suit, a Common Cause lawsuit and two congressional investigations continued, but phase one of media coverage was running out of steam at the end of 1972. The media retold stories, summed up unanswered Watergate questions, dug out biographies of the burglars and others named in investigations. Hunt's wife Dorothy was killed with 46 others in a plane crash in Chicago just before Christmas. She was carrying $10,000 in $100 bills, which spurred another round of investigative reporting, but the money could not be tied to Watergate. For a time, the coverup worked.

Phase two began in January 1973, when Senate Majority Leader Mike Mansfield appointed Senator Sam J. Ervin, Jr., 76, the Democratic "country lawyer from North Carolina" and Harvard Law School, to head the Senate Select Committee on 1972 campaign practices, bypassing the normal inquiry through the Senate Judiciary Committee, which was headed by Nixon loyalist James Eastland of Louisiana.

Ervin, erstwhile defender of Senator Gravel, selected for his committee Democrats Joseph M. Montoya of New Mexico, Herman E. Talmadge of Georgia and Daniel K. Inouye of Hawaii, and Republicans Howard Baker of Tennessee, Edward J. Gurney of Florida and Lowell P. Weicker of Connecticut. Georgetown University Professor Samuel Dash was appointed majority counsel, to play a prosecutor's role, with authority to hire two-thirds of the committee staff members.[15]

Prominent Dash appointees were Terry Lenzer, an open enemy of Nixon since he had been dismissed as head of the Office of Legal Assistance for the anti-poverty program in 1970 and once a defense attorney for the Berrigan brothers, and Scott Armstrong, who had been best man at Bob Woodward's wedding. It was obvious that the pretense of a fair, full and impartial hearing would not last long. How the deck was stacked with the enthusiastic cooperation of the media, recipients of leaks from the majority staff, was told by Fred Thompson, chief minority counsel, a 30-year-old Tennessee lawyer new to Washington, who found himself outnumbered and outgunned.[16]

Coincident with the formation of the Ervin Committee, the *Times'* Seymour Hersh delivered a blockbuster implicating Mitchell, redeeming Hersh's reputation as a ruthless investigator. He quoted Watergate burglar Frank Sturgis as saying that the burglars still were being paid, and were under pressure to plead guilty, with the promise of hush money.

Hersh, it turned out, had pirated the story, wrecking the book its author was selling. Andrew St. George, the one-time companion of Castro in the Sierra Maestra, fallen on hard times, had submitted to Random House and Harper's Magazine Press a confidential outline of the biography he was writing with Sturgis, in which Sturgis tied Mitchell to Watergate. Hersh, whose books were published by Random House, startled St. George with a call asking to see him about the confidential outline. At their meeting, St. George charged, Hersh told him he had the outline and would publish its revelations unless St. George got him an interview with Sturgis, guaranteed off the record, with identities protected.

Hersh met with St. George and Sturgis, then revealed both their names in his story. Hersh said later,

> . . . I never had the outline. I bluffed him out of his pants. I pretended I had it all the time. He was so hot to get his name into the *Times*. The only time Sturgis talked to me was when Andrew St. George was upstairs taking a leak. I never received the outline of that book. I give you my goddamn word. I thought the article was fair. He thought it was terrible. He called up Rosenthal, begging him to put it off. I hated to do it to the guy, but I never had the outline. He had the Watergate story and couldn't do anything with it. Why? Because he's Andrew St. George.[17]

Far behind despite Hersh's enterprise, the *Times* brought back from freelance work J. Anthony Lukas, the Pulitzer Prize winner for his sympathetic portrayal of rebellious youth and admirer of the Chicago

Seven, to draw together all the Watergate threads in a magazine series of unlimited length. The series eventually became *Nightmare, the Underside of the Nixon Years,*[18] one of the most effective anti-Nixon polemics.

The full Senate approved the Ervin Committee, 77 to 0, in early February 1973 after Republican attempts to include the 1964 and 1968 elections in the inquiry were beaten down. The trial of the Watergate Seven had just ended in guilty verdicts, all but Liddy and McCord pleading guilty, but without answering the questions: who hired the spies and why? Judge John Sirica gave Liddy 20 years plus eight months for contempt, and delayed sentencing of the others. The Ervin Committee asked for records of the trial and grand jury investigations. Sirica rebuked Prosecutor Earl J. Silbert for not calling enough witnesses during the trial, and Silbert, stung, asked for another grand jury to study high-level suspects.

While the Ervin Committee got its act together, two Watergate bombshells exploded in March: McCord and Pat Gray made confessions.

McCord, facing a sentence of up to 40 years, wrote a six-page letter to Sirica on March 19 asking for a private meeting with the judge. He did not trust prosecutors working for the Justice Department, and he had evidence that political pressure was being put on the defendants for their silence; there had been perjury. McCord was taken to Dash, and told him that Magruder and Dean were involved in the break-in and coverup. Nevertheless, Sirica sentenced McCord and the four Miamians to 40 years, and Hunt to 35 years, conditional on their talking. The media agreed with the suspension of the Constitution's provisions against cruel and unusual punishment and self-incrimination.

As McCord broke, Patrick Gray III, the new FBI director, was being grilled at his Senate confirmation hearings. Gray conceded that he had given raw FBI reports on Watergate to Dean at the White House, and that Kalmbach had told him of giving $30,000 to Segretti at Chapin's request. Gray further said he had loaned to Dean the original Dita Beard memo to her ITT boss so Dean could have it tested for authenticity, and finally Gray said that Dean probably had lied in saying that he didn't know of Hunt's office in the Executive Office Building.

The coverup was unraveling. Woodward and Bernstein piled on the pressure, reporting that Mitchell's aide Fred LaRue had handled hush money payments to the Watergate Seven.

The March bombshells sent Dean and Magruder, each without the other's knowledge, and without informing Haldeman or Ehrlichman, off to find criminal lawyers to bargain for them with the Ervin Committee's Dash. Hunt, too, was attempting to bargain for immunity from further prosecution and to relieve his tentative sentence.

For a month, a quasi-legal battle raged in the media over Nixon's statement that he would invoke executive privilege and not allow his aides to testify, specifying that Dean had both executive privilege and a lawyer-client relationship with the staff. The folksy Ervin on national television said that White House aides must appear; he would "send the Senate's Sergeant at Arms down to the White House and arrest everybody."

Magruder and Dean were confessing to Ervin's lawyers, and Gray further admitted he had destroyed evidence on Dean's instructions— fake cables that Hunt had constructed trying to tie Kennedy more directly to Diem's assassination, and Hunt's report on Teddy Kennedy's conduct at Chappaquiddick. In late April, Gray resigned from the FBI; Magruder resigned from his new post as Assistant Secretary of Commerce; Strachan resigned as counsel to the United States Information Agency. Hunt's secret testimony revealed his raid with Liddy on the office of Ellsberg's psychiatrist. Attorney General Kleindienst told Nixon that Ellsberg's trial judge in Los Angeles would have to be informed of the 1971 Fielding break-in.

In his confidential, unsworn talks with Dash's men while negotiating for immunity, Dean was accusing Haldeman, Ehrlichman and his one-time father figure Mitchell of masterminding the coverup. On April 8, Dean called Haldeman in California and said he thought he needed an experienced criminal lawyer. From that, Haldeman suspected that Dean was negotiating, and Nixon called Dean to the Oval Office on April 15, then again the next day to say he would like to have Dean's signatures on two letters, one resigning and the other asking for a leave of absence. Going into the office on April 16, Dean had seen Ehrlichman and Haldeman emerging laughing, then turning sober when they saw him. The sight strengthened Dean's suspicion that he would be made the scapegoat for Watergate. Dean told Nixon he would not resign unless Ehrlichman and Haldeman resigned, and he would write his own letter. The scene replayed the start of Dean's career as a lawyer, when he had been fired and also insisted that he resigned first.

Dean reported in his book that Bernstein of the *Post*, pressing for an interview, got word to him with the advice that he should tape-record his story and put it in Bernstein's possession, for use only if the President had Dean murdered. Dean wrote that he took the suggestion that he might be assassinated seriously, but he didn't see Bernstein. Still, Woodward and Bernstein reported Dean's secret testimony to Dash in detail on April 27 and April 29, while Nixon was at Camp David escaping Washington. Their stories may have settled it; Nixon called Haldeman and Ehrlichman to Camp David for their strained parting. Nixon henceforth would be alone in defending himself, his presidency and the Vietnam settlement. It was one month after the last GIs had left Vietnam, almost unnoticed by the media, to be welcomed home as "baby killers."

Nixon addressed the nation on April 30, announcing the resignations of Haldeman, Ehrlichman, Dean and Kleindienst. The White House had self-destructed. Nixon's speech contained the last-stand defense that he would hold to the end: he was responsible, but he had not known until Dean told him March 20 of the coverup.

Nixon said, "Today, in one of the most difficult decisions of my presidency, I accepted the resignations of two of my closest associates in the White House, Bob Haldeman and John Ehrlichman, two of the finest public servants it has been my privilege to know." It was not an implication of wrongdoing, he said:

> They agreed with me that this move was necessary. . . . Because Attorney General Kleindienst—though a distinguished public servant, my personal friend for 20 years, and with no personal involvement in this matter—has been a close personal and professional associate of some of those who are involved in this case, he and I both felt it was necessary to name a new Attorney General. The counsel to the President, John Dean, has also resigned.

Nixon said he was appointing Defense Secretary Elliot Richardson, who had just taken over the Pentagon when Melvin Laird moved to the crumbling White House staff, to be Attorney General, and Leonard Garment would replace Dean. Richardson would have power to appoint a Watergate Special Prosecutor. Photographers were barred from the speech, while Nixon left close to tears.

Nixon's slightly incoherent and hastily composed speech was the poorest he had given since his concession in the California gubernatorial race. The *Washington Post* said it was "not enough to repair ten months of temporizing, evasion and deceit."

The next day, the *Times'* Hersh reported that government investigators planned to indict Haldeman, Ehrlichman, Mitchell, Magruder, Dean and LaRue, and were pursuing Chapin, Strachan, Herbert Porter, Kenneth Parkinson and Kalmbach. Hersh reported that Hugh Sloan, the former CRP treasurer, confirmed his account. Mitchell and Stans at the same time faced the Vesco trial in New York.

The *Times* at this point broke with Kissinger, who had asked that there be "no orgy of recrimination." The *Times* editorialized that "Mr. Kissinger seems to be transferring guilt from those who instigated Watergate to those who have exposed it," although Kissinger had made no accusations. The editorial said that when Kissinger asked for compassion "in the tragedy that has befallen so many people," could be "really be insensitive to the tragedy of those who remain without hope for amnesty from this administration for having broken the law, not in pursuit of political power, but in protest against a war they regarded as immoral?"[19] The Vietnam war was, for the *Times*, as ever the issue, and those violently opposing it had not been in pursuit of political power. The break with Kissinger later would become a vendetta.

Dean had turned over to Judge Sirica the keys to a safe-deposit box in Alexandria, Virginia, containing documents that may have included the Huston Plan which he had saved from the first days of his White House employment.

Hunt's testimony to the grand jury on the Fielding break-in was read at the Los Angeles trial of Ellsberg and Russo, and Judge Byrne dismissed all charges against them, stipulating that the case was so contaminated that they could not be tried again. Byrne later said that Ehrlichman, scouting for a replacement for Pat Gray, had twice talked to him about the FBI directorship.

Through the month of May, Dean held out for immunity, staving off a subpoena from the grand jury, where he had decided he would have to take the Fifth Amendment rather than testify in a closed hearing without immunity.

Senator William Proxmire, Democrat of Wisconsin and the successor to Joe McCarthy, who had urged Nixon to appoint a Special Prosecutor, complained on the Senate floor that "some of the statements made by the press concerning the Watergate affair have, in my judgment, become grossly unfair to President Nixon." Protesting the leaks of Dean's testimony, Proxmire said that Nixon "is being tried, sentenced and executed by rumor and allegation. . .based on a charge that certain unidentified investigators for the grand jury have elicited from a witness. . . .I find this kind of persecution and prosecution without trial McCarthyism at its worst."[20]

Television reporters had contributed little to the Watergate exposé except for leaks to Daniel Schorr and Leslie Stahl of CBS, supplementing the "hemorrhage of leaks" from the Ervin Committee's preparatory interrogations to print journalists, who now hunted the Senate corridors literally in packs.

Television's day dawned on May 17, when Ervin opened public hearings, "the greatest show on earth," before an audience of millions, saying that "the survival of our form of government is at stake." Weicker, the anti-Nixon Republican on the panel, sharpened the national audience's appetite, promising they would see "the men who almost—almost—stole America." For three months the hearings would saturate the air waves, far surpassing the previous greatest show, the Army-McCarthy hearings. Television generated more newspaper coverage, and Watergate filled page after page in newspapers.

The Ervin Committee hearings started sedately, but on the second day the first dynamite witness, James McCord, described the bugging of the Watergate offices, implicating Magruder, Dean, Mitchell and Haldeman. Ervin cautioned the audience that McCord's testimony was hearsay, inadmissible in court, derived from Liddy and Hunt. McCord also implicated Caulfield, who appeared before the committee to say he had offered McCord executive clemency at Dean's direction "from the highest level of the White House." McCord had not believed it, and further had written to Helms at CIA, before Helms was transferred, warning that Nixon would try to blame the agency for the break-in. McCord also wrote Caulfield to pass on the word that if the CIA were implicated, "every tree in the forest will fall."

McCord's former attorney Gerald Alch, angry that McCord had impugned his integrity, appeared before the committee to charge that McCord's new attorney, Bernard Fensterwald, who also headed the left-wing Committee to Investigate Assassinations, had told him, "We are out to get the President of the United States." McCord's testimony became increasingly compromised.

The print media was in a kind of frenzy that made the Communist *Daily World* and radical left *Guardian*, noted for hyperbole, look much like the *Times* and *Washington Post*, from which the Communist publications borrowed lavishly.

Gus Hall, head of the Communist Party, addressed a crowd of about 1,000 at the Hotel Diplomat in New York, with a speech that could have been given by any liberal politician. "Nixon promised to bring us together," Hall chortled to the crowd.

In the *Village Voice*, Paul Hoffman interviewed in Chicago Sherman Skolnick, who charged that the White House had murdered Dorothy Hunt and the 45 others on her plane. The story noted that Skolnick lived on lecture fees and the sale of Julius Moder's *Who's Who in the CIA*, published in East Berlin (the story did not say by the SSD), and *Farewell America*, by James Hepburn, which charged Kennedy's murder to CIA employees, published in Luxembourg.

The *Times* accepted a full-page ad demanding impeachment from the Citizens' Committee for Constitutional Government, headed by

William Meyers, Joseph H. Crown and Peter Weiss of IPS. The *Times* also published a news report that was an advance promotion for the movie, "Executive Action," to star Burt Lancaster, dramatizing the same theme as Hepburn's book, Kennedy's murder by ex-CIA hands, written by Dalton Trumbo of the Hollywood Ten, Donald Freed and Mark Lane.[21]

In Congress, Representatives McCloskey and Abzug spoke on impeachment proceedings to an almost empty chamber.

Before the Ervin Committee and a hypnotized television audience, Hugh Sloan told of disbursing $199,000 to Liddy without asking how it was to be spent. Herbert Porter confessed to perjury, telling the committee that Magruder had asked him to lie to the grand jury to avoid endangering the President and to corroborate Magruder's testimony, and he had complied. Magruder testified that Mitchell had authorized the Watergate break-in and had helped plan the coverup.

As the Ervin Committee moved to its climax—Dean's testimony— Dean took the Fifth Amendment repeatedly before the grand jury to preserve the "use immunity" the Ervin Committee had granted him. What Dean said before the committee could not be used against him, but he still could be prosecuted on the testimony of others. The softened *Times* story did not use the guilty-sounding expression "Fifth Amendment" in its lead, and the headline read, "Dean Is Silent Before Grand Jury."

The *Times* did print a European view, of columnist Bernard Levin in *The Times* of London, who had come to the United States to be shocked by the "Senatorial inquisition." Levin wrote:

> . . . it is just about the most scandalous violation of every standard of justice to take place in a free society since the Southern gentry abandoned lynching as their favorite outdoor sport. . . the conduct of the chairman, Senator Sam Ervin, is so deplorable that the lack of any serious protest against his behavior is in itself a measure of the loss of nerve on the part of so many distinguished Americans in the press, the academic world and politics itself. . . . Ervin and others— especially the ridiculous and maudlin Lowell Weicker, who looked several times as though he was going to cry at his own benignity— fell over themselves to congratulate Magruder on being a fine, up- standing young man with a splendid future in front of him despite this setback. . . . The technique, of course, was exactly the one used by Senator Joseph McCarthy. . . .

Fred Thompson, the committee's minority counsel, agreed that the hearings became "legalized atrocities." He grew increasingly upset at the drift into unfair treatment of witnesses, particularly Ervin's badgering of Stans, Haldeman and Ehrlichman. He wrote:

> . . . the 'public' was being avenged; it did not seem to matter that the witnesses were at a far greater disadvantage than someone accused of murder. . . . Our witnesses were not entitled to a bill of particulars. . . . They had no right to discover any evidence in the possession of the government that might help them. They were confronted with hearsay accusations of prior witnesses. They were not given an opportunity to face their accusers.[22]

The committee withheld evidence. William C. Sullivan, the former FBI No. 3 man, had met with Dean in April 1973, not knowing that Dean was negotiating for immunity, but distrusting him on sight. Sullivan did, despite his distrust, write a careful memo to Dean giving advice on handling Watergate, and he volunteered to appear before the Ervin Committee to testify on previous political intelligence operations in which earlier Presidents had used the FBI. Sullivan said he thought his testimony would help the Nixon administration, telling Dean that the administration had been spartan in its requests for FBI surveillance in comparison with Johnson's administration. Committee lawyers interrogated Sullivan but refused to call him publicly on the technicality that the scope of the investigation had been limited by the Senate to 1972. For the same reason, the committee's transcript refers to Sullivan documents but does not print them with the transcript, keeping Sullivan's evidence a secret. Sullivan was killed in a hunting accident in November 1977.

Before Dean's public testimony, Nixon issued a 4,000-word statement conceding that there had been unethical and illegal efforts in the White House, stemming from national security considerations that began with the Cambodia incursion riots in 1970. Nixon said he had contributed to the atmosphere that caused illegal actions, but the coverup exceeded his directives. He said that the cancelled Huston Plan was not subversion, but had been considered because of FBI failures.

Nixon's statement again set the limits to what he would admit. He said, in summary:

> One—I had no prior knowledge of the Watergate bugging operation, or of any illegal surveillance activities for political purposes; two—long prior to the 1972 campaign I did set in motion certain internal security measures, including legal wiretaps. . . three—people who had been involved in the national security operations later, without my knowledge, undertook illegal activities in the political campaign of 1972; four—elements of the early post-Watergate reports led me to suspect, incorrectly, that the CIA had been in some way involved. . . five—I sought to prevent the ex-

posure of...covert national security activities, while encouraging those conducting the investigation to pursue their inquiry into Watergate itself. I so instructed my staff, the Attorney General and the acting director of the FBI; six—I also specifically instructed Mr. Haldeman and Mr. Ehrlichman to insure that the FBI would not carry its investigation into areas that might compromise national security activities or those of the CIA; seven—at no time did I authorize or know about any offer of executive clemency...neither did I know, until the time of my own investigation (March 1973) of any efforts to provide (the defendants) with funds.

Nixon's partial admissions did not go far enough. The nation wanted to hear John Dean. For many hours, Magruder's testimony had implicated Mitchell, Haldeman and others, but he could draw no direct line to the President. Dean might.

Times editorials thundered that Nixon had tried to subvert America:

> ...The Watergate scandal is a profoundly sinister event because in so many aspects it reflects an authoritarian turn of mind and a ready willingness on the part of those at the highest levels of government to subvert democratic values and practices.... Mr. Nixon's guiding philosophy is that the ends justify the means...Watergate was a series of crimes and conspiracies against individual liberty, against the democratic electoral policy, against lawful government...[23]

Senator Hugh Scott, Republican of Pennsylvania, had just made a similar charge against the *Times*: "The Pentagon Papers were stolen documents. The Pulitzer Prize was given for action which was based on theft and thievery, and a great newspaper has argued continually that the ends justify the means...."[24]

Well before Dean testified, partisans anticipating his testimony were praising or condemning him. Woodward and Bernstein commended him first in their leaked reports of his secret testimony, and their followers accepted Dean as a sinner who had seen the light. Dean was a hero to columnist Mary McGrory and to television commentators before he spoke in public.

Dean arrived at the Ervin Committee June 25 with his attractive second wife Maureen, quickly adopted as "Mo" by much of the television audience, and a prepared statement he had worked on for two months. The committee had prepared a truckload of copies of his 245-page statement to be distributed to reporters.

Dean took the whole hearing period to read his statement, saying that Nixon, Haldeman, Ehrlichman and Mitchell had participated in the coverup for eight months, and that Nixon continued the coverup after

Dean's March 21 warning that there was "a cancer on the Presidency" and appeal to come clean.

Because Dean had been granted use immunity, it was to his advantage to get everything on the record, so that an overlooked offense could not be used to prosecute him. His charges sprayed out like machine gun bullets: the Huston Plan, wiretaps on Pentagon Papers suspects, the talk of a raid on the Brookings Institution, Caulfield's Chappaquiddick inquiry, Gemstone, Watergate, the destruction of evidence, laundered campaign funds, soliciting the CIA to break off the FBI investigation, hush money for the burglars, turning off a subcommittee investigation by Representative Wright Patman's investigators, Segretti, solicitation of IRS pressure, a Nixon offer of clemency to Hunt, plans to balk the Ervin Committee, the Vesco case, the Fielding break-in, the attempt to get Dean to sign a scapegoat resignation, ending with Dean's suspicion that the White House taped its visitors.

Dean's sworn statement pictured him as resisting participation in illegal actions, rather than instigating and directing them. It would, if accepted as credible, convict Haldeman, Ehrlichman, Mitchell, Magruder, Krogh, Strachan, Kleindienst, Kalmbach, Caulfield, Colson, Deputy Attorney General Robert Mardian, Chapin, LaRue, and stray bullets and riccochets struck others, including Nixon's congressional liaison William Timmons, CIA deputy chief Vernon Walters and Judge Charles Richey, who presided over the Democrats' civil suit against Mitchell. The *Times*, now regularly using three-deck, eight-column banner headlines equal to those that had been devoted to Hungary and Suez combined, covered more than five pages with Dean's testimony.

The Senate had voted an order to halt bombing in Cambodia, and as Dean testified, it failed to muster a two-thirds majority to override Nixon's veto of the bombing ban. The test vote showed that almost two-thirds of the Senate would not support Nixon.

After Dean's devastating first-day testimony, there could be only one main news story in subsequent days: Was Dean credible?

As Dean returned before the committee for questioning by friendly Senators (Ervin and Weicker), skeptics (Baker, Inouye and Talmadge) and the hostile Senator Gurney, a catalogue of contradictions appeared. Dean had thoroughly implicated the President, Haldeman and Ehrlichman in the coverup, but now he said that before September 1972 he did not know of their involvement "for a fact, and do not know of it today." Almost all of his testimony on subsequent days softened his opening statement, except for one grenade he still was holding to fire on retreat.

Dean had said he told Kleindienst and Henry Petersen at Justice that he didn't think the White House could stand a wide-open investiga-

tion. Now he added, ". . . in an election year," a drastic change that de-
flated the gravity of the original statement.

Dean had given the impression that, straining to uncover the coverup, he had warned the President in March of a cancer on the Presidency, then waited for Nixon to take action, and on April 8 called
Haldeman in California to tell him he was going to the prosecutors.
Haldeman had replied, "Well John, once the toothpaste is out of the
tube, it's awfully hard to get back in."

Thompson elicited from Dean that he did not in fact tell Haldeman
that he was going to the prosecutors. Instead, he had engaged an attorney on March 25, four days after first telling the President of the scope
of Watergate, and his attorneys negotiated for his immunity from
March 30. Dean saw the prosecutors himself on April 8. Dean had said
he tried to get Nixon to step forward on April 15, but now conceded
that he had not told Nixon on that occasion that he already was talking
with the prosecutors.

Dean had been the activist at the center of the coverup. He had recommended Liddy, but after Gemstone, he made no suggestion that
Liddy was a political menace, apparently failing to tell responsible
higher-ups that Liddy had offered to kill Jack Anderson. Dean had suggested that Hugh Sloan take the Fifth Amendment, although Sloan was
uninvolved. It was Dean's suggestion to Ehrlichman and Gray that
Gray take some of the documents from Hunt's safe, which Gray destroyed, along with his future. Dean retained some of Hunt's documents covertly. It was Dean who repeatedly summoned Vernon
Walters of the CIA to suggest CIA involvement in Watergate and to
press the CIA to turn off the FBI. It was Dean's suggestion—he said relayed from Mitchell—to bring the CIA to the rescue. Dean had 25 contacts with Gray, pressing the idea of CIA involvement, which was to
panic McCord into breaking ranks. Dean coached Magruder to commit
perjury. Dean asked Caulfield to promise McCord executive clemency,
which McCord did not believe. Dean asked Kalmbach to raise hush
money. Dean told Liddy to get Hunt out of the United States. No wonder Dean feared being made the "scapegoat."

Part of Dean's whirlwind activities came out in cross-examination
before the Ervin Committee, but more came out later before the House
Armed Services subcommittee on intelligence in its inquiry into the alleged involvement of the CIA in Watergate—when the media was no
longer interested in Dean. In the subcommittee hearings, it emerged
that General Vernon Walters had told Gray he might resign: "I'm not
going to let these kids kick me around any more." Walters told the subcommittee, "This man (Dean) called me in and tried to get me to ac-

cept blame for my organization, and I refused."[25]

That still was in the future when Thompson drew from Dean on television that he got raw FBI 302 reports from Gray by telling him the President wanted them, but did not show the 302s to Nixon, Haldeman or Ehrlichman, only telling them that the FBI investigation was "vigorous." Dean did show the reports to Mardian, who had moved from Justice to CRP, although he had pledged to Gray that no one except the President would see them.

Pressed hard, Dean said that he and his lawyers had worked out a Phase I for his defense: "I would discuss with the prosecutors everything I could remember, everything I could tell them, and the evidence would not be used against me, so they could assess what they wanted to do with that."

Stories leaked to the press earlier had made much of 40 meetings on Watergate Dean allegedly had with Nixon, but Dean's handful of meetings and late rise to prominence emerged in cross-examination. After some evasion and confusion, Dean said he had discussed Watergate with Nixon first on September 15, 1972, and then not again until February 28, 1973, then subsequently on March 13, March 20, March 21, March 22 and April 15—a tardy series of reports.

Under prodding, Dean admitted he had evaded committee rules in giving an off-the-record interview to *Newsweek*. The interview had resulted in a vivid report in which Nixon leaped out of his chair in consternation.[26] Details, including the leaping, were false, he conceded.

The story of Dean's borrowing from White House funds came out painfully over three days. In sum: $22,000 had been made available to Strachan for Liddy's intelligence operations. Liddy had spent $6,800 of it on Watergate. Strachan and Richard Howard delivered the remaining $15,200 to Dean, the defacto intelligence chief, to put in his safe. Dean took what he thought was $5,000—actually $4,850—and said he put his personal check and an IOU in its place, returning the money later. When Hunt's demands for financial help arrived, it was decided to make the White House fund whole, and Dean arranged for Mitchell to send over $22,000 in campaign funds. He did not contribute or mention the $15,200 of the funds in his possession, explaining that he did not want it to be part of hush money. Eventually, it emerged that Dean returned the $4,850 in April 1973, when he already was bargaining for immunity, and on the date he said he had put in his check, his bank balance stood at slightly over $1,600.

Similarly, the story of Dean's firing from his first job with a legal firm came out over two days. At first, Dean said he had not been fired and produced a letter praising Dean's honesty that appeared to explain the affair as a personality clash with his ex-boss. Eventually Dean was required to describe a 1965 television franchise for St. Louis that he was working on, a conflict of interest with a client seeking the franchise. His boss had said, "You're fired," and Dean had responded, "You can't fire me, I've resigned."

Such cross-examination of Dean had damaged his credibility with that part of the television audience paying attention, but television is ephemeral; it vanishes, quickly in the case of legalistic language. Reading the newspaper of record, a historian will never know that Dean stumbled.

The nation wanted to know if Dean had lied or told the truth. The answer of *Times* reporter James M. Naughton stressed "Mr. Dean's steadfast adherence to accusations," and the headline writers wrote, "Ex-Counsel Is Firm."

On the question of credibility, the *Times* recounted an exchange with Talmadge: " 'Well Senator,' Mr. Dean replied, 'I have been asked to come up here and tell the truth. I have told it exactly the way I know it.' The way Mr. Dean told it presents clear and sharp discrepancies with Mr. Nixon's Watergate statements. . . . "[27]

For the *Times*, the issue of Dean's credibility did not arise; the never-changing issue was Nixon's credibility. The *Times* printed two pages of transcript text on Dean's second day, with no sign of Dean's exchanges with Thompson and Senator Gurney. On the third day, when Gurney bore in on Dean's handling of the $15,200 entrusted to him, the *Times'* Douglas Kneeland reported there had been a "verbal fencing match for more than three hours today, but if any blood was drawn it could probably have been sopped up by a Band-Aid." Kneeland implied that Dean won the match, writing: " 'I thank the Senator for his questions,' Dean said, in what may have been a final thrust for touché. 'I think they were very good.' "[28] Dean had emerged unscathed, according to the *Times*. On Dean's second day of testimony, a *Times* headline over a profile said, "A Calm and Cool David."

In contrast with the *Times* view, Senator Scott called Dean a turncoat, an embezzler and "this little rat." Columnist Joe Alsop called him "a bottom-dwelling slug." William Safire, who had left the Nixon administration to fulfill a lifelong ambition and became a *Times* columnist (and its fig-leaf conservative), wrote that "Gunga Dean" had betrayed a far better man than himself. Author Patrick Anderson, who was writing Magruder's book for him, in the process researched Dean's early life and concluded that he was a chameleon, whose aim was never to displease a boss. He quoted a classmate as saying that Dean was an idea thief who had "no guiding principle."

Dean, not a resourceless guerrilla fighter, had saved one blast which, although specious, would distract headline writers from any slip-ups he had made. By prearrangement with Weicker he produced the "enemies lists" and the media was enthralled. As Dean produced document after document that he called enemies lists, and reporters and editors scrambled to put them together into coherent lists, the media concluded that there was one "main list" of 20 persons and other lists adding up to more than 200 persons. Ervin commented to Baker, "I'm going to demand a recount; there are more enemies than we got votes." Everyone enjoyed the enemies list except the *Times* and *Post* columnist Kraft, who concluded it was one more proof of the police state Nixon had been constructing.[29]

The enemies lists emerged this way: Weicker was questioning Dean, asking him to refresh his memory and see if he could come up with new charges. Weicker asked if the FBI, the Intelligence Evaluation Committee or the IRS had been asked to perform any other illegal activities. Dean said he knew of no illegalities by the Intelligence Evaluation Committee (the Huston Plan substitute).

Then he added in a non sequitur:

> I do of course know, and as I have submitted it in documents, other agencies were involved in seeking politically embarrassing information on individuals who were thought to be enemies of the White House.
>
> I might also add that in my possession is a rather, very much down the line to what you are talking about, is a memorandum that was requested by me to prepare a means to attack the enemies of the White House. [That inverted sentence is obscure; we'll see why.]
>
> There was also maintained what was called an enemies list, which was rather extensive and continually being updated.

Dean's use of the passive voice tended to obscure that "there was maintained" by him lists ordered by him and called by him "enemies lists."

The transcripts and various memoirs show this context:

When the *Times* began publishing the Pentagon Papers, Colson's office and the new Plumbers attempted to identify persons who might have been involved, listing Ellsberg's known contacts. As the media lined up against the administration on the issue of the Pentagon Papers, Colson's office compiled a list of "opponents" who should not be given interviews or favors. The list was sent to Dean and to press aides, along with a covering memo signed by Colson's aide George Bell, on June 24, 1971, the day the Supreme Court agreed to hear the *Times'* case against injunction.

On August 16, 1971, Dean, striving to win the status of his predecessor Ehrlichman and actively soliciting business among the White House staffers, wrote and circulated a memo to selected personnel on "Dealing with Our Political Enemies." Dean asked the staffers to submit names of hostile persons and suggestions on "how we can best screw them; e.g., grant availability, federal contracts, litigation, prosecution, etc." The memo that raised warnings of fascism from critics as different as Joseph Kraft and William F. Buckley, Jr. was Dean's own. To the average staffer, the implication of the memo was that Dean was using fierce language to suggest ways to discourage grants of federal or foundation funds or federal contracts to persons deemed saboteurs, including court action if necessary, and to seek redress where tax exemptions had been abused. Replying to the memo, Strachan used the word "enemies" in quotation marks, setting it off as Dean's word, not his. If usage had been general, Strachan would have written enemies without quotation marks; he was quoting back Dean's intemperate language. Other respondents in Dean's collection of documents referred to "your opponents list."

It is apparent from Dean's first taped conversation with Nixon on September 15, 1972, that Nixon had not previously ordered a list of opponents. Nixon asked, "What about watching the McGovern contributors and all that sort of thing?" It is clear from the context that Nixon was talking about watching contributors' compliance with the new election funding law. The talk then branched off into Nixon's anger at the lawsuits by Larry O'Brien, Common Cause and others pressing investigation of the Watergate break-in.

Nixon said:

> I want the most comprehensive notes on all those who tried to do us in. Because they didn't have to do it. ('That's right,' Dean said.) They didn't have to do it, I mean, if they had a very close election, everybody on the other side would understand the game. But now they are doing this quite deliberately, and they are asking for it, and they're going to get it—we have not used the power in this first four years as you know. ('That's right,' Dean said.) We have never used it. We haven't used the Bureau and we haven't used the Justice Department, but things are going to change, and they're going to get it right. ('That's an exciting prospect,' Dean said.)

Nixon, of course, had legions of real enemies. To catalog them and assign rank would have taken a large, full-time staff. Dean said that as the responses to his request came in, he simply put them in a file. Someone would send him, for example, a newspaper clipping featuring signatures of a group or committee demanding Nixon's impeachment over Cambodia. That was a "list." A roster of the staff members of McGovern's campaign was a list. A group of fat cats contributing to Muskie's campaign was a list. Members of the businessmen's peace organization that introduced Ellsberg to *Los Angeles Times* editors constituted a list. Jane Fonda and friends who appeared at peace rallies made up a list. The Kennedy faction of Senators was a list. Some congressmen appeared both on lists of hostile black Representatives and of left-wing Representatives. Labor leaders Harry Bridges and Cesar Chavez organized the National Labor for Peace, a list. Richard Barnet and Marcus Raskin of IPS made the same list as the Black Panthers' Hughie Newton and the Brookings Institution's Leslie Gelb.

The list of news reporters and editors appeared random and wholly out of proportion to their activities and attitudes. Because so many Californians were in the White House, Ed Guthman, managing editor of the *Los Angeles Times* and Robert Kennedy's friend and one-time spokesman, who had turned the *LA Times* from pro to anti-Nixon, was named on at least three lists, while certified enemies of Nixon on the *Times* and *Washington Post* failed to make any list at all.

Colson apparently believed that Dean was sorting the stuff, and he diligently kept adding names to "the list."

Dean occasionally would write a memo reminding that "the list" had to be kept to about 20 persons while he conferred with the powers about action against them. Dean produced two priority lists of 20 persons each, not quite the same. They were terrible lists, unrepresentative of real mortal enemies, and any news reporter could have made better lists. One list was headed by Arnold M. Picker, United Artists Corporation; then came Alexander E. Barkan, AFL-CIO; Ed Guthman; Maxwell Dane, a public relations man credited with sinking Goldwater's campaign; Charles Dyson, an associate of Larry O'Brien who ran radio spots against Nixon; Howard Stein, a McCarthy bankroller; Allard Lowenstein, a dump-Nixon leader for 18 years; Morton Halperin; Leonard Woodcock of the United Auto Workers; S. Sterling Munro, Jr., an associate of Senator Jackson; Bernard T. Feld, funder of left-wingers; Sidney Davidoff, a John Lindsay aide; Representative John Conyers, the leading black anti-Nixon spokesman; Samuel M. Lambert of the National Education Association; Stewart Rawlings Mott, funder of leftists; Dan Schorr, "a real media enemy"; S. Harrison Dogole, a Humphrey contributor; actor Paul Newman; and Mary Mc-

Grory, who wrote "daily hate-Nixon articles." The final prime list dropped a few of these names to substitute Eugene Carson Blake; Leonard Bernstein; Lloyd Cutler, who pushed the Common Cause lawsuit; Thomas Watson of IBM; Tom Wicker of the *Times*; and Clark Clifford, who had joined McGovern's campaign.

On September 11, 1972, four days before his first private meeting with Nixon, Dean took the second list, which he apparently believed contained persons susceptible to an investigation of tax irregularities, to IRS director Johnnie Walters. Walters showed the list to Treasury Secretary George Shultz, who told him to do nothing with it.

Several newsmen reported that their 1972 tax returns were audited. So was mine, and I was not anti-Nixon; I had claimed an exemption for overseas residence under the wrong paragraph.

In subsequent days before the Ervin Committee, Dean filled out his testimony with explanations of the enemies lists, which he had kept before Nixon remarked to him, "I hope you are keeping a good list," but without claiming a creator's credit and skillfully evading Senator Baker's questioning about whether he ever went to the IRS.

Reporters and editors could see that, except possibly for the top-twenty list that Dean took to Walters, the lists were not significant, but they made entertaining copy. Publications ran stories with multiple photos of Carol Channing, Joe Namath and Barbra Streisand, knowing that some diligent drudge had volunteered their names to Dean for appearing at a rally or signing a petition. Reporters boasted that they were "high on the enemies list," or chagrined that they had been overlooked. Dean had scored another media coup.

Dean would not be strongly disputed until John Mitchell, Haldeman and Ehrlichman faced the Ervin Committee later in the summer. Mitchell denied ordering the Watergate break-in, and noted that Dean had said Magruder pushed Liddy into it. Mitchell testified that he consistently had withheld from Nixon the "White House horror stories" to avoid damage to the President's re-election. Mitchell denied authorizing an intelligence plot, denied that he had told Dean he would have to use part of a $350,000 fund to pay hush money, denied discussing clemency for Hunt with Dean, denied assuring Ehrlichman that Hunt had been bought off.[30]

Mitchell's testimony in July was quickly topped. Dean, who hung out with the Ervin Committee's majority staff with such eager cooperation that a desk name plate for him was put on a lawyer's desk, had told the staff that Alexander Butterfield should be questioned about the possible taping system installed in the Oval Office, which he had mentioned vaguely at the end of his opening statement. The legal staff in confidential session pried out of Butterfield the admission that he was in charge of the taping system, then put Butterfield before the committee and the television cameras. Butterfield said that virtually all conversations in the Oval Office, Nixon's EOB office and on two White House telephones had been preserved on tape.

The media and the Ervin Committee was rejuvenated with a new war cry: "Nixon bugged himself! Deliver the tapes!"

Revelation of the taping system meant a reprieve for the Ervin Committee, whose personnel had clung to television stardom long after their audience had begun to drift away. The case against Nixon, even with the pursuit of the tapes, had lost momentum by the end of the summer, and Nixon was able to hold two lengthy press conferences, even though all of the questions were hostile.

By early fall it appeared that Nixon would serve out two more years, then retire under a cloud. The Ervin Committee had not produced a basis for impeachment, but perhaps the tapes themselves could be that basis. Leading Democrats, including Kennedy and McGovern, insisted that if Nixon refused to surrender the tapes of his Watergate talks with leading staff members, it would be reason for impeachment, an obstruction of justice.

While the battle of the tapes dominated the news in late summer, the newly appointed Special Prosecutor, Archibald Cox, was preparing trials for the implicated White House staffers.

The new Attorney General, Elliot Richardson, yanked from the Pentagon just as he was studying up as Defense Secretary, pledged to Senators at his confirmation hearings that he would allow the Special Prosecutor complete autonomy in ferreting out the whole Watergate story, that he would not intervene.

Testing the rolling waters of public opinion carefully, Richardson let it be known that he was considering four prominent jurists for Special Prosecutor; he was not going to be stuck with a choice that could be criticized. All four choices turned him down; a Special Prosecutor might be the President's executioner in a white-hot and perhaps irrational political climate.

Richardson then settled on Cox, former Dean of Harvard Law School, idealistic and *weltfremd,* who had been an original member of the Kennedy for President team in Hyannis Port in 1958. Cox's original task for Kennedy had been to coordinate the candidate's speech writers, a job at which he failed, according to Arthur Schlesinger, Jr., because Cox could not keep under control Kennedy's individualistic writers. Cox similarly would lose control of the Special Prosecutor's activist staff. Neither Kennedy nor Johnson had been able to fit Cox into a high government post, and both had made him Solicitor General, a job with more title than substance. Richardson inadvertently had created a leaderless Cox's army that would be out for the blood of all Nixonites.

After John Dean's testimony, in which he had touched all bases including events before he reached the White House, the scale of Watergate misdeeds was well known. Dean had specified dates of his talks with Nixon in the six months of his membership in the inner circle, so that tapes of those dates were pinpointed. The Ervin Committee had not answered Senator Baker's famous question, "What did the President know and when did he know it?" What remained to be done was to fix responsibilities precisely, to find where the devil was buried in the details, and to discover the spot at which the President held a smoking gun.

The testimony of McCord, Magruder and Dean, although tainted and subject to challenge, had wiped out the White House staff, reshuffled the Cabinet and major departments, frustrated the planned governmental reorganization and wrecked Nixon's second term. The only remaining question was impeachment. Although Representative (Father) Robert F. Drinan of Massachusetts had introduced a resolution of impeachment at the end of July, neither Congress nor the public was ready to go along. Drinan had been elected in 1970, running against the Cambodia incursion, and his resolution charging Nixon with genocide in Indochina had no chance. But the tapes could bring impeachment, in the view of Senators Kennedy and McGovern, if Nixon refused to surrender them. There the battle was joined.

Of the hundred or so varied personalities in the White House and Executive Office Building who worked for Nixon, no more than a handful had any serious interest in foreign affairs, and therefore little notion of the heart of Nixon's presidency; Kissinger's National Security Council staff was isolated from Watergate.

Dean and Magruder had become experts on domestic politics, but they were typical Americans in that their horizons were limited to California and Washington, D.C. Both had come to the White House late, not members of the original team, and Nixon's concerns were not theirs.

Neither Dean nor Magruder believed there was a revolution going on in the United States; things had been unruly for the last eight years, most of their adult lives, and government-by-demonstration appeared normal to them. In their books, neither mentions foreign affairs, and both mention interests that are symbolic of success in the American system of values: the importance of clothing and the size of one's office. Dean felt awkward when he first went to San Clemente wearing a suit to find Bob Haldeman wearing a sport coat, but he was relieved to see they were both wearing the same wing-tipped shoes. Magruder, who admired Dean, was pleased to find that they both patronized the same Washington men's shop. With their limited interest in the rest of the world, they did not see any connection between the revolutions—Marxist-Leninist, Maoist, anti-colonial, religious, nationalist—that had been revising the world since World War II and symptoms of revolution in the United States, such as the assassinations of leaders, urban and racial violence, intellectually motivated violent splinter groups. Tending to ignore international events, the backbone of *The New York Times*, they gave about equal political weight to the *Los Angeles Times*, the local power in their California homes.

When Dean made his first dramatic appearance before the Ervin Committee and the rapt nation, his first words were that Watergate was an "inevitable outgrowth of a climate of excessive concern over the political impact of demonstrators, excessive concern over leaks, an insatiable appetite for political intelligence, all coupled with a do-it-yourself White House staff, regardless of the law."

Pondering that opening statement for two months, and believing that concern about demonstrations and leaks was excessive, Dean did not have a clue that publication of the Pentagon Papers was a political assault on the President's conduct of foreign affairs, any more than the Supreme Court majority had understood it to be a political issue, thinking it was a civil rights issue instead.

In this, Dean and Magruder were not much different from the nation's news editors, almost all of whom saw Watergate as a purely domestic affair and something that every American readily understands, a detective story. In the vast nation, only one detective, Sanford J. Unger of the *Washington Post*, noticed that the Pentagon Papers had been in the possession of the Institute for Policy Studies, which was bent on changing the political system, long before the *Times* received the papers, or noticed that there was something peculiar about the quashing of the Boston grand jury through delaying tactics by Senator Gravel and Leonard Rodberg. Ungar's discoveries were not followed up by others. The army of journalist-detectives never discovered, or showed much interest in, the identity and motives of Deep Throat, while some, at the same time, proclaimed that Deep Throat had saved the nation.[31]

During the Watergate period the nation was oblivious to foreign affairs, hardly noticing that the war in Vietnam was in abeyance and perhaps over.

As Special Prosecutor Cox's army closed in on Nixon, yet another scandal broke in August—kickback charges against Vice President Agnew, the first traditional corruption tied to the White House.

Then a foreign event intruded on the media's preoccupation. In the Middle East, an area more directly vital to American interests than Indochina, the October War erupted.

Chapter XIX
The October War and the Saturday Night Massacre

"They say, best men are molded out of faults, and for the most, become much more better by being a little bad."

—Shakespeare, *Measure for Measure*

No one was surprised when Nixon's ventures into the Middle East in 1969 and 1970 made little headway. The surprise was that he attempted an activist policy there while his resources were being drained in a two-front war in Vietnam and at home.

The Middle East exercises in 1970 had been educational. The Rogers-Sisco temporary ceasefire interrupting the War of Attrition remained in force, but only because Nasser died, and the new man in Cairo, Anwar Sadat, had other plans.

The Rogers plan, the overture to Egypt in December 1969, had at first backfired, being met and raised by the Soviets, who sent pilots to Egypt four months later. Nixon had been forced to improvise, suspending deliveries of Phantoms to Israel in the spring of 1970, then shifting gears and sending them when he needed Israel during the revolt in Jordan. When the revolt ended, Nixon inspired a request to Congress for $500 million in aid to Israel, the silent partner in the Jordan venture. The United States still had no relations with Egypt, but a handful of American diplomats occupied the American Embassy in Cairo, and Egyptian officials visited Washington.

In December 1970, Dayan visited Washington, where he was pressed by Nixon, Kissinger, Rogers and Defense Secretary Laird to renew mediation talks through United Nations envoy Gunnar Jarring, talks which had been broken off by Israel at the time of the Jordanian revolt.

Dayan had other concerns at the meeting. Although Nixon had resumed deliveries of military equipment to Israel, Egypt's Foreign Minister, Mahmoud Riad, had just announced in Washington that the United States had promised to suspend arms for Israel again for the duration of talks on a Suez Canal disengagement plan that Sisco was pushing. Dayan pointed out Riad's remarks to Nixon, and thought it odd that Nixon looked surprised and turned to Laird for confirmation. At the end of Dayan's round of consultations, he left Washington feeling that a new arms suspension would remain in effect, and therefore Israel would not be talking with Jarring. Before he left New York, he received a call from Sisco. There had been a reconsideration, and Israel would get the military supplies. Evidently Nixon had intervened, and his stock went up with Dayan, as it would later rise with Golda Meir.

The revolt in Jordan did not end when it disappeared from American newspapers, and the PLO remained in north Jordan. In early 1971, Hussein's army opened a month-long, low-key campaign and drove 7,500 guerrillas out of the country, most of them into Lebanon via Syria, about 100 fleeing into Israel to surrender there.

In Syria, Attassi's government had fallen to a coup by Hafez Assad, author of the Moscow arms deal after the Six Day War. In April 1971, Assad had himself confirmed president with 92% of the vote in a referendum.

In Egypt, Sadat was an unknown quantity. He had been at Nasser's side since the overthrow of King Farouk, first as a ruthless security chief. James P. O'Donnell recalled that Sadat in those days carried a pistol with notches cut in the butt. After the Six Day War, Sadat silently had broken with Nasser. An Egyptian nationalist, he was wary of Nasser's ambition to lead the Arab world, and it was apparent that Nasser's socialism was a prescription for bankruptcy. He distrusted Nasser's pro-Soviet intimates, former Wing Commander Ali Sabry and *Al Ahram* editor Mohamed Heikal. But Sadat carried out Nasser's orders assiduously, in a manner so self-effacing that some called him Nasser's poodle.

Sadat's hold on the country was tenuous, and he moved first to consolidate his relations with the military. When the temporary ceasefire on the Canal came up for renewal in February, Sadat accepted the proposal to allow Israeli ships to use the Canal after an Israeli pullback, with a view to signing a peace agreement with Israel. Rogers congratulated Sadat on his flexibility, politically hazardous in the Arab world. Meir commented that Sadat's offer was "very nice," but not a substitute for negotiations between Israel and the Arabs.

In a candid interview with *Newsweek's* Arnaud de Borchgrave,[1] Sadat went farther, saying he would sign a peace treaty and would recognize the territorial integrity of Israel in exchange for Israeli withdrawal to the 1967 borders. De Borchgrave took Sadat's views to Meir in Israel, starting a series of interviews that almost became a dialogue, but Meir dashed cold water on a settlement without direct negotiations. Sadat proclaimed 1971 "the year of decision," in which Arab armies would attack and overwhelm Israel. Everyone dismissed his threat as hyperbole.

Although De Borchgrave thought a chance for peace was lost through Israeli overconfidence, few in the Middle East thought Sadat was in a position to negotiate. Shortly after Sadat made his peace proposal officially to Jarring, he crushed a coup plot by Ali Sabry, bringing an alarmed President Podgorny from Moscow to Cairo to reconfirm the 15-year-old treaty of cooperation and friendship. Sadat then conducted a sweeping purge of the army and bureaucracy that included a start on dismantling Nasser's socialism, spurring the first unrest at Cairo university. Sadat visited Moscow in October and announced a new arms agreement.

Early in 1972 a second thin chance for peace appeared. Jordan was free of guerrillas, and contrary to media and State Department prophecy, Hussein was not regarded as a butcher; rather his popularity appeared secure. Israel's border with Jordan saw active traffic, and the West Bank was quiet. In March, Hussein proposed a federated state with the West Bank and a joint administration of Jerusalem with Israel. The proposal was not acceptable to Israel, and the suggestion isolated Hussein in the Arab world. Sadat broke relations with Jordan, and the Gulf states withheld Hussein's subsidies until he recanted.

Sadat's relations with the Soviets deteriorated through two visits to

Moscow in early 1972, in part because the Soviets did not deliver the arms promised the preceding October and insisted on supervision of weaponry in Egypt. In July Sadat ordered the Soviet military out of Egypt, and 12,000 Soviet soldiers manning missile sites and 200 pilots left. By the end of July, 40,000 Soviet personnel, including dependents, had left Egypt, leaving about 2,000 technicians and advisers. Sadat's efforts to solicit Western arms foundered, however, on his anti-Jewish statements—"a mean, traitorous and treacherous people"—and on the Munich massacre of 11 Israeli Olympics athletes by Fatah guerrillas.

Sadat's break with the Soviets, although not complete, gave the Israelis a feeling of relative security, and when Meir visited Nixon in March 1973, she remarked, "We've never had it so good."

The 1973 upheaval in Washington, centered on the Ervin Committee hearings, was regarded with uneasiness in Israel but with interest in Egypt. Leaders of neither country regarded Nixon as endangered in the summer of 1973, but the American version of a purge had left the White House and government in disarray. There was a new Defense Secretary, James Schlesinger; a new CIA chief, William Colby, and Rogers was about to leave, to be replaced by Kissinger. Sadat had worked for two years reorganizing the Egyptian military and pressuring the Soviets into no-strings deliveries of modern weapons, including the new SAM-6 missiles. The Watergate furor was an additional element making the time to strike opportune. In May, Israeli intelligence reported an Egyptian attack was imminent, and Israel partly mobilized at some expense for a false alarm.

In June, as the media build-up to John Dean's testimony dominated news in the United States and the *Times* editorialized that Watergate was "profoundly sinister," Brezhnev arrived in Washington for a return summit negotiation. Nixon and Brezhnev signed a declaration of principles on June 21 that included a renunciation of force by the two superpowers against third nations. It would later provide a rationale for the U.S. nuclear alert against Soviet intervention in the October War.

Nixon flew with Brezhnev on Air Force One across the country to San Clemente, a flight that gave Brezhnev a personal impression of the size of the country, the heavy traffic and efficient roads: the sight of a country difficult to invade and hold by conventional armies, just as the immensity of the Soviet Union precluded successful military occupation by a foreign attacker.

Brezhnev insisted on staying at Nixon's home, in Tricia's small bedroom, apparently so that he could summon Nixon to a midnight conference along the lines of the threatening dacha harangue on Vietnam. The Middle East was Brezhnev's subject, and an acrimonious dispute ensued, Nixon assuring Brezhnev that the United States "will not let Israel go down the tubes."

As Nixon and Brezhnev conferred in San Clemente, Israeli intelligence warned Meir that Sadat planned an attack across the Canal in the autumn. Only Major General Benjamin Peled, the Israeli air force commander, took the warning seriously, pleading for a preëmptive campaign against SAM missile sites. He was turned down.

Brezhnev flew home to Moscow on June 25 as Dean, reading his catalog of Watergate charges, held the Americans hypnotized. The House that day endorsed a Senate bill cutting off funds for bombing the North Vietnamese buildup in Cambodia, which would leave the South Vietnamese entirely on their own. Two days later, Nixon vetoed the bill, and the Senate passed the rider on another bill immediately.

Senate Majority Leader Mike Mansfield said he would continue to attach the rider "again and again, until the will of the people prevails." Mansfield had his way, and, by August, Congress had barred Nixon from any use of American military forces in Indochina. Nixon wrote an angry letter on August 2 to Democratic leaders of Congress charging them with "abandonment of a friend," but as of midnight August 14, 1973, there was an absolute cutoff of American funds, new or old, "to finance directly or indirectly combat activities by United States military forces in or over or from off shore of North Vietnam, South Vietnam, Laos or Cambodia." Nixon had been declawed in Indochina.

Clashes in the Middle East had stepped up after Meir's confident conversations in Washington in March. In April, Israeli commandos raided Beirut, destroying the headquarters of Hawatmeh's Popular Democratic Front. In August, coincident with the first heavy fighting between North Vietnamese and South Vietnamese, who were now on their own, there also was fighting between the PLO guerrillas and the Lebanese army, a prelude to civil war in Lebanon. In September, Israeli jets shot down 12 Syrian jets in two air battles, losing one Mirage. The air clash was reminiscent of the prelude to the Six Day War, but it drew little attention in the United States, where the media was absorbed in Watergate and newspapers had space for only one foreign story, the overthrow of President Salvador Allende in Chile.

In late September, the CIA reported indications that the Egyptians and Syrians were preparing an attack on Israel, and Soviet ships unloaded 3,000 Moroccan soldiers in Syrian ports. The CIA conducted a more thorough analysis, and withdrew the warning on October 5: the Arab troop movements, clear on satellite and overflight surveillance, appeared to be routine maneuvers, nothing to worry about. That day, Israelis learned that the Soviets were evacuating dependents from Egypt and Syria.

On Saturday, October 6, 1973, I was in West Berlin, idled for months by American absorption in Watergate. In early afternoon, a German radio bulletin reported artillery fire at the Suez Canal. Dayan was quoted briefly as saying it was not a mere clash, "It is all-out war." Then both Egyptian and Israeli censorship clamped down, and for hours there was no more news than that. While I booked a call to New York and packed a suitcase, my New York office was calling me. The *News* had Joe Fried in Israel; I was told to try for Cairo. Within an hour of the radio bulletin, I was at Tempelhof.

I asked the attractive German girl at the Pan Am counter if she could check whether Cairo airport was open. She made a call and said it appeared to be closed, but no one was sure; what had happened? I told her of the radio bulletin.

"Who fired the first shot?" she demanded. I didn't know. Her reaction was representative of most instant opinion in the West, I reflected. It would be assumed that Israel was staging another preëmptive attack, but if it turned out to be Egypt, the matter would be dropped.

Flying on the first leg to Frankfurt, I felt queasy, skin prickly, as I realized that Israel already had lost the war. There was nothing for Israel in this war except casualties. Israel could not think of occupying the vast city of Cairo, which had several times Israel's population. Holding to its 1967 gains too long, Israel could not even threaten to reconquer territory. It held no threat for the Arab nations. Sadat had started the war, a bold and brilliant coup, and he could hardly lose, whatever the military outcome.

There are no unbiased reporters, and bias is sharpened in the Middle East. On a sentimental level, the first time I saw Israel before the 1967 war it was an exhilarating, miraculous little country, intellectually stimulating and innovative, the first to build a city based on desalinated water, revolutionary in its agriculture, brave, humane and thoroughly democratic. On a practical level, no Arab nation could be destroyed in the war; Israel could be.

My bias did not mean I was anti-Arab. The Arab nations are as ethnically diverse as Swedes and Greeks; Nasser remarked that an Arab is anybody who thinks he's an Arab. Altogether, they are intriguing and original, creators of superlatives including the world's best architecture; a case can be made that Arabs invented journalism. The cultural fall out of Islam, or Submission, gave me trouble, especially the notion that truth is what is good for Allah, a concept that had contaminated politics beyond the norm. I was not always sure when Arab political statements were to be taken as true, or when they were to be understood to be discountable. The world would be a poor place if either Arabs or Israelis were subtracted from it, but in 1973 only the Israelis faced subtraction.

A phone call in Rome confirmed that Cairo was out of reach and Beirut was open, so I flew on to try to get to Damascus. Syria also was in the war.

Beirut was apprehensive and hostile. Even the Saint Georges Hotel, my favorite in the world—until it was destroyed later by the PLO—had a sullen atmosphere. A few days later at the American Embassy, which had been rocketed by guerrillas and was protected by Lebanese army armored cars, I learned that the Israeli counter-offensive on the Golan Heights had been frustrated by the arrival of Iraqi troops—a division plus a brigade—in the middle of the Israelis' pincer movement. The Iraqis inflicted few casualties, but they stalled the Israeli attack as ammunition was expended knocking out 80 Iraqi tanks. As usual, the only hard information was coming out of Israel, while the Arab media proclaimed victories.

At the newspaper *An Nahar*, despite the victories, Arab newsmen dropped their usual courtesy and were abrupt or emotional. One waved a wet photoprint, crying, "Look at this, what your Jew friends have done to Damascus." Damascus had been the Garden of Eden. Israel had bombed its television transmitter after a telecast had displayed, against a background of fierce threats and wildly strident music, the humiliation of captured Israeli pilots. Three bombs fell at the junction of the television station, the War Ministry and the Soviet Embassy. According to the wet photoprint thrust at me, the damage had been craters in the street.

The concern over Damascus was not entirely on the level. Lebanon had been at odds with Syria over Syrian promotion of the PLO in Lebanon. This war was more menacing than earlier ones, and Lebanese were worried not only about Israeli bombs but about the prospect of a victorious Syria taking over Lebanon, too. Syria never had exchanged embassies with Lebanon on the ground that it was historically part of greater Syria. In attempts to get into Syria through Lebanese official contacts, it became apparent that relations between the two countries were abysmal.

Beirut was intimidating in 1973, and a thin source of news. Syria admitted only a few correspondents known to them. The only way to Cairo was through Libya and the 1,000-mile Benghazi Express, Libyan taxis following the World War II El Alamein-Tobruk route. Libya's Moammer Khadafy admitted no travelers whose passports were not written in Arabic, so I embarked with a photocopy of my passport with Arabic translations written over it, hoping to pass with the help of a questionable visa-note grudgingly released by the Libyan consul. I did not know that Sadat had asked Khadafy to relax his rule for Western correspondents, whom he wanted in Cairo, and was surprised to be admitted at Benghazi airport. From hostile Lebanon through hostile Libya, where a Dutch television team and I were temporary prisoners of vigilante children at the taxi stop, I entered into comparatively friendly Egypt.

The coordinated Egyptian-Syrian attack on Israel at 2 p.m. on October 6, Yom Kippur, was miraculously kept secret, in part because Sadat's secret notification of Arafat was ridiculed in Beirut when it promptly leaked to the Arab press. The attack represented masterful planning.

Sadat had no intention of sending his army across the Sinai to Israel as Nasser had done in 1967; Israel would be left to Syria. Sadat's plan was to seize the length of the Canal and penetrate into the Sinai no more than 12 miles, re-establishing Egyptian self-respect. That would keep his troops and armor under the umbrella of the batteries of SAM-2, SAM-3 and SAM-6 missiles strung along the Canal that had aggravated the War of Attrition. If the Israeli air force attacked and was destroyed by the missiles, then Sadat's army would advance under cover of Egypt's husbanded air force. The strategy partly succeeded. When war broke out, Benny Peled was caught with many of his jets on the ground undergoing reconfiguration to enable rocket attacks on the SAM sites. He was forced to switch back to bombing configuration because rockets had no effect on the heavy Soviet pontoon bridging equipment across the Canal.

Both the Syrians and Egyptians employed innovations, well-drilled troops and tactics suited to the different situations on the Canal and on the Golan Heights.

Syria had 1,700 Soviet-built tanks in readiness and threw 500 tanks and 45,000 men into the assault on the first day against 117 Israeli tanks and 5,000 men on the Heights. Syria added 300 more tanks on the second day. Syrian artillery blasted the Israeli observation camp on

Mount Hermon, covering an unprecedented landing by Syrian helicopter-borne troops.

The main thrust of the Syrian attack came south of Kuneitra, the only town on the Heights, instead of at the town itself, where the Israelis had expected it. Israel, not yet mobilized, was forced to throw ready troops onto the Heights, once again up those torturous roads, rather than drive immediately toward the Canal.

The Israeli-occupied territory on the Heights is a complex killing ground, about 15 miles by 40 miles of rugged ground full of ditches, hedgerows and scrub forests that make natural ambushes. By the third day of the war, Israeli troops had knocked out 900 Syrian tanks but still were reeling from the force of new and varied Soviet weaponry, with several of the key Israeli commanders dead. At one point, Syrian bridging equipment almost reached the Jordan River, where the road to Haifa would have been open. At the time of the Israeli counter-offensive on the fifth day, when a Jordanian brigade and Saudi troops had joined Syria, the northern front was touch-and-go. Major General Keegan said later that, if Soviet officers flying overhead in helicopters had possessed more sophisticated communications equipment and had succeeded in coordinating Syrian forces on the ground, Israel would have lost the war.

Egypt had drilled and trained its troops for specific exercises, practicing for months the use of bridging equipment on dry-land ramps, testing out hydraulic pump teams on rafts to wash through the ridge of sand barrier on the Israeli side of the Canal with high-pressure hoses. The Egyptian attack sent the Second Army and part of the Third Army across the Canal along its length, using rafts, inflatable boats and massive bridging equipment that had been assembled behind the sand barrier ridge on the Eqyptian side of the Canal.

Of Israel's 16 strongholds along the Canal banks, the Bar-Lev line of forts made of heavy concrete, girders and thick steel mesh, 15 fell on the first day, each manned by Yom Kippur holiday crews of only 20 to 30 Israelis. One stronghold south of Port Said held out for several days, long enough to surrender. With 2,200 tanks in readiness, Egypt put 300 tanks across the Canal on the first day, overwhelming the handful of Israeli tanks stationed at a few of the strongholds. When the Israeli air force knocked out a pontoon bridge section, a new section was floated into place within hours.

Israel required 72 hours to mobilize the 120,000 reserves who were called up only hours before the attacks on October 6. By the time a part of them could begin moving across the Sinai, Israel had lost to Egypt's SAM missiles 50 planes, almost a quarter of its jet fighter-bombers, the key weapon. Egyptian armor did not try to seize the Mitla and Gidi passes, but only made shallow penetrations into the Sinai, covering infantry that dug in. When 2,000 Egyptian and Israeli tanks clashed in massive tank battles later, thousands of Egyptian infantrymen emerged from foxholes firing two-mile-range Sagger anti-tank missiles and the small, 375-yard-range RGP-7, the Soviet rocket grenade that later became the favorite weapon of the PLO.

Both Egyptian and Syrian troops carried the one-man Strela, or SAM-7 anti-aircraft missile. Both held in readiness 55-mile-range Frog-7 missiles and 180-mile-range Scud missiles with 1,200-pound warheads. Both Arab armies were fighting, not retreating, even at night with new optical equipment.

In the first five days of the war, when Israel was on the defensive and almost losing the Golan Heights, its fate became enmeshed with the political warfare in Washington over Watergate as well as with Arabist factions in both the State and Defense Departments.

The beleaguered Nixon was in retreat before the Hydra-headed Watergate charges, particularly two campaigns that were coming to flash point, the Agnew case and the battle over the tapes.

On August 29, Judge Sirica had granted a petition by Special Prosecutor Cox to subpoena nine tapes pinpointed by John Dean's testimony. Nixon had taken the case to the Appeals Court, arguing that a President must have confidentiality. He expected to lose the appeal, but he hoped to limit the delivery to those portions of the tapes dealing with Watergate conversations.

Nixon therefore had his secretary, Rose Mary Woods, transcribing the tapes, and she reported that she had lost four to five minutes from one tape through accidental erasure.

Simultaneously, through August and September, Vice President Agnew had been the target of a Justice Department investigation for fraud and bribery while Governor of Maryland, fighting back against leaked stories to the *Times* and *Washington Post* that treated him as convicted. Nixon, his legal counsel, Fred Buzhardt, and his new White House chief of staff, General Alexander Haig, became entangled in Agnew's defense because the threat of impeaching a Vice President offered stimulation toward impeaching the President. On October 5, the eve of the October War, Agnew's attorney signaled that Agnew was ready to capitulate and resign. Buzhardt agreed to speak about plea bargaining with Attorney General Richardson, who was pushing Agnew's prosecution vigorously. They were to meet October 6, decision day for Agnew.

Early that morning Ambassador Kenneth Keating, the former New York Senator defeated by Robert Kennedy, reported from Israel that Meir expected an Egyptian-Syrian attack within hours and would appreciate anything the Americans could do to forestall it. Nixon in Washington and Kissinger and Sisco in New York, where the United Nations General Assembly was meeting, were all awakened with the report.

In Washington the Special Action Group of leaders from the State and Defense Departments, Joint Chiefs and CIA director, met in contact with Kissinger by telephone. Damascus radio first announced the fighting, saying that Israel had attacked Syria, and part of the Special Action Group believed that Israel had moved preëmptively. Within an hour it was apparent that Israel was under double attack, but Washington's perception of the war was fatalistic rather than alarmed. Washington regarded Israel as invincible in the region, and the main concern was keeping the Soviets from reaping benefits from the war. No Washington administration ever has appreciated that Israel's capacity to accept casualties is limited.

Neither Nixon nor Kissinger recognized that Israel had lost the war politically with the first shot, but some Israelis did, including Meir and Dayan. Dayan later would be criticized in Israel for indecision and his initial impulse to pull back from the Canal. Chaim Herzog wrote, "The shock of the war caused something to snap in Dayan."[2] But Dayan was retreat-oriented well before the war broke out. He had not wanted to seize the Canal in the Six Day War, and for several years had pushed for a political settlement. The attack confirmed his apprehensions.

When Kissinger learned of Egypt's demands on the second day of the war in a message from Hafez Ismail—Israel's surrender of all occupied territories—he still blithely thought the United States could let the Israelis "beat them up for a day or two and that would quiet them down." Israel's Ambassador Simcha Dinitz seemed to Kissinger not unduly alarmed. Dinitz asked that the United States stall any United Nations order for a ceasefire until Israel's mobilization had time to take hold. But on day three, with catastrophe near on the Golan Heights, Israel asked for a resupply of weapons, stunned by its air losses.

Nixon admired the Israelis, resented their distrust of him, resented more the enmity of many of their American Jewish backers, and took an unsentimental view of the crisis. He did not want the Arabs crushed, throwing them further into the arms of the Soviets. He did not want either side to win, but rather to reach an equilibrium, "even an equilibrium of exhaustion," as a foundation for reaching an enforceable settlement.

During the third day of the war, Israel was told it could have two

Phantoms to replace the 50 jets it had lost, a token that dismayed Dayan. In both the State and Defense Departments, warnings were sounded of Arab oil power, and talk centered on keeping any aid covert. Pilots of a few Israeli commercial El Al planes who arrived to transport ammunition were told they could land at U.S. Air Force bases only after their Star of David insignia had been painted over. By the end of the day Israel had lost 1,000 men.

Agnew visited Nixon on October 10, a traumatic meeting in the political wreckage of the White House, already swept of Haldeman, Ehrlichman, Dean, Colson, Strachan, Krogh and others, then tendered his resignation to the new Secretary of State, Kissinger, as the law would have it. As Agnew went off to face court like the others, Nixon was receiving anxious messages from Meir.

Nixon's response was foreordained. Seventeen years before, as Vice President, he had been assigned to defend the decisions of his mentor, John Foster Dulles, at Suez, and he knew that Dulles' decisions had begun the debacle that was still with him. Nixon ordered Kissinger to replace Israeli military equipment losses on a one-for-one basis, telling Kissinger to work out the logistics. It was a response well beyond the hopes of Israelis.

On October 12 Nixon nominated Representative Gerald Ford to become Vice President, just as the Court of Appeals ordered Nixon to deliver nine tapes to Judge Sirica. The Defense Department still was delivering nothing to Israel except ammunition on the El Al planes. Defense Secretary Schlesinger had solicited commercial charter planes to transport supplies to Israel, finding none were able and ready to do so. Meanwhile Soviet Antonov-22 transports loaded with munitions flew regularly over the Cairo Hilton Hotel, and on October 11, Soviet ships that had been loaded at Black Sea ports before the outbreak of war were unloading in Syrian harbors.

The Western Allies refused landing rights for U.S. Air Force C-130 planes, and now the Portugese Azores also barred from landing the C-130s that Schlesinger sent. Chancellor Willy Brandt informed the United States that NATO supplies stocked in West Germany could not be transferred legally out of the NATO area, and could not be loaded in West German ports for shipment to Israel. Nixon signed a stiff note to Portugal that reopened the Azores, and on day four of the war ordered Kissinger and Schlesinger to get the supplies to Israel "on anything that flies."

On October 13, three C-5A Galaxy transports, giant planes under fire in Congress for cost overruns and inefficiency, flew nonstop to Israel. Two days later the United States publicly confirmed the airlift, and eventually 72 Galaxys flew 560 sorties to Israel carrying tanks, artillery, helicopters, ammunition and communications equipment. Phantom jets, replaced on a one-for-one basis, depleting Air Force stocks, flew nonstop to the war, refueling in the air. They arrived in the middle of the major Egyptian tank push in the Sinai, at the same time that a flanking attack led by Israeli Major General Ariel Sharon crossed the Canal to invade Egypt's Deversoir region at the northern end of the Great Bitter Lake.

The next day Kissinger and Le Duc Tho were awarded the Nobel Peace Prize for the settlement of the Vietnam war, Tho refusing his honor, declaring that the war was not over. Kissinger would return his when Saigon fell in 1975. That day six Arab nations of the Organization of Petroleum Exporting Countries announced a 17% increase in oil prices, the first step toward skyrocketing increases that would cripple Western economies. The oil squeeze had been in the cards, war or no.

For correspondents, Cairo was a physically comfortable place to sit out the war in frustration. Unlike Israel, which warned correspondents that they were responsible for their own safety and then let them rent cars from Hertz and go to whatever battlefield they could get to, Egypt kept correspondents in Cairo where officials would not speak with them. Egypt had its reasons for the blackout of information; in ten days the Arab armies had run out of steam, and the national mood was stoic anticipation of another defeat. Kosygin came to Cairo and left without correspondents knowing it. Occasionally, a busload of correspondents was taken to a hospital where they could interview civilian casualties, but not military casualties. Of about 300 correspondents in town, about 100 managed to make one or two guided tours of the Canal front, mostly to see the devastation Israel had inflicted on Ismailia during the War of Attrition. On one tour, we heard descriptions of total Egyptian victories at the strongholds and saw bodies of Israelis rotting in shattered armored cars, left there for the jackals, at another point a segregated military cemetery.

If a correspondent unearthed a scrap of news, running between various embassies, it was eliminated from his copy by the censors. Any newspaper reader in a Western country knew more about the progress of the war than correspondents in Cairo, who got their news from the BBC via shortwave.

The only correspondent permitted to leave Cairo was *Newsweek's* De Borchgrave, who accompanied an Egyptian officer friend to the

Southeast front. Six months before the war, De Borchgrave had published another in his series of Sadat interviews in the candid language they had established.[3] Sadat had said then that "the battle is now inevitable." The Nixon administration had sided entirely with the Israelis, and negotiations were hopeless: "Everything was discouraging. Complete failure and despair sum it up," Sadat said. "Israelis are quite happy where they are. It's hopeless to change it." Sadat warned of the American refusal to take into account Arab psychology. De Borchgrave, sold on Sadat's sincerity, had outlined the coming war to Kissinger. He was not able to get across either in Washington or with the Pulitzer committee, which awarded that year's prize to Hedrick Smith of the *Times* for reporting from the Soviet Union.

During the war, even De Borchgrave's contacts produced only scraps in Cairo. At the end of October, in his only wartime appearance before the media, Sadat apologized for the primitive public relations, while himself speaking in arabesques: Egypt had responded to aggression on October 6; there was only an insignificant pocket of Israeli troops near Suez; most of the Third Army was not encircled but poised to strike at the Israeli rear.

With nothing of significance to report, a few of us were heartened to be summoned to the office of Ashraf Gorbal, Sadat's media coordinator. Gorbal, normally courteous, was grimly angry. When we were seated, he rose and strode stiff-legged to a map on the wall to point out El Arish, the former Egyptian air base in the Sinai, where I had seen MiG wreckage during the Six Day War.

"The United States," Gorbal said, "is flying Phantom jet aircraft directly into El Arish, into territory that has been Egyptian for a 1,000 years, and turning them over to Israeli pilots on the battlefield. There never has been a more flagrant violation of international law."

Already, the United States had delivered 35 Phantoms to the Israelis in El Arish, Gorbal said. "We are not anxious to be at loggerheads with America. We hope that America has not reached the point of no return. Do you think the flights are in the interest of peace?" He dismissed us.

Egypt regarded the deliveries as grave, and Gorbal would have been disappointed that it made me light-hearted. Leaving his office, I said to Joe Morris of the *Los Angeles Times,* that was a story I could believe. It had Richard Nixon's fingerprints all over it, like the bombing of Hanoi and mining of Haiphong. Morris was noncommittal; characteristically, he did not say that he was ill. He vanished a few days later, evacuated to West Germany to be treated for lymphatic cancer.

There was later a controversy in the American Jewish community and among foreign policy intellectuals over who was responsible for the airlift to Israel. The airlift generally was approved in the United States, although it hastened the oil boycott of October 20, just as King Faisal of Saudi Arabia had warned on October 13, the day the first Galaxy took off. Faisal also told Washington not to send the scheduled ambassador to Saudi Arabia.

The media tended to credit Kissinger with the airlift. His stock had risen with his Nobel Prize, and commentators remarked that it was a pity Kissinger had been born outside the United States; he seemed to be the author of the opening to China and SALT-1, and he, instead of Nixon, should have been President.

The first full account of the airlift was by Marvin and Bernard Kalb, then of CBS, in their book *Kissinger*,[4] and it was promptly challenged. The Kalb brothers' theme was that, while Nixon eventually cut through the delays, Kissinger had played a vital role in his one-man fight against Pentagon officials allied with oil interests to get the airlift moving. In the Kalbs' version, Schlesinger played the heavy. Tad Szulc challenged that version in a magazine article that absolved the Pentagon of foot-dragging and blamed Kissinger for the initial delays and insistence on "low profile" deliveries of weapons.

The two versions, pro-Kissinger and anti-Kissinger, were examined by Edward Luttwak and Walter Laqueur in *Commentary*,[5] noting that in both versions, the impression was given that Nixon, rendered passive by Watergate and Agnew's resignation, went along with Kissinger's policy until Israel was on the ropes, when he intervened. To the media, it was unbearable that the airlift could have been Nixon's work.

Golda Meir thought otherwise. She wrote Nixon, "Early this morning I was told of the decision you made to assure us the immediate flow of U.S. material. . . . We are fighting against heavy odds, but we are fully confident that we shall come out victorious. When we do, we will have you in mind."[6]

Chaim Herzog did not regard the delays in delivering weapons with the seriousness that Dayan or the American Jewish community did, calling the American resupply "generous and unexpected." Herzog wrote:

> Only the United States appreciated the significance of Israel's struggle. Paradoxically enough, the courageous and unequivocal American stand in favor of Israel gave the United States a standing in the Arab world such as it had not known before, and showed the countries of Western Europe in their craven and abject surrender to the Arab sheikhs to be the weak, leaderless and divided community they are.[7]

(When the war subsided, Willy Brandt, in the spirit of the U.S. dove Senators, declared, "In our hearts we were not neutral.")

Those controversies still were in the future on October 20, when Saudi Arabia, Algeria, Libya, Kuwait and Abu Dhabi, encouraged by the Soviets who were pressing Algeria to join the war, imposed a total oil boycott on the United States and The Netherlands, whose leaders had dared express sympathy with Israel as the victim of a surprise attack. Except for Holland, Western Europe was not boycotted, but oil supplies were curtailed, and the subtraction of Rotterdam's refineries left Western Europe harder hit than the United States; weekend driving was banned for months in Europe.

Kissinger on the day of the boycott was in Moscow, in response to an ultimative message to Nixon from Brezhnev, negotiating terms of a Middle East ceasefire that the United States and Soviet Union would push through the United Nations Security Council. Nixon sent to Congress a request for $2.2 billion in aid to Israel.

Simultaneously with the oil boycott and Kissinger's negotiations in Moscow for a ceasefire that would not dictate terms to Israel, Nixon's battle to retain control of the White House tapes reached a climax. Nixon had attempted to negotiate a compromise, under which transcripts of those parts of the tapes dealing with Watergate would be verified by a referee, Senator John Stennis, and turned over to Sirica, Nixon retaining the actual tapes with other conversations on them. Special Prosecutor Cox held a press conference to declare that he was "not out to get the President," but he insisted on having the tapes.

The *Times* brought out its eight-column banner type:

NIXON TO KEEP TAPES DESPITE RULING;
WILL GIVE OWN SUMMARY; COX DEFIANT
Israel Reports 10,000 Men and 200 Tanks Across Canal.[8]

A *Times* editorial saw hope in the Soviet offer to Kissinger of a plan for an international peacekeeping force backed by big-power guarantees. The editorial was not helpful, undercutting Kissinger's efforts toward direct Israeli-Arab negotiations.

Cox's statement that he was not out to get the President, and his modest apology that he might be "getting too big for my britches," was at least the equal of Nixon's dissimulations. Cox was, of course, out to get the President, and his men were opening an investigation into whether Bebe Rebozo used influence to exclude competition for his small bank in Key West. Nixon ordered Cox fired. Haig telephoned Richardson to ask him to dismiss Cox, telling him it was "an order from your Commander in Chief." Richardson refused and said he would have to resign; he had given guarantees to Senators during his confirmation hearings that he would not interfere with Cox.

At a tense meeting in the Oval Office, Richardson submitted his resignation to Nixon, declining to delay it until the Middle East crisis was over. His deputy, William Ruckelshaus, resigned with him rather than fire Cox. The Solicitor General, Robert Bork, agreed to fire Cox and then resign later. Seven FBI men sealed Cox's office, barring entry to his staff. The media's charges ranged from a fascist coup to insanity. The *Times* bannered:

> NIXON DISCHARGES COX FOR DEFIANCE;
> ABOLISHES WATERGATE TASK FORCE;
> RICHARDSON AND RUCKELSHAUS OUT
> Kissinger Meets Brezhnev on Mideast Cease-Fire Plan.[9]

While Kissinger flew back from Moscow with the ceasefire agreement, Haig cabled him en route that the Washington situation was "at white heat," and that "an impeachment stampede" might develop in Congress unless Kissinger could meet with Congressional leaders and stress Nixon's accomplishments in the Middle East crisis.

Two days after the Saturday Night Massacre, the Soviets and Americans rammed through Resolution 338 in the UN Security Council, ordering a ceasefire in the Middle East just as an Israeli attempt to capture Ismailia failed. Egypt and Israel accepted the ceasefire immediately on October 22, Syria some hours later, but like all Middle East ceasefires, violations occurred on all sides. Hours after the ceasefire, Sharon's troops completed encirclement of Egypt's Third Army at Suez.

On October 23, the House Democratic leader, Thomas P. (Tip) O'Neill, a Kennedy stalwart from Massachusetts, forwarded an impeachment resolution to the House Judiciary Committee for "speedy and expeditious consideration." It was one of 23 impeachment resolutions circulating in the House. Father Drinan, Tip's Massachusetts colleague, had submitted a resolution in July charging aggression against Cambodia, but O'Neill was a professional; he had lined up support.

Faced with a revolt of Republican congressmen, Nixon agreed to surrender the tapes to Sirica. The next day, he vetoed a War Powers Bill that would have tied his hands in the Middle East conflict.

Nixon was near the end of his stamina. He told Kissinger:

> They are doing it because of their desire to kill the President. And they may succeed. I may physically die. . . . What they care about is destruction. It brings me sometimes to feel like saying to hell with it. I would like to see them run this country and see what they do. The real tragedy is if I move out, everything we have

done will crumble. The Russians will look for other customers, the Chinese will lose confidence, the Europeans will—. They just don't realize they are throwing everything out the window. I don't know what in the name of God. . . .[10]

Israel's encirclement of the Third Army at Suez represented a military victory and a powerful bargaining chip—35,000 Egyptian military men at Israel's mercy—but it also represented the Arab humiliation that neither Nixon nor Kissinger wanted. Sadat appealed to the Soviets, proposing a joint Soviet-U.S. peacekeeping force even as UN truce officials arrived in Egypt. On October 23, Brezhnev sent a stiff message to Nixon charging the Israelis with attacking the Third Army in violation of the ceasefire and implying American collusion with the Israelis. A second ceasefire went into effect October 24, but the Soviets had decided to follow up Sadat's request; they would have a third party propose a Soviet-U.S. peacekeeping force in the Security Council, where the United States would be forced to go along or veto it.

Sadat made public his call for a Soviet-U.S. peacekeeping force on October 24, just as Nixon wrote him asking him not to do so. The United States had known since October 11, when Israeli troops were counter-attacking in Syria, that the Soviets had three airborne divisions on alert. There were now seven Soviet airborne divisions on alert and 85 Soviet ships in the Mediterranean. A Soviet task force including landing craft and helicopter carriers was nearing Alexandria.

That day Brezhnev sent two messages to Nixon, increasingly harsh, charging Israel with attacking the Third Army, which had attempted a small breakout, and demanding immediate U.S.-Soviet intervention. Brezhnev warned that the Soviets were considering going into Egypt unilaterally. Nixon told Haig and Kissinger to work out a response that included action to deter the Soviets.

Nixon was at the end of his rope. He was now committed to delivering the nine subpoenaed tapes to Sirica, and two of the tapes never had been recorded. Because he did not usually go to his hideaway office in the Executive Office Building on Saturdays, the Secret Service had not replenished the tape recorder there for his conversations with Haldeman, Ehrlichman, Petersen, Kleindienst and Dean on April 15, 1973, and the tape ran out in the middle of his talk with Ehrlichman. On one of the tapes that existed, Rose Mary Woods said she had inadvertently erased a part when she was interrupted by a telephone call for four or five minutes while she was transcribing the tape. Nixon anticipated that the roof would fall in when that became public. The impeachment process had begun in the House.

When Kissinger collected his aide, General Brent Scowcroft, Haig,

Schlesinger, JCS Chairman Admiral Thomas H. Moorer and CIA Director Colby in the White House situation room, Nixon did not attend. Kissinger and Haig, his confidants during the Vietnam crises and throughout the Middle East crisis, knew his requirements, and Nixon probably did not trust himself to dominate the meeting if he attended. The situation room consultants unanimously recommended that Nixon call a world-wide Defense Condition Three alert of nuclear and strike forces, one step up from the Defcon-4 readiness alert but below Defcon-2, imminent attack. At the same time messages would be sent to Sadat and Brezhnev warning against any superpower intervention in the Third Army crisis.

Nixon later wrote in his memoirs that he sent that night messages to Sadat and Brezhnev. To Sadat, referring to his earlier message, he said, "I asked you to consider the consequences for your country if the two great nuclear countries were to confront each other on your soil. I ask you further to consider the impossibility for us undertaking the diplomatic initiative which was to start with Dr. Kissinger's visit to Cairo on November 7 if the forces of one of the great nuclear powers were to be involved militarily on Egyptian soil. We are at the beginning of a new period in the Middle East. Let us not destroy it at this moment."[11]

Nixon's message to Brezhnev said in conciliatory language but conveying unmistakable intent that the proposal to send joint U.S.-Soviet forces into Egypt was "not appropriate in the present circumstances," and denying there were any ceasefire violations to justify it. The message said that "we must view your suggestion of unilateral action as a matter of gravest concern involving incalculable consequences." The message did not rule out possible U.S. and Soviet participation in a United Nations peacekeeping force, but it said, "You must know that we could in no event accept unilateral action."[12]

Kissinger notes in *Years of Upheaval* that this message was delivered to Ambassador Dobrynin at 5:40 a.m., about six hours after the Defcon-3 alert, when it was presumed that the Soviets would have monitored the alert. Kissinger wrote that it was sent "in Nixon's name," implying that he wrote it. Kissinger may have written both messages, which would not invalidate Nixon's claim to authorship; diplomats are hired to write messages.

Within a few hours of the midnight Defcon-3 alert, it had leaked and was on radio bulletins at 6:30 a.m., spurring alarmed activity at the United Nations.

That evening the *Times* bannered:

U.S. FORCES PUT ON WORLDWIDE ALERT
LEST SOVIETS SEND TROOPS TO MIDEAST;

CRISIS EASED AS U.S. SETS UP A PATROL.[13]

This time the European press joined in with doomsday headlines. Israel quickly agreed to permit 100 trucks to carry food, water and medical supplies to the Third Army. Sadat sent Nixon a message through Hafez Ismail saying he would settle for an international United Nations force. Brezhnev sent Nixon a message that he would dispatch 90 observers to the Middle East, omitting any mention of troops.

A sizeable part of the American media believed that Nixon had ordered the nuclear alert in a desperate and perhaps insane effort to divert attention from impeachment.

Kissinger called a press conference at noon, at which he was at his jaunty best. He began with a rundown of the crisis leading to the alert and the Soviet moves toward intervention, disclosing as much as he could prudently. When a reporter posed a question in the framework of something Kissinger had written, he remarked, "You are quoting my favorite author" (laughter). Kissinger said that Nixon had been "in complete charge" at all times, but had not been at the meeting formulating the response. Still, he was asked repeatedly questions that implied the alert had been phoney, one questioner saying, "You are asking the American people to accept a very dramatic military alert on the basis of a handful of snow, without telling them or us exactly why."

Kissinger's replies to the barrage of questions were:

> It is a symptom of what is happening in our country that it could even be suggested that the United States would alert its forces for domestic reasons. . . . It is up to you ladies and gentlemen to determine whether this is the moment to try to create a crisis of confidence in the field of foreign policy as well. . . . There has to be a minimum of confidence that the senior officials of the American government are not playing with the lives of the American people.

The next day Nixon faced a press conference to try to explain his firing of Cox, still seething at press reports of a Gestapo takeover of the Special Prosecutor's office and media doubt about the validity of the alert.

Dan Rather of CBS asked for his thoughts on the impeachment movement. Nixon replied:

> Well, I'm glad we don't take the vote of this room, let me say. . . . As a matter of fact, Mr. Rather, you may remember that when I made the most difficult decision of my first term on December 18, the bombing of—by B-52s—of North Vietnam,

that exactly the same words were used on the networks that were used now: tyrant, dictator, he's lost his senses, he should resign, he should be impeached. But I stuck it out, and as a result of that we not only got our prisoners of war home, on their feet rather than on their knees, but we brought peace to Vietnam, something we didn't have for over 12 years. It was a hard decision and one that many of my friends in the press who had consistently supported me on the war up to that time disagreed with.

Now, in this instance, I realize there are people who feel that the actions I've taken in regard to the dismissal of Mr. Cox are grounds for impeachment. I would respectfully suggest that even Mr. Cox and Mr. Richardson have agreed that the President had the right—the Constitutional right—to dismiss anybody in the Federal government.

The events of this past week, I know, for example, in your head office in New York some thought it was simply a blown-up exercise, there wasn't a real crisis. I wish it had been that. It was a real crisis. . . .

A reporter said, "You once wrote too many shocks can drain a nation and even cause a rebellion to get progressive change and progress. Do you think America is at that point now?"

Nixon replied that if a revolt occurred, the electronic media might be a contributing cause.

I have never heard or seen such outrageous, vicious, distorted reporting in 27 years of public life. . . . Perhaps what happened is that what we did brought it about, and therefore the media decided they would have to take that particular line. But when people are pounded night after night with that kind of frantic, ·hysterical reporting, it naturally shakes their confidence. . . .

A *Times* news analysis by Reston commented that Nixon's attack on the television networks had spoiled an otherwise masterful performance:

He looked healthy and vigorous. Considering what he had been through in his crises with the Russians in the Middle East and the courts and Congress at home, and the disgrace of his Vice President and the challenge of Elliot L. Richardson, Archibald Cox and William D. Ruckelshaus, he was remarkably calm and lucid.

He was answering the main question on everybody's mind: how was he holding up under the pressure. Almost all the way through, he was not only holding up very well, but was defending his positions on the courts, Congress and the Middle East with remarkable serenity and skill.

Then, suddenly, and almost precisely as he had done in that famous farewell news conference in Los Angeles 11 years ago, all the controlled rage of this most private and controlled man burst out against the television networks. . . .

. . . he had been so provocative and even vicious in his criticism of the networks that he was asked why he was so angry about them. And then he made the old mistake that has hounded him throughout his political career.

'Don't get the impression,' he said, 'that you can arouse my anger. You see, one can only be angry with those he respects.'

It was about the most vicious remark any American President has made about his critics. . . .

Reston's notion of what constitutes viciousness—disrespect for media commentators—was bizarre, but Reston did have reason for his own smouldering anger. The issue was Israel, the most neuralgic point on the *Times'* anatomy.

Almost everything that Nixon said or did enraged the *Times,* but none of his offenses surpassed the affront of his support of Israel throughout the October War. Israel had been a burden and a source of danger and frustration to the *Times* since 1946, two years before its existence. The *Times* was an American, not a Jewish, newspaper, with a constituency of the Northeast and Washington intellectual elite, but the *Times* also had a proprietary interest in American Jews, some of whom already distrusted *Times* policy toward Israel and the Middle East.

Throughout the October War, the *Times* had done its usual thorough reporting job, but its editors consistently had played down the threat to Israel, making the war a secondary story to the siege of Nixon. Nixon, not threatened Israel, got the banner headlines and almost daily lead editorials: "One-Man Law," "The Tape Cover-Up," "Beyond the Tapes," "The Mysterious Tapes," "Moral Paralysis," "Road to Impeachment," "Defiant President," "Impeachment," "The Missing Tapes."

Secondary *Times* editorials on the war urged an early ceasefire, when Israel would have been in the position of a militarily defeated nation. *Times* news stories stressed Sadat's statements that he did not want to destroy Israel, without noting that was Assad's department. Now, Nixon's implied claim to have ordered the nuclear alert to save Israel from a real crisis amounted to attempted subversion of a core *Times* constituency. That Nixon could have had any part in helping Israel was impermissible.

Just as the *Times* was on shaky ground with Jews, Kissinger too had a problem. He was required to display candor and solicitous friendliness to Arabs while shuttling between Cairo, Tel Aviv and Damascus after he met Sadat in Egypt on November 7 and renewed American-Egyptian diplomatic relations. There were murmurs already that he had dragged his feet, or at least not shown sufficient urgency, during the delays in getting the arms airlift started. At the global level, Brezhnev was angry at publicity surrounding the American alert, and it was in Kissinger's and America's interest to play down the seriousness of the Soviet threat in order to soften the challenge of the alert to the Soviets.

On November 21, David Binder of the *Times* Washington bureau wrote a definitive Page 1 piece on the background to the alert, the main source of which appeared to be Kissinger, under the headline, "An Implied Soviet Threat Spurred U.S. Forces Alert."

The story said that the Soviets never had made an actual threat, only an implied one, and it suggested that the Soviets were in part justified: Israel had surrounded the Third Army after Kissinger stopped off in Israel on his way home from Moscow with the ceasefire agreement, and Kissinger felt a sense of betrayal by the Israeli action. The Soviets then had taken advantage of the opportunity to establish a large Soviet presence in the Middle East, and a second Brezhnev message hinted at unilateral action, so Kissinger and Schlesinger decided to call the alert, contacting Nixon by telephone upstairs at the White House.

Binder's story, with a minute-by-minute timetable, said:

> President Nixon remained in charge throughout, his aides say, but he was also remote, staying the entire night in his White House apartment and receiving the telephone messages of Mr. Kissinger and Mr. Schlesinger. Mr. Nixon empowered them to manage the crisis on their own, the Cabinet official said, leaving them to conceive and carry out the various moves.

It said that Haig operated as a go-between and had no decision-making role.

Kissinger also notified the British Ambassador, the NATO Council in Brussels and Ambassador John Scali at the United Nations, then drafted a reply to Brezhnev saying the United States would not tolerate a Soviet unilateral move, then went upstairs to receive ratification of his moves by Nixon.

Times editors liked the story so well that Binder was asked to write it again for the Sunday edition, where the new version appeared under the headline, "The Action was Downstairs; the President was Upstairs," changing the emphasis from downplaying the seriousness of the alert to Nixon's inactivity. In the second story, no one said that Nixon was in charge.

Binder wrote that it might never be known what Nixon did upstairs at the White House on the night of October 24, but that Kissinger conceived the alert and Schlesinger ordered it: "...it is now certain that both the timing and exact nature of the alert were acted upon without the President's specific prior approval. Mr. Kissinger and Mr. Schlesinger acted alone getting the President's earlier, general approval over the phone for an American policy that included both a firm political response and a military signal."

On the basis of talks with Kissinger and others, Binder reported that it appeared to have been "less a full-blown crisis than a firm test of superpower wills and tactics."

The report said that, since Nixon was upstairs, and there was no Vice President and no Director of the Office of Emergency Preparedness, the decisive meeting in the situation room consisted of the Secretary of State, National Security Adviser and Defense Secretary: "Kissinger, Kissinger and Schlesinger." They were joined belatedly by Moorer and Colby. The story did not mention Scowcroft or Haig, the person in direct contact with Nixon.

Binder concluded: "From all of this, it seems clear that there was no actual crisis, but a potential crisis. . . . Only after news of the alert was broadcast did Mr. Nixon decide to dramatize it as a crucial personal faceoff against the Russians."[14]

In Cairo, there had been no Western newspapers available since October 6, when the *International Herald-Tribune* arrived containing Binder's story. Read in Cairo, it appeared to be plausible, with most of its various facts probably unassailable, yet it did not jell, a compilation of little truths that did not add up to a true story. The Soviet intentions had been real, not tentative. That Nixon did not sit up all night in the situation room, as Lyndon Johnson would have done, did not remove his well-known intentions from the decision-making. Nixon at his healthiest was not one to hover over the situation room discussing how many B-52s were stationed on Guam or the time it would take the 82nd Airborne Division to get under way. Binder reported that any threatened commander can order a Defcon-3 alert, which was low-level, but that situation did not arise, so the minimization was gratuitous and irrelevant. The stress on Nixon's being *non compos mentis* following the Saturday Night Massacre apparently did not qualify for Reston's definition of viciousness.

The story omitted the crucial factor: Brezhnev believed the alert because it was "in Nixon's name." In Kissinger's name it would have been meaningless. Nixon had tangled personally with Brezhnev over Israel, and he had bombed Hanoi, mined Haiphong harbor and strafed Soviet ships in the process. The Soviet Politburo would not have been impressed by an alert called in the name of George McGovern, Hubert Humphrey or Edmund Muskie over the issue of the Israelis and the Third Army, and it is safe to say that none of these would have called the alert or allowed their top aides to do so in their names. Muskie later had an opportunity as Secretary of State to lead crisis management during the hostage situation in Iran, and he solved it by agreeing to Iranian demands. Had there been a dozen Kissingers and no Nixon in October 1973, the alert would not have been called, and there would not have been a South Vietnam or an Israel much after that date. Meir knew it, if the *Times* did not.

After the October War tapered off in the truce signed by generals at Kilometer 101, the point of Israeli advance 60 miles from Cairo, a political constellation existed for the first time for peace in the Middle East. Sadat had won politically, achieving his main goal of redeeming self-respect, and he was eager to get on with a settlement. Hussein still was indebted to Nixon and had not burned his bridges with Israel, having lent assistance to Syria (which earlier had tried to kill him), but not attacking Israel directly and keeping his air force grounded. Negotiations would be wearying and dicey, but Israel too had a more urgent need for peace. To Sadat, the Americans had looked better then the Soviets in the crisis, and less dangerous. For one day, December 21, the foreign ministers of Israel, Egypt, Jordan and Syria actually met in one room together in Geneva, even though each side called the other mass murderers before Syria walked out. At the United Nations, Syria always walked out before Israel spoke.

American resupply had permitted Israel to regain dominance in the air, the critical factor protecting Israeli population centers, and the first large-scale American aid to Israel was a signal that Israel was a permanent country; never before had it had a meaningful ally.[15]

A settlement was tantalizingly close. It is difficult to believe it, but momentum stalled and the chance was lost because the American force that determined the outcome of the war, personalized in Nixon, was shot down by an 18 1/2-minute humming noise on a tape recorder, a tape gap that proved to be of little or no real significance.

From the end of August until late October, the day Israel and Egypt accepted a ceasefire, Nixon had fought off subpoenas for the nine tapes. To give up the tapes would open the door to a goldfish-bowl Presidency, but the media agreed that to refuse them would prove Nixon guilty of criminal complicity.

Three days after firing Cox, Nixon agreed to give the tapes to Judge Sirica on an ears-only basis. Nixon's counsel Fred Buzhardt had the difficult task of telling Sirica that two subpoened tapes did not exist, triggering new accusatory headlines and repeated editorials in the *Times*.

One untaped conversation was Nixon's first talk with Mitchell after the Watergate break-in, a brief telephone call on June 20, 1972, in which Mitchell said he apologized for losing control of the CRP staff, and Nixon said he jokingly signed off the talk, "Don't bug anybody without asking me." The tape machine had not been switched into the telephone.

The second non-tape was Nixon's conversation with Dean on Sunday night, about 9 p.m., April 15, 1973, in which Dean told Nixon that he was going to the prosecutors, but not that he already had done so. It was later verified that the tape had run out over the Saturday-Sunday period, when the machine normally was not serviced.

Alfred Wong, deputy assistant director of the Secret Service, later testified that the nine tape recorders used in the White House and Executive Office Building cost only $2,800, and some were previously used Secret Service equipment. Wong said the machine in Nixon's EOB office was serviced daily Monday through Friday, but not on weekends when the office was seldom used. Two six-hour tapes had been installed on Friday the 13th. Nixon on April 14 and 15 had held five hours, 26 minutes of conversations before seeing Dean, and the first tape switched out. The switch that should have shifted the second tape into operation malfunctioned, and the Dean conversation never was recorded. Logs of service visits to the EOB and Wong's check of the tapes on the machines indicated that no surreptitious tape switches were involved.

By the time the two "missing tapes" were explained, the media was committed to anticipating discovery of tape tampering. Sirica complained that there were numerous gaps in the tapes, which were readily explained: the voice-activating mechanism picked up random sounds, such as a pen scratching on paper, activating the machine to record silence for a few minutes before shutting down again. But suspicion fueled speculation about tape switches and splicings, none of which ever materialized.

On November 21, Sirica announced the bombshell: there was an

18 1/2-minute gap on a crucial tape of Nixon's first recorded conversation with Haldeman on Watergate, on June 20, 1973. Sirica demanded all of Nixon's tapes to ensure their safety.

The media exploded, *Newsweek* noting that no single discovery had so imperiled Nixon. The purported importance of the tape gap was that the erasure appeared to be a prima facie case of subpoenaed evidence having been destroyed.

The real importance was in the timing of the news story, when the media needed something new. Nixon had withstood for 18 months multiple investigations by the Washington press corps, a dozen agencies and Congressional committees, the Sam Ervin Show, the trials and impending trials of his White House staff. The public was satiated with repetitive evidence, and the House Judiciary Committee was gearing up impeachment hearings without solid evidence of an impeachable offense, its 38 members inclined against impeachment 20 to 18.

Rose Mary Woods volunteered that she had erased part of the tape inadvertently on October 1, 1973, when she was interrupted by a five-minute phone call. She had immediately told Nixon, who was not alarmed, believing that the tape she had been transcribing was not one of those that had been subpoenaed. She could not account for the whole 18 1/2 minutes.

Virtually every columnist, cartoonist and editorialist in the nation took a crack at the tape gap, a natural for cliché humor. Sirica appointed a panel of six electronic experts, one each nominated by the White House and the Special Prosecutor, and the FBI was sent to investigate the circumstances of tape handling in the White House. The media was able to keep the tape gap story alive for seven months, from November 1973 until June 1974.

In January the six-expert panel delivered to Sirica its first report on its testing of the tape and Woods' Uher 5000 recording machine. The report was all but incomprehensible to a layman except for its main conclusion: there were five, or possibly nine, start up marks of the erase head, indicating at least five manual attempts to erase. All major newspapers and the news magazines published the experts' diagram of the buzz section of the tape, showing sections of loud buzz, soft buzz, markings of erase and record heads, etc.

The experts were challenged by Allan D. Bell, a former general and head of Dekor Counterintelligence and Security, Inc., who had on his own tested Uher recorder characteristics. *Science* magazine also challenged the experts, charging slipshod work in their two months of testing and noting that scientific etiquette required their publishing their data at the same time as their conclusions. While the White House

Uher was being tested by the experts, a transistor had failed and had been replaced, indicating that the machine was faulty. Bell said that his tests showed that the erase-head marks could have been caused by fluctuating current and the defective transistor.

It was not until June that the six experts submitted their complete report with data, and they had dug in to defend their original conclusion: five manual erasures, and no possibility that malfunction of the machine could have caused them. Sirica had authorized a new group of experts from Stanford University to submit findings to the court, and the Stanford group disagreed with the six experts' certainty of exclusive manual responsibility.

Although the country was inundated with technical jargon on tape recorder mechanics, the main point remained unexplained: How did a long stretch of 18 1/2 minutes get erased?

In one of the experts' reports there was a passing mention, overlooked by most of the media or tacked on near the bottom of stories, that the Uher recorder will erase on high-speed rewind, requiring 20 seconds to wipe out 18 minutes, if the record button and rewind button are held down at the same time.

In my first use of a Uher recorder, borrowed from the *Chicago Tribune's* Larry Rue in 1970, I taped a speech in Bonn from the radio, ran it back, started it up, and nothing was on the tape. Rue's assistant and later successor, Alice Siegert, not realizing she was speaking to a mechanical idiot, had instructed me on how to start the recording: "Hold down those two buttons at the same time." Vacantly, I also held down two buttons on rewind and erased a 30 minute speech in about a minute. Technically, I do not know if my action engaged the erase head or over-recorded silence with the recording head while the tape sped through rewind. Rose Mary Woods testified that on one occasion Nixon visited her while she was transcribing, and pushed some buttons on the machine. Nixon also spent a day listening to the tapes, and no doubt rewound patches to hear them again, as the EOB recordings especially are almost inaudible. Nixon swore he did not erase any tape, but it is possible that he did so without knowing it, on rewind, as I had done.

What is unquestionable is that the experts' certainty of manual erasures was overdrawn, unscientific—as certainty often is—so strongly challenged as to be worthless, yet devastating to Nixon.

While Haldeman was in prison, no longer a Nixon loyalist and naturally at his most bitter, he racked his brain, consulted his sketchy notes and Nixon's telephone logs for clues to that day to jog his memory. He could not remember anything incriminating that Nixon had said dur-

ing the erased conversation. Haldeman recalled that Nixon had speculated that Colson must have triggered the break-in (which was not the
case), said that Colson denied it, then added that Colson had telephoned Magruder about getting something on Larry O'Brien and
might possibly have mentioned the President. The talk Haldeman
could recall was too speculative to be incriminating to Nixon, and
leaned more to the exculpatory, in that Nixon didn't know who ordered the Watergate break-in. Haldeman was in no mood to lie in his
book to protect the already disgraced Nixon.[16] The erased evidence
that fascinated the media for seven months was not relevant, but it
would go a long way toward impeaching the President.

Chapter XX
Impeachment

"Can a king be saved once he has been brought to trial? He is dead when he appears before his judges."

—Danton

When Watergate came along to act as a lightning rod for revolutionaries and an Eastern establishment that had come to believe in its right to power, the revolution of 1964-1972 had gone into remission. Nixon's election victory in 1972 was overwhelming, and the departure of American soldiers from Vietnam in the spring of 1973 deprived the New Left of its catalyst. No cities were burning, and after the mass arrests of the Mayday Tribe in 1972, government-by-demonstration became less attractive.

By late 1973, when formal impeachment proceedings began against Nixon, the public was satiated with Watergate, the revolution diminished to surly weariness. The detective story had been solved long since, and polls indicated that a sizeable majority believed Nixon had been involved in the coverup from the beginning, as the Washington press corps had assumed all along. At the time, a majority of about

60% did not want Nixon impeached; that is, a majority considered his offenses onerous but not sufficient for impeachment. What polls do not register is the intensity of commitment, and the minority demanding impeachment included the intense revolutionaries, intense political opponents and the *gleichgeschaltete* media.

The Sam Ervin Show in the summer of 1973 further reduced the small number of Nixon supporters in the major media, now in a war of attrition with the President. The media had come to regard Nixon's defenders as the media's enemies, and an enemy within the media was a traitor. The media itself put an end to free expression.

In August, a retired Orthodox rabbi in Reheboth, Massachusetts, Baruch Korff, spent $1,200 of his own money to publish a newspaper advertisement, "An Appeal to Fairness," although he was living on a $3,500-a-year pension from his congregation. Korff asked solicitations for his National Citizens' Committee for Fairness to the Presidency, and within two months he had 50,000 contributors nationwide, their small contributions going to pay for more advertisements.

As Korff's impromptu organization grew, the puzzled Nixon wrote to thank him, then gave Korff a long, tape-recorded interview which the rabbi wrote into a book, *The Personal Nixon: Staying on the Summit.* Publishers, of course, rejected it, so Korff formed Fairness Press and published the book himself, although he had no facilities for distributing it.

To the media, Korff had curiosity value, particularly because he turned out to be good-humored and amusing. He was repeatedly asked, "How does Nixon know you're not a kook?" Korff laughed, "He doesn't."

The *Times* knew about Korff. He was a Ukranian-born Zionist ("the worst kind," as W.C. Fields said of the Chinese laundryman). He had been ridiculed in a series of *Times* reports in 1947 when he was arrested in France for agitating for the creation of Israel.

The *Times* published a letter from Rabbi Simeon J. Maslin of Chicago that was intended to put an end to Korff's mischief. Maslin wrote that Korff's appeals were "so maudlin and so filled with distortion and fantasy" that he was moved to identify him. Korff was a "mock heroic rabbi" who had made an "abortive attempt to bomb London" in 1947 and had staged a "highly melodramatic interview" with an alleged Stern Gang leader; in sum, a headline grabber.[1] The letter did not say "bomb London with leaflets."

Angry letters flowed into the *Times.* Rabbi Nathan N. Rosen, who disagreed with Korff on Nixon, nevertheless had known Korff for 40 years as "a highly sensitive and compassionate human being," scion of an illustrious Hasidic family, who had been "a one-man rescue squad" in saving Jews from Nazi Germany. Rosen wrote, "Permit me to say that it ill befits the *Times* to print an obviously erroneous view when its own unlimited resources could have established a more accurate view of the 'President's Defender.'"

Rosen suggested that Korff was defending Nixon because "U.S. aid to Israel during President Nixon's first four years exceeded the combined aid given to Israel under Presidents Truman, Eisenhower, Kennedy and Johnson...."[2]

Korff himself said:

I will not speculate on the President's guilt. They have not established a single point against him...but hell—and the word hell by the way is in the Bible, so don't tell anyone that I use bad language—what government agency doesn't run a covert operation? If they didn't, we'd be out of business. George Washington did....So what's perjury? People commit perjury every day, wittingly and unwittingly. It's a catchall. It is this holier than thou attitude that kills me....There isn't a President worth his salt who hasn't done things for which an ordinary citizen would go to jail. I don't actually say the man is a saint. Nor am I claiming King David is a saint. King David sent his general into battle so he could steal his wife, but we recite the psalms of David every day. But Nixon is one of the most straightlaced Presidents ever. He's not sophisticated like Kennedy. He was brought up a Quaker. Were he more sophisticated and cunning, it never would have reached this stage. Nixon is not gregarious. He's not engaging...here is a man who can send a love letter to someone and sign it 'sincerely yours.' Even so, I regard him with the highest esteem, as my President, a man who has been vilified, savaged, brutalized, whose blood has been sapped by vampires. I see him holding out against willful people who are unworthy of polishing his shoes.[3]

Korff said he had voted for Kennedy, Johnson and Humphrey: "I voted against Nixon when I was a prisoner of the media—I have since been liberated." The rabbi eventually would receive more than two million contributions, poured into advertisements, but in the end was alone. The grave risks he had taken as a young man in ransoming 39,000 Jews from German-occupied countries gave him the assurance to withstand ridicule and hostility, serving his own God.

Media reaction to the Saturday Night Massacre at the height of the

October War caused House Majority Leader Tip O'Neill to recognize with some enthusiasm that an impeachment proceeding was viable.

If O'Neill's friend Jimmy Breslin can be believed, O'Neill's misunderstanding of foreign affairs was total, and he had little interest in the Middle East or Indochina.

Breslin recounted in his book, *How the Good Guys Finally Won,* that O'Neill believed Nixon was able to mine Haiphong harbor and bomb Hanoi because he had arranged beforehand for Soviet and Chinese permission. O'Neill reached this interpretation when Nixon had told a group of Congressional leaders that the Middle East settlement— ceasefire apparently is meant—"couldn't have been made without the help of the Russians." Nixon allegedly had said, "We needed their help. It was the same with Vietnam. We couldn't have done anything unless we had been able to make an agreement with Russia and China before we went ahead at the end."

O'Neill, and Breslin, interpreted this to mean that Nixon had cleared the mining of Haiphong and bombing of Hanoi with the Communist superpowers, thereby invalidating any Nixon claim to bold decision-making, and Breslin reported O'Neill telling him, "I'm taking notes while he's talking and I just say to myself, 'Oh boy!' " On the basis of this nonsense, Breslin applied to Nixon a quotation he attributed to Kierkegaard, "No temple-robber, toiling in shackles of iron, so vicious as those who pillage among sacred things; and even Judas, who sold his Master for thirty pieces of silver, is not more despicable than those who traffic in great deeds."[4]

Morally armed with Breslin and Kierkegaard, O'Neill forwarded an impeachment resolution written by Representative Jerome Waldie of California, an IPS intimate, to the House Judiciary Committee and began pressing its new chairman, Peter W. Rodino, Jr., of New Jersey, to get moving on organizing Nixon's impeachment.

At the same time, O'Neill repressed Father Drinan's resolution of impeachment over Cambodia because it had no chance of being passed and might defuse the impeachment momentum when it was defeated. The *Times* ran a laudatory profile of Rodino, a little known North Jersey machine politician, on October 24, while Nixon and Brezhnev exchanged messages that led to the nuclear alert.

Pressed by O'Neill to get a special counsel before the Christmas recess, Rodino settled on John Doar, a former Assistant Attorney General under Robert Kennedy, who had made a reputation for courage and tenacity in prosecuting the killers of civil rights workers in Mississippi. Doar was ideal in the prosecutor's role. He was a Republican, albeit a John Lindsay-Nelson Rockefeller Republican, who had for 15 years worked for the Bedford-Stuyvesant Restoration Corporation in New York, a Robert Kennedy project. Doar was Robert Kennedy's kind of Republican.

Doar and his staff set to work on a prodigious project, compiling a narrative from the Ervin Committee testimony, previous grand jury secret testimony, trial records of Watergate defendants, tapes, documents and White House transcripts of tapes. Doar produced 38 volumes of narrative, virtually an oral history of Nixon's incumbency minute by minute, subject to possible manipulation by deletion and other techniques previously practiced on the Pentagon Papers, and omitting only the real business of the Presidency, such as foreign affairs.

The 38 members of the House Judiciary Committee were not, the media conceded, actually representative of Congress. As the committee geared up in early 1974, 18 members, almost half, were committed to impeaching Nixon, while the House as a whole was only one-quarter to one-third in favor of impeachment. David S. Broder commented that women, blacks and urban liberals were overrepresented on the 21 Democrat majority, compared with their proportions among the 248 House Democrats. Southerners, conservatives and rural constituencies were underrepresented. The Republicans on the committee were weighted the other way, more conservative, but their votes would count only for cosmetic purposes if all Democrats voted for impeachment. The vote for impeachment would be decided at the moment that the three Southern Democrats, Walter Flowers of Alabama, James R. Mann of South Carolina and Ray Thornton of Arkansas, joined the other Democrats.

The committee Democrats were weighted in still another way. Most of them had been fervent opponents of the Vietnam war, associates of the left fringe influenced by the Institute for Policy Studies, and some had been agitating for impeachment since the Cambodia incursion.

Robert W. Kastenmeier of Wisconsin had brought Marcus Raskin of IPS to Washington. Waldie was an anti-war activist, as was Father Drinan of Massachusetts. John Conyers of Michigan was on a number of John Dean's enemies lists and usually agreed with Charles Rangel and Elizabeth Holtzman of New York and anti-war activist Don Edwards of California. Firmly committed to impeachment from the beginning were Rodino, Jack Brooks of Texas, William Hungate of Missouri, Barbara Jordan of Texas and John Seiberling of Ohio. They were joined by Joshua Eilberg of Pennsylvania, Edward Mezvinsky of Iowa, Wayne Owens of Utah and Paul Sarbanes of Maryland, who would win a Senate seat after becoming an impeachment leader during debate.

Among Republicans on the committee, Nixon's defenders were limited to Edward Hutchinson of Michigan, Charles W. Sandman, Jr. of New Jersey, Charles E. Wiggins of California, Trent Lott of Mississippi, Joseph J. Maraziti of New Jersey, Delbert L. Latta of Ohio, Carlos Moorhead of California, Wiley Mayne of Iowa and David W. Dennis of Indiana. Henry P. Smith III of New York would vote against impeachment passively; he was not running for re-election.

All of them would pay for being on the losing side, and some would leave politics permanently.

On the committee staff, Doar's 39 lawyers were heavily Ivy League and Democrat-oriented. William Patrick Dixon, a 29-year-old attorney working for Representative Kastenmeier and for the staff at large, not for Doar, had been an original McGovern campaign volunteer and said he had spent three years working for Nixon's impeachment before he leaked committee memoranda to the press to build up impeachment fever. Dixon was praised in a profile in the *Times,* "Leaked-Memos Author."[5] The committee's Republican counsel, Albert Jenner, was dropped after he was quoted in a Texas newspaper as favoring impeachment, to be replaced by Samuel Garrity.

The House Judiciary Committee's scenario differed greatly from the Ervin Committee's investigation. Most of the real work would be done by Doar and his staff of investigators and archivists. The congressmen were to study up, debate briefly and vote. Their time in the television sun would be brief but intensely dramatic, so the Democrats insisted on opening public hearings in the evening, at prime time.

The scenario called for the committee to recommend proper articles of impeachment—the vote a foregone conclusion—then for the House to vote by simple majority to impeach—presumed likely at the beginning of 1974—and then for the Senate to try Nixon, dismissing him if a two-thirds vote were achieved. The full scenario could not be completed without more momentum.

Such a drama builds its own momentum, and the more likely Nixon's Senate trial became, the more menacing loomed the next November's Congressional elections, a situation foreseen by Tip O'Neill. Any defender could anticipate carrying part of Nixon's official disgrace by November, and Sandman commented later, "It changed from nonpartisan to highly partisan. . . one of the darkest moments in American history."

The business of government must go on, and in early 1974 Nixon delivered his State of the Union message and his budget message to Congress. The nation was going into recession; the oil shortage was acute, and the economic outlook "highly uncertain." In Wall Street newsletters, doomsday predictions began to appear. At the same time, Nixon wrote Senator Ervin refusing to comply with subpoenas for hundreds of tapes and documents, writing that it would "destroy any vestige of confidentiality of Presidential communications." Nixon hired James St. Clair to replace Buzhardt as his personal counsel, and William Saxbe was sworn in as still another Attorney General.

One item of unfinished business was the Vietnam war. To win President Thieu's agreement to a ceasefire, Nixon had pledged "swift retaliatory action" in the case of a major North Vietnamese violation of the truce, and had kept the pledge until Congress forbid any form of intervention after August 14, 1973. At the beginning of 1974, Thieu reported that the North Vietnamese, violating the agreement, had built up forces in South Vietnam to 400,000 troops and were planning an offensive. In Saigon, Ambassador Graham Martin cabled Nixon directly a request for $1 billion in aid.

In February, *Times* correspondent David K. Shipler reported from Saigon that American aid was prolonging the war, in a Page 1 story headlined, "Vast Aid from U.S. Backs Saigon in Continuing War."

Shipler wrote that Saigon's war machine was kept going by 2,800 American technicians, employed by private companies under contract to the Defense Department,

> . . . one facet of a vast program of American military aid that continues to set the course of the war more than a year after the signing of the Paris peace agreements. . . . Whether the United States is breaking the letter of the agreements could probably be argued either way, but certainly the aid directly supports South Vietnamese violations and so breaks the spirit of the accords.

Shipler suggested that the true cost of aid was higher than official figures, with salaries of some specialists "hidden in the vast budgets of the United States Air Force, Army and Navy and not labeled 'Vietnam.' " He added that "Furthermore, the American-financed military shield has provided Mr. Thieu with the muscle to forstall a political settlement," and that the United States continued aerial reconnaissance, prisoner interrogation, training, supply and transportation.[6]

Ambassador Martin, incensed at Shipler's report, cabled Kissinger warning that Hanoi was attempting to use "remnants of the American 'peace movement' to bring influence to bear on selective susceptible, but influential, elements of American communications media and particularly on susceptible Congressional staffers." Martin rebutted the

Shipler article paragraph by paragraph, charging inaccuracies and half-truths. Senator Kennedy, engaged in a campaign to cut off military aid to Saigon, wrote an angry letter to Kissinger saying that Martin's cable raised "the worst kind of innuendo" about congressional criticism of military aid.

Meanwhile, the *Times'* James M. Markham had spent a week in Viet Cong-controlled areas, reporting in a series of articles in February that Communist morale was high, anti-Americanism strong and the organization of life superior to that in areas under the Thieu government. In Cambodia, where Communists controlled 60% of the country but not the capital, the *Times'* Sydney Schanberg reported from Phnom Penh pervasive corruption in the government of Lon Nol.

The Congressional campaign to cut military aid to Cambodia and South Vietnam proceeded relentlessly in tandem with the impeachment proceedings. In March Nixon asked for a $2.4 billion aid package. In April a caucus of Democrats in the House rejected any increase in aid. In May the Senate voted 43 to 38 to refuse the additional aid request, and on May 22 the House cut aid to South Vietnam by $474 million. The Soviets meanwhile stepped up aid to North Vietnam.

Parallel with South Vietnam's deteriorating situation, the Palestine Liberation Organization opened a new terrorist campaign aimed at frustrating the peace negotiations that Kissinger was attempting to get underway in the Middle East. A series of PLO raids into northern Israel, killing mostly women and children, began April 11 at Kiryat Shmona, then continued May 15 at Ma'alot, June 13 at Shamir and June 24 at Nahariya. Golda Meir had been replaced by Prime Minister Yitzhak Rabin on April 22.

For American policy, the only hopeful sign in the Middle East was that Sadat had decided that, while the Soviets could provide arms, "only the Americans can bring peace," and had decided to throw in his lot with Washington. As Sadat permitted relations with the Soviets to deteriorate, Nixon asked Congress in April for $250 million in aid for Egypt.

In March, a grand jury under the new Special Prosecutor, Leon Jaworski, indicted Haldeman, Ehrlichman, Mitchell, Mardian, Parkinson, Colson and Strachan. Jaworski demanded 64 tapes and documents of the President's conversations with the indicted men, touching off a new court battle over tapes. Already jailed or facing prison were Liddy, Hunt, the four Miamians, Krogh, Magruder, Segretti, Porter, LaRue and Kalmbach, with Chapin and Stans facing other trials.

James L. Buckley of New York, counted as a Nixon friend, became the first Republican Senator to go public with a plea that Nixon resign. Nixon declined, just as he was ordered to pay almost a half million in back income taxes and penalties, a telling point with the public.

In April, the House Judiciary Committee subpoenaed 42 tapes and dictabelts. The demand, differing from Jaworksi's in that they were not for the purpose of evidence in a criminal trial, was the first such demand by Congress on a President in history. Nixon refused, but released instead 1,308 pages of edited tape transcripts. In the early days of May, the *Times* filled up 11 newspaper pages daily with the transcripts, almost twice the volume of the huge Pentagon Papers installments.

Doar immediately charged that the White House transcripts were inaccurate, although he said he did not mean that they were doctored. He conceded that some tapes were scarcely audible, but his staff had been able to pick up parts of conversations marked "unintelligible" in the White House transcripts. Some of the improved versions from tape sections obtained from the Ervin Committee and a grand jury were helpful to the President, but most of the discrepancies were damaging to him.

Rodino pressed the demand for more tapes, and Nixon continued to refuse. Rodino charged that Nixon had edited out of the transcripts evidence that he had learned of the coverup earlier than March 21, 1973.

In June, Nixon embarked on a tour of the Middle East, where Kissinger had been shuttling off and on since the end of the October War, achieving an Israeli-Syrian disengagement agreement on May 31. Nixon received enthusiastic welcomes in Egypt and Jordan, a cordial welcome in troubled Israel, subdued but correct welcomes in Syria and Saudi Arabia. Considering the ravages of the recent war, it was a triumphal tour, but Nixon arrived home to be greeted by details of the transcript discrepancies, leaked to the media by William Dixon of Kastenmeier's staff.

The strain was telling on everyone, even the urbane and poised Kissinger. Touring with an entourage of generally friendly correspondents, Kissinger held an angry, emotional, impromptu press conference in Salzburg, Austria, on June 11 to threaten that he would resign unless he were cleared of Watergate-related charges in the media and Congress. Unidentified Congressional sources had tied him to the 1971 national security wiretaps that followed publication of the Pentagon Papers. The Senate Foreign Relations Committee voted an endorsement of Kissinger to prevent his resignation.

Correspondents traveling with Nixon in the Middle East noticed his limping, which became more pronounced during his follow-up visit to the Soviet Union. Nixon was breaking down with phlebitis.

At the end of June Nixon was in Moscow conferring with Brezhnev on the SALT-2 treaty Kissinger had been negotiating off and on since the end of March. Once again he returned to the United States as the House Judiciary Committee released, officially this time, its differing transcripts of the White House tapes. In the Supreme Court, Jaworski and St. Clair presented oral arguments on the issue of executive privilege protecting the tapes.

The impeachment process was approaching a climax on July 9 when Doar released the most damaging discrepancy in the versions of what the tapes said. A passage that had been marked inaudible in large part by the White House now had the President saying to his aides on March 27, 1973, just after Dean had warned of a cancer on the Presidency:

> I don't give a shit what happens, I want you all to stonewall it, let them plead the Fifth Amendment, coverup or anything else if it'll save it, save the plan. That's the whole point. On the other hand, I would prefer, as I said to you, that you do it the other way (they had been talking of a limited hangout). And I would particularly prefer you to do it that other way if it's going to come out that way anyhow.

As the House Judiciary Committee prepared for its televised debate and dramatic voting on the impeachment resolutions, the Supreme Court ruled 8 to 0 on July 24 that Nixon must deliver 64 tapes and documents to Jaworski as evidence in the forthcoming Watergate coverup trial. Republican attempts to delay the televised debate until the tapes could be examined were voted down. Nixon, from San Clemente, said he would comply with the court ruling, ending fears of a Constitutional crisis. That night the House Judiciary Committee began televised debate on the first article of impeachment.

The verdict was known in advance, as Washington handicappers had predicted since late spring that all of the Democrats and a few Republicans would vote for impeachment. Republican Lawrence J. Hogan, who was running for Governor of Maryland, made it certain by announcing he would vote for impeachment. The remaining suspense lay in how many Republicans would join the Democratic majority. The morning line of Washington media analysts guessed that the vote would be about 29 to 7 for impeachment, with two undecided. The developing debate would pinpoint how the members would vote.

Jerome Waldie, since the previous September a leader of the impeachment movement, used his allotted 15 minutes, then continued to recount the long list of charges in three-minute segments as other Democrats yielded to him their three-minute rebuttal periods. Father Drinan railed at the "concealment of clandestine war in Cambodia," although the other Democrats did not want that issue in the debate. William Hungate called Nixon "inhuman," "profane" and "devious."

The already-decided debate would have been a charade except for Charles Sandman, Charles Wiggins and Edward Hutchinson. Sandman said:

> There are sufficient votes here for an impeachment resolution; this everyone knows. I wonder what the prosecutor in the United States Senate is going to do for witnesses. He is going to plead his whole case on tapes, because he cannot use any of (the nine witnesses heard by the committee). Because every one of them testified no act of wrongdoing on the part of the President.

Wiggins said, "The law requires that we decide the case on the basis of the evidence, not on the material, 38 books of material. My guess, Mr. Doar, is that you can put most of the admissible evidence in half of one book. Most of this is just material and not evidence."

The committee voted on July 27 to approve the first article of impeachment, nine counts of obstruction of justice: making or influencing false statements to lawful officers, withholding evidence from lawful officers, counseling witnesses to give false statements, attempting to interfere with investigations, paying for the silence of witnesses, attempting to misuse the CIA, informing suspects of information that investigators had about them, promising favored treatment to potential convicts to buy their silence. The vote was 27 to 11, Republicans Thomas Railsback of Illinois, Hamilton Fish, Jr. of New York, Lawrence L. Hogan of Maryland, M. Caldwell Butler of Virginia, William S. Cohen of Maine and Harold V. Froelich of Wisconsin voting with the majority.

The committee subsequently voted 28 to 10 that the President had abused his power, Republican Robert McClory of Illinois joining the majority. The five counts were: attempting to misuse the IRS, misusing the FBI unrelated to national security to violate citizens' civil rights, using a secret investigative unit which was illegally financed and misusing CIA resources to prejudice a fair trial for Ellsberg and Russo, allowing subordinates to cover up actions including Watergate, buggings, the Fielding break-in, improper testimony in the confirmation of Attorney General Kleindienst and regarding CRP financing practices, and interfering with various investigations.

On July 30, the committee voted a third article, 21 to 17, charging defiance of the committee's subpoenas. As a last act, the committee rejected Drinan's article on aggression against Cambodia by a vote of 28 to 10.

As a legal matter, Nixon was guilty of some of the counts of the first two articles of impeachment, although several counts were redundant or of questionable gravity. The third article was legally obscure and therefore no grounds for the drastic action of impeachment. But the issue never had been one of legality; it always had been political, and it was decided on the basis of transient political pressures, as in a revolution.

The real issue was sounded at the height of the debate when Hutchinson, in an anguished voice, burst out, "But consider the *context!* This country was on its knees when he was elected!" The context was what Watergate was all about, but the context could not be summarized in 15 minutes, and there was no Republican organization to pool allotted speaking time. (The *Times* published pages of excerpts from the debate, but I could not find Hutchinson's dramatic interjection in them.)

Probably no orator could have given the context of Watergate even if allotted the whole evening. He would have had to refute media misrepresentations over a 20-year period that had accumulated and become dogma.

Nixon had been hired by the electorate to reverse a slide into revolutionary anarchy caused in part by the profligate waste of American global influence by an egocentric Kennedy administration that had been adored by the media. The media wrecked Johnson's administration, not out of malice and despite the media's approval of his contribution to social change, but out of resentment that he was not the martyred Kennedy. Nixon had done the job he was hired to do, despite a media that was relentlessly hostile.

Nixon's offenses were defensive actions against threats that the media perceived as directed against Nixon but actually were threats directed against the country. The FBI under Hoover would not investigate Halperin or Ellsberg, and it was years later than the FBI learned from Cuban and Soviet defectors that Cuban instructors of the Weathermen had instigated the Chicago Days of Rage. The IRS would not examine the tax-exempt status of ideological propaganda foundations, and later big media continued to cover up some of the ideologists' direct connections with Cuba and Vietnam. The CIA balked at writing a psychological profile of Ellsberg because he was a U.S. citizen, and eventually produced one saying that his motive was misguided patriotism, a sympathetic profile.

Ellsberg, a hawk who changed his mind and insisted that the government change its mind with him, enlisted the aid of the Institute for Policy Studies and *The New York Times* to attempt to dictate policy on Indochina, won Supreme Court endorsement and then was imitated within the Washington bureaucracy. The CIA spied on the White House, and the Joint Chiefs spied on the National Security Council. Individuals from both groups leaked secrets to Jack Anderson and the *Times* to promote their personal foreign policies. Anderson published grand jury transcripts, and Carl Bernstein solicited grand jurors to break their oaths. The rules were changed on Nixon in mid-term in regard to both tax deductions and campaign contributions.

The Justice Department found difficulty in prosecuting Ellsberg or violent revolutionaries, with long trial delays, mistrials, grand juries dismissed without completing investigations. The justice system moved efficiently, however, in prosecuting anyone allied with Nixon, in concert with the media.

A few of the impeachment leaders were revolutionaries; more were cynical politicians, counting votes and seeing that power was being offered to them. Some, like the liberal John Doar, nurtured at Bedford-Stuyvesant on *The New York Times,* believed the *Times'* nightmare, that Nixon was engaged in a calculated fascist overthrow of the United States government. That notion was reinforced by liberal commentators like Joseph Kraft, outraged at being bugged, who wrote "There was a systematic effort to set up what amounts to a police state." There was nothing of the sort; Nixon was constantly on the defensive, placed in the bull's-eye of the media and the bureaucracy first by the Cambodia incursion, then by the Pentagon Papers.

Harrison Salisbury was accurate in saying that through the Pentagon Papers case, the *Times* literally became the Fourth Estate, and that without the Pentagon Papers there could not have been the debacle of Nixon's Presidency. Salisbury was perhaps too modest; with the abdication of the rest of the media to *Times* leadership, the *Times* became the government.

When the House Judiciary Committee, solemn, visibly suffering at the painful task of summoning the strength of its collective conscience to purge the revered Presidency at the end of July 1974, the tyrant was all but dead. He still had to be buried.

The possibility still existed that Nixon could survive trial in the Senate, a process that could have taken two to six months, scraping up somehow a one-third minority. Senator Barry Goldwater and others put the idea to rest. In a drawn-out fight, the political reality was that a dwindling minority would take Nixon's place in the media's bull's-eye. There already was talk of disbanding the Republican Party and forming a new one, an idea later pushed by William F. Buckley.

Alexander Haig was one of those who persuaded Nixon to give up, although Nixon was breaking down physically in any case. Many marveled that he still was on his feet, under unremitting tension since the Saturday Night Massacre ten months earlier. Muscular and nerve tension did not go to his heart but to extremities of his vascular system, and his phlebitis was inflamed.

On August 5, Nixon released transcripts of three conversations of June 23, 1972, revealing his early complicity in the coverup. He had in effect ordered that the FBI investigation be shut off. The transcripts were called the "smoking gun," produced after the verdict.

Nixon resigned the Presidency on August 8, and the next day Gerald Ford was sworn in as the 38th President of the United States.

On September 8, Ford granted Nixon a full pardon for any crimes committed in office, and immediately Ford's press secretary, Jerald terHorst, resigned in protest. TerHorst was rewarded for his loyalty to the media with a syndicated column, which, however, proved so provincial that big city subscribers, including the *Daily News,* dropped it as soon as they could do so without embarrassment. Two days after the pardon, a *Times* poll said that Ford's support already was waning because of it. For the first time in history, a President went to Capital Hill to testify before a Congressional committee. Ford wanted it unmistakably on the record that he had not promised Nixon a pardon in order to become Vice President.

On September 19, Nixon, in San Clemente, was subpoenaed to testify at the trial of his top aides in Washington. His attorneys pleaded illness, which the media did not believe. On September 25, doctors began attempting to dissolve a clot on his lung caused by his phlebitis. As the trial of Mitchell, Haldeman, Ehrlichman, Mardian and Parkinson opened, the Dow-Jones Industrial Average bottomed out below 590.

Meanwhile the media heavens sang with praise for the House Judiciary Committee. A new era had begun, and the United States had a new Pantheon of heroes: Senator Sam, Peter Rodino, Sam Dash, John Doar, Archibald Cox, Leon Jaworski, Elliott Richardson, Daniel Ellsberg, Carl Bernstein, Robert Woodward, Ben Bradlee, John Sirica.

A key hero, Deep Throat, without whom the bureaucracy and responsible political leaders could not have enlisted the power of the media to penetrate the Watergate maze, remained modestly underground. The media showed little interest in his identity or motives; it was enough that he had done his duty and saved the Republic.

A new Congress was elected, overwhelmingly Democrat and progressive, eliminating those tarred with the Nixon brush.

Two months after his subpoena, Nixon still claimed to be too ill to testify at the Washington trial. Judge Sirica took medical testimony on his condition, pondered the results and finally on December 5 excused Nixon from testifying.

With Nixon eliminated, the *Times* turned its attention to new miscreants, and on December 22 published a massive exposé by Seymour Hersh of CIA domestic spying. William Colby, caught in the Watergate pressures and considering Hersh as one of the *Times* men with whom the CIA kept good relations, had given to Hersh the CIA's "family jewels." The family jewels had been ordered by James Schlesinger, a report of CIA activities of dubious legality, for internal use in reforms. It led to the lengthy investigation by Senator Frank Church's Senate Intelligence Committee, which unearthed far more CIA misbehavior under Kennedy than under Nixon. A purge of the CIA paralyzed it for years.

As 1975 opened, a Washington jury convicted Haldeman, Ehrlichman and Mitchell on multiple counts of obstruction of justice and related coverup offenses. It also convicted on one count Robert Mardian, the *Times'* reviled adversary during the Pentagon Papers trial, and acquitted Kenneth Parkinson. That day, a major Communist drive was reported under way in Cambodia, and the Ford administration airlifted military supplies.

In American political tradition, politicians sometimes have gone to jail for venal offenses, but now men were sent to prison for political behavior, not monetary gain. They included Haldeman, Ehrlichman, Mitchell, LaRue, Magruder, Strachan, Mardian, Porter, Krogh, Colson, Chapin, Segretti, the almost unknown George A. Hearing (for campaign dirty tricks), Kalmbach, Hunt, McCord, Barker, Martínez, Gonzáles and Sturgis.

John Dean, who expected a suspended sentence, was shocked to receive one to four years; he served five months. Liddy served more than four and a half years in some of the nation's worst prisons. Stans and Kleindienst were among several fined but not sent to jail. The careers of dozens more, including the political careers of Nixon's defenders on the committees, were aborted.

Senator Gurney, Nixon's only defender on the Ervin Committee, was accused by the *Miami Herald* of having an illegal Boosters' Fund, and Gurney charged that the story was fabricated by Ervin Committee investigators who resented his role. Gurney was cleared after two trials.

If Nixon had been tried and imprisoned, the seed would have been planted for the right-wing coup that the left said it feared, not immediately and not under Nixon sympathizers, but one day when the full effects of the purge had sunk in. The system had not worked because it depended not merely on a cantankerous press, but on a varied press independent of any leadership.[7]

During the climax of the impeachment process, the rest of the world had difficulty understanding what was going on in the United States. Overseas, the shock of Watergate was not so much sordid behavior in the White House; it was that the United States' vaunted democracy was revealed as parochial politics, as bitter and thoughtless as in a banana republic. Impeachment was a matter of grave concern to nations dependent on the United States, which now included Anwar Sadat's Egypt and King Hussein's Jordan, as well as Israel, digging in its heels under Rabin at the prospect that its only ally was unstable.

Two months after Nixon's resignation, King Hussein, a necessary key to any comprehensive settlement in the Middle East, went to Rabat, Morocco, his decision made to make his peace with the Palestine Liberation Organization. PLO fortunes would rise with the retirement of the United States into isolationism, and the impeachment signal was unmistakable; that was where the United States was headed. Hussein, before an Arab League summit at Rabat, finally and irrevocably renounced claim to the West Bank of the Jordan River, accepting the PLO as the sole legitimate representative of the Palestinian nation. In November, Arafat made a triumphant appearance at the United Nations in New York, just before terrorists raided the Israeli village of Beth Shean, and the United Nations Education, Scientific and Cultural Organization barred Israeli delegates. The chance for a Middle East peace was gone again.

Chapter XXI
The Fall of Saigon
and the
Scourging of Nixon

"Before the Hate had proceeded for thirty seconds, uncontrollable exclamations of rage were breaking out from half the people in the room. . . . In its second minute the Hate rose to a frenzy. People were jumping up and down in their places and shouting at the tops of their voices. . . . In a lucid moment Winston found that he was shouting with the others and kicking his heels violently against the rung of his chair. The horrible thing about the Two Minute Hate was not that one was obliged to act a part, but, on the contrary, that it was impossible to avoid joining in."

—*George Orwell, 1984*

By early 1975 the millenium, somehow, had not arrived. Nixon had been banished to isolation in San Clemente, and the purge of Washington's dangerous rightists was at its end. The United States was at peace and no longer the world's gendarme. A new, liberal Congress was sworn in, dominated by Senate doves, one more handsome than the other. Democrats had picked up more than 40 seats in the House to win two-thirds representation. The *Times* enthused that the 94th Congress at last had a "working majority." The media preened itself for saving the nation, but there were bugs in the harvest.

The economy was in steep recession, and neither President Ford nor Representative Al Ullman of Oregon, the new chairman of the House Ways and Means Committee, could get agreement on an energy policy. Populism ruled, and Congress felt that the people demanded 60 cent gasoline. Detroit produced cars to guzzle it. The social phenomenon was the "me generation."

No one had given much thought to foreign affairs during the Watergate years, and the media made it formal: correspondents were brought home. The evacuation of correspondents had started with the fall of the debased dollar, and by 1975 correspondents overseas were reduced to one-third the number of a decade earlier. Newspapers filled space once given to world news with columnists and new People Pages, although the personalities portrayed tended to look alike. Broadway was without individuality, booked with revivals; popular music was simplistic and repetitive, and Hollywood, finding reality distasteful, produced movies about ghosts and spacemen. Uniformity of thought had made the nation gray.

The country's mood was mean spirited. Patricia Hearst, kidnapped and kept 57 days in a closet for the pleasure of homicidal sociopath rapists, was sent to jail by a San Francisco jury for consorting with criminals. War veterans were considered drug addicts responsible for much of the burgeoning crime. The country would resist accepting refugees from a former ally.

The *Times*, to its credit, kept the flag flying, withdrawing few correspondents, maintaining men overseas at great expense and consolidating its position as leader in foreign affairs. Since other newspapers dropped correspondents, the *Times* was more than ever the custodian of opinion of world matters.

Indochina was unfinished business, surprisingly still there two years after the American pullout. South Vietnam was in better shape than had been expected, Cambodia in worse, with two-thirds of the country occupied by North Vietnamese and Khmer Rouge troops.

At the end of 1974 President Ford had asked substantial aid for the Indochinese allies, but in the continuing battle over aid, Congress had set a ceiling of $700 million for South Vietnam in 1975 and $377 million for Cambodia, imposing restrictions on its use.

Congress also had cut off military aid to Turkey because it invaded Cyprus after an attempted Greek rightist coup there.

In early January 1975, North Vietnamese troops overran Phouc Binh, the first provincial capital lost in South Vietnam since the taking of Quang Tri province in the aborted 1972 offensive. Ford asked Congress for $300 million more in emergency aid. Reporters' questions at Ford's press conferences reflected the opinion of Congress that the state of the economy would not permit more aid.

The *Times* had been attacking Thieu consistently for intransigence and ceasefire violations, and its defense analyst, now the interchangeable man Leslie Gelb, reported that Congress would not support Ford's request. Gelb wrote: " 'Just think,' a Senatorial aide said, 'One of the first things this new revolutionary Congress will be asked to vote on is whether to give $300 million to President Thieu.' "[1]

Thieu and the South Vietnamese military had been apprehensive since August 1973, when Congress barred any further U.S. bombing or naval support, and dismayed at Nixon's fall. Still, Thieu could not believe that there was not a way around the bombing ban if it should become a life-or-death matter. He misjudged the strength of pacifist sentiment in Congress.

In February, with Communist troops battering Phnom Penh and Cambodia near collapse, Ambassador Graham Martin flew from Saigon to Washington to plead for a three-year "final" aid package for South Vietnam. He returned to Saigon empty handed. The CIA was reporting that the Communists were interested in negotiations, and in Washington Colby was suggesting that the critical period was six months away.

Kissinger conceded privately to reporters that Cambodia might be doomed even with additional aid, since there was no chance that the United States would reenter the war.

The *Times* had been an influential player in Indochina since the undermining of Diem in 1963, and since 1965 had preached with increasing passion that a Communist victory in Indochina was inevitable. Passion had overflowed with the Cambodia incursion in 1970, when the first hints toward an impeachment of Nixon surfaced. In 1975, a minority in the United States still credited Nixon with some foreign policy gains, and the continued existence of South Vietnam and the Lon Nol government in Cambodia constituted a kind of battered monument to the disgraced President. *Times* columnists began a sustained attack on Ford's aid requests, on the theme sounded by Senator Mansfield: "Additional aid means more killing and fighting."

At the time of the October War nuclear alert, the *Times* had promoted Kissinger as a means of demonstrating Nixon's fecklessness, but now Kissinger was committing two offenses: he was pressing for aid to Indochina, and he would not publicly denounce Nixon, although he might drop a slurring remark in private conversation.

Columnist Anthony Lewis, whose polemics on Vietnam from London had been imaginative compared with his bland reports from Hanoi when he finally visited there, turned his attention on Cambodia and his fury on Kissinger, the Watergate survivor.

Lewis urged Congress to reject further aid in a series of columns that developed these themes: Kissinger's insistence on maintaining Cambodian and South Vietnamese governments that could not stand on their own meant cruel, perpetual warfare fed by U.S. money, and Nixon and Kissinger—not the Communists—had brought war to Cambodia in the first place. Lewis derided Nixon's claim in 1970 of a "successful operation" in Cambodia, without mentioning that Nixon was barred by Congress from following it up. He described a "Kissinger doctrine:" if a government comes to power in a coup and takes its country into the U.S. orbit, Washington will do anything to prevent any change from that government, no matter how little popular support it has, no matter how terrible the cost to its people.[2]

Times editorials duplicated Lewis' themes, charging Ford with "blatant disregard" for human suffering in Cambodia and an intention to keep the war going to the bitter end rather than permit a political transition. The Cambodian pawns had suffered long enough; aid would only prolong their misery.[3] Only columnist William Safire noted that "political transition" was a euphemism for surrender by non-Communists, but Safire, still angry at being wiretapped, joined in castigating Kissinger as devious.[4]

Correspondent Sydney H. Schanberg was reporting graphic and touching descriptions of Cambodia's ordeal: half the nation now refugees facing starvation, "coughing children, weeping children, silent children too weak to respond any more." Lewis quoted Schanberg's reports, and Russell Baker, normally a humor columnist, contrasted quotations from Schanberg's reports with quotations from Ford and Kissinger in a column headlined, "An Offering of Bullets."[5]

Supporting fire for Lewis' themes came from columnist Tom Wicker, who wrote that one hundred times the $222 million additional aid Ford was requesting would not bring an anti-Communist victory in Cambodia. Wicker suggested that the Nixon administration had been involved in Prince Sihanouk's overthrow, which was untrue, and joined in the charge that the 1970 incursion, not the Communists, had brought war to Cambodia.[6]

Lawrence Eagleburger wrote the *Times* to protest the "malicious attacks" on Kissinger by the columnists, noting that Lewis' language— "cynical brutality," "monstrous futility," alleged insensitivity to maimed human beings—constituted an attack on Kissinger's character, not a disagreement rationally argued. He recalled that the *Times* once had opposed McCarthyism, but now the *Times* was "prepared to be the vehicle for attacks which bear a strong resemblance in tone, content and tactics to the sordid phenomenon it once courageously opposed." Eagleburger said Kissinger had not seen his letter, and he had waited until Kissinger left for the Middle East before writing it, so he would not be accused of being Kissinger's agent. The *Times* published the letter as an Op-Ed page column under the headline: "In Defense of Kissinger: an Aide Replies."[7] A footnote identified Eagleburger as Kissinger's executive assistant.

Wicker stressed a new theme: warnings of a bloodbath were a hoax. Describing Ford as "the man who pardoned Nixon," Wicker attacked the credibility of Ford's aid request

> . . . to allow Lon Nol's government to survive, to reach a negotiated settlement and avoid a 'bloodbath' in Cambodia. None of those things are likely to happen, even if Congress provides the money right away. The trouble with that is the bloodbath now going on. . . bloodbath theories have been advanced so often to justify disastrous policies in Southeast Asia that some skepticism is in order. . . .[8]

(The *Times* had not made much of the very real bloodbath at Hué in 1968.)

Ford pressed on, writing to House Speaker Carl Albert: "Are we to deliberately abandon a small country in the midst of its life and death struggle? Our national security and the integrity of our alliances depend upon our reputation as a reliable partner."

A *Times* editorial responded: "President Ford's increasingly threatening remarks about the future of Cambodia are only serving to make a bad situation worse." The editorial said the issue of United States reliability was not germane; the United States had no defense commitment to Lon Nol; Congress repeatedly had disclaimed any such commitment. The *Times* suggested that Ford "is only confusing and possibly demoralizing allied governments around the world which have more solid reasons for relying on the United States."[9]

The aid controversy brought two Congressional fact-finding teams to Indochina, one representing the House, led by John Flynt of Georgia, the other an independent mission of Senator Dewey Bartlett of

Oklahoma and California Representative McCloskey, Daniel Ellsberg's friend. They cut a wide swath of activity in South Vietnam, demanding to interview political prisoners and conferring with opposition politicians.

At least two of the Representatives, Bella Abzug of New York and Douglas Fraser of Minnesota, were IPS clients and fans of the Indochinese Resource Center's Don Luce and Fred Branfman, high on the enemies list of Ambassador Martin. Abzug and Fraser candidly said they were gathering ammunition for their well-known anti-war positions. The touring congressmen also spent eight hours in beleaguered Phnom Penh. Flynt, Abzug and Fraser returned demanding that Ford recall Ambassador Martin, the *Times* reported with some satisfaction.

On the return of the official team, they briefed a House Democratic caucus, which voted 180 to 49 on March 12 to oppose any further aid for Cambodia, dooming Ford's request. A *Times* editorial proposed phasing down aid to South Vietnam, geared to "the minimum military support that Saigon needs to avert the deterioration that occured in Cambodia," and with the aim of forcing Thieu into a political settlement.[10] The *Times* believed, with the CIA, that the Communists wanted to negotiate.

The *Times* had asked Prince Sihanouk, in asylum in Peking, for a comment, and printed his reply on the Op-Ed page. Sihanouk appealed to the United States to no longer involve itself with the Lon Nol regime that had overthrown him. "Since 1970 the United States has spent more than $7 billion for the destruction of Cambodia and the genocide of the Cambodian people," Sihanouk wrote. (Aid in the period had been $1.7 billion.) "But even if the United States spends billions of dollars more, our national resistance will not die. It will end in victory."[11] Sihanouk sent a similar cable to Tom Hayden and Jane Fonda.

By mid-March Cambodia was written off, although Ford would continue appeals for aid, and attention turned to the identity of the prospective victors there. The CIA did not know who led the Khmer Rouge, tending to believe it might be Khieu Samphan, whom Sihanouk had once banished from his government and sentenced to death. CIA analyst Frank Snepp, writing after the fall of Cambodia, said the CIA had known for years that Khieu Samphan intended to raze the cities and make Cambodia a rural estate, his theme since his student days. He already had systematically depopulated every town the Communists had taken.[12]

Times correspondent Schanberg reported from Phnom Penh a wrap-up of what could be learned of the rebels. Although he underlined that the material was sketchy—"it has been jokingly called the world's most mysterious successful revolutionary movement"—much of what Schanberg wrote became dogma in the Cambodia post mortem. Under the headline, "The Enigmatic Cambodian Insurgents: Reds Appear to Dominate Diverse Bloc,"[13] Schanberg found nationalists and moderates as well as Communists in the leadership.

Schanberg first discussed Sihanouk; then the apparent top man, Khieu Samphan, listed as Deputy Premier, defense minister, commander-in-chief of the armed forces and member of the politburo of the Khmer Communist Party; then Ieng Sary, a Hanoi-inclined Communist; next Saloth Sar, Secretary General of the Communist Party; then Hou Youn and Hu Nim, former cabinet ministers to Sihanouk, both considered more nationalist than Communist. Schanberg's article was cautiously optimistic. The insurgents had promised that no one would be executed except "seven traitors," starting with Lon Nol, and that everyone who switched sides would be pardoned.

Schanberg wrote that "most non-Cambodian observers—foreign diplomats and military experts—view the bloodbath debate as essentially irrelevant because they believe that an insurgent takeover is certain and that the wisest and most realistic approach would be to bend all efforts to make it as orderly and humane as possible." Khieu Samphan was "a nationalist with a reputation for integrity, incorruptibility and concern for the peasants and who is highly respected among non-Communist Cambodians." Schanberg believed that the North Vietnamese were only advisers, not main troops, and although he mentioned reports of villagers killed, he accepted the opinion of his diplomatic sources that "such behavior has not been widespread."[14]

The *Times* also had access to differing reports, such as one from the Reverend Robert Charlebois of Catholic Relief Services, who said he expected a bloodbath if the Khmer Rouge won, and had "documented evidence" of atrocities, but such reports were buried and downplayed.

Representative McCloskey told a Senate Foreign Relations subcommittee that he feared the Khmer Rouge might take vengeance "because Lon Nol's army makes a practice of taking no prisoners," and because refugees had told grim stories of Communist brutality. McCloskey also blamed Nixon's 1970 incursion for bringing Cambodia into the war, and said, "We could not have a greater sense of guilt to any nation in the world than what we have done to these poor people." He advocating giving aid until June 30, and then cutting it off to force a surrender, with Lon Nol leaving. Columnist Lewis praised McCloskey's argument in a column, "Avoiding a Bloodbath."[15]

What was left out of the various analyses was that Khieu Samphan was not the leader of the Khmer Rouge; Saloth Sar was, and he was to become Pol Pot. His brother-in-law Ieng Sary—they married sisters—was not a pro-Hanoi Communist, but like Pol Pot a Hanoi-hating Communist, and both had been ready to turn on their Vietnamese masters long before 1970. They had planned a blood purge of Cambodia for years.

Although the *Times'* Schanberg did not believe in a bloodbath, he had become an expert on Oriental corruption. His article, "Cambodia's Regime: As Corrupt as People Say," led the Sunday Week in Review section almost on the eve of the bloodbath.[16] Schanberg reported that many Cambodians had grown enormously rich on the war by embezzling from the hundreds of millions of aid dollars, selling artillery ammunition to the enemy, officers pocketing the wages of as many as 100,000 nonexistent soldiers, officials selling draft exemptions, school graduation certificates, visas to leave the country and automatic rifles that started out as aid material. Contrasts between rich and poor were "grotesque": refugees stirring garbage to find a scrap; wounded jamming the hospitals wall to wall, then emerging as amputees to join the thousands of beggers. He noted that Sihanouk's regime had been corrupt too, but the effects were more reprehensible in wartime. Schanberg quoted an unnamed diplomat: "They don't deserve to win this war. The Communists may be no better. . . but this side has treated its people so badly and so corruptly that it has forfeited all right to govern them."

Wicker that day quoted Schanberg's dispatches—"of proven reliability"—to warn that the Ford administration was playing with fire in trying to use the two scare words, "surrender" and "bloodbath," to bully Congress into more aid. Wicker wrote that if anybody "lost" Cambodia or was responsible for its likely "surrender," it was the Lon Nol government, "corrupt, inept, unpopular, ineffective and in power only by a military coup to which the CIA contributed encouragement at least." Wicker underlined Schanberg's points that Communist burnings of villages had not been widespread, that most observers in Phnom Penh did not expect a bloodbath and that the insurgent forces were not all Communists.[17]

At that point, the siege of Phnom Penh was driven out of the headlines by the momentum of the North Vietnamese offensive in South Vietnam. Without informing the Americans, Thieu decided to pull back his troops to more defensible perimeters. On March 18 a South Vietnamese army fled the central highlands in disarray toward the coast.

On Kissinger's return to Washington on March 24, Ambassador Martin, who was in the United States for dental surgery, urged at a high level meeting that the Soviets be told detente was at stake in the North Vietnamese offensive. Hué was being evacuated, and it fell to the Communists the next day.

Left out of the aid debate was the principle of human anticipation. No one appeared to understand the toll that gradual abandonment had taken on the South Vietnamese since the Congressional cutoff of bombing in August 1973, later translated into total abandonment by the stalling on aid. Congress was giving Thieu and Lon Nol the treatment administered to Diem by the Kennedy White House. No one evaluated the stimulating effect it was having on the North Vietnamese.

Kissinger told a press conference on March 26 that when the Vietnamese ceasefire was reached, "There never was any proposition that the United States would withdraw and cut off aid, and those agreements were negotiated on the assumption that the United States would continue economic and military aid to South Vietnam, and also that there would be some possibility of enforcing the agreement. . . ." Nixon had written Thieu on November 14, 1973, promising "swift and severe retaliatory action" if North Vietnam attacked the South.

"The problem we face in Indochina is an elementary question of what kind of people we are," Kissinger said. "For 15 years we have been involved in encouraging the people of Vietnam to defend themselves against what we conceive as external danger. To abandon them now, therefore, would be tantamount to betraying a sacred trust."

Within the Ford administration Kissinger had opposition, including some of his own aides and Defense Secretary Schlesinger, who believed the time had come to cut losses. The anti-war movement's conviction that South Vietnam could not be held was fulfilling itself.

Four days after the public appeals by Ford and Kissinger, Danang, South Vietnam's second-largest city, packed with more than a million refugees and rioting South Vietnamese troops, fell to the Communists. The next day Lon Nol left Cambodia, ostensibly on a diplomatic mission.

Martin flew back to Saigon with General Frederick Weyand, still bent on defending the shrunken core of South Vietnam. Thieu asked for B-52 support, still unable to believe that bomber strikes had been ruled out absolutely.

Disasters piled up rapidly. A C-5A Galaxy transport took off from Saigon April 4 with 325 persons aboard, 243 of them Vietnamese orphans, and crashed when a cargo door blew off, killing at least 150 persons. On April 8 a South Vietnamese pilot, Nguyen Thanh Trung, bombed the Presidential Palace. Air Marshal Nguyen Cao Ky, who still thought that the United States might call on him to replace Thieu, denied any knowledge of the attack. Hanoi radio said that Trung had been a long-time Communist agent.

President Ford appealed to Congress at a joint night session on April 10 to approve quickly $722 million in military aid and $250 million in economic and humanitarian aid for South Vietnam, the military aid figure recommended by General Weyand. Ford also asked for authority to use the U.S. military to protect evacuation if necessary. As Ford spoke, a hiss was heard from the Democratic side of the house, and several Democrats walked out.

Someone leaked to the *Times* that of $700 million in aid previously authorized, as of February 28 only $158 million had been delivered, another $369 million was in the pipeline, and the rest not yet obligated; the new aid request was more psychological than a material necessity. Kissinger's staff blamed Schlesinger's staff for the leak undercutting Ford's morale-boosting request.

The day after Ford addressed Congress, American diplomats began evacuating Phnom Penh in Operation Eagle Pull. While Kissinger still attempted to contact Sihanouk in hopes of bringing him into a settlement, 36 giant CH-53 helicopters evacuated 82 Americans, 159 Cambodians and 35 allied nationals from Phnom Penh to Thailand, Ambassador John Guenther Dean leaving with the American flag under his arm.

Former Premier Sisowath Sirik Matak, Lon Nol's partner in the coup against Sihanouk, wrote Ambassador Dean:

> Dear Excellency and Friend: I thank you sincerely for your letter and your offer to transport me to freedom. I cannot, alas, leave in such a cowardly fashion. As for you, and in particular your great country, I never believed for a moment that you would have the sentiment of abandoning people who have chosen liberty. You have refused us protection, and we can do nothing about it. You leave, and it is my wish that you and your country will find happiness under the sky. . . . I have only committed the mistake of believing in the Americans.

Sirik Matak also cabled Ford, saying:

> We will struggle now alone without your support. The Khmer people have already paid a very heavy sacrifice in human lives for you Americans to enable you to disengage from South Vietnam. Your policy of abandonment of a poor country, decided brutally without warning or preparation, puts us in a position of heart-

breaking betrayal . . . there will be in this capital of two million a terrible carnage. The Communists will find only ruins and desolation. We will die on our soil achieving our last desire—to die in freedom. I lay on the American conscience all Khmer deaths present and future.

The *Times* reported the cable buried deep in its story. In an editorial, it congratulated the "admirable sense of duty" of Premier Long Boret, who also declined to leave.[18] Sirik Matak and Long Boret were refused asylum at the French Embassy, and were executed a few days later.

Schanberg, with several Western correspondents, remained behind, expecting to stay at the Red Cross-protected Hotel Le Phnom. He was quickly disabused, forced by the conquering Communists to move on the run to asylum in the French Embassy compound, which became the international sanctuary.

Schanberg won the Pulitzer Prize for his courage in staying behind and his reporting on the Communist takeover when he was evacuated to Thailand three weeks later. His first report from Thailand was agonized, describing the sudden mass evacuation of perhaps four million Cambodians from the cities, with no exceptions for age or illness, hospitals emptied, relatives carrying the dying wounded on their backs.

Schanberg wrote that everyone had looked ahead with hopeful relief to the collapse of the city's defenses and the end of the war, believing that the suffering would be largely over. "All of us were wrong," he wrote. "That view of a future Cambodia—as a possibly flexible place where changes would not be extreme and ordinary folk would be left alone—turned out to be a myth." Yet he remained so stunned that he continued to deny the predictions of a bloodbath, reporting that "none of this will apparently bear any resemblance to the mass executions that had been predicted by Westerners." Still attempting to look at Cambodia through the eyes of the revolutionaries, he speculated that perhaps the rebels saw the evacuations as a "harsh necessity," that there was no way to "build a new society for the benefit of the ordinary man . . . without literally starting from the beginning."[19] No one could know that as he wrote, mass executions were mounting.

Just before Cambodia fell, a small firestorm blew up in the American media over Kissinger's references to Nixon's pledge of support to Thieu at the time of the ceasefire agreement. The media professed surprise and outrage, although the sense of the pledge had been reported at the time, if no one had been interested in securing precise quotations. The *Times'* Leslie Gelb telephoned Senator Church, asking his reaction to White House declarations that Nixon's pledge was not news, and Church said he would have his Foreign Relations Committee look into Nixon's bypassing Congress. Church told Gelb that White House explanations that the Nixon pledge was known were part of the "double-talk, deception and deceit that have been endemic to our whole Vietnam policy at every stage." The *Times* reports were heavy ammunition for Congressional critics of Ford's aid requests.

On April 14, two staff investigators for Church's committee, Richard Moose and Charles Meissner, returned to Washington from Saigon and briefed the committee, urging accelerated evacuation of Americans from South Vietnam. Moose and Meissner had been briefed privately by their friend, CIA analyst Snepp, who regarded South Vietnam as lost and whose concern now was saving the Americans and Vietnamese who had committed themselves to the United States. The entire Foreign Relations Committee went to see Ford in the Oval Office. He declined to set a deadline for evacuation.

Ambassador Martin believed that a premature exodus of Americans would touch off a bloody mutiny such as had occurred at Danang. He placed hourly telephone calls from Saigon to friendly Congressmen, lobbying for the largely symbolic $722 million in military aid. To keep the American press in Saigon under some kind of control, Martin authorized a secret airlift of 600 Vietnamese dependents and employees of the press corps on Air America flights, the kind of secret reporters could keep. The U.S. military was running its own black airlift without informing Martin.

By April 17 the CIA had learned the worst: there would be no negotiations. Hanoi wanted unconditional surrender. General Van Tien Dung intended to celebrate Ho Chi Minh's birthday in Saigon on May 19. The CIA station chief in Saigon, Thomas Polgar, clung to the possibility of a political deal if Kissinger could find leverage to use on the Soviets.

Kissinger met with Anatoly Dobrynin, who went through the motions of forwarding his messages to Brezhnev, while Soviet sources in Moscow misled *Times* reporters there, telling them that North Vietnamese resources were too thin for total victory at that time.

The *Times* had brought Malcolm Browne back to Saigon from Belgrade as bureau chief, and Browne worked closely with Polgar, members of the International Commission on Control and Supervision of the truce, and the local Communist truce representative, the Provisional Revolutionary Government's Colonel Vo Dong Giang. As late as April 19 Browne was reporting that the Communists might hold off an onslaught on Saigon to allow a peaceful transition of power. Giang said the two conditions were that Thieu resign and that American military advisers disguised as civilians leave the country. Browne later told me that the Communist contacts deceived him and everyone else at every turn. Snepp wrote that Hanoi could not have put together a better disinformation team than Browne and Polgar.[20]

An indignant *Times* editorial castigated Ford:

> In a desperate effort to shore up his request for a massive new dose of military aid to Saigon, President Ford has now told the world that the Soviet Union and Communist China honored their commitments, while the United States failed to do so. It is as incredible as it is inaccurate for the President of the United States to justify a bankrupt policy by portraying the two Communist superpowers as more trustworthy than the United States.[21]

In a separate editorial the same day, the newspaper said that the fate of Cambodians now rested with Prince Sihanouk and the "other insurgent leaders." Sihanouk had sent the *Times* a victory message from Peking via the Red Cross, and the *Times* chided him: "To say that the Phnom Penh leaders who had offered to step down 'deserve nothing but the gallows' is irresponsible and inflammatory at this tense moment," the *Times* said. Columnist Lewis, meanwhile, praised Congress for ending aid. "Congress was often dismissed as inept," Lewis wrote, "But compared with what? Compared to the record of our Presidents and Secretaries of State in Indochina, Congress shines. . . ."[22]

The *Times* editions of April 18, as Phnom Penh surrendered, might be collector's items. The editorial looked ahead:

> Must the futile battle of Phnom Penh now be duplicated, at far greater cost in lives, in a fight to the finish in Saigon? . . . Nothing that is said or done in Washington now will change the military disaster that has befallen President Thieu's government. . . . North Vietnam is obviously acting in massive violation of the military provisions of the 1973 truce, but President Thieu has just as clearly violated the political provisions of that accord—the procedures for establishing a coalition National Council to create a new political constitution for South Vietnam.

On another page, Ambassador Martin was reported conducting "business as usual," that Representative McCloskey questioned the state of Martin's health (read "sanity"), and a story recalled that on March 5 several sources had said that Representative Flynt had told Ford, "One thing we all agree on is that your Ambassador in South Vietnam is a disaster." Martin now was a target, as Ambassador Nolting once had been.

An article from Santa Monica quoted Tom Hayden as saying, "I see this as something we've all been working toward for a long time. Indochina has not fallen, it has risen. What has fallen is the whole cold war establishment. We now have the opportunity to define a new policy." His wife, Jane Fonda, said, "The suffering and turmoil have been going on for decades—this is just a pittance. Obviously we care about the suffering, but unless the United States stops channeling the wherewithal to the Thieu government to permit him to continue the military struggle, then the other side is going to escalate."

A new portrait of Cambodia's prospective leader Khieu Samphan said he had already "put his economic and organizational skills to work to forge both a growing army and the rudiments of an economic base to feed it . . . ." A news analysis said that the Ford administration's talk of moral obligation was a charade, aimed at gaining time to evacuate Americans. It suggested that Ambassador Martin had been holding the Americans hostage for a continuing commitment to the Saigon government.

The crown jewel in that edition of the *Times* was a large article taking up half the Op-Ed page, received through the mail from Bernardine Dohrn, the fugitive Weather Underground leader who was on the FBI's ten-most-wanted list. Under the headline, "Of Defeat and Victory," Dohrn heralded the victory of the Students for a Democratic Society in their ten-year struggle "to end the war in Vietnam, and to change the institutions which created it." She wrote:

> The need to pacify and control the people at home has produced an orgy of 'Communist bloodbath' rumors. These completely fabricated and unsubstantiated horror stories are designed to manipulate the 78% of the American people who now oppose their government's Indochina policies. . . . In the liberated areas, the revolutionary program will begin to improve the lives of the Vietnamese people. . . .

President Thieu resigned after ten years in office on April 21 in a two-hour speech on Saigon radio. He said he had accepted the settlement of 1973 only on Nixon's assurances, but that since then, Watergate had destroyed America's resolve. American aid always had been critical and had saved the country in 1972; without it, he was only an obstacle. Vice President Tran Van Huong would succeed him.

The next day, as Huong attempted to negotiate through the ICCS and PRG, South Vietnamese troops evacuated Xuan Loc, linchpin of Saigon's defense line.

South Vietnam's air force tried a last foray, dropping 15,000-pound Daisy Cutter bombs, designed to clear helicopter landing pads in jungles, and landing one CBS-55 bomb on headquarters of the 341st Division near Xuan Loc, killing more than 250 North Vietnamese.

Air Marshal Ky still thought the Americans might turn to him to try to rally the army, but instead American emissaries asked him not to attempt a coup. He understood; they had again chosen General Duong Van Minh.

Big Minh, who had ordered Diem killed 12 years earlier, succeeded Huong. He would surrender to Communist troops in the Presidential Palace he had once attacked with American encouragement.

Malcolm Browne, who had continued to report hopeful signs from the Communist side and a slowdown in fighting, finally reported to Polgar that they, the negotiators, had been doublecrossed. Giang said that Big Minh was totally unacceptable.

Saigon fell on April 29, when a heavy rocket and artillery attack struck Tan Son Nhut airport and its adjoining military headquarters complex as 81 U.S. Navy helicopters evacuated about 1,000 Americans and 5,500 South Vietnamese to aircraft carriers offshore. Ambassador Martin, barely on his feet with fatigue, savaged in the American press, was among the last to leave. For his bravery in taking on an assignment that became hopeless with the fall of his President, he would face, as Senator Church had promised the *Times,* a humiliating grilling in Congress before being discarded like other Americans who would not compromise integrity—Nolting, Keating, Clay, Harkins, Krulak, Higgins, Keegan, Sisco.

In the United States a silence fell over the usually vociferous commentators. The *Times* solicited comment from Americans who had been engaged for or against United States involvement, but found most of those who had supported the American effort too bitter or anguished to respond. Ambassador William J. Porter did reply:

> All of my worries of all these years about how it was going to end have materialized. We didn't understand the place; we didn't know how to fight there. . . . There are lessons to be drawn from it, very clear lessons. We should never have tried to get by with half measures, because you can't do that and control the outcome. The national moral is that you apply power if you have it.

Most who replied disagreed with Porter and agreed with the *Times.* Anthony Lake:

> I'm glad the fighting is coming to an end, but I feel shame that it took so long and that we played the role we did in extending it for so long. It has been inevitable that they would win the war for so many years. Now here's a chance to figure out what kind of

foreign policy we should have instead of having Vietnam rip us apart. . . .

Morton Halperin:

I'm relieved that it's over and that we didn't go back again. My fear was that Vietnam was a film that would just keep running backwards and forwards and would never end [an image often used in speeches by Ellsberg]. Then dismay that people talk of losing Vietnam or the fall of Vietnam. That country has not fallen, and we didn't have it to lose. Vietnam will now be independent.

Cora Weiss:

It's a very exciting and tragic moment at the same time. Exciting because no more lives will be wasted, because the people of Vietnam will be able to determine their lives without foreign interference. Tragic because one can't forget the needless death and destruction. For 25 years the United States has tried to control 23 million people on a tiny strip of land and we couldn't do it and we should never try to do it anywhere else.[23]

The *Times* editorial showed neither anguish nor the satisfaction that might have been expected, but a continued peckish irritation at the anti-Communist Ambassador Martin:

The United States left Vietnam with the same confusion and lack of direction that took this country there in the first place. . . . There is still no convincing explanation why the administration and Ambassador Graham Martin allowed thousands of American personnel to remain on the spot in Saigon long after their functions had become superfluous. Even when evacuation had started, a thousand American officials remained and became by their presence a force to obstruct the political bargain that might have prevented a final rout. . . . What could have been an orderly transfer of power by procedures internationally agreed upon in the Paris accords of 1973 now appears to have become a simple takeover by force. . . . Why this (American) change of heart came about is another question which cannot now be answered.[24]

The *Times* editorialists still had one or two balls left to juggle: Ford and Kissinger had warned that U.S. credibility was at stake with other allies, and that the defeat would send the United States into isolationism.

In a series of editorials the *Times* rebutted both themes. Ford confounded U.S. credibility with allies and with the "discredited and ineffectual clients" Lon Nol and Thieu. The United States was not reverting to isolationism; it was only learning the limits of its power. No serious observer believed that the status of the United States was entwined with the fate of Lon Nol or Saigon's defenses. As witness, the *Times* quoted serious observer Willy Brandt, who had been discredited and deposed because of his close friendship with East German spy Günther Guillome, who had been planted in his chancellory.

Although the *Times* sometimes favored defense cuts and Senator Mansfield's annual call to bring the troops home from Germany, it now thought it best to slow defense cuts for the moment, and was glad that Mansfield and Tip O'Neill were shelving their resolutions to bring the boys home. It quoted approvingly Senator Walter Mondale: "The Congress decided against war in Vietnam. We did not vote to become an isolationist country." American power was not at issue, the *Times* insisted; the new agenda was not isolationism. "The Secretary of State need have no doubt that the American people will support an active foreign policy...."[25]

The *Times* erred. The American people stopped the world and got off on April 29, crawling back into the womb of isolationism they had left 34 years before, trying hard to pretend it was December 6, 1941. Allied trust in the United States, damaged through the 1960s and dwindling fast since 1973, all but vanished. Since America would not fight, its Ambassadors became targets for terrorists, starting with Cleo A. Noel and his deputy, George Curtis Moore, in Khartoum in 1973, to be followed by Ambassador Francis E. Meloy, Jr. and his aide, Robert O. Waring, in Lebanon in 1976. President Ferdinand Marcos of the Philippines sent notice that American occupancy of Clark Field and Subic Bay would have to be renegotiated. Panama demanded the return of the Canal.

Among the revolutionary movements revived by the North Vietnamese success from Puerto Rico to Africa, the Palestine Liberation Organization was riding highest, wielding more influence in the United Nations than any nation except the superpowers. Its state-within-a-state status in Lebanon touched off a murderous civil war that raged for two years and then simmered on indefinitely. In 1958 Eisenhower had landed Marines in Lebanon, but in 1975 the American media and government looked the other way.

Ford was unable to follow up SALT-1 with any substantial arms reduction negotiations with Brezhnev. The Soviet Politburo, confident that an isolationist Congress would restrict American defense spending, accelerated a vast strategic arms build-up aimed at achieving superiority rather than parity, including the new blue-water navy Khrushchev had begun after the Cuban missile crisis.

Middle East peace negotiations remained stalemated through the American elections of 1976, when Jimmy Carter, endorsed by the *Times* and carrying New York State decisively, succeeded Ford. The *Times* rejoiced at the new Secretary of State, Cyrus Vance, and the new chief arms negotiator, Paul Warnke, whose copy of the Pentagon Papers it had printed through the agency of IPS and Ellsberg, but was disappointed that the Senate failed to confirm Theodore Sorensen, the one-time draft resister, as head of the CIA.

The Eastern establishment architects of the disasters of the 1960s were back in the saddle. Carter's policies would be the opposite of Nixon's. Plans to produce the B-1 bomber and enhanced radiation weapons went the way of Skybolt. Two months in office, Carter spoke out for an independent Palestinian state. Israelis then ousted their permanent Labor government in favor of Menachem Begin, who could not be intimidated.

George Ball, the *Times* favorite who had welcomed the Berlin Wall as a stabilizing factor, advocated quarter measures instead of half measures during the Cuban missile crisis and in Vietnam and had signed the Cable of August 24 that doomed Diem, had become wealthy as an investment banker and did not join the Carter administration. He appeared often on television shows, his advice solicited respectfully, never grilled.

In 1976 Ball proposed in *Foreign Affairs* that the United States and the Soviet Union impose a settlement on the Middle East. Vance, meeting with Andrei Gromyko, announced on October 1, 1977, that the superpowers were summoning the participants of the October War, plus the PLO, to a renewed Geneva conference before the end of the year.

Anwar Sadat, who had staked his life on easing the Soviets out of the Middle East, was as appalled as the Israelis were. Sadat scuttled the Geneva conference with the bold stroke of going to Jerusalem in November. Subsequently the American media unanimously credited Carter, who never had been to the Middle East and knew the Pyramids only from picture postcards, with the Camp David accords.

A year later the Carter administration consulted Ball on the burgeoning Iranian revolution, which had been simmering since 1967 under Marxist leadership but in 1978 was being hijacked from the Marxists by the Islamic zealots of Ayatollah Ruhollah Khomeini. Ball advised dropping the Shah, which was done, and another American ally went the way of Eden, Adenauer, Macmillan, Diem, Thieu, Lon Nol and Park Chung Hee, soon to be murdered by the Korean CIA chief. Iran executed thousands—far more than the inflated death toll of the revolution as reported in the American media—and became the main threat to the Persian Gulf, instead of its protector.

In May 1977 the disgraced Nixon had been silent for almost three years, but there was disquieting news. Although no American television network news personality wanted to speak with Nixon, nor was any American network willing to carry Nixon interviews, a British interloper, David Frost, was interviewing Nixon for a television series. The *Times* mobilized to meet the threat as though, columnist William Safire remarked, they feared he might return from Elba.

Frost had been in Sydney, Australia, when he saw Nixon's resignation speech on television in August 1974. He thought that Nixon would be "the most intriguing man in the world to interview," but he did not think he had a chance against the expected competition from American commentators. To Frost's surprise, his bid was the only one Nixon had received. More surprising, Nixon was willing to give Frost control of methodology and content of the interviews. Then Frost discovered that no American television network or advertising agency would touch his project.

Reading Frost's candid book about the interviews[26] is to see the wheels spinning in the Frostian head as he realized the virulence of hatred for Nixon in the American media. He had gone into the project interested in the complete Nixon, including China, the Middle East, the Soviets, the Vietnam disaster. He quickly realized that the project depended on America's acceptance of it, and therefore it would have to center on Watergate. That meant he would have to nail Nixon's hide to the barn door.

The team Frost assembled for his project, mostly recruited on the recommendation of Joseph Kraft, included no one except himself who could be construed as tolerant of Nixon's side of the story. John Birt, from London Weekend Television, quickly concentrated on Nixon's guilt. James Reston, Jr. already had collaborated with Frank Mankiewicz on two books damning Nixon. Bob Zelnick, from Public Television, was anti-Nixon, and Phil Stanford had worked with I. F. Stone, *The New York Times Magazine* and the *Saturday Review,* all passionate Nixon opponents.

Frost was warned repeatedly, even by Nixon himself, that he risked being tarred with the Nixon brush if he should appear to be an objective, naive patsy. Frost's friend Clay Felker, the New Journalism publisher of *New York Magazine,* warned that the media establishment in New York thought that Frost was in over his head in tangling with Nixon, a warning that was published as a news item in the *Washington*

Post. Columnist Kraft, who watched the first day's film, told Felker that Nixon had been in control.

Commenting on the first rough-cut rushes of film, Felker told Frost, "I thought it was good in parts, but you have to realize how many people are out there, lying in wait for these interviews. If you put a foot wrong, they'll kill you."

Before the project got under way, the *Times* demanded in an editorial that Frost present "full disclosure" of the "personnel of the 'international consortium' that is to be Mr. Nixon's financial angel," at a time when Frost did not have financing for the project. Frost reported in his book that the *Times* editorial closed down opportunities for finding financing and required him to make a quick flight to London to secure short-term money to cover funds he had raised from reluctant bankers in New York. Since the networks would not show Nixon, Frost put together a network of independent stations.

The steady growth of the *Times'* influence through the 1960s and 1970s impressed many editors, among them Michael J. O'Neill, who reached the top at the *New York Daily News* in 1975, succeeding Floyd Barger. Editors at the *News* were required to "match" any story that made Page 1 of the *Times*, and O'Neill hoped to make the paper a kind of tabloid version of the media leader. In view of the new isolationism, the *News* did not invest in foreign coverage, the backbone that had made the *Times* powerful, but instead acquired a number of columnists, including Jimmy Breslin, Pete Hamill, Michael Daly, Jack Anderson and Liz Smith, all left of center and all comfortable with *Times* views.[27] As one of six foreign correspondents done away with, I was assigned to the New York desk during the Orwellian Hate Week in May 1977.

On the night of April 30, the Washington press corps was assembled in tuxedos for the annual Gridiron Club dinner when the *Times* and *Washington Post* first editions came out with a Nixon story. The *Times* headline said:

NEW TAPES LINK NIXON
TO WATERGATE SCHEME
3 DAYS AFTER BREAK-IN
In Talk With Colson Then He Called
Cover-Up a 'Dangerous Job.'

At the *News*, the expression "new tapes" galvanized editors into action. A call went to the Washington hotel hosting the press dinner, and the *News'* managing editor, Washington bureau chief and correspondents were hauled out to match the *Times*. They could not get the "new tapes" instantly, but they could copy parts from the *Washington Post,* journalistic etiquette preventing us in New York from simply pirating them from the *Times*. As the *News* team slipped out of the dinner in Washington, an editor in New York, otherwise an intelligent and reasonable man, rubbed his palms together and announced, "Now to perpetrate a little journalism." Perpetrating journalism at the *News* had come to copying the *Post* in Washington to imitate the *Times*.

On the telephones to Washington, a hitch developed. A Washington correspondent complained, "Hey, this is all old crap." One of them said, "Okay, here's something new. Get this down. This is a quote of Nixon telling Dean that the Supreme Court justices are boobs. He says. . . ."

Having heard that story somewhere before, I interrupted to ask what the context of the statement was; why was Nixon calling them boobs? "What difference does it make?" the correspondent demanded. "He's insulting the Supreme Court, isn't he?" It was the conversation about the Supreme Court's decision on the Pentagon Papers, and my own reaction when I heard the court decision had been the same as Nixon's, "Well, what can you expect? Potter Stewart's a boob; Brennan's a boob. . . ." The insults got into the *News*, years late, without saying what they were about. But the *News'* circulation was falling.

The *Times* scoop, by James M. Naughton and Anthony Marro, contained nothing new, and the *Times* conceded, buried on the jump page, that the "new material, which lawyers on all sides in the case have been aware of for years, does not alter the basic facts. . . . Yet it shows. . . . the calculation and callousness of Nixon White House discussions."

The "new tapes," then, were a fraud, transcripts that had been kicking around the Watergate trials for two years, now being orchestrated to deflate in advance Frost's interviews and create a proper atmosphere for Hate Week. The *Times*, in its story, was candid about its purpose: "The material was made available to *The New York Times* in the wake of widespread speculation that Nixon had refused, for the most part, to concede culpability in the Watergate affairs in interviews with David Frost that are to be telecast nationally beginning Wednesday night."[28] The *Times* quoted "one source" as saying that Nixon had stonewalled the interviewer much of the time.

On the same day, the *Times* published a story by Les Brown suggesting that *Time, Newsweek* and *TV Guide* were letting down the media team, making deals of questionable ethics to obtain parts of the interviews for advance cover stories. The *Times'* objection was that publicity from the stories would spur Frost's sale of advertising spots in the interviews, which "could add about $500,000 to the profits." The story said that the "11th hour publicity blitz" had added 28 stations and swelled the impromptu network to 155 outlets, after the networks had refused the series. The *Times* listed advertisers who had bought spots as though they were a rogues' gallery. An earlier *Times* story, suggesting that a group of San Diego investors might have a hand in editing the interviews, was retracted.

Frost began taking abuse from the American media before the interviews started. Once into the interviews, he realized he would be finished in American television unless he got through Nixon's defenses. To force a confession of guilt from Nixon, he resorted to a tactic that would be unfamiliar to BBC audiences. Frost compiled a list of 16 Nixon quotations from the tapes that would be incriminating when presented out of context, and, once Nixon was softened up by lead-in questioning, threw all of them at Nixon at once:

> One, 'You could get a million dollars and you could get it in cash. . I know where it could be gotten.' Two, 'Your major guy to keep under control is Hunt.' Three, 'Don't you have to handle Hunt's financial situation?' Four, 'Let me put it frankly: I wonder if that doesn't have to be continued?' Five, 'Get the million bucks, it would seem to me that would be worthwhile. . . .'

As Frost paused after his questions, Nixon said:

> Let me stop you right there. Right there. You're doing something here which I am not doing, and I will not do throughout these broadcasts. You have every right to, you were reading there out of context, out of order. . . . Read the last sentence. The last sentence which says, after that, 'You never have any choice with Hunt, because it finally comes down to clemency.' And I said six times in that conversation—you didn't read that in your ten things—six times I said, 'You can't provide clemency.'

Nixon probably had gone into the interviews wanting to confess in some degree, but to confess in context. While denying that he had committed an impeachable offense, he conceded, "I let down my friends. I let down the country. . . . I, I let the American people down, and I have to carry that burden with me for the rest of my life."

The television was on in the newsroom at the *News*, but no one appeared to be watching it. The news editor, a strong personality, turned his back to the set, announcing grimly, "I can't stand the sight of the son of a bitch," and curious copyboys drifted away from the set. I did not know then that the news editor's brother, a *Times* man, had assisted the Boston transfer of the Pentagon Papers from Ellsberg to Sheehan.

The *Times* story that night, by Naughton, began with Nixon admitting "he had 'let the American people down' by lying, disregarding his constitutional oath and abetting the Watergate coverup while in the White House." But Naughton found that his apologia was "nonetheless more rueful than remorseful," and Nixon had refused "to concede that his conduct had amounted to obstruction of justice."

A news analysis by David E. Rosenbaum charged Nixon with continued lying, listing discrepancies between what he told Frost and the tape transcripts, but the story strained to find factual discrepancies; Nixon did not refute Frost's charges, he had disputed the interpretation of the facts.

A *Times* editorial headlined, "The Trial of Richard Nixon—and of America," displayed nostalgia for Judge Sirica and Senator Sam:

> The judge: He was not the Chief Justice, not a Congressional committee chairman, not even an American. The moral magistrate of Richard Nixon's guilt was, finally, a British journalist who, like the defendant, stood to gain great profit from the trial. . . .
>
> The defendant: That Richard Nixon had been unseen for three years was startling in itself. For many of us, our entire adult lives can be calibrated by his six (or was it sixty?) crises. . . . How minutely, thus, we inspected the deepened seams on the mask of his face, and wondered whether he thought even a million dollars could compensate him for the self-degradation of each new (telltale?) fluff, fumble and evasion. . . . [29]

The *News* had become dedicated to following *Times* judgments, and the ferocity of the *Times* attacks on Nixon had to be "matched." Columnist Breslin compared Nixon unfavorably with Britain's great train robber, then in the headlines, calling the ex-President, without using his name, a thief, a coward and a whore. Hamill called Nixon "this crook," "this son of a bitch," "the Bela Lugosi of American politics, lying out there in the crypt in San Clemente and rising into the darkness at night." James Wieghart, the Washington columnist, warned any persons in the media who might be thinking of deviating with a pro-Nixon word that they would be regarded as "fawning sycophants" and "venomous spear-carriers." [30]

Frost's second interview, telecast May 12, concerned foreign policy and inevitably some Nixon successes. The *Times* was up to the challenge. Naughton's lead said, "Richard Nixon said...tonight that Henry A. Kissinger was an intellectual giant, but he described the former Secretary of State as moody, secretive, capable of outrageous private remarks and intensely protective of official perogatives...."

The story was a continuation of earlier prodding by the *Times*, "Let's you and him fight," which Kissinger had resisted.

Naughton wrote, "...the refrain that ran throughout the telecast was Mr. Nixon's stress on his personal stewardship of big-power diplomacy while minimizing Mr. Kissinger's role and influence, as though the former President was trying to salvage a place in history at the expense of his administration's Nobel laureate." Naughton reported, "A spokesman for Mr. Kissinger said he would have no comment on Mr. Nixon's remarks."

A sidebar by Bernard Gwertzman, "Nixon Talk Reflects Fascination With Soviets," revived the *Times'* version of the October War alert. Gwertzman blamed Israel for breaking the ceasefire in the Suez area, causing the Soviet threat, and reported, "This led to the American decision to put forces on a low-priority alert." Naughton noted that neither Frost nor Nixon had mentioned that the alert came about after the Saturday Night Massacre when "contemporary reports suggested that Mr. Nixon had approved rather than initiated the alert."

The *Times* reporters ignored the point that Frost thought most striking in his foreign policy interview. Nixon had told him that he had written Thieu because he wanted him to know that "he had my commitment, my personal commitment, to take whatever action I could as President, having in mind of course the reservation that he knew I always had to have in mind....I'd have to have congressional support on the appropriations side." Frost objected that renewed bombing for a peace that had been won was a contradiction in terms. Nixon replied that he would have ordered air strikes, and he would have gotten public support. "I would have broken the case strongly. It would have been swift. It would have been massive. And it would have been effective." Nixon said, "....the Congress lost it. And that's the tragedy and they have to take responsibility for it."

Frost's third interview, scheduled for May 19, was leaked to the *Times* in advance "from Mr. Frost's production company." The headline read: "Nixon Says a President Can Order Illegal Acts Against Dissidents; In Frost Interview Tonight He Cites an Inherent Power for Burglaries and Wiretaps."

Naughton's story said that Nixon told Frost, "Well, when a President does it, that means it is not illegal."

The *Times* used that quotation six times in headline type: twice on May 19, three times the next day plus once in a photo undercaption, and again in the Sunday Week in Review. Nixon never said it. It was a misrepresentation of a give-and-take dialogue with interruptions and digressions. It might be compressed by rational editing to read, "If a President does it . . . because of the national security . . . or because of a threat to internal peace of significant magnitude . . . it is not illegal."

A Hate Week cannot be conducted properly without backup from television, so the MacNeil/Lehrer Report on Public Television had a panel ready to discuss the first interview. The panelists were Carl Bernstein, Robert Woodward and Dr. David Abrahamsen, M.D., author of the psychobiography *Nixon vs. Nixon: an Emotional Tragedy.*[31] All three had profited from books pummeling Nixon, but the scurrility of Dr. Abrahamsen's effort embarrassed even Woodward and Bernstein. Abrahamsen on television resembled an infuriated S. Z. (Cuddles) Szakall, the gentle, jowly commedian. With apologies to Central Europe, it is not possible to convey his performance without touching on his genuine psychiatrist's accent: "But look vot he did to Jerry Voorhis," Abrahamsen said, bouncing up and down in his chair. ". . . he hass had a criminal mentality zince childhood." Abrahamsen's book was thoroughly specious long-distance psychoanalysis; he never met Nixon, and diagnosed Nixon's mother from the grave as a castrator who had made Nixon's father an egocentric tyrant. For good measure, Abrahamsen referred to Alger Hiss as Nixon's victim and suggested that Hiss' grand jury indictment was fixed.[32]

Robert MacNeil replied to my protest: "I have to agree with you that our Nixon follow-up show was one sided . . . Charles Colson was a virtually firm guest until the last minute . . . we feel we cannot let the refusal of one side in effect veto a program."

David Susskind, however, dug up three persons advertised as "Nixon die-hards" for his Metromedia television show June 5. When former White House staff member Bruce Herschensohn gave an unruffled defense of Nixon, ignoring Susskind's invitations to attack Kennedy and Johnson, Susskind burst out, "But he is fundamentally evil!" Still, Susskind was the only television performer in the New York area to permit a pro-Nixon voice to be heard.

The edgy anxiety the *Times* had displayed before the Frost-Nixon interviews recurred in the spring of 1978 as Nixon's book, *RN,* went to press.

As in the case of the television interviews, Nixon's memoirs were attacked in advance: the book contained nothing new; it had been called in for revision in the light of Haldeman's book (untrue); Nixon had not written the book (untrue—he had written 1.5 million words pared down by editor Bob Markel of Grosset & Dunlap); Nixon would receive too much money for it. A young lady sued to have Nixon deprived of any proceeds, and a boycott was organized at the Atlanta Book Fair. Bumper stickers were distributed, "Don't Buy Books from Crooks." *Washington Post* columnist Haynes Johnson declared on Public Television that he would not buy the book, a pledge widely seconded.

When *RN* reached the bookstores in New York, the *Times* reported the book was a flop. The *New York Post,* recently under the management of Australian Rupert Murdoch, who did not understand the local rules, reported in its Page 6 column that the book was too selling, the first contradiction of the *Times* in New York since the Pentagon Papers.

On June 4 *RN* appeared on *The New York Times* list of non-fiction bestsellers in the Number 4 position. The *Times* explained in a footnote:

> Hardly had *RN* appeared on the stands when a spate of *TV and wire service stories* pronounced the book dead on arrival. [My italics; the wire service stories no doubt were picked up from the *Times* and distributed to TV stations.] The publishers, Grosset & Dunlap, had denied that the book was a flop, calling the reporting 'selective and emotional' . . . . our own poll indicated that the book does poorly in the East—anti-Nixon country?—but very well elsewhere.

The *Times* still had not reviewed the book. *The New York Review of Books* published the first review in the area, by John Kenneth Galbraith, a long-time Nixon enemy. The first one-fourth of the review discussed Galbraith's adventures in the Office of Price Administration in 1942, where he did not meet the temporary employee Nixon, and the minor tax deduction Galbraith took ($4,500) for papers he gave the Kennedy Library. The review established Galbraith's close association with John Kennedy and his wife, Adlai Stevenson, Arthur Schlesinger, Jr., W. Averell Harriman and Nathan Marsh Pusey.

When Galbraith got around to the book, he charged that Nixon had not written it: "As committee work goes, this book is not badly written." Galbraith read the book the way the media scanned tape transcripts, looking for something that made Nixon appear stupid or evil: "One gets caught up in the game—looking for flaws in his explanations."

The *Times* finally reviewed *RN* on June 11, 1978, when it was the

Number 2 bestseller. A footnote remarked that it was selling less than half as well as Number 1, *If Life Is a Bowl of Cherries, What Am I Doing in the Pits?* by Erma Bombeck. The reviewer, Professor James MacGregor Burns, a biographer of Presidents who had eulogized the Kennedy team's alibi books, dutifully followed the *Times* line. Psychologically, the book showed that Nixon was divided against himself. Nixon "spews out torrents of invective" such as "State Department jerks." Nixon paints "an especially unflattering portrait of Henry A. Kissinger as an inveterate hardliner, emotionally unstable, constantly in need of tutoring and bucking up by his chief, although immensely talented." Once again, the *Times'* theme, "Let's you and him fight."

Burns had done a great deal to contribute to the fame of Roosevelt's strong presidency, as in *Roosevelt: The Soldier of Freedom,* but the decisiveness he applauded in Roosevelt's battle against Germany, Japan, fascism, anti-war pacifists, he found reprehensible in Nixon's battle against the North Vietnamese, communism, terrorists and the same anti-war pacifists. He did not touch on the book's substance.

Throughout the ideological assaults on Nixon's television interviews and his book, the *Times* repeatedly editorialized that it was long-since time to forget the Nixon era, bury it. By 1977 the world knew that the Khmer Rouge were committing genocide in Cambodia, that the China Sea was full of Vietnamese refugees, and the danger arose that someone might remember that the *Times* consistently had disparaged the scare talk of a bloodbath. In the midst of the Frost-Nixon interview, on May 20, a *Times* editorial furiously blamed Nixon again for the genocide the Khmer Rouge were committing.

Help arrived with the publication of *Sideshow: Kissinger, Nixon and the Destruction of Cambodia,*[33] by William Shawcross, the young British reform-Marxist journalist and author who had believed that Alexander Dubček was the prophet of a new, benign form of communism. As in the case of the Pentagon Papers, Shawcross had obtained *documents* to prove his case, this time legally through the Freedom of Information Act.

To the *Times, Sideshow* was the greatest book ever written. Its conclusions were the same as those of Anthony Lewis during the fight against continuing aid before Cambodia fell: Nixon had introduced the war to Cambodia, forcing the North Vietnamese back into that country, touching off its destruction. The *Times'* promotion of *Sideshow* was unprecedented, with Page 1 stories on its conclusions before publication, multiple ecstatic reviews, resumés of its arguments by columnists and editorialists. In 1979 the *Times* published articles and commentaries, some of them lengthy, on Shawcross' book on February 6, May 3, May 13, May 15, July 15, July 23, August 5, September 23, September 24, October 4 and December 30. The *Times* made Shawcross an international figure as it once had made Castro an international figure, familiar to viewers of NBC's Today Show.

Since Nixon was disposed of, the *Times* praise of Shawcross centered in an attack on Kissinger, who did not reply to it. Kissinger was about to publish *White House Years,* and the *Times* reported in a story covering half a page, "Kissinger Revised His Book More Than He Reported." The story, by Wolfgang Saxon, reported that comparing Kissinger's book with his corrected galley proofs showed "many additions, deletions and change of phrases and paragraphs bolstering his contention that aerial bombardments of Communist base camps in Cambodia in 1969 did not force the North Vietnamese to move deeper into Cambodia." It cited several paragraphs it said were added to refute the Shawcross thesis.

Kissinger did not respond to the *Times'* attack, but he did write to the *Economist* of London, which had called Shawcross' book propagandistic, misleading and unfair. Kissinger wrote:

> . . . . The basic point of Mr. Shawcross' book which simply omits that (1969) Vietnamese offensive is that our 1969 bombing of the sanctuaries (to a depth of around five miles) and the eight-week ground assault against them in 1970 (to a distance of 21 miles) explain or justify the Khmer Rouge massacre of two million to three million Cambodians in 1975. I find this obscene. The genocidal horrors perpetrated by the Khmer Rouge in Cambodia in 1975 have obviously been profoundly disquieting to antiwar critics who for so long advocated that we abandon Indochina to its fate. . . .

Kissinger wrote that it was Hanoi that invaded Cambodia in the middle 1960s; it was Hanoi that organized the Khmer Rouge and was

> . . . trying to strangle Cambodia in the month before our limited attack, and it is North Vietnamese troops who have overthrown the Khmer Rouge in 1978-1979. Had we not invaded the sanctuaries Cambodia would have been engulfed in 1970 instead of 1975. . . . The Shawcross thesis is essentially that resistence to totalitarianism in Indochina was immoral and the Communist gulags in Indochina essentially the fault of those who tried to prevent them.

The *Times* picked up the letter from the *Economist* and printed it as a column, "By Henry A. Kissinger," on its Op-Ed page on September 23, keeping the Shawcross story alive.

Although Kissinger would not reply to the *Times*, Martin Herr, who had been minister at the U.S. Embassy in 1970, did reply in a blistering letter accusing Shawcross of "a giant mystification of the public about the sequence of events in Cambodia in 1970." Herr noted that the *Times* itself had reported the North Vietnamese offensive toward Phnom Penh in March 1970, a month before the incursion supposedly pushed them into the interior.

Shawcross appeared at the Overseas Press Club in New York at the beginning of October 1979, appearing defensive although the audience consisted of friendly *Times* readers. His lecture was not centered on his book, but on the current horrors of starvation in Cambodia and the efforts of agencies like Oxfam to relieve it, making himself a defender of starving Cambodians. Asked about Kissinger's reply, Shawcross, like the *Times*, said that Kissinger had been forced to revise his memoirs extensively, adding the charge, "Kissinger has manufactured a North Vietnamese threat to Phnom Penh in 1970 which cannot be substantiated."

Shawcross received one challenging question. A woman rose to say she had lived in Indochina for six years, including several months in Cambodia, working with Indochinese while out of touch with the news, but all of them had told her they thanked God for the Americans, and if they left, a holocaust would occur. Her question was, "Did the bombing of the Vietnamese on the border make any difference to Cambodia's fate?" Shawcross, agitated, said he had not made the bombing a central issue; Kissinger had done that in his letter to the *Economist*. His book, he said, underlined that the issue was not the bombing or the 1970 incursion, but the period 1971 to 1975, "when Cambodia was grossly neglected." Kissinger "does not address that issue at all," he said. "By 1975 the Khmer Rouge had grown to 70,000; they were children; they came to power in a vacuum." Besides, he added, the question was hypothetical. He did not appear to be aware that the neglect of Cambodia was Congress-imposed.

An element neglected by Shawcross was the state of relations between the Khmer Rouge and the North Vietnamese Communists who ruled them, a relationship that denied nationalism and mixed Marxism-Leninism with Oriental, master-vassal feudalism.

Just after Shawcross' appearance at the Overseas Press Club, Ieng Sary, deputy premier and foreign minister of Democratic Kampuchea, appeared at a news conference at the United Nations. It was sparsely attended. Although Ieng Sary was a certified monster, his credibility was so low that the American media ignored his statements. He was closely questioned by a Communist Polish journalist who had been to Cambodia, seen "thousands of skeletons" at the village of Prey Veng, and wanted to know what had happened to Hu Nim, once high in the regime of Pol Pot and named as a prospective leader by the *Times*.

Ieng Sary gave the standard evasions: It was good to get questions from Poland, because relations with Poland always had been friendly, and Poles who were on the truce commission in Vietnam knew Cambodia well. Hu Nim had been minister of information, but he turned to betrayal so he was jailed. Ieng Sary didn't know what happened to him because he was a foreign minister, not a minister for security. Ieng Sary had visited Prey Veng and had found no skeletons, no bones. "Maybe skeletons were carried there to show you. Maybe they came from fighting in 1975 when the Vietnamese killed many people. Maybe it was true that there was a massacre at Prey Veng, but Kampuchea had no time for the administration or urbanization of cities." Ieng Sary conceded that while the new agricultural campaign was under way, some acts occurred without the knowledge of the leadership; people died of malaria; mistakes were made by village cadres who made people work day and night.

Then he made some revealing remarks. "We wanted good relations with China, but the (North) Vietnamese always interfered, created obstacles. The Vietnamese did not want us to have relations with foreign countries."

Ieng Sary told of being a student in Paris at the time of the 1954 Geneva conference when he was recruited by a Ho Chi Minh agent named Vien Tang Tung, who also recruited Saloth Sar. Very early Ieng Sary and Saloth Sar realized that the Vietnamese Communists "wanted to keep us away from foreign contacts to prevent our having foreign relations." Starting in 1952, the Vietnamese Communists were "recruiting Cambodian intellectuals for mobilization in the maquis." The Cambodian Communists realized early that relations with China and with the Soviets were "the only way to prevent the Vietnamese from swallowing us, but the Soviets backed the Vietnamese. The Soviets and Cuba were in the present war (between Cambodia and Vietnam) from the beginning."

The theme of Ieng Sary's unreported press conference—it did not appear in the *Times*, and the *News* did not use my piece—has been hammered ever since in publications of Pol Pot's regime: the Vietnamese Communists never intended to leave Cambodia, rather, to infiltrate millions more Vietnamese. The war with Vietnam had been inevitable, with the Cambodian Communists following the Chinese model as Hanoi turned increasingly to the Soviets.

Chou En-lai died in January 1976, followed by Mao in September, and within a year China turned on its Vietnamese clients, cutting off aid in retaliation against Vietnam's seizure of Cambodia and mistreatment of the Chinese minority in Vietnam. Then China massed an army at the border and poured rocket and artillery fire into Vietnam, as the Soviets established themselves at Danang. The breakup of alliances came too late for South Vietnam.

Correspondent Henry Kamm won a deserved Pulitzer Prize for the *Times* in 1978 with his persistent revelations of the bloodbath at sea of the boat people.

Kamm also visited Prince Souvanna Phouma, under a kind of house arrest in Vieng Say, Laos, the country that Eisenhower had told Kennedy was the key to Indochina. The former premier, Kamm reported, "appeared to regret that the United States had not pressed the war in Indochina all the way." Tucked away at the bottom of the story was Souvanna Phouma's comment, "The United States is a bizarre country. The United States has terrible weaknesses. Everything had to go through the Congress. The President of the United States has almost no power."[34]

Chapter XXII
A Monopoly of Virtue

*"Hermotimus, I cannot show what truth is, so well as
wise people like you and your professor, but one thing
I know about it, and that is that it is not pleasant to
the ear; falsehood is more esteemed."*

—Lucian of Samosata, Skeptic

During the 1960s and 1970s, while the *Times'* fortunes and influence
rose like a star over West 43rd Street, the progressive degeneration of
New York City centered a block away on 42nd Street west of Times
Square. By the Bicentennial year 1976, the most likely place in the city
to be mugged was in the shadow of the nation's protector. Forty-
second Street was ruled by porno shops, drug pushers, pimps,
prostitutes—female, male and child—psychotics, three-card monte
dealers, pickpockets, derelicts and youths with knives. During the
blackout riots of July 1977, a *Times* editorial hinted at the rationale behind the newspaper's concern for peace, humanitarianism and pragma-
tism in cautioning against shooting the looters and arsonists who

destroyed the business district of Bushwick in Brooklyn: "Do you know how many hoodlums out there have guns?" the *Times* warned the police.[1]

Except for surrendering the city to the barbarians inside the gates, the *Times* was on top of the world in 1977. It had won the two great arguments of the epoch, Vietnam and Watergate, and for sheer power no institution could rival it.

For two decades, praise for the *Times* had accumulated. Richard Rovere of *The New Yorker* informed the British in a London magazine in 1959 that "without the *Times*, no one with any professional concern with events as they unfold can function in his accustomed way.... there are few writers on public affairs who do not work on the comfortable assumption that the *Times* will call to their attention anything they want called to their attention."[2] Going into the 1960s, Joseph Kraft estimated that the *Times* readership included 44% of all government officials in Washington, 30% of the nation's college presidents, 60% of American newspaper editors and 28% of banking executives.[3]

One who took exception was George Lichtheim, a professor at Columbia and Stanford, who wrote:

> To the foreigner who spends some time in the United States, few features of the local scenery are more surprising than the general esteem in which *The New York Times* is held.... as a reliable source of information about the world outside America's borders, the *Times* is inadequate and misleading.... Within the journalistic profession it has long been accepted that the *Times* is not to be relied upon for the kind of reporting that readers of the more prestigious European newspapers take for granted.... What it persistently fails to do is to acquaint its readers with the real drift of affairs abroad, notably when that drift—and this is where a kind of censorship appears to come in—runs counter to the editorial frame of reference.... The overall impression—a compound of ignorance, provincialism and plain incompetence—remains the same year after year. Inexhaustible it may be, the relevance of its coverage leaves something to be desired.[4]

By the late 1970s the Lichtheims had been routed. A movie thriller of the period, "Three Days of the Condor," drew its theme from Seymour Hersh's stories on the CIA's family jewels. Villain of the murderous plot was the CIA deputy director for covert actions. Confronted by the CIA researcher who discovered the power-mad scheme, a CIA executive confirms that it will be covered up. The loyal

American is alone, what can he do about it, since the CIA will kill him? Their encounter takes place on the sidewalk of 43rd Street, and the hero replies, "Don't you know where you are? They know it all. I gave them the story." He gestures to the doorway. In Old English typescript, the door's glass panes proclaim, "The New York Times." Fadeout.

The *Times* did not rise to its position of final arbitrator of the nation's problems accidentally, or because Americans are boobs who will buy anything well-packaged. Lichtheim notwithstanding, the *Times* earned its prominence in the 1940s by investing heavily in foreign reporting, the most neglected field of journalism, and continuing the investment when others dropped out. It is not the *Times'* fault that others abdicated the field. The *Times* built the largest, if not the best, staff of foreign correspondents, and it printed their dispatches at length whether their cables were relevant or not. The correspondents, when they came home, filled the Washington bureau and the editors' slots with men who could silence their adversaries with the remark, "Well, have you been there?"

The *Times'* reputation for a global outlook, justified by the sheer volume of its foreign reports, helped it survive as the number of New York newspapers dropped from 11 to three. When the *New York Herald Tribune* lost Homer Bigart to the *Times*, began skimping on foreign reporting, turned to "writers" rather than reporters, and died, the *Times* no longer had a competitor. As it gained absolute power, it followed absolutely the law of intellectual corruption.

Some of the *Times* correspondents rank with the world's best, but they cannot run the newspaper from the field, and they don't always fit into management positions. The correspondents became hostage to the *Times'* slide into ideology. In the home office and Washington bureau, John Oakes on the editorial page, columnists Reston, Wicker and the two Lewises, editors of the *Magazine, Book Review* and later Times Books, offered upcoming *Times* staffers the key to advancement. Everyone on the staff understood what was wanted after the promotions of Herbert Matthews and David Halberstam.

The *Times* is located at the center of the book publishing industry, and its *Book Review* exerts leverage amounting to veto power over which books are published and which succeed. Writers on contemporary history are obliged to refer to the *Times Index* of news stories, the most complete of its kind, often picking up *Times* philosophy along with dates and speech texts. There are about 200 universities in the *Times* circulation area, among them Columbia, where the School of Journalism was part of the *Times* farm system and whose Pulitzer committee cannot overlook the *Times*. Associated Press and United Press

International are headquartered in New York and rely heavily on the *Times*, as do *Time, Newsweek* and other magazines. Because the United Nations is in New York, a *Times* story immediately reaches the representatives of more than 150 nations.

Television networks potentially have greater power than the *Times*, but television seldom discovers or initiates news; it magnifies news that others have discovered. Television news is uncomfortable with paradox or contradiction, especially because its personalized presentation requires that every newscaster and correspondent be entirely self-assured, whether or not he understands the subject at hand. Part of their assurance is the *Times*.

At CBS and NBC network headquarters in New York, research files are based largely on *Times* clippings. A television crew arriving in Tehran or San Salvador typically arrives carrying a batch of *Times* data to identify the players, accepting the *Times'* judgment on which are the good guys and the bad guys. They had better accept the *Times'* judgment, because their product will be checked by editors against the *Times'* product at headquarters. The *Times* has a special relationship with CBS, conducting joint polls, and CBS correspondents overseas often work with *Times* correspondents.

When the *Times* "became the Fourth Estate" with the publication of the manipulated Pentagon Papers, other newspapers that once had superlative correspondents were dying off, among them the *Herald-Tribune, Chicago Daily News* and *Washington Star.* The *Times* syndicate wire became so pervasive that front pages of newspapers across the nation from the *Boston Globe* to the *Seattle Post-Intelligencer* began to look identical. A few newspapers with independent foreign correspondents, like the *Baltimore Sun* and *Los Angeles Times*, were off the main route of communications traffic.

Although the *Washington Post* has special leverage as the capital's dominant newspaper, it cannot rival the *Times* because it is not at the communications hub, and in any case it is on the same ideological wave length. For years the *Times* and *Post* have exchanged frontings—Page 1 leads and headlines—just before first edition time, once by telex, later by telephotos of Page 1 proofs, so each can catch up on the other's main stories and coordinate their impact. At 9 p.m., when the *Times* radio station WQXR broadcasts frontings, the leads were taken down verbatim at the *New York Daily News*, where editors were required to match *Times* Page 1 stories, if only with a paragraph or two, regardless of the night editor's judgment of the worth of the stories.[5]

When the *Herald-Tribune* died in 1966, it put up for grabs a crown jewel, the *Paris Herald-Tribune*. The *Times* had attempted a competing European edition under Sydney Gruson in Amsterdam, but it failed to dent the *Herald-Tribune's* popularity. Now the *Times* and *Washington Post* moved in, dominating the *International Herald-Tribune*, with its entrée to European political and media circles. More than ever *Times* correspondents in Europe were accorded treatment equal to the U.S. Ambassador's because they had commensurate power.

In Washington the *Times'* reputation for global expertise created a caste of *Times*-government interchangeable men who can be a disruptive influence. As the media-government adversary relationship melded with *Times* ideology, some of the interchangeable men became something like a fifth column in the bureaucracy, especially in Republican administrations. Cyrus Vance, never criticized in the *Times*, resigned from the *Times* board of directors to become Secretary of State and rejoined the board when he resigned from the Carter administration over the attempt to free American hostages in Iran.

With the media falling into lockstep behind the *Times*, it is not surprising that public figures avoid direct challenges to *Times* judgments. Only one has taken on the *Times* frontally and won, Daniel Patrick Moynihan, aided by Punch Sulzberger's aversion to Bella Abzug.

Moynihan incurred the *Times'* wrath when he was a domestic adviser to Nixon and used the expression "benign neglect" in advising Nixon that race relations could use a period of cooling off to digest the advances made in the Johnson administration. In November 1970, a *Times* editorial vetoed Moynihan's first nomination to be United Nations Ambassador, under the headline, "Wrong Man for the Job."

In his book, Moynihan observed that if he was "not qualified," neither was chief editorialist John Oakes.[6] Moynihan wrote:

> Oakes' chief characteristic was that he was almost entirely predictable. The *Times* had become, and remained, the greatest newspaper in the world. . . . But the editorial page retained a distinct New York provincialism. It was as ethnic an editorial page as that of *Il Progresso*, the *Jewish Daily Forward*, *La Prensa* or the *Irish Echo*. Its universalist, even deracinated air was its most distinctive ethnic characteristic, the mark of German Reform Judaism of that particular branch that so flourished in, and has so influenced, the City of New York.

Moynihan wrote that *Times* news columns are impeccable but not infallible, "and something of Oakes' editorial page opinions eventually seeped into the news reporting."[7]

Five years after the first *Times* veto, Moynihan did become President Ford's United Nations Ambassador over the *Times'* objections.

While Moynihan was at the UN, W. Averell Harriman circulated his opinion in Washington that Moynihan had "lost Africa" for the United States, and Moynihan blamed the *Times* for its ally's sniping. Moynihan was forced out of the UN post at Christmas 1975 by a James Reston column charging that he had "provoked the Soviets, affronted the European allies and outraged the Secretary-General of the United Nations and the new nations of the Third World." Moynihan also had been a champion of Israel at the UN, stepping on the *Times*' corn. Still, against *Times* sniping, Moynihan defeated by a hair the abrasive Bella Abzug for the Democratic nomination for Senator in 1976, then won the election handily.

Times ideology appears to derive from two nightmares, fear of a fascist takeover of Washington and fear of a Jacquerie by the underprivileged. The fascists are to be combatted and the mob placated.

Fear of fascism repeatedly has led the *Times* into error, often taking the nation with it. In the 1950s the *Times* portrayed McCarthyism as a menace rivaling Nazism or the Mongol invasion, exaggerating a minor demogogue suffering from alcoholism into the equivalent of Tamerlane. Americans were not very anti-Communist in the 1950s, but Senator Joseph McCarthy detected that they were anti-devious. Communists were pretending not to be Communists, and their deception made an inviting target. When Abbie Hoffman was on the run after his arrest for trying to sell $36,000 worth of cocaine to U.S. agents and had jumped bail, he was interviewed secretly on Public Television. "I'm a Communist," Hoffman said. "I'm sure Dr. Spock and Dave Dellinger are Communists, but there's a hangup in this country about saying you're a Communist." Abbie had a point; if Communists said they were Communists, there couldn't be McCarthyism.

In the 1960s the *Times* was sure that a Neo-Nazi revival threatened in Germany. American editors went along with the *Times* because there was nostalgia for Hitler in the 1960s, when politics had become too complex. Editors longed for the good old days when they had an absolute, 100% villain, and Hitler had fit the bill perfectly. The Neo-Nazi revival was a fraud, and the West Germans got instead the other end of the political spectrum, Willy Brandt, a German whom the *Times* approved.

In the 1970s the *Times* mobilized all of its resources to prevent Richard Nixon from taking over the government in a fascist coup and turning America into a police state. The media joined in because few in it had ever liked Nixon much, but the big police state issues—the Huston Plan, Gemstone, enemies lists, persecutions through federal agencies, massive political sabotage—were frauds. The *Times*' basic premise cannot be supported; the most precise item in J. Anthony Lucas' book was its title: *Nightmare*, a nightmare being emotional terror taking place in the mind of its dreamer.

Times editors appear to see the Third World and black Americans in the same picture frame, to be placated, patted on the head, solicited, so they won't rise up in bloody revolt against privilege. *Times* editors apparently believed Frantz Fanon, the apostle of Marxism, violence and vengeance from Martinique and the Algerian revolution, when he wrote in *The Wretched of the Earth* that the colonized (underprivileged) do not want to share the farmland; they want the farm, the farmer chopped to bits and the farmer's wife for a slave. Fanon evidently gave the *Times* a delicious fright. His hatred, possibly influenced by his early cancer, was a slander of the Third World, most of whose people want anything but revolution, just as the great majority of black Americans are hard working and want progress with tranquilty.

The *Times* became the champion of any and all revolutions, most of which were power struggles between factions, even when a disastrous outcome could be forseen. *Times* editorialists and columnists deny any distinction between authoritarian and totalitarian regimes, even in countries with cultures that demand strong leaders. All authoritarians must be deposed, to quell fascism and placate the revolution, whether they are Franco, Batista, Diem, Pahlavi, Somoza, Park Chung Hee, Marcos, King Hassan or Menachem Begin. Leaders to be preserved, allegedly representing heroism or moderation, have included Castro, Mugabe, Ho Chi Minh, the Alexander Dubček group, János Kádár, Wladyslaw Gomulka and Erich Honecker.

No one can discuss the *Times* without recognizing its ambivalent attitude toward Israel, the state the Ochs family never wanted and wished would go away. If there had to be an Israel, the *Times* would explain to it what its responsibilities were.

The *Times'* worst fears were realized in 1977 when Menachem Begin, a real, honest-to-Jehovah Jew, incorruptable and fearless besides, was elected prime minister. The *Times* set about to annul the election of the only democracy in the Middle East. But in its assault on Begin, the *Times* was drawn into precisely the quagmire it always had avoided, intramural Jewish politics in both Israel and the United States.

A medium for the *Times* assault was the Peace Now movement, launched in March 1978 by the successors to earlier pacifist groups on the left fringe. In 1978 Peace Now had a logical momentum following the October War and Sadat's visit to Jerusalem. Shortly after the movement's founding, the *Times* published on Page 1 a report that 37 prominent American Jews, including Nobel laureates, had sent a letter of support to Peace Now. The signatures had been solicited by Leonard Fein, editor of the American Jewish magazine *Moment*, and a couple of the signatories either rescinded their endorsements or denied having made them, so that the epistle is variously referred to as "the letter of the 35" or "the letter of the 36."

Chaim Herzog, then retiring as Israel's UN Ambassador, commented:

> So there were 36 people who didn't agree with the government of Israel, who went public. I can produce letters from many more than 36 equally brilliant people who support the Israeli government, and I guarantee that this would not be published on the front page of *The New York Times*. Just because the letter of the 36 panders to what certain members of the editorial board feel should be Israel's policy, that doesn't necessarily mean you've got a major division in American Jewry, or in Israel.[8]

In October 1979, the Israeli magazine *New Outlook*, the mobilizing center of earlier pacifist movements, sponsored a conference, not in Israel but in Washington, that drew together backers of Peace Now, including many of the New Left components of the Institute for Policy Studies. By the end of the conference the far left appeared to have captured Peace Now, and its influence further diminished in Israel.

Nevertheless, the *Times* and Leonard Fein did it again. Fein held a press conference in Israel to announce that 56 prominent Americans had endorsed a statement condemning Begin's government as extremist, and suggesting a major split between American Jews and Begin. The Page 1 story was unsigned.[9] Rabbi Alexander Schindler and Theodore Mann, ex-chairmen of the Conference of Presidents of Major Jewish Organizations, denounced Fein in a *Daily News* story for using their names and questioned his motives, and the *Times* gave Fein a column on the Op-Ed page to explain that his criticism was not malicious.[10]

The *Times* repeatedly has been forced to pull back from its reporting on Israel. After quoting a National Lawyers Guild investigating team, despite the guild's low credibility, on the serious charge, "The Israeli government implements a policy of torture for the annexation of the occupied areas," the *Times* was required to correct with an Op-Ed piece from one of the many Jewish teams that swarmed into Israel looking for torture and finding none. *Jewish Week*, the largest Jewish weekly in the country, was so incensed that it published a special supplement devoted to *Times* bias in Middle East news.[11]

At the Mizrachi Women's Annual Convention in New York on June 21, 1978, Israeli Deputy Consul Yosef Ben-Aharon remarked in a speech that the *Times* "has mismanaged news, failed to reflect the basic difference between Israel and the Arab world, permitted its editorial policy to determine its portrayal of news and presented its readership with a thoroughly unrealistic picture of Arab policies and motives." The *Times*, he said, "is the most dangerous enemy of Israel in the United States." One of the women got up and left, muttering audibly, "I can't stand any more of this," demonstrating her loyalty to the *Times*.

By March 1982, when the *Times'* opposition to Begin was five years old, Professor David Sikorsky of Columbia University noticed that heavy *Times* coverage of riots on the West Bank following Israel's removal of the mayor of El Bireh greatly exceeded *Times* coverage of Iran's massive counterattack against Iraq in Khuzistan. Sikorsky analyzed *Times* coverage of the two events for each day of the week of March 22 to March 27—more than 1,000 lines of report and commentary plus photographs on the West Bank clashes compared with 130 lines on the fateful Iran-Iraq war. "The awareness of the lack of balance of the major, traditionally liberal media, including paradigmatically *The New York Times*, has only slowly filtered into the resisting consciousness of their readers and viewers," Sikorsky wrote.[12] He charged that exaggerating the West Bank disturbances into a major calamity revived anti-Israel activity in Washington and in the United Nations.

As Sikorsky noted, Israel was getting a terrible press in the United States in early 1982.

By June 1982, when Israel invaded Lebanon in pursuit of the PLO, the ground had been prepared for a debacle of American journalism that dragged President Reagan's administration along in its wake. Secretary of State Alexander Haig, never a media favorite as a survivor of Watergate, was fired for declining to condemn Israel. During Israel's drive through southern Lebanon and its 80-day siege of West Beirut, media commentators widely called the military action unwarranted and excessive, exaggerated casualty figures, declared Begin devious and unworthy of support, painted the PLO guerrillas (now "fighters") as victims, misreported Middle East sentiment and recited in oracular tones the dire litany that relations between the United States and Israel were undergoing a profound change.

This time, however, the far-away events were on territory familiar to many Americans, including some with dual American-Israeli citizenship, and some of the unanimous media mistakes were spotted quickly. Television news was heavily censured, and for the first time in a decade even the *Times* was criticized, not merely by small-circulation publications and newsletters, but also by the *Wall Street Journal*, the *New York Post* and by former allies such as Norman Podhoretz in his influential *Commentary.*[13]

With television under fire, ABC organized a series of open meetings moderated by Ted Koppel, to permit the public to let off steam. Unfortunately, the series was broadcast after bedtime in the East, where it was most needed.

On the ABC audience-participation shows, most media participants took refuge in the idea that the fault lay in television's natural characteristic of focusing on a graphic display of war's horrors. Koppel himself knew better, and several times interjected in response to a charge of misleading news, "It's the context again!" Television did not or could not present the context of a protracted news event, and neither was the print media providing a context.

When Lebanon's enduring civil war reached its climax in 1975-1976, during the period of America's amnesia following its rout by the North Vietnamese, Lebanon was not considered an area where the United States had interests. The context of the war never was reported in the American media. As the Muslim-Christian modus vivendi in Lebanon broke down into divided clans of Christian Arabs, Sunni Muslims, Shi'ite Muslims, Druse feudal-socialists and Palestinian refugees, the Palestine Liberation Organization, heavily subsidized to buy Soviet automatic weapons, barrage rockets and rocket-propelled grenades, easily outgunned everyone else. PLO ascendency provided both a pretext and a cover for Syria's moving into Lebanon, where it never had established an embassy because it considered Lebanon part of greater Syria.

The first great bloodletting of Lebanon's civil war occurred in January and February 1976, when the PLO and its allies shelled and overran the Christian town of Damour, consolidating a large, contiguous bloc of PLO turf. On January 21, after the first days of the battle of Damour, Abu Musa, head of Asifa, the military branch of Fatah, said his men had killed 500 Phalange militiamen. Lebanese air force planes, the Syrian army and the PLO took part in the destruction of Damour, the dead running into thousands. The slaughter could not be blamed on a maverick faction, as is the PLO's custom; Yasser Arafat was directly responsible for Asifa, the spearhead of the attack.

As Damour fell in February 1976, fighting had spread in Beirut, where the Hilton, Phoenicia and Saint Georges hotels were blown away, attracting more attention in the United States than Damour.

By June 1976 Syria, now openly in Lebanon and no longer under the cover of Palestinian organizations, worried that the heavily armed PLO would take over the country. The Lebanese army had disintegrated, and Syrian troops advancing into Lebanon clashed with the PLO at roadblocks and in turf disputes. On June 16, U.S. Ambassador Frances E. Meloy, Jr., his economic adviser Robert O. Waring and their driver, Zoheir Moghrabi, were shot to death and left on a garbage dump. President Ford ordered the evacuation of Americans.

In mid-June the Christian Phalange attacked Tal Zaatar, a key PLO stronghold, and Syrian troops either stood back or assisted in the siege. Tal Zaatar fell in August, with thousands dead. Now the American media paid some attention. The PLO won sympathy for Tal Zaatar, while the Christians had received none for Damour.

In October 1976 an Arab summit meeting in Riyadh announced a ceasefire to be policed by an Arab peacekeeping force—which turned out to be the Syrian army already in place—and ordered the separation and relocation of factions, a hint of partition. Throughout the period only one voice managed to be heard in the United Nations and the American media defending Lebanon's right to independence, that of Chaim Herzog, Israel's UN Ambassador.

That November, after Syrian troops entered Beirut, the PLO foreign minister-designate Farouk Khaddoumi visited the United Nations. With Arnaud de Borchgrave, then of *Newsweek*, I met Khaddoumi at a Libyan cocktail party. De Borchgrave remarked that the PLO had fallen on hard times; what would it do next?

Khaddoumi was interested in De Borchgrave as a friend of Anwar Sadat, and he spoke candidly. "We are going south," he said, grinning. In Fatahland, southern Lebanon, he said, "We will use our weapons as catalysts," that is, to provoke a war between Israel and the inconstant Syrians. The next 14 months saw a PLO arms build-up in southern Lebanon and increasing raids and rocket attacks on Israel, all aimed at civilian targets.

The PLO in southern Lebanon was a strategic asset to Syria, provided it did not provoke an Israeli invasion. Syria by then occupied part of the Bekaa Valley, enabling it to outflank the barriers of the Golan Heights and Mount Hermon. The Golan Heights escarpment is difficult to descend with heavy military equipment even if Syria could recapture the Heights, but there are no serious physical barriers between the Bekaa Valley and Haifa. The moves so far had left Syrian troops overseeing Lebanon, "down from the Golan," and with a PLO buffer.

In March 1978 a dozen PLO raiders landed on Israel's northern coast, seized a busload of picnickers and killed 37, wounding scores more before Israeli troops caught up and wiped them out. Three days later Israel drove into southern Lebanon for the first time on March 15, after 30 years of respecting Lebanon's neutrality.

At the United Nations, U.S. Ambassador Andrew Young was known as a single-issue diplomat, devoting most of his time to problems of southern Africa. He was circumspect in allowing a southern Africa issue to reach the Security Council only after foolproof preparation. But in the case of Israel's thrust into Lebanon, announced as limited and temporary, Young was instantly before the Security Council proposing a UN peacekeeping force. The Security Council approved the ill-fated force, Unifil, on March 19, with a vote of 12 to 0.

Unifil did not attempt to expel the PLO from southern Lebanon; rather, it supplied the PLO with food and water, unannounced. When I reported the clandestine supply in the *New York Daily News*, a UN spokesman blandly said it was temporary pending the PLO's organization for departure. Unifil later became a screen protecting the PLO from Israel and from Christian Lebanese Major Saad Haddad, Israel's borderland ally.

Although Israel captured large stores of weapons in southern Lebanon in 1978 and established that Tyre was a major PLO weapons port and depot, its incursion was judged capricious, and with a drumbeat of anti-Israel resolutions in the UN General Assembly, the atmosphere was prepared to allow President Carter to sell F-15 jets to Saudi Arabia and Egypt. The *Times* editorially advised Carter to conclude the sale, and in Haiti where I was vacationing, that settled the issue. The Port au Prince newspaper headlined, "New York Times Okays Sale of F-15s to Saudis."

In May 1978 I reported a sharp debate between Begin and George Ball at a dinner of the Economic Club at the Hilton Hotel in New York, which I thought the outspoken Begin won. Ball's last words, choked out in some emotion (probably anger) were, "Nevertheless, the United States should sell F-15s to Saudi Arabia, and I will so testify tomorrow before the Senate Foreign Relations Committee." The *Times* had a reporter present but published nothing on the dramatic clash until its repercussions continued the following day.

Lebanon's civil war did not end with the Riyadh summit of October 1976, but rather moved, with flare-ups of fighting, in the direction of partitioning Lebanon into about nine PLO, Christian and Muslim ministates, supervised by Syria. PLO weapons poured into Beirut and into southern Lebanon through Tyre and Sidon. Intramural assassinations and bombings killed leaders of several factions, including the Druse Kamal Jumblat and Zuhair Mohsen, Syrian head of Saiqa and a rival for Arafat's leadership of the PLO.

In April 1981 the Christian city of Zahle came under siege again, this time by Syrian troops, and once again no Western television cameras were present for close-ups. Zahle's defenders surrendered their weapons in July after three months of shelling and bombing by Syrian jets, holding out longer than the PLO would hold out in West Beirut under American restraints of Israel in 1982.

Syria needed Zahle to consolidate its hold on the Bekaa Valley. During the siege, Israeli jets shot down two Syrian helicopters that were rocketing Zahle, and Syria answered with SAM missiles, the first seen in the Bekaa Valley.

Israel was not going to repeat the experience of 1973, when Egyptian SAMs decimated the Israeli air force in a few days, and Begin announced that Israel would destroy the SAMs in the Bekaa. In apparent preparation for a land drive, Israel bombed PLO positions in southern Lebanon. At the same time, Israel learned that Iraq's nuclear reactor was nearing completion.

When Israeli jets bombed Iraq's French-built nuclear reactor and uranium-separation centrifuge near Baghdad on June 7, much of the media was bemused, not sure what to think. Nobody wanted nuclear arms in Iraq's hands. Iraq had taken advantage of Iran's revolutionary convulsions to invade Iran's oil fields.

The *Times*, however, knew what to think. It brought out its banner headline type, condemned Israel in a series of editorials, and the outrage of columnists Reston, Anthony Lewis and Flora Lewis exceeded Iraq's. Flora Lewis called Begin an unattractive and bigotted terrorist, and advised Washington to work against his re-election.

Israel now was certain to move against the SAM missiles in the Bekaa Valley, and President Reagan dispatched Ambassador Philip Habib to the Middle East to demand a ceasefire in Lebanon. Israeli jets pinpoint-bombed PLO headquarters in Beirut, Israel's first air strike at the city.

The effect of Habib's first mission to Lebanon was to leave the SAM missiles in place and to protect the PLO in southern Lebanon. From Israel's point of view, his mission was another disaster comparable to Andrew Young's intervention three years earlier.

Early in 1982 the *Times* was reporting, repeatedly and accurately, that Israel was preparing an invasion of southern Lebanon. On February 26 Israel's Ambassador to Washington, Moshe Arens, warned that the large-scale PLO build-up of arms might provoke an invasion. American press and television commentators suggested, suspiciously, that Israel was looking for an excuse to renege on its scheduled pullout from the Sinai, a speculation that was unfounded and proved erroneous.

Between March 9 and April 29, Anthony Lewis published seven columns in the *Times* attacking Begin, praising peace-lovers in the area—including PLO moderate Dr. Issam Sartawi, who subsequently was murdered by a PLO gunman in Portugal—attacking American Jews who supported Begin and assailing Israel's suppression of West Bank demonstrators.

On April 3, Israeli diplomat Yacov Barsimov was murdered in Paris, where anti-Jewish bombings were frequent. On April 22, Israel's air force attacked PLO bases in southern Lebanon, and three days later Israel withdrew the last of its soldiers from the Sinai, razing Israeli settlements there to keep the settlers from returning.

On June 3, Israel's Ambassador to London, Shlomo Argov, was shot and critically wounded, and the next day Israeli jets pounded PLO positions in southern Lebanon again.

President Reagan heard of the Israeli jet raid in Versailles, where he was attending his first Western summit. Aware that 30,000 Israeli troops were poised on the border, Reagan conferred with Haig, called in Philip Habib and sent Begin another well-publicized warning not to invade southern Lebanon.

The next day Israel launched its long-delayed full-scale invasion, driving past 7,000 Unifil troops to Tyre, Sidon and the Crusader-built Beaufort Castle, the PLO's high-ground fortress. The *Times* deplored Israel's Operation Peace in Galilee both in an editorial, "Ever Greater Israel," and in an Anthony Lewis column on June 7, as Reagan sent Habib on his second mission to demand a ceasefire in Lebanon.

Haig advised against U.S. intervention, and at first Reagan did not intervene strongly, only disassociating the United States from Israel's invasion. The *Times* drew attention to the lack of American condemnation of Israel in a headline on June 8.

On June 10, with Reagan still in Europe, Arab ambassadors met with Vice President George Bush, expressing anger at U.S. silence, and Reagan sent another "firm call" to Begin to stop fighting and get out of Lebanon. The *Times* published on June 11 an Op-Ed page guest column, "Begin's Zionism Grinds On," by PLO member Professor Edward Said, a frequent contributor.

Habib achieved another ceasefire on June 12 as Israel's armor in hot pursuit cut off West Beirut, trapping the PLO leadership there between Israelis and the Christian Phalange. The next day King Khaled of Saudi Arabia died, succeeded immediately by Prince Fahd.

A week after the invasion began, during the ceasefire pause, with Begin scheduled to speak at the United Nations and then visit Washington, the world media began publishing casualty figures attributed to the highly credible International Red Cross. The reports said that in southern Lebanon 10,000 civilians had died and 600,000 persons made homeless. The figures, it turned out, came from the head of the PLO's Red Crescent, Arafat's brother.

As Begin left for the United States on June 16, unidentified Reagan administration officials suggested that the President would not meet with him if Israeli troops seized West Beirut. Israelis already had been welcomed into Christian East Beirut. State Department spokesman Dean Fischer, choosing his words carefully, told reporters that the United States had been assured that Israel did not intend to occupy Beirut. The *Times* editorial that day was headlined, "A Place for Palestinians."

Two thirds of the world's delegates boycotted Begin's address before the United Nations disarmament conference as the *Times* reported that Reagan would see Begin after all, since Israel had given assurances that its troops would not seize Beirut. No source was given for the report of Israeli assurance, and Israel denied one had been given. In Beirut, the PLO was giving conflicting signals: it would leave Beirut; no, it wouldn't but would make it the Stalingrad of the Arabs. National Security adviser William P. Clark, who had amused the Washington press corps by his failure to know the name of the prime minister of Zimbabwe (the widely publicized Robert Mugabe), but then had taken a beginner's course in foreign affairs as Under Secretary to Haig, objected to Haig's meeting with Begin at the UN in New York. The Washington press corps now appeared to find some merit in Clark.

Reagan received Begin as the *Times* reported on June 20 estimates by "Lebanese authorities" that nearly 10,000 persons had been killed and 600,000 made homeless. Reston, despite 40 years experience of murky Middle East casualty figures, was more precise in his column that day: "9,583 dead, 16,000 wounded and still counting." The *Times* that day published a full-page advertisement that aroused nostalgia for the halcyon days of the Vietnam war:

DEATH AND DEVASTATION
IN LEBANON
40,000 people killed and wounded
700,000 people homeless.

The ad of the Ad Hoc Committee in Defense of the Palestinian and Lebanese People was signed by more than 200 familiar peace-seekers from the Vietnam era, among them former Senator James Abourezk, Eqbal Ahmad, Richard Barnet, Daniel and Philip Berrigan, Julian Bond,

Ramsey Clark, Noam Chomsky, Barry Commoner, Dave Dellinger, Nat Hentoff, the Reverend Jesse L. Jackson, William Kunstler, Representative Pete McCloskey, Pete Seeger, I. F. Stone, William Styron, Studs Terkel, Peter Weiss and two newcomers, Professor Edward Said and Professor Mansour Farhang, who for a time had joined the government of Ayatollah Ruhollah Khomeini and defended the seizure of American hostages in Iran.

The ad of the activists charged, falsely, as it turned out, that "virtually every population concentration of Palestinians and Lebanese east and south of Beirut has been subjected to terror bombing, with consequent death and dreadful injury . . . indescriminate use of fircpower . . . wanton destruction . . . ."

Some of the ad's sponsors signed another ad in the *Times* on July 25, which compared Beirut with Dresden, Warsaw and Hiroshima, along with new signers including former Mexican President Luis Echeverria Alverez, Sean McBride, the new Greek Minister of Culture Melina Mercuri, the Reverend William Sloan Coffin, Jr. and Andrew Young.

If Americans believed Lebanese politics to be labyrinthine, what were Lebanese to think of American politics and the Byzantine manner in which it now entered the conflict?

All of the signers of the ads in the *Times* were natural and fervent adversaries of Reagan, who now appeared to adopt their recommendations.

Haig had been advising Reagan that Israel's purging of the PLO from Lebanon would remove a main roadblock to peace. Haig also objected to a series of actions that had undercut him, including Reagan's communications with Habib that involved Clark but bypassed him. Haig also suspected that Clark and Bush—who had attended the funeral of King Khaled in Saudi Arabia—had opened a back channel with the Saudis that was reassuring the PLO and stiffening their resistence in Beirut, prolonging bloodshed. Haig told Reagan on June 24 that he was resigning, and Reagan accepted his written resignation the next day. Most of the media reported that the major disagreement was over European cooperation in the Soviet gas pipeline project, apparently reluctant to give Israel any implied backing from Haig.

On June 26, while Haig's resignation was the sensation of Washington, Israeli planes dropped leaflets over West Beirut warning civilians to flee an impending attack. Someone in authority told Reagan's spokesman Larry Speakes to inform the media that Begin had deceived Reagan in their talks, and had promised not to take Beirut. In Jerusalem, Israeli officials again denied any such pledge.

The charge of deceit stunned Jerusalem, and Israel announced another ceasefire immediately. Twice Reagan had held back Israeli forces. Arafat's reply was to warn again that American interests in the Middle East were doomed by American collusion with Israel.

Reagan permitted four days to pass—during which the allegation of Begin's deception was repeated in the American media to poisonous effect—before saying, in answer to a question at his news conference on June 30, that Begin had given him no such pledge, but only had said that Israel did not want to assault West Beirut. Reagan stressed that Israel had been given no green light to invade.

Begin had been called many things, but he had not been called deceptive. Rather, the standard epithet was intransigent: immovable from a stated position, or the opposite of devious. Begin became prime minister after almost 30 years in opposition because, whatever liabilities he had, he possessed credibility, so the charge of deceit was particularly pernicious.

Despite his increasing isolation, Begin pressed on, charging that the PLO was stalling and did not intend to leave Beirut. Israel finally resorted to heavy bombing of PLO and Syrian guns in West Beirut, and to shutting off food, water and electricity to force civilians to move across town and out of the line of fire. The media painted the intermittant and limited siege as ruthless, something of an exaggeration to survivors of real sieges in Leningrad, Warsaw or Budapest. Reagan wrote Begin twice in early August demanding that "the bloodshed must be stopped" and warning that sanctions were being weighed.

American television nightly showed West Beirut apartment buildings blazing under Israeli bombs or crumbling under shells, seldom noting that the target buildings were hollow shells from seven years of civil war. Reagan was so disturbed by a photograph front-paged in the *Washington Post* of a bandaged little girl, who, according to the UPI caption, had lost both arms to Israeli munitions, that he protested to Foreign Minister Yitzhak Shamir. UPI retracted the caption after Israeli investigators found the little girl. She had been hit in East Beirut, normally the target of PLO rockets and shells, and her broken arm had been exaggerated to the loss of both arms. Reed Irvine of Accuracy in Media detailed that other photographers present with the UPI man had not heard mention of two arms being lost.

On July 11, the *Times* published another misleading advertisement, as did the *Washington Post, Chicago Tribune, Atlanta Constitution* and *Dallas Times-Herald*. The ad of Concerned Americans for Peace implied endorsement by the American Red Cross, CARE and other relief organizations. The *Christian Science Monitor* declined the ad when the agencies said that use of their names had not been authorized. This time the *Times* investigative reporters failed; they could not track down the persons who placed the ad. Reed Irvine noted that when he placed ads in the *Times*, he was required to document virtually every statement, concluding that the *Times'* senior officials liked the ads the newspaper printed.

The *Times* Op-Ed page twice published contributions from George Ball, who had made many contributions to U.S. foreign policy, each time, as luck would have it, leaving the situation worsened. Ball now offered his unfailing touch in an article headlined, "Recast Ties to Israel."[14] He urged the Reagan administration to talk with the PLO, charged Begin with expansionist policies and with planning a system for the West Bank "that remarkably resembles apartheid," and advised Washington to stop permitting Israel to shape American foreign policy. If the Israelis would not get on with negotiations that contemplated self-determination for the Palestinians, the United States should terminate its relationship of indulgent Big Brother, Ball wrote.

A month later Ball was on the Op-Ed page again, headlined, "Divert Aid for Israel to Rebuild Lebanon."[15] Ball put the annual "U.S. subsidy" to Israel at "$2.7 billion—$750 per head for Israel's 3.5 million people. It is as if every American family of five gave Israel $70 a year." Angry readers disputed Ball's figures, noting that Israel repaid loans, and Norman Podhoretz reluctantly examined whether Ball could be called anti-Semitic. Anti-ally would be easier to document.

In early September, as the PLO left Beirut spurred by Israeli munitions, new Secretary of State George Shultz's new approach to the Middle East surfaced. The Reagan administration, having done all it could to prevent Israel from getting the PLO out of Beirut, would now take over, accept the opportunity created by Israeli soldiers who had died and Israeli political leaders who had taken all the risks, to exploit the new opportunity for peace.

Meanwhile, as the American media stressed demonstrations in Israel against Begin, his approval rating in Israel rose to 62%, a figure American Presidents can only dream of.

By September scores of foreigners had gone through southern Lebanon, including American congressmen and scholars. Almost unanimously they agreed with Bayard Rustin that media reports of widespread devastation were false, and that virtually all of the Lebanese they had talked with freely, whether Christian or Muslim, had damned the PLO. When the visitors met with Western reporters in East Beirut, they found their accounts greeted with hostility. The reporters would hear nothing favorable about Israeli conduct.

Through the months of June to September, and prepared by the media's turning against Israel earlier, the Reagan administration was influenced by coverage of the war that was so one-sided that Reed Irvine headlined a report about it, "Lies About Lebanon."[16]

Yasser Arafat, who had directed the fighting against King Hussein in 1970 and tried to organize the secession of north Jordan, whose Black September group had killed Israeli athletes in Munich in 1972 under the direction of his aides Abu Hassan and Abu Daoud, and whose Asifa had wiped out Damour to start the chain of reprisal slaughters, meanwhile was greeted as a hero by Greek Premier Andreas Papandreou, by the leaders of the Arab summit at Fez, Morocco—where he and King Fahd hugged and raised arms together in Winston Churchill's victory salute—and by Pope John Paul II in the Vatican.

The ambiguous outcome of Arafat's military defeat no doubt encouraged the bombers who killed Lebanon's new president, Bashir Gemayel, along with two dozen of his aides. The bombers of Gemayel also could draw comfort from American media descriptions of Gemayel as a fascist, a reminder often interjected into the reports of ABC's Peter Jennings. With Gemayel's death, Lebanon was again leaderless, and Israel moved quickly into West Beirut to silence the leftist Muslim militias and stay-behind PLO men who had inherited, contrary to the ceasefire agreement, heavy PLO weapons that were supposed to have gone to the Lebanese army. The Reagan administration again charged Israel with deception and with breaking the ceasefire, as though blowing up Gemayel and two dozen aides had been adherence to the ceasefire.

By mid-September the Reagan administration and the media were almost as much on the defensive as Begin was. The erosion of American public support for Israel was turning around.

The massacre of Palestinians in the Shatila and Sabra camps in West Beirut by Christian militiamen was the kind of outrage that might have provided a smoke screen for the media's earlier errors, if they hadn't overdone it by attempting to make Israel directly responsible.

In the first days of the invasion, the *Times*, the main background source for the rest of the media, had let an error slip into a dispatch from correspondent John Kifner. Kifner, or one of his editors, wrote that Israeli troops were approaching the major remaining PLO base, Damour. The story said that Damour, originally mostly Christian, had been sacked in the 1975-1976 civil war "in retaliation for the right wing siege of the Palestinian camp at Tal Zaatar and has been since occupied by guerrillas and refugees."[17] There had been, in fact, an earlier inconclusive siege of Tal Zaatar, but the story left an erroneous impression that the slaughters started at Tal Zaatar. The error was fixed in the

Times library, and by September 20 the sequence of the Damour-Tal Zaatar massacres was reversed in a dispatch by Thomas L. Friedman, now an egregious error that would be repeated by others. Friedman's report said that suspects of the massacre at Shatila included the Damour Brigade, "made up of many of the sons of Christian families massacred by the Palestinians in Damour in February 1976 in retaliation for the Christian massacre of Palestinian civilians at the Tal Zaatar refugee camp." In fact, the PLO started the bloodbath sequence at Damour; the retaliation was at Tal Zaatar five months later. Not to be outdone, NBC correspondent Rick Davis put together television film of previous atrocities, mostly by the Phalange—"which many considered fascist"—stressing film from Tal Zaatar. Damour was not mentioned.[18] No one mentioned that Shatila had been a training school for international terrorists.

For a week or so the media had a replay of My Lai, which had become a key propaganda justification to abandon Indochina, before sobriety began to return. Unlike My Lai, the assassins at Shatila were not "ours." Still, for a time, Israel's defenders in the United States were silenced by Shatila and Sabra.

When the American media adopted the *Times'* judgement on the Vietnam war in the early 1970s and agreed that United States ties with Indochina had to be severed, there was a corresponding gain in influence by the Institute for Policy Studies.

The alliance between the *Times* and IPS, bonded at about the time of the Pentagon Papers and the *Times'* hiring Seymour Hersh from Dispatch News Service, came to flower during the Carter administration. Associates of IPS entered the government again, including Patricia Derian, wife of State Department spokesman Hodding Carter III, whose Human Rights division in the State Department had input into Cyrus Vance's policies. Other administration figures close to IPS included chief disarmament negotiator Warnke, domestic policy adviser Stuart Eizenstat, Kissinger's one-time wiretapped aide Anthony Lake and Treasury official Gene Godley.

The *Times* promoted IPS even more than did the *Washington Post*, where editor Bradlee had a soft spot toward the think tank since the tentative contacts over the Pentagon Papers. His foreign editor, Karen de Young, who spoke at IPS seminars, had reported on Nicaragua's Sandinista revolutionaries in such glowing terms that Reed Irvine's Accuracy in Media suggested that she be named successor to Herbert Matthews.

The *Times* Op-Ed page is an ideal platform for Eastern think tanks that seek to reach the audience the *Times* serves, but IPS has been represented on the Op-Ed page more than all the others combined, becoming "virtually a *Times* institutional columnist."[19] Rael Jean Isaac, author of *Israel Divided*,[20] noted that during three months between March 1 and June 1, 1979, the *Times* Op-Ed page published an article by Peter Weiss on March 2, five articles by Eqbal Ahmad on March 28, April 15 and 25, May 13 and 23; an article by Fred Halliday on May 18, an article co-authored by Marcus Raskin on June 1, and the *Times Magazine* featured Richard Barnet on April 1. She had been drawn to study IPS because it was "a veritable hive of anti-Israeli activists."

When IPS challenged her first report in *Midstream* on the think tank, she checked the *Times* again and found columns by IPS associates on the Op-Ed page on October 1, 2, 15, 26, 28 and November 13, 1979. On the *Times* Op-Ed page, IPS competition almost wiped out the liberal Ford Foundation, the liberal Brookings Institution and the leftist Carnegie Endowment for World Peace, sometimes unkindly referred to as Alger Hiss' old outfit.

For years the Washington press corps, including wire services, used IPS sources without informing the public of the institute's leftist ideology, except for an article in *Esquire* in 1971 and two articles in *Barron's* in 1978. Finally in 1981, prodded by Isaac's articles, the *Times* published a fairly comprehensive piece, "The Think Tank of the Left," by Joshua Muravchik.[21]

IPS appearances on the *Times* Op-Ed page became less frequent after Isaac published a series of articles on IPS in *Midstream, Jewish Week* and the newsletter of the National Committee on American Foreign Policy. She charged that IPS had "consistently advocated policies that accord with the Soviet line, whether the issue is disarmament (for the West), abolition of nuclear power (for the West), support of Soviet-linked revolutionary groups, apologetics for Soviet expansion, etc." She cited Brian Crozier, then director of the London Institute for the Study of Conflicts, as noting that IPS "is the perfect intellectual front for Soviet activities which would be resisted if they were to originate openly from the KGB."

The most thorough outline of IPS and its spinoffs appeared in *Midstream* of June/July 1980, in an article by Isaac headlined, "Empire on the Left."[22] It caused a ruckus and drew a response from IPS director Borosage and board chairman Weiss that made the follow-up *Midstream* edition of February 1981 a revealing debate on IPS. In attempting to demolish Isaac as a McCarthyite red-baiter, Borosage and Weiss inadvertently demonstrated the key objection to IPS, its devious equivocation. The spinoffs were completely independent of IPS, its leaders explained, and the *Times, Harper's* and prestigious professors were cited to prove that IPS scholars were respectable; Raskin "once served" on the board of *CounterSpy's* funders; nobody supported the PLO; Weiss himself was a "life-long Zionist;" Tariq Ali (barred from entering the United States) was "probably the leading figure in Britain's student protest meetings of the Sixties;" Eqbal Ahmad was "a respected Pakistani scholar with a broad international following;" Barnet was "one of the country's leading experts on U.S.-Soviet relations."

Twice during the Johnson and Nixon administrations the Internal Revenue Service audited IPS—in 1967 and 1970—after Senator Strom Thurmond declared, "By giving a tax exemption to an organization like the Institute for Policy Studies, our government is allowing tax exemption to support revolution." Although the 1970 audit stretched into 1971, IPS was ruled a research and educational organization, and the tax exemptions of its far-flung empire were original targets of the Nixon White House's investigations.

William F. Buckley wrote in 1981, comparing IPS with the anti-Semitic Liberty Lobby:

> IPS people tend to be more literate, more erudite. They're not as literate or erudite as Lenin or Trotsky. But they are as despicable, notwithstanding which dozens upon dozens of Washington bureaucrats and congressional aides associate in various ways with IPS, and such Senators as Mark Hatfield and journals as the *New Republic* send valentines to the IPS.

Buckley's attack was a rare exception to the rule of immunity that IPS enjoyed for more than a decade. In the *Times, Washington Post* and perhaps in the Carter Justice Department, the exemption of IPS to criticism extended to covering up an IPS connection to the Cuban Directorate General of Intelligence (DGI) through Orlando Letelier, head of the IPS-allied Transnational Institute and former foreign minister of Salvador Allende's Marxist government in Chile.

In September 1976 a bomb exploded in Letelier's car on a Washington street while Letelier was driving with IPS Fellow Michael Moffitt and his wife, Ronni Karpfen Moffitt, 21, also an IPS employee. Letelier and Ronni Moffitt were killed, and Michael Moffitt injured, an important story that filled columns in the *Times* and *Washington Post*. For several years Reed Irvine of Accuracy in Media attempted to get the *Times* and *Post* to publish evidence found in Letelier's briefcase that he was a Cuban agent receiving $1,000 a month via Beatriz (Tati) Allende, daughter of Allende, who was married to Louis Ferdinand Ona, a ranking Cuban intelligence officer, and that he had been in contact with numerous Soviet and Cuban officials as well as key congressional aides.[23]

With its contacts to the *Times, Washington Post*, Random House, Times Books and others, IPS has been able to influence American policy significantly over a broad range.

IPS associates in and out of government played a role in President Carter's pressing for a Palestinian (PLO) state when he was eight weeks in office. They also influenced Carter's initial decision to withdraw troops from South Korea, and although Carter rescinded the decision when it became apparent that it was destabilizing South Korea, his change of heart did not occur early enough to deter the assassination of President Park Chung Hee in May 1980. Too Chin Paik, the long-time speaker of South Korea's Assembly, told me in August 1979 that the *Times'* hostility to Park and its championing of Kim Dae Jung, charged at the time with orchestrating fanatic and fatalistic youth demonstrations, contributed materially to "causing chaos" in South Korea. For a time, the *Times* correspondent, Henry Scott-Stokes, was barred from South Korea.

IPS influence on the media continued during the Reagan administration, dramatically in the IPS-orchestrated defeat of Ernest Lefever when he was denied Senate confirmation to succeed Patricia Derian at the State Department. Big media went along as various IPS spinoffs painted Lefever, their old foe, as an enemy of human rights and a lackey of international corporations with a barrage of false charges. Lefever's Ethics and Public Policy Center had reprinted in booklet form Rael Jean Issac's exposé of IPS.

Lefever also had written, as a Brookings Institution scholar, a two-year study that refuted the orchestrated Communist campaign to defame Dan Mitrione, the United States police adviser who was kidnapped and murdered by Uruguay's Tupamaros. The *Times*, in a column on its Op-Ed page by A. J. Langguth, had described Mitrione as a torture instructor to the Uruguayan police and strongly implied he was a CIA agent.[24] Lefever insisted that Mitrione "never had anything to do with the CIA," and "never taught or advocated methods of torture." The *Times* celebrated Lefever's defeat in the Senate with an Op-Ed column by IPS's Borosage and William Goodfellow of the Center for International Policy headlined, "Rights 1, Lefever 0."[25] The same Op-Ed page featured two questionable articles on the alleged torture in Argentina of Jacobo Timerman, one by Timerman himself and one by Anthony Lewis.

Ten years after the *Times'* publication of the Pentagon Papers, almost to the day, pollster Louis Harris reported: "Peoples' trust in the accuracy and truth of the news they get from television and the newspapers declined during the last decade. They are most wary about news eminating from Washington, D.C. Only 21% say they 'very much' trust TV news from the nation's capital, and an even lower 13% 'very much' trust such news in their newspapers."[26]

The collapse of public trust in the media during the period of the *Times'* ascendency was no secret to media executives. In 1973 the National News Council was established "To serve the public interest in preserving freedom of communication and advancing accurate and fair reporting of the news." It has failed dismally. Most of the public complaints the council investigated were trivial and were "found unwarranted." The council is wary of reaching judgment on serious cases of news manipulation, including the 1973 case that helped cause its creation, the Nixon administration's charges of bias. The council complained that it could not get from the White House specific instances to support Nixon's charge of "outrageous, vicious, distorted" reporting—and of course it could not, especially while Watergate fever was running. Why should a President, just forced from office, invite a new deluge of calumny by fighting a lost battle? So the council piously ruled, "We believe it is seriously detrimental to the public interest for the President to leave his harsh criticism of the television networks unsupported by specific details that could then be evaluated by an impartial body."[27] The cop-out continued, as the Harris Poll indicated seven years later.

Let me repeat: it is not the *Times'* fault that the rest of the media abdicated leadership to it. The *Times* was more enterprising, spent more, thought more—if not well—about foreign affairs, and it pushed its philosophy as anyone has a right to do. It had the country's best foreign correspondent (Henry Kamm), the most entertaining columnist (Russell Baker), the best art critic (Hilton Kramer) and the only large-format Sunday magazine. If the rest of the media accepted the accompanying distortions and disinformation, the *Times* can't be wholly blamed. As more newspapers die and information is increasingly entrusted to television, the only hope is that some independent-minded reporters will appear to keep the media from bringing on the calamities the *Times* fears or favors.

Most news editors throughout the country have no experience outside the United States, and there was nothing much an editor could do in 1978 when the *Times* and the wire services agreed that the possible savior of Iran was something called the National Front, led by the elderly Karim Sanjaby. An editor could, however, get sore after being swindled in this fashion a few times.

Similarly, when the *Times* editorialized that to sell F-5 fighter jets to King Hassan II would be "The Wrong Coin for Morocco," because the jets would be used against the Polisario Front and possibly provoke conflict between Morocco and Algeria, an editor might pause to give the matter a moment's thought. One does not need to know a lot about Morocco to notice that the total population of the Western Sahara in 1960 was less than 24,000 souls, mostly Berbers, like most Moroccans. That few persons cannot constitute a new nation, and any editor or State Department official could be sure there was something fishy about Polisario. The Carter administration did refuse aid to Hassan, and the impoverished Polisario then turned up with T-54 tanks, SAM-7 missiles, lots of Kalashnikovs and RGP-7s along with British Land Rovers, once the Carter administration's signal had given the Libyans and the Soviets a go-ahead.

An editor might exercise his common sense when the *Times* syndicate wire delivers the information that the Hungarians have grown to love János Kádár after 25 years of his rule, or that Cuba "has become a showcase among Communist and third world countries for its achievements in providing social services to its 10 million citizens."[28] While cultural differences sometimes are baffling, some human basics remain constant, and an editor upon hearing that "the Palestinians" all want to live under Yasser Arafat, might ask himself if he would like to live under Arafat and his crowd.

When the American public was misled in 1982 by an almost unanimous media insistence that a majority of El Salvadorans sympathized with the guerrillas, los Muchachos, only to be startled by a 60% right-of-center vote in elections monitored by respectable observers, the media had received much of its erroneous information from the *Times, Washington Post* and IPS-linked organizations and individuals.[29]

The El Salvador election embarrassment caused some soul searching in the media, but television newscasters quickly shifted attention to an American ground swell demanding a nuclear weapons freeze, a grassroots movement that was as genuine and spontaneous as Astroturf. It came right after a Soviet call for a freeze in deployment of nuclear weapons in Europe, where the Soviets had plenty, and guidelines for the American movement had been laid out years earlier by organizations as varied as the left-alligned churches, the Foundation for National Progress, the Center for National Security Study and the American Friends Service Committee.

The United States is traditionally an isolationist country, except for its brief heyday as world leader between 1945 and 1960 and its ad hoc interventions in the Caribbean and Central America. Relatively few Americans follow foreign affairs closely or worry much about foreign policy until a crisis arrives, and then they sometimes believe a solution can be found by referendum. The country possesses some foreign policy brains in the State Department and the CIA, but both agencies have an institutional bias toward the liberal Eastern establishment from which they came and regard conservatives as aliens.

The media, whose editors gradually adopted the *Times*-IPS view of the Vietnam war and then opted out of foreign affairs entirely, supplies the reverse of a corrective: it shoves the country further along the *Times*-IPS track. Some bankers, oil company employees and individuals in universities are well-informed on foreign affairs, but often on a single country or region, and they have no organization or media platform.

Foreign policy is complex, affects everything in domestic politics, and its problems usually can be only ameliorated, not solved in one fell swoop as the media would have it. The United States cannot have a foreign policy like that of The Netherlands or Denmark because it can't deny its power or its responsibilities.

The first duty of foreign policy is to preserve the nation's security, which can be done only with a sensible view of how the world works. The Atlantic and Pacific Oceans have allowed Americans a loose, pluralistic democracy which cannot be imposed on nations of different cultures that do not have Atlantic and Pacific Oceans protecting them. The United States can't remain curled up in an isolationist cocoon behind its oceans, nor can it be recklessly interventionist or rule the world.

The United States cannot survive without friendly nations, and it must accept that some regimes have no desire to be friendly in the forseeable future. It must make a distinction between friends and enemies, realize that there are qualitative differences in friendliness and enmity. It must above all stop the practice of double-crossing or abandoning friends at a moment of trouble when the United States is needed.

Since 1956, in the face of the world revolution which would have abated if we had stopped encouraging it, Americans have behaved like Siberians fleeing in a sled, tossing to the wolves nation after nation, hoping to keep the pack from our borders. We have used as an alibi the charge, in part generated by our own left, that the United States is domineering. Periods of history when Americans have been domineering have been brief and often traumatic, and for the most part the world does not perceive the United States that way; rather, the world holds against us our irresolution. It is no accident that almost every speech by a Soviet leader uses the word "resolute" to describe his nation, especially when contrasting his system with that of the United States.

Soviet foreign policy has been resolute, although with declining energy as the Politburo aged. The Soviets consistently defend their empire employing the Leninist political science of getting and keeping power, using any means, and they consistently conduct a Marxist offensive of destabilization in the rest of the world.

A basic interest of the United States must be stability in the non-Communist world, not encouragement of revolution, and there are few nations that would profit from a revolution. To that extent, American foreign policy must be counter-revolutionary.

We have come full circle, back to the themes of John Foster Dulles before he went off the track at Suez. Some day the nations of central and eastern Europe will be sovereign again, their talents unleashed, and one way or another Germany will be reunited. Someday Arabs may realize that they have squandered their wealth and their futures for an obsession, and Africa will pass from its stage of anti-colonialism to something else. The United States has the duty of influencing the outcomes by supporting those who choose to be friends. The media has the duty to recognize disinformation.

NOTES

1. Leonard Mosley, *Dulles, a Biography of Eleanor, Allen and John Foster Dulles and Their Family Network* (New York: Dial Press/James Wade, 1978), 386.

2. Townsend Hoopes, *The Devil and John Foster Dulles* (Boston: Little, Brown and Company, 1973) 340.

3. Moshe Dayan, *Moshe Dayan: Story of My Life.* (New York: William Morrow and Company, 1976), 183.

4. Anthony Eden, *Full Circle, the Memoirs of Anthony Eden* (Boston: Houghton Mifflin Company, 1960), 488.

5. Dayan, *Story of My Life,* 216.

6. Ibid., 218.

7. Ibid., 229.

8. General Reinhard Gehlen, *The Service* (New York: World, 1972), 229.

9. Radio Budapest, 30 June 1956, midnight. From *Rundfunk-Dokumente,* privately published by Jozef Gert Farkas, Munich, February 1957.

10. Ed Clark and his wife Catherine, then an NBC stringer, smuggled out of Yugoslavia Milovan Djilas' manuscript of *The New Class.*

11. See note nine above.

12. Herman Finer, *Dulles Over Suez* (Chicago: Quadrangle, 1964), 334.

13. Ibid., 319.

14. Mosley, *Dulles,* 417.

15. Ibid., 415-416.

16. Interview with Major General George Keegan, Jr., (ret), May 1978.

17. Daniel Ellsberg, *Papers on the War* (New York: Simon and Schuster, 1972), 284.

18. Nixon was the only Western politican to visit Hungarian refugees in Austria during the revolution. The Austrians were behaving admirably and wanted someone to see it, so despite their misgivings at having regained their sovereignty only a year before, they welcomed him demonstratively. On December 20 and 21, Nixon put in 15-hour days

talking with refugees in camps and with relief officials, and in the middle of the night rode a tractor-drawn wagon through the ice to a farmhouse at Andau with William P. Rogers, Representative Bob Wilson and Robert L. King. The party returned with two women refugees, a banner headline in the *Daily News* but only a sentence in the *Times*.

The next day Nixon went to the U.S. refugee center in Salzburg, where he met with young Hungarians coming down from their emotional highs at having initially routed the Soviets. Nixon's provocative questions ignited sharp counter-questions from the Hungarians, who wanted to know why the United States had only reluctantly raised its visa quota to 20,000, why RFE broadcasts had said help was coming, why refugees who escaped before the revolt were barred from the United States. A spirited discussion developed, and Nixon left for home saying, "We'll do some powerful thinking on the way back. Some of my ideas have changed. I didn't realize the complications. This has been an education for me. Continuing these kids' education is one thing I'm going to bat for. They are top people...."

Nixon's report to Eisenhower impressed the *Times,* which published the full text on 2 January 1957. Nixon reported that 88,000 of the 155,000 refugees at that time had gone to other countries, while the United States had admitted 15,000. Over congressional resistence, about 38,000 Hungarians eventually were admitted to the United States under parole provisions, almost half owing their visas to Nixon's efforts.

The trip remained alive to Nixon; in his memoirs he wrote: "I was disappointed by the hardhearted attitude many Americans seemed to have toward the Hungarian refugees. I felt the same way when there was similar resistence to the Cuban refugees in 1959 and the Vietnamese refugees in 1975."

19. *The New York Times,* 28 June 1956.

20. Townsend Hoopes was a member of the foreign policy establishment having served in Truman's Defense Department and as a consultant to Eisenhower's State Department, a deputy assistant Secretary of Defense for international security affairs in the Johnson administration, member of the Council on Foreign Affairs and contributor to *Foreign Affairs.* The *Times* liked Hoopes' book, reviewing it twice. Christopher Lehmann-Haupt praised it on 9 November 1973, and Alfred Kazin acclaimed it on December 30. Harrison Salisbury wrote for its dust jacket that it was "a magnificent job," and W. Averell Harriman called it a "fascinating and penetrating account," noting that Dulles had "diverted President Eisenhower from his natural inclination to try, after Stalin's death, to compose some of our differences with the Soviets...."

21. Hoopes, *The Devil and John Foster Dulles*, 323.

22. Ibid., 374.

23. *Times* coverage was comprehensive, but there were plenty of nits to pick. The newspaper gave a small Page 1 headline to the most significant event of the Suez crisis, Nasser's announcement that he had accepted Soviet arms. There was an excuse: the *Andrea Doria* had just sunk, preëmpting the banner type, but the *Times* remained more sanguine than other newspapers about the Soviet introduction of arms into the Middle East. Similarly the *Times* gave large amounts of space to Hugh Gaitskell, leader of Britain's Labor Party, in the campaign against Eden after the attack on Suez, tending to obscure popular British support for Eden before the United States pulled the rug from under him.

24. Eden, *Full Circle*, 512.

25. When Nikita Khrushchev arrived in Budapest on April 2, 1958, most Hungarians were in rags and gaunt from 17 months of strikes and slow-downs. Some of the nation's best youth had been executed after show trials or deported to Siberia, and the fates of Imre Nagy and Pal Maléter were unknown. Khrushchev came to cajole, clown a little, make promises, and also to browbeat and threaten the suicidal nation. Budapest's population was ordered to György Dózsa Avenue on April 4 for a show that had been rehearsed through the night. Through a narrow alleyway in the packed crowd, 32 Soviet tanks clattered at top speed in a roar of exhausts as Soviet jets screamed down the avenue at the height of the four-story rooftops. Behind the reviewing stand, howitzers with overcharges blasted a 21-gun salute, shaking the ground and shattering a few windows across the street. Khrushchev spoke to a stony-silent crowd on a subject that did not interest them: Eisenhower's alleged refusal to enter into nuclear test ban negotiations.

When Khrushchev's speech was broadcast, applause was dubbed in; in the Soviet Union, movie houses showed the crowd cheering with closed mouths. In speeches at Dunapentele, Cegléd, Szolnok and Karcag, Khrushchev solicited and bullied thin crowds. At Tatabánya, where a crowd was marched in groups to the soccer field, Khrushchev warned, "You must advise amateurs of provocation that we don't recommend any more provocations. If any provocations occur, they will be met with all the strength of all Socialist countries, and the Soviet Union's armed forces will be at their disposal."

The crowd began drifting away, and Khrushchev shouted, "If you don't like it, swallow it anyway! Be vigilant and don't relax your grip, so that we have to help you again. You miners made some mistakes in 1956, too. You called it a revolution, but it's as easy to tell a revolution from a counter-revolution as it is to tell a rooster from a hen. There is a law. You must beat the enemy or he will beat you. We tell others not to poke their noses—their pigs' snouts, we Russians say—into our business. I know there are counter-revolutionaries still among you. I know you are out there; now why don't you stick up your heads, and we'll knock them off!" The crowd continued filing out. Western reporters got Khrushchev remarks twice softened through Hungarian-to-English translations, but Vincent Latève, of Agence France Presse, whose mother tongue is Russian, provided me with direct translations.

After the Tatabánya walk-out, Khrushchev held no more outdoor rallies, speaking at Csepel Island inside a factory with reporters barred. His visit produced colorful and revealing news stories, and when I howled that all my stories had been shorted, my editor, Hugh Schuck, replied, "What are you complaining about? We used a story every day. The *Times* wasn't even running the story." The *Times* did lead the paper with one story on Khrushchev's visit. Elie Abel filed from Budapest Khrushchev's April 4th speech challenging Eisenhower to join in the moratorium on nuclear tests the Soviets had announced unilaterally on March 31—Stevenson's 1956 idea. Then Abel returned to Vienna, perhaps because his visa expired, and the *Times* did not report Khrushchev's intimidating speeches or the Hungarian walk-outs.

Chapter II

1. Herbert L. Matthews, *The Yoke and the Arrows* (New York: Braziller, 1957).

2. Herman Dinsmore, *All the News That Fits* (New Rochelle, New York: Arlington House, 1969), 46.

3. *The New York Times*, 6 May 1956.

4. Testimony before the Senate Judiciary Subcommittee hearings on *The Communist Threat to the United States Through the Caribbean,* 29 March 1961.

5. Colonel Pérez-Chaumont, commandant at Moncado barracks in 1953, was Cuban military attaché in Mexico City in 1957, when he monitored Castro's contacts with Mexican Communists, the Soviet Embassy and the Czechoslovakian commercial attaché. He reported to Ambassador Robert Hill and others at the U.S. Embassy, including political affairs counsellor Raymond Leddy, often complaining that Washington appeared to ignore the reports. On 22 August 1959, after Castro had been in power eight months, Leddy informed Dr. Milton Eisenhower, the President's brother, during an airplane ride in Mexico, that Castro was pro-Communist and his government was falling under Communist influence. William Wieland was aboard the plane and disagreed throughout the 90-minute discussion, saying Castro was not a Communist and there was no evidence that anyone in his government was a Communist. Hill and U.S. Army Colonel Benoid Glawe entered the discussion, agreeing with Leddy. Glawe said to Leddy, "I disagree with Mr. Wieland. In my mind, he is either pro-Communist or a fool." (Leddy's testimony to the Senate Judiciary Subcommittee on *The Communist Threat,* 1 June 1961.)

6. Mario Llerena, *The Unsuspected Revolution* (Ithaca, New York: Cornell University Press, 1978), 63.

7. Teresa Casuso, *Cuba and Castro* (New York: Random House, 1961), 94-95.

8. Ruby Hart Phillips, *Cuba, Island of Paradox* (New York: McDowell, Obolensky, (undated)), 296.

9. Felipe and Javier Pazos both served Castro in his government, then went into exile, Felipe Pazos under threat of death from Che Guevara.

10. Hugh Thomas, *The Cuban Revolution* (New York: Harper and Row, 1971), 133.

11. In April 1959, Castro embarassed Matthews by gleefully describing the deception, in Matthews' presence, to the Overseas Press Club

in New York. Matthews forgave him, saying that Castro had a childish side.

12. Llerena, *Unsuspected Revolution,* 94.

13. He later wrote *M26, the Biography of a Revolution* (New York: Lyle Stuart, 1961).

14. Llerena, *Unsuspected Revolution,* 99.

15. Ibid., 104.

16. Ibid., 108.

17. Thomas, *The Cuban Revolution,* 178.

18. *The Communist Threat to the United States Through the Caribbean,* Senate Internal Affairs Subcommittee, 12 June 1961.

19. *The Communist Threat,* testimony of 8 September 1960.

20. Thomas, *The Cuban Revolution,* 173.

21. Earl E.T. Smith, *The Fourth Floor* (New York: Random House, 1962), 21.

22. *Human Events,* 17 August 1957.

23. *New York Herald-Tribune,* 15 November 1957.

24. *The New York Times,* 25 February 1958.

25. Smith, *The Fourth Floor,* 58-59.

26. Shortly after the arms cutoff to Batista in March 1958, Ambassador to Honduras Whiting Willauer wrote a report to Secretary of State Christian Herter warning of Communist infiltration in the Caribbean. Willauer, an Asia veteran, wrote, ". . . . The Edgar Snows of Chinese communism are replaced today by the Herbert Matthews of Caribbean Communists. . . the trouble with this type of journalism is that it is carrying the banner for a cause, and, in its hate of the dictators, it is blind to the nature of the forces of communism which are infiltrating the legitimate revolutionary forces. . . ." Willauer said he repeatedly sent detailed reports to Assistant Secretary Rubottom detailing steps in the Communist takeover in Cuba. On 9-11 April 1959, when Castro had been in power more than three months, 14 U.S. ambassadors to Caribbean nations met in San Salvador, El Salvador, under the supervision of Under Secretary Loy Henderson and Rubottom. Several of the ambassadors, including Hill and Willauer, insisted that Castro was a Communist, while Ambassador Philip Bonsal defended Castro. The report of the San Salvador meeting was rewritten in the office of Wieland and circulated through the State Department, causing a formal complaint from Hill that it had been falsified. (Willauer's testimony before the Senate Judiciary Subcommittee on *The Communist Threat,* 27 June 1961.)

27. *New York Daily News,* 21 April 1975.

28. Smith, *The Fourth Floor,* 93-94.

29. *The New York Times,* 14 April 1958.

30. *The New York Times,* 2 November 1958.

31. *The Communist Threat,* 8 September 1960.

32. Thomas, *The Cuban Revolution,* 154-155.
33. *The New York Times,* 11 December 1958.
34. Thomas, *The Cuban Revolution,* 260.
35. Phillips, *Cuba, Island of Paradox,* 369.
36. Thomas, *The Cuban Revolution,* 262.
37. *The New York Times,* 2 January 1959.
38. Smith, *The Fourth Floor,* 193-194.
39. *The New York Times,* 4 January 1959.
40. *The New York Times,* 12 January 1959.
41. *The Communist Threat,* testimony of 30 August 1960.
42. Llerena, *Unsuspected Revolution,* 183.
43. Depending upon whose figures are accepted, there were between 500 and 700 executions. While Castro was in the United States, 28 took place.
44. Richard Nixon, *RN* (New York: Grosset and Dunlap, 1978), 202.
45. *New York Daily News,* 21 April 1975.
46. *The New York Times,* 16 July 1959.
47. Tad Szulc and Karl E. Meyer, *The Cuban Invasion* (New York: Ballantine Books, 1963), 20.
48. Howard Hunt, *Give Us This Day* (New Rochelle, New York: Arlington House, 1973), 98.
49. James Monahan and Kenneth O. Gilmore, *The Great Deception* (New York: Farrar, Strauss and Company, 1963), 153-154.
50. Casuso, *Cuba and Castro,* 241. Castro ignored an offer by the Hotel Commodore of free lodging, arranged by Secretary-General Dag Hammerskjold.
51. Ibid., 15.
52. Theodore Draper, *Castro's Revolution—Myths and Realities* (New York: Praeger, 1962), 210-211.
53. Llerena, *Unsuspected Revolution,* 248.
54. Herbert L. Matthews, *Fruits of Fascism* (New York: Harcourt, 1953), prologue.
55. Herbert L. Matthews, *Half of Spain Died* (New York: Charles Scribner's Sons, 1973).
56. Ibid., 25.
57. Ibid., 22-23.
58. Theodore C. Sorensen, *Kennedy* (New York: Harper & Row, 1965), 169.

1. See Theodore H. White's *The Making of the President* (New York: Atheneum, 1961), and Sorensen's *Kennedy,* particularly Chapter XII, for a discussion of Kennedy's sophistication in public relations.

2. *The New York Times,* 14 October 1960.

3. *The New York Times,* 26 August 1948.

4. *The New York Times,* 4 August 1948.

5. John F. Kennedy, *Why England Slept* (New York: W. Funk, 1940).

6. *The New York Times,* 7 October 1960.

7. *The New York Times,* 20 October 1960.

8. Peter Wyden, *Bay of Pigs* (New York: Simon and Schuster, 1979), 67.

9. In *A Thousand Days,* Schlesinger goes to some length to deny that Kennedy was briefed about the Cuban invasion before the election. He reported that the October 20 statement on giving aid to Cuban freedom fighters was drafted by Goodwin and cleared by Sorensen and Salinger without Kennedy seeing it because the candidate was asleep. He cites Allen Dulles' denial in March 1962 (responding to Nixon's book, *Six Crises*), and quotes Kennedy telling Goodwin if he wins the election, then he, Kennedy, won it, but if he loses, then Goodwin lost it. At the time of decision on the invasion, he told Goodwin, "Well Dick, we're about to put your Cuban policy into action." But these quotes are sophisticated banter, and the literal-minded Schlesinger was not good at banter or interpreting it. It is not plausible that a basic policy statement would be sent to the *Times* Page 1 casually in a tightly run campaign. Nixon, as shown in his memoirs, was sure Kennedy was briefed. Kennedy also knew from other sources of the impending invasion. William Attwood, one of his speech writers, made several calls in mid-October to Andrew St. George, who was in Florida with photographer Hank Walker working on a *Life* story of Cuban exiles in training. St. George told Attwood they would not be ready to go before the election. See David Wise and Thomas B. Ross' *The Invisible Government,* (New York: Random House, 1964), 341-342. The word was passed to Bobby Kennedy, who had thought of a possible speech before the election to neutralize the political effect of the invasion if it occured before the vote.

10. Harrison E. Salisbury, *Without Fear or Favor* (New York: Times Books, 1980), 139.

11. *The New York Times,* 14 October 1960.

12. *The New York Times,* 22 October 1960.
13. *The New York Times,* 26 October 1960.
14. *The New York Times,* 2 November 1960.
15. Sorensen, *Kennedy,* 205.
16. *The New York Times,* 4 November 1960.
17. *The New York Times,* 2 November 1960.
18. *The New York Times,* 2 April 1960. Writing *The Cuban Invasion* with Karl Meyer, Szulc revised that opinion, concluding, "Getting the 'Maximum Leader' to embrace the Russians was like bribing Don Juan to have a date with Venus." (p. 150).
19. *The New York Times,* 10 January 1961.
20. Salisbury, *Without Fear or Favor,* note, 145.
21. Wyden, *Bay of Pigs,* 95.
22. Thomas, *The Cuban Revolution,* 570.
23. Wyden, *Bay of Pigs,* 33.
24. Schlesinger, *A Thousand Days,* 305.
25. Thomas, *The Cuban Revolution,* 508.
26. Ibid., 525.
27. Hunt, *Give Us This Day,* 175.
28. Sorensen, *Kennedy,* 296.
29. Schlesinger, *A Thousand Days,* 225.
30. Thomas, *The Cuban Revolution,* 530.
31. Wyden, *Bay of Pigs,* 160.
32. *The New York Times,* 6 April 1961.
33. Salisbury, *Without Fear or Favor,* 153-154.
34. Schlesinger, *A Thousand Days,* 261.
35. *The New York Times,* 7 April 1961.
36. Szulc, *The Cuban Invasion,* 86.
37. Salisbury, *Without Fear or Favor,* 151-152.
38. *The New York Times,* 11 April 1961.
39. *The New York Times,* 12 and 14 April 1961.
40. Wyden, *Bay of Pigs,* 170.
41. Sorensen, *Kennedy,* 296.
42. Wyden, *Bay of Pigs,* 199 (from Cabell's unpublished autobiography).
43. AP version as published by *The New York Times,* 19 April 1961.
44. *Pravda* and *Izvestia,* 19 April 1961.
45. Schlesinger, *A Thousand Days,* 176.
46. Kennedy did assign Bobby to deal with the CIA. After telling Bissell he would have to go, the brothers kept him dangling until the following December, charged with coming up with a way to eliminate Castro. Bissell did not succeed, and in November 1961 Operation Mongoose was inaugurated under Colonel Edward G. Lansdale. It greatly increased sabotage in Cuba as part of a plan to incite an uprising, and it included efforts to kill Castro. Bissell was told in December

he was through, and he finally was fired in 1962.

47. The media showed little interest in the four Alabama Air National Guard pilots who died, Leo Baker, Riley W. Shamburger, Jr., Wade Carrol Gray, and Thomas Willard Ray. Their deaths were covered up until Senator Everett Dirksen (R-Illinois) revealed their fates on 25 February 1963. Kennedy then conceded at a news conference on 6 March 1963, that they had died "serving their country" while on "a volunteer flight." Other details of the Bay of Pigs took longer to surface, such as the loss of ten of the original 16 B-26s with their ten Cuban pilots, which had required the CIA to solicit National Guard help to man eight more B-26s. (*The Invisible Government,* 84-88.)

48. Nixon, *RN,* 234-235.

49. Unconfirmed casualty figures invariably are exaggerated, but Castro's losses certainly were heavy. Given the relative credibility of the accounts, Castro's casualties must have run into the hundreds, and were an indication that control of the air was decisive.

50. David Halberstam, *The Best and the Brightest* (New York: Random House, 1969), 66-67.

51. At Tarawa, Shoup's forces lost 990 dead and had 2,300 wounded, while the entire Japanese force of about 7,000 men was killed.

52. *The New York Times,* 20 April 1961.

53. The *Times* already considered Krock, the last conservative on the newspaper, a dinosaur in 1961, although he had contributed four Pulitzer Prizes to the paper's reputation. Kennedy told his friend, Ben Bradlee, on hearing that *Newsweek* columnist Ken Crawford planned to knock Krock in a column, "Tell Ken to bust it off on old Arthur. He can't take it, and when you go after him, he folds." See *Conversations With Kennedy* (New York: W. W. Norton, 1975), 141. Krock was obviously isolated on the *Times,* and Art Buchwald wrote in his syndicated column, "There are only four of us writing humor from Washington these days, Drew Pearson, David Lawrence, Arthur Krock and myself." Krock was deeply discouraged at the failures of the Kennedy and Johnson administrations in meeting the challenges of world revolution and domestic disorder. He closed his *Memoirs* (New York: Funk & Wagnells, 1968): ". . . Only I have contracted a visceral fear. It is that the tenure of the United States as the first power in the world may be one of the briefest in history."

54. Sorensen, *Kennedy,* 301.

55. Kennedy's attitude toward Castro was equivocal throughout, even when his brother Robert was pressing for Castro's assassination. Before the 1960 election, Kennedy had written in *The Strategy of Peace* that Castro was "part of the legacy of Bolivar," and in his Cincinnati speech he appeared to agree with Castro to some degree, saying, "We used the influences of our government to advance the interests and increase the profits of the private American companies which dominated

the island's economy." French journalist Jean Daniel, of *L'Express,* said he interviewed Kennedy in 1963 and Kennedy asked him to pass this message to Castro, off the record: "I think that there is not a country in the world, including all the regions of Africa and including any country under colonial domination, where the economic colonization, the humiliation, the exploitation have been worse than those which ravaged Cuba, the result, in part, of my country during the regime of Batista.... In a certain sense, it is as though Batista were the incarnation of some of the sins committed by the United States. Now we must pay for those sins...." Mario Lazo wrote in *Dagger in the Heart* (New York: Funk & Wagnells, 1968), 79-80, that Daniel's "shocking disclosure once more reminded me and others close to Cuban affairs of the abysmal ignorance in the United States with respect to Cuba, even in the highest official circles." Lazo said that Cuba had profited enormously from its U.S. connection, and he was astonished that the myth of exploitation was so easily swallowed.

56. Wyden, *Bay of Pigs,* 325.
57. Sorensen, *Kennedy,* 301.
58. Wyden, *Bay of Pigs,* 202-206.

Chapter IV

1. Khrushchev intended to be threatening at the Paris press conference, which was set up with Communist correspondents filling the first four rows of seats, where their applause would be seen on television, but he did not intend to blow up. Béla Fábián, a former Hungarian parliamentarian who had been in Hitler's concentration camps and in the Soviet Gulag (and whom Khrushchev called "Dr. Hooligan"), stood on a chair in the rear and shouted charges. Krushchev erupted, cursing and threatening, and his television coup was ruined for Soviet audiences. De Gaulle had permitted Fábián's small group of Hungarians to enter with press passes.

2. The *Times* bought magazine pieces on Germany from Britons during the period. An article by Labor Party luminary Barbara Ward in the *Times Magazine* of 2 October 1949, was headlined, "Is Germany Still A Menace to Peace?" Ward wrote: "It is incredibly dangerous (to build up Germany as a potential ally), for, however subsidiary their role may be now, when they are defeated, disarmed and divided, the Germans are still a menace to peace and will remain so in any forseeable future" because the line of ideological cleavage in the world ran through Germany.

The British often took the position that things were not so bad in East Germany, which eased the immorality of Germany's division. A Labor Party defense secretary, Emanuel Shinwell, reported that all of East Germany's soldiers were volunteers; he knew because he had asked them.

By 1960, the *Times* was reporting in a similar vein. Flora Lewis reported from East Germany in the *Times Magazine* of 20 March 1960: "Refugees still sneak away to the West—at a rate of about 100,000 a year, far less than the exodus of the mid-fifties but still enough to hurt. But the number of people moving east from West Germany has climbed sharply from the 10 per cent of westbound migrants that had held for years. They included both West Germans crossing the border for the first time and East Germans returning to their homes. There is no firmly reliable statistic, but there are indications that the eastward movement may have reached 50 percent of the reduced flow westward. More important, among those who stay in East Germany, the common refrain is a toneless, resigned, "One can live here."'

Lewis' report caused some stir, especially when her statistic, half as many West Germans moving east as East Germans moving west, was quoted by Walter Lippmann in his column, Lippmann being so anti-German that he would not set foot in Berlin as a matter of principle. A reporter in the *Times* Bonn bureau, Arthur Olsen, went to East Berlin and asked to see the reception center for West German refugees and was told they were all out getting inoculations. Olsen later left the *Times* to join USIS, then moved to the diplomatic service.

3. *The New York Times,* 19 April 1949.

4. *The New York Times,* 10 August 1949.

5. *The New York Times,* 14 Agusut 1949.

6. Kennedy, "A Democrat Looks at Foreign Policy," *Foreign Affairs* (October 1957).

7. Konrad Adenauer, *Errinerungen, Volume 4* (1959-1963—*Fragmente*) (Stuttgart: Deutsche Verlags Anstalt, 1968), 91-99.

8. Kennedy and Adenauer were opposites in many respects, but both were politicians. Kennedy's success through charisma came early, while Adenauer, at the age at which Kennedy became President, was only the perennial mayor of Cologne. Although Adenauer had no charisma, he acquired a pithy style of speaking without speech writers that went to the heart of the matter. Once, when De Gaulle asked Adenauer what he thought of speculation that Britain might open a drive to join the Common Market, expecting a discourse on the complex prospect, Adenauer replied in a sentence, "I wish Macmillan knew what he wanted."

Adenauer had seen so much that his bursts of temper were brief, and he neither got mad nor got even. Months after the Wall went up, Adenauer did not resent Kennedy. He visited De Gaulle in December 1961, and De Gaulle remarked that he had received very early a bad impression of Kennedy from his campaign speeches and inaugural address. De Gaulle predicted that Kennedy would go adventuring in Africa, Asia and the Caribbean, neglecting the more vital Europe.

Adenauer replied that Kennedy had been "forced to fight with all his strength in all directions at once," and deserved some understanding. Kennedy had suffered defeats in Laos and Cuba before Berlin, Adenauer said, and had difficult social, racial and educational problems at home. Adenauer wrote in his memoirs (Volume 4, p. 127) that De Gaulle finally promised to find an occasion to say something nice about Kennedy and the Americans.

9. In "Konjev Liess Aufmarschieren," *Der Spiegel* magazine (No. 34, 1966) quoted what appeared to be minutes of the Warsaw Pact summit meeting of March 29, which probably came indirectly from the *Bundesnachrichtendienst.* When the Wall was built, Gehlen's BND drew up a report to prove to West Germany's parliament that it was not

caught napping, but had reported every stage of preparations. The secret document was given to Eugen Gerstenmaier, who showed it to key members of parliament. *Der Spiegel*'s book-length, three-part series in 1966 on the background to the Wall, *"Konjev Liess Aufmarschieren,"*'drew on the leaked Gehlen document, as well as on interviews and the Sorensen and Schlesinger books.

10. Schlesinger, *A Thousand Days*, 343.

11. The *Times* had a team of reporters on hand. Seymour Topping came to Vienna from the Moscow bureau and wrote the curtain-raiser on June 2, saying that Khrushchev was under pressure to make peaceful coexistence work in the face of criticism from hard-line critics in Communist China: "Mr. Khrushchev is thus deeply committed in the senior councils of the Communist bloc to the value of the meeting with Mr. Kennedy and to the theory that it can be exploited. This personal involvement is expected to make Mr. Khrushchev a cautious negotiator who will be determined to find some common ground with Mr. Kennedy to justify future negotiations on what he regards as central issues: Germany and disarmament. . . . If he is rebuffed, Premier Khrushchev in all probability will make known his determination to go ahead with the signing of a peace treaty with East Germany. . . . The Western powers would be told that the East Germans are prepared to negotiate reasonably on access rights. . . . "

12. Schlesinger, *A Thousand Days*, 348.

13. Charles E. Bohlen, *Witness to History* (New York: W.W. Norton & Company, 1973), 481.

14. Nikita Khrushchev, *Khrushchev Remembers* (Boston: Little, Brown & Company, 1974), 500-501.

15. *The New York Times*, 5 June 1961.

16. *The New York Times*, 6 June 1961.

17. *The New York Times*, 7 June 1961.

18. *The New York Times Magazine*, 15 November 1964.

19. On June 6, Wallace Carroll, Reston's aide in Washington, wrote in the *Times* that Khrushchev gave Kennedy "a strong indication that he was determined to settle the Berlin question by the end of the year." His story, buried on Page 15, was headlined, "Soviet Deadline on Berlin Hinted." But more prominently the next day, a *Times* editorial commented on Kennedy's report to the nation, saying: "He spoke with calm firmness and dignity, taking the American people into his confidence. But he dared to look boldly at the stark facts of the great conflict of our day, the conflict between communism and freedom."

20. See "That Special Grace," *Newsweek*, 26 November 1963.

21. Benjamin Bradlee, *Conversations With Kennedy* (New York: W.W. Norton & Company, 1975), 125.

22. *Der Spiegel*, No. 34, 1966.

23. *The New York Times*, 16 June 1961.

24. *The New York Times,* 23 July 1961.

25. In *Khrushchev Remembers,* the Soviet leader reported that Konev was appointed to answer Clay's appointment, saying that Kennedy had put a pawn on the board, "so we advanced a horse." Actually, Konev had been recalled from retirement and began running the build-up in East Germany shortly after the Vienna summit, well before Clay was thought of in Washington. Khrushchev did not always remember so good.

26. George Bailey is the author of *Germans—The Biography of an Obsession* (New York: World, 1971).

27. I was the chastised questioner.

28. James O'Donnell went to Berlin to work with Clay. He quit the government when Clay's mission ended, remaining in West Berlin for the next 19 years, researching the Hitler era and writing magazine articles and *The Bunker.* Once an ardent Kennedy supporter, O'Donnell sometimes showed visitors to Berlin what he called "the John F. Kennedy Memorial Wall."

29. *Der Spiegel,* No. 35, 1966.

30. Egon Bahr, speaking on television in 1970, recalled, "The reality then (August 1961) was that the Governing Mayor of Berlin had to wait for a relatively long time before Allied patrols came. It also took a long time before a mere protest was sent to Moscow." Bahr later told Viola Herms Drath: "More than anything else this experience made us realize that entry permits to East Berlin were available only by cooperation with Moscow—this actually happened two years later." (*Willy Brandt, Prisoner of His Past* (Radnor, Pennsylvania: Chilton, 1975), 94.)

31. *The New York Times,* 15 August 1961. Adenauer could not cut East-West German trade unilaterally, which would have involved the Allies in a new blockade of Berlin. Britain especially would not support economic retaliation, and some left-wing members of Britain's Parliament, such as Ian Mikardo, ran businesses largely based on trade with East Germany. Mikardo regularly had a prominent stand at Leipzig Trade Fairs and maintained close relations with East German officials.

32. Gehlen, *The Service,* 239.

33. Arthur Krock, *Memoirs* (New York: Funk & Wagnalls, 1968), 370.

34. Sorensen, *Kennedy,* 621.

1. *The New York Times,* 14 September 1962. Matthews said he wrote virtually all editorials on Latin America in the period.

2. Krock, *Memoirs,* 378-379. Thiraud de Vosjoly had visited Cuba, moving easily there with his French diplomatic status. At some point he also briefed Kennedy on his missile evidence. An anti-Communist, he became embroiled in an intrigue with an alleged Soviet spy in the entourage of President De Gaulle, was forced out, and moved to Canada. He was the model for Leon Uris' novel *Topaz.*

3. Elie Abel, *The Missile Crisis* (New York: Lippincott, 1966), 17-18.

4. *The New York Times,* 1 September 1962.

5. *The New York Times,* 5 September 1962.

6. Schlesinger, *A Thousand Days,* 798.

7. Victor Lasky, *It Didn't Start with Watergate* (New York: Dial Press, 1977), 81.

8. Schlesinger, in *A Thousand Days,* wrote that McCone could not have been too concerned about his missile theory, since he went on his honeymoon, but he does not mention the "honeymoon telegrams."

9. Krock, *Memoirs,* 379. McNamara gave the job of consolidating intelligence to a deputy, Cyrus Vance. Vance called in Benjamin Civiletti, asked if he knew anything about intelligence or had read the appropriate legislation, and receiving a negative answer, said, "Good. You and I are going to reorganize it." Henry L. Trewhitt, *McNamara* (New York: Harper and Row, 1971). Reorganizations of intelligence often go astray. Although reorganization was spurred by Kennedy's distrust of the CIA after the Bay of Pigs, McNamara's Defense Intelligence Agency resulted in giving the CIA more, not less, authority, in that it expanded analysis staff and assumed responsibility for National Intelligence Estimates.

10. *The New York Times,* 7 September 1962.

11. *The New York Times,* 9 September 1962.

12. *The New York Times,* 9 September 1962.

13. Mario Lazo, *Dagger in the Heart* (New York: Funk & Wagnalls, 1968), 210.

14. Interview.

15. Abel, *The Missile Crisis,* 24.

16. Ibid., 31.

17. Oleg Penkovskiy, *The Penkovskiy Papers* (New York: Doubleday-Avon edition, 1966), 324.

18. The missile gap had been speculated earlier by James Gavin in *War and Peace in the Space Age* and by Senator John F. Kennedy on the Senate floor on 14 August 1958, but Hilsman was the first to suggest specific figures showing a gap.

19. *New York Herald-Tribune,* 19 December 1958.

20. Penkovskiy, *Papers,* 327.

21. Ibid., 241.

22. Sorensen, *Kennedy,* 617.

23. Abel, *The Missile Crisis,* 57-58.

24. Schlesinger firmly planted the idea that the Jupiters and Thors were obsolete and vulnerable in 1962, and their removal from Turkey and Italy made no difference. In *A Thousand Days* (807), he reported that their removal had been recommended in 1961 by McNamara and the Joint Congressional Committee on Atomic Energy. Hilsman reported in *To Move a Nation* (202) that an angry President Kennedy had long before ordered dismantling the missiles in Turkey, "obsolete, unreliable, inaccurate and very vulnerable—they could be knocked out by a sniper with a rifle and telescopic sights," and he had ordered Rusk in May 1962 to raise the issue at a NATO meeting, but the Turks "objected on political grounds." Hilsman said Kennedy again "ordered" their removal in August 1962. Sorensen, the only one of the three Kennedy insider historians who attended Excom meetings, is less vehement. He reported in *Kennedy* that the President had long before asked McNamara to review the overseas Jupiter missiles.

By contrast, General Curtis LeMay, who was Air Force Chief of Staff at the period, said in *America Is In Danger* (New York: Funk & Wagnalls, 1968), 200, that the missiles in Turkey "became operational just before the Cuban missile crisis," that the cement of their installations had just dried, and they represented a very expensive answer to 750 Soviet IRBMs targeted on Europe. "I did not accept the explanation that the missiles had become obsolete so quickly," LeMay wrote, "nor did any other military man I know." He wrote, "The precipitous action smacked of a deal . . . we definitely came out on the short end of the bargain in a confrontation which has been hailed as a great American diplomatic victory."

25. *Newsday,* 1 November 1963.

26. According to David Detzer in *The Brink* (New York: Thomas Y. Crowell, 1979), Kennedy told Max Frankel, the *Times* bureau chief in Washington, that he had ordered a blockade of Cuba, but asked him to call his publisher and see if the *Times* story could be held up for a day or two, so that the Soviets would not preëmpt with some drastic act. Detzer wrote that Frankel called Kennedy back and asked him to give his word to the *Times* that he would "shed no blood and start no war during the period of our silence," and Kennedy agreed.

27. Thomas, *The Cuban Revolution,* 636.

28. *Daily News,* 31 October 1962.

29. Neither Keating nor McCone ever revealed precise sources of their missile information. Keating, along with Dodd, often chaired the Senate Judiciary subcommittee that conducted a running investigation for years, published by Congress as *The Communist Threat to the United States Through the Caribbean.*

Keating often interviewed knowledgeable witnesses before and after their formal testimony. His suggestion that missiles might remain in caves was ridiculed by part of the media, but a number of witnesses before the subcommittee had testified that the Soviets had elaborate underground military installations in natural caves that honeycomb several Cuban mountain areas. After Keating had lost his Senate seat, Paul Bethel, who had been press attaché at the U.S. Embassy under Ambassador Smith and was a White House consultant on Cuba until the Bay of Pigs, described to the subcommittee reports of an elaborate tunnel system the Soviets had built out of the natural caves. Bethel had spent six years interviewing Cuban exiles for his *Latin American Report* before giving that report in testimony 7 March 1967.

30. Shocking as it was to the *Times* to discover that the Soviets might have tried to manage news in the Soviet Union, it had not passed unnoticed that the White House, Defense Department and CIA had been managing news on an unprecedented scale under Kennedy. Kennedy's photogenic and theatrical qualities had been put to use in striking photographs of the President, in half-silhouette, pensive at the window of the Oval Office, shoulders slightly bowed under the world's weight, yet with a firmly planted stance—a photo that made the cover of *Life.* The first insider account of the missile crisis was written by Charles Bartlett and Stewart Alsop in the *Saturday Evening Post* with data provided by Kennedy himself and the CIA's Ray Cline. It painted Kennedy as the hero, Stevenson as a weak-kneed pacifist, and Kennedy's refusal to refute the story publicly embittered Stevenson until his death.

31. *The New York Times,* 20 October 1964.

32. UN Security Council, 2026th Meeting, 31 August 1977.

33. Khrushchev, *Khrushchev Remembers,* 504.

1. Harold Macmillan, *At the End of the Day* (New York: Harper and Row, 1973), 335-348.
2. Ibid., 343.
3. *The New York Times,* 12 December 1962.
4. Richard E. Neustadt, *Skybolt and Nassau* (Boston: sanitized manuscript in the Kennedy Library), 101.
5. *The New York Times,* 18 December 1962.
6. Neustadt, *Skybolt and Nassau,* 101.
7. Ibid., 209.
8. Adenauer, *Erinnerungen: Volume 4,* 201-202.
9. Interview in Oxon Hill, Maryland, 22 August 1978. On 22 December 1962, the Air Force announced a successful Skybolt test and was quickly slapped down by a Defense Department denial.
10. Neustadt, *Skybolt and Nassau,* 122.
11. Correspondence, 23 April 1982.
12. Rael Jean Isaac, "New Left Input into U.S. Foreign Policy," *Newsletter of the National Committee on American Foreign Policy,* February 1980.
13. *Midstream,* February 1981.
14. Marcus G. Raskin, *Being and Doing* (New York: Random House, 1971).
15. *Ramparts* commented in 1968: "When the improbable student rebellions of West Berlin, Morningside Heights and the Sorbonne broke out this spring, all agreed that Herbert Marcuse was the Marx of the children of the new bourgeoisie." Well, not all. Marcuse was the guru of American student rebels, but European youths had better-entrenched idols, including Marcuse's colleague in pre-Hitler Germany, Theodor Adorno of Frankfurt University. Adorno, like Marcuse, Bertolt Brecht and others, fled Hitler for the United States in the 1930s. In New York, Adorno helped Max Herkheimer found the New School for Social Research. He returned to West Germany—not to East Germany like Brecht—and developed the "Frankfurt School" of "third-way" socialism, more revolutionary than West Germany's Social Democrats had become, and similar to Leninist socialism "before the Stalinist aberration." Among Adorno's students or class auditors were Yasser Arafat, Angela Davis and Karl Dietrich Wolff, head of West Germany's *Sozialistisches Deutsche Studentenbund.* Wolff got part of his revolutionary training at the University of Michigan as an exchange student,

where he took a "freedom ride" into the American South. Back in Europe, Wolff and his brother established ties with Dani (The Red) Cohn-Bendit, who touched off the Paris riots that followed the West Berlin shooting of Red Rudi Dutschke. Adorno's "Frankfurt School" was seminal for other German universities, and when Adorno died the *Times* gave him a long obituary befitting a founder of New York's New School, but it never mentioned that he taught Marxism or had any political leanings at all.

16. *Time,* 1 April 1979.

17. Richard J. Barnet, *The Giants* (New York: Simon and Schuster, 1977).

1. Hans Kapfinger incurred the wrath of Social Democrats by publishing excerpts from a book by Susanne Sievers, a former mistress of Willy Brandt. Sievers was a bright, tall divorcee, socially in demand in Bonn, where she ran a newsletter, when she met Brandt in 1951. She was arrested on a visit to East Berlin in 1952 by SSD men who grilled her on her relationship to Brandt and suggested an espionage arrangement. Months later she was sentenced to eight years as a spy for the Social Democrats' *Ostbüro*. Released after four years, she reported that she spent 24 hours trying to see Brandt, and when she did, was given a 100 marks and a plane ticket to West Germany. Broke and now friendless, she got some help from Strauss. In 1961, as the Wall went up and Brandt challenged Adenauer in the elections, she published *There Also Was a Girl* under the pen name Claire Mortensen. It sold out instantly and became a collector's item. Kapfinger obtained a copy, which included some of Brandt's love letters. Christian Democrats charged that Social Democrats tried to buy up the book edition; Social Democrats charged that Strauss incited the book; Christian Socialists charged that Social Democrats incited Nada Illmann to charge Kapfinger with sexual extortion. One of the Social Democrats suspected of inciting Illmann was an editor on the *Süddeutscher Zeitung* in Munich who soon thereafter was charged with sexual extortion of one of his copy girls, a plot much like Arthur Schnitzler's play *Reigen,* which became the French movie, *La Ronde.* Sievers' story is found in *Willy Brandt, Prisoner of His Past,* by Viola Herms Drath.

2. "Uncle Aloys" was Aloys Brandestein, who was broke and taken in after World War II by the Zwicknagl family, where Marianne as a little girl had called him uncle. Eventually Brandestein worked for Backhaus K.G., a firm that repaired tank treads for the *Bundeswehr.* The 12-page *Der Spiegel* article was illustrated with pictures of lavish summer homes of munitions dealers, and the casual headline reader would get the impression that Aloys was the uncle of either Strauss or his wife, and that his relationship with Strauss accounted for the firm's success. The spongy article suggested that a suitcase of money had been destined for Strauss, although it was not delivered, and said in a footnote that Strauss secretly negotiated with a Bad Godesberg real estate agent to buy for cash the $375,000 Casa Roccavispa villa in Switzerland. The real estate agent testified in court he had been surprised to read the entirely false story in *Der Spiegel,* but he welcomed the pub-

licity.

3. One of the officers, Colonel Adolf Wicht, was the Hamburg office chief of the *Bundesnachrichtendienst,* and his arrest raised speculation that General Gehlen had sabotaged Strauss through the article because Strauss' Defense Ministry had coöpted some of his best men. Wicht was said to have "reviewed" the article before publication, objecting to only one item which was deleted. The magazine reported that Adenauer was ready to arrest Gehlen and kept him overnight in the Chancellery (*Der Spiegel,* 14 November 1962.) The police raiders found a note that appeared to be from Wicht warning *Der Spiegel* manager Detlev Becker of the impending raid. Gehlen refuted all of these charges, writing that Wicht had not "reviewed" the article but that *Der Spiegel* had presented him with a list of ten detailed questions, which Wicht forwarded to Pullach, where they were answered by a press officer on the basis of previously published material (*The Service,* 253-254). Gehlen believed that *Der Spiegel* was attempting to ruin Strauss and incriminate the *Bundesnachrichtendienst* at one blow, and that the note found by police was a *Der Spiegel* plant intended "to conceal the identity of the prominent Defense Ministry official who was the real culprit—the official who supplied the secret documents" (*Ibid.,* 256). Gehlen wrote: "Why should I have tipped off a magazine I was increasingly coming to recognize as a hostile instrument?" (*Ibid.,* 255). Unmentioned was that Wicht once had been a potential rival of Gehlen, when the British briefly considered building their own German espionage organization around him. (See *Gehlen, Spy of the Century,* 149.)

4. The *Times* registered "surprise" at the Bavarian results on 26 November 1962.

5. *The New York Times,* 4 November 1962.

6. *The New York Times,* 10 November 1962.

7. *The New York Times,* 11 November 1962.

8. *The New York Times,* 13 November 1962.

9. *The New York Times,* 21 November 1962.

10. *The New York Times,* 22 November 1962.

11. *The New York Times,* 13 December 1962.

12. *The New York Times,* 23 November 1962.

13. *The New York Times,* 30 November 1962.

14. Schlesinger, *A Thousand Days,* 403.

15. *Die Welt,* 18 May 1962.

16. Donovan also had helped Lieutenant General Reinhard Gehlen draw up his contract with the incipient CIA in Washington, under which Gehlen preserved his independence and his option to put his organization wholly at the disposal of a German government later. (See *Gehlen, Spy of the Century,* by E. H. Cookridge (New York: Random House, 1972), 135.)

17. In his book *Strangers on a Bridge* (New York: Atheneum, 1964), Donovan said he obtained Pryor's release as a bonus in negotiations with East German attorney Wolfgang Vogel and Ivan Schishkin, an official in the Soviet Embassy in East Berlin. Donovan apparently did not know that Beitz earlier had put the Pryor family in touch with Vogel and had a representative in Berlin working on the case.

Pryor was arrested in East Berlin in August 1961. Three weeks later I learned that an unnamed American was being held, and identified him by ringing doorbells at the Free University. He had just completed a thesis on a dispute between economists in East Germany over the centralized economic system and was a serious published scholar. His family was appreciative of my story in the *News,* as the State Department had not informed them of the arrest. The Pryors promised to alert me if and when he was to be released, and they did so. But when I went to Berlin on the morning of his release, all of them had vanished.

Tipped that Beitz had been involved, I flew to Essen, where Beitz told me in his home, "Just a few hours ago my man from Berlin was sitting in that chair, where you are sitting. He told me he brought Pryor out on the Friedrich Strasse S-Bahn to the Bahnhof-am-Zoo station in West Berlin, at which point they were surrounded by Americans who took Pryor away from him." Beitz said he would deny the story if I used his name, because everyone in West Germany would want to enlist his help in getting a relative out.

It seems apparent that the East Germans, ready to release Pryor anyway, convinced Donovan through a difficult sham negotiation that Pryor was a bonus to the release of Powers. Kennedy, however, was told that Beitz had been involved, and Beitz was the last West German to visit Kennedy before he was assassinated in Dallas.

18. Sorensen, in *Kennedy,* 318, said that the President "only rarely planted questions at press conferences."

19. Correspondents from Washington accompanying Kennedy later identified the questioner: "Oh, that's Marianne Means. She's a friend of his. He met her out in the boondocks when he was campaigning, and now she's working for Hearst Headline Service. Every once in a while a Secret Serviceman comes around and takes her in to see him." "Now I know why they call you guys hard-nosed," I told them. "It's from bouncing balls off your noses while you clap your flippers." *Time* reported on 12 October 1962 that "Marianne Means, 28, could claim the title as the only White House correspondent to have got her job through the President." *Time* said that Kennedy met her in Lincoln, Nebraska, in 1957, and later asked Hearst's national editor, Frank Coniff, "Are you going to send Marianne to the White House?" At this writing, Means writes a syndicated column.

20. In *Kennedy,* 601, Sorensen replaced this line with an elypsis.

21. When the Soviets resumed nuclear testing in August 1961, Ken-

nedy "warned" that the United States would resume testing too, but there was not much to test. It was not until 1 March 1962, that Kennedy could announce on television, after touching base with Macmillan and Hugh Gaitskell, that the United States would resume testing, and the first blast did not occur until 15 April 1962. Sorensen reported that the U.S. tests received as little publicity as the President could "manage." (*Kennedy,* 624.)

22. John Kennedy, *The Strategy of Peace,* Senator J. F. Kennedy's edited speeches (New York: Harper and Brothers, 1960).

23. In the summer of 1972 Brandt's first government suffered internal conflict over *Ostpolitik.* The budget did not pass parliament, and Economics and Finance Minister Karl Schiller quarreled with Brandt and resigned. *Quick* magazine published a letter from Schiller to Brandt charging Brandt's government with fiscal irresponsibility, and Brandt called Schiller "a mental case." On 10 August 1972, police of the State of North Rhine-Westphalia raided *Quick* offices in Bonn, Munich, and Hamburg, looking for evidence of tax fraud, bribery of public officials and breach of security. Brandt's government said the press raid was the state's idea, and there was no international fuss.

24. To placate the unruly students, the West Berlin government gave them a clubhouse, a downtown building that became known as the Republican Club. It teemed with life, young men and women seeking adventurous politics and somebody to shack up with. Decorated with posters of Ho Chi Minh, Che Guevara and Rosa Luxemburg, it became a center for organizing demonstrations that sometimes turned into riots. Reporters looking for Horst Mahler, Gudrun Ensslin or Fritz Teufel checked the Republican Club, and so did plainclothes police in hippy costume. Police thereby managed to preëmpt an attack on Vice President Hubert Humphrey with bags of pudding, during a visit to Berlin in April 1967, that probably would have provoked Secret Service guards to shoot.

Chapter VIII

1. Kennedy, *The Strategy of Peace*, 57, 59.
2. General de Gaulle, *Le Salut, Memoirs de Guerre* (Paris: Library Plon, 1959), 195.
3. Ibid., 192 & 195.
4. Bernard Fall, *The Two Vietnams* (New York: Praeger, 1967), 137.
5. Marguerite Higgins, *Our Vietnam Nightmare* (New York: Harper & Row, 1965), 14.
6. Ibid., 158, 69.
7. Fall, *The Two Vietnams*, 246.
8. Edward Geary Lansdale, *In the Midst of Wars* (New York: Harper & Row, 1972), 308-309.
9. Fall, *The Two Vietnams*, 249.
10. *The Pentagon Papers,* all versions.
11. *Pentagon Papers,* Defense Department version (not in the *Times'* version).
12. The Joint Chiefs, spanning the two administrations, were not enthralled with the revival of the Green Berets. Marines and airborne troops already existed, and another elite troup added to morale problems of the infantry. The 5,000 Green Beret East Europeans, whose use had been denied to the CIA's Frank Wisner during the Hungarian revolt, had dwindled to 1,800 men stationed at Bad Tölz, West Germany, when Kennedy assumed office. Now guerrilla and counter-insurgency training was added to the curricula of service academies and the War College.
13. Roger Hilsman, Jr., *To Move a Nation* (Garden City, New York: Doubleday, 1967), 419 and note, 439.
14. Few elections in the Third World have evenly matched candidates, and patronage also plays a role in some U.S. elections. In 1977, New York City elected a new mayor, with no clearly marked favorite among four candidates. Democrats, who control patronage in New York, received 91% of the vote for two candidates (one running as a Liberal), to 9% for two Republicans (one running as a Conservative). No New York newspaper commented on the 91% phenomenon.
15. *Pentagon Papers,* Defense Department version (not in the *Times'* version).
16. Ibid. (not in the *Times'* version).
17. A careful reader of the *Times'* document on Lansdale's team might note that it consisted of only a dozen American officers, ten of them

rushed in to beat the Geneva accords' freezing of military assistance personnel as of 11 August 1954. Eisenhower's administration honored the accords to that extent, at least. The team's mission was a temporary one to assist the Vietnamese in unconventional warfare to allow Diem time to stabilize his government. It managed to devalue North Vietnam's currency and increase the refugee flow to the south through forged leaflets purporting to be instructions to the Vietminh, prevented a coup against Diem and began pacification and training programs. The oil-contamination caper was minor, but it involved volatile chemicals, not sugar in gas tanks.

18. *Pentagon Papers,* Defense Department version (not in the Times').

19. *Pentagon Papers,* Senator Gravel Edition (not in the *Times'*).

20. In July 1962, the *Times of Vietnam* reported on the conclusion of the Laos negotiations that the United States (Harriman) had "fallen into a Communist trap." American correspondents took it as an insult and blamed the story on Mme. Nhu. One of them (unnamed) charged into the Saigon office of press officer John Mecklin demanding a comment on the story. "We had none," Mecklin wrote. The reporter raged, "Doesn't the United States have any dignity left at all?" The *Times of Vietnam* proved accurate. (*Mission in Torment,* 141.) The Kennedy in-house historians insisted Harriman's negotation was a success and reported it helped his star rise in the administration. Nolting, however, said the Embassy agreed with Diem: "As a consequence of the lack of safeguards in the Agreements on Laos signed in 1962, the 40,000 or so North Vietnamese troops in the Eastern provinces of Laos stayed there, and the Ho Chi Minh trail became what some have called the 'Harriman Memorial Highway.'" (*Many Reasons Why,* 64, 65). Nolting thought that 40,000 North Vietnamese stayed; Colby of CIA thought about 7,000.

21. William Colby and Peter Forbath, *Honorable Men* (New York: Simon & Schuster, 1978), 191-198.

22. *Pentagon Papers,* Defense Department version (not in the *Times'*).

23. Ibid. (not in the *Times'*).

24. Michael Charlton and Anthony Moncrieff, *Many Reasons Why* (New York: Hill & Wang, 1978), 79-80.

25. John Mecklin, *Mission in Torment* (Garden City, New York: Doubleday, 1965), 141.

Chapter IX

1. Newsweek, 17 September 1962.

2. Peter Braestrup, *Big Story* (Boulder, Colorado: Westview Press, 1977), 5.

3. David Halberstam, *The Making of a Quagmire* (New York: Random House, 1964, 1965), 43-56.

4. Six years after the Buddhist immolations, the self-immolation by fire of Jan Palach, 19, in Wenceslas Square in Prague, made him the hero of Czechoslovakia following the Soviet crushing of the Prague Spring.

5. Higgins, *Our Vietnam Nightmare,* 19.

6. From *The Pentagon Papers,* Senator Gravel Edition (not in the *Times'* version). In the *Times* version of the Pentagon Papers, Hedrick Smith summarized Nolting's prediction of *feuding factions* if Diem were deposed as Nolting arguing that Diem's overthrow would "plunge Vietnam into *religious civil war.*" (My italics.) This misleading paraphrase supports Halberstam's theme of religious conflict; the document does not.

7. *Pentagon Papers,* all versions.

8. Vietnamese Buddhism is so informally organized that disputes continued between those supporting Halberstam's estimate of 70% of the population and Higgins' 15%. A clue may be found in the elections of 1967 in South Vietnam, when 4,735,404 persons voted out of an eligible 5,853,251. Of the 11 tickets on the ballot, the Thieu-Ky ticket got 34% of the vote and later received parliamentary support from parties representing 35% of the vote. The An Quang (Buddhist) party, opposed to Thieu and Ky and neutral in the war effort, got 10.8%.

9. Halberstam, *Making of a Quagmire,* deleted from later editions; see note, 276.

10. Higgins, *Our Vietnam Nightmare,* 167-168.

11. Ibid., 124-125.

12. Halberstam, *Making of a Quagmire,* 228. Published versions of the Pentagon Papers mention meetings of the generals with and without Nhu, but do not mention a "raze the city" quotation. "Raze the city with artillery" is the kind of language we newspaper people like, but editors should be wary of it. Razing is harder than it sounds, re-

quiring inordinate quantities of heavier artillery than the Vietnamese possessed at that time. Israel razed the emptied small city of Ismalia with artillery during the War of Attrition that Nasser provoked, but it took more than a year. In the real life coup in Saigon on 1 November, the Vietnamese army could not even raze the Presidential Palace in 14 hours. It is implausible that Nhu said it, even as hyperbole, after living at war for 20 years and having become a military expert.

13. Halberstam, *Making of a Quagmire,* 231-232.

14. Ibid., 237.

15. Richardson was "reassigned" at Lodge's request to demonstrate to the Ngo brothers that they no longer had a sympathetic channel through which to communicate directly with the American government and bypass the U.S. Embassy, according to William Colby in *Honorable Men, 211.*

16. *The New York Times,* 23 August 1963.

17. Halberstam, *Making of a Quagmire,* 243.

18. *Pentagon Papers,* all versions.

19. *New York Herald-Tribune,* 24 September 1963.

20. *New York Herald-Tribune,* 3 October 1963.

21. Lodge's proposals are included in the Senator Gravel Edition of the *Pentagon Papers,* Document 135 (not in the *Times* version). Thuc did leave for the Vatican after talks with Lodge, the Italian ambassador and the Papal delegate. On September 9, Mme. Nhu left for Europe and the United States, seeking support for the Diem government. So gestures were made to appease the U.S. government.

22. *Pentagon Papers,* all versions.

23. *Chicago Sun-Times,* 22 June 1971.

24. *Pentagon Papers,* Senator Gravel Edition, Document 137 (not in the *Times* version).

25. *The New York Times,* 4 September 1963.

26. *The New York Times,* 5 September 1963.

27. *New York Herald-Tribune,* 5 September 1963.

28. *Pentagon Papers,* all versions.

29. *Newsday,* 1 November 1963.

30. *Pentagon Papers,* all versions.

31. Diem's death caused little remorse in the American media. A characteristic comment was that of Michael J. O'Neill in his column in the *New York Daily News* of November 2: "It might be flattering to our national ego if the U.S. could claim it called all the shots in Ngo Dinh Diem's sudden eviction from his Gia Long Palace. But, unhappily or otherwise, this is not exactly the case." O'Neill reported that Washington was only trying to reform Diem, not eliminate him. O'Neill later became editor of the newspaper.

32. Higgins, *Our Vietnam Nightmare.*

33. The Kennedy men eased out by Johnson all turned vocally against

the war, beginning with Hilsman, followed by Ball when he left after brief service as United Nations Ambassador. A frankly opportunistic statement on the switch was made by John Kenneth Galbraith on BBC's Third Program. Galbraith told interviewed Michael Charlton: "Sometime in 1966 or early 1967, Arthur Schlesinger and Richard Goodwin, William vanden Heuvel and I all had lunch together, and I remember Arthur saying, 'If this thing gets worse in the last seconds before final destruction, we'd better be able to say that we opposed it.' We all committed ourselves at that time to really working against the war, which meant breaking with the administration. I identified myself for a time with something called 'Negotiations Now,' then we had a great struggle within the ADA (Americans for Democratic Action) and brought ADA down solidly against the war. Then I began what was a long and fascinating, I may say, association with the man who deserves more credit than anybody else for bringing our involvement to an end, and that's Eugene McCarthy." (*Many Reasons Why,* 161.) Johnson said in an interview with Walter Cronkite on CBS on 2 May 1969, that "a cult" of unnamed Kennedy aides systematically undermined his Vietnam policy.

34. *Chicago Daily News,* 13 November 1964.

35. From 1980 correspondence with Beech, then *Los Angeles Times* correspondent in Bangkok.

Chapter X

1. Unlike Halberstam and Browne, Neil Sheehan did not immediately write a Vietnam book. Sheehan did, however, write an introduction to the English-language translation of Jules Roy's book, *The Battle of Dien Bien Phu* (New York: Harper & Row-Pyramid, 1966). Sheehan's theme was that American officials in Vietnam were blindly repeating the French errors of a decade earlier. Sheehan took the occasion to attack an enemies list similar to Halberstam's. Sheehan wrote that Diem was "a plump little man who waddled like a duck when he walked. . . sitting in his air-conditioned office in the presidential palace isolated from the people by his own choice, surrounded by sycophants and security policemen and convinced he ruled by divine right." Nhu was "a French-educated intellectual" who "spoke in a low, rasping voice," and "had become a victim of his own talent for intrigue. . . and of his contempt for the rest of the human race." Mme. Nhu "fancied herself the rightful empress of Vietnam" and "goaded Nhu and her brother-in-law deeper in their folly. . . ." Ho Chi Minh "is still the greatest nationalist leader in the country to much of the peasantry, and the Communists drew deeply and successfully on this credit. . . . ." Sheehan ridiculed Ambassador Nolting for telling journalists that Diem was "widely respected in the countryside," and that the regime was rallying its people in "a great national movement" to sweep the Viet Cong from the country. General Harkins and his staff "sat in their air-conditioned offices in Saigon and waxed optimistic on the same kind of supposedly impressive statistics the French had confronted themselves with during the first Indochinese war." Higgins' dispatches "faithfully reflected the official point of view."
2. Halberstam meanwhile had worked in Poland.
3. *The New York Times,* 21 November 1965.
4. *The New York Times,* 24 November 1965.
5. *The New York Times,* 28 November 1965.
6. A month before the Berlin Wall.
7. *The New York Times,* 14 October 1965.
8. *The New York Times,* 31 October 1965.
9. *Reader's Digest,* February 1964.
10. *The New York Times,* 9 June 1967.
11. *The New York Times,* 14 June 1967.
12. Exclusive article by Hilsman, Long Island Press, 21 February 1970.
13. Charlton and Moncrieff, *Many Reasons Why,* 89-91.
14. Ibid., 92-93.
15. *Newsday,* 29 November 1963.

Chapter XI

1. Testimony, Senate Government Operations Committee, 13 May 1969.
2. Johnson wrote: "I did not believe that the nation would unite indefinitely behind any Southerner. One reason. . . was that the metropolitan press of the Eastern seaboard would never permit it. My experience in office had confirmed this reaction. I was not thinking just of the derisive articles about my style, my clothes, my manners, my accent, and my family—although I admit I received enough of that kind of treatment in my first few months as President to last a lifetime. I was also thinking of a more deepseated and far-reaching attitude—a disdain for the South that seems to be woven into the fabric of Northern experience. . . . To my mind, these attitudes represent an automatic reflex, unconscious or deliberate, on the part of opinion molders of the North and East in the press and television." (*The Vantage Point,* 95.) It did not get better: a Reston column attacking Johnson for hanging on in Vietnam and declaring erroneously that he had begun his re-election campaign was headlined: "Washington: 'My Fellow Amurricons.' " From *Times,* 30 June 1967.
3. Lyndon Johnson, *The Vantage Point* (New York: Holt, Rinehart and Winston, 1971), 19.
4. Lady Bird Johnson, *A White House Diary* (New York: Holt, Rinehart and Winston, 1970), 734.
5. Johnson, *The Vantage Point,* 3.
6. Lyndon Johnson, "The Tug of World Events," *1969 Encyclopedia Britannica Book of the Year.*
7. *The New York Times,* 2 April 1963.
8. Berkeley had a long tradition of Jack London-esque radicalism, London having started as an oyster pirate in nearby Oakland. In a house a block from the campus, shared by a psychologist, a trombone player, an agitator for Harry Bridges' longshoremen's union and myself, frequent visitors were members of the Society for the Arts, Sciences and Professions, who were organizing the presidential campaign of Henry Wallace in 1948. Hugh DeLacy, the Washington state Congressman who was considered the only Western pro-Communist in the House, lost his re-election bid and visited us with an assortment of

Hollywood and Midwest Communist figures. Unused to drinking, De-Lacy proclaimed one night that he was Gideon, ready to lead a res-urected Gideon's Army.

9. *The New York Times,* 21 November 1964.

10. Three city commissioners of Birmingham filed a $1,500,000 libel suit against the *Times* on 6 May 1960, for a story by Harrison Salisbury that the *Times* headlined "Fear and Hatred Grip Birmingham." Later city commissioners of Bessemer and Montgomery, the governor of Alabama and two private citizens sued, and total damages threatened to reach $6,150,000. The *Times* and Salisbury lost initially, and suits involving $300 million were filed against other news media. The Supreme Court ruling in *Sullivan vs. The New York Times* on 9 March 1964, that libel had not been committed and that the suits struck "at the very heart of the constitutionally protected area of free expression," freed the *Times* and Salisbury of liability and opened the South to the same freedom of reporting as the North.

11. *The New York Times,* 5 December 1964.

12. *The New York Times,* 17 August 1965.

13. *Pentagon Papers,* all versions.

14. For Raskin's court testimony on the Tonkin Gulf resolution, see Jessica Mitford's *The Trial of Dr. Spock* (New York: Alfred A. Knopf, 1969), 159.

15. Charlton and Moncrieff, *Many Reasons Why,* 108-109.

16. *Ramparts,* April 1972.

17. Dong Hoi was described as a peaceful fishing village by Wilfred Burchett in *Vietnam North* (New York: International Publishers, 1966).

18. *The New York Times,* 9 February 1965.

19. *The New York Times,* 10 February 1965. Coincident with the *Times* editorial shift to flatly opposing the war, Marcus Raskin of the Institute for Policy Studies looked up Bernard Fall, who had not been against the war but was critical of Diem's handling of it. Fall began to "adopt my view of it," Raskin reported, and they collaborated on editing *The Vietnam Reader* (New York: Random House, 1965). Their anthology gave the appearance of balance, including a Lyndon Johnson speech, a long Senator Dodd speech, and excerpts from Walt Rostow, Dean Acheson, Robert McNamara and McGeorge Bundy, all mild or weakly discursive selections, with the bulk of the book given over to Raskin, Barnet, I. F. Stone, Mao Tse-tung, etc, all firey. *The Vietnam Reader* "had an immediate and powerful impact in university circles" and was the "primary source material for the many study groups and teach-ins that sprang up across the country in 1965," according to anti-war activist Jessica Mitford in *The Trial of Dr. Spock,* 45, 49.

20. Salisbury joined the *Times* to become its Moscow correspondent from 1949 to 1954, the last years of Stalin's rule. His Moscow reports were in conflict with the darker view of *Times* resident Soviet expert

Harry Schwartz, resulting in enmity between the two. Salisbury had wanted the *Times* to label his dispatches "censored," but the editors declined. He later wrote in *Journal* (Chicago: University of Chicago Press, 1961), 17 that all dispatches from Moscow are automatically biased and misrepresent the news. "These dispatches are printed in the *Times* with no indication that they have been tampered with. Yet the fact is they represent, first, my effort to anticipate the censor and phrase the dispatch in terms which he will pass; second, the censor's effort to slant the story into the Soviet line by judicious editing."

On his return in 1954, Salisbury wrote an enormous 14 part series, stressing that it was his first opportunity to write free of censorship. The acclaimed series won a Pulitzer Prize and made Salisbury celebrated, although the dispatches proved perishable. Two of the long articles predicted that the post-Stalin junta would liberalize the Soviet Union. Salisbury described Georgi Malenkov as "full of old-fashioned grace," Krushchev as "a hail fellow well-met," Lazar Kaganovich as "liking his liquor," Nikolai Bulganin as "handsome and witty" and Mikoyan as "probably the sharpest and cleverest of all."

Salisbury warned that speculation over a power struggle between Malenkov and Khrushchev was dangerous wishful thinking. His sources told him that "Malenkov is top dog and would take Khrushchev in any showdown." One long article speculated without sources that Stalin had been murdered; another reported that Lavrenti Beria held the capital after Stalin's death, but he hesitated, lost, and probably was executed in Lubianka; another said that Marshal Zhukov's army took the city back from Beria.

Salisbury was the first American correspondent to visit Siberia, and he reported the MVD's slave-labor empire, with the caveat that Siberia always had served as a penal camp. Free of censorship, he wrote, "It should not be supposed that the prison labor seen working everywhere in the north and east shows any particular marks of oppression or hardship. The work crews this correspondent saw were healthy and robust looking, particularly the women, as is usually the case in the Soviet Union. They look like hardy peasants who were accustomed to rough work and tough life. They did not appear to be more harshly treated than other work crews engaged in similar physical occupations...prison gangs can be seen fairly frequently in the Caucasus, usually in units of twenty-five or fifty men and women, working on the highways with two or three lackluster MVD lads guarding them."

Not everyone at the *Times* was overwhelmed by Salisbury's series, which ran from September 19 to October 2, 1954. Members of the Washington bureau called him "Rasputin" (*The Kingdom and the Power,* 138), and Salisbury was considered an enemy by such Soviet emigrés as Alexander Solzhenitsyn, Andrei Amalrik and others. Lev

Navrozov, who arrived in the United States in 1972 and wrote *The Education of Lev Navrozov* (New York: Harper & Row, 1975) became a dedicated enemy of the *Times*. In a review in the *Yale Literary Magazine* (Volume 149, No. 4, 1981), Navrozov wrote, *"Without Fear or Favor* is a live modern *Tartuffe,* complete with an excellent title and told by a protagonist of mercurial hypocrisy, unlimited opportunism and effortless mendacity . . . ."

21. Gay Talese, *The Kingdom and the Power,* (New York: World, 1969, Bantom edition), 514.

22. *The New York Times,* 27 December 1966.

23. Wilfred Burchett reported through Tass that he accompanied Salisbury on his tour, according to Herman H. Dinsmore in *All the News that Fits* (New Rochelle, New York: Arlington House, 1969), 138. Salisbury did not mention Burchett either in his dispatches or in his book, *Behind Enemy Lines-Hanoi* (New York: Harper & Row, 1967).

Burchett had been accused of threatening American prisoners of war in North Korea during the Korean War. Any doubt about the charges should be dispelled by Burchett's book *Vietnam North* in which he describes his questioning of three prisoners of the North Vietnamese. By his own account, Burchett badgered the prisoners, charging them with bombing hospitals and leper colonies and referring to their status as war criminals, since no war had been declared. Navy Commander (later Senator) Jeremiah Denton did not take Burchett's intimidation and told him that all targets were military and "during the last 20 years there have been no declarations of war. In Korea there was not. At Suez there was not. In this case there were plenty of warnings. No underhanded methods. No sneak attack." (*Vietnam North,* 41.)

24. *The Vantage Point* is strewn with Johnson's resentment of De Gaulle.

25. Johnson did not pursue Castro as the Kennedys had done, and he may not have known about the plots against Castro and Trujillo by earlier administrations. CIA Director Richard Helms said that, in a meeting with Johnson on 10 May 1967, Johnson's conversation with him went: "Then you're not responsible for Trujillo?" "No." "Diem?" "No." "Castro, he's still alive, okay." Johnson later told Howard K. Smith, "Kennedy was trying to get Castro, but Castro got him first." In 1971, Johnson told Leo Janis of *Atlantic* that when he came into office, "We were running a damn Murder Incorporated in the Caribbean." The Johnson-Helms discussion is put together in *The Man Who Kept the Secrets*, by Thomas Powers (New York: Alfred A. Knopf, 1979), 143, 156-157.

26. Ray Cline, *Secrets, Spies and Scholars* (Washington: Acropolis Books, 1976), 213.

27. By May 19 it was clear to me that there would be a war, as I happened to be vacationing in Eilat. A visiting Soviet artist, who was hold-

ing an exhibit in Tel Aviv, also was in Eilat, sketching the port facilities. A large group described as Israeli Boy Scouts set up camp on the beach and made excursions into the Negev (and presumably the Sinai), all of them with rather heavy five o'clock shadow to be Boy Scouts. Everyone in town knew that, "Here we go again." Nevertheless, the *Daily News* insisted that I leave Israel to conduct an editor around Berlin, and I barely got back on 2 June before the airport closed on 5 June.

28. Dayan, *Story of My Life,* 346.
29. Ibid., 377.
30. Talese, *Kingdom and Power,* 111-112.
31. Salisbury, *Without Fear or Favor, 30.*
32. *The New York Times,* 6 October 1946
33. *The New York Times,* 9 November 1956.
34. *The New York Times,* 5 June 1967.
35. *The New York Times,* 6 June 1967.
36. *The New York Times,* 8 June 1967.
37 *The New York Times,* 11 June 1967.
38. *The New York Times,* 17 July 1967.
39. *The New York Times,* 5 June 1967.
40. *The New York Times,* 4 June 1967.
41. The draft-resistence movement was run by Americans who in most cases denied being Communists but had little or nothing against communism. It had some foreign Communist connections through the Cuban Mission to the United Nations and the meetings with North Vietnamese in Bratislava in 1967, Budapest in 1968 and Cuba throughout.

In February 1968 FRITA, a European draft-assistance group (Friends of Resisters Inside the Army), claimed 600 American deserters in France, Holland and Sweden. U.S. Army Headquarters in Europe in Heidelberg said there were about 40 deserters. K. D. Wolff, head of German SDS, supplied me in Frankfurt with Paris addresses given to prospective deserters which I checked out before looking up deserters in Paris. It included the Marxist French National Vietnam Committee, the Soviet-sponsored Mouvement de la Paix, the publishers of *Drapeau Rouge*, the offices of attorneys representing the French Communist Party and the Quaker Center.

At 35 rue de Clichy, one of the addresses, was a Soviet import-export firm, whose proprietor told me no deserters had been seen there. He did, however, write out an address where I might get information: 114 bis, rue de Vaugirard, the Quaker Center. It housed PACS, the Paris-American Committee Against War, led by Maria Jolas, then 70. At the Quaker Center, Tony Clay told me to leave my hotel number and I might be contacted. That night Mr. Cook, contact man for FRITA, called, and after suitable discussion and insults, said a courier might pick me up to interview several deserters.

The interview, in a clandestine atmosphere, was held in an expensive apartment, divided by a bed sheet over the archway, with two deserters who eventually came through the sheet to talk while Cook recorded the conversation. They were Phil Wagner, 25, from Felton, California and Richard Perrin, 19, from Springfield, Vermont. I asked if they were not concerned that their protectors and financial supporters might be KGB. Perrin asked, "KGB? What's that?" and Cook snapped, "Don't answer that! KGB—Soviet CIA. Mr. Braley, many members of this organization are not Communists, and the lady in whose house you are a guest is not a Communist, and your question is out of order. The *New York Times* correspondent would never ask a question like that."

When De Gaulle resigned in 1969, Mr. Cook turned out to be Tomi Schwaetzer, an Austrian citizen. Paris police, unleased by the lack of central government, picked him up and tried to ship him to Vienna, but the Air Austria pilot refused to take him. So police put him on a plane to Corsica. Schwaetzer's friends got him back into France briefly, then he moved to Heidelberg and set up a news service specializing in U.S. Army scandals. He told me he frequently sold material to the *Times* bureau in Bonn. When the *Daily News* published my deserter series, all references to Communists were taken out, and Schwaetzer telephoned my wife to say how pleased he was.

42. Mailer became famous in his 20s by capturing the mood of the nation (or the critics) with *The Naked and the Dead* shortly after World War II while he was at Harvard. Read today, the novel is embarrassing. It has the stock soldier characters of a B movie: The tough sergeant, the kid from New York, the hillbilly, etc., as background actors to the conflict between the fascist commanding officer and his young Marxist aide, who discuss political philosophy after the model of Wolf Larsen and his captive poet in Jack London's *The Sea Wolf*.

43. Norman Mailer, *The Armies of the Night* (New York: Farrar, Strauss & Giroux, 1968, Signet edition), 307.

44. Arthur Waskow, "Ghandi and Guerrilla," *Liberation,* November 1967.

45. *Subversive Involvement in Disruption of the 1968 Democratic Party National Convention, Part 3,* Senate Judiciary Committee Hearings 4-5, December 1968.

1. Sir John Glubb was writing of the Mamluke Empire, around 1500. The quotation appeared in *Soldiers of Fortune* (New York: Stein and Day, 1973), 301.

2. See Tad Szulc's *Czechoslovakia Since World War II* (New York: Viking Press, 1971).

3. Zdeněk Fierlinger is thought to have been a Communist disguised as a Social Democratic leader who delivered the country to the Communists through his coalition agreement. In 1968 he still was alive and a vocal Stalinist. His case is not unique. East Germany's Otto Grotewohl led his Social Democrats in a parade that merged symbolically with Walter Ulbricht's Communists into the Socialist Unity Party; Social Democrat Jozef Cyrankiewicz became president of Communist Poland and lived like royalty; Social Democrat György Marosán became the ruthless interior minister of Kádár's rump government that put down the remnants of the 1956 Hungarian revolution. In present Socialist and Social Democratic parties of Western Europe, it is easy to speculate which leaders would be most likely to throw in with an invading Red Army, although it is considered red-baiting to do so.

4. Szulc's valuable book, *Czechoslovakia Since World War II*, centers on the Prague Spring. It is detailed as an account of liberalization and the invasion, and is put in context regarding developments in other countries of East and Central Europe. His emphasis on "Socialism with a human face" might be misplaced, considering that non-Communist Czechs are all but ignored. He predicts an inevitable revival of liberalism within the Communist system.

A year after the Prague Spring, the student Jan Palach committed suicide in Prague as "Torch No. 1," bringing on the scene a new reporter who published his book before Szulc could complete his. William Shawcross, 24, a British liberal, produced a *tour de force* for so young a journalist in *Dubček* (New York: Simon & Schuster, 1970). It is a dazzling analysis of inner-party relationships of Czechs and Slovaks before, during and after the Prague Spring, but it glorifies the reform Communists and romanticizes Dubček: "For anyone now to pretend that the ideals and promises of Prague Spring were not Dubček's own is quite absurd. Given his unexpected but unswerving commitment to these ideals, it is impossible to pretend any longer that he was just a fig-urehead, an unthinking tool in the hands of the intellectuals. For alone among the leading reformers, Dubček has refused to make any criti-cism of his aims in the spring. . . . Dubček will always be remembered as the one man who did more than anyone else to make of commu-nism a system of government fit for people—ordinary people with or-dinary human faces." (240-241.)

5. *The New York Times,* 6 January 1968.
6. *The New York Times,* 16 March 1968.
7. *The New York Times Magazine,* 31 March 1968.
8. *The New York Times,* 27 May 1968.
9. *The New York Times,* 19 May 1968.
10. *The New York Times,* 14 and 22 July 1968.
11. *The New York Times,* 22 July 1968.
12. *The New York Times,* 23 July 1968.
13. *The New York Times,* 24 July 1968.
14. Ibid.
15. *The New York Times,* 26 July 1968.
16. *The New York Times,* 18 July 1968.
17. *The New York Times,* 1 August 1968.
18. *The New York Times,* 4 August 1968.
19. *The New York Times,* 5 August 1968.
20. From Bratislava I filed a report saying that the Czechoslovaks had lost. The party jargon in the communique, dismissed in the West, in-cluded pledges to observe democratic centralism, to reimpose press censorship, to resume control of the population without further eva-sion. Dubček could not honor the solemn pledges he had signed in Bratislava, I wrote, and the Soviets would impose compliance. The *New York Daily News* did not print my dispatch, in the face of con-trary opinion stemming from Jiří Hájek and flowing in from the wire services, but editorialist Reuben Maury saw it and mentioned it in an editorial, saying "We will withhold our cheers." (*Daily News,* 5 August 1968). When the Soviets invaded, someone dug out my old, unused dispatch and printed part of it, "As the *News* reported. . . ."
21. *The New York Times,* 11 August 1968.
22. *The New York Times,* 12 August 1968.
23. *The New York Times,* 18 August 1968.
24. Ibid.
25. *The New York Times,* 1 September 1968.
26. *The New York Times,* 2 September 1968.
27. *The New York Times,* 3 September 1968.
28. Don Oberdorfer, who was in Saigon for Knight newspapers during Tet and then moved to the *Washington Post,* concluded in *Tet!* (New York: Doubleday, 1971) that everyone lost the Tet offensive, the Com-munists on the battlefield and the United States politically. His battle

death figures from United States and South Vietnamese sources were 3,895 American officers and men; 214 officers and men from Korea, Australia, New Zealand and Thailand; 4,954 South Vietnamese officers and men; 14,300 South Vietnamese civilians, and 58,373 officers and men of North Vietnam and the Viet Cong.

The Communists put an estimated 67,000 of their most experienced fighters into Tet and lost almost all of them, he reported. The people of the cities did not rise up and join them, and Tet consolidated the Saigon regime, which was able to double its military strength from 670,000 men to more than a million after the offensive. But Tet apparently convinced Oberdorfer that the United States did not belong in South Vietnam. Oberdorfer called the *Times'* disputed scoop on Westmoreland's request for 206,000 troops "the most dangerous and damaging leak of (Johnson's) administration," apparently without knowing that it came from Ellsberg via Kennedy. (309.)

29. Braestrup, *Big Story.*
30. Ibid., 705.
31. Ibid., 722.
32. Ibid., 706.
33. Of the media represented by correspondents in Saigon, only the *Times* was markedly dovish in 1968, according to Braestrup. He reported that during February and March 1968, the height of the Tet offensive, the *Times* gave the Hanoi government more attention than it did the Saigon regime, of which it disapproved, publishing four major Agence France Presse stories from Hanoi on Page 1 and 43 stories from Hanoi or by its emmissaries on inside pages. He cited such headlines as "Hanoi Says Aim of Raids Is to Oust Saigon Regime" (2 February) and "Hanoi Indicates It Is Still Ready to Discuss Peace" (9 February).
34. Braestrup, *Big Story,* 340.
35. Ibid., 284.
36. Ibid., xxxii.
37. *Washington Post,* 28 September 1975.
38. The disputed military estimates of Communist armed strength in South Vietnam figured in Ellsberg's trial in Los Angeles, when CIA analyst Samuel A. Adams testified in Ellsberg's defense that the Pentagon deliberately clung to a low estimate of Communist forces by excluding some classifications of the Viet Cong, and that JCS Chairman General Earle Wheeler insisted that the Communists had "peaked forces at 240,000 just before Tet." Adams testified that the military resisted his figures, which showed that Communist forces actually were 440,000 and could be as high as 600,000. (At Tet the Communists committed 67,000.) A normal headline for the story of such a dispute would have been something like, "CIA Analyst: Army Estimate of Foe's Strength Erred." Actual headlines were: "Ellsberg Witness Asserts Military Falsified Reports" (*The New York Times,* 7 March 1973), and "Viet Report

Falsified, CIA Analyst Says" (*New York Post,* 7 March 1973).

These news stories and headlines apparently confused Harrison Salisbury, who wrote in *Without Fear or Favor* (62) that Ellsberg leaked to Sheehan "a story about the Vietnamese order of battle and how it had been phonied to justify the new troop escalation. It had, for practical purposes, been doubled." It had not, of course, been doubled, but had been previously underestimated by half, if the analyst's estimate is accepted, and therefore could not have been phonied to justify troop requests. In January 1982, CBS revived the story in a 90-minute documentary, "The Uncounted Enemy: A Vietnam Deception," that pilloried General Westmoreland and became the subject of a libel suit against CBS.

39. W.W. Rostow, *The Diffusion of Power* (New York: Macmillan, 1972), 519-520.

40. Publishers-Hall Syndicate, in the *Washington Post,* 7 July 1971.

41. Thomas Powers, *Diana, the Making of a Terrorist* (Boston: Houghton Mifflin, 1971), 125.

42. *The New York Times,* 18 August 1968.

43. *The New York Times,* 1 September 1968.

44. Ibid.

Chapter XIII

1. Edith Efron, *The News Twisters* (Los Angles: Nash, 1971), 50.
2. Ibid., 155.
3. *The New York Times,* 25 July 1968.
4. See Chapter XIX.
5. *The New York Times,* 6 October 1968.
6. *The New York Times,* 3 November 1968.
7. All citations, *The New York Times,* 7 November 1968.
8. Ibid.
9. *New York Times,* 9 May 1969.
10. Henry Kissinger, *White House Years* (New York: Little, Brown and Company).
11. Charlton and Moncrieff, *Many Reasons Why,* 190-191.
12. Lieutenant William Calley was sentenced to life in prison in March 1971. The White House received a large volume of protest mail, and Nixon commuted Calley's sentence to be served confined to military headquarters pending appeal. The sentense was later reduced and Calley was paroled after Nixon left office in 1974.
13. "Dare We Develop Biological Weapons?" *The New York Times Magazine,* 28 September 1969.
14. *The New York Times Magazine* published a long letter (2 December 1970) praising Hersh's biological warfare esposé from Paul O'Dwyer, New York's left-wing former city council president, who was running unsuccessfully for the U.S. Senate. O'Dwyer, a strong supporter of the Irish Republican Army, became an attorney for the Islamic Republic of the Ayatollah Ruhollah Khomeini during the period in 1980 when American Embassy personnel were being held hostage in Iran, ending O'Dwyer's political aspirations.

   Hersh finally saw Vietnam briefly in July 1979. He did not investigate current news—the boat people and genocide in Cambodia—but sought condemnations from Communist leaders to attack Kissinger in *The Price of Power* (New York: Summit, 1983).
15. *The New York Times,* 16 October 1969.
16. *The New York Times,* 15 October 1969.

17. The *Times Book Review* had high praise for *My War With the CIA* by Prince Sihanouk and Wilfred Burchett (New York: Pantheon Books, 1973) at the height of Watergate (26 August 1973). The reviewer, James C. Thomson, Jr., did not identify Burchett as an employee of the KGB, but commented, ". . . far greater than any crime of covert complicity in Sihanouk's overthrow is what happened next: the overt American invasion of Cambodia on April 30, 1970. By that senseless act the Nixon administration destroyed all that Sihanouk had achieved: the shielding of Cambodia from the Indochina war and the preservation of Cambodia's independence. By that act, and its sequel, the obliteration bombing of Cambodia, the Nixon administration has gone far toward the destruction of the Khmer civilization. Of all the 'high crimes' this President is accused of, that may well rank among the highest."

18. Jean Lacouture, French biographer of Ho Chi Minh, suggests that Sihanouk left Cambodia because of the Communist Vietnamese build-up. "Like everyone else, Sihanouk was aware of the growth of Vietnamese presence in his country. It is possible that in order to avoid having a direct confrontation with his associates, who were beginning to threaten his neutrality, he wanted to stand aside, leaving to General Lon Nol the chore of 'cleaning out' Cambodia of the Vietnamese presence, to come back later with his hands clean and his country freer." *Cambodia—The Widening War in Indochina* (New York: Simon & Schuster, Washington Square Press, 1971) 15-16.

19. Nixon, *RN,* 450.

20. *The New York Times,* 30 April 1969.

21. *The New York Times,* 1 May 1970.

22. Nixon, *RN,* 454.

23. *The New York Times,* 2 May 1970.

24. Ibid.

25. *The New York Times,* 3 May 1970.

26. On April 30, some hours before Nixon's television announcement of the Cambodia incursion, National Guardsmen at Ohio State University, not far from Kent State, had fired birdshot at rioters, wounding 13, and 73 others were injured in fights with Guardsmen. The rioting was unconnected with Indochina. That day 4,000 federal troops were flown to New Haven, Connecticut, to guard against riots at the murder trial of Black Panther leader Bobby Seale, who had been separated from his other trial in Chicago for leading riots at the Democratic Convention.

27. *The New York Times,* 10 May 1970.

28. *The Newsletter on the State of the Culture* of 30 July 1969, published by The Smith, surveyed all 1968 issues of the *Times Sunday Book Review* and reported that top advertisers commanded the attention of reviewers, while smaller advertisers generally received disproportionately less notice. Its statistical table showed that the Random

House combine (Random, Knopf, Pantheon) was at the top, and received more individual reviews than its total number of ad pages, leading in both categories. "The Newsletter does not believe the *Times* is guilty of first degree corruption," it said. "Rather, the content of the book review proves the axiom that the books backed by major advertising are the ones which are noticed by the reviewers." It noted that the editors "frequently assigned reviews to well-known literary friends or enemies of the authors."

29. Sir Robert Thompson, *Peace Is Not at Hand* (London: Chatto and Windus, 1974).

30. The *Times* published 40 editorials on Cambodia in 1970, many of them repeating the "quagmire" theme of the Halberstam era and flat assertions that the war could not be won. As early as 31 March, the *Times* warned that the new Cambodian government's willingness to permit South Vietnamese cross-border raids into Vietnamese sanctuaries could draw the United States into a wider war, and it warned repeatedly against U.S. military aid for Lon Nol (April 17, 21, 27). In the expression of the *Times Index,* editorials "scored" Nixon's widening of the war (30 April, 1 May), and warned that the "perilous breach of self-restraint" might make the Communist superpowers react (they did not). Editorials deplored the attack by construction workers on anti-war demonstrators, praised the Moratorium demonstrations, repeatedly supported the Cooper-Church amendment to limit the President's war powers (May 8, 14, June 24, July 1). An editorial derided Nixon's "glowing" claims of success in the Cambodia incursion (July 1).

31. *The New York Times,* 6 May 1970.

32. *The New York Times,* 7 May 1970.

33. *New York Times,* 10 May 1970.

34. Ibid.

35. *The New York Times,* 12 May 1970.

36. Theodore H. White, *Breach of Faith* (New York: Atheneum-Reader's Digest Press, 1975), 129.

37. Dan Schorr turned up in Bonn as CBS correspondent in 1959, a self-made man who had gone to Holland after World War II and learned Dutch as a way of breaking into the correspondent's trade. In Bonn, he set up a cooperative arrangement with Sidney Gruson of the *Times,* who was receiving special attention from the goverment. Adenauer had been at loggerheads with Gruson's predecessor, M. S. Handler, over Handler's messianic anti-Nazi stories, which Adenauer felt stimulated the far right rather than discouraged it. Gruson was admitted to inner circle briefings at the Foreign Ministry, with top German reporters Dieter Schwarzkopf and Günter Muggenberg translating the proceedings for him.

Schorr paid Gruson back with a scoop at Christmas 1959: Nazis had smeared swastikas and the slogan "Juden raus" in Cologne, Adenauer's stronghold. CBS carried the story as though Hitler had returned, and Gruson's story made Page 1, triggering a wave of reports worldwide that Nazism was reviving in West Germany. My editors demanded an anti-Nazi story, and I reported that the neo-Nazi parties were minuscule; Germans had had it with the lunatic fringe. But when the Cologne swastika-smearers were caught, the world media covered their trial in February 1960 as though the culprits were major menaces.

They turned out to be Arnold Strunk, 25, a baker's apprentice, and Paul Schönen, 25, an office clerk, who had been blind drunk. They received 14 and ten months respectively for graffiti that was mild by New York City standards, their case irresponsibly blown into an international incident. Interior Minister Gerhard Schröder reported on February 17, 1960, that in six weeks the publicity inspired 685 cases of swastika smearing, of which only 73 were by politically motivated persons including agents under East German direction. The Schorr-Gruson scoop triggered imitation anti-Semitic incidents from Antwerp, Belgium, to Argentina via Leeds, England and Milan, Italy.

38. W. Mark Felt, *The FBI Pyramid* (New York: G.P. Putnam's Sons, 1979), 79.

39. William C. Sullivan with Bill Brown, *The Bureau—My Thirty Years in Hoover's FBI* (New York: W.W. Norton and Company, 1979), 207-209.

40. Ibid., 212.

41. See Chapter XVIII.

42. Sullivan, *The Bureau,* 211. Mark Felt agreed, saying, "It was Sullivan's plan."

43. White, *Breach of Faith,* 136.

44. John Dean, III, *Blind Ambition* (New York: Simon and Schuster, 1976), 276.

45. *The New York Times,* 7 June 1973.

46. Dean, *Blind Ambition,* 37.

Chapter XIV

1. Nixon's charge that dove Senators were thin reeds of support for Israel was borne out repeatedly during the Carter administration's efforts to pressure Israel into a Middle East settlement. One case was the Senate's controversial vote to sell F-15 Eagle jets to Saudi Arabia in May 1978. Many Senate doves, traditional friends of Israel, voted for the sale, which paved the way for further arms sales to the Saudis, including AWACS surveillance planes. Shortly after the Senate approved the F-15 sale, both the Saudis and Anwar Sadat stiffened their demands on Israel, Sadat saying on 30 July that there would be no more negotiations unless Israel was prepared to withdraw totally from occupied lands. The dove Senators thereupon wrote letters to Secretary of State Cyrus Vance protesting, in effect, that they had been tricked into voting for the F-15 sale, with copies of the letters to *The New York Times,* which printed their protest. The weak reeds had managed to have it both ways, jeopardizing Israel while blaming it on Carter administration trickery.

2. Nixon, *RN,* 481-482.

3. As Habash was leaving the Intercontinental after freeing his hostages, I got out of a taxi in front of him on my first visit to Amman. Several correspondents came out of the lobby to shake the hand of the stocky man with a Mussolini jaw standing in shirtsleeves beside an Arab officer in a splendid mustard-colored general's uniform. These were obviously important persons, so I too stuck out my hand, saying my name and the name of my newspaper. At the hotel entrance I asked Eric Pace who the VIPs were. Pace said, "You just had the honor of shaking hands with George Habash. The general is Saleh Mahdi Amash, vice president of Iraq." The applause for Habash from his victims was my introduction to the Middle East's journalism-by-intimidation. I would discover that much of the reporting from Beirut, then headquarters for most Middle East correspondents, was colored pro-PLO by intimidation.

Intimidation works best when alloyed with a rational reason for behavior, such as a correspondent's natural sympathy for refugees, and in the Middle East some correspondents who would angrily deny they could be intimated became strongly pro-PLO, unaware that they were subjects of a technique as old as the Turks' creation of Janissaries.

During the October War in 1973, American employees of banks and oil firms in Beirut staged an anti-Israel demonstration in front of the

U.S. Embassy, possibly certain in their own minds that their sympathy for the Arabs was genuine (although Sadat and Assad launched the war). The suggestion that they were displaying Arab bias in order to preëmpt further intimidation probably would outrage them.

4. *The New York Times,* 11 June 1970.

5. *The New York Times,* 13 June 1970.

6. *Der Baader-Meinhof Report, aus den akten des Bundeskriminalamtes, der "Sonderkommission, Bonn" und dem Bundesamt für Verfassungsschutz* (Mainz: Has and Kohler Verlag, 1972), 41-42.

7. Forced to leave Jordan by the outbreak of the September revolt, the Red Army Faction returned to West Germany and embarked on a series of bombings and bank robberies. Among the first they killed were U.S. Lieutenant Colonel Paul Bloomfield—with a bomb at the Frankfurt Officers Club—and Captain Clyde R. Bonner, Specialist Ronald Woodward and Specialist Charles Peck at the U.S. Army Headquarters for Europe in Heidelberg with a car bomb planted by Meinhof. Their companion on the Middle East trip, Michele Rey, once a Coco Chanel model, then a Viet Cong sympathizer who sold her jungle adventures to *Life,* was married to Konstantinos Costa-Gavras, director of the pro-Marxist film "Z".

8. *The New York Times,* 15 September 1970.

9. Britain freed skyjacker Leila Khalid, who returned to Beirut to lecture at the American University and to marry Bassam Sherif. After the Munich massacre of Israeli athletes in 1972, a Fatah-Black September enterprise, a series of letter bombs sent by the Popular Front maimed a number of prominent Jews in Europe. Bassam Sherif received a letter bomb in return, half-blinding him and crippling his hand.

10. Abu Hassan had overall direction of Black September, which sent an assassin to Cairo to kill Jordanian Prime Minister Wasfi Tal, a Palestinian, and publicly drink blood from his gunshot wounds. In January 1979, Abu Hassan was blown up by a car bomb in Beirut. Daoud Oudeh, or Abu Daoud, who was the on-the-scene manager of the Munich massacre, was shot five times in the coffee shop of the Warsaw Intercontinental Hotel in August 1981, and survived.

11. *The New York Times,* 17 September 1970.

12. *The New York Times,* 20 September 1970.

13. *The New York Times,* 21 September 1970.

14. Casualties in the Jordanian revolt were widespread and never precisely determined, but were close to Hussein's estimate of less than 2,000 dead, far less than the PLO figure of 10,000 dead given prominence in the *Times* (26 and 30 September 1970).

15. *The New York Times,* 26 September 1970.

16. The *Times* explained that Hussein's victory was a loss in three stories, on September 24, 25 and 27, but that did not excuse my own error along the same lines. In the *Times* of September 27, John L. Hess,

who may have talked to the same U.S. diplomat that I did, reported from Beirut, "...The big loser, paradoxically, may be King Hussein...he cannot erase from Arab minds the fact that, as many newspapers have observed, he killed more Palestinians than the Israelis ever did...the Jordanian tragedy is viewed by Arab militants as confirming the thesis of Dr. George Habash, the chief of the Popular Front for the Liberation of Palestine, who has insisted that to defeat Israel the Arabs must first overthrow their 'reactionary' governments."

17. Nixon, *RN,* 485.

18. The *Times* characterized Nixon's role in the Jordanian revolt as "the principal brinksman" in a roundup written in Washington by Hedrick Smith (30 September 1970). Nixon by then was on a tour of Europe, and Max Frankel reported from Naples that Marshal Tito's decision to permit Nixon to visit Yugoslavia as scheduled was helping Nixon to "salvage some significance from his visit around the fringes of Europe." The headline on Frankel's story read, "Saving an Awkward Day, Tito's Decision to Keep to Schedule Helped Nixon to Reduce His Losses" (30 September 1970).

19. Eric Rouleau later became a contributor to the *Times* Op-Ed page, and through that introduction a guest on American television shows, including PBS. He was pronouncedly pro-PLO, and later a confidant of the revolutionaries who overthrew the Shah of Iran.

20. *The New York Times,* 26 September 1970.

21. William Safire, *Before the Fall* (New York: Doubleday, 1975), 327.

1. According to United Nations figures, 37,522 Americans died in combat and 103,284 were wounded in the Korean War. South Korea's military lost 70,000 dead and 150,000 wounded. Chinese and North Korean armies suffered about 2 million casualties, of which 60% were Chinese, and an estimated 3 million North Korean civilians and a half million South Korean civilians died from war-related causes.

2. *Rolling Stone,* 6 December 1973. Interview with Jann Wenner.

3. Daniel Ellsberg, *Papers on the War* (New York: Simon and Schuster, 1972), 284 (Touchstone edition).

4. Ibid., 285.

5. Apparently following Kissinger's axiom, "An expert is a man who has read a book nobody else has read," Ellsberg repeatedly relied on his study of the Nuremberg trial record to compare it with the Pentagon Papers in the early 1970s. Nobody ever said, "Aw, come on, Dan." Documents of the War Crimes Trials described Hitler's revolutionary government, dictatorial, vengeful and single-minded, bent on conquest. The Pentagon Papers picture decades of internal governmental disputes, bureaucratic infighting, more plans scrapped than implemented, while essentially seeking stalemate. Nor did the media recall that Western jurists and statesmen had grave doubts about the Nuremberg trials, even to the French name given the German site. Robert Murphy, the State Department veteran, thought less damage would have been done if the defendants at Nürnberg had faced a Roman Circus instead: a straight thumbs-up or thumbs-down from the populace. The trials established retroactive law, punished surrogates instead of the actual criminals in some cases and mixed the incompatible legal systems of the Soviet Union and the Western Allies. The Soviet legal system emerged unscathed, but the U.S. Constitution's provision that Congress declares wars was rendered obsolete by the precedent. The American media never noticed, and throughout the Vietnam war asked why it was not declared.

6. Ellsberg, *Papers on the War,* 14. See General Keegan's remarks, Chapter V.

7. McNamara report to President Johnson, 16 March 1964, in the *Pentagon Papers,* all versions.

8. *Rolling Stone,* 6 December 1973.

9. At this writing a major Soviet navy base.

10. *Pentagon Papers,* stressed as Document 79 in the *Times* version.

11. Charlton and Moncrieff, *Many Reasons Why,* 175.

12. General Westmoreland said that the huts ignited on the CBS television film camouflaged pill boxes, adding that "it was reported at the time that the Zippo lighter was given to a Marine by the reporter or a camera-man." William Small, head of CBS News, denied it to the BBC in Charlton and Moncrieff's *Many Reasons Why,* 152-53.

13. Ellsberg, *Papers on the War,* 305.

14. Charlton and Moncrieff, *Many Reasons Why,*169.

15. Ibid., 169.

16. Barry Farrell, "The Ellsberg Mask," *Harper's* October 1973.

17. Felt, *The FBI Pyramid,* 145. The eighteen national security wiretaps did not turn up much information, but they made enemies for Nixon and Kissinger. Those tapped were Morton Halperin, Helmut Sonnenfeldt, Daniel Davidson, Anthony Lake, Winston Lord, Richard Sneider and Richard Moose of Kissinger's staff; William H. Sullivan and Richard F. Pederson of the State Department; James W. McClane of the White House Domestic Council; John P. Sears, Deputy Counsel to the President; Laird's aide Lieutenant General Robert E. Pursley; speechwriter William Safire; William Beecher and Hedrick Smith of the *Times;* Henry Brandon of the *London Sunday Times;* columnist Joseph Kraft and CBS correspondent Marvin Kalb.

18. *The New York Times,* 9 October 1969.

19. The name of Vu Van Thai surfaced early in 1972 at Ellsberg's trial in Los Angeles, where he was named an unindicted co-conspirator. He was found in Dakar, Senegal, working as a consultant for the United Nations Development Program, and he declined comment on the case without an agreement and authorization from the UN Secretary-General. He said that Ellsberg was an old friend, but "I used to be in the service of Vietnam, but now I am in the international civil service and no longer concern myself with Vietnamese affairs."

20. Ellsberg, *Papers on the War,* 35. Ellsberg's italics.

21. *Rolling Stone,* 8 November 1973. Interview with Jann Wenner. It was unusual that Kissinger took Morton Halperin on as a member of the National Security Council staff because his philosophy was classically anti-anti-Communist. Halperin said later, "At one level, Nixon is totally undercutting anti-communism. Only a few people in government still believe in anti-communism. But the notion that communism is evil is being fought in Vietnam." Halperin believed that anti-communism arose from a commitment to reconstruct Europe, and "the rhetoric got out of hand." (*Los Angeles Free Press,* 30 March 1973.)

22. Raskin confirmed that "it was about that time, late 1969" that Ellsberg gave the papers to IPS. Telephone interview, 11 December 1980.

23. *Washington Post,* 30 April 1972.

24. *Washington Plans an Aggressive War* (New York: Random House,

1971).

25. Ellsberg, *Papers on the War,* 192.

26. Ibid., 215.

27. *The New York Times,* 7 November 1970.

28. *New York Daily News,* 10 June 1973. Taped interview with Michael McGovern.

29. *Rolling Stone,* 8 November 1973.

30. Daniel Ellsberg, "What Nixon is Up To," *The New York Review of Books,* 11 March 1971.

31. Salisbury, *Without Fear or Favor,* 85-86.

32. Jellinek later became head of Times Books.

33. Ellsberg, *Papers on the War,* 34.

34. Salisbury, *Without Fear of Favor,* 82.

35. Ibid., 96.

36. *Boston Globe,* 7 March 1971.

37. Salisbury, *Without Fear or Favor,* 36.

38. Nat Hentoff in the *Village Voice,* 20 May 1971.

39. Sanford J. Ungar, "The Papers' Papers," *Esquire,* May 1972.

40. John Leonard had just become *Times Book Review* editor when Sheehan submitted his review of 33 books. Leonard also had reviewed and praised Mark Lane's *Conversations With Americans,* discovering later from Sheehan that many of Lane's reports of GIs' statements about Vietnam were false. Leonard considered himself a radical novelist. He had been at Berkeley during the student revolution, and was proud of having worked for Pacifica Radio Station KPFA in Berkeley, when it was investigated as a Communist front by the Senate Internal Security subcommittee, and had been an anti-war organizer. (Interview with Nancy Henderson, *Writers' Digest,* May 1975.)

41. Charlton and Moncrieff, *Many Reasons Why,* 183.

42. Salisbury, *Without Fear or Favor,* ix.

43. Ibid., 186-187.

44. *New York Daily News,* 10 June 1973. Interview with Michael McGovern.

45. Nixon wrote that after the *Times* publication of the Pentagon Papers, "we received a report that the Soviet Embassy in Washington had received a set of the Pentagon Papers before they had been published in *The New York Times.*" Nixon's *RN,* 513.

46. *The Stages of War and Duplicity* (Moscow: Publishing House of Political Literature, 22 July 1971), 12.

47. *Granma* (Havana), 12 June 1971.

Chapter XVI

1. *The New York Times,* 13 June 1971.
2. The *Times Book Review* took a suspicious view of the Defense Department's 12-volume *United States-Vietnam Relations, 1945-1967.* The reviewer, Yale historian Gaddis Smith, began, "Historians of modern international relations frequently must rely on documents which, although authentic, were selected and released as political weapons." He found the Defense Department's work was so excised by the "Pentagon censor." Deep in the review, Smith conceded that the *Times'* version contained few documents and the Defense Department version had many hundreds, four times as many as the *Senator Gravel Edition.* To recapitulate: the *Times* published a house-written, tendentious version with little documentation as a political weapon; then Gravel published a hodge-podge version; then the Defense Department filled in serious omissions in the two pirated publications—and was accused of censorship.
3. Sanford J. Ungar, "The Papers' Papers," *Esquire,* May 1972.
4. Ibid.
5. *Washington Post,* 14 June 1971.
6. *Esquire,* May 1972. *The New York Review,* less fastidious, published part of the IPS manuscript, "Kennedy's Private War," by Stavins, 22 July 1971.
7. *The New York Times,* 14 June 1971. The unhappy *Post's* copycat headline: "Air War Plans Set Before '64 Election."
8. *The New York Times,* 21 June 1971.
9. *The New York Times,* 15 June 1971.
10. Nixon, *RN,* 125. Nixon did not mention it, but one member of a batch of persons denied security clearance by Otepka was Harding Bancroft.
11. "Press Versus Nixon; Now It's All-Out War," *The Times* (of London), 20 June 1971.
12. *The New York Times,* editorial, 16 June 1971.
13. *Washington Post,* 15 June 1971.
14. The long-continuing FBI telephone tap on Morton Halperin probably had nothing to do with his campaign activities for Muskie. Halperin remained in contact with Ellsberg, who, as it turned out after

the tap was discontinued, had retained other secret documents. Halperin simply remained a suspect for a long time.

15. *New York Post,* 17 June 1971.

16. *The New York Times,* 18 June 1971.

17. Sidney Zion and Warren Hinckle III had disagreed before as co-editors of *Scanlon's.* The January 1971 edition was printed in Quebec after the lithographers' union at Barnes Press in New York refused to print it, as did the union in San Francisco. The edition, entitled *Guerrilla War in the USA,* reported that the revolution had reached a stage of "armed propaganda," and cited 1,000 guerrilla attacks overlooked in Senator John McClellan's report on 4,330 bombing incidents between January 1969 and June 1970. The edition included interviews with the Weather Underground, Daniel Berrigan, Huey Newton, urban bombers and Army mutineers, along with directions for assassinations, kidnappings and making fire and chemical bombs.

Zion, in a commentary, expressed contempt for the guerrilla war: "Its intellectual base is empty, its practical sense burlesque, its vision as appealing as a parade of basket cases. . .treacherous and despicable as they are sad-assed and hopeless. A dose of Marx, a touch of Trotsky, a drop of Castro, a splash of Fatah—in sum, a cornucopia of despotism."

Hinckle wrote that it was presumptious "for a noncombattant to endorse or condemn a war that is going on in his own country when he isn't out there fighting on either side," and that if dynamite was forcing Melvin Laird and the Bank of America into rethinking, "it was dynamite well set off." Of guerrillas, Hinckle wrote, "Personally, I think those I've met are all right, and I refuse to beat them up."

It is noteworthy that the *Times* cited the pro-violence, IPS-related Hinckle in attacking Zion. Eventually Zion made it back into the *Times'* good graces. With *Ma'ariv* correspondent Dan Uri, he sold the *Times Magazine* a solid background piece on the Sadat-Begin breakthrough in the Middle East.

18. *The New York Times,* 26 June 1971.

19. Salisbury, *Without Fear or Favor,* ix.

20. Ibid., 5.

21. *International Herald-Tribune,* (Paris), citing *Times,* 1 July 1971. See Chapter VII.

22. *Chicago Sun-Times,* 23 June 1971.

23. *The New York Times,* 15 June 1971.

24. *Newsweek,* 21 June 1971.

25. *Los Angeles Times,* 22 June 1971.

26. *Associated Press,* 6 July 1971.

27. *Los Angeles Times,* 18, 23 and 21 June 1971. Three years after publication of the Pentagon Papers, Edward Jay Epstein described their manipulation in *Commentary* of April 1974: "Since the *Times* decided not to print the entire study. . .or even substantial parts of the

narrative, which was complex and academic, sections of the material had to be reorganized and rewritten along a theme that would be comprehensible to its audience. The theme chosen was duplicity: the difference between what the leaders of America said about the Vietnam war in private and in public. The Pentagon study, however, was not written in line with this theme. . . . To convert this bureaucratic study into a journalistic expose of duplicity required taking certain liberties with the original history: outside material had to be added and assertions from the actual study had to be omitted. . . ."

28. *Washington Post,* 26 June 1971.
29. *New York Daily News,* 15 June 1971.
30. *Human Events,* 26 June 1971.
31. *The New York Times Magazine,* 12 December 1971.
32. Ibid.
33. *Publishers' Weekly,* 18 August 1971.
34. The *Times Sunday Book Review* gave it Page 1 treatment under the headline, "So that what changed him would change America."
35. *Publishers' Weekly,* 15 July 1972.
36. *The New York Times,* 3 June 1973.
37. Sanford J. Ungar, *The Papers & the Papers* (New York: E.P. Dutton & Company, 1972), 260.
38. Senator Gravel's intervention in the Pentagon Papers case proved politically profitable, and he was re-elected in 1974, the year of Republican eclipse after Nixon resigned. During Gravel's second term publicity turned unfavorable. The Justice Department investigated charges by Elizabeth Ray (who said she was the mistress of Representative Wayne Hays of Ohio) that she had a sexual encounter with Gravel aboard the houseboat of former Representative Ken Gray of Illinois. Gravel denied the charge. The *Wall Street Journal* did a Page 1 number on Gravel on 8 August 1980, charging him with high-pressure fund raising and noting that his net worth doubled to $528,030 during his first five years in the Senate, and that in 1973 he paid heavy mortgage and loan payments on a gross income of $57,360. In the 1980 Democratic primary in Alaska, Gravel was defeated by Clark Gruening, son of the Senator Gravel had defeated in 1968.
39. *Congressional Record,* 22 November 1971, E 12550.
40. Dr. Leonard Rodberg, *The Pentagon Watchers* (New York: Doubleday, 1970).
41. *Anatomy of an Undeclared War* (New York: International Universities Press, 1972).
42. Kissinger, *White House Years,* 730.
43. Sullivan, *The Bureau,* 238-239.
44. *Washington Post,* 31 March 1975.
45. *The New York Times,* 23 July 1971.

Chapter XVII

1. *The New York Times,* 6 February 1972.
2. *The New York Times,* 15 May 1972.
3. Nixon, *RN,* 613.
4. Charlton and Moncrieff, *Many Reasons Why,* 197.
5. "How Kissinger Did It," *Foreign Policy,* No. 15, Summer, 1974.
6. Charlton and Moncrieff, *Many Reasons Why,* 198.
7. Ibid., 204.
8. *Public Opinion,* November 1981. A study under the auspices of the Research Institute on International Change, Columbia University.
9. As late as 1982, CBS News was attempting to show that Sam Adams' estimate of enemy strength in South Vietnam had been correct and that General Westmoreland had conspired to keep the true facts from President Johnson. CBS aired the 90-minute documentary, "The Uncounted Enemy: A Vietnam Deception," on 23 January 1982, and the show was promoted editorially by the *Times,* since it supported the original (and challenged) Ellsberg-to-Kennedy-to-Sheehan leak. The CBS show drew an angry rebuttal from Walt Rostow in a letter to the *Times* declaring that Johnson had been well aware of the dispute, and Reed Irvine's *Aim Report* of February 1982 called on CBS to fire Mike Wallace for "atrocious journalism." Westmoreland's suit against CBS was pending at this writing.
10. Lawrence V. Cott, in *Human Events,* 17 August 1974.
11. *The New York Times,* 24 January 1973.
12. *The New York Times,* 6 February 1973.

Chapter XVIII

1. Interview with Felt, 17 November 1982.
2. G. Gordon Liddy, *Will* (New York: St. Martin's Press, 1980).
3. Dean, *Blind Ambition,* 85.
4. Gordon Liddy's limited version of Watergate events appears to me more plausible than Dean's partly because Liddy wrote his own book, while Dean's, according to Richard Rovere, was assembled from Dean's almost incoherent manuscript by Taylor Branch. In Dean's book, the author portrays himself as a clean-cut, ambitious young American seduced by the dazzling perks and power of the White House. Liddy appears to recognize his own neuroticism, portraying himself as a romantic but principled zealot with a high I.Q. and a streak of masochism.

Liddy was responsible for part of the Watergate wreckage. His description of the Fielding break-in reads like teenagers raiding a bakery for the pastry, not the cash register. Breaking his own rigid security code, he told McCord more than the wireman needed to know, used McCord on the Watergate break-in after promising Magruder not to involve CRP personnel and blabbed to Dean about the Fielding break-in. Liddy also talked about his volunteering to kill Jack Anderson, the origin of rumors out of Miami's Cuban community that Nixon employed assassins. (Note that Robert Kennedy did employ assassins, but it was unknown at the time of Watergate.) Liddy also wrote that he was willing to kill Dean and his one-time buddy Hunt, if he had received orders from a responsible leader to do so, as he thought such murders could be justified. Liddy did not kill anybody. Liddy ascribes his respect for Hitlerian ruthlessness to a German maid his parents hired when he was a child. Presumably, if they had hired a Japanese maid, Liddy would have committed hari-kari after botching the Watergate burglary.

While awaiting sentence, Liddy was asked by Henry Petersen, the request confirmed by Mitchell, to cooperate with the prosecutors. Because the request did not come directly from Nixon, Liddy suspected it and refused.
5. See H. R. Haldeman with Joseph DiMona's *The Ends of Power* (New York: Times Books, 1978).
6. See Fred Thompson's *At That Point in Time* (New York: Quadrangle, 1975), 220-230.
7. Bradlee, *Conversations With Kennedy,* 201.
8. See Maurice Stans' *The Terrors of Justice* (New York: Everest

House, 1978).

9. Dick Tuck's exploits included planting a spy on Nixon's campaign train, and pulling the train out of the station as Nixon began addressing a crowd. During the 1962 California campaign, Tuck backgrounded a Nixon Chinatown rally with signs in Chinese that translated, "What about the Hughes loan" to Nixon's brother. In Miami in 1968, Tuck hired a women's picket line for Nixon's hotel, each picket carrying a sign, "Nixon's the One," and each of them black and visibly pregnant. Most people, including Republicans, thought that Tuck was vulgar but sometimes funny.

10. Carl Bernstein and Bob Woodward, *All the President's Men* (New York: Warner Books, 1975), paperback edition, 141 and 227.

11. *The New York Times,* 4 April 1974.

12. White, *Breach of Faith,* 295.

13. *City News* (a New York strike newspaper), 24 August 1978.

14. Jeb Stuart Magruder, *An American Life* (New York: Atheneum, 1974), Chapter XII.

15. The Ervin Committee was past its peak in August before the committee's chief investigator, Carmine S. Bellino, was charged with having bugged Nixon's campaign in 1960. George Bush, Republican national chairman, produced three affidavits charging Bellino and two others with bugging Nixon's hotel room before a debate with Kennedy. Bellino and the two others named denied it, and the media didn't like the story. After a committee investigation, the Senators voted along party lines, resulting in Bellino's exoneration. The Republicans said there was no proof that Bellino bugged Nixon, but that the evidence was equivocal, and that he should not have been in the position of chief investigator.

16. See Thompson's *At That Point in Time.*

17. Philip Noble, "How the New York Times Became Second Banana," *Esquire,* May 1975.

18. J. Anthony Lukas, *Nightmare, the Underside of the Nixon Years* (New York: Viking Press, 1976).

19. *The New York Times,* 28 April 1973.

20. *Congressional Record,* 8 May 1973, S 8417-8418.

21. *The New York Times,* 12 June 1973.

22. Thompson, *At That Point in Time,* 103.

23. *The New York Times,* 17 June 1973.

24. *Congressional Record,* 8 May 1973, S 8420.

25. Committee report of 23 October 1973.

26. *Newsweek,* 14 May 1973.

27. *The New York Times,* 27 June 1973.

28. *The New York Times,* 28 June 1973.

29. Columnist Joseph Kraft, in the *Washington Post* of 1 July 1973, used the enemies list as his major exhibit to prove, "not from hearsay

but from solemn documents" that "this country was being pushed in the direction of a police state." Kraft dismissed Dean as a mere *apparatchik,* without mentioning that Dean originated the "screw our enemies" memo, or that the lists were Dean's. Kraft wrote: "Begin with the lists of White House 'enemies' which the committee unearthed last week thanks to the courageous determination of the young Republican Senator from Connecticut, Lowell Weicker. Those lists were part of an action to mobilize the full power of darkness available to the federal government against the political opposition. The purpose, as one of the covering memos acknowledged, was to 'use the available federal machinery to screw our political enemies.'" Kraft did not use the full quote from the memo or ascribe it to Dean. Kraft had been bugged in Paris during the Pentagon Papers investigation, and he pressed hard for impeachment.

30. Like the traveling salesman with the farmer's daughter, the Ervin Committee worked its will with the accused witnesses until it ran into Pat Buchanan. The President's rough-hewn speechwriter had written some bloodthirsty memos about Democratic candidates, and majority counsel members leaked to the media the unfounded suspicion that he was the wellspring of dirty tricks. Buchanan was shown a few of his memos and ordered to appear before the committee to explain them.

On the eve of Buchanan's appearance before national television, minority counsel Thompson discovered that Buchanan was to be mousetrapped. He would be questioned on memos and correspondence that he had not been shown, and surely his groping and hesitation would mark him as guilty. Thompson phoned Buchanan and late into the night read him the surprise documents that would be sprung on him, refreshing his memory.

Buchanan appeared before the committee, his Irish temper seething but under control, and turned accuser, making clear the unethical attempt by Dash and Lenzer at entrapment. Well prepared, Buchanan rattled off blithe and specific answers to Dash's questions, giving the committee what one of the Senators conceded was a "practical lesson in political hardball," and abruptly wrenching the committee out of its pretended idealism into the real world. Pressed to answer the accusatory question of how far he would go in political tactics, Buchanan replied, "What tactics would I be willing to use? Anything that is not immoral, unethical, illegal or unprecedented in previous Democratic campaigns."

Even the partisan cheering section in the Senate Caucus Room guffawed. Buchanan had made the committee appear ridiculous, "an unmitigated disaster," according to Talmadge, who urged Ervin to wind up the proceedings.

31. Haldeman reported in *The Ends of Power* (135) that Bob Bennett's CIA case officer all but pinpointed Bennett as Deep Throat, but Woodward denied it, and Haldeman agreed. Haldeman's candidate was Fred

Notes 651

F. Fielding, Dean's staff assistant. Fielding, at this writing, is President Reagan's counsel, making Haldeman's charge dubious. Fielding convincingly denied being Deep Throat in a letter to the author on 17 January 1983, and noted that Haldeman had retracted the charge, unreported by the media. John Dean, in 1982, just after Alexander Haig was eased out as Reagan's Secretary of State, suggested that Haig was Deep Throat, apparently to win publicity for Dean's new book, drawing a properly indignant denial from Haig.

The most publicized candidate to be Deep Throat, W. Mark Felt, wrote in his book, *The FBI Pyramid,* that he was not, and met Bob Woodward only once, in Felt's office with an aide present, to refuse Woodward's proposal that he sort out accurate from inaccurate data in Woodward's possession.

Felt told me when the suggestion that he was Deep Throat first appeared in the press, shortly after his retirement in 1973, he was "more amused than angry; I thought at the time that Deep Throat had made a contribution." In 1982 Felt had changed his mind, and surprisingly agreed to my suggestion that Nixon should not have been forced out of office, despite Felt's troubles with the Nixon White House.

In one of the ironies of the post-Watergate era, Felt, the enemy of Sullivan the subversive hunter, was himself tried, along with Pat Gray and Edward S. Miller, for violating the civil rights of Weather Underground sympathizers, and Nixon testified that Felt had been doing his duty properly. After Felt's conviction during the Carter administration, President Reagan pardoned him as one of his first presidential acts.

Evidence appeared to be accumulating that there was no Deep Throat. Felt said it was possible that an agent of the FBI Washington Field Office gave Woodward part of the information attributed to Deep Throat, out of resentment at the outsider, Acting Director Pat Gray. All of the agents of the Washington Field Office were grilled on the question, which caused more resentment and produced no answer. If Deep Throat does not exist, then pure fiction was introduced into Woodward's and Bernstein's fateful reports.

Chapter XIX

1. *Newsweek,* 22 February 1971.
2. Chaim Herzog, *The War of Atonement* (Boston: Little, Brown, 1975), 280.
3. *Newsweek,* 9 April 1973.
4. Marvin Kalb and Bernard Kalb, *Kissinger* (Boston: Little, Brown and Company, 1974).
5. *Commentary,* September 1974.
6. Nixon, *RN,* 924.
7. Herzog, *The War of Atonement,* 284.
8. *The New York Times,* 20 October 1973.
9. *The New York Times,* 21 October 1973.
10. Henry Kissinger, *Years of Upheaval* (Boston: Little, Brown and Company, 1982), As cited in *Time,* 1 March 1982.
11. Nixon, *RN,* 938-939.
12. Nixon, *RN,* 939-940.
13. *The New York Times,* 26 October 1973.
14. David Binder's second account of the Defcon-3 alert stressing Nixon's inactivity might have suffered from editing and headline writers' treatment, as Binder was not particularly anti-Nixon. Six months later, while visiting West Germany, Binder appeared with a panel discussing Watergate on the popular Sunday morning television show *Frühschoppen.* He mildly corrected the host, Werner Höfer, who had implied that Nixon was taking credit for Kissinger's foreign policy successes: the foreign policy was Nixon's, Binder said, carried out efficiently by Kissinger. Binder also guessed that Nixon might escape impeachment, recalling that the media had been hostile to him since the 1968 election campaign, when its miscalculation of Nixon's voter appeal caused commentators to invent "the next Nixon" as an alibi for the media's earlier misjudgment during the campaign. Binder reported that the atmosphere in Washington was poisonous, and he appeared to blame equally Nixon's tendency toward fanaticism and the counter-fanaticism he inspired in the media.

I was a member of the same television panel, recalling in my broken

German that the first call for impeachment came with the Cambodia incursion, that many American publicists had committed their credibility to the proposition that the Vietnam war was unwinnable, and that if Watergate had not occured, they would have had to invent it. I contended that the impeachment proceedings were a residue from the Vietnam war, an occasion to discharge emotions and frustrations from the war and the polarization it had encouraged. (Transcript, *Frühschoppen,* West Germany's First Program, Cologne, 16 June 1974.)

15. The October War was the most deadly of the Israel-Arab wars. The Arab air forces lost 514 planes, while Israel lost 102, almost all to SAM missiles. In air combat, Israel lost five aircraft to the Arab forces' 334. Israel lost 2,521 dead and 7,056 wounded, of whom 3,500 were maimed—more than three times the comparative American dead in 12 years of the Vietnam War. Egypt and Syria did not publish figures of war dead, but Egypt reported 7,500 dead and wounded, Syria 7,300, both figures lower than Western estimates.

16. One of the most Byzantine episodes of Watergate was the publication of *The Ends of Power,* which Haldeman had not intended to write until Times Books sent co-author Joseph DiMona to talk him into it. The *Washington Post* pirated Haldeman's conclusions, publishing them before its ally, the *Times.* Then the *Times'* reviewer, Elizabeth Drew, author and television commentator, slammed the book and Haldeman, who "unlike Nixon, is not an interesting villain." Drew found that Haldeman "did not understand how our system of government was designed to work . . . had no sense of history, of governing, of the moral implications of his acts." In condemning the *Times'* book, Drew sounded the *Times'* theme strongly, however: " . . . our constitutional system was threatened, our liberties were in danger. Perfectly sensible people had begun to worry about the dangers to our system before Watergate was ever broken into; many of them experienced a fear, without precedent, of their own government." (*Times Book Review,* 12 March 1978.)

Chapter XX

1. *The New York Times,* 8 October 1973.
2. *The New York Times,* 22 October 1973.
3. *Washington Post,* 19 July 1974. Interview with Sally Quinn, headlined "Rabbi Korff's Angle: 'Using the Media to Castigate the Media.' "
4. Jimmy Breslin, *How the Good Guys Finally Won* (New York: Viking Press, 1975), 56.
5. *The New York Times,* 21 June 1974.
6. *The New York Times,* 25 February 1974.
7. With Nixon's disgrace complete, his last defenders in the media admitted their guilt, pleading that he had deceived them. Columnist James J. Kilpatrick drank his hemlock in a widely noted column, "My President Lied." William F. Buckley suggested in his *National Review* that perhaps Nixon's crimes were not so grave, received 200 cancellations of subscriptions, and decided that the magazine would publish no more exculpatory material on Nixon, castrating his publication. Buckley became "Mr. Conservative," a title bestowed by Eastern establishment media liberals. At the *Daily News,* editorialist Reuben Maury, still itching to fight, was retired.

Chapter XXI

1. *The New York Times,* 24 January 1975.
2. *The New York Times,* 20 and 22 January 1975, and 10, 13, 20, 17 February 1975.
3. *The New York Times,* 2 and 3 March 1975.
4. *The New York Times,* 3 February 1975.
5. *The New York Times,* 2 March 1975.
6. *The New York Times,* 25 February 1975.
7. *The New York Times,* 5 March 1975.
8. *The New York Times,* 9 March 1975.
9. *The New York Times,* 11 March 1975.
10. *The New York Times,* 16 March 1975.
11. *The New York Times,* 2 March 1975.
12. Frank Snepp, *Decent Interval* (New York: Random House, 1977), 340.
13. The *Times* Page 1 of 13 March 1975, was almost exactly duplicated seven years later, on 18 March 1982. The page layout was identical—a three-column picture at the top of the page, with headline underneath. In 1975:

> The Enigmatic Cambodian Insurgents;
> Reds Appear to Dominate Diverse Bloc.

In 1982:

> Salvador Rebels: Five-Sided Alliance
> Searching for New, Moderate Image.

In both cases guerrilla armies were described as broad coalitions, apparently led by Communists, but perhaps really more nationalist, with a likelihood that moderates would prevail if the United States would permit negotiated settlements, both stories said.
14. *The New York Times,* 13 March 1975.
15. *The New York Times,* 17 March 1975.
16. *The New York Times,* 18 March 1975.
17. *The New York Times,* 16 March 1975.
18. *The New York Times,* 16 April 1975.
19. *The New York Times,* 9 May 1975.
20. Snepp, *Decent Interval,* 381.
21. *The New York Times,* 17 April 1975.

22. *The New York Times,* 17 April 1975.

23. *The New York Times,* 30 April 1975.

24. *The New York Times,* 30 April 1975.

25. *The New York Times,* 4, 9, 10, 15 and 29 April 1975.

26. To review David Frost's *I Gave Them a Sword,* (New York: William and Morrow Company, 1978) the *Times* chose one of those Clay Felker had warned Frost would be out there lying in wait, J. Anthony Lukas, author of *Nightmare.* Lukas wrote that when he watched the first interview, "My first reaction, as I recall, was barely contained rage. 'So this is the way it all ends,' I growled. 'For two years he stonewalls the press, covers up from Congress and lies to the public. Then, once Ford has guaranteed him against prosecution, he sells his story to a British showman for $600,000 plus 20 percent of the profits.' " Lukas reported that most of the material in the book "is a regurgitation—in excruciating detail—of the 28 hours of videotaped interviews" containing "little news" and "long gray patches of dialogue." Lukas did like spots in the book, quoting Frost's assistant Birt as snapping at a Nixon aide, "We can't plea-bargain with you," and Public Television's Zelnick, when Frost has Nixon on the ropes, saying, "Move in, tear the s.o.b. to pieces."

27. The strategy of *Daily News* editor Michael J. O'Neill of following the *Times* lead succeeded in the sense that it rid the newspaper of conservative readers. Jack Anderson's column failed to produce exclusives and was dropped. Pete Hamill was dropped despite a small protest demonstration led by attorney William Kunstler, later brought back to contribute fiction. Michael Daly was dropped for fabricating a story from Northern Ireland which gave the impression he had been on patrol with brutal and callous British troops. Clay Felker, who was hired as managing editor of the afternoon edition *Tonight,* resigned when the edition lost millions and folded. In early 1982 the Chicago Tribune Company put the *News* up for sale, and in May 1982 O'Neill resigned "to resume a love affair with writing."

28. *The New York Times,* 1 May 1977. For some reason, the "new tapes" story is omitted from the extensive "Watergate" section of the *Times Index of 1977.*

29. *The New York Times,* 5 May 1977.

30. *New York Daily News,* 5 May 1977.

31. Dr. David Abrahamsen, M.D., *Nixon vs. Nixon: An Emotional Tragedy* (New York: Farrar, Straus & Giroux, 1976).

32. Dr. David Abrahamsen's book, *Nixon vs. Nixon: An Emotional Tragedy,* was a straightforward attack under its unctuous title, but the *Times Book Review* took its cue and reported that the book was "a considerable achievement.... It will make even an inveterate Nixon-hater feel a measure of sympathy." John Dean called it "an important book... answers the unanswerable questions about the Nixon presi-

dency." Columnist Harriet Van Horne found it "full of dazzling insight and perception." It surely was the most repulsive of all the Nixon books.

33. William Shawcross, *Sideshow: Kissinger, Nixon and the Destruction of Cambodia* (New York: Simon and Schuster, 1979).

34. *The New York Times,* 24 March 1979.

Chapter XXII

1. *The New York Times,* 16 July 1977.
2. *Spectator* (London), 2 January 1959.
3. *Esquire,* April 1961.
4. *Commentary,* September 1965.
5. The *Daily News* effort to match the *Times* sometimes produced grotesque results. When Alex Haley's saga *Roots* became an international television hit, the London *Sunday Times* published a dispatch from a correspondent in Western Africa reporting that Haley had been taken in by local witch doctor conmen, who led him to believe that he was a descendant of one Kunta Kinta. The *Times* London bureau picked up the story and it appeared on Page 1. So at 9 p.m. a *News* editor dutifully called AP and UPI and asked them to match it. Since the London *Sunday Times* story was readily available at London bureaus of both agencies, both had the story on their wires within the hour. Every newsroom in the United States received simultaneous AP and UPI stories on Haley's alleged misadventure, so an inconsequential story, actually an anecdote, received splash treatment nationwide. Haley never claimed his saga was history, and stressed that it was a novel.
6. Daniel Patrick Moynihan with Suzanne Weaver, *A Dangerous Place* (Boston: Atlantic-Little, Brown, 1975).
7. Ibid., 64 and 66. John Oakes, Punch Sulzberger's cousin, once had been a candidate to become publisher of the *Times.* Oakes and Sulzberger clashed over whether to support Abzug or Moynihan for the Democratic senatorial nomination, Sulzberger insisting on burying the hatchet and endorsing Moynihan. Partly as a result of the clash, Max Frankel replaced Oakes as editorial page editor in late 1976. After retirement, Oakes continued to write by-lined articles for the Op-Ed page.
8. *New Leader,* 19 June 1978. Interview with Gertrude Samuels.
9. *The New York Times,* 2 July 1980.
10. *The New York Times,* 6 July 1980. When some criticism of Leonard Fein by Rabbi Schindler and Theodore Mann did get published, the *Times* gave Fein space for a column to reply on the Op-Ed page. Fein's apologea, under the headline "Criticism Is Not Fatal," stressed his devotion to Israel, and said that even harsh critics of Begin "reject as preposterous the notion that Israel's policies represent the principle barrier to peace in the Middle East." (*Times,* 19 July 1980.)
11. *Jewish Week,* 28 May 1978.
12. "Balance and Responsibility in the Media, the New York Times on

the Iran-Iraq War and the West Bank Clashes," *Midstream,* June-July 1982.

13. See "J'Accuse," *Commentary,* September 1982.

14. *The New York Times,* 18 July 1982.

15. *The New York Times,* 25 August 1982.

16. *AIM Report,* Vol. IX, No. 17, September 1982.

17. *The New York Times,* 9 June 1982.

18. NBC News, 19 September 1982.

19. *Midstream,* February 1981.

20. Rael Jean Isaac, *Israel Divided* (Baltimore: Johns Hopkins University Press), 1979.

21. *The New York Times Magazine,* 26 April 1981.

22. Spin-offs from IPS included the Transnational Institute (TNI) in Amsterdam; the Corporate Data Exchange in Washington; the Center for National Security Study (a linchpin of the anti-Pentagon lobby); the Foundation for National Progress, publisher of *Mother Jones,* successor to *Ramparts*; the Bay Area Institute in San Francisco, which founded Pacific News Service; the Internal Security Project of 1971, which gave birth to the Organizing Committee for the Fifth Estate, publisher of *CounterSpy,* which at first relied heavily on renegade CIA agent Philip Agee; the Middle East Research and Information Project, publisher of pro-PLO *MERIP Reports*; the Cambridge Institute, founded by IPS Fellow Gar Alperovitz; the Southern Institute in Atlanta, publisher of *Southern Exposure;* and the Government Accountability Project, which encourages selective whistle-blowing by members of the government bureaucracy. IPS denies that it created Members of Congress for Peace Through Law, the dove caucus which at one time numbered 155 members of the House and Senate, but IPS speakers dominated its seminars. IPS contributors appear in the *Village Voice, In These Times,* the *Guardian,* the *Progressive* and *The Nation.*

23. See *AIM Reports,* October 1980, No. 19.

24. *The New York Times,* 11 June 1979. A. J. Langguth, a former *Times* reporter, had published a year earlier his book, *Hidden Terrors* (New York: Pantheon, Random House, 1978), which was promoted in a lengthy news story in the *Times* on 7 May 1978. The report from Washington, without a by-line, was headlined, "U.S. POLICE PROGRAM IS CALLED C.I.A. COVER," and said the book accused the United States of encouraging the torture of political prisoners in Brazil and Uruguay. On 4 June 1978, another Langguth column appeared on the Op-Ed page praising Philip Agee and other CIA defectors and encouraging more CIA employees to defect.

25. *The New York Times,* 14 June 1981.

26. Harris Poll, 29 June 1981.

27. *In the Public Interest,* The National News Council, 1975.

28. *The New York Times,* 26 April 1981. A special to the *Times* from Kenneth A. Briggs in Havana.

29. *Times*-IPS cooperation was illustrated in an Op-Ed page article on El Salvador on 15 June 1980. "The Aid for El Salvador Is Called Non-Lethal" was written by Thomas Conrad of the American Friends Service Committee's National Action/Research on the Military-Industrial Complex, and Cynthia Arnson of IPS. Documents obtained under the Freedom of Information Act indicated that the Carter administration sent to El Salvador "7,500 CS tear-gas grenades, 250 'Manpack' field combat radios, thousands of batteries and an unspecified number of tear-gas-grenade launchers," it charged. The authors especially questioned 50 portable PFS-2B night-vision devices and 14 "image intensifiers" used for night targeting. It warned that U.S. support for the ruling junta fostered repression and could sow anti-Americanism. In sum, the article, by innuendo and harmless facts made sinister by citing withheld documents, reached a conclusion that was refuted by El Salvador's voters in the election of the spring of 1982.

INDEX